Religion in America

ADVISORY EDITOR

Edwin S. Gaustad

*P*RESIDENT *W*ITHERSPOON

Varnum Lansing Collins

TWO VOLUMES IN ONE

ARNO PRESS & THE NEW YORK TIMES

New York 1969

Reprint edition 1969 by Arno Press, Inc.

*

Library of Congress Catalog Card No. 78-83416

*

Reprinted from a copy in the
Columbia University Libraries

*

Manufactured in the United States of America

PRESIDENT WITHERSPOON

VOLUME ONE

LONDON:HUMPHREY MILFORD

Oxford University Press

PRESIDENT

WITHERSPOON

A BIOGRAPHY

BY
VARNUM LANSING COLLINS

DEO JUVANTE

VOLUME ONE

PRINCETON
PRINCETON UNIVERSITY PRESS
1925

PRINTED AT THE PRINCETON UNIVERSITY PRESS
Princeton New Jersey United States of America

PREFACE

A LETTER TO EDWARD DICKINSON DUFFIELD

My dear EDWARD:—

MORE years ago than it is exhilarating to count, an under-graduate at Princeton composed an oration which he entitled "Scotch Granite," his fanciful name for President Witherspoon. Delivered on every sort of occasion,—prize contests, "chapel stage," extempore speaking in Hall, and I do not know where else (there must have been more time for oratory in those days than now),—the oration as you doubtless remember acquired campus fame beyond the average. And it deserved the applause it received, for it was good.

You were the orator; and I, by some happy chance, was often one of your listeners. I say happy, because I have ever since been glad that my curiosity was stirred by your enthusiastic delineation of the great President's character. But when in later years I tried to learn more about him I found only desiccated sketches in biographical dictionaries, a funeral sermon, a notice prefixed to his collected writings, and a brief memoir or two. So I resolved to gather the materials and myself attempt the story of his life.

This is the story. It has been a long time in the making, for I have been busied about many other things while it was growing; and now to give it to the printer seems like parting from an old friend. Yet I hope it will not be found to have suffered for the delay. Such as it is, this unassuming narrative of the life of one whom I think you rightly called a great American I dedicate to you, not only because you were its original source of inspiration, but also (and even more gratefully) because of our long and loyal friendship.

It is not with false modesty that I call this book unassuming. Do not let the notes and references deceive you with any simulation of erudition; on the contrary, some of them are merely corroborations of the text, others are details that hardly belong in the higher company of larger print, while the rest are intended to do nothing more than name my sources to those readers who may wish to know them. Dr. Witherspoon's life was part of a movement greater far than he, and it is not impossible therefore that the materials of this story may serve other purposes than mine. Moreover, the single biography of the President, published since this book was begun, contains neither notes nor references, and not having even an index is a difficult book to use. That in such a method of writing there are advantages to the author I am ready to admit; but I cannot see any advantage to the reader, who sometimes may have entirely innocent motives for wanting the authorities. Perhaps it had been better if my book had imitated its predecessor more closely in this respect; but when one questions century-old traditions as I have found myself doing more than once, and when one is compelled to doubt what others have accepted as facts, it is fairer to the reader as well as safer for oneself to fortify conclusions with page and chapter, even though one's book be only biography and not a doctoral dissertation.

It is a simple enough tale that is told, in spite of its being the life of a man who was a born leader and therefore half the time a fighter. Some of the fighting may seem a trifle dull to you; and yet it was anything but dull to him—or to his opponents; controversies that look trivial now appeared epochal then. After all, must you not take the meat in a man's life as he leaves it, the lean with the fat? I have tried at any rate to avoid the danger to which Lord Rosebery alluded in the preface to his life of Chatham —the danger of forgetting "that the province of history and biography, though they often overlap, are essentially distinct." The life of a man, he reminds us, is not his public life—"we want to know how a master talked, and if possible, what he thought, what he was in his hours of ease, what he enjoyed, how he unbent; in a word, what he was without his wig and bag and sword, in his dressing-gown and slippers."

Dr. Witherspoon was inseparably concerned at first with an ecclesiastical struggle in Scotland and later with educational, political, and ecclesiastical developments in America, and his life cannot be recounted without constant allusion to these movements; they were his "wig and bag and sword," and they have not all grown trivial with the passing years. His management of the college over which he presided was so peculiarly characteristic, its misfortune during the Revolution and its labored recovery were so personal to him that here also the story of his life is an inextricable part of another and longer narrative—that of the College of New Jersey in the last quarter of the eighteenth century. You cannot tell the one without relating to some extent the other; he dominated and permeated the place; to the public outside he was the place; and it has been my effort to justify contemporary opinion. But I have fallen wretchedly short of my intention if I have let the larger life of his times, in which he moved so vigorously, or even the story of his administration at Princeton, overshadow the "dressing-gown and slippers," the qualities that brought him into prominence, and the lovable personality that held him there and gave him the influence he wielded.

My indebtednesses are so many that it is not possible even to name all who have given me their aid so generously; my thanks are offered to them no less heartily because it must be done in this general manner. Especially am I under obligation to the former minister of Paisley's Abbey Church, the late Reverend Dr. Gentles, whose cordial hospitality to the American stranger within his gates more than a decade ago makes that visitor almost ashamed now to write this belated public acknowledgment of his interest and genial courtesy. And similarly, another debt that cannot now be fully repaid is the one I owe to President Witherspoon's great-great grandson, the late General Alfred A. Woodhull of Princeton, who not only never failed to satisfy my importunity but so graciously for many years also gave me the honor of his intimate friendship and the benefit of his resourceful suggestions and great stores of information. I must acknowledge too, the assistance of Mr. J. Harvey Witherspoon Phillips of Tampa, Florida, who lent me valuable records and inconvenienced himself by carrying out investigations beyond my reach; and also the help of the Rev. G. H. Ingram of Trenton, until lately clerk of the Presbytery of New Brunswick, who gave me access to the remarkable manuscript minutes of that body. My particular and warmest thanks are extended to Dr. John E.

Peters of Camden, New Jersey, as learned and indefatigable in his researches into Presbyterian and Princeton history as he is generous in sharing the results of his persevering and well-nigh inerrant labors.

When I consider the libraries in Scotland, England, and the United States whose staffs I have pestered with requests, I am filled with dismay; I owe them so much. But if one staff may be singled out above the rest, it is that of the Library of Princeton University—*quorum pars fui*—and I would here remember with gratefulness the innumerable and uniformly helpful courtesies and privileges accorded to me by that staff since I left its membership. Frequent and special favors have likewise been shown me by the staff of the Library of Princeton Theological Seminary and those of the Pennsylvania Historical Society and the New Jersey Historical Society. Libraries and librarians seldom receive just due from makers of books; their aid is taken, as it were, for granted. This is the appreciation of one who knows somewhat of their unceasing and often thankless toil.

And thus, my dear Edward, with these totally inadequate acknowledgments I withdraw from the scene; and, unrecognizable perhaps to you in his latter-day dress, your "Scotch Granite" takes the stage. But under his new trappings I hope you will find the same great heart you described to us years ago.

V. L. C.

CONTENTS

VOLUME ONE

ILLUSTRATIONS

VOLUME ONE

PRESIDENT WITHERSPOON

VOLUME ONE

CHAPTER ONE

THE EARLY YEARS

FOUR miles southeast of Haddington in the Scottish shire of that name, by a road that winds over rolling country, lies the village of Gifford in the parish of Yester. It consists of a group of low stone cottages clustering on the bank of a little stream known as Gifford Water, a stream that wimples still on its way to the Tyne at Haddington as merrily as it did when the smooth turf on its banks was the bleaching ground of the newly formed British Linen Company.

Starting from the village cross, one branch of the single street runs parallel with Gifford Water and loses itself in a long avenue of ancient elms leading to Gifford, or Yester Castle, whose magical history is alluded to in *Marmion*. The other branch of the street in a few hundred paces brings one to the ivy-covered kirk in a yard shaded by trees as picturesquely venerable as itself. Close by, a cosy modern manse stands near the site of its eighteenth century predecessor. Latter-day improvements, which even sequestered spots like this may not escape, have swept away all trace of the humbler home where former ministers of Yester Parish lived, and where John Witherspoon was born.

Spelled in a variety of ways, the name Witherspoon occurs frequently enough in Scottish records; but it has not been the fortune of the writer to discover how directly the ancestors of John Witherspoon were connected with the original spearmen whose wooden pikes or spears, burned at the points for hardening, gave them the name of "wooden spon," whence came the early "Wotherspon" and the later varieties of the name.[1] The family was of old and honorable descent. The Witherspoon arms are or, a cross ingrailed betwixt four crescents, gules.[2] The crest is a dexter hand holding a garland of laurel all ppr., with the motto *"Deo juvante."* The arms are not in Sir James Balfour Paul's *Ordinary*

---

[1] H. A. Long, *The Names We Bear*, p. 104, 210.
[2] Alexander Nisbet, *System of Heraldry*, Edinburgh, 1816, vol. I, p. 123; Burke, *General Armory* (ed. of 1883) adds "a mascle ar."

of Arms[3] and it is safe to assume that they are not legitimately borne by any Scottish Witherspoons today. They date, however, at least from 1451, when an Alexander Witherspoon, as witness to a deed confirmed by James I, is mentioned in the Register of the Great Seal of Scotland as a scutifer. At that time the family seems to have been Glasgovian. Forty years later a James Witherspoon was burgess of Glasgow and procurator of the lepers in the hospital, and from him the line is fairly traceable.

It is a line which has its full quota of public officials and clergymen. The records of the period name a James Widderspune who, between 1496 and 1507, at the court of James III of Scotland, ministered to the moods of royalty by being now "a fithelar and teller of tales" and now a "fowler" to the king;[4] but it is unlikely that he and the Glasgow burgess are identical. Among the latter's children was William who moved to Linlithgow and became burgess of that city and owner of the Brig, or Bridge, House estate in Torpichen Parish. His son Robert was bailif of Linlithgow in 1539 and provost of the city from 1542 to 1554. But William's most interesting child was James, who, with a sister Katherine, was the subject of letters of legitimization issued by the queen in 1543. Under date of 1559 John Wetherspone and "James Wetherspowne of Brighouse," a natural son of William mentioned above, are named as witnesses in one of the Laing charters owned by the University of Edinburgh;[5] and a few years later James for a moment enters the story of Scotland's unhappiest queen. For in March, 1565, he was commanded with others to appear before the king and his spouse and their privy council to answer to the charge of complicity in the murder of David Riccio, her majesty's secretary. In August, 1571, he was forfeited, but in the following May he signed allegiance to the crown, and thereafter lived in peace, so far as the records show, until the closing year of his life when, in August, 1579, his bellicose disposition got him into his last earthly trouble. Found guilty of hav-

[3] Second ed., Edinburgh, 1903.
[4] *Accounts of the Lord High Treasurer of Scotland*, ed. Sir J. B. Paul, Edinburgh, 1877–1901, vols. I, II, III.
[5] *Calendar of the Laing Charters*, ed. J. Anderson, Edinburgh, 1899, nos. 695, 707; also *Register Great Seal of Scotland*, vol. XXIX, p. 172.

ing done bodily hurt to two other gentlemen he was ordered to pay a heavy fine or else languish in Edinburgh jail. But he neither paid the fine nor darkened the prison door, for the unassailable reason that he was lying "bedfast, deidly seik" at Linlithgow; and by January 19, 1580, he was dead.[6]

William of Linlithgow's great grandson John was a signer of the Solemn League and Covenant in 1648, and this John's son Alexander, a Glasgow merchant, seems to have been father of the Reverend James Witherspoon who in turn was the father of Princeton's President.[7] Ministers, chaplains and vicars are scattered plentifully through the family history but no vindication has been found of the claim that there was an unbroken line of ministers behind Dr. Witherspoon extending back to John Knox.

During the end of the sixteenth century and through the seventeenth the valuable Witherspoon estate of Bridge House is frequently mentioned in deeds and charters; but, direct descendant though he is believed to have been, the Reverend James Witherspoon seems to have had no share in them. His will leaves no property save a paltry month's salary due him as a King's chaplain.[8] Born in 1691, he was graduated from Edinburgh University in April, 1709, studied theology, and is lost sight of until November, 1719, when he was presented to Yester Parish. Installed at Gifford in March 1720, he entered immediately on this charge, remaining there until his death forty years later. On October 21, 1720, he was married at Gifford, to Anna, or Anne, daughter of the Reverend David Walker and Margaret Paterson, his wife. Mr. Walker was minister of Temple Parish, County of Edinburgh. The alleged descent of the Walkers from John Knox is the source of the oft-asserted but unproved claim connecting President Witherspoon with the reformer.[9]

---

[6] *Register, Privy Council of Scotland*, vol. I, p. 437; vol. II, p. 738; vol. III, p. 206; *Calendar, State Papers rel. to Scotland and Mary Queen of Scots*, vol. III, p. 669.
[7] Some genealogies give David as the father of the Reverend James.
[8] *Commissariot of Edinburgh.* Testaments, CXVIII.
[9] It may be well to state at once the facts on which the conclusion implied above is based. John Knox was twice married. He left no children by his first wife. By his second wife, Margaret Stuart, daughter of Lord Ochiltree, he had among other children a daughter Elizabeth born about 1570 who married in 1594 the Rev. John Welsh of Ayr. She died in 1625 three years after her husband. They had three sons and two

The date of Mrs. Witherspoon's birth is no longer of record, but the baptismal register of Temple parish shows that she was baptised July 19, 1696, and it is safe to assume that her birth did

daughters, of whom only the second son, Josias, and his younger sister, Louise, are concerned in the present matter.

Josias Welsh was the father of the once celebrated John Welsh, the deprived minister of Irongray, Dumfries. A Reverend John Blackader in his manuscript memoirs (Wodrow MSS., Advocates Library, Edinburgh) mentions the fact that he was acquainted with a young woman in Fife who was "a cousin of John Welsh of Irongray." This was approximately in 1674 when this John Welsh was making a preaching tour in Fifeshire.

Louise Welsh, the second daughter of Elizabeth Knox and John Welsh, the elder, was born at Jonsac in France in May, 1613; but after 1625, when she appears as a witness to her mother's will, all trace of her is lost. She is supposed to have returned to Scotland, to have married, to have settled in Fifeshire, and to have become the mother of the unidentified "young woman" of the Blackader manuscript. Moreover, this "young woman" is supposed to have married one of the two brothers, David or James Walker, farmers at Leslie, in Fifeshire, and thus to have become the mother of the Reverend David Walker, minister of Temple Parish. The Leslie birth and marriage records afford no light, as they do not antedate 1673 and 1729 respectively.

It is scarcely necessary to point out that genealogical claims based on suppositions like the above cannot be accepted seriously.

With David Walker the descent gets back to firm ground again. He married Margaret Paterson and was the father of Thomas and Anne (or Anna) Walker, the latter of whom married the Reverend James Witherspoon and became the mother of President Witherspoon. Her brother Thomas, in his day a well-known Scottish ecclesiastical writer, is the earliest of the alleged Knox descendants to claim the ancestry in print. This he does in his *Vindication of the Discipline and Constitution of the Church of Scotland* (Edinburgh 1774, p. 379). Assuming that he derived his information from his father, the Reverend David Walker of Temple, the Knox kinship is carried back close enough to the time of John Welsh of Irongray and the unknown cousin to acquire at least an air of possibility; but here again the evidence is lacking.

Dr. David Laing (Knox's *Works*, edited for the Bannatyne Club, Edinburgh, 1865, vol. 6, p. LXXIII) considered it extremely doubtful that any descendants of Knox were existing. Dr. Charles Rogers (*Genealogical Memoirs of John Knox and the Family of Knox*, edited for the Grampian Club, London, 1879, p. 147) makes no reference to descendants although admitting that "it is not improbable" Louise Welsh may have been the mother of the young woman described as the cousin of John Welsh of Irongray. William Crawford, (*Knox Genealogy*, Edinburgh, 1896, p. 5) thinks it doubtful if any lineal descendants of the Reformer exist. Dr. D. Hay Fleming of St. Andrews, the historian and modern authority on Knox, in a letter to the author of these lines, admitted that the claim could not be lightly set aside, but had no fresh evidence in its support; while the authorities of H. M. Register House at Edinburgh frankly expressed to the writer their disbelief in the claim.

Finally it may be added that President Witherspoon himself does not appear to have ever claimed descent from the Reformer.

The most generous conclusion that can be reached, after examination of all available sources, manuscript and printed, is the Scottish one of "not proven."

not precede this date by many days. Of her personality and character our only knowledge is derived by inference from the facts of her ministerial parentage and her marriage to a lowland parish minister, and from the early training she gave her children. In an entry made November 11, 1744, by her husband in his manuscript "Separate Register of the Presbytery of Haddington," he describes himself as a widower, and in the absence of any official register for the parish it will probably be impossible to get nearer to the exact date of Mrs. Witherspoon's death. Her grave is no longer marked in Gifford churchyard.

She was the mother of six children, born within ten years— John, the future president of Princeton, baptised February 10, 1723 (date of birth not recorded but said to be February 5), David, baptised February, 1725, Susan, baptised March 20, 1726, Josias (or Joseph) born February 9, 1729, baptised February 23, 1729, James, baptised October 29, 1730, and Margaret Ann born December 31, 1732. The little that is known of all save the first-born of these children is quickly told. David seems to have been the favorite brother of Dr. Witherspoon. The draft of a letter written to him in 1761 by the President and seen in later years by Dr. Ashbel Green but now lost, shows that he engaged in mercantile business in the West Indies and was unfortunate. Through his older brother's influence with the Marquis of Tweeddale a lieutenancy was obtained for him on a British warship of 60 guns in which he sailed once more for the West Indies, and there he disappears from record. The President's son David was named after him—"your namesake is a comely thriving boy," says the letter already alluded to, "he is to be weaned in a few weeks." It will be seen later that the nephew shared his uncle's spirit of adventure and to some degree also his fate of unsolved mystery.

Susan Witherspoon married James French who was for nearly thirty years master of the High School at Edinburgh and their son James was at one time the tutor of Sir Walter Scott. Of Josias, all we have is a personal relic in the remnant of President Witherspoon's library at Princeton in the shape of a volume of Buchanan's poems bearing the inscription in a hand as boyish as its spelling is uncouth: "Josias Wederspan his Bugha nan Psalms febreyary on a seterday 1740." Of James nothing is known save that he died before November, 1744; and of Margaret Ann the sole records are the date of her birth and a casual mention of her in President Witherspoon's letter of 1761 to his brother David.

As for the father of this family, the Reverend James Witherspoon of Gifford, the sources of information besides being fragmentary are also conflicting. In general he is said to have filled his charge with exemplary fidelity. According to Dr. Samuel Stanhope Smith, who wrote the memoir for Dr. Rodgers' funeral sermon on President Witherspoon, and whose source of information must originally have been the President himself, the Reverend James Witherspoon was notable for his piety and for the accurate learning displayed in his writings and pulpit utterances, a statement evidently borrowed by the author of the memoir of Dr. Witherspoon in the Edinburgh *Christian Instructor* of October 1829.[10] But how much this filial opinion is indebted for its tone to a dutiful observance of the fifth commandment, or how far it may be trusted as a critical judgment, we have no sermons or other writings of the Reverend James Witherspoon whereby to judge. The only comment on him as a preacher is an early one by the celebrated Robert Wodrow, who under date of May 13, 1728, writing from Edinburgh, mentions Mr. Witherspoon preaching there during a meeting of the General Assembly.[11] His text was the significant one "Contend earnestly for the truth," and he very naturally introduced Assembly topics into his discourse; but, ignoring his obvious authority for proper warmth, he "explained very softly, and much overlooked earnestness, recommending moderation and charity. Those who were mistaken, said he, may yet be right at heart; such as preach nowadays are sure to be misunderstood by one side or the other," and, adds Mr. Wodrow feelingly, "it's no desirable province." From this fleeting glimpse one infers that the minister of Gifford was a peaceable man, not eager in wrangle and dispute, theological or otherwise. In later years, if one may put any trust in a

---

[10] The memoir is signed by "Presbyterian of the West" and is dated from Paisley. Ashbel Green's manuscript life of Dr. Witherspoon shows that the author was Thomas Crichton of Paisley.

[11] *Correspondence, Wodrow Society,* Edinburgh, 1843, vol. III, p. 365.

youthful impression, this peace-loving disposition got somewhat
the better of him and developed into slothfulness. The portrait
of Mr. Witherspoon in the autobiography of Dr. Alexander Carlyle—"Jupiter" Carlyle of Scottish ecclesiastical history—is anything but flattering. But figs do not grow on thistles, and in more
ways than one Dr. Carlyle was a very Scotch thistle. Flattery is
not to be sought in his pages, and least of all when he is commenting on his early contemporaries. Principal Tulloch has pointed
out that Dr. Carlyle's portraits are rough character sketches
thrown out as it were off-hand, rather than attempts at elaborate
description. But this view while charitable does not take into
consideration Dr. Carlyle's avowed intentions. He began his
autobiography when almost a decade past his alloted three-score
years and ten, and in his opening paragraph declares that, having observed how "carelessly and consequently how falsely" history is written, he intends to set down certain facts within his
knowledge for the use of the future historian, "to keep him within the bounds of truth and certainty." The venerable author fell
foul of the very bounds he had erected, for a strict regard for
"truth and certainty" leads inevitably to the suspicion that some
of his early recollections are of dubious reliability. With this caution in mind we may then read that when, during his undergraduate days, young Carlyle was wont to go to Gifford manse in the
summer to visit his college-mate John Witherspoon, the two boys
used to fish all day under the trees that arched Gifford Water, in
order to be out of reach of the Reverend James "who was very
sulky and tyrannical, but who being much given to gluttony, fell
asleep early, and went always to bed early, and being fat as a
porpoise was not to be awaked so that," continues the breathless
sentence, "we had three or four hours of liberty every night to
amuse ourselves with the daughters of the family and their cousins who resorted to us from the village when the old man was
gone to rest." Again, Dr. Carlyle recollects that in 1744 when he
was entering his ministerial career, and according to custom had
to visit the clergy of Haddington Presbytery singly for examination before admission to trials for a charge, he went to Gifford to
call on Mr. Witherspoon. But besides having very few topics to
examine on, the ponderous gentleman, we are told, was too lazy

to engage in anything so arduous as the examination of a divinity student—"how to eat and drink and sleep being his sole care, though he was not without parts, if the soul had not been buried under a mountain of flesh." On the other hand it should be noted that in this very year, 1744, Mr. Witherspoon was appointed to a royal chaplaincy, a post with more honor perhaps than salary, but nevertheless a post of some distinction. He was frequently sent to the General Assembly and usually placed on important committees, and in 1742 he preached the annual sermon before the Lord High Commissioner. The manuscript session record of Yester parish has preserved for us a characteristic of his methods. He was accustomed to note therein the name of each Sunday's preacher with the text used, and thus is revealed his own but by no means exceptional habit of delivering a series of sermons from the same text. For instance, on Romans viii,33, he preached eight successive Sundays, and seven on Ephesians v, 15. His son John is named for the first time as occupant of his father's pulpit on October 11, 1746, when he had been three years in the ministry. Twelve years later, on October 15, 1758, a much talked of man, the son preached in the same place for the last time during his father's incumbency. Mr. Witherspoon's constant prayer was that he might not outlive his usefulness and it is said that he prepared to preach one Sunday morning in August, 1759, was taken ill before church time, and by noon was dead. He was in his sixty-eighth year and left his eldest son his sole executor. His grave is in Gifford churchyard.[12]

The birth register of Yester parish for the beginning of the eighteenth century has followed the unknown path of the death

[12]On his tombstone now lies a memorial tablet added during the World War and bearing this inscription:
"JOHN WITHERSPOON, D.D., LL.D., SON OF THE ABOVE,
PRESIDENT OF PRINCETON, NEW JERSEY, U.S.A.,
MEMBER OF CONGRESS AND
SIGNER OF THE DECLARATION OF INDEPENDENCE 1776.
BORN IN THE MANSE HERE 5 FEBRUARY 1723
AND DIED IN HIS ADOPTED COUNTRY 15 NOVEMBER 1794.
AN UPHOLDER OF LIBERTY
HIS LIFE NOW TAKES ON
A NEW SIGNIFICANCE 1918."
The story of the recovery of Mr. Witherspoon's grave and of the addition of the inscription quoted above is told in the *Princeton Alumni Weekly* of January 22, 1919.

register; but happily the parish baptismal record is preserved at His Majesty's Register House in Edinburgh, and from it we learn that John Witherspoon was baptised at Gifford on February 10, 1723, the date of birth not being given. There appears to be no documentary authority for the traditional birth-date, February 5, 1722, adopted in all but one of the sketches of John Witherspoon that have come under observation. Prevalent Scottish custom required children to be baptised within two weeks of birth,—indeed usually within one week; and that the minister of Gifford should have allowed his first-born son to live over a year unchristened is incredible; such paganism would have stirred his austere parishioners to righteous indignation. February 5 may have been the day of John Witherspoon's birth; the year was certainly 1723.[13]

Of his childhood we have little record. He used to say that his early training was given him by his mother, and that he was able to read the Bible at the age of four. Compelled to memorize portions of it, at one time he could repeat nearly all the New Testament; Watts' *Psalms and Hymns* were learned in the same way. Judged by modern standards he was a remarkable boy, but in the group of men who gave distinction to eighteenth century Scotland he was not exceptional. His home life and training were probably not very different from that of hundreds of boys of his generation, save that as a parish minister's eldest son his future was more carefully planned. Precocious he may have been; a prig he was not. If the heather hills left on his mind no mark, and Scottish woodlands had for him no spell,—none at least to be reflected later in his writings—yet he knew the charm of angling in running waters; somehow he learned Scotland's ancient and honorable game; mastered also the tricks of curling; and the passage

[13] The Rev. John Thomson, author of the article on the parish of Yester in the *New Statistical Account of Scotland by the Ministers of the respective Parishes*, (Edinburgh, 1845), was the first to call attention to the error in the traditional date. Corroboration is found curiously in an American diary. One evening in October, 1770, Dr. Ezra Stiles of Yale was President Witherspoon's host at New Haven, Conn., and drew from his guest a brief resumé of his life, recording the information in his diary. The dates of Dr. Witherspoon's matriculation at Edinburgh, of his ordination, and of his receiving an honorary degree from St. Andrews, are accurately given. The date of his birth is recorded as 1723. There seems to be no reason for assuming that this date is wrong.

already quoted from Alexander Carlyle's autobiography shows that he profited by having sisters. The clerical bent of his mind, however, must have received its first impulse at home; he was destined for the church and that marked him. And yet beneath his seeming austerity we shall find that he kept a glowing vision —a love of liberty as free as the air of the hills among which he grew up.

He was early entered at the ancient grammar school of Haddington, and as a sturdy youngster probably tramped twice each day the four miles thither from Gifford. Founded before the Reformation, the Haddington Grammar School had given John Knox, the Maitlands, the Cockburns, and other famous Scotsmen, their early education. A stone's throw from the ruined abbey and the inky Tyne, the schoolhouse still stands with the Yester coat-of-arms, a goat rampant, on each gable. Clad in a modern coat of whitewash and closely shouldered by modern buildings, it is used now as a municipal lodging house for the poor. One John Lesley was master in Witherspoon's boyhood, and during his rough and ready régime the school was typical of its kind and age. Scholars were drilled in the conventional elements of mathematics, English, and the classics, the only relief to the monotonous curriculum being the performance of plays on certain occasions, the epilogue and prologue once being written by none other than Allan Ramsay, the Shepherd Poet. Cock fights were a common sport; but the great event in the school year was the football match on Fastern's Even, in which masters and scholars all joined—the latter rejoicing savagely in their one well-earned opportunity to square accounts with their tyrannous pedagogues.

At this school, spurred on by parental admonition, young Witherspoon paid strict attention to his studies and by degrees acquired among his fellows a reputation for soundness of judgment and mental alertness due more rightly perhaps to the seriousness of his home training, and when at the age of thirteen he was pronounced ready for the University he was considered advanced for his age.

According to his own statement made to Ashbel Green in later years he understood Latin and Greek and French at this time as well as he ever did; but his youthfulness on entering the University was not extraordinary; David Hume and Principal Robertson both entered at eleven, Thomas Reid and James Beattie, the philosophers, at twelve and fourteen respectively. Destined as he was for the ministry there was but little glamor attached to his entrance into university life. It merely meant another step toward the goal set up before him, and if his heart burned with any imaginings they probably were only of the time when he should look down from the eminence of a pulpit upon the upturned faces of a listening congregation.

The arts course at Edinburgh in those days theoretically extended through four years, the first being spent in Latin, the second in Greek, the third in Logic, and the fourth in Natural Philosophy. In addition there were professors of mathematics and moral philosophy, attendance on whose lectures was optional. Thirty-odd years before, the tutorial system, whereby a professor led his pupils through the various years and finally saw them graduated, had given way to the professorial system whereby each lecturer was concerned principally with his own subject and it became nobody's business to bring the students up to graduation. They attended what courses they pleased and graduation fell into disregard. In 1704, for example, sixty-five came up for their degree, and 104 in 1705, while in 1749 the number had dropped to three. When Witherspoon went up to Edinburgh some trace of the old tutorial system was lingering in the custom of matriculating under a given professor; and so it happens that in the manuscript book of matriculations for 1704–1762 preserved in the university archives, under the formidable heading "Discipuli Domini Johanni Stevenson qui subscripserunt die vicesimosexto mensis Februarii MDCCXXXVI" may still be seen the already formed and unmistakable signature "Jo. Witherspoon." His handwriting at this time is the best evidence of his maturity.[14]

[14] In the Witherspoon Collection in the Library of Princeton University is the Horace (Utrecht, 1713) he purchased shortly before matriculation, bearing his autograph on the title-page, and on the fly-leaf this entry also in his hand: "Joannes Wederspan (written over the name *Witherspoon*) est hujus Liber Legitimus Possesor Februarii Die quarto An: Dom: Milesimo septingentismo trigesimosexto." This autograph is the earliest example of his habit of writing his name on the title-page of each book in his library.

Whatever one may think of the faculty of Edinburgh University at that time—and the general opinion is that it was made up of men able in their day like Drummond in Greek, and Stewart in natural philosophy, but now past their prime—the young student could scarcely have chosen a more inspiring instructor than Professor Stevenson. Even Alexander Carlyle grows almost enthusiastic about him. He was one of the most successful teachers of his day. Logic was the chief subject of his professorship but rhetoric had been added to it and for many years remained a part of his field of instruction, and it has been said that no one in a chair at Edinburgh did more to turn men to the love of letters. It should be remembered that English at this time was still a written and not a spoken language in Scotland. Even by the middle of the century there was plenty of work for tutors in English pronunciation. Charles Townshend, the English statesman, attending a meeting of the Select Society of Edinburgh is alleged to have slyly suggested that the Society employ an interpreter for the benefit of visitors like himself. Professor Stevenson had occupied his chair but six years when Witherspoon became his pupil; he was still in his full vigor and enthusiasm, and had not yet become the venerable figure of the touching scene depicted in Graham's *Scottish Men of Letters*.[15] His influence was the strongest, outside of family circles, that the future president of Princeton carried with him through life. Years after, when a striking similarity was noticed between Dr. Witherspoon's lectures on composition and taste and Hugh Blair's lectures on rhetoric and belles lettres, the President declared to Ashbel Green that he had never exchanged a word with his college-mate, the future rhetorician, and Dr. Green suggests with every probability of correctness that the similarity of their views was due to their common education under Professor Stevenson. To the latter's teaching may surely be traced President Witherspoon's love of good literature, his insistence on form and style, his interest in the English language, and the influence that he subsequently exerted in these directions in America.

For a village boy like him, however, in whose veins good blood was flowing but who had never enjoyed the opportunity of city

[15] p. 100.

life, residence at the capital should have exerted influences in some ways perhaps more potent, because more subtle, than even association with a rare character like Stevenson. That keen-witted combination of worldliness and piety, Alexander Carlyle, recognized these subtle influences and made the most of them— the historic traditions of the city, the benefit of meeting the world, the cultivation of taste, and the gaining of "a certain manner and address that can only be obtained at the capital." John Witherspoon would not have considered Carlyle's "manner and address" ideally ministerial; but it is probable that he never recognized the latent qualities and values of urban atmosphere. Tradition, and the romance of life in an historic city, never caught his sympathies. His sober upbringing had made him old beyond his years; he had never known the golden age; almost at a bound he had leaped from infancy into the full noon of life; since the time he had recited his prayers at his mother's knee he had been trained to remember that he was a minister's oldest son and that on his shoulders before long would fall his father's mantle; it was serious business this matter of preparing himself for such a responsibility, and little or nothing else engaged his attention while at the University. Here in part is to be sought the explanation of the sober strain that marked his character.

The university buildings at Edinburgh were wretched, looking more like almshouses than halls of learning; they were "low and ruinous," consisting of ancient dwellings remodelled into lecture halls; classrooms were small, dark, and low ceilinged.[16] Living was cheap and good; but plain though it was it did not produce high scholarship; application to study seems to have been unfashionable. Dr. Erskine in his funeral sermon on Principal Robertson gives the impression that the University at this time abounded with youths of conspicuous talent and "indefatigable application to study." The youths and their talents were there, and in a handful of cases there were indications of application to study, but evidence of a general interest in the major purpose of a university career is lacking.

Dr. Witherspoon has left no recollections of his undergraduate

[16] Principal Robertson in Graham, *Social Life in Scotland*, vol. II, p. 206.

days and our only actual knowledge of them is derived from Dr. Carlyle's autobiography. The two students lodged together in the same house, halfway down the Lawnmarket. With them were John (afterwards Colonel) and Alexander Maxwell, while Sir Harry Nisbet and John Dalrymple (afterwards Sir John of Cranstoun) used to come in to prepare their work with Carlyle's tutor. There were no better names than these on the university rolls and it may be assumed, therefore that young Witherspoon's social standing was unassailable. He took virtually the same studies as Carlyle though not always under the same instructor, and in view of his subsequent academic work in America we may glance for a moment at the course of study they pursued.

Carlyle's recollection is that the first year was spent in the humanities class under Professor Kerr, continuing his Latin and beginning higher mathematics with Euclid. Being an exceptional Greek student he seems to have dropped that subject. In his second year besides continuing mathematics with Professor McLaurin and attending Kerr's private Latin class in which Juvenal and Tacitus were read and the "beauties and peculiarities of the Latin tongue were opened up," he joined Professor Stevenson's class in logic and rhetoric, reading at 8 a.m., Aristotle's *Poetics* and Longinus *On the Sublime*, and at 11 a.m., Heineccius' *Logic* and an abridgement of Locke's *Essay*. At 2 p.m., Stevenson read to his class a "compendious history" of ancient philosophy. Examination or quizzes in all subjects were held thrice a week. Carlyle took French instead of Greek, and during the session the class advanced so well that its members learned to read French easily, and actually prepared Molière's *Médecin malgré lui* for performance on the college stage, though the play was not given. Young Witherspoon, as we have seen, had learned French before coming to Edinburgh. His father is said to have been a close student of the French Calvinist writers and from him the boy received his knowledge of the language.

In his third year at the University, besides continuing McLaurin's mathematics and Kerr's private Latin class, Carlyle attended Sir Robert Stewart's lectures on natural philosophy and took up dancing, the *Spectator* having recently led his father to think that a course in dancing would make him more graceful in

[16]

the pulpit. Young Witherspoon, however, being a minister's son of the stricter sort, was not allowed to use this interesting but profane method of acquiring the grace that his Creator had neglected to give him.

The fourth year was spent in moral philosophy and mathematics, to which McLaurin was adding astronomy and a course of experiments in mechanics, with a few general lectures in natural philosophy to make up the deficiencies of Sir Robert Stewart's course, deficiencies due to the old age of the professor. Carlyle then joined the class in divinity and found the professors very "dull and Dutch and prolix." They formed no school of theology but preferred to allow their students to do their own thinking, a practice which is adduced as the reason for the advanced views and liberal accomplishments of the younger Scottish clergy of the time. A sixth year having been spent in divinity, finally in his seventh winter at Edinburgh Carlyle delivered a Latin discourse and was graduated in theology.

In general, this course was the one followed by Witherspoon though with one marked difference at the conclusion of its undergraduate portion. The University, as has been said, had abandoned the tutorial system for the professorial or lecture system, with the result that each student attended only such lectures as he pleased, and graduation with its attendant Master's degree had come to be considered of no importance. In November, 1738, Witherspoon and four fellow students, one of whom was Hugh Blair, represented to Principal Wishart and some of the professors that they desired to receive their degrees and to that end were willing to print theses and defend them in public. Grasping at any idea howsoever novel or even revolutionary to rescue graduation from its discredit, the authorities, far from resenting this undergraduate suggestion, willingly agreed to allow their petitioners to earn their degrees as proposed; and in order to encourage others to adopt the same course they further agreed to remit for such students certain university fees. On February 23, 1739, accordingly, in the university common hall before a large audience attracted by the novelty of the occasion, each of the five theses in Latin was defended by its author and impugned by the other four candidates. Witherspoon's dissertation of twelve quarto pages had for its subject *De Mentis Immortalitate* and was dedicated to the Marquis of Tweeddale. The most remarkable thing about the production in modern eyes would probably be the fact that its author had just passed his sixteenth birthday. On February 26, 1739, three years to a day from the date of his matriculation, he was laureated Master of Arts.

Of his personality at this period Dr. Carlyle's autobiography, which is again our only source of information, says that although he was a good scholar and a very sensible and shrewd boy, yet he had a disagreeable temper, a flat voice, and an awkward manner, "which prevented his making an impression on his companions of either sex that was at all adequate to his ability." Carlyle further asserts that these defects remained with him and so roused his envy that they forced him to "take a road to distinction very different from that of his more successful companions."

It is generally agreed that President Witherspoon's voice was poor, and that he was not a graceful speaker; and it is also true that his road to distinction was different from that of his college-mates. But Carlyle's implication that his removal to America was due to envy is altogether erroneous. Whatever one's opinion as to the comparative success of his career and those of his contemporaries at the University of Edinburgh, one fact this book, it is believed, will render finally incontrovertible—Dr. Witherspoon did not leave Scotland because of jealousy nor because he felt himself to be a prophet without honor in his own land.

On receiving his degree he remained at Edinburgh to pursue his theological studies. These he might have completed in three years and thus have received at nineteen a licence to preach, but either on the advice of his father and friends, or in deference to a rule of the Assembly which opposed such early licensure, he continued as a student over four years. Carlyle again supplies a glimpse of him here. It was the custom of divinity students of the University and the younger ministers of the district to spend their summer in East Lothian and generally to assemble at Haddington on presbytery day. Finding presbytery dinners too dreary, with their strictly limited supply of wine—two bottles for the whole company—these young men got into the habit of hiring a room for themselves at another tavern and meeting there ear-

Disputatio Philosophica,

QUAM

FAVENTE NUMINE,

Ut in artibus liberalibus & disciplinis Philosophicis magister rite renuncietur,

Ex Auctoritate Reverendi admodum VIRI,

D. *Gulielmi Wishart*, S. T. D.

Academiæ *Edinburgenæ* Præfecti,

NEC NON

Amplissimi Senatus academici, & nobilissimæ Facultatis artium decreto, Publico eruditorum examini subjiciet, ad Diem 23 *Februarii*, hora decima antemeridiana,

JOANNES WEDERSPAN, *A. & R*

EDINBURGI:
In Ædibus Jo. PAXTON, M. DCC. XXXIX.

ly in the afternoon, and with other ministers dropping in, used to keep up until bedtime what they called an "enlightened conversation." The discussions we are told were entirely theological and philosophical, but there was as might be expected more freedom and friendliness than at the sedater presbytery gatherings. Witherspoon never failed to be one of the company, continues Carlyle; but the latter's impression of his fellow student at this time is no pleasanter than the earlier one. To the free and easy autobiographer Witherspoon seemed "close, and suspicious, and jealous, and always aspiring to a superiority that he was not able to maintain." The accuracy of this impression is impeached by Carlyle's admission that he remained on intimate terms with him and was glad enough to continue his visits to Gifford to spend the days fishing and the evenings with sisters and cousins. In return he used to invite his alleged disagreeable companion to his own home at Prestonpans. The society of the fair sex Witherspoon "loved of all things," says Carlyle, and at Prestonpans he had greater opportunity to enjoy it because there were more girls, "and no restraint from an austere father," so that sixty years later, Carlyle, thinking it over, considers the "austerity of manners and aversion to social joy" which he asserts Witherspoon subsequently affected, were the "arts of hypocrisy and ambition; for he had a strong and enlightened understanding far above enthusiasm and a temper that did not seem liable to it." Whatever that last sentence may mean, one cannot help suspecting that Carlyle's entire recollection is controlled first by disapproval of Witherspoon's course in the church of Scotland, secondly by hostility to his American career, and finally by ignorance of the fact that for many years he was the victim of a nervous complaint which compelled him to keep the strictest check on himself. As a young man he could not have been altogether the churlish individual that the description implies, and Carlyle's acknowledged friendship with him during these years is the best proof thereof. Dr. Witherspoon's American contemporaries found him a distinctly sociable person, and to his death he retained the warmest friendships even in Scotland. The truth seems to be that Carlyle and Witherspoon were as different types of men as ever studied for the same profession. The one was brilliant, pleasure-loving, liberal in conduct, popular; the other was quiet, serious-minded, plain-spoken and slow of friendships. It was not extraordinary perhaps that they should have been intimate in youth; it would have been very singular had they maintained that intimacy when maturer years came on; and it was the complete dividing of their ways, a dividing that began at least spiritually in undergraduate days, with the ensuing difference of mental attitude and point of view, that misled Dr. Carlyle in his old age into leaving on record what he mistakenly considered a truthful portrait of his boyhood friend.

At Edinburgh the young divinity student met his first love, Miss Anna Hogg, a "pious and intellectual" girl who refused him her hand, but who remained single and corresponded with him regularly until his death. She it was who, after he left Scotland, kept him informed as to his family and friends and the state of religion in his native land; she rarely touched on politics and it was only when England was threatened by French invasion that she broke her curious rule and gave her correspondent a description of the political spirit of Great Britain at that time. Twelve of her letters to Witherspoon were in Dr. Green's possession when he was writing the President's biography but only one is now with the Green manuscript. The tone of that letter corroborates the general impression that Dr. Green received of her character.

In 1743 Witherspoon's theological studies at Edinburgh came to a close, and on September 6 he was licensed to preach by the Presbytery of Haddington. It is said that he was invited to assist his father at Gifford with the right to succeed him eventually, but the evidence of this invitation has not been found and it was not until three years later that he preached for the first time at Gifford, if we may trust the elder Witherspoon's manuscript parish record. The living at Beith in Ayrshire happened to be vacant, the celebrated Dr. Leechman having just left it to take at Glasgow University the chair of divinity which he was to make famous. The Earl of Eglinton, patron of the Beith living, being a minor, his mother the countess recommended John Witherspoon and three other candidates to the Presbytery of Irvine within whose jurisdiction Beith lay, that they might be called to preach "in order to give the parish a free choice and that the merit of the

preacher might be best argument of the settlement." This un-
usual procedure resulted in Witherspoon receiving the call in
January, 1745, signed by a large majority of the heritors and
elders, and consented to by a large number of heads of families.
But before he could be ordained, a protest was lodged against
him on the score of unorthodoxy. It was decided to proceed with
his trials and in March they were heard at Irvine, when he defended once more the principles of his precocious Edinburgh thesis which seems to have been the *casus belli*. Meeting approval,
and no further objection being raised to his "Doctrine, Life, or
Conversation," the date of his ordination was set for April 11,
1745. Thus at last, a young minister of 22, he found himself in
charge of a parish that dated back to the Reformation, in a
neighborhood full of romance and historic interest, yielding an
annual stipend of seventeen pounds, twelve shillings and six-
pence, and seventy-nine bolls of meal, with a glebe of thirty-one
acres hard by the village.[17]

But no parish, however romantic in associations and generous
in salary, could have entirely absorbed this vigorous young Scot.
Already he was developing into a man whose interests were not
bounded by his daily tasks, but to whom were coming calls to activity other than that for which he received a salary. He assumed
charge of his parish the victor in an ecclesiastical skirmish; he
had not been there six months before he found himself in a far
more realistic fray, and not victorious.

When in 1745 the invasion by the Young Pretender threw the
country into excitement, the loyal presbyteries of the Church of
Scotland did not hesitate to consider the matter in their sessions
and the majority passed resolutions similar to those that were
entered on the records of the Presbytery of Irvine. There we read
that on January 7, 1746, after spending considerable time in
prayer, the Presbytery proposed to follow the example of other
presbyteries and agree upon a method of signalizing their abhorrence of the rebellion:

Upon which the Presbytery unanimously Resolved, primo, to do all
in their power for influencing such as are within their Bounds to exert

[17] Sir John Sinclair, *Statistical Account of Scotland*, Edinburgh, 1793, vol. VIII, p. 316.

themselves in support of the present Government; Secundo, That they will in conjunction with their own parishes contribute for raising some Volunteers for that purpose if it be found necessary; Tertio, if the Duke of Cumberland shall come to Scotland, They will, on being informed thereof, meet to appoint some to wait upon him,

and a committee was appointed to notify the other members of the meeting.

Needing only some such ecclesiastical countenance as this, the young pastor, whose ancestral fighting blood had been stirring within him since the first news of the rebellion, drew up on behalf of the owners and tenants of the barony of Broadstone in his parish, a subscription paper for the purpose of defraying the expenses of a party of Beith militia, at the head of which he proposed to march to Stirling to join the royal forces, "for the support of our religion and liberty, and in defence of our only rightful, and lawful Sovereign, King George, against his enemies engaged in the present rebellion." [18]

The amount he collected was eighty-eight pounds fifteen shillings, and the militia men, to the number of about a hundred and fifty, were engaged to serve thirty days from the date of their departure from Beith. But on reaching Glasgow, they were informed by the military authorities that their services would not be needed and that they might retrace the twenty miles home. Nevertheless their leader did not propose to go thus far and have the experience come to naught. Dismissing his little band, he pushed on to the scene of conflict, accompanied by his beadle bearing a trusty sword, still preserved and dearly prized by that gentleman's descendants. And on January 17, 1746, these two indispensable officers of the parish of Beith appeared as spectators at the battle of Falkirk. It was no fault of the minister that he was not a participant in the fray, and his companion was evidently not less willing; but he had only himself to thank for the predicament in which he fell before the day was done. The warlike accoutrement of the devoted beadle gave the lie to the min-

---

[18] *Cochrane Correspondence*, p. 120 (Maitland Club Publications) Glasgow, 1836. It is said that the preamble is in Mr. Witherspoon's handwriting; a receipt for part of the money collected is signed by him.

ister's clerical garb; and, on suspicion, the Reverend Mr. Wither-spoon was seized by the Pretender's forces. For a week he was carried hither and yon until, on the twenty-fifth of January, with ten other civilians and five members of an Edinburgh company of volunteers, he was put into Castle Doune, near Stirling, as a prisoner of war. The castle was already in ruinous condition but at the top of the western tower, under the battlements, a "large, ghastly room" was found in which the prisoners were placed. At one end of the apartment were two recesses, one of which Witherspoon and the volunteers, with two Aberdonians taken as spies and threatened with halters, used as a sleeping-room. The second cell was occupied by the other seven persons who also declared that they too had come to Falkirk merely to witness the battle. Straw and blankets purchased in the village were the sole furniture the prisoners had at their disposal. Being allowed by their Highland guards to climb up on the battlements the volunteers decided to attempt escape by making a rope of their blankets and the Aberdonians agreed to join in the attempt. Mr. Witherspoon prudently declared he would see how they fared and if they were successful would probably follow. Lots were drawn for the order of descent and about one o'clock on the last night of the month, by bright moonlight the party began their effort. The first four got down safely, but the fifth "who was very tall and big, coming down in a hurry, the rope broke with him just as his feet touched the ground." The next man persisted in going down notwithstanding, and boldly dropped the twenty or thirty feet that the rope now lacked, fell on his companions, broke several ribs, and dislocated an ankle. This party got away safely, carrying the injured man to the house of a friendly farmer. The seventh had even worse luck. Seeing the accident he pulled up the rope, repaired it with blankets still left and then started down. All would have gone well had he not so thickened the rope against mischance that when he came to the repaired section his hands slipped and he fell to the ground sustaining such injuries that he shortly after died from the effects. Mr. Witherspoon did not make the venture, and a few days later his prudence received its reward in his release. The whole experience had a most serious effect on his constitution and he never fully recovered from the exposure and nervous strain. Apparently he did not care to talk about it; for instance he told Dr. Ashbel Green that he had suffered a shock to his nerves soon after ordination but he never related the circumstances, and Dr. Green did not know the Castle Doune story until he read it long after in the sketch of the President in the *Christian Instructor*. For at least three years after this adventure Mr. Witherspoon had a nervous affection of the most distressing kind which sometimes took the form of a sudden and overwhelming presentiment in the midst of a service that he would not live to finish his task; and he told Ashbel Green that he would not have felt able to persevere in his chosen calling except for his father's urging and insistence. During the rest of his life his nerves were easily disturbed.

On his release from Castle Doune he hastened back to his anxious parish, arriving in time to endorse with a very genuine earnestness the resolution adopted by the Presbytery of Irvine on February 11, 1746, appointing a committee to wait on the Duke of Cumberland and inform him "how joyful it is to the presbytery that His Grace is come to our country to oppose the present Rebellion," and to wish him all safety and success. A month later when it was reported that written commissions were necessary before humble members of a Scottish presbytery could gain access to an English duke, the commissions were drawn and Mr. Witherspoon was added to the delegation. Thirty years were to elapse before he was to have his next military experience and in the meantime he was to acquire a more appropriate reputation in the less sanguinary arena of ecclesiastical conflict.

True to his early training he seems to have been a hard student at Beith if we may trust the traditions gathered by one of his biographers. The number of books he bought and the number of candles he burned were the source of much local comment. But he was no mere bookworm; he was a good horseman and golfer; he still went fishing; and he had the reputation of being the best clerical curler Beith had ever seen.

On September 2, 1748, two and a half years after the Castle Doune adventure, he was married to Miss Elizabeth Montgom-

ery, daughter of Robert Montgomery of Craig House, near
Beith. She was twenty-seven and he twenty-five years of age.[19]

[19] There were ten children by this marriage: (1) Anne or Ann, born at Beith, July 23,
1749, died April 1, 1817, at Princeton, N. J.; (2) Christian, a daughter, born at Beith,
August 13, baptised August 14, 1750, died at Beith, December 10, 1756; (3) James,
born at Beith, November 17, 1751, died at Germantown, Pa., October 4, 1777; (4)
Robert, born at Beith, April 3, 1753, died at Beith, July 1754; (5) Barbara, born at
Beith, February 18, baptised February 20, 1756, died at Paisley, August 1, 1763; (6)
John, born and baptised at Beith, July 29, 1757, died at sea, 1795(?); (7) Frances,
born at Paisley, August 16, baptised August 26, 1759, died December 14, 1784 at
Charleston, S. C.; (8) David, born at Paisley, September 22, baptised September 27,
1760, died 1801; (9) George, born at Paisley, March, died at Paisley, July 27, 1762;
(10) a son still-born at Paisley, June 16, 1763. Parish manuscript records of Beith
and Paisley.

CHAPTER TWO

TWENTY YEARS IN THE SCOTTISH CHURCH

PRESIDENT Witherspoon's twenty years of aggressive life in the Church of Scotland can scarcely be estimated without some understanding of the conditions prevailing in that body when he entered its councils. He came on the scene at the opening of a new age in Scotland—an age which, as Professor Mathieson has pointed out, was no less remarkable on its secular side for the industrial awakening of the country than notable on the ecclesiastical side for the brilliant though short-lived triumph of liberalism, and for the sudden outburst of literary activity which was at least one reflection of that triumph and which must remain the unchallenged boast of Scottish historians.[1]

With the industrial awakening he was not immediately concerned. His interest lay in the spread of liberalism and the ensuing decadence of spirituality. But he was not blind to the literary efflorescence that marks the middle of the eighteenth century in Scotland, since the most famous names in that movement were also those of leaders in the contemporary liberal or Moderate party in the church, whose eager antagonist he became. It is an interesting fact, noted by Professor Mathieson and paralleled in literary histories other than Scotland's, that the men who carried those names were born very nearly together—Hugh Blair the critic and rhetorician, in 1718, Robertson the historian and Smollett the novelist, in 1721, John Home the poet, in 1722, Adam Smith the economist, in 1723. The exception was David Hume who was seven years older than Blair. The latter and John Home were prominent members of the Moderate party of which Robertson became the leader; while to Witherspoon, probably the brainiest man in the Popular party, as the opponents of the Moderates were called, fell the distinction of heading the opposition.

When, in 1747, Witherspoon sat for the first time in St. Giles as a member of the General Assembly, Francis Hutcheson, the

[1] W. L. Mathieson, *The Awakening of Scotland*, Glasgow, 1910, preface.

[26]

philosopher whom he was to handle so severely later and who was to remain his favorite object of attack, had but recently died, leaving behind him the fruitful memory of brilliant lectures whose easy optimism, born of the Earl of Shaftesbury's teachings, was revolutionizing religious thought and life among the younger generation of ministers; Hume had issued his *Essays Moral and Political* and was reading the proofs of his *Essay concerning the Human Understanding*; John Home was writing his first tragedy; Robertson was filling notebooks with materials for his first historical work; Adam Ferguson, as chaplain of the Black Watch, was not yet the popular lecturer on ethics but was gaining first hand acquaintance with that civil society whose historian he was to become; Hugh Blair was beginning to draw crowds to hear his polished discourses—discourses that Dr. Samuel Johnson declared he loved, even though their "dog of an author" was a "Scotchman and a presbyterian and everything he should not be;" Adam Smith was lecturing on literature but musing over the principles he was soon to lay down in his *Wealth of Nations*; and Thomas Reid was preparing to publish his *Inquiry into the Human Mind on the Principles of Common Sense*, the philosophy of which Witherspoon was to be the leading early exponent in America. Remembered now chiefly as historic milestones in the progress of human intelligence, these names and others like them[2] show that literary activity was in the air, that a creative spirit was abroad, in other words that Moderatism in this respect was only another expression of the general stir of intellectual liberty of the eighteenth century.

But the vitality of a Church is not to be estimated by its output of literature, least of all if that literature be almost entirely secular. It was the effect of this activity on the ancient spirit of the Church that called into life the criticism of the conservative Popular party—and this was the party with which by birth, by early training, and by conviction Dr. Witherspoon on entering the Church allied himself. He had no quarrel with good literature —he had listened to John Stevenson too attentively for that; but he refused to admit that the pulpit was the place for its exploitation.

[2] Fuller lists may be found in Mathieson and Grahame.

By fostering a taste for refinement and polite learning, and by substituting the preaching of a pure morality for doctrinal and evangelistic sermons, Professor Hutcheson, according to some critics,[3] had attempted to make the Church a more attractive career for the sons of the upper classes who had been steadily deserting it for other walks in life. But in the eyes of the older generation he had succeeded only in sensualizing and degrading the ancient teachings and in producing a type of younger ministers who were sadly different from their fathers.

Witherspoon, in a satire presently to be noticed, attacked the general influence of Hutcheson, and held up to ridicule the contemporary tendency toward intellectual superficiality. He had heard a clergyman say that any student might get in six weeks as much divinity as he would ever need; everything was now "more compendiously taught, and more superficially understood, than formerly. . . . In the very mechanic arts, laborious diligence gives way to elegance and ease. . . . Every year gives us a shorter method of learning some branch of knowledge. In short, in these last days the quintessence of everything has been extracted, and is presented us, as it were, in little phials. . . . Agreeable to all this, have we not seen," he asked, "many students of divinity, brought up in hot-beds, who have become speakers in General Assemblies, and strenuous supporters of a falling church, before their beards were grown, to the perfect astonishment of an observing world."

It seems harsh to say, as Professor Mathieson implies, that the Popular party proposed to saddle the awakening energies of Scottish literature and art with the incubus of theological nightmare and the fanaticism of an earlier age.[4] Witherspoon's party believed that sermons should be more than graceful expositions of morality, or opportunities for quotations of poetry, and that the Christian Church and especially that branch to which he belonged, irrevocably stood for certain great dogmas which no amount of progress, intellectual or material, and no hunger however keen for literature could permit ministers of the Church to ignore in their pulpits. It was this ignoring or glossing of fun-

[3] e.g., McCosh, *Scottish Philosophy*, pp. 67, 82.
[4] Mathieson, p. 199.

damental dogmas and the general lowering of the ancient standards of personal conduct that shocked the stauncher adherents
of orthodox faith. In other words, once more was being fought
the eternal feud between the old and the new, between the ancient theology, the fanaticism if one insists, of a sterner generation and the newer, more comfortable philosophy of a more cul-
tured age. The ministers of the new school were looked upon with
suspicion; they were called not unfairly "paganized Christian divines;" it is even admitted that as a class they were humanists
rather than divines, citizens rather than churchmen, men of the
world rather than dogmatic preachers.[5]

On the other hand as Dr. McCosh[6] remarks it must also be admitted that their opponents, the evangelicals of the Popular
party, in opposing the culture and liberal sentiments of the Moderates came perilously near to proving themselves incapable of
appreciating the apostle's command to follow whatsoever things
are true and honest, just and pure, lovely and of good report.
The difficulty was that they could not see any trace of these
qualities in the Moderate preaching and manner of life.

But Moderatism had another side. Not only was it allied to
the intellectual spirit of the times, not only was it productive of
relaxed personal religious life and a more complacent attitude
toward fundamental Presbyterian doctrine, but it was an ecclesiastical policy whose chief instrument was the enforcement of
the obnoxious law of patronage. This was the law that placed the
disposition of church livings in the hands of patrons. The patronage party was growing stronger each year as more ministers,
who were accepted beneficiaries of the system, came into the Assembly,[7] while the people on the other hand were growing more
obstinate for what they claimed to be their right to choose their
own spiritual shepherds. Each session of the Assembly, therefore,
became the scene of debate and oratory that in brilliance compared favorably, so we are told, with the speaking in the Houses
of Parliament at London. But at synod meetings the surround-

[5] Mathieson, pp. 197, 240.
[6] *Scottish Philosophy*, p. 87.
[7] In 1769 the number of benefices in the Scottish Church exceeded 900. Mathieson, p. 146.

ings were less imposing and proceedings less decorous. Samuel Davies, the trustee and later president of the College of New Jersey, was a visitor at the meeting of the Synod of Lothian and Tweedale in the spring of 1754 and comments in his diary on the "prodigious ferment" of the session, expressing his surprise and grief at the altercations, the "intolerably severe reflections" passed, and the "inhumanity and persecution" he witnessed; there appeared to be, said he, but little of the spirit of serious Christianity among the younger clergy. The effect of the struggle that was going on fell most heavily of course on the parishes themselves. Not only are the minutes of the General Assembly and of the Synods for that period records of bitter wrangles and of tactics that savor more of ward politics than churchly procedure, but much of the contemporary history of Scottish parishes reveals a state of affairs little short of amazing. We read of ministers forced on parishes by aid of armed soldiery, of bloody riots at attempted inductions, of heresy charges discouraged, of ministers guilty of immoralities going unpunished while others were deposed for obedience to conscientious scruples against countenancing inductions unwanted by parishes. One has but to glance over the pages of a volume like Graham's *Scottish Men of Letters of the Eighteenth Century*, or Dr. Carlyle's *Autobiography* to feel that, whatever the rank and file of the clergy were doing, many if not most of the ablest and most prominent ministers of the day were leading lives scarcely marked by what the world ordinarily understands as piety. And yet these were the men whose writings undeniably added lustre to Scotland's name. There seems just ground, therefore, for the criticisms of the Popular party.

The Moderates advocated the supremacy of church authority and the strict exercise of the Church's judicial powers, and in the Assembly at Edinburgh upheld the steady support of the law of patronage, while in Parliament at Westminster they petitioned for its repeal. Patronage had long been unpopular. By an Act of 1592 the patron of a vacant parish could present to the presbytery any person duly qualified as a minister, and the presbytery was compelled to ordain and settle him after certain trials and examinations had been undergone, and provided there were no technical objections to his personal character and doctrine. The fate of Presbyterianism during the Restoration developed a spirit of independence which made it difficult for ministers, after the Revolution of 1689 had restored Presbyterianism and patronage, to return to the old order of things. Appreciating the new feeling, the church courts did not altogether disregard the law but contrived to render it largely ineffectual by declaring that a presentee must have a "call" from the parish before he could accept the charge, and the whole attitude of the Church grew to be, in the words of Dugald Stewart, one that "implied a greater respect for the call than the presentation." The call did not have to be unanimous nor even that of a majority. Each case seems to have depended on the strength and violence of the opposition; and favoring the opposition, presbyteries were sometimes declining to settle appointees even in the face of orders from their synods.

The crying need of better stipends and the refusal of Parliament to give this need consideration because of the laxness of the Scottish Church in its observance of the law, led the younger group of Moderates to advocate and enforce a tightening of the reins of government; and although the people as a whole opposed the policy, the Moderate party built up a majority in the Assembly which carried out the policy under the leadership of William Robertson, subsequently principal of the University of Edinburgh, and the historian. The policy was highhanded, but highhandedness is often not far from statesmanship. It has been said that Dr. Robertson was a man who seldom made a joke and never a blunder; and Raeburn's portrait of him at the University is in full accord with whatever truth lies in the saying. There are the clear, calm, calculating eyes with their steady unsmiling gaze, the long lean nose, the thin dry lips; even the slender hand drooping idly over the chair arm has something steel-like in its suppleness and clean-cut strength; it is what one imagines the hand of an ecclesiastic and statesman should be. This was the man who declared that if the will of the majority in the Assembly was to be openly flouted, and temporizing was to take the place of obedience, the result would inevitably be chaos and disintegration, and the Church would be exposed to the contempt and scorn of the world as a church without union, order, or discipline, destitute of strength to support its own constitution and falling into ruins by the abuse of liberty.[8]

Dr. Robertson's policy triumphed; it brought order into the Church; it crushed the revolt of the presbyteries, and for a while at least it silenced popular clamor. With its ultimate fate at the close of the century we are not here concerned; but even in the golden days of its supremacy it gradually alienated masses of people from the Establishment. By 1765, three years after Robertson openly assumed the leadership he had tacitly held for ten, and three years before Witherspoon left Scotland for good, the number of dissenters from the Establishment had grown to more than 100,000 with 1200 churches of their own.

It will have been gathered that Dr. Robertson's opponents in the Popular party were the more austere in dogma, more evangelical in the pulpit, more tender of the early piety; they fought against the blind operation of patronage, against the forcing of ministers on people who did not want them; they fought for the right of personal conscience. And at the same time that Robertson was assuming virtual though as yet unacknowledged leadership of the Moderates, Dr. Witherspoon was coming to be regarded as the champion of the Popular or orthodox party. One cannot be very wide of the mark in seeing in his enlistment on the side of the people in this slow ecclesiastical contest some presage and explanation of the attitude he was to take in the coming political struggle on the other side of the Atlantic. His attitude was already that of the American, Samuel Davies, who under date of June 15, 1754, writes in his diary:

I find a great number of the clergy and laity have of late carried church-power to an extravagant height, denying to individuals the right of judging for themselves, and insisting upon absolute universal obedience to all the determinations of the general Assembly. I heard sundry speeches in the House on this head which really surprised me. The nobility and gentry who are lay-elders, are generally high flyers; and have encroached upon the rights of the people, especially as to the choice of their own ministers. Violent settlements are enjoined by the authority of the General Assembly and there is no prospect of redress.

[8]Quoted by Dugald Stewart.

The two parties were brought face to face in what is known in Scottish ecclesiastical history as the Gillespie case, in which Mr. Thomas Gillespie, minister at Carnock, was deposed in May, 1752, by the General Assembly for allowing his conscientious scruples to keep him away from the ordination of a Mr. Andrew Richardson at Inverkeithing. The ordination had been strongly opposed by the people of the parish, and owing to this opposition the presbytery of Dumferline, to which Inverkeithing belonged, had refused to ordain Mr. Richardson, who had thereupon appealed to the Assembly. The case had come before the Assembly commission or standing committee, and after a brisk fight the presbytery had been ordered to carry out the ordination. This the presbytery did not do and at the March, 1752, meeting of the commission the issue was fairly met as to how far members of inferior judicatories were bound to give effect to the sentences of superior courts in opposition to the dictates of their private judgment and conscience. Manifestos embodying the principles at stake were issued by both sides. The Moderates asserted that the presbytery had not carried out the commission's injunction, a fact which was promptly acknowledged. But when a vote of censure was put, the Moderates could not control a majority and the vote failed of passage. Thereupon they gave notice that they would protest to the Assembly itself and would publish their *Reasons for Dissent* from the commission's failure to censure. The Popular majority at once appointed a committee to draw up their *Answers to the Reasons for Dissent.* The two pamphlets duly appeared, and for those who are sufficiently interested in Scottish ecclesiastical history to wish to examine in detail the differences between the two parties, these manifestos are among the earliest and most authoritative as well as the most eloquent expositions of the principles under controversy. Dr. Robertson is believed to have written the manifesto of the Moderates, while Dr. Witherspoon, though not a member of the committee in charge, was mainly responsible for that of the Popular party. In the Assembly that May, Robertson carried the day, and when a scapegoat was sought on whom the new policy of vigorous rebuke should be inflicted, Mr. Gillespie, a devout and innocuous member of the rebellious presbytery, was deposed for disobedience to the mandate of the Assembly. By many the action was considered unwarranted and cruel. Sermons were preached on it; prayers were offered on the issue involved; the case was discussed in every presbytery, and synod, and manse; and an unsuccessful effort was made to reinstate the victim.

Dr. Robertson's ascendancy had now begun. Until his time none but men of advanced age and established reputation rose to address the Assembly unless called on by the moderator. This tacit closure deterred if it did not actually prevent younger men from speaking. Before the meeting of the Assembly of 1751 Robertson, Carlyle, Home, Blair, and others at a secret conclave had resolved to fight leniency in a case of censure, and when the case came up Robertson broke through the ice of tradition and unbidden by the moderator addressed the Assembly and was followed by the other younger men of his side. From that moment we are told debate became freer and keener. Dr. Witherspoon's reference to beardless divinity students speaking in the General Assembly has already been mentioned; it was not misunderstood in the General Assembly.

He had come strongly into prominence for the first time by preaching that year's annual sermon before the Lord High Commissioner. The opportunity to strike a blow for the Popular party was approaching. Early in 1753 appeared an anonymous pamphlet entitled *A Just View of the Constitution of the Church of Scotland* defending the Assembly's action in the Gillespie case and vindicating the policy of the Moderates. It purported to represent a certain set of ministers as agitators of the people and as acting not on conscience but on love of popularity. It was asserted in the pamphlet that Mr. Gillespie's presbytery was supported and countenanced in its disobedience by ministers who had little or no claim to esteem and it was hinted that the action of the commissioners in not censuring "was manufactured in a certain place and by certain hands, while others were employed as the dupes to propose and support it." Vague though the allusion was it was generally conceded to be aimed at Dr. Alexander Webster of Edinburgh, an orthodox leader, and a warm friend of Witherspoon, as the "manufacturer," and at Witherspoon himself as one of the "dupes." The latter had been a close observer of the state of affairs in the Church, and as we have seen had already taken his stand. He had further been revolving in his mind a sketch of the various parties in religion and learning in Scotland, but this notion had gradually faded during 1751 and 1752 before the conviction that religious interest was waning in the churches, and moreover that a public neglect of religion was resulting from the abuse of church authority in the rebuking and disposition of ministers who did not think themselves in conscience at liberty to assist in the ordination of pastors who had no willing people. Perceiving how the wind was blowing in the General Assembly, he resolved to attack the other side with the subtler weapon of ridicule by publishing a satirical description of its policy and methods, and in May, 1753, he had intended to put forth a half sheet of "moderate" maxims under the ironical title of *A List of Self Evident Truths*. But the appearance of the attack on Dr. Webster and himself led him to give up his original plan and to expand his "List" into a pamphlet of *Ecclesiastical Characteristics* which was published anonymously at Glasgow.[9]

Moderation, the author declares in a preliminary paragraph, is an excellent thing and particularly the noblest character of a churchman; and it is no small presage of the glorious and blessed state of the Church that so many of our young men are "smitten with love of moderation and generally burn with desire to appear in that noble and divine character." This has inspired him with the ambition of training up in this most useful of all sciences as many as desire it. But there is no complete system of moderation in print. He had "earnestly intreated several of the most eminent men of the moderate stamp among us, those burning and shining lights of our Church," to undertake the preparation of such a guide; but one and all were "so busied in acting moderation, that they could not have time to write upon it." Besides what would become of us "if any of the expert steersmen of this ecclesiastical vessel of ours should retire from the helm?" Hence he will proceed with the task himself and enumerate all the maxims upon which moderate men conduct themselves, with an "illustration

[9] The introduction to the Glasgow edition of 1754 states that the first edition appeared in October, 1753. The essay was noticed, however, in the September issue of the *Scots Magazine*, (vol. XV, p. 472).

and confirmation" of each. He warns his readers that he will make but very little use of Scripture, because "that is contrary to some of the maxims themselves."

Maxim I lays down the fundamental proposition that "All ecclesiastical persons, of whatever rank, whether principals of colleges, professors of divinity, ministers, or even probationers, that are suspected of heresy are to be esteemed men of great genius, vast learning, and uncommon worth; and are by all means to be supported and protected." The discussion of this opening broadside is full of direct hits; of which the casual remark that "I never knew moderate men in my life that did not love and honor a heretic," may be taken as a specimen.

Maxim II declares that "When any man is charged with loose practices or tendencies to immorality, he is to be screened and protected as much as possible; especially if the faults laid to his charge be, as they are incomparably well termed in a sermon preached by a hopeful youth that made some noise lately, 'good humoured vices.'"

Maxim IV states the rules for the moderate preacher; his subjects must be confined to social duties; he must recommend them only from natural considerations, viz., the beauty and comely proportions of virtue, and its advantage in the present life, without any regard to a future state of more extended self interest; his authorities must be drawn from heathen writers, none, or as few as possible, from Scripture, and finally he must be very unacceptable to the common people.

Maxim VI asserts that "It is not only unnecessary for a moderate man to have much learning, but he ought to be filled with a contempt of all kinds of learning but one, which is, to understand Leibnitz's scheme well; the chief parts of which are so beautifully painted and so harmoniously sung by Lord Shaftesbury, and which have been so well licked into form and method by the late immortal Mr. Hutcheson." These references to authorities gives Mr. Witherspoon the opportunity to "subjoin a short catalogue of the most necessary and useful books, the thorough understanding of which will make a truly learned moderate man." To give further proof of his deep concern for the edification of ingenuous youth, he has extracted "the sum and substance of the above library" and presents it to the world "under a name which is not without a meaning, though not intelligible to all"—his "Athenian Creed," which is worth quoting in full:

I believe in the beauty and comely proportions of Dame Nature, and in almighty Fate, her only parent and guardian; for it hath been most graciously obliged (blessed be its name) to make us all very good.

I believe that the universe is a huge machine, wound up from everlasting by necessity, and consisting of an infinite number of links and chains, each in a progressive motion towards the zenith of perfection, and meridian of glory; that I myself am a little glorious piece of clockwork, a wheel within a wheel, or rather a pendulum in this grand machine, swinging hither and thither by the different impulses of fate and destiny; that my soul (if I have any) is an imperceptible bundle of exceeding minute corpuscles, much smaller than the finest Holland sand; and that certain persons in a very eminent station, are nothing else but a huge collection of necessary agents, who can do nothing at all.

I believe that there is no ill in the universe, nor any such thing as virtue absolutely considered; that those things vulgarly called sins, are only errors in the judgment, and foils to set off the beauty of Nature, or patches to adorn her face; that the whole race of intelligent beings, even the devils themselves (if there are any) shall finally be happy; so that Judas Iscariot is by this time a glorified saint, and it is good for him that he hath been born.

In fine, I believe in the divinity of L. S———, the saintship of Marcus Antoninus, the perspicuity and sublimity of A———e, and the perpetual duration of Mr. H———n's works, notwithstanding their present tendency to oblivion. Amen.

After Maxim VII has informed us that "A moderate man must endeavor as much as he handsomely can, to put off any appearance of devotion, and avoid all unnecessary exercise of religious worship, whether public or private," Maxim VIII gets at the heart of one phase of the problem in the Scottish Church by informing us that "In church settlements, which are the principal causes that come before ministers for judgment, the only thing to be regarded is, who the patrons and the great and noble heritors are for; the inclinations of the common people are to be utterly despised."

"Thus," concludes the author after thirteen maxims, of which those quoted are fair examples,

I have laid down and illustrated these excellent maxims, not without labour and expense of thought; and I think carried them so far as to make a complete system for the education and accomplishment of a moderate clergyman, for his guidance in public judgment, and his direction as to private practise. And now, courteous reader, as a traveller after having gone through the different parts of a country ascends some eminence to review the whole, let us stand still and rejoice over the happy state of our mother-church of Scotland, in which moderation so greatly prevails; and let us rejoice in hope of what improvements she may yet arrive at, by adhering to these maxims, now digested into such admirable form and order. O what noble, sublime, and impenetrable sermons shall now be preached! What victories and triumphs shall be obtained over the stupid populace by forced settlements, which never have such a beautiful and orderly form as when finished by soldiers, marching in comely array, with shining arms, a perfect image of the church-militant! And what perfectly virtuous and sinless lives shall be led by these clergy, who with steady eyes, regard the good of this vast whole, which never yet went wrong! There is nothing indeed that any way tarnishes the beauty of this prospect but the miscarriage of the augmentation scheme over which I could now lament in elegiac strains but that my hope is not yet quite extinct; for who can tell whether when we shall have driven away the whole common people to the Seceders who alone are fit for them, and captivated the hearts of the gentry to a love of our solitary temples, they may not be pleased to allow us more stipends, because we shall have nothing to do but to spend them?

Nothing could have succeeded better. The satire was the sensation of the hour. It took the Popular party by storm and went into edition after edition. The Moderates gnashed their teeth in wrath; they called the unknown author all manner of opprobrious names; threatenings and slaughter were breathed against him; the pamphlet was contrary to the interests of religion; no good man could have written such a thing; it was the work of an evil heart, a firebrand, a violent and contentious person, a man unfit to be a member of any peaceable society. Even a few of the Popular party were not quite sure that they should give it countenance though it made them chuckle with glee in their low-roofed cottages. As one good soul expressed the doubt: "Alas! would it not have been better to have had recourse to prayer than satire?" The minister of Beith was the last man to doubt the efficacy of prayer, but he also had good scriptural authority for the belief that there is a time for everything, and from his point of view this was not exactly the time for prayer. So the sales went on. The second edition appeared in the middle of December, 1753, a second "corrected and enlarged" edition in 1754, a third with an additional maxim in May, 1754, an edition is mentioned in the *Gentleman's Magazine* as published in London in September, 1754, a fourth in February, 1755, the fifth in 1763 and the sixth in 1765, the seventh edition appeared in 1767, and finally in 1842 still another, making, exclusive of a Dutch translation, ten editions, of which the first five appeared in two years. Its authorship was never acknowledged in print by Dr. Witherspoon, even the *Apology* of 1767 being anonymous. To be sure, in 1765 when his London publisher issued his *Essays on Important Subjects* and included the satire and its defence, the title-page of the former states that they were inserted by the publishers and are only "generally ascribed to the same Author" as the essays; and in his preface to the volume Mr. Witherspoon says that "the liberty which the publishers seem resolved to take of adding to this collection two anonymous Treatises is what I could not prevent; and therefore if there be anything in them improper or offensive, they alone are to answer for it." It was left to American printers, the Bradfords of Philadelphia, in their edition of 1767 to place the author's name unequivocally on the title-page; but as late as 1774 Scottish conservatism, crystallized in William Gray, the Edinburgh publisher, was still listing *Ecclesiastical Characteristics* and its *Apology* among anonymous publications and separately from the other works of their then well-known author. The Bodleian Catalogue for some now inscrutable reason ascribed both to "the Reverend Mr. Buchanan of Somersetshire."

In Scotland the satire made too palpable a hit to remain long in anonymity. The fact that it was from Witherspoon's pen soon leaked out. "There is a piece published," wrote Mr. Samuel Davies in his diary in June, 1754, "under the title of 'Ecclesiastical Characteristics,' ascribed to one Mr. Witherspoon, a young minister. It is a burlesque upon the high flyers under the ironical name of moderate men; and I think the humour is nothing inferior to Dean Swift." In some quarters it was declared, however, that Witherspoon had merely aided in its composition, lacking the skill to be its sole author.

Hard hit though they were, the Moderates were too discreet to attempt any reply; but it gave a country schoolmaster and student of divinity in Edinburgh University, Andrew Moir by name, cause to think that he could benefit the reading public by an attempt at authorship. He called his production a *Letter to the Author of the Ecclesiastical Characteristics* and had it printed at Glasgow in the spring of 1754. It purports to be written by the president of a club of Moderate divinity students and describes their mode of life under the maxims of Witherspoon's satire. Allusions to the members are pointed by initials now unidentifiable.[10] Mr. Moir had read Witherspoon's production with delight and in his own effort attempted to gild the lily. Dreary, if not pathetic, reading at best, it deserved little but contempt when it appeared; but the initials whetted public curiosity and caused somewhat of a stir, much to the satisfaction of its impulsive author who had made no secret of his authorship. For his pains he was expelled from the University and also from the Presbytery of Edinburgh. He promptly countered with another production *Moderation without Mercy*, and then informed a long-suffering world that he was the author of a recent ghastly performance called *The Deist stretched on a Death Bed, or a Lively Portraiture of a dying Infidel*. The wonder now is that the University and the Presbytery should have taken any notice whatever of the productions of this man, but the *Letter* was considered calumnious, his *Moderation without Mercy* scurrilous; and anything then ap-

---

[10] In the copy owned by the Edinburgh Public Library these initials had been filled out in the margins by some former owner, but a cheerfully careless binder trimmed those margins so that the identifications are mutilated beyond deciphering. The copy in the Library of Princeton University belonged to Witherspoon himself and is unmarked.

pearing on the controversy between the two parties in the Church secured immediate attention.[11]

The *Ecclesiastical Characteristics* was not Mr. Witherspoon's first anonymous appearance in print. The *Scots Magazine* for April, 1753, contains an essay by him on Lord Kaims which, while not of surpassing merit, is nevertheless interesting as his earliest published defence of the philosophy of common sense and was claimed by him in later years to have antedated the work of Reid. John Erskine of Edinburgh had lent Witherspoon a copy of a book by Dr. Joseph Bellamy of New England "with which he was much pleased," and to keep Mr. Bellamy informed on the development of this "valuable young minister," Mr. Erskine forwarded to his American correspondent the anonymous essay of his younger friend.[12] This was the latter's introduction to American readers.

Mr. Witherspoon was sent to the Assembly of 1756 and appointed on two important committees, one of them being the annual commission. At this Assembly he undoubtedly heard read a letter from the trustees of the College of New Jersey in America returning thanks for the collection granted to that institution. Whether he had met Messrs. Gilbert Tennent and Samuel Davies when they visited Great Britain on behalf of the college a year or two earlier is not known although, as we have seen, Mr. Davies knew him by reputation; but he little dreamed that in a dozen years or so his own name would be permanently associated with the college which they represented.

In the spring of 1756 the Laigh Kirk or Low Church, at Paisley, a few miles north of Beith, found itself without a minister.

---

[11] The facts in the case are to be found in the first edition of the *Edinburgh Review* for January, 1755, p. 56, (or in the 1818 reprint, p. 49) in an article whose authorship is ascribed, in a pencil note in the British Museum copy of the reprint, to Dr. Jardine of Edinburgh. The *Scots Magazine* for April, 1754, contains the report of Moir's trial before the University and his formal expulsion and repudiation. The report signed by the rector was ordered printed. Mr. Moir's escapade does not seem to have definitely ruined his career. In Dr. Witherspoon's library is a sermon by Mr. Moir printed at Edinburgh in 1761 on *The Babbler, or the Fate of the faithful Minister of Christ*, whose title page shows that he was pastor of a parish, and whose contents are colored with his personal experiences as an enemy of moderation. Mr. Moir had a gift for curious titles.

[12] *New Jersey Historical Society Proceedings*, vol. VI, p. 170.

Witherspoon's fame was rising; the second edition of his *Essay on Justification*[13] had appeared at Edinburgh, and he seemed best fitted to fill the vacancy. Accordingly in June the magistrates and town council, patrons of the living, resolved to call him and having found that the citizens of the borough as well as the church session concurred in their choice, they ordered their clerk to make out the necessary documents. The presentation duly signed was transmitted to Beith for Witherspoon's acceptance, and the patrons, "willing to give all suitable encouragement," bound themselves and their successors to pay him the yearly salary of twenty-four pounds eight shillings and tenpence and two-thirds sterling more than the thousand marks scots and twenty pounds sterling for manse and glebe already provided for their minister. Owing to an error in the presentation a fresh copy had to be prepared, and on Witherspoon's acceptance a committee was ordered to take the documents to presbytery and apply for the moderation of a call. Again there was delay; for in August the Paisley Council learned that the presbytery, without assigning reasons, had refused to grant the call. It developed that the presbytery had taken umbrage at the *Ecclesiastical Characteristics* of which the candidate was the alleged author, and which according to the presbytery was harmful to the interests of religion,

---

[13] The first edition was issued at Glasgow earlier in the same year. The work was based on two sermons "now thrown into the form of an essay, lest the despised title of a sermon should offend some." The essay also admits of the addition of notes, some of which "regard the philosophical principles which have of late been published among us, of which I propose in a short time a fuller discussion." Mr. Witherspoon never fulfilled this intention. The introduction refers to the disinclination of the present age to listen to the Gospel; but on the contrary to "despise and deride the message because of the meanness of the messenger, or the homeliness of the terms in which it is delivered. . . . From a certain love of ease and luxury of mind, they despise and trample upon all distinctions, which have not something pleasing and insinuating in their ideas and form." The most special or plausible objection to the doctrine of Justification by imputed righteousness is that it "loosens the obligation and practice," and that is what he has particularly applied himself to refute in the following essay. It is addressed to the Reverend Mr. Hervey, rector of Weston Favell in Northamptonshire, England, in testimony of Mr. Witherspoon's esteem for his excellent writings, as a public declaration of his espousal of the same sentiments as Mr. Hervey, his ambition to contribute to the support of the same cause, and also that thereby "It might appear to all that no external distinction, or smaller differences, ought to be any hindrance to a cordial esteem and affection between the sincere servants of our common Master."

and injurious to the characters of many ministers of the church. The council appealed to the Synod of Glasgow and Ayr and before its bar Witherspoon appeared and right willingly defended himself in a speech which he later amplified into his *Apology*. He made the strong opening point that, without a hearing in his own behalf or even a chance to see his accusations, he had been condemned as the author of a pamphlet with which the presbytery did not find itself in sympathy; and the town of Paisley was now awaiting redress. He did not pretend, nor had he ever pretended, to any connection with the pamphlet in question and he would not yield his present point by discussing that production. But he would consider a little whether the crime of which he was accused was so safely to be taken for granted as to allow presbytery to assert it in their minutes and associate his name with it, without allowing him opportunity to be heard. Did not the people of Paisley know the rumor of his authorship when they sent him their unanimous call? Were they so abandoned that they would call an enemy to watch for their souls? Did not the presbytery know that he the suspect had been member of an adjoining presbytery ever since the suspicion began to exist? that he had been a member of the Synod with themselves? that he had been a member indeed of the General Assembly? Did not the presbytery know that a large majority of people found no fault with the pamphlet and that prominent divines like the bishops of London and Oxford and Gloucester had given it their approval? By the hastiness and partiality of presbytery's sentence it looked to him as if the members felt themselves struck at in the pamphlet and if they did so feel, was it just that they should constitute themselves his judges? He does not pretend to the "polite and courtly" style, but believing that the wrath of man worketh not the righteousness of God he would examine the whole situation calmly and simply. And into every phase of it he proceeds to go, in a long and able argument full of clear close reasoning and subtle thrusts at the Moderates, proving pretty conclusively that the Paisley presbytery, which had no jurisdiction over him, had been guilty of irregular procedure and flagrant injustice in passing sentence on his character, in finding relevancy without examination, and in appointing a committee or, as he terms it, an inquisition, to discover the facts directly in the face of law and equity.

The speech is a brilliant piece of adroit pleading and a perfect example of the argumentative and tactical skill that made its author so redoubtable a debater on the floor of the Assembly. And the delicious humor of the situation lay in the fact that all the parties concerned were quite aware that the speaker was the author of the satire in question. It was evident that the Moderates had made a blunder. Long and heated discussion of the "Paisley affair," as it was called, ensued and the Synod directed a committee to see if the parties could not settle the matter out of court. At length it was agreed that the Synod should order the presbytery to moderate a call without discussing the latter's right to enquire into the *fama clamosa* relative to *Ecclesiastical Characteristics*, and without approving or disapproving the presbytery's action in the case. The members of the presbytery, by no means of one mind on the subject and glad enough now to settle the matter as speedily as possible since Dr. Witherspoon had won all the laurels, agreed to the arrangement if the Synod would vindicate them from the injurious reflections thrown out against them "as if their conduct had been inquisitorial and hurtful to the Liberties of Mankind." Hurt feelings being thus healed, the Synod appointed December 9, 1756, as the date of the moderation and the Reverend Archibald Smith as preacher, on which occasion the Paisley records assure us a most harmonious call was issued. It bore the names of the magistrates, town council, and the kirk session, the concurrences signed by the incorporators within the borough and by other proprietors of the sittings, the heritors, heads of families, and a number of burgesses and citizens. There could be no doubt of the cordial welcome Dr. Witherspoon was receiving from his new charge. But the end was not yet. It now remained to get the documents in the case formally laid before the Presbytery of Irvine to which Beith belonged and to secure his release, an apparently simple matter which required six months more to negotiate. And long before it reached a consummation, in fact a week after the events just related, social, literary, and clerical Edinburgh was thrown into intense excitement over a play performed for the first time in public on December 14, 1756, at the Canongate Theatre, the same house that Allan Ramsay had been compelled to close, thanks to the puritanical tone of the Edinburgh public. The play was *Douglas* and its author the Reverend John Home, Witherspoon's former college-mate and his fellow prisoner at Castle Doune, now a minister in the Church, and up to this time in good standing.

It is not difficult to understand the stir if we can appreciate the curiosity aroused as to what sort of play a Scotsman, a minister of the Established Church, would write. Garrick at London had declined the manuscript but that did not dampen the hopes of literary Edinburgh, and it is said that when the play was finally produced the town was actually in an "uproar of exultation" that it should have proved to be of the first order. A racy account of the whole episode is given by Dr. Carlyle, who with several ministerial friends attended the performance, much to the hurt of stricter brethren. The clerical authorship of *Douglas* gave it greater interest than its patriotic subject. Antagonists and champions rushed into print and for the next few months the bookshops were flooded with bitter sermons on one side, abusive essays on the other, and alleged verse satirizing both. The stage was attacked in doggerel and defended with the same weapon; personal abuse was conspicuous; and, as might be expected, the two parties in the Church lined up on opposite sides of the question.

The best type of the antitheatre essay is John Witherspoon's *Serious Enquiry into the Nature and Effects of the Stage*, published originally at Glasgow. It summed up as soberly, and really as fairly as the times permitted, the orthodox position on the question "Whether supporting and encouraging stage-plays, by writing, acting, or attending them, is consistent, or inconsistent, with the character of a Christian."

The primary object of the drama, says the essayist, is pleasure and amusement, whereas man's one and only obligation is "supremely and uniformly to aim at the glory of God." If a sense of this obligation were in men's minds "stage-plays, nay, and a thousand other amusements now in use would never have been heard of. The truth is, the need of amusement is much less than people commonly apprehend, and where it is not necessary, it must be sinful." Even as an amusement or recreation the stage is unnecessary and expensive. It is an unlawful recreation because it agitates the passions too violently and interests too deeply, and therefore is not recreative in effect. The Christian character implies "self-denial and heavenliness of mind," neither of which is induced by the drama. For these reasons, the theatre may not be supported by professing Christians.

The author next considers "the modern pretence" that the stage is useful and instructive. He finds that it is unauthorized by Scripture and that it does not tend to support the interests of religion. There are "noble and excellent" sentiments in some dramas but "much fewer than is commonly supposed," and there is a great difference between these sentiments and "the solid and profitable truths of religion." In fact, the majority of plays have a pernicious tendency. "They commonly turn upon the characters most grateful, and the events most interesting, to corrupt nature. Pride under the name of greatness of mind, ambition and revenge under those of valour and heroism, have been their constant subjects; but chiefly love; love, which is the strongest passion and the most dangerous in the human frame, and from which the greatest number of crimes, and crimes the most atrocious, have sprung, was always encouraged upon the stage."

Further, the drama "in its most inspired state is a picture of human life and must represent characters as they really are." If a dramatist did not depict real life he would transgress the fundamental rules of the art. The majority of characters represented on the stage are bad, and the impression made on the audience is hurtful.

No one can contribute to the encouragement of the stage, without "being partaker of the sins of other" in that he helps to support "the players in that most unchristian occupation" and encourages by example "those to attend all plays indiscriminately, who are in most danger of infection."

Nor is the drama necessary to education. "Without it young persons of rank think they cannot have that knowledge of the world which is necessary to their accomplishment." But why should the world "or anything else be known, but in order to our spiritual improvement?" Where can plays be found—at least comedies—"that are free from impurities, either directly or by allusion and double meaning?" And even when plays are "more reserved" themselves, they are sure to be "seasoned with something of this kind in the prologue or epilogue, the music between acts, or in some scandalous farce with which the diversion is concluded." The author pretends to no firsthand knowledge of these things "but from printed accounts and the public bills of what plays are to be acted." He affirms that no woman of "reputation (as it is called in the world), much less of piety who has been ten times in a playhouse, durst repeat in company all that she has heard there." And the essay ends with an inevitable parting shot at the reverend author of *Douglas*.

The *Scots Magazine*[14] in its review of Witherspoon's essay, the only one written during the controversy that is noticed at length, was glad that he had put his name on the titlepage and wished other writers would follow his example; it would be a pledge for decency, said the reviewer, a quality sadly lacking in the "immense quantity of profane drollery and personal abuse" which had been published for and against the stage during the past few months and which, by the way, Mr. Witherspoon deemed strong evidence of the immorality of the theatre. It is only fair to say that a pamphlet entitled *Morality of Stage-Plays Seriously Considered*, written by Adam Ferguson, defended just as calmly the liberal position, laying down the proposition among others that it was the duty of Christians to support the theatre and thus raise its moral tone. This was promptly answered by a still longer effusion *Some Remarks on a late Pamphlet entitled The Morality of Stage Plays Seriously Considered*. Equally anonymous, and making up in scurrility what they lacked in dignity, were satires in verse like *Douglasiana*, consisting of five songs arranged to popular airs and ridiculing the ministers defending the play, and *The Seven Champions of the Stage*, subtitled "an excellent new oldfashioned song," which was indeed new and may have been oldfashioned, but which only blindest partisanship could have called excellent. Both are in the Witherspoon Collection at Princeton.

[14] vol. XIX, p. 143.

"Home and his friends", says Professor Mathieson,[15] "by extorting such an avowal (as Witherspoon's essay), from their opponents had raised a far larger question than one of clerical decorum; and the Church, which had dallied with humanism whilst professing to maintain its Puritan tradition, had come at last to the parting of ways." And Professor Mathieson thinks that Dr. Alexander Carlyle did not greatly exaggerate the significance of the crisis when he said he could not help numbering the production of *Douglas* and the circumstances attending it among the most remarkable occurrences that had ever taken place in Scotland. The Church at large, or at least so much of it as was immediately concerned, lost no time in setting forth its opinion of the advanced wing which supported Home and his play. The Presbytery of Edinburgh issued an *Admonition and Exhortation* to all within its bounds which was speedily ridiculed in parody and song. A light sentence was inflicted on one member of the presbytery, who being summoned before it for having been present at the opening night, pleaded guilty and offered the extenuation that he had stood in a corner out of general view. Others were rebuked by their own presbyteries. John Home, to save his head, delivered a tearful farewell sermon and resigned his charge. Even Dr. Carlyle found himself in hot water, being accused of keeping company with players, attending rehearsals, directing the actors, and appearing at the playhouse and turning some gentlemen out of a box in a disorderly manner. The fact that these gentlemen were usurpers of the box, and hilariously drunk at that, did not mitigate the main offence, and on appeal the case went through the Synod up to the General Assembly which confirmed the lower court's condemnatory sentence. Two years later, however, Dr. Carlyle was elected to preach before the Lord High Commissioner; in 1770 he became Moderator of the Assembly, and in 1789 just failed of election to its chief clerkship, one of the responsible permanent offices within its gift; so that the victory of the orthodox party in his case would seem to have been slight indeed.

At this Assembly (May, 1757,) Dr. Witherspoon fought one of his losing battles against the Moderates, leading a band of eight

[15] *Awakening of Scotland*, p. 199.

dissenters from the vote of the majority to accept the commission of elders who had not qualified according to the technical church law. The Patronage Act required elders to be strict in the observance of the Sabbath and in family worship. The elders in question confessedly failed of these qualifications and Witherspoon used the logic of the situation against the Moderates who claimed to stand for the strict adherence to law. Regarding personal religion as of indispensable importance to eldership under the law, he demanded that the commissions from six or seven presbyteries be thrown out. But for the moment the Moderates seemed to think that the one thing needful for a pastor was that he should be presented and for an elder that he should have political backing. It is suspected that the practice of running in lawyers and other shrewd laymen as elders to fill the Moderate ranks and sit in the Assembly to argue for their side and to introduce courtroom methods, is traceable to this period. Witherspoon's dissent pointed out the evil consequences of such a practice, consequences which have not altogether failed of realization. There seems to be no question that the *Reasons for Dissent* on this occasion were drawn up by him; they bear strong marks of his style and they were read by him before the Assembly. The preamble admits that there are decisions from which it would be unnecessary, if not improper, for a minority to dissent. But the present decision is fraught with so much danger that the dissenters feel it requires as strong and public disapproval as possible. They declare, therefore, that the acceptance of faulty commissions is a manifest violation of the standing law of the Church's constitution; it opens the way to further and greater breaches of that constitution; as a decision from the highest tribunal of the Church it is especially dangerous, and in view of the fact that the method of selecting elders for the Assembly is carefully protected by the constitution, a breach thereof in admitting unworthy men when the decay of personal religion is so great and so visible, is deplorable. But the protest was ordered to lie on the table, and there it still remains.[16]

In the meantime the cumbrous formalities connected with the

[16] The text of the *Dissent* may be found in Morren's *Annals*, vol. II, p. 103–108. It was also separately printed.

call to Paisley had been complied with, and in June, 1757, the Reverend Mr. Baine, minister of the beautiful and historic abbey at Paisley, was able to report to the town council that the papers had been served on the Presbytery of Irvine, and on the sixteenth, no objections having been registered, the new pastor was inducted into office at the Laigh Kirk. Mr. Baine preached the installation sermon, which from its misdated imprint, its misspelling of the new minister's name, and the odd "advertisement" serving as a preface, is altogether a curiosity.

"It will perhaps occur," says this preface, "that something else than its merit brings this little performance to light; and now that it appears in public the question is not if it be weak but is it strong? is it truth in season or ill timed invective? The studied and not unacceptable brevity of the sermon made some further illustration of it necessary and if any of the subjoined notes have assumed a spirit and colour different from the original discourse; if in any of them bold superlative folly is exhibited in its proper dress, the gentle reader, 'tis hop'd, will not take offence." [17]

To a man of less buoyant spirit than Witherspoon the sermon would have seemed more chilling than the proverbial wet blanket. The text was that exquisite fifteenth verse of the tenth chapter of Romans, and the preacher appeared to wish to remind at least one of his hearers that it was a gospel of peace and not of discord and wrangle of which they both were the messengers. But the only beauty in the sermon lies in its text. A careless piece of composition throughout, it ends abruptly though not before it advertises its orthodoxy by getting in a hard hit at the stage and of course at the author of *Douglas*.

The Laigh Kirk at Paisley had been opened for worship in 1738 when the population of the town was about 3500. It contained over 1300 sittings of which nearly three-fourths were retained by those who had subscribed the £1934 the building had cost. When Witherspoon was called to the church, Paisley had a population of 12,000 and was still growing. In 1733 its streets

[17] A Sermon preached at the Translation of the Rev. Mr. Wotherspoon, from Beith to the Laigh Church at Paisley, June 16, 1757. By James Baine, M.A. Minister of the Gospel in Paisley. Glasgow: Printed by Archibald M'Lean, MDCCVII, pp. 18. 8vo.

had been narrow and dirty, its houses mean in appearance, and its people slovenly in dress and manners. Fifty years later its streets were "spacious and well paved," its houses mostly "new and elegant," its people "gay and polite," and its servant girls in their "caps, gauzes and white stockings were better dressed than citizens' wives" of the earlier generation. The change was due almost entirely to the success of the weaving trade which had been taken up late after the Reformation and which was now drawing to the place crowds of strangers from all quarters bent on business. The town was in a transition stage when Mr. Witherspoon settled there and he entered fully into the needs and hopes of the community. He was able ultimately to boast in the General Assembly with Mr. Baine that the oversight of morals in Paisley was unsurpassed in any town of its size in Scotland. He speedily won the regard and respect of the municipal authorities and he must have made his position sure when he lent the council a hundred pounds within nine months after his arrival. The great majority of Scottish livings at the time were worth under £70 so that Witherspoon's salary of more than a hundred pounds at the Laigh Kirk, the same as Mr. Baine's at the Abbey, was considerably above the average.

Change of pastorate did not mean, however, any relaxation in attitude toward the Moderates. On the contrary the new minister's first year at Paisley saw him delivering on special occasions sermons that showed clearly his intention to maintain the stand he had taken as the avowed champion of orthodoxy, in opposition to the increasing liberalism of the other party. These sermons are the group he later published at London in the first collection of his writings as most truly expressive of himself and of the message he felt he bore for the times. The first of them was preached in January, 1758, at Edinburgh before the Society in Scotland for Propagating Christian Knowledge.[18] In printing the sermon, which opens with a phrase aimed directly at the Moderates as men "who disguise or alter the gospel in order to defend it," or who "often endeavour to give such views of Christianity as will render it palatable to a corrupt worldly mind, and instead

---

[18] *The Absolute Necessity of Salvation through Christ.*

of abusing will soothe and gratify the pride of man," Dr. Witherspoon added a long note on charity. He was aware that the sternness of the doctrine he preached would make him likely to be called uncharitable; but he held that no charity should be shown to errors in teaching fundamental doctrines. The Scriptures had no such meaning in their use of the word. And as he had anticipated, this view of charity at once met serious objections, and when he prepared a second edition of the sermon, as he was soon compelled to do, he sent with it an essay on the *Scripture Meaning of Charity*.

In February, 1758, on the day appointed for the annual public fast he took as his subject the inseparability of religion and national prosperity and painted a dark picture of the times.[19]

Every class and denomination of men among us, every party and faction, however unwilling each may be to acknowledge its own share of the guilt, and however prone to load its adversaries with the blame of procuring it, is yet willing to acknowledge that we are at present in a distressed, and in an contemptible state. . . . We have not only had for sometime past repeated threatenings of scarcity and dearth, but vast multitudes have been afflicted with famine in its rigor. . . . We have been long engaged in war with a powerful and politic enemy. And has not the providence of God sensibly frowned on us, and visibly frustrated almost every one of our attempts—we have turned our backs faint-hearted before our enemies in almost every encounter; and the greater and more formidable our preparation for any enterprise, the more pitiful the issue, and the more shameful our defeat and disappointment. . . . Is not this nation, once in a manner the arbiter of the fate of Europe now become the scorn and derision of her neighbours and all that are round about her? . . . How numerous and expensive, but how useless and inactive have been our fleets and armies! And how deplorable is the condition of our colonies abroad! They are the chief theatre of war, because indeed, they are the subject of the contest. Surely it is affecting to think of the unnatural barbarity and cruelty that there is often exercised when no age or sex is spared. . . .

If it please God to suffer our enemies and continue their progress, it is hard to say how far the desolation may extend, or how universal it may prove.

As for the religious side of national life, as a people and as a

[19] *Prayer for National Prosperity.*

Church they had fallen low; infidelity was gross and prevalent, many persons of high rank were deserting the house and the worship of God, and openly treating His service and His servants with contempt.

So great, said the preacher, is the prevalence of irreligion, contempt of God, sensuality and pride, that many of the grossest crimes are not only practised but professed, not only frequent but open, not only persisted in, but gloried in and boasted of; insomuch that it requires no small degree of fortitude and resolution, steadfastly to adhere to the principles and character of a disciple of Christ, in opposition to the spirit and stream of fashionable conversation. In place of the purity of faith and strictness of morals which was the glory of the Reformation, we have substituted a pliant and fashionable scheme of religion, a fine theory of virtue and morality, a beautiful but unsubstantial idol, raised by human pride, adorned and dressed by human art and supported by the wisdom of words.

He exhorts his hearers to mend their ways; he begs them to pray for "our gracious sovereign King George, under whose mild and legal government, we have long enjoyed as much happiness as our national quiet would allow," that the Lord may give him wise understanding, protect his person, direct his councils, and prosper his arms. A review of history shows that God has supported his people and his cause when things were at the lowest ebb.

Let no Christian, therefore, give way to desponding thoughts, though infidelity unresisted spread its poison . . . though there are few to support the interest of truth and righteousness, though we have seen a new thing on the earth, a minister of Christ leaving the pulpit for the stage, let us not be discouraged. We plead the cause that shall finally prevail.

Another important and characteristic discourse was delivered in the Abbey at Paisley on September 7, 1758, at the ordination of Mr. Archibald Davidson as one of the ministers of that church.[20] Its purpose was to find out why upright and faithful ministers meet with calumny, and are called seditious and factious breeders of trouble, enemies to Caesar and turners of the world upside down. What is there, asks the preacher, in true re-

[20] *Charge of Sedition and Faction against good Men.*

ligion that gives rise to this accusation and makes society so prone to believe it? It is because the servants of God are and must be the objects of the resentment of those who will not follow in their steps; they will not and dare not comply with the sinful commandments of man; and they are often obliged to bear witness against the sins of others and reprove them.

There seems to be an under current of personal feeling in certain passages of this sermon as if the speaker were drawing on his own experience: "Are there not some," he asks, "who cannot endure such strictness as is inconsistent with conformity to the gay and fashionable world? . . . Do they not consider every reprover as an enemy to their State? Do they not hear with secret pleasure and spread with apparent triumph, every report to the prejudice of such troublers of Israel?" Cautious persons must beware of being misled by the persecuting cry. Ministers in particular must be careful not to give any real ground for it; they should conduct their zeal with steadiness, but also with meekness; avoid intermeddling with civil affairs; finally should bear the charge with patience.

In the charge to the new minister Dr. Witherspoon reiterates the necessity of preaching the "grand and leading truths of the gospel, original sin, Christ's imputed righteousness, justification by free grace, the necessity of regeneration, and the operation of the Spirit." Any minister in the Scottish Church who, having subscribed to the Confession of Faith, did not preach these truths was guilty of perjury. This was a straight thrust at his opponents besides being a summary of his own theological views; and when he goes on to say that he would have sermons carefully prepared but not "dressed up with excessive elegance, and a vain ornamental foppery of style," one is inclined to ask whether he was thinking of his college-mate, Hugh Blair, then in the full glory of his oratorical powers. Such sermons, he said, reminded him of painted windows which with their fine colors made a brave show but kept out the light and rendered the house comfortless and dark. He had evidently noticed the beautiful ancient glass which is still the glory of Paisley's Abbey. It indeed made a brave show, and perhaps kept out some light, but to a more liberal mind it would scarcely have seemed to "render the house comfortless." On the contrary, to such a man the happier thought would have occurred that those glowing windows were relics, in this Romanist abbey turned Presbyterian kirk, of a lost art, an art in its day lovingly practised and piously dedicated to the glory of God and of His Church Invisible.

The most interesting passage in the sermon, however, in view of the preacher's subsequent career, is his declaration that ministers should avoid meddling with civil affairs—they should be separate and set apart for their work, consecrated to their office; it is sinful and dangerous for them "to desire or claim the direction of such matters as fall within the province of the civil magistrates." These words were spoken in September 1758. Twenty years later the preacher was completing the second of five separate years of service as a member of the American Continental Congress. More than that, when he found after the American Revolution that the constitution of the State of Georgia contained a provision that no clergyman of any denomination should be a member of the Legislature, he wrote a letter to the public press asking for the reasons of this disqualification, depriving the clergy as it did of one of their "most important rights" as citizens.[21] By that time both he and his enemies in Scotland had forgotten the sermon in Paisley Abbey.

As moderator of the Synod of Glasgow and Ayr, in October, 1759, he opened the session with a sermon on the "Trial of Religious Truth by Its Moral Influence," the last of his great doctrinal sermons, and here again he insists on all the old orthodox points, and gives a gloomy description of the religious decadence of the country, closing with a frank statement of the weakness and intellectual dishonesty only too prevalent in the ministry, whereby "an unsubstantial theory of virtue" was being preached in place of "the great and operative views of the gospel."

He had lost no time in joining hands with Mr. Baine and doing what he could to lessen the burden of his older colleague. It was thought that the organization of two church sessions instead of the existing one would be a step in that direction, and

[21] *Works*, vol. IV, p. 227, (edition of 1800).

in April, 1758, the two ministers applied to the presbytery of Paisley to erect them. When the presbytery refused the request they appealed to the synod and there the presbytery's decision was reversed. But the presbytery promptly appealed to the General Assembly and another petty fight was on. It mattered not that the magistrates and council of Paisley agreed with the ministers that the two sessions would tend to greater comfort and efficiency in the two churches; the presbytery had not forgotten the lashing the younger minister had given it not so very long ago when his call to Paisley was under discussion. The town officials desired only peace and sent a propitiatory committee to the presbytery signifying their concurrence in the ministers' proposition and praying for the presbytery to withdraw the appeal to the Assembly and to grant the application. But the presbytery refused to hear the petition, and the town then directed Mr. Baine and Mr. Witherspoon, the latter as moderator of the session, to appear at the bar of the Assembly and prosecute a counter appeal against the presbytery. The two ministers published their case in a quarto pamphlet[22] wherein they went into full, and (to modern readers) tedious, detail. But the opposition was too strong and at the Assembly the synod's authorization for the erection of a second session at Paisley was reversed, and the erection of any new session for the Laigh Kirk was forbidden until that part of the town should be legally disjoined and formed into a parish.

Paisley had enjoyed Mr. Witherspoon's pastorate for two years when there came a call for his services elsewhere. In July, 1759, one of the ministers of the Scottish church at Rotterdam was made emeritus, and application was made to Dr. John Erskine and Mr. Robert Walker of Edinburgh for names of candidates to fill the vacancy. Their first choice declining to leave Scotland, they named the junior minister at Paisley as possessing all the requisite qualities, besides being one of the most esteemed men in the church. He was approached and took the proposal under consideration. Without waiting for his decision, the

[22] See Appendix I.

Rotterdam church elected him unanimously; but his ties were already too strong and he declined to break them.[23]

At the meeting of the Assembly of 1760 he delivered another powerful speech on the old subject of compelling a parish to accept a minister against its will. The Earl of Balcarras, patron of the living at Kilconquhar, had presented it to Dr. John Chalmers of Elie, and the people objected to him. The Assembly voted that Dr. Chalmers should be installed in the face of the parochial protest. From this decision Witherspoon and five others dissented, and it was in defence of this action that he delivered the speech referred to.[24] It is a dispassionate statement of the case from the Popular party's point of view. He had long had the deepest sense of the dishonor and loss of authority that the Church was suffering and the injury that the souls of men had suffered by many settlements in which a pastor was installed without a people. He was aware that many worthy and faithful ministers looked upon these cases as of necessity under the law of patronage, but he feared that from the habit of doing so when there was necessity the Assembly was continuing to do so when there was no necessity. Could a pastor, he asked, be of service to a flock that did not want him and would not listen to him? There was strong opposition to Dr. Chalmers on good grounds; his settlement at Kilconquhar was not a necessity, and the speaker called on everyone within hearing to judge seriously whether this settlement would be for the glory of God and the good of mankind. It would offend not only the people of the parish and those in the lower class of society but many also in all stations of life; and it was these people who were led to treat with derision a minister's concern for his usefulness and to declare that it was for nothing more than the desire of a comfortable benefice and a

---

[23] W. Steven, *History of the Scottish Church at Rotterdam*, Edinburgh, 1832, p. 192. Although Mr. Witherspoon did not visit Holland until 1768 when he was preparing to leave Europe for America, he seems to have been much interested in the Dutch Church, and we shall see that he made an effort to secure the emigration of a Dutch professor of theology for the Colonies. Several of his works were translated into Dutch and were published in Holland, his *Essay on Regeneration* being issued under the editorship of Paul Chevalier, Professor of Theology at the University of Gröningen.
[24] *Works*, vol. IV, p. 327.

salary for life. As for himself he would be sorry to see the day come in Scotland when they would learn from England how to leave the people and the work entirely out of consideration, and so call their charges no longer "parishes" but frankly "livings."

The editor of the *Annals of the General Assembly* notes that in transportation cases it had been the Assembly's custom to engage in prayer, but the manuscript record says nothing of such procedure on this occasion.

At the meeting of the General Assembly of 1761 Witherspoon was at last to taste the fruits of victory in the cause that was enlisting his most persistent energy, the cause of the people against ecclesiastical high-handedness. During the preceding autumn the magistrates, council and kirk session of Paisley had perfected, after much deliberation, a scheme whereby the office of English schoolmaster and session clerk should be combined, a plan which incidentally sheds some light on prevalent educational conditions. In September they had elected to the clerkship the incumbent of the mastership, one William Adie who, however, was opposed to the union of duties. Although entirely approved of by the presbytery the scheme had to receive the sanction of the Synod and in October for reasons of its own that body vetoed the plan and forbade the union. Paisley decided to carry the matter higher and accordingly at the Assembly in 1761 Witherspoon led the fight against the Synod. He made it clear that by the decree of erection of the parish the magistrates and council of the town were well within their rights in the proposal and he argued the opposition to a standstill so that the Assembly was forced to reach the wary verdict that it "could not disapprove" the conduct of the Paisley Kirk session in sanctioning the plan, and it furthermore could see nothing in it injurious to the session, and that therefore it reversed the sentence of the Synod, sustained the election of Adie as session clerk, and ordered the session to admit him accordingly. And Mr. Witherspoon went back to Paisley for once a victor. It was a novel sensation.

The popularity Mr. Witherspoon enjoyed at Paisley was strikingly illustrated in the following spring when the town of Dundee moderated a call to him and applied to the presbytery of Paisley to have him transported. At the hearing set, the patrons of the

Laigh Kirk produced a strong resolution against his departure concluding in these terms:

And as the Magistrates and Council are much satisfied with the said Mr. Witherspoon and are greatly against his transportation, and likewise judging such a transportation would be much to the hurt of the Community and Lay them under very great Hardship and Inconveniencys, Therefore they hereby resolve to oppose the said Transportation to the utmost of their Power.

For this purpose they appointed a committee to appear at the Presbytery not only to oppose but to prevent the transportation. With the municipal resolution went one of even greater significance from the "Society of Weavers, Taylors, Shoe Makers and Wrights in Paisley" also protesting against the transportation. The whole town stood behind its representatives in opposing the move, forming a unanimous and remarkable tribute to the man. The documents[25] filed in the case were numerous and wordy and the matter was too difficult for the presbytery to settle, especially as it appeared to the members that the reasons favoring transportation preponderated, while Witherspoon himself was unwilling to go. To the Assembly naturally, therefore, the case was referred and in May, 1762, from Dundee appeared two representatives of the magistrates and council with three ministers of the presbytery, and a lawyer, while from Paisley appeared two members of its council, with a lawyer, and Witherspoon himself. Both sides were heard, Witherspoon being also interrogated, and after debate the Assembly to the joy of Paisley decided that its pastor should stay where he was. The story of the Dundee call and especially a consideration of the documents filed by Witherspoon's constituency at Paisley form the best possible refutation of the allegation so persistently made that he left Scotland dissatisfied and disappointed.

Zeal for the interests of good morals was responsible, however, for his entanglement at this time in an unfortunate affair known as the Snodgrass case, which, while it did him no great harm at Paisley or among his friends elsewhere, nevertheless because of certain personal elements injected into it and because there can

[25] Paisley MS. town records.

be little doubt that for once Mr. Witherspoon allowed himself to be carried away by his zeal, did not place him in the best light before the world at large. At the meeting of the Assembly which considered his call to Dundee there was lying on the table a protest from the Presbytery of Paisley and John Snodgrass, a Paisley sheriff's clerk, and others, against Witherspoon and the kirk session. It seems that two months earlier, on the evening before the administration of the Sacrament of the Lord's Supper, Snodgrass and five other young men of the town met in a private room on a frequented street and held a drinking bout, in the course of which they not only became noisy and profane, thereby causing a crowd to collect, but, so it was alleged, mimicked their ministers and went so far as to hold a mock celebration of the morrow's sacrament. The story reaching Witherspoon's ears he reported it to the session who called the accused and began an examination. While this was in progress Mr. Witherspoon preached a sermon in which he represented the defendants as men of vicious habits and character, especially naming young Snodgrass who he alleged had contracted his habits in student days at Edinburgh. The session having concluded its investigation found the accused guilty, and sentenced them to public rebuke before the congregation and to whatever further censure the presbytery might inflict. At the presbytery Witherspoon, evidently still under strong emotion, threatened to print his sermon with names and evidence, unless the presbytery's censure were what he deemed adequate to the enormity of the offense. But after examining the documents the presbytery decided that the sacrilegious celebration was not proven, and, therefore, merely ordered the moderator to rebuke the culprits before the bar of presbytery. Witherspoon at once protested against the decision and declared that he would appeal to the Assembly, and in May, 1762, he printed his sermon and placed it on sale at three bookshops in Edinburgh, two at Glasgow, two at Dumfries, and one each at Stirling, Perth, Dundee, Kilmarnock, Greenock, and Ayr. It was dedicated to the Town Council at Paisley, and its preface states that although "considerable alteration and additions were made in transcribing the sermon for the press" yet it is substantially the same, and "the passages complained of are

[60]

printed precisely in the terms in which they were delivered." [26]

At this juncture, it is said, cooler heads advised Dr. Witherspoon that his action was not only injudicious but unjustifiable, and he went, therefore, to some pains to gather together all copies he could find and actually stopped the sales until the meeting of the Assembly was over. He subsequently denied this, explaining that the non-distribution of the sermon was due to the fact that he had suspended the sales until after a decision had been reached by the Assembly on his Dundee call lest it should exercise undue influence in the decision of the greater question of his transportation. That matter settled, the sermon was put on sale immediately after the Assembly adjourned. As a result the complainants found themselves odious in Paisley and their lives and persons even endangered on the streets. They, therefore, sued the minister in the civil courts for criminal libel and asked damages to the amount of one hundred pounds each and one hundred pounds costs. The case came up in June, 1764, and five months later the opinion was handed down that, though the preaching of the sermon was justifiable, the printing and publishing of it, with an explanatory preface wherein the plaintiffs were charged by name with the actions described in the sermon, was illegal, unwarrantable and injurious, and that, therefore, the defendant was liable for damages and costs; but inasmuch as the preaching was occasioned by improper conduct on the part of the plaintiffs—two of the young men concerned had hastily left Paisley, and another had apologised before the session for his conduct—and the publication of the sermon was due to intemperate zeal rather than to malicious and deliberate intent to injure, the damages were set at only thirty pounds and the costs at eighty-eight pounds, ten shillings. On appeal, the higher courts increased the damages to one hundred and fifty pounds and granted full costs. The case dragged on until February, 1776, when it was settled by compromise. Dr. Witherspoon must have deeply regretted his impetuosity even though his motives were unimpeachable. The full manuscript report of the case is in the archives of His Majesty's Register House at Edinburgh, where the reader (if there ever be another) who struggles

[26] *Seasonable Advice to Young Persons.*

through the reams of legal foolscap, will find at least one bright spot in the closing sentence of the plaintiffs' argument which quotes in extraordinary French a sentence from Molière's *Le Tartuffe* wherein is distinguished the character of true and false zeal. The association of Witherspoon's name with that of Molière's hypocritical imposter sufficiently indicates the personalities employed.

Ashbel Green never heard him allude to the case although it was rumored in America that Dr. Witherspoon had been prosecuted and severely fined, and that friends had settled the claims against him. It was even said that strong opposition had developed against his leaving Scotland because of these unsettled claims. In a memorandum book now lost but which Dr. Green found among the President's papers, there was a record of contributions, many of them anonymous, sent to Witherspoon to help him out of his difficulty. The total was some forty pounds sterling. Dr. McCosh implies that the Snodgrass case influenced Witherspoon in his decision to leave Scotland—his enemies were making Scotland "too hot" for him; but Dr. McCosh's statement is merely a paraphrase of earlier and mistaken writers.

In 1764 while this case was pending, young Snodgrass ran foul of his pastor once more, Witherspoon accusing him of evil conduct, it being alleged that he was seen in compromising circumstances with a notorious woman. But before presbytery he proved his innocence and was exonerated; his accuser had been misled by local gossip.

The entanglement in which his sermon *"Seasonable Advice"* had got him was undoubtedly viewed with joy by his enemies and there must have been expressions of satisfaction that at last the author of *Ecclesiastical Characteristics* had been seriously checked. This production had been by no means forgotten—successive editions were keeping it alive—and it is likely that it was held up against him whenever the opportunity seemed good. Whatever may have been the reason, Mr. Witherspoon decided to defend the satire and especially as he was meditating a return to that form of writing. In 1763, therefore, he rewrote a portion of his synod defence of 1756 and issued it anonymously as a

Serious Apology dedicated to the "Nobility and Gentry of Scotland particularly such of them as are elders of the Church, and frequently members of the General Assembly," without whose leadership and aid he believes "every attempt for reviving the interest of religion is quite hopeless." In this defense of his famous pamphlet, he discusses it as to subject, literary form, and usefulness. It had been asked if any good resulted, and whether a veil would not have been more charitable and have served the cause of religion better. But he believed on the contrary that the good was served by showing up the clergy if they were at fault. He resented most the accusation that the satire was not the act of a pious man. This was the old accusation against Pascal's *Provincial Letters* in their day, but he points out that now these "ironical witty papers" are not counted against Pascal's piety. The criticism is not sincere. For, where have the enemies of the *Ecclesiastical Characteristics* protested against writing directly leveled at religion itself and published but recently, "taking away the very foundation of morality . . . and bringing in doubt the very being of a God?" Does not this tempt one to repeat Molière's remark in connection with the protest against his *Tartuffe*, that a man may write what he pleaseth against God Almighty in perfect security: but if he write against the character of the clergy in power, he is ruined forever.[27] As for the form of his attack men had said why not attack the situation seriously if at all? Were it not better to consider an evil gravely and becomingly, rather than merely to hold it up to ridicule? In defence of the use of satire he cites the Scriptures as well as uninspired writers; but he says that it was the prevailing taste of the age that chiefly induced him to adopt the form he did—"a certain levity prevails at present among all ranks." Indeed he feels that not one-twentieth of the readers of the *Characteristics* will read the *Apology*; they will deny it is by the same author, its style being

---

[27] Evidently referring to the remark of the great Condé quoted by Molière in his preface to the first edition of the *Tartuffe*. The king having wondered why those who were so scandalized by this play raised no objection against *Scaramouche*, the prince replied: "The reason is that *Scaramouche* makes fun of Heaven and religion, about which they don't care; while Molière's play makes fun of themselves, and that is something they cannot stand."

so different. Men do not care to think; the age is one of mental sluggishness—"Authors of periodical publications such as reviews, magazines, and even common newspapers" all cater to this taste for diluted literature; and to the same cause may be ascribed the "inundation" of novels in recent years. Did the clergy deserve the satire? The laity almost unanimously agreed on its truth and many of the clergy of England gave evidences of their favor. Among them he names the bishops of London, Oxford, and Gloucester. But the strongest proof is the Moderates themselves; the outcry they made with their malice and resentment proved without doubt that his shot had gone home. He goes further in his justification and examines the state of the Church in regard to doctrine, discipline and government, and easily makes out his case. He declares that this *Serious Apology* is due entirely to the unwearied endeavors of many to represent his performance as evidence of an unchristian disposition. He has "not the smallest reason to repent of it on account of the nature, its design, or its effects upon the public." He ends by beseeching all to exert themselves with zeal and activity for the preservation and recovery of the Church, and not despair; and he closes with the final paragraph of his fast sermon in 1758 on *Prayer for National Prosperity.*

The demand for his essay on *Justification* which had appeared first in 1756, coupled with a sense of the prevailing decay of religion that seemed to him to mark the age, induced him in 1764, when on a visit to London, to arrange with the Dilleys to issue a three volume edition of his essays and doctrinal sermons, of which the third volume was a treatise on *Regeneration,* now for the first time printed. In this collection his aim was to establish what he conceived to be the fundamental doctrines of Christianity. The preface is dated June, 1764, and the third volume is imprinted the same year, but the other two volumes bear date of 1765, although the collection as a whole was reviewed in the *Scots Magazine,* the *Gentleman's Magazine* and the *Monthly Review* before the end of 1764.

He was gaining in fame abroad and losing none of his popularity at home. In June, 1764, the University of St. Andrews conferred on him the honorary degree of Doctor of Divinity,[28] and the Paisley town records of April, 1766, contain this entry:

Act for a Compliment to Mr. John Witherspoon. The said Day the Magistrates and Council considering the Good Services done To ye Community by the Reverend Mr. John Witherspoon minister of ye Gospel in ye Laigh Church Hereby agree To give ye said Mr. Witherspoon a Compliment of fifteen pounds Stirling and authorize ye clerk to draw a precept for ye said sum on ye Treasr which shall be allowed ye Treasr in his accounts.

And in October of the same year the council added twelve pounds sterling to his salary.

At the Assembly of 1766 he was fighting again on behalf of his parish. The presbytery having refused to admit two elders on commissions from Paisley, Dr. Witherspoon protested and the case was referred to the higher court. Both sides were heard by the Assembly and after a lively debate lasting two days the Assembly reversed the presbytery's decision. But Witherspoon's victory was only momentary, for the Assembly further declared that inasmuch as the presbytery had excluded constituent members from voting, the entire election from Paisley was null and void, and, therefore, ordered the names of all Paisley representatives struck from the roll. With the tables now unexpectedly turned, Witherspoon protested against this action vehemently but unavailingly and the engrossed minutes for the year contain no Paisley delegation. Thus Dr. Witherspoon was in the outcome defeated but the debate had good results as it occasioned the passage of a new act on the form of commissions. His disgust must have been supreme, however; for the report of the Assembly's special committee on schism was on the docket for this meeting, and in the great debate that ensued, he was compelled to watch his rival Dr. Robertson lead the Moderate cohorts while he himself, having no standing on the floor, could take part only as a spectator.

[28] "St. Andrews June 26, 1764. Sederunt—Rector, Mr. Morton, Dr. Hadow, Mr. Watson, Mr. Wilkie. Conferr'd the Degree of Doctor in Divinity upon the Reverend Mr. John Witherspoon, minister of the Gospel at Paisley." University Minutes (MS.) vol. VII, p. 49.

The position he occupied in the esteem of his parish indicates that, while his public appearances may give the impression that his career was one of constant wrangle, this was hardly the case. He had carried to Paisley the personal qualities that he had shown at Beith although there seem to be no traditions lingering about his ministry in this commercial town. It is only fair to acknowledge that Dr. Witherspoon dearly loved an argument, and it is most probable that he was often and easily baited. One of his own presbyters admitted subsequently that he often opposed him in order to hear what he would say, a statement indirectly supported by the memoirs that somewhat remarkable man, Dr. Somerville of Jedburgh.[29] Somerville in his autobiography says that there were few weightier speakers in church courts than Witherspoon, and although his manner was "inanimate and drawling" yet the depth of his judgment, the solidity of his arguments and the aptitude with which they were illustrated and applied "never failed to produce a strong impression on the Assembly."

Dr. Witherspoon had been considering a second venture into the field of satire and in 1765 he issued, anonymously again, a piece of fiction or satirical allegory to which he gave the name of a *History of a Corporation of Servants*. It is a satire on the history of the Christian Church and of the Scottish branch in particular.

The scene is laid in the interior of Brazil whither the survivors of a vessel belonging to Lord Anson's squadron of 1741, cast away on a desert island in the South Seas, finally made their way. They lived here many years as slaves in the court of a powerful prince and at last two of them acquired such favor that they made their way back to Great Britain. One of them described to the author the extraordinary condition of the servants of this realm. The story consists of twelve chapters with an Introduction and a Conclusion, and the key to the whole is found in the idea that the servants are the clergy and the corporation of servants is the Church. With this key in mind the reader understands that the first three chapters relate the growth of the Papacy up to the Reformation, or the formation of the "servants' corporation." At this time "the lands lay uncultivated, the people were

[29] Thomas Somerville, *My own Life and Times*, p. 99.

reduced to the greatest misery imaginable, they were sorrily clothed and worse fed, nobody prospered but the servants, or rather the upper classes of them, the noble and honorable servants, the overseers and arch-overseers." And if anyone dared to raise an accusation against the corporation he was "carried to a dreadful subterranean place and there put to the most horrid and shocking torture which at length ended in death." This the reader will recognize as the Inquisition. Chapter four tells how at last one of the lower servants resolved to open the eyes of the public, and by dint of preaching his notions got some to join him and resolve to return to the old primitive system of service. And thus is the Reformation described. The result was a long series of struggles between the old and the new until finally in a northern province (unnamed, but of course Scotland) the reformers evolved an admirable system of service. The next chapter depicts the prosperity of the northern provinces under the new scheme, until the establishment of a law empowering great men to nominate servants to inferior families (the law of patronage), when degeneration set in. One party of servants (the Moderates in thin disguise) used all manner of arts and force to appoint servants in families, and "matters drove on heavily for a while." The next two chapters describe the unfitness of many so-called servants under the conditions now prevalent, and particularly owing to the ridiculous methods of testing them and examining their credentials and testimonials, the allusion here being to Witherspoon's opinion of the younger clergy of the day. The eighth chapter brings the story up to the publication of *Ecclesiastical Characteristics*. The good and bad servants were distributed over the country and one of the good servants, who was an opponent of prevalent conditions, fell upon the singular device of drawing

a picture of the droll or ludicrous kind, in which by enigmatical characters he represented the various impositions of the servants in general; he also took off the likeness of the principal and most active leaders of the corporation, and put them in the most comical postures imaginable,

and the postures are described. The furore that the picture created is then portrayed. A whole chapter is devoted to an account of a debate in the corporation on the propriety of driving out all the "strange cattle" (the schism of 1763), and mending the fences which were in so sorry a condition, a debate which was futile in its results. The following chapter discusses the ambition and covetousness of the servants and their interest in a multitude of other things than their duties, and cites as an example one who was most successful at story-telling, and especially stories of heroic action of his people's predecessors; he immediately gave over all work in the family to which he belonged, and when he was civilly put in mind of his neglect he told his critics that they might go about their business for they were a pack of seditious slanderers. Thus might Principal Robertson the historian, whose first work had been a history of Scotland, have seen himself caricatured. The two closing chapters of this curious work are given over to depicting the attitude of the people in view of the proceedings of their servants.

In a way the story is clever, especially in the parallel which is well sustained; but it is undeniably heavy; and it seems to have fallen flat. One is of course immediately put in mind of Gulliver and it is very possible that Dr. Witherspoon got his idea from Dean Swift with whose writings he was familiar. It would be interesting to know whether he had read Voltaire's *Micromegas* which was still new. The work lacks the spontaneity of the *Ecclesiastical Characteristics*, and although its purpose is the same as that of the earlier effort, the chastening of the Moderates, public interest in the struggle between them and the Popular party was on the wane. In regard to that controversy, the public at large, like the people of the north provinces in the story, "rubbed on as well as they could."

Dr. Ashbel Green, whose interpretation of the work has been followed in the account given above, found several other pieces of satire among Dr. Witherspoon's unpublished papers, which he destroyed as they were of local concern or about individuals long dead. Dr. Witherspoon's next publication of the sort belongs to his American period. The *Corporation of Servants* is his only preserved effort of prose fiction, and his most ambitious piece of imaginative writing.

During the summer of 1766 he received a call to Dublin which he declined; but a few months later a very different call was coming, which decline as he would, he could not evade, and which ultimately he was to accept as a summons to higher responsibility and greater opportunity than hitherto had been his lot.

CHAPTER THREE

ON July 17, 1766, the Rev. Dr. Samuel Finley, fifth President of the College of New Jersey at Princeton, died in Philadelphia whither he had gone for medical treatment. For a month past his recovery had been despaired of, and in anticipation of his death the trustees of the college must have given thought to the choice of his successor. But no formal decision had been reached when they adjourned after their regular meeting at Commencement in September; and a special meeting was called in November at which to choose the man who should be their sixth President.

The colonial period, first of the four great periods into which the history of Princeton University divides itself, was ended, and the second—the Revolutionary period—was beginning. Each of the five colonial Presidents had contributed something to the character of the institution during the twenty years of its existence. Jonathan Dickinson, the leading Presbyterian clergyman of his day, had assisted at its faltering inception; the Reverend Aaron Burr had given it material body and the color of his own piety and graciousness; Samuel Davies had lent it an incipient nationalism and a certain element of culture; even the brief hour of Jonathan Edwards' rule had brought it lustre; and these foundations Dr. Finley had strengthened with his firm though stolid qualities. Through two decades these men, one after the other, had toilingly planted and watered, and their successor, a greater than they, was to take up their effort and give it breadth and flexibility, virility and permanence, and in an administration of more than a quarter of a century was to gather the real first-fruits.

A precedent that was to remain unbroken until the twentieth century insisted that the head of the college be a Presbyterian clergyman; the labor of the task required of him physical and mental robustness; the aims and young traditions of the college

demanded that he be of unquestioned piety, preferably of reputation as an author, and possessed of as broad culture and wide
scholarship as the age provided. And there did not appear to be
in the Synod of New York and Philadelphia, nor even among the
New England friends of the college, any man of such acknowledged attainments, such long standing in the ministry, and such
general weight of character, as to satisfy these requirements.

On November 19, the trustees reassembled at Princeton with
minds made up, and although the minutes of the meeting state
that only after "mature deliberation" did they elect to the vacant presidency the Reverend Dr. John Witherspoon of Paisley,
in Scotland, yet it may be assumed for reasons which shall appear, that most of the deliberation had taken place before the
meeting. Whose was the bold suggestion, the flash of eternal wisdom, that first brought the Scotsman's name into consideration
we shall perhaps never know, but the decision was no blind lucky
leap in the dark. Dr. Witherspoon's career since the publication
of *Ecclesiastical Characteristics* must have enlisted the approval
of most if not all American Presbyterians. Very probably for
once they would have agreed even with the Unitarian, Dr. John
Lathrop of Boston, that in the famous satire could be found
"many characters in this part of the world, painted out very exactly," and they would have endorsed his wish that every minister in America "would read it once a month." [1] Dr. Witherspoon's attitude was the one they would have taken on the vital
questions of patronage, abuse of power, and degeneration of religious life. His name must have been frequently on the pens of
those Scottish divines who periodically exchanged with their
transatlantic brethren interminable epistles on the state of religion; and although no American edition of his writings had as
yet appeared his treatise on *Justification*, his *Inquiry into the
Stage*, and possibly his latest essay—that on *Regeneration*—not
to mention his doctrinal sermons, had crossed the ocean and won
admiration. Some Americans at least had read in the *Scots Magazine* his early essay in reply to Lord Kames on the philosophy of
common sense, for the Reverend Mr. Bellamy who first had it

[1] Sprague, *Annals*, vol. VIII, p. 71. Letter of June 28, 1768.

called to his attention had no reason to keep its authorship a secret. It is certain that Dr. Witherspoon's position in the Church of Scotland and a corresponding anticipation of his potential influence in America had more weight with the trustees of the College of New Jersey than any educational qualifications he may have possessed. Dr. Francis Alison, an honorary graduate of Princeton and vice-provost of the University of Pennsylvania, or the College of Philadelphia, declared to the Reverend Ezra Stiles of Connecticut that the Princeton trustees knew nothing of Witherspoon's academic abilities; he was esteemed as a "keen satirical writer," but whether he could teach anything but divinity "was hard to say." Dr. Alison's reference[2] to him as "one Wetherspoon, a minister in Paisley in Scotland" indicates neither acquaintance nor cordiality on his part, but rather the note of academic disdain for an outsider. In all the extant letters relating to the election the emphasis is placed on Witherspoon's ecclesiastical rather than his educational value to the colonies. Nevertheless, there could have been little question that his university training was of the best, that his success as a minister of the gospel was a fact and his piety beyond suspicion; and he was entering the prime of manhood. Added to these qualities was the belief that he would prove a tower of strength in the episcopate controversy through which the Colonies were at that time passing; and back of it all, intangible but by no means unimportant, there lay in his favor the attraction and prestige that British birth and British training and experience still held in the eyes of American colonials. The choice of this man for their President was not only an act of excellent common sense on the part of the trustees of the College of New Jersey, but it proved to be a stroke of unexpected genius.

A copy of the minute of election together with a letter praying acceptance, signed by the Honorable William Peartree Smith, acting president of the board, was sent to Dr. Witherspoon, addressed in the care of Mr. Richard Stockton, a lawyer of Princeton and a graduate and trustee of the College, who happened to be in London.

[2] Stiles MSS., Yale University Library. Alison to Stiles, December 4, 1766.

THE CALL TO PRINCETON

Nassau Hall, Princeton, New Jersey.
November 19th, 1766

Revd Sir

The Trustees of the College of New Jersey, actuated by the most sensible concern for the future welfare of that rising Seminary, (already become of unspeakable importance to Religion, and the Presbyterian cause in North America) under the late afflicting Providence, in removing by death their President, the Rev^d & Worthy Dr. Samuel Finley, have employed their anxious thoughts, for several Months past, in looking out, both at Home & abroad, for a Gentleman, properly qualified, to succeed him in that important & conspicuous Station.

Having maturely considered the various & important interests, which, under God, appear in a great degree, to depend upon the future Prosperity of the College of New Jersey; and having considered also the character You Sir sustain in the Church of Scotland & in the learned World—the Trustees, (this Day convened for the purpose of election,) chearfully proceeded to elect and did elect Dr. Witherspoon to the President's Chair. Inclosed is a Copy of the Minute of the transaction, extracted from their Record of Proceedings.

You will immediately perceive, S^r that there are very weighty reasons which have led this Board to request you to undertake the disagreeable task of breaking from your present Connections & undergoing the difficulties of a Voyage to a distant Country. We trust, however, the noble Cause you will promote in this Station of first Eminence in the Church in these Southern Provinces, and the great Ends your Compliance will answer to Religion & Learning in general thro' out all the Colonies will afford You a more than proportionable degree of Satisfaction. And this Board do assure you that nothing in their power shall be wanting to render your Life here comfortable and happy.

The Situation of the College is in a very populous, agreeable & healthy Country, upon an elevated tract of Ground, in a clear and wholesome Air; the latter appears from the uncommon State of Health which hath always been remarkable among the Students & Inhabitants of the Village. The Loss of four Presidents in the Compass of a few Years, hath been owing to Singular circumstances, & occasioned by a variety of Infirmities which attended them previous to their removal to Nassau Hall. Mr. Burr, the first who had presided, was a gentleman of infirm Constitution, almost worn out before he came to the College. Mr. Edwards dyed of the Small Pox. Mr. Davies constitutionally prone to inflammatory disorder being let Blood, on a Cold he had taken, an inflammation seized his Arm, which brought on a fever, & proved mortal. Dr. Finley dyed of a Schirrous Liver & consequent Dropsey, the foundation of which disorder was laid some years before his appointment. These things are so particularly mentioned to you S^r, to remove any apprehension of the insalubrity of the Climate, which we can assure you is as healthy here as in any part of N. America.

The Stated Salary annexed to the Office is £250 Curr^y equal to £146 Sterl^g (exch. generally being at 70 p c^t) A large hansome & commodious Dwelling-House is provided for the use of the President, together with a good Garden & sufficient Quantity of Land to furnish him Winter-Fuel & Pasturage. The Perquisites, *communibus annis*, may be about £40 Curr.^{y} The whole, upon moderate valuation, being estimated at £350 Curr^y equal to 206 Ster^g. The trustees are sorry that the state of the College Funds puts it out of their power, at present, to offer you a more ample Reward. They further agreed & have Voted, to allow (in case of your Acceptance) One hundred Guineas for defraying Expences of your removal & Voyage; and that the Salary commence on the Day of your Arrival in America.

We ardently pray, that Providence may make your way plain before you, for the acceptance of their choice trusting in the great Head of the Church, that He will make the eminent Talents he hath afforded you, much more eminently & conspicuously useful to the general Cause of Christianity & the Interests of Virtue & Literature at the Head of this Seminary, than in the Station now assigned You.

We have by this Opportunity written to Richard Stockton Esqr a Member of this Board, now in London on his private Affairs, praying him, if his Business will permit, to wait upon You at Paisley, as soon as he conveniently can. He is a Gentleman of Fortune & Figure in his Profession of the Law, of distinguished Abilities, & Influence here, and a warm Friend to the interests of Religion & Learning. He is thoroly acquainted with the State of our Affairs religious & political, capable of giving the most authentic informations, and answering the minutest Enquiries. In him therefore S^r you may place absolute Confidence. The printed Account of the College inclosed will also give you more ample Information than can be contained in the bounds of a Letter, of the State of the Institution.

We would not impolitely urge a too hasty Resolution in an Affair of such importance to Dr. Witherspoon; But as he will necessarily reflect that the College of New Jersey must, while unprovided of a

Head, labour under great Difficulties & Disadvantages, his Determination with all convenient Dispatch will be highly acceptable to the Board.

By order & in Presence of the Trustees of the College of New Jersey, Signed by Reverend S^r.

Your most Obedient, and
very humble Servant
Wm. P. Smith Pres^{dt} of Trustees[3]

With this letter was forwarded a copy of the official *Account of the College of New Jersey* published in 1764. Duplicates of these documents were sent to Mr. Dennis DeBerdt, the London agent of the province of New Jersey, to be used in case Mr. Stockton were not in the city. Mr. Stockton was also informed that the board would defray his expenses if he would go to Paisley and present the election to Dr. Witherspoon in person and urge him to accept.

It cannot be said that Dr. Witherspoon's election was hasty; but there was no waste of time, and the reason for prompt action is found in the ecclesiastical politics of the time. The American Presbyterian Church was divided into two parties, the Old Side and the New. With the latter the college had been associated since its origin and the other party had never been allowed any real share in its control. On the whole the college had risen steadily in reputation until by the time of President Finley's death it was unquestionably the leading American institution of higher learning having Presbyterian affiliations. Old Side candidates for the ministry were, however, meeting at their trials such "hard measures from the ministers in ye favor of Jersey college under a pretence of examining their style," says Dr. Alison, that they were finding it almost impossible to pass those trials and Anglicans were advising them to leave the Presbyterian fold with its "narrow persecuting bigots" and cast their lot with them.[4] To obviate these circumstances the Old Side party had recently resolved to send all their boys to Princeton, "very persuaded that, were all students bred under the same professors in the same col-

[3] Green MS., the original received by Dr. Witherspoon. A copy is in the Minutes of the Board.
[4] Stiles MSS., Alison to Stiles, December 4, 1766.

lege, our disputes would end." [5] But the college needed a larger faculty; the business of the Presidency, added to a heavy schedule of teaching, was too much for one man to handle; tutors, efficient or otherwise, were constantly on the move, and the college naturally suffered from so many changes in its teaching staff; in fact, the opinion was alleged to exist in some circles that the college had been on the decline ever since Mr. Burr's death and that the students were not getting a fair return for their time and money spent at Nassau Hall. Moreover, a suspicion that the Anglican Church was endeavoring to get control of American educational institutions of learning, its achievement in this direction in New York and Philadelphia, and indications that Governor Franklin of New Jersey was trying to bring about similar results at Princeton, together with the underlying fear of the establishment of an American episcopate which would further hamper the liberties of non-Anglican bodies, made it evident that the sooner Presbyterians buried their differences and united their forces the better would be their position to cope with that branch of the Christian Church which they called "the enemy."

Therefore as the College of New Jersey was now without a President and was sorely in need of funds, the Old Side deemed the time ripe for an effort to win by fair bargain an adequate share in the management of the institution with whose fortunes they believed the destinies of American Presbyterianism to be inevitably involved. An overture was accordingly prepared in Philadelphia looking toward this end, and at the special meeting of the board of trustees of the College in November, 1766, accompanied by a group of lawyers and other prominent citizens who were to support it with their presence and their oratory, there appeared a delegation of ministers appointed by the Old Side party in Philadelphia to lay before the trustees a petition and a letter—"a very strenuous letter"—bearing twenty-six signatures and outlining the Old Side's proposition. This included, besides the election of a President, the appointment of at least three

---

[5] Alison to Stiles, *loc. cit.* This is the probable explanation of the sudden doubling of the graduating class in 1765 and 1766. The size of the average class from 1760 to 1764 had been sixteen; in 1765 and 1766 it was thirty-one; during the interregnum of 1767 it dropped to eleven.

other professors, one of divinity and two of the sciences, who should cover other subjects in the curriculum; and in return the petitioners proposed not only to establish funds but also to open subscriptions for a number of years to increase those funds. And recognizing the unhappy differences existing in the Church, the petitioners suggested that the President and one of the professors should be elected from the Old Side and the other two professors from the New Side. Acceptance of the proposal would mean an immediate increase of students, faculty, and funds. Altogether the proposal from several points of view was a generous one and bade well to end the dissension in the Church, besides promising distinct advance in the efficiency of the College; it would have been more generous had the choice of an Old Side President not been one of its terms.

According to Mr. Samuel Purviance, Jr., a Philadelphia merchant closely sharing Old Side counsels, the plans were kept secret until the last moment, a copy of the memorial being sent to the trustees only just before the meeting.

So Sensible are we of the narrow Biggotry of our Brethren ye New Lights, wrote he to Ezra Stiles, that we dare not disclose these our benevolent & generous views for fear of defeating our Intentions; by apprizing them beforehand Schemes wd. be laid to oppose us in this most Salutary Measure; so that we hope to take our Friends off their Guard; on this Acct the Design is intedd to be kept private amongst us until near the Time of Election; If this looks like Cunning, I'm sure its such as you'll approve where the Intention is so good. Its needless to point out to a Person who can so readily see, how many Advantages wd. naturally arise from this scheme; It wd. in general kill ye Seeds of Narrow Principle, Unite our at present divided Strength, Raise a Number of able Labourers for ye Vineyard & Render us a formidable Barrier agst both Civil & Religious Encroachers. I can hardly suffer myself to despair of success in these noble Aims. . . . . If we succeed in Uniting our Strength in the Jersey College & the intended Union with our Friends in N: Engd I shan't much regard what our Enemies can do agst. Us.[6]

Judging by the background of ecclesiastical politics suggested in this very frank exposition of the plan, Dr. Witherspoon, if not

[6] Stiles MSS., Letter of November 1, 1766.

exactly stepping from a Scottish frying-pan into an American fire, nevertheless must have found himself in an element not altogether unfamiliar when he transferred his allegiance from the parent Church to its colonial offspring.

The scheme described by Mr. Purviance leaked out; the trustees of the College were not taken off their guard; and the Old Side promoters found that they had sadly miscalculated the strength of their fellow ministers' pride. Even the gain to the general cause of Presbyterianism against the feared encroachments of Anglicanism was not sufficient to carry the day. Despite the reunion of the rival synods, the wounds of the old schism which had split the Church were not quite healed; the College was still too personal an asset for the New Side group to share, and the trustees with less charity perhaps than good luck forestalled their petitioners as we have seen by nominating as President a man whose affiliations were neutral to be sure, but who nevertheless was a man of their own choosing, and elected in such a way as to intimate with more firmness perhaps than delicacy, that they would brook no interference; and then they received the Philadelphia delegates. The latter acknowledged themselves disconcerted by the election that had just taken place, their proposal being contingent on a vacant presidency, and they hastily retired, declining to engage for the future conduct of their constituents. Privately, they complained that their reception had been cold and very impolite and their memorial treated with contempt.[7]

After the Philadelphians had withdrawn, the trustees passed a somewhat superfluous resolution to the effect that while they would gladly do everything in their power to bring about harmony among all the patrons of religion and sound learning and would welcome the increase of the faculty of the College, yet they did not feel warranted in electing additional professors until they saw the means of paying their salaries. It may be added, to conclude this none too creditable story, that negotiations were generously renewed by the Philadelphians the next year, waiving all

[7] Stiles MSS., Alison to Stiles, December 4, 1766, and Purviance to Stiles, December 13, 1766.

party considerations, and a compromise was effected whereby one Old Side trustee was elected to the board and three professors to the faculty, John Blair, Dr. Hugh Williamson of Philadelphia, and Jonathan Edwards, Jr., already a tutor in the College. Of these Mr. Blair alone entered on his duties. The Old Side promised aid in securing funds for the maintenance of these chairs but after the arrival of Dr. Witherspoon the plans were annulled by the board, the funds not having materialized. With the resignation of Professor Blair in 1769, the new President had a free field, and two years later fresh plans for enlarging the faculty were taken up similar in scope to those of 1766 and, thanks to the strength of Dr. Witherspoon's personality, free from party trammels, but only to be brought to naught by the Revolutionary War.

Dr. Francis Alison, who had been slated for the presidency in case the Old Side proposal were adopted, was one of the first to admit that Witherspoon's acceptance would be a likely way to reunite the Presbyterian body; but by certain other members of his party the action of the trustees was bitterly resented, and a contemptible effort seems to have been made by the irreconcilables to wreck the effort to get Dr. Witherspoon. A letter was written from Philadelphia to the President-elect, seeming to encourage his acceptance but really calculated to produce the opposite result. And it partially succeeded. Mr. Stockton declared that this "artful, plausible, yet wickedly contrived letter" more than anything else originally deterred Dr. Witherspoon from entertaining serious thoughts of accepting his call to America.[8]

At first Mr. Stockton was disinclined to make the trip to Paisley. It was February, 1767, when he received the trustees' commission of the preceding November and he found it difficult to decide which was worse, the weather or the roads. Persuaded at

---

[8] No copy of the letter appears to have been preserved. The documents on which the account given above is based are in Hageman, *History of Princeton*, vol. I, p. 79, Field, *Provincial Courts of New Jersey*, vol. I, pp. 288, 386, and the *Henley Smith Papers* in the Library of Congress. Maclean says the letter was written from Princeton, but Mr. Stockton saw the original and could hardly have been mistaken in dating it from Philadelphia. Benjamin Rush also speaks of it as coming from Philadelphia.

length to go to Paisley he discovered that, in spite of letters urgent and descriptive sent to Dr. Witherspoon from America,[9] neither he nor his friends had "any Tolerable idea" of the place to which he was invited, nor did they have any notion of the importance of the college over which he was asked to preside. One and all opposed his acceptance. Mr. Stockton was able to overcome the effect of the Philadelphia letter and to remove Dr. Witherspoon's own objections and he even took upon himself, in view of an unaccountable discrepancy as to salary discovered in the trustees' letter, to stand by the sum therein named—three hundred and fifty pounds proclamation money and perquisites, instead of the two hundred and fifty pounds proclamation and perquisites originally voted.[10]

The following letter written on the last day of February by Dr. Witherspoon to Mr. Archibald Wallace, an Edinburgh merchant, and now among the manuscripts in the Presbyterian Historical Society at Philadelphia, alludes to this important question, but is more particularly interesting because of the hint it contains as to the chief, and hitherto unmentioned, obstacle in the way of his acceptance.

Dear Sir:

Mr. Stockton would inform you how he found matters here. Though no material alteration has happened since he left us yesterday having so important a matter under consideration I read over again the Trustees' letter this morning and observed a circumstance which I had overlooked before, that they mention the fixed Salary of the President to be £250 Currency, and the perquisites about £40 Currency, and yet make the whole amount to £350 Currency, £206 Sterling. From my not being accustomed to comparing Currency & Sterling I did not observe that particular when at Edinburgh, but now perceive that they must have estimated the House and Pasturage to make up the

---

[9] One of the most charming of these communications was from the Reverend Dr. John Rodgers of New York, written on Christmas Eve, 1766. He sits down at midnight—the ship sails in the morning—to seize the opportunity to send a few lines, to tell Dr. Witherspoon who Mr. Stockton is, and to say that young Benjamin Rush will call upon him, and finally to give him some idea of the position to which he had been called. The original is in the papers with the Green MS.

[10] President Finley's salary had been four hundred pounds proclamation but the poor financial condition of the College had necessitated the reduction.

sum total. Now this is so greatly inferior to the offer which I refused from Dublin last summer, where the work is less burdensome, that when I came to explain matters with my wife and friends, I knew not what to say to it.

I have writ this because I expect Mr. Stockton will not leave Edinburgh on Monday, so that you may have an opportunity of speaking to him in case I have yet committed any mistake.

From the persuasion of you and the other friends at Edinburgh, and what Mr. Stockton has said of the state of religion in America, I find a pretty favorable inclination in my own mind to the proposal, though many difficulties lie in the way.

My wife recovered her spirits a good deal yesterday night after Mr. Stockton left us, and spoke a good deal in praise of him as a man of excellent sense and fine behaviour, but whether this arose in part from expectation that the affair was wholly over, I cannot say.

I believe I need scarcely beg your Sympathy and the assistance of your prayers on this weighty occasion, as I dare say they will not be wanting. I would have writ more but am straitened in time.

I am with compliments to all friends, dear Sir

Your's &c

Mr. Stockton was not able to win over Mrs. Witherspoon in spite of the good impression he made on her, an impression he left behind him wherever he went. But in this case his eloquence, his wit, his good looks and polished manners, his air of brains and breeding, were of no avail. In London he had been received by Government with every mark of respect; the corporation of Edinburgh had given him a public dinner at which the freedom of the city was presented to him, and it is said that the town of Paisley did him similar honor. His mission to North Britain was common talk, and the rumor even got abroad in Edinburgh that Dr. Witherspoon had accepted, that he was already collecting books for the college library, and that he would sail for America in the spring. But none of these things moved Mrs. Witherspoon; and early in March Mr. Stockton paid a second visit to Paisley for the specific purpose of converting her. Again he had counted without his hostess. She was a quiet, home-loving body with a numerous family; she disliked change of abode; she had in fact objected to her husband's removal from Beith to Paisley; still more strenuously then did she protest against this unheard-of transatlantic migration. Even the crafty suggestion that she would find it easier to live in Princeton than at Paisley, the former "being the cheapest place in America"—a distinction it has long since ceased to earn—had not influenced her, and she would not so much as see the smooth-speaking American lawyer the second time. Nothing daunted, Mr. Stockton resorted to strategy and proselytised, so he says, all the eminent clergy of Edinburgh and Glasgow by putting the case of the College of New Jersey before them in such a way that they not only changed their own minds as to the oughtness of Dr.Witherspoon's acceptance of the presidency, but even agreed if necessary to attack Mrs. Witherspoon in her own entrenchments and take her position by storm. March went by, however, and no decision had been reached. From London in April Mr. Stockton wrote once more asking for an answer, as he proposed leaving England by the first of May; he knows how seriously Dr. Witherspoon had been taking the matter into consideration and what attention he has given to the facts in the case; he hopes the obstacles which at first showed themselves have not been insurmountable; what shall he say on his return to America if Dr. Witherspoon refuses, and what will his fellow-trustees do? "Shall we turn to our old antagonists and thereby let them in by wholesale or shall we make them greater enemies than ever before by totally neglecting them? I am pained when I think of the consequences of your determining against us." [11]

But the lady in the question had been holding out bravely and her husband finally capitulated. The matter he said had given him such uneasiness—"the greatest that ever anything of the kind did"—that he could not dismiss it from his mind. And on April 18, 1767, he wrote to Mr. Stockton that the family difficulties were insurmountable although he himself was inclined to favor the plan. "My wife continued in such distress on the subject that for some weeks after you left us she was scarcely ever half a day out of bed at a time till I told her at any rate to make herself easy, for whatever inclination I might have to it, the Removal was of such a nature that I could not insist upon it unless she could be brought to agree to it." Since then they had talked

[11] Presbyterian Historical Society MSS. Letter of April 14, 1767.

about it, and he had hopes sometimes it might go through; but now he had little or none. "It has been a time of utmost anxiety and difficulty to me," he concluded; he could not have stood any longer the state of uncertainty and suspense, and he had therefore decided to write his declination as soon as Mr. Stockton would tell him to whom it should be addressed.[12]

The formal letter of declination sent to the trustees has not been preserved. Benjamin Rush, a graduate of Princeton, at that time studying medicine at Edinburgh, on hearing the news wrote a despondent letter to Dr. Witherspoon beginning: "And must poor Nassau Hall indeed be ruined?" Three quarto pages of hysterical language follow, foretelling what will happen to the College; he hopes its dissolution will not be laid to Dr. Witherspoon's door:

O Nassau Hall, Nassau Hall, in vain rescued and cherished by every Lover of religion, since thou art to fall into the Hands of some—but I cannot express it—my Heart bleeds within me—O Nassau Hall, Nassau Hall.

After this amazing outburst the young medical student got control of himself again and concluded his epistle with an apology: "Pray excuse the Freedom I have assumed and attribute it to my Zeal for the College." [13]

With more practical sense Dr. Witherspoon, unable to go to America himself, now devoted his attention to naming a substitute, and when in May he received a visit from Rush, who was acting the part of Mr. Stockton's understudy, he suggested an old friend, the Reverend Charles Nesbit of Montrose, whose name had already been mentioned in the connection. To Nesbit Witherspoon wrote urging acceptance if called, and to Mr. Stockton he sent a long and fine letter of recommendation of the new possibility.[14]

[12] Green MS. The original letter.
[13] Green MS. The original letter.
[14] The letter is among the papers with the Green MS. It can hardly be necessary to do more than dismiss again with contempt the legend mentioned by Dr. Alexander Carlyle, and similarly dismissed by him, to the effect that Nesbit was Witherspoon's natural son. Dr. Nesbit's parentage is easily authenticated in the Scottish parish records.

But Dr. Nesbit appears to have totally refused to consider the question although he did call on Rush; and his name was never formally brought before the trustees. A week later Rush wrote to his classmate Jonathan Bayard Smith a letter which indicates that he had not yet given up hope. The letter, moreover, furnishes corroboration of the assertion that an attempt was made from America to deter Dr. Witherspoon, and it also gives us the only contemporary description of Dr. Witherspoon that we have.[15]

Doc[r]· Witherspoon has not yet determined any way with Regard to ye College.[16] His Mind I know has a Strong Biass to America but Alas! he is Obliged as yet to plead yt. he has married a Wife and cannot come. I have dined and supped frequently w[th]· him here in Edinr; and am charmed with his Behaviour. he appears to be Mr. Davies and Dr. Finley revived in One man. in point of Genius he is equal to ye first, and in Knowledge I believe he is superior even to Dr. Finley himself, more especially in y[t]· Branch of Knowledge which is now a days so much admired viz: the Belles-Lettres. I have heard him preach twice, and can truly say he exceeds any Preacher I have heard since I came to Scotland—indeed I have heard few Preachers in ye Course of my Life that were equal to him. his Voice has much of that mellody in it w[ch]· we used so much admire in the late Mr. Bostwick. his Appearance in the Pulpit is Solemn and gracefull. his Sermons are loadned w[th]· good Sense, and adorned at y[e] same time w[th]· all the Elegance and Beauty that Language can give them. And what above all enhances these Accomplishments in him as a Preacher is, that he never carries a Note w[th]· him in the Pulpit, so that I am in hopes sh[d]· he go to the College he will by his Example put an End to the too common Practise of reading Sermons in America, more especially among our young ministers. May that Providence w[ch]· has formed him w[th]· such great Endowments, and w[ch]· I trust directed y[e] Eyes of y[e] College towards him, remove all Obstructions from Out of his Way, and make y[e] path of Duty clear before him. I think the College of New Jersey would flourish as much under him as ever it has done under any of his Predecessors. He is the Homo factus ad Unguem, and is admirably calculated for overthrowing all the Stratagems of those who have hitherto combined to ruin our College. I have wrote to him twice, and plead with him to embrace the Offer in as strong Terms as if I was

[15] Library of Congress. *Henley Smith Papers*, Letter of April 30, 1767.
[16] Rush is mistaken. Witherspoon had decided by April 18.

pleading for my Life. I took ye Liberty of sending him a Copy of that part of your Letter wch. related to his Election, and to the Schemes of Govr. Franklin, Dr. Allison &c wth. Regard to the College. I was very happy in finding it exactly coincide wth. what I had told him before,— here my Friend I could unfold a Secret to you that would excite your manly Indignation, and rouse up all ye Jersey Scholar in you. good Mr. Tulford the Seceding Minister in Philada. and one Mr. Clash a Seceding Minister in New York, each of them wrote to Dr. Witherspoon and urged his embracing the Call from the most benevolent & disinterested motives. they likewise wrote to several of their Friends here to use their utmost Influence to prevail wth. ye Doctor. may Heaven reward them for their Piety and Public-Spirit: the Case was widely different from this wth. certain Gentlemen in Philada. happy for the College Mr. Stockton had it in his power fully to refute all ye Aspersions that were thrown upon it, and to obviate the Accounts that arrived here (wth: ye Acct. of ye Doctor's Election) of y^e "Bigotry"—"Faction"—"Ignorance," "Narrow Views," "little Management"—"want of Discipline," "raw Tutors," "weak illiterate Presidents," and entire Loss of Reputation, wch. have hitherto prevailed at the College of New Jersey. Methinks I see your Cheeks redden wth. Resentment; but for a while suspend your Rage my Friend. they did this from the most friendly Motives, and from a real Desire to advance ye Interest of ye College, it was wth. a view of prevailing upon Doc^r. Witherspoon to come and rescue the unhappy College from ye Hands of Bigotry—Superstition and Ignorance. May heaven reward them for their Piety and Public Spirit! Remember my dear Jonathan this is only inter Nos. Mr. Stockton will unravel the whole Secret to you. in ye mean time let w^t I have hinted to you remain a profound Secret in y^r. own Bosom. May ye College of New Jersey be overwhelmed wth. an earthquake on ye day in wch. Dr:——— or Mr. ———get a Footing there!

Dr. Witherspoon's letter of declination was read at the trustees' meeting at Princeton in October, 1767, and they at once, and rather hastily, elected to the vacant presidency the Reverend Samuel Blair of Boston, a graduate of the class of 1760; and the first act of this academic comedy closed.

But in the meantime at Paisley a change had taken place. Having gained her point in May, Mrs. Witherspoon had straightway weakened. During the early summer Rush spent several days at Paisley and Mrs. Witherspoon at last had given him a calm hearing and had argued the whole matter out with him, until finally he had talked away her fears and objections, and in August she had given her consent to the move, if now her husband should be re-elected.[17]

The Reverend Charles Beatty, a trustee of the college, visiting Scotland that summer took the opportunity to go to Paisley and was agreeably disappointed in the wife of the Laigh Kirk's minister. Instead of the "poor, peevish, reserved, discontented" lady he had expected to find, he met a "well-looking, genteel, open, friendly woman—which perhaps you will be surprised at." She regretted her rudeness to Mr. Stockton, and explained it by saying that "she was in a weak state of health and that in that situation things appeared very gloomy to her—crossing the sea, and that her husband might soon die, and she be left in a strange land &c."[18]

Benjamin Rush at Edinburgh had gone into ecstasies over the new turn of affairs. On the twenty-third of October he sent this letter to Dr. Witherspoon (the enclosure referred to has not been preserved):

My dear Sir:

Last night I received the enclosed letter from one Mr. Smith in Philadelphia, a gentleman of distinguished worth, and one whose strong attachment to the College of New Jersey, renders the intelligence contained in the letter such as may entirely be depended upon. I thought it best to send it to you, as I could not conveniently extract those passages more particularly which relate to that College.

You will see that the Trustees, so far from being in the least irritated against you for your refusal, are pleased with your extensive views and just notions of the importance of the College. You will likewise see in what dangers and difficulties that College is involved, how thick and fast its enemies increase, and how much the hearts of its pious friends are trembling for fear the united forces of civil and religious Combinations will end in the ruin of the College.—

Oh, Sir, does not your heart expand with unutterable sentiments of love and benevolence when you think that you are to be the means of

[17] Green MS. Archibald Wallace to Mr. Stockton, August 22, 1767; also Biddle, *Memorial of Benjamin Rush*, p. 29.
[18] C. Beatty to R. Treat, October 15, 1767, in *Scotch Irish in America*, 9th Congress, 1900, p. 72; Maclean, vol. I, p. 385.

rescuing so important a Seminary from ruin? Don't you some time Anticipate the transport of being received with ten thousand wel-comes the moment you land in America? and of being at the head of an Institution on which the spreading of the Gospel through the wide extended continent of America now entirely depends?—to preside over that College methinks is a Province worthy of an Angel! I am very Confident the Trustees cannot have a President till four months after they receive your refusal, not only from what I know of the laws of the College, but from what I heard Mr. Stockton say when in Edin-burgh. The law was strictly adhered to in Mr. Davies' case. Four months elapsed between the time of his refusal and second election. The ship you enquire after sailed from London to New York the 2nd. of September. You need not send the enclosed letter to town till you come yourself. My best compliments to Mrs. Witherspoon.[19]

Mr. Archibald Wallace, the Edinburgh merchant, had already hastily dispatched a letter to Mr. Stockton informing him of Mrs. Witherspoon's surrender; and Dr. Witherspoon himself had immediately written, discreetly hinting that a re-election would meet with a favorable answer. To this Mr. Stockton replied November 5, explaining the election of Mr. Blair.

Princeton, Nov. 5, 1767

Rev. & dear Sir

Your two letters dated in August last came to hand a few days agone—the pains you have taken in endeavoring to find out, and in recommending a proper person for the president of New Jersey Col-lege as mentioned in your first Letter shows your attention to its In-terests: but your consent to become its president yourself as hinted in your last, altho' an unexpected, yet is a much stronger and more acceptable evidence to the Trustees of your regard to that institution. You will perhaps suppose it unhappy that before the agreeable ac-count of Mrs. Witherspoon's consent and your determination thereon had reached us, that we had filled the place by electing Mr. Blair; but by a strange coincidence of circumstances, it is hoped that the elec-tion will only seem to manifest the regard of the Govrs of the College to that Gentleman, and at the same time not prevent them from final choice.

The Trustees doubted not of Mr. Blair's acceptance when they elected him, and supposed that as one of the professors was his uncle, altho the President was so young he the uncle being satisfied would

[19] Presbyterian Historical Society MSS.

[87]

influence in conciliating the others. But whether true or false it seems Mr. Blair has been informed that his youth will make him inadmissible among his Brethren upon such terms as he would chuse, and therefore before we heard from Scotland it was generally said that Mr. Blair was so much disgusted that he certainly would not come in; but now every one says that as he is as famous for his modesty as for his Learning and other valuable "Qualifications" he will not hesitate to declare in the negative. If that should be the case the Trustees will meet immediately and re-elect you; and there is not the least doubt but it will be unanimous; for the News of your Consent to come apparently inspires every friend of the College with Joy—they say it will effectually make up the ancient quarell among the presbyterians here, will open a more easy & advantageous communication with North Britain &c. &c. &c. in short your coming seems now the common Topic of conversation and every one is pleased with the prospect. My present hurry prevents my being very particular and as I expect we shall have Occasion of writing you soon again there is less need of it.

You'll please tell Mrs. Witherspoon if she comes to Princeton both Mrs. Stockton and I will take great pleasure in endeavouring to make the place agreeable to her and that I doubt not she will soon like America full as well as she does Scotland.

My respects to your worthy colleague Mr. Muir, to Mrs. Witherspoon, your daughter and other branches of your family.

I am Dr Sir

Your respectful friend & ob. Serv.

It turned out as Mr. Stockton had hoped. Mr. Blair, realizing that his youth—he was only twenty-seven—was regarded as a serious drawback to his efficiency, seized the obvious opportunity to avoid an awkward predicament, besides insuring his reputation for modesty and generosity, by sending forthwith to the trustees the declination on which he had already resolved. The situation being thus cleared, at the meeting of the board in December when Mr. Blair's letter was read and his declination accepted, Mr. Stockton produced the letters he had received from Scotland and informed his colleagues that if Dr. Witherspoon were re-elected he would esteem it "a duty to enter into this public service." The news was heard with "peculiar satisfaction" says the record. Dr. Witherspoon was promptly re-elected (December 9) and Mr. William Peartree Smith was once more directed to transmit a copy of the vote of election, and to request Dr. Witherspoon to hasten his coming. A copy was also sent to Benjamin Rush for use in assisting the President-elect in the difficult task of cutting loose from Paisley.

The good news that Dr. Witherspoon was again a presidential possibility had spread rapidly and its effect we have already seen in Mr. Stockton's letter of November 5. The Reverend George Duffield told Mr. Beatty that "no sooner did the Letters arrive here from Scotland that Mrs. Witherspoon like another Sarah was willing to follow her husband, than Witherspoon's name dwelt upon every Tongue, and the very air of Princeton for Weeks together resounded with Nothing but the name of Witherspoon." [20] Rush had been keeping Dr. Witherspoon buoyed up until the news of his formal re-election should arrive. Already in December he was suggesting wealthy persons who might be disposed to give Dr. Witherspoon books for the college library; he explained away the election of young Mr. Blair and the circumstances of his declination.

"The College must have sunk into Disrepute wth. so young a man at the Head of it. But wt. could be done? better far to make choice of him than Dr. Allison. You see my dear Sir how Opportune, nay how indispensable your Offer was. Say has not the immediate Hand of Providence over-ruled this most important Event? The Hearts of the College were trembling with Fear when they saw the Object of their Hopes entrusted to the feeble Hands of an inexperienced Youth. But you have banished all their Fears, & they once more exult & triumph in the prospect of seeing their darling seminary the Bulwark of the Religion & Liberty of America; for my part I am transported every time I think of it:

Redeunt Saturnia Regna
Aspici et Omni Saeclo venturo laetentur [21]

Dr. Alison wrote a little later to Mr. Stiles:

Dr. Wetherspoon is expected at Princeton and great things to be

[20] Green MS. Rush to Witherspoon, April 30, 1768, quoting Mr. Duffield's to Mr. Beatty, which he had seen.
[21] Green MS. Rush quotes the half line correctly (Vergil, *Eclogues* IV, 6) but the second line (*Eclogues*, IV, 52) should read "Aspice, venturo Laetentur ut omnia saeclo."

done. The only want that they feel there is want of money. The trustees are bad Oeconomists and have squandered away much money and are not able to maintain a President and professors, and as they will not share the management with the Synod of Philadelphia I fear they will not have much help from that quarter, but all have high expectations from the Scots Doctor. I wish he may have skill to heal all our divisions.[22]

That closing sentence makes amends for the somewhat ungracious tone of the rest of the paragraph. In fact the only dissenting note in the chorus of public approval seems to have been a half jocular remark by young William Paterson, the future Associate Justice of the Supreme Court, then a student of law at Princeton. He was writing to his chum John Macpherson, also a former Nassovian, and was attempting to be playful: "Witherspoon is President. Mercy on me! we shall be over-run with Scotchmen, the worst vermin under Heaven." And he later alludes to the new comer as "the Scotchman." But Paterson was partly Scotch himself, as was his correspondent; and elsewhere writing to the same friend he speaks of his filial affection for Scotland and his loss of patience when he hears people rail against it.[23]

Dr. Witherspoon's letter accepting his election is no longer in existence. With characteristic energy he at once began to prepare himself for his new duties. Knowing that the grammar school at Nassau Hall, which had been discontinued shortly after President Finley's death, would be reorganized under his care and that, besides being considered a legitimate perquisite of the presidency it could be made a powerful feeder for the College and a model for colonial secondary education, he made use of a trip to London late the following February (1768) to visit eminent teachers and get hints as to methods and textbooks. His private memorandum book, seen by Ashbel Green, contained the notes of his itinerary, but Dr. Green does not quote from it and the book has disappeared. Remaining over two weeks he secured by purchase or gift large accessions to the college library and then paid a visit to Holland to form acquaintance with prominent men in the Dutch Church and to discuss a plan for sending to

[22] Stiles MSS. Letter of June 4, 1768.
[23] Mills, *Glimpses of Colonial Society*, pp. 48, 88.

Princeton a professor of divinity from Holland under whom Dutch candidates for the ministry in America might pursue their theological studies.[24]

After a stay of two weeks in Holland, Dr. Witherspoon returned to Paisley in April and on the twelfth of that month at the meeting of the presbytery announced that he had received a call to America which he thought he would accept, and he, therefore, begged that a special meeting be called at which he might with due formality present his resignation. It will be remembered that his settlement at Paisley had been attended by extraordinary difficulty; the procedure in his leaving was to be no less complicated. In fact, the path of a minister entering or leaving any Scottish parish in those days seems to have been strewn with as many formal obstructions as could possibly be imagined.

May 10, at Paisley, Dr. Witherspoon read the following letter addressed to the moderator of the presbytery:[25]

Rev. Sir:

It is not unknown to the members of this Presbytery that I have received a Call to the College of New Jersey in America. This after much deliberation I have come to a resolution of accepting of. The reasons inducing me to this is unnecessary to trouble the Presbytery with: it is sufficient to say that no dissatisfaction either with the Church of Scotland or my present Charge has in the least contributed to it. On the contrary I part with all my connections in Scotland with

[24] In 1766 a plan had been laid before the trustees of the College looking toward this end but the board came to the conclusion that the time was not ripe for such a professorship and had tabled the proposal. Soon after, the Classis of Amsterdam had suggested to the two parties in the Dutch Church in America that they bury their differences, give up for the present the effort to organize a separate college, and unite in procuring from Holland a professor of divinity who should be located at Princeton by courtesy of the College of New Jersey and who should perhaps give courses in the College. This seems to have been the reason for Witherspoon's visit to Holland. At Rotterdam he was in frequent conference with John H. Livingston, the future well-known divine who at this period was a student of theology at Utrecht. The plan came to naught as the American churches objected to a local union with Princeton and a few years later a charter was obtained for Queens, now Rutgers, College. The history of these developments is found in Alexander Gunn's *Memoirs of J. H. Livingston*, in Corwin's *Manual of the Reformed Church in America*, 4th edition, p. 119, and in the history of the founding of Queens (Rutgers) College. The accounts of Jonathan Sergeant, treasurer of the College of New Jersey, show that the institution paid Dr. Witherspoon's expenses for the trip.

[25] Presbytery of Paisley MS. records, May 10, 1768.

the greatest Reluctance and shall ever retain a grateful sense of the obligations I ly under to my Brethren in the Ministry in this Presbytery and elsewhere as well as to a very affectionate Congregation the care of which I am now to surrender. I do therefore hereby demit my Charge in this place hoping the presbytery will receive it and Conceive their Sentence in such terms as it may plainly appear to be of the nature of a Translation and that I depart in full Communion with the Church of Scotland.

I am Rev. Sir your Affec^e Brother and obedient
humble servant

Jn° Witherspoon

After Dr. Witherspoon had addressed the presbytery on the subject, Benjamin Rush was introduced to lay before the meeting the minute of the trustees of the College of New Jersey which had been sent to him, dated December 9, 1767, showing that Dr. Witherspoon had been unanimously elected President of the college. Rush having withdrawn, a minute dated May 9, 1768, was then read from the magistrates and town council of Paisley.[26]

The Magistrates & Council being informed that the Reverend Mr. Witherspoon minister of the Laigh Church in this place is to give his Demission to the Presbytery of Paisley tomorrow the tenth day of May seventeen hundred and sixty eight years, Do hereby appoint Baillie John Storie & Baillie John Sclater two of their number in their name to attend the Presbytery and signify to them that though they have Lived in the Greatest harmony with Him since he was their minister and Could have wished that he had Continued in his present Charge, Yet since he has seen it his duty to Accept of another Office from Respect and friendship for him they Resolve to give no opposition But are willing that the Presbytery accept to his Demission.

John Storie
John Sclater

A committee of elders from the kirk session then appeared and presented the following extract from the session minutes dated May 10, 1768:[27]

At Dr. Witherspoon's desire the Moderator represented that after mature deliberation he had been prevailed upon to accept of a call

[26] Paisley Council MS. records.
[27] Presbytery of Paisley MS. records.

from the College of New Jersey in North America and that he intended to give in his demission of his pastoral Charge to the presbytery of Paisley to meet this day. But as the time fixed for his departure would not admit of delay he desired that the Session would appoint a deputation of their number to wait on the Presbytery and in their name express their assent to the acceptance of his demission. The session having considered the above requisition nominated and appointed [names left blank] to wait on Presbytery and in their name represent that though they have always had reason to esteem Dr. Witherspoon very highly in love for his own and his works sake and feel the strongest reluctance at the dissolution of his pastoral relation to them yet since he hath seen it his duty to accept of the call to New Jersey and expresseth a desire that the Revd Presbytery may accept of the demission he proposes to exhibit, they are determined to make no opposition but to acquiesce in what deliverance the Presbytery shall be pleased to give on the Cause.

Robert Burns was not yet born, but Dr. Witherspoon was already quite familiar with the spirit of his future countryman's famous line concerning the plans of mice and men. He did not doubt that he was called to America under Providence and he had accepted the call in that spirit; but at the same time he could not avoid the fear that, as this is at best an uncertain world, something might happen to necessitate a change in his plans even at the eleventh hour and he had no intention to fall, providentially or otherwise, between the two stools of the Princeton presidency and the Paisley pastorate. With excusable prudence, therefore, he asked to be heard again in his own behalf, and then requested Presbytery to consider his demission under the restriction that his ministry should not cease until the date of his actual departure from Scotland, lest any unforeseen circumstance prevent him at the last moment; and that in the meantime he be given leave to depart in case the ship on which he proposed to take passage should sail between then and the June meeting of the presbytery. This was granted by unanimous consent, and it was also voted that upon any person appearing at Presbytery with a written letter from him asking final acceptance of his resignation, or on receipt of authentic evidence of his having sailed, Presbytery would accept the same and find the pastoral relation with Paisley dissolved from that date. And in the event of his departing thus

The Presbytery Did and hereby Do Recommend him as a minister in full Communion with the Church of Scotland whose character and Conduct Justly Intitle him to all due respect and encouragement from the Synod of New York and Philadelphia, and their other Brethren in America who have the esteem of and are friendly to the constitution of this Church.[28]

The opinion has been expressed [29] that Dr. Witherspoon left Paisley a persecuted and disappointed man. But the documentary evidence in the case is quite to the contrary. The resolutions, letters, and other records connected with his call to Dundee, with his money presents and increases of salary at Paisley, and finally with his departure for America, admit of only one view of his place in the affection and esteem of his parishioners and of his own feelings toward the community and his position in the church at large. And his words in his first sermon at Princeton and in subsequent letters home show beyond possible doubt that he was speaking with perfect candor when he assured his colleagues of the Presbytery of Paisley in his letter of May 9, 1768, that he was not leaving Scotland on account of any dissatisfaction. As for his alleged sacrifice of valuable estates on leaving Scotland, as alleged by Graham and others, it yet remains to be proved that he ever owned or was likely to own any. There are indications that he had rich relatives, and Ashbel Green reports the rumor that one of these offered Dr. Witherspoon a large sum to remain in Scotland; but no facts have come to light in support of this rumor.

Already on April 16, the Sunday after he had announced to the Presbytery his forthcoming departure, Dr. Witherspoon had preached the first installment of his farewell sermon, *Ministerial*

---

[28] Presbytery of Paisley MS. records.

[29] For example, Hew Scott, *Fasti*, vol. II, part I, p. 203, says he was "soured and embittered;" James Peterson, *History of the Counties of Ayr and Wigton*, vol. III, part I, p. 67, says that Paisley became "too hot" for him; James Graham, *Social Life in Scotland*, vol. II, p. 444, says that "harassed by long persecution . . . he sacrificed valuable estates and left Scotland in disgust," and Dr. McCosh in his *Scottish Philosophy* follows in general these opinions.

Fidelity.[30] On May 15 he delivered the remainder, and the next day after reading the last proofs of his volume of *Discourses* and dating the Introduction, he and his family left Paisley for Greenock, the port of Glasgow, where the brigantine *Peggy*, a fine stout vessel "well found with good accommodations," according to the *Pennsylvania Gazette*, and commanded by Captain Robert Spier, was riding at anchor in the Clyde. With delightfully unconscious humor the Edinburgh *Caledonian Mercury* of the following Saturday sapiently informed its readers that

On Monday last the Reverend Mr. John Witherspoon a late minister in Paisley, set out for Greenock to take upon him the office of President of the College of that place.

On the eighteenth, as the ship was going down the river, Dr. Witherspoon wrote the following to the moderator of the presbytery by whom it was introduced at the June meeting:[31]

From on board the Peggy in
Greenock road, May 18, 1768.

My dear Brother

We are Just getting under Sail therefore please to intimate this to the Presbytery at their next Meeting According to the Tenor of their Minute and tell them I am sensible of their Civility and Kindness in the manner of expressing their Sentence and hope they will now without delay find the Vacancy that Steps may be taken for its supply. I shall remember you daily before God. I expect the same from you and that you will give orders as to the publick prayers the first Lords Day in your own church and the first day there is Sermon in the Laigh Church after that let any Minister do as he pleases. Let Brother Alice know I think of him and all other friends.

I am Dear Sir your affece· Brother &c

Jn° WITHERSPOON

Baillie Storie of the Council then appeared and prayed the Presbytery to accept the demission and declare a vacancy ac-

[30] The memoir published in the *Christian Instructor* for October, 1829, states that this sermon was published in separate form for Dr. Witherspoon's parishioners; but no such copy has been found. The earliest edition seen by the present writer is in the *Discourses on Practical Subjects* published at Glasgow in 1768; the sermon is also in the *Practical Discourses* published at Edinburgh in the same year.

[31] Presbytery of Paisley MS. records.

cording to previous resolution, which was done. And thus at last ended John Witherspoon's official connection with the Church of Scotland.

During the monotonous weeks that succeeded each other after the purple hills of Ireland had faded below the horizon, Dr. Witherspoon must have spent many hours musing over the step he had taken. Its seriousness he had well weighed during the past two years, and when he finally accepted his call he did so only with grave misgivings as to his fitness for his new task, misgivings which even the extravagant joy of Benjamin Rush had not dispelled. In the last letter he received from this enthusiast before sailing, the latter reminded him of Young's line: "'Tis impious in a good man to be sad," and pointed out that "a uniform Chearfulness of Temper" would at the present juncture throw lustre on everything he did in entering upon his charge at Princeton. There is sufficient hint here of the state of Dr. Witherspoon's feelings when the final wrench came, on leaving Scotland.

Difficult enough as such a step would be in these days of space and time annihilation, a hundred and fifty years ago it was one before which a stouter heart than his might well have quailed. Not only was he leaving his native land and lifelong associations, but he was casting over a devoted charge upon which he exerted an ever-widening influence, and he was deserting ecclesiastical circles wherein he had won enviable reputation. His interest in America to be sure was no new thing; he had long looked upon that country as the solution of Scotland's pauper problem and he was soon to acquire land in the New World with the intention of encouraging Scottish emigration. But he was not going to America either as a landowner nor as a promoter, although we shall hear more of his property later. Nor could financial reasons have swayed him, for in purchasing power the Princeton salary was not much larger than the one he was receiving at Paisley, and in any case it seemed altogether probable that he would have been offered better livings than Paisley had he remained in Great Britain; the Dundee and Dublin calls were already instances. Nor had he found his labors irksome nor his associations unpleasant. He was deeply attached to his parish and never ceased to think of his people kindly and to regret the breaking of pastoral relations with them. His people loved and honored him. The frictions he had encountered in his gusty career were scarcely other than those any virile character might reasonably have expected to meet. Like other men of vigorous temperament he had made his mistakes and had suffered for them. As for the rest, he had rather enjoyed the give and take.

So that he seemed to have had everything to lose and very little or nothing to gain by exchanging his Paisley charge for the precarious headship of an educational establishment of dubious permanency with a quarreling clientele, and in a distant colony. He had no experience in administration of that sort unless we except what he had gathered as a clerical visitor at Scottish parochial schools, and with the best of intentions this could scarcely prove of much assistance in directing the fortunes of an American college. For that matter, if he wished to teach there was ample opportunity to begin at home, where in a Highland parish of his day not more than three persons on an average could read or write.[32]

As for the college to which he was going, until his first election to its presidency whatever knowledge he had of it was derived entirely from secondary sources. He was of course aware of the collections taken up for the College by the Reverends Gilbert Tennent and Samuel Davies some fourteen years before, and he may have seen the meagre account of the institution which they distributed along their way, as rare a pamphlet now as it was meagre then; but there is no indication that he met the oddly mated pair from Princeton. In the reports of the Society in Scotland for Propagating the Gospel which were in his library he had come across allusions to the work of the College in educating Indian students; his copy of the *Official Narrative* of the Indian Charity School conducted at Lebanon, Connecticut, may have given him further light on this subject; and he had surely heard of the visit to Great Britain paid by a young Princetonian, the Reverend Nathaniel Whitaker, in company with that good Indian, though alive, Samson Occom. He owned a copy of Jonathan Edwards' *Remarks* on John Home's *Essays on the Principles of*

[32]Graham, *Social Life in Scotland*, vol. II, p. 157. Even as late as 1821, it is said, half the population of 400,000 could not read.

Morality and Natural Religion; he possessed Edwards' *Life of David Brainerd;* and he had subscribed for a copy, "on fine paper, not coarse," of Edwards' *Treatise concerning Religious Affections,* so that he knew something of at least one of his predecessors; and finally Blair's *Account of the College of New Jersey,* the only satisfactory sketch of the institution yet printed, had been sent to him on his election. But it seems altogether probable that until Mr. Stockton and Benjamin Rush visited him he had never talked with anyone who knew the college from personal experience as student or officer—it will be remembered that Stockton found he had "no tolerable" notion of the place. According to Ashbel Green, George Whitefield, who was thoroughly familiar with the earlier history of the college, wrote to Witherspoon urging him to accept the call to Princeton, telling him that in a new country like America "every gownsman was a legion in the cause of religion," but there is no evidence that they ever met, and Whitefield's letter does not seem to have been preserved.[33]

To a Scottish Presbyterian of his antecedents and training there was in the Princeton call one attraction clearly paramount. From the letters quoted it is obvious that the emissaries of the College of New Jersey had pleaded the missionary phase of the enterprise they laid before him and had placed the gain to American Presbyterianism and the cause of religion by the side, if not actually in front, of the gain to American education. As we have seen, there was very little said about education. Dr. Rodgers for example, in the close of his midnight letter of Christmas Eve, 1766, had said that Witherspoon's coming would enable the trustees to enlarge the course of study by erecting additional professorships, this to be effected when the President's chair was filled; but the emphasis in the letter is distinctly laid on the fact that the eyes of Presbyterian churches in seven provinces looked to Princeton alone to supply their pulpits; the President would have the power not only to serve the Church as a whole in the widest and most efficient way by training its ministry, but would also be the revered head of Presbyterian interests in the Middle Colonies, a thought echoed by the irrepressible Benjamin Rush in a phrase more vigorous than Presbyterian,

[33] Ashbel Green, *Autobiography,* p. 336.

when by way of illustration he told the Doctor that President Davies of Princeton had been as it were "a bishop among the Churches." [34]

The College was described as a school of prophets, and although it was absolutely unsectarian in charter it was evidently strongly Presbyterian in tone. American Presbyterianism seemed in no small danger of disintegration; the existence of the College itself was threatened; the influence that such an institution might develop in supplying the ministry with consecrated men, educated and trained along the same line, and the insistence of its friends, coupled with Witherspoon's own half-timid conviction that he was the man to save the institution and probably the Church from being shattered by faction, constituted, unless one is very much mistaken, the imperious note in this cry from Macedonia to which he knew not how to turn a deaf ear.

Lurking in his mind, moreover, however little others may have thought of it or he himself have realized just then, was the belief that the function of such a college was not merely to educate candidates for the ministry, but also to send out into the widening spheres of colonial life Christian gentlemen and scholarly men of affairs. Stockton, Rush, and Beatty must have so depicted its possibilities in spite of its reverses, and so described educational conditions in the Middle Colonies, with Princeton in the strategic position halfway between New York and Philadelphia where both colleges were under Anglican influence, and halfway between William and Mary in the south and Harvard and Yale in New England, that he could not have failed to see the beckoning of half-veiled opportunity for a strong man of brains, common sense, and energy, to mould the lives of some of the best youth that this new country was producing. Dr. Rodgers had referred to this, while Rush with Edinburgh University in mind had pointed out that there were many modern ideas that Witherspoon might introduce into the College inasmuch as the trustees, according to his estimate, were mostly "very contracted in their Notions of Education, & want a man of Spirit to give them more extensive Views to all their Schemes." [35] Events were

[34] Green MS. Letter of March 25, 1767.
[35] Green MS. Letter of December 29, 1767.

to show that thanks to Dr. Witherspoon's influence in unexpected colonial developments this particular "school of prophets" was to become for a brief but brilliant hour a school of very practical politics, and to be quite as notable for the men it graduated, able and eager to take their place as leaders in secular affairs, as for the ministers of the gospel who listened within its walls to their first lectures in divinity. It was not Dr. Witherspoon's fault but his good fortune that he soon found himself making more men of affairs than men of the cloth; and it was a regrettable day for Princeton when she let go the advantage he then gave her.

Nevertheless if we seek in a single phrase of his own the one dominant reason for his coming to America we may find it in the closing paragraph of his first Princeton sermon. One would not guess that this discourse is the maiden utterance of the new President of an institution of learning. The headship of the College carried with it the pastorate of the Princeton village church and it is scarcely the eager master mind seizing a splendid chance for achievement, it is not the President, but the modest, and almost timid, pastor, who is speaking:

I make no merit at all, of having left country, and kindred, and connections of the dearest kind, in order to serve the interest of the Church of Christ in this part of the globe; for I consider with pleasure the oneness of his body, and the extent of the Catholic Church. . . . But when I consider the respect and affection so much above my desert, that have been shown to me since my arrival in this place, and the testimonies of joy and satisfaction which have been given by all ranks I am filled with the greatest concern because it plainly implies an expectation of duty and service from me, which I fear I shall be ill able to perform. . . . Pray that an all sufficient God may give strength from above, and pour down his blessing on the public institution in this place. . . . Pray that success may attend the ministry of the gospel in this place; and that if it please God the esteem and affection shown me by all to whom I stand now related may not be less than it is, for I have not the least reason to desire, nor indeed the courage to hope, that it can possibly be greater.[36]

The grip of the past was still strong upon him, and therefore, it was still as the pastor that he ended his sermon with one brief additional sentence:

[36] *Works*, vol. II, p. 531.

And once more pray that my beloved charge whom I left in Scotland, and will never forget, may by the special conduct of divine providence be supplied with a faithful pastor, who may feed them with knowledge and understanding.

—a poignant sentence full of a very human touch of regret as it casts back for a single wistful moment to the crowded church across the sea, where every Sabbath twelve to fifteen hundred persons sat dutifully at his feet, in contrast with the "thin and negligent" congregation of college boys and colonial villagers he was that day addressing for the first time.[37]

[37] It was in these terms that Dr. Witherspoon, in his introductory lecture on divinity, reverted to his feelings on his first appearance before a Princeton audience. (*Works*, vol. IV, p. 10).

CHAPTER FOUR

THE MAKING OF AN AMERICAN

O N Sunday, August 7, 1768, the gallant *Peggy* reached her moorings at Philadelphia after a tedious voyage of twelve weeks. She had been reported in the river the day before and several gentlemen had gone down to welcome her distinguished passenger. The flutter of excitement that marked his landing on American shores was not unnatural. The general public was familiar with the somewhat sensational circumstances of his two elections, and the newspapers had widely spread the news of his coming. By thoughtful persons for whom the progress of higher education in New Jersey and in the Colonies at large held any concern, the experiment of importing a foreigner for an American educational executive position would be watched with the utmost interest; while for those to whom the cause of religion, and especially of Presbyterianism and religious freedom, was the principal concern, his coming was fraught with the most far-reaching possibilities. The Bradfords of Philadelphia had published a new edition of his celebrated *Ecclesiastical Characteristics,*—and had done their share to fan Presbyterian interest. The opinion prevailed that if he proved to be the man of the hour his presence would indeed mean not only an end to the feud between the two factions in the Church and their guidance into the way of peace, but also the probable reorganization of the Church along better administrative lines and the creation of a unified front wherewith to face the struggle for existence. It was not strange, therefore, that before he was fairly ashore, the President found himself the cause of a good natured rivalry whose object was to secure him as guest for the few days he and his family were to spend in Philadelphia recovering from the effects of three months' confinement in the cramped quarters of a little ship. Mr. Andrew Hodge, the prominent merchant, was the lucky host, and for the best part of the next week his house was the Mecca of all ranks and persuasions coming partly to pay their respects to a divine of such repute, and partly it must be suspected to get a glimpse of this stranger who had quit his native land for the presidency of the College of New Jersey.[1]

They saw a heavily built man of medium stature, a man in the full power of his forty-six years. His blue eyes, under strikingly thick brows, immediately caught attention—they were the clear, quick-kindling eyes of an active mentality; his hair was brown, his complexion fair; the cheekbones were high, the mouth mobile, the nose and ears noticeably large; his face, grave in repose but lit by gleams of humor when he talked, was strongly modelled and somewhat heavy, but not stern or severe; character was stamped in every feature. He had that indefinable quality called presence. His voice was disappointing and he spoke with a very marked Scottish accent, but one listened to him inevitably, confident that here was a man who did not speak save when he had something worth saying. With him were his wife, a gentle looking woman of forty-eight, and five children, Ann, the oldest, now in her twentieth year, James, a stripling of seventeen who had already been four years a student at the University of Glasgow, John, who had just passed his eleventh birthday, Frances, just reaching her ninth, and David the youngest, his father's pet, a precocious and lovable boy of eight. Two other daughters and three sons he had left sleeping in the low-walled churchyards of Beith and Paisley.

On the twelfth the Witherspoons set out for Princeton. At Trenton the party was met by a number of ladies and gentlemen and by trustees of the College, living in the neighborhood. At the old province-line, a mile or so from Princeton, the undergraduates, and the faculty consisting of Vice-president William Tennent, and the three tutors Joseph Periam, James Thomson, and Jonathan Edwards, Jr., were awaiting their new head. When the triumphal procession reached Princeton, the President's House on the campus not being ready Mr. Richard Stockton threw open his hospitable doors and entertained the new-comers at "Morven," his stately ancestral home, which with its spacious apartments and cool wide halls, its formal gardens and its wealth of trees and lawn must have been a glad relief after the heat of Philadelphia, as well as a revelation to a family that hitherto had

[1] *Scots Magazine*, October, 1768.

dwelt in a humble Scottish manse. And that night the undergraduates, only too ready to celebrate, illuminated Nassau Hall with tallow dips in every window, while the village (and indeed the whole countryside) united in an effort to emphasize the welcome. The glow of those simple lights could be seen for miles—Princeton is set on a ridge, and the trees that veil her now were not yet planted, so that Nassau Hall was a landmark against the sky. The lights denoted the beginning of a new era in the annals of the College; and, more important still, they marked the advent of a new force into the history of the province and of the American people. Dr. Witherspoon was as much surprised and pleased as he was touched by the enthusiasm of his reception. Its very fervor was almost pathetic. Things were not done so at home where men were less close to nature, less frank of their feelings; and if he had any remaining doubts as to the sincerity of his call or as to the wisdom of his acceptance they must have been swept away by the enthusiastic greeting he received on every side. The words of his first sermon show how deeply he was stirred. He realized now that the bounds of his influence were not to be the walls of Nassau Hall but that he held their setting within his own hands; and he faced his new associations confident that he would not fail.

On August 17 at a special meeting of the board of trustees he took the oaths of office; there was no public inaugural ceremony.[2] During the few days between his arrival and his inauguration he had had ample opportunity to look over the College and its environment. He had found the village consisting of perhaps some fifty houses clustered along the high road, most of them modest enough though set amid ample orchards and gardens. On the outskirts of the village were three or four homes of more substantial style belonging to older and richer families. It was a sunny, healthy spot; and lacking urban distractions and temptations (save as they were echoed at the few but excellent taverns that catered to the wants of travellers or met the accustomed

---

[2] Ashbel Green, *Presbyterian Magazine*, vol. IV, p. 467, was mistaken in his address to the Princeton Alumni Association in 1840 on Witherspoon's administration, when he said that the President delivered an inaugural when he was inducted into office. He delivered it at commencement, a month later.

View of Nassau Hall, Princeton.

From the Engraving by Amos Doolittle

needs of genial villagers), it seemed to him an admirable locality for an institution such as he believed the College of New Jersey should be—not a quiet, comfortable, dreaming place, but a training school wherein to prepare men's hearts and minds to meet the clash and challenge of the world. Lying on the border between two counties of the province, the village was gaining importance as the common meeting ground of both; and the President learned that during the ten years the College had been here, its presence had brought to the village growing interest and reputation.

In the *Account of the College of New Jersey*, he had read what may be called the official description of the College, and from the frontispiece drawn by the versatile Vice-president, the Reverend William Tennent, and engraved by Dawkins, he had obtained a fair notion of the appearance of its buildings. He was not surprised, therefore, to find them better looking than anything at the University of Edinburgh. Nassau Hall, the finest edifice in the province, was a severely plain stone edifice 176 feet long and 54 deep, consisting of a basement and three stories, surmounted by a low belfry,[3] and situated in an unfenced plot of ground some four and a half acres in extent facing north on the highroad—the fence so carefully drawn in the Dawkins plate was only the artist's "embellishment." The building itself was just ten years old and still bore the garish look of newness. The yard in front of it —or campus, as it was first called in Witherspoon's time, was bare save for a row of young buttonwoods, recently planted along its northern boundary. It would be difficult for modern Princetonians to imagine this space without its arching elms, its cool deep shade, and its close cropped turf; but in 1768 it was still a veritable "yard." The President's House stood at the northwest corner of the lot; east of Nassau Hall was a kitchen building and steward's house, and south of it were the college outhouse and a shed in which were kept the fire-engine and leather buckets. Counting three students to a room, the building was estimated to accommodate one hundred and forty-seven. The forty-nine rooms or suites consisted of a central study some

[3] The present cupola dates from the restoration after the fire of 1855.

twenty feet square, with two large closets for bedrooms, each containing a window. On the north front of the building there were three entrances, each approached by a low flight of steps leading into the first floor; two of these were duplicated on the southern side of the building. Over the main front entrance was a bust of Homer, the only external adornment the building had. Passing through this entrance one crossed the long hall that pierced the building from end to end and came into the prayer-hall or chapel, cool in summer but cold as a tomb in winter, the largest apartment in the building, being about forty feet square with a low gallery on the western side containing the organ, "small tho' exceeding good" as the official account hath it, and according to Dr. Ezra Stiles of New Haven the first to be used in any American Presbyterian house of worship. Opposite the gallery was the rostrum used by college declaimers on weekdays, and on which stood the high pulpit, where prayers were offered every morning and evening and sermons delivered on Sundays. Over the rostrum was a life-size portrait of His Majesty King George II; above the gallery, and surmounted by his carved and gilded coat of arms, hung a picture of Jonathan Belcher, late Governor of the Province and patron of the College. A series of small portraits of British sovereigns completed the decoration of the hall. Above the main entrance on the second floor was the library whose contents in 1764 numbered only 1200 volumes, but which by 1768 probably approached 1500, thanks to the acquisitions brought over by Dr. Witherspoon. In the basement were recitation rooms, and a dining-room large enough to hold faculty, students and grammar scholars. The building was lighted by candles and heated by woodfires. Water was obtained from two good wells behind Nassau Hall.

Under President Finley the curriculum of the grammar school had consisted chiefly of the elements of Latin and Greek, arithmetic, penmanship, reading, and declamation. The twenty-two "Rules and Orders to be observed by all the Members of the Grammar School at Nassau Hall" had long ago been printed as an appendix to the *Complete Introduction of the Latin Tongue* . . . "published principally for the use of the Grammar School at Nassau Hall," [4] and many of the requirements in matters of conduct applied to undergraduates. Graduation from the grammar school carried with it admission to the College without further test.

As for the College, the entrance requirements dated from 1748 and consisted of proficiency in reading, writing, spelling, and English composition, a knowledge of the rules of simple arithmetic (added in 1760), ability to write Latin prose, to translate Vergil, Cicero, and the Greek gospels, and a commensurate acquaintance with Latin and Greek grammar.

The curriculum in College was what might have been expected of such foundations and entrance requirements. Freshman year was spent in Latin and Greek—Horace, Cicero, Greek Testament, Lucian and Xenophon. In sophomore year the classics were continued and geography, rhetoric, logic, and higher mathematics, were begun. Juniors continued mathematical studies and went through a course in natural and moral philosophy, metaphysics and chronology, and those who expected to enter the ministry began Hebrew. Senior year was devoted to a review of the classics, arts, and sciences, and to composition; and in a course, which seems to have been one of criticism and which was usually given by the President, the graduating class re-read Homer, Horace, and Longinus, with comments on aesthetic points by the professor. A weekly course in disputation begun in junior year was continued, and on Sundays Seniors delivered public disputations on religious subjects. Once a month was "oration day"—an institution which, later known for obvious reasons as "chapel stage," died a lingering death in the last decade of the nineteenth century—when Seniors delivered harangues of their own composition. Every evening, except on Saturday and Sunday, the members of the three lower classes pronounced declamations or delivered selections from the great classical orators or from the English poets.

[4] The Princeton copy is the second edition, published at Woodbridge, N. J., in 1760. A facsimile of the titlepage, with the rules themselves, was published in an edition of one hundred copies by C. L. Traver at Trenton, N. J., in 1893. No reprint seems to have been issued during Witherspoon's time.

The rising bell rang at five and morning prayers were said at five-thirty, when a Senior usually read a chapter of the Bible from the original into English, after which the President proposed a few questions on the reading and then commented at large. Between morning chapel and breakfast, which was served at eight, came an hour's study. Recitations began at nine and lasted until one, the dinner hour. From three until five, when the bell rang for vespers, were study hours. Evening prayer was introduced by what contemporary terminology called "psalmody," but in spite of the assistance of the organ and official assurance that care was taken "to improve the youth in the art of sacred music," and notwithstanding the inspiration that should have been derived from the memory of James Lyon, who prepared his early American hymn-book *Urania* while an undergraduate in Nassau Hall and whose compositions were used at commencement, the youth in question do not seem to have made much musical progress. After vespers they were free again until seven when supper was served; and at nine the curfew called every one back to his room. Of spare time there was little; of athletics none. The high purpose of a college education in those sterner days precluded reference to sports in the accounts of college life; in fact the records, official or private, antedating the Revolution, mention this frivolous subject only once. But the tacit official disapproval of sports did not deter students from working off superfluous energy in childish pranks which were the contemporary substitutes for better forms of exercise, and of which an instructive catalogue has been left to curious posterity by Philip Vickers Fithian of the Class of 1772.[5]

The board supplied in the college refectory was theoretically as good as the neighborhood afforded, an official claim of which the truth was never proved to the satisfaction of the boarders. Most of the insurrections in the College then and thereafter had their root in the refectory. Tea and coffee were served at breakfast, and dinner, so we are gravely informed, saw every variety of meat and fish that could be obtained—and "sometimes pyes." Cider and small beer were the customary drink at dinner, milk and chocolate taking their place at supper; and after vespers any

[5] *Journal and Letters*, p. 256.

undergraduate might, if he cared to, "brew himself a dish of tea" in his room—an official permit belonging of course to pre-Revolutionary days. The total cost per annum approximated twenty-five pounds, six shillings, made up of the following items: tuition, four pounds, board and service, fifteen pounds, room-rent one pound, washing three pounds, wood and candles two pounds, sundries six shillings.

With many of the students looking forward to the ministry, it was to be expected that the formal religious tone of the College should be marked. Attendance at chapel was compulsory, especially on Sundays when the students listened to two sermons, one in the morning at the Presbyterian Church and another in the middle of the afternoon at the college chapel. Early morning prayers were said in chapel on Sundays as on other days, and at the same hour. Not content with this, a religious society, composed of any who cared to join, held meetings on Sunday evenings where the program consisted of prayers and hymns and the reading of a sermon by a tutor. In addition each class had its prayer meeting.

Thanks to the care of Mr. Tennent, who had been Acting President since Dr. Finley's incapacitation, Dr. Witherspoon found things less disorganized than might have been expected, but he plunged into his work with an energy as startling as it was successful. Such energy had no precedent in the history of the College and was to remain unparalleled until another Scotsman, exactly a century later, came to occupy the presidential chair.[6]

Beginning with fundamentals the President at once took hold of the grammar school. It will be remembered that he had made an effort in Great Britain to get advice in regard to the conduct of such a school. The hints he obtained during this brief course in

[6] It cannot be out of place here to refer once more to the curious parallelisms that mark the lives of Dr. Witherspoon and Dr. McCosh, first pointed out by Dean West and repeated in the writer's sketch of the history of Princeton (New York, 1914). Both were by birth Lowland Scotsmen, and students at the University of Edinburgh; ministers of the Scottish Church at important crises, one heading the opposition to the Moderates, the other aiding in the establishment of the Free Church; both coming to America, Witherspoon in August, 1768, McCosh in August, 1868, to do as Presidents of Princeton perhaps their greatest work; both living the last twenty-six years of their lives in Princeton, the one dying November 15, 1794, the other November 16, 1894. Academic history has seldom repeated itself so completely.

pedagogics, miscellaneous though they must have been, were so well ordered in his mind and what he called his "scheme" was so well thought out, that within one week after his inauguration he had completed his plans, obtained the sanction of the trustees, chosen a member of the senior class, William Churchill Houston, as master, and published an advertisement in the papers stating that the school would open in November, on the day the college winter term began. Improvements were already announced; he had procured a "Terrestrial Globe" so that the scholars might learn geography "at some Hours of Leisure"—it had hitherto been taught in sophomore year in the College; writing and arithmetic would be taught daily; cheap lodgings had been arranged in the village and the pupils could board in the college refectory.[7]

As for the curriculum of the College, that was a matter not to be meddled with hastily, and for the present Dr. Witherspoon

[7] The announcement, (*N. J. Archives*, 1 ser., vol. XXVI, p. 269,) is dated Princeton, August 25, 1768, and reads as follows:

The Trustees of the College of New Jersey, give Notice to the Public, That whereas the Grammar School which used to be kept under the Direction of the President as a Nursery for the College has been discontinued for some Time, on Account of the long Vacancy of that Office, That the Chair being now filled by the Arrival of the Gentleman last chosen from North-Britain; The School is to be opened under his Direction, precisely on the 7th Day of November next, being the Beginning of the Winter Term in College. The PRESIDENT, has already provided a Person to teach it; and has undertaken to the Trustees to lay down a Plan of proceeding to the Teacher, to have it under his constant Inspection; and take Care that it be conducted on the very best Principles. This he hopes to be able to do with the greater Success, for that, being acquainted, before he left Home, that such a Thing would be expected from him, he took Care to perfect his Scheme, by conversing with some of the most eminent and approved Teachers in Great-Britain. Parents are desired to take Notice, that their Children being properly founded in the Languages, is of the utmost Importance to their Subsequent Studies in College being easy, pleasant, and successful. Several reputable Householders in Princeton, have engaged to the Trustees, to take Boarders at as cheap a Rate, it is presumed, as in any Town in this Province, where a public Grammar School is taught: And if the Parents of any of the Children should decline to have them boarded in the College, the Trustees have consented to their being taken in and supplied as the Scholars are. There is a Terrestrial Globe provided for the School, that they may be taught Geography at some Hours of Leisure; they will also have an Hour each Day appropriated to Writing and Arithmetick without any additional Expense, which it is of Importance that they learn early. This Notice is given so long before the Time of opening School, that Parents may have their Children there seasonably; and it is particularly desired that such as have Children to begin the Latin, would send them, if possible, upon the very Day above mentioned; that they may neither suffer any Loss themselves, nor be the Means of retarding others.

made no changes. But within a few weeks of his arrival at Princeton he did announce a reduction of college expenses. The idea had gained credence that an education at Princeton, besides being the luxury that a college education anywhere was in those days, was unnecessarily costly, and in order to wipe out the grounds of this charge, the President had devised a new plan. The high charge for board was due to the remissness of parents and guardians in paying students' college bills; the steward had to buy on credit at advanced prices. Now, in order to enable him to pay cash and thus secure more reasonable rates it was proposed to require part payment of college fees in advance, a simple expedient which apparently had not occurred previously to the financiers of the College. According to the new plan board would cost six shillings and sixpence New Jersey proclamation money per week; each student on admission would deposit with the steward seven pounds in advance for board and at commencement or at the beginning of the following term would be required to pay up all his arrears in tuition fees and room-rent, or cease his connection with the College. The total expenses per year were thus calculated to amount to twenty-three pounds thirteen shillings, or one pound seven shillings less than in Dr. Finley's time. The announcement stated that:

Upon the Plan above adopted the Expence of living here, will be within a few Shillings, more or less, as follows;

To 1 Year's Board (deducting the Vacation Weeks at Spring and Fall) at 6s. 6d. per Week	£ 13.13.	O
Fire Wood and Candles, about	2.10.	O
Washing, about,	2.10.	O
Tuition and Chamber Rent	5.00.	O
	£ 23.13.	O

Every student to pay one Shilling per Week, for every Week's Absence after the Vacations are ended, to indemnify the Steward, who pays Wages to Servants for their Benefit.

Of far greater significance, not only from the viewpoint of American educational history but also from that of Dr. Witherspoon's own conception of his task and opportunity, though of less immediately apparent importance, was the announcement, made at the same time, of the arrangement of graduate courses for those who wished to continue their studies, whether for the learned professions or merely to acquire such liberal accomplishments in general which in the pertinent phrase of the advertisement, "fit young Gentlemen for serving their Country in public Stations." In this Dr. Witherspoon was re-asserting one of the two principal aims of the founders of the College and one which was in danger of being lost sight of in the demand made on it to produce ministers of the gospel. It is worth while to quote this portion of the advertisement in full, coming as it undoubtedly did from President Witherspoon's own pen, and giving such clear evidence of his attitude toward the higher purposes of academic training:

The Trustees further give Notice, that they have made Provisions for the Encouragement of young Gentlemen, who have finished the ordinary Course of Philosophy, to return and pursue their Studies at College, and fit themselves for any of the higher Branches, to which they shall think proper chiefly to devote their future Application, whether those called learned Professions, Divinity, Law and Physic, or such liberal Accomplishments in general, as fit young Gentlemen for serving their Country in public Stations. For this purpose, the Professor of Divinity, besides what Attention he may give to the Instruction of the Senior Class will give regular Lectures upon the System. The President also has engaged to give Lectures twice in the Week, on the following Subjects (1) On Chronology and History, civil as well as sacred; a Branch of Study, of itself extremely useful and delightful, and at present in the highest Reputation in every Part of Europe, (2) Critical Lectures on the Scripture, with the Addition of Discourses on Criticism in general; the several Species of Writing, and the fine Arts, (3) Lectures on Composition, and the Eloquence of the Pulpit and the Bar. The President will also endeavour to assist every Student by Conversation according to the main Object, which he shall chuse for his own Studies; and will give Lists and Characters of the principal Writers on any Branch, that Students may accomplish themselves, at the least Expence of Time and Labour. For the Attainment of their Ends, a very valuable Addition to the Public Library was brought over with the President, another large collection of the most standard Books, is newly arrived; and a Third is very soon expected from London. So that this College, which had before all the Advantages for Study, that a retired healthful Place could possess, is now well furnished with a valuable Public Library, which will be improved by continual Additions. It is to be observed that from those, who after their ordinary Courses, shall return to College, in order to pursue their Studies with those Advantages, no Tuition Money will be required, except that the French language will be taught, if desired, for a very reasonable Gratuity.[8]

It was this prompt, masterful grasp of the reins government this quick infusion of new ideas, and the immediate uplift of an invigorating personality that produced the general feeling naïvely expressed in a letter by Mr. Sergeant, the college treasurer:

The arrival of Doctor Wetherspoon to our College is very agreeable to its Friends, and are in hopes of much good being done to its Interest by so great & good a Man as he appears to be.[9]

On September 28 the first commencement procession led by the new President went from his door, capped and gowned according to a rule passed at the first meeting of the trustees that he attended, to the Presbyterian Church where he opened the exercises with a "learned & elegant Latin Oration on the Connection & mutual influences of Learning & Piety." This was his inaugural address, an address that has disappeared. Ashbel Green saw the manuscript several years later while he was an undergraduate, but it was not found among Dr. Witherspoon's papers at the time of his death and Green throws no light on its contents.

The most pressing need of the College was more money and more students, and the President seems to have taken very naturally to the task of securing both. He may have been a novice in the business of education, but he had ordinary sense enough to know that a college cannot be maintained only on good intentions and a curriculum; and he lost no time, therefore, in starting his quest for both money and students. Recognizing instantly that he was his own best advertisement, before the sensation of his arrival had died down he seized the opportunity to strike while interest was still excited, and to see and be seen. Early in September he had visited New York, where in Anglican circles at any rate he fell short of his reputation: "The celebrated Dr.

[8] *New Jersey Archives*, 1 ser., vol. XXVI, p. 306. This is the first time French was offered as a study at Princeton.
[9] To Mr. Carey of Boston, September 15, 1768. Princeton University Library.

Witherspoon is arrived," wrote the Reverend T. B. Chandler from Elizabeth, N. J., to ex-President Johnson of King's College, New York, September 9, 1768, "and all I hear of him is that he makes but an indifferent Figure in the Pulpit." [10] But now that the long vacation was on, he made a trip through New England with Dr. Rodgers, preaching wherever he was invited, appearing for example in four Boston pulpits in three days.[11] His visit was not unheralded. As long ago as May 9 the *Boston Chronicle* had quoted the statement of a passenger on a vessel just arrived from Scotland, that Dr. Witherspoon had sold his furniture and preached his farewell sermon, and was soon to sail for America; and undoubtedly his name had occurred more frequently than ever in ministerial correspondence of the late summer. His visit to New England must have been successful for he brought home for the College in cash and promises the sum of one thousand pounds proclamation money, and left in its place the favorable interest he had set out to create. The Reverend Charles Chauncey wrote to Ezra Stiles after this visit that Dr. Witherspoon was

a gentleman of good learning, strong powers, and a catholic, charitable Spirit. We are highly pleased he has come over to be president of the Jersey-College. We are persuaded he will do better than any who have gone before him. He is no friend to the grand and distinguishing Tenets of Mr. Edwards wch. have been almost universally imbibed in that part of the Country.[12]

And the practically minded Mr. Sergeant wrote again to Mr. Carey:

I am glad the Rev. Dr. Witherspoon met with so good acceptance in your parts, & hope he will prove a great Blessing to our College. He is got safe home.[13]

But by the time this strenuous and keen-eyed Scotsman had "got safe home" he had secured much besides a mere exchange of

[10] Yale University MSS.
[11] "Last Monday," said a Boston news item of October 24, "came to town the Reverend Dr. Witherspoon, president of the College of New Jersey. On Monday he preached the weekly lecture, on Friday he preached at the Rev. Mr. Pemberton's, yesterday forenoon at the old brick, and in the afternoon at the old south meeting-house."
[12] Yale University Library, Stiles MSS. Letter of November 7, 1768.
[13] Princeton University Library, Letter of November 19, 1768.

money and "good acceptance." He had seen and learned more about the American colonies than most of his sovereign's cabinet ministers, three thousand miles away, ever cared to know. He had come to America not unready to be surprised; Americans whom he had met in Scotland and England had given him presumably a better notion of the new world than could be derived from the occasional colonial newspapers he may have seen or from the columns of the monthly magazines for which he was a subscriber. But the knowledge he obtained of country and people with his own eyes and ears during the first two months of his life in America had overstepped the bounds of all his imaginings.

Not the least surprising fact was one he learned on his first journey, that it was possible and even customary to travel in America without fear of molestation by footpads and highwaymen—a possibility and a custom almost unknown in Great Britain. Economic conditions were equally contrasting. In Scotland, outside of the largest towns, the people were poor and miserable; living, as Benjamin Franklin observed three years after this date, "in the most sordid wretchedness in dirty hovels of mud and straw, and clothed only in rags." With the exception of a few successful merchants, the lower classes of the inhabitants, farmers and others, were precluded from improving their political status.[14] A few acquired a little money, but they could never acquire any new privilege or rise to have any sort of weight in the legislature of the land. Excepting the 1500 or 2000 voters who elected the representatives of the thirty Scottish counties no farmers nor even landed men were of any political consequence.

In Scotland not only the peasantry but many persons of landed property have no representation at all nor the shadow of a representation. . . . In fact, the lower classes of the people in North Britain, who pay a great proportion of all the taxes imposed on the nation, are as really without representation in parliament as the British colonies in North America,[15]

continues the anonymous pamphlet already quoted. Poverty and wretchedness were common enough to go almost unnoticed;

[14] *Candid Enquiry into the Causes of the Migrations from Scotland.* Glasgow, n. d.
[15] *Candid Enquiry.*

beggars abounded; love of country was slight because there was so little about it that appeared worth loving.

Far different had Dr. Witherspoon found it in America. What Philadelphia, New York, and Boston lacked in size and age and substantiality, they made up in attractiveness and order. None was so picturesque of course as Edinburgh, still in its medieval dress, but on the other hand none was so squalid. Such contrasts and extremes in welfare did not exist, or if they existed were not so obvious. Glasgow, for example, in spite of its growing commercialism probably still retained much of its freshness and charm of thirty years earlier. But the city pavements were reserved for strutting tobacco magnates, men whom no inferior trader ventured to accost,[16] and the haughty pride of quick wealth must have been galling to the less fortunate, and to the poor intolerable.

Along the highroads in America, however, were thriving little villages; beggars were nowhere to be seen; men squared their shoulders and took on a new self-reliance in this land where, as one Scotsman put it, the air was "ever sweet and clear," where there was "no such black foul weather as at home; but a fine pure sky and bright heavens;" no one could "imagine a climate so fine and healthy." Is it any wonder that an immigrant, a former parishioner of Dr. Witherspoon's, has left it on record that the sky in America appeared much further away than at home and was not continually falling in moisture! As the President for the first time traversed New Jersey that September he must have perceived why it was called the "garden of America." [17] His ridings led him past a succession of prosperous farmlands and enticing orchards. In the villages the profusion of flowers and fruit astonished him, and though his turn of mind and his view of the physical world about him were economic and practical rather than aesthetic, yet he could not have been quite blind to the russet and gold of the turning autumn woods, nor totally unconscious that above it all was spread the glory of an Indian-summer sky. And when he observed the comfort in which the small

[16] Mathieson, p. 244.
[17] Alex. Thomson, *News from America*, Glasgow, 1774. An excellent sketch of this immigrant is found in the *Pennsylvania Magazine*, vol. VIII, p. 315.

farmers lived, and noticed that even servants and laborers and mechanics were well clothed and well fed, his mind must have reverted to the dismal lot of the lower classes in misty Scotland. He returned to Princeton more than ever resolved to do what lay in his power to encourage the poor farmers among his own people to try their lot in this new country where hope and opportunity seemed to be had for the asking. Silent testimony to his interest in Scottish emigration is plentifully found even still in the remnant of his library, and the course of this narrative will show further his practical interest in the problem.

He came back also a wiser man. For, beside the physical appeal of the land, he had received subtler impressions which shaped themselves before long into definite convictions and as such were to have larger results than even his lately gained enthusiasm for the pleasant places in which his lines had fallen. He wrote some time later that a man would become an American more easily and surely by residing in the country three months, than by reading or hearing about it three years. He penned these words on the authority of experience. Just now he was learning what an American was, and unconsciously but none the less surely his own metamorphosis had begun. One might admire the beauty and fertility of the country, be at once impressed as he was by its spaciousness, and yet dismiss these things with the explanation that they were the works of nature, the gifts of God. But the difference between an American and a Briton was a subtler matter and not so easily accounted for. Though Americans spoke of Great Britain as "home," and were proud of their British descent, though they copied British fashions, called their counties, townships, and estates by British names, and sent their sons over sea, when they could afford it, to finish their education in British universities and schools of law and medicine,[18] yet Dr. Witherspoon soon found that there was a distinct spirit of Americanism abroad in the land, that Americans had a solidarity, and homely loyalties, and ways of thinking especially in matters political, which they had worked out for themselves, of

---

[18] This is virtually Dr. Witherspoon's own language in his "Letter on the Contest between Great Britain and America," *Works*, vol. IV, p. 301, where he is speaking of the attachment of the people of America to those of Great Britain.

which he had heard but little and of whose origin and growth he knew less. Most novel to him was their un-British conception of representative government. Like the majority of Britons he had believed—if he had thought enough about them to have beliefs at all—that the difficulties between the mother country and her precocious colonies had been to a large extent smoothed out by the repeal of the Stamp Act. His belief would have been that of Mr. John Adams, though phrased less lyrically, to the effect that the repeal of this measure had "hushed into silence almost every popular clamor, and composed every wave of popular disorder into smooth and peaceful calm." But Dr. Witherspoon found in 1768 that Charles Townshend's Revenue Acts had stirred the controversy up afresh. At Boston between sermons he had not failed to hear the story of the riot in June when Mr. John Hancock's sloop *Liberty* was seized by custom officials for not complying with the regulations; he must have learned that in August, the very month he landed at Philadelphia, the Boston merchants had signed a non-importation agreement, that in September almost a hundred towns in Massachusetts had met in convention to adopt measures, that the inhabitants of Boston had assembled in Faneuil Hall and solemnly resolved that "at the utmost peril of their lives and fortunes they would maintain and defend their rights, liberties, and privileges and immunities," and that on the very day he was presiding over his first commencement at Princeton, two additional British regiments had arrived at Boston to maintain order. He learned too that the merchants of New York had agreed to the non-importation proposal. Little else was being talked about just then in this remarkable country where the average citizen seemed better educated, conversed more intelligently and with greater confidence, and had a wider, keener knowledge of the history as well as of the administrative law of his country than his fellow in Scotland or England. And somehow involved with the present grievance was a question of rights which were not so called in Great Britain—certainly not in Scotland—but which had grown up by imperceptible degrees and were jealously clung to by Americans, and among which certain notions continually asserted themselves; to wit—that whatever the original settlers' reasons may have been for coming to America, the one point on which all were agreed was that they considered themselves as having brought their liberty with them, and as entitled, therefore, to all the rights and privileges of freemen; that the colonists looked upon it as the foundation stone of British liberty that the freeholders or proprietors of the soil should have the exclusive right of granting money for public use; that the Colonies considered themselves as not directly subject to the British Parliament, but as separate independent dominions under the same sovereign.[19] And it must have dawned on him that he was meeting on every hand adherents to a radical political philosophy not understood in England, nor even accepted universally in the Colonies, but whose democratic features were singularly appealing to a dominant strain in his own nature.[20] It never entered his mind at this time, of course, that separation between Great Britian and the American Colonies was inevitable, still less that it was in sight. Nothing was farther from his expectations than the civil war that was to come within a decade.[21]

Even in the orations delivered in September from the Princeton commencement platform there was a strong flavor of current politics. The salutatory of young Mr. Pierpont Edwards of Connecticut was on "Civil Liberty" and the fact that it was in Latin did not prevent it from being considered "spirited." Among the theses defended on the rostrum were these portentous propositions: "It is to the interest of any nation to have the trade of its new countries as free from embarrassment as possible," and "It is lawful for every man, and in many cases his indisputable duty, to hazard his life in defence of his civil liberty," while the valedictorian took "Patriotism" for his subject. Commencement orations in our less rhetorical twentieth century are seldom of interest save to the speakers' devoted friends and relatives; but

[19]"Memorial and Manifesto of the United States," *Works*, vol. IV, p. 218. This is very nearly the language of Governor Bernard of Massachusetts who had said in a report home in 1765: "In America, they (the colonial governments) claim to be perfect states, no otherwise dependent on Great Britain than by having the same king."
[20]He was receiving current pamphlets on these matters, sent to him by his new friends in Boston and elsewhere, which he carefully grouped together and bound in volumes for his library.
[21]"The Druid," in *Works*, vol. IV. p. 167.

the eighteenth century American public really seems to have enjoyed them; they were the earliest "fruits of academical education" as a contemporary critic called them, the first outward and visible signs of inward and spiritual graces derived from a college education at a time when a college education was still a distinction. But these Princeton orations had a deeper significance and President Witherspoon, as he laid aside his gown and bands after the echoes of the day's oratory had blown away, must have done some hard thinking. If Princeton undergraduates seriously discussed these questions of the hour, what was to be expected of their fathers? What indeed was to be expected of these boys themselves when they should reach maturity? Hardly in a more striking way could he have realized how much to heart America was taking what British cabinet ministers thought of lightly or not at all.[22]

For the time being, however, he kept his thoughts to himself. With open eyes and keen ears, but with his mouth shut tight as to politics, he tended his own business and it prospered. Ever present and especially pressing just now was the problem of secondary education on which he plainly saw that higher education rested; and so we find in the *Pennsylvania Journal* of March 2, 1769, a second delightfully frank advertisement of the grammar school at Nassau Hall, wherein the President takes the public comfortably into his confidence. The previous advertisement had met with flattering response; the number of pupils had exceeded all expectations; the President was directing the school in person; he was introducing European methods, and Mr. Houston was taking his orders. In Latin he was applying the pedagogical method of the Glasgow public grammar school (which must have sounded extremely up-to-date); he was also using "a book of classic maps to point out the places spoken of," and the master was being coached by the President on classical antiquities so that he might explain allusions to manners, customs and laws of the ancients. The "terrestrial globe" was in frequent use and

---

[22] A recent writer has pointed out that after 1770 for three years the Colonies were hardly mentioned in Parliament, and a page or two of the *Annual Register* was thought sufficient to chronicle American doings. Becker, *Beginnings of the American People*, p. 231.

geography was being taught "by occasional exercises for amusement rather than for a task." Nor were grammar, reading, and spelling neglected, and every Sunday evening the boys were instructed in the principles of religion. The new President's aim seems to have been to do away with as much unnecessary drudgery as possible in elementary studies and to enlist the attention of his scholars by securing their interest. The best guarantee of the work done he soon perceived would be the ranking of his pupils who entered the College upstairs from the school in the basement of Nassau Hall, when compared with that of boys admitted from other schools; it would be "a terrible reproach," he concedes, if his own boys proved inadequately prepared; and, therefore, "it is expected, and even hoped, that other schoolmasters will by a laudable emulation keep us hard and close to our duty." This characteristic document reads in full as follows:

Nassau Hall, Princeton, Mar. 2, 1769

In terms of the advertisement formerly published, the Grammar School at Princeton was begun precisely on the 7th of November last. The numbers considering the shortness of the time, have exceeded expectation. The design of this present notice is to assure the public, that according to my promise to the trustees, I have undertaken the conduct of it; that the young man who teaches it receives his whole directions from me, and has hitherto given the greatest satisfaction by fidelity and diligence in the execution of them. He is furnished with a book of directions for masters to form their pupils to a thorough knowledge of the Latin language, drawn up by one who was long Rector of the public grammar school in Glasgow, the seat of one of the universities in Scotland, and taught it with as great reputation and success as any that ever appeared in that country. He is furnished with a book of classic maps, to point out the places spoken of in any author the scholars may happen to read, and it is particularly recommended to him to study the Roman & Greek antiquities, that he may be able to explain any word that refers to the customs and manners of the ancients or the constitutions of their several states. He is also furnished with a terrestrial globe, that they may be taught Geography, by occasional exercises for amusement rather than a task. One hour every day is spent in writing and arithmetick; And it is proposed to have a weekly exercise of reading in English authors with propriety and grace with remarks on the grammar and spelling of the English tongue. Every Lord's day evening since the school began, the scholars have been convened, and instructed in the principles of religion. This is done for the sake of those whose parents live at a distance, and will be carefully continued. On the whole the public may rest assured that no pains will be spared to make the instruction at this school complete and accurate: and indeed they have a pretty sure pledge of our fidelity, because the scholars who enter college from this school must be a sort of standard for the qualifications of those who are to be admitted from other places. It would be a terrible reproach to offer insufficient scholars brought up within our own walls, and it is expected and even hoped that other school masters will by laudable emulation keep us hard and close to our duty.

J. WITHERSPOON [23]

In May, 1769, he issued a further notice which plainly indicates his interest in the relation between the College and the grammar schools and his insistence that teachers be thoroughly familiar with Princeton's entrance regulations. In the first place the requirement of four year's residence for the bachelor's degree which was to have gone into effect in September, 1769, had been totally repealed, so that admission was upon the same footing as before. He informs the public that a strict and impartial entrance examination will be held in each case, and in order "that no schoolmaster, or others concerned in the scholars, may have reason to complain of advantage being taken against them" he reprints the 1748 and 1760 entrance requirements. He then announces that a candidate for entrance into any class except the freshman will pass the final public examination of the next lower class, or if by mishap he came too late for this ordeal three members of the class he proposes to enter will be drawn by lot, and by "fair comparison" with them in a special examination he will be either "admitted or degraded"—a novel and not altogether inadequate device. Furthermore it is expected and desired that masters sending a number of boys to college come with them and be present—and assist—at their examination. This co-operation between school and college examiners in entrance tests is a fair anticipation of the characteristic feature of the present College Entrance Examination Board. "By this means," says the notice,

[23]*New Jersey Archives*, I ser. vol. XXVI, p. 384.

the schoolmen "will have the opportunity of seeing justice done to them, and all suspicion of unfairness and partiality will be effectually prevented." [24]

Meanwhile the light of the President's ecclesiastical prominence in Scotland could not be hidden under any number of bushels in the shape of American educational problems, and he had fallen quickly and naturally into his right place in the American Presbyterian Church. The Presbytery of New Brunswick, to which he had neglected until April, 1769, to present his letter of dismissal from Paisley, had received him warmly and he found himself a delegate to the annual meeting of the Synod of New York and Philadelphia. At this meeting (May, 1769,) the President could have had no adverse criticism to make of his reception for he was accorded every mark of honor—if indeed it were unqualified honor to be put on eight separate committees at his first appearance. He was appointed, moreover, to head the delegation from the Synod to the convention with the Associations of Connecticut to be held at New Haven in the following September and to open the convention with a sermon. His foreign connections were likewise responsible for his being added to the committee to revise the letters which the Synod had ordered written to the Church in Holland, Switzerland, Scotland, Ireland, etc.

The College of New Jersey occupied an extreme share of the Synod's attention at this meeting. In 1768 an application from the trustees had been read requesting that a part of the annual collection recently ordered for the promotion of Christian knowledge be appropriated to the support of a divinity professor at Princeton. The request was refused but the sum of fifty pounds was loaned to the corporation for the purpose named, and it was agreed to make a special collection for the same object. The funds proving insufficient, in May, 1769, a fresh application was made by the trustees requesting assistance in raising money for the support of the College. Learning of the low funds of the College, the Presbytery ordered subscriptions to be gathered and although the results were incredibly slow nevertheless by April, 1772, nine congregations had subscribed the sum of £662.14.2

[24] *New Jersey Archives*, 1 ser., vol. XXVI, p. 426.

of which only £367 had been collected. Dr. Witherspoon, Professor Blair and Mr. William Peartree Smith were directed to draw up a statement of the condition of the College for distribution among the several congregations, and five hundred copies of their report were ordered printed for that purpose.[25] Furthermore, twenty-five members of the Synod were appointed agents in Pennsylvania, Maryland, New Jersey, Virginia and South Carolina, to "use their utmost endeavors to obtain subscriptions." To Dr. Witherspoon in particular, assisted by two others, was assigned Philadelphia and Bucks County, Pennsylvania; and with the Reverend James Caldwell, who had already made a successful begging tour in Long Island and adjacent parts of New Jersey, he was further directed to visit the southern parts of Virginia.

There is no doubt that his presence had given fresh force to the claims of the College. From various parts of the country reports began to come in of subscriptions set on foot. Dr. John Rodgers, the New York trustee, went to South Carolina to collect the benefactions there awaiting an authorized agent; Mr. Caldwell, elected a trustee that autumn and not content with Virginia as his sole field of operations, became agent in Maryland, the two Carolinas and Georgia, and gathered in a thousand pounds above his expenses. The subscriptions in Georgia were paid chiefly in produce and the College went temporarily into the shipping business, chartering a small vessel to proceed to Georgia and bring the produce up from the south.

Our Jersey College, wrote Dr. Alison to Mr. Stiles in none too generous a strain, is now talking as if she was to be a bulwark against Episcopacy. I should rejoice to see her Pistols like honest Teague's, grown up into great Guns. The President is an active man, a good Preacher: and has done much to procure funds; but still they want able professors, and ye college is in statu quo, save only that he is constituted a professor of Divinity; this they greatly wanted, and this Department he will, I expect, convince the world was fittest for him. I hear no great things of his Superior Knowledge in any Branch of

[25] No copy of this document, manuscript or printed, has been traced.

Philosophy. But I think he will do better than any that they have had of late years, or could have chosen in the Bounds of our Synod.[26]

Contemporary observers of American academic occasions must have found the Princeton commencement of September, 1769, unusually interesting. Besides being the first time that the honorary degree of doctor of laws was conferred in America, a particular curiosity was attached to the recipients of this degree and of an honorary master's degree conferred the same day. The doctorates fell to Mr. John Dickinson, author of the well-known *Farmer's Letters* and also of the *Liberty Song* which had recently gone the rounds of the colonial press, and to the Honorable Joseph Galloway, speaker of the Pennsylvania Assembly, and later the author of the *Speech* urging the king to resume the powers of government, a production which Mr. Dickinson severely criticized. The master's degree was conferred on Mr. John Hancock of Boston, already a public hero thanks to the adventure of his sloop, the *Liberty*. College commencement platforms bring together oddly contrasting personages; but in view of recent events this was a curious trio to watch and the manner of Mr. Galloway and Mr. Dickinson toward one another must have been especially worth observing. Nor is the group less interesting from the vantage point of subsequent history: Galloway, on purely intellectual grounds finding himself in a few years forced into loyalism and exile, Dickinson becoming a conservative and unpopular patriot, and Hancock rising to be a leader of the revolutionary party, and the president of the Continental Congress that resolved on independence. Even if the expectations of the board of trustees were mistaken in the case of Mr. Galloway, the honoring of Dickinson and Hancock showed frankly whither the sympathies of the College of New Jersey were tending.

Immediately after commencement Dr. Witherspoon set out on his first trip to Virginia. "Doct^r Witherspoon's business to Virginia," wrote young James Madison of the sophomore class

---

[26] Stiles MSS. Letter of August 1, 1769. In order to release part of the funds used for his salary, Professor Blair that spring had resigned the professorship of divinity to which he had so recently been elected, and Dr. Witherspoon had assumed the duties of the chair in his place, with an additional salary of fifty pounds.

to his father in a letter which the Doctor himself bore, "Doct^r Witherspoon's business to Virginia is nearly the same, as I conjecture (i.e., collecting funds) and perhaps to form some acquaintance to induce Gentlemen to send their sons to this College." At Williamsburg in Virginia, one Sunday afternoon late in October, the visitor drew such a concourse of people that no building was large enough to hold his audience and he preached in the capitol yard which was crowded. After the sermon a collection was taken up amounting to sixty-six pounds to which the governor added another twenty. In the following February Dr. Witherspoon was back in Virginia evidently on college business, for when he returned the College owed him some thirty-two pounds for expenses. He was revealing unsuspected powers of adaptability and was finding himself as much at home in Virginia as in Massachusetts. He admired the northern Colonies, especially Pennsylvania and New Jersey, and welcomed the impartiality with which every denomination was treated, and he himself could in his turn be as impartial when he came into Colonies where influence other than Presbyterian prevailed. He soon learned to expect in the aristocratic South and particularly in Virginia a welcome and a hospitality that in warmth and lavishness equalled if it did not exceed anything in the North. Pleasant though he had found New Jersey, there were provinces pleasanter still—where the first question in the catechism, for instance, did not sternly approach the matter of man's chief end, but satisfied itself with merely asking his name, provinces where an old-world courtesy and chivalry existed toward women and strangers, and where life's enjoyment in the open-handed, happily careless fashion of the plantation was in marked contrast with the more business-like though not less genuine kindness of the compacter and more commercial North. He noticed, however, that the southern Colonies "blessed as they are with a superior soil and more powerful sun," were greatly inferior to Pennsylvania and New England "in numbers, strength, and value of land in proportion to its quantity." And he "easily solved" the question of causes. The constitutions of the northern Colonies were "more favorable to universal industry," and we need go no further he said, "to have the full force of liberty" illustrated.[27]

From trips to these parts of the country the President never returned empty-handed. Even when he brought back no money —which was seldom—he brought back new friendships with wealthy planters and so not only strengthened the foundations of the marked southern affiliations that Princeton was to have during the rest of the eighteenth and the first half of the nineteenth century, but also created the wide acquaintance which he personally enjoyed and which during his later American career he turned to his adopted country's good account. It was in this way for example that he met the Madisons, the Lees, and the Washingtons. James Madison had entered Princeton in the summer of 1769 but his father had never met President Witherspoon. In October, 1771, young Madison hopes that his father will meet the Doctor during the latter's visit to Virginia—"I am persuaded that you would be much pleased with him & that he would be very glad to see you."[28] At what date he met the Lees we do not know, but that he was on friendly footing with the family is evident from the following letter to Colonel Henry Lee which also suggests the attitude of parental oversight that he assumed towards boys entrusted to his care.

Princeton, Dec. 28, 1770

Sir

I wrote you by post, on the receipt of your letter by Joseph Cross, and now have drawn out your Account, that it may be ready to go by him, who has promised to call on his return. You cannot judge perfectly of what will be their Expense till the year is completed, for the inclosed Account contains not only the necessaries for Henry's Chamber at first coming to College, but his College board for the whole year, which will by order of the Trustees be paid every six Months in advance. At the expiration of the year I will send you the necessary Acct.

I have nothing to add to what I writ formerly of the behaviour of your Sons, and their progress in their Learning. It has always been in all respects agreeable. John Wilkinson is very well, seems to be happy

[27] "Reflections on public affairs," *Works*, vol. IV, p. 202.
[28] *Writings of Madison*, ed. G. Hunt vol. I, p. 8. One of Madison's brothers followed him to Princeton but was not graduated.

and has begun his studies with alacrity. The School is to be publicly examined by the Officers of the College, and some neighbouring Gentlemen on Monday next. If Joseph Cross does not pass before that time and anything happens worth communicating shall add it to this letter.

There is a French Gentleman come here lately from St. Domingo, who proposes to stay about 6 months to study the English Language. This will be a happy opportunity for acquainting our young people with the pronunciation and giving them a habit of Speaking french which I was before introducing here.

I learn from Mess[rs] Madison & Wallace how much we are indebted to you for your favourable opinion and friendship, the continuance of which we will do a lot to deserve.

Please offer my respectful Compliments to Mrs. Lee and your family & believe me

Dear Sir

Your most Obed[t] humble Servant

JOHN WITHERSPOON

Col. Henry Lee [29]

There seems to be no record of President Witherspoon's first meeting with Washington. The latter's favorable acquaintance with Princeton probably antedated that occasion, however, for in 1769 he had offered to pay the entire college expenses at Princeton of his kinsman William Ramsay, Jr., "a youth fond of study & instruction, and disposed to a studious life." Washington authorized the boy's father to depend on him for the lad's support as long as would be necessary to complete his education, and in case of his own death the letter in which this offer was made was to be obligatory upon Washington's heirs or execu-

---

[29] Crimmins Collection. The Henry mentioned in the first paragraph of this letter is the future "Light Horse Harry" of Revolutionary fame, Governor of Virginia, and father of General Lee. A few weeks before this his brother-in-law, Dr. William Shippen, Jr., of Philadelphia had written of him to Richard Henry Lee in the following language: "We are much disappointed in not seeing you here with your son or sons on your way to Dr. Witherspoon. . . . I am persuaded there is not such a school on the Continent. Your cousin Henry Lee is in College and will be one of the first fellows in this country. He is more than strict in morality; he has a fine genius and is too diligent. Charles is in the Grammar School and the Dr. expects much from his genius and application too." (*Southern Literary Messenger*, vol. XXVII, p. 443) Part of this letter is quoted in Fitzhugh Lee, *General Robert E. Lee*, p. 8. Henry Lee was graduated in 1773, Charles in 1775.

tors.[30] Washington very speedily valued Dr. Witherspoon's advice. His stepson, John Parke Custis, had at this time as his tutor the Reverend Jonathan Boucher, an Anglican clergyman, and it would appear that Washington, probably thinking of college for him, asked Dr. Witherspoon on one of his early trips to Virginia to examine the boy. The President did so and found him scholastically wanting. On Washington reverting to Boucher, the latter, irritated by the criticism of a Presbyterian minister of three years teaching experience, replied somewhat tartly. Dr. Witherspoon had said that the boy should have begun Greek. "This Business of Education is a complex & extensive Subject," Mr. Boucher would have his patron understand, "& a man should be well acquainted with it, before He ventures to pronounce how far another has or has not done his Duty;" [31] Witherspoon's criticism must have been made at random; it was not possible for him to have found out what Mr. Boucher ought to have done, in the few questions he put to the boy; if the Doctor had examined him "candidly & fully," he would have found him, to be sure, not full of "dry, useless & disgusting School-boy kind of learning fit only for a Pedant," but he would have found him not ill accomplished, considering his manners, temper, and years, in that liberal, manly, and necessary knowledge befitting a gentleman; at any rate, if Washington contemplates a change, Mr. Boucher begs he will not send the boy to Princeton; William and Mary is better in every respect; if not there, then to King's College in New York,[32] for the unexpressed reason that both of these were good Anglican institutions. The Princeton matriculation lists are incomplete and we do not know whether young Custis ever entered Princeton or not. He was never graduated. But a quarter of a century later Washington sent John Custis' son, George Washington Parke Custis, to Princeton under Witherspoon's successor, President Smith, and in his correspondence with this attractive but negligent youth may be found further indications of Washington's attachment to the College of New Jersey.

[30] *Writings of Washington*, ed. Jared Sparks, vol. II, p. 350.
[31] In Witherspoon's Library is Boucher's copy of the *Plan of Education at Mr. Elphinston's Academy, Kensington*. Did the tutor send the pamphlet to the President so that the latter might learn something about this complex business of education?
Letters to Washington, ed. S. M. Hamilton, vol. IV, p. 83.

Dr. Witherspoon was not breaking altogether new ground when he made his first southern tours in the interest of the College—indeed, at that time he could not have ventured far in any direction without coming across a Princeton trail, a fact which would have readily occurred to him on his first appearance at the Synod of New York and Philadelphia had he been familiar with the Princeton alumni lists. For, of the forty-eight ministers and elders present, sixteen were graduates, four were honorary graduates and four were officers of the College, while of the seventy absentees whose names were recorded in the minutes thirty-five were graduates or officers. Accordingly, when he struck south from Philadelphia he found a Princeton tradition already sprung up, planted by alumni from the earliest classes down to the present. For the most part they were ministers of the gospel, many of them serving widely scattered charges in remote and unexpected settlements—men like James Hunt of 1759 in Maryland, and Thomas Martin of 1764 from whose school Princeton received James Madison; or John Brown of 1749, and his classmate James Todd, both keeping alive in Virginia the influence of Samuel Davies in turning likely young men toward Princeton; or itinerant missionaries like Hezekiah Balch of 1762, who had been teaching ever since graduation and was now preaching through Virginia and North Carolina. Had Dr. Witherspoon visited the latter province, he would have found the Princeton influence astonishingly strong, spread by men like Hugh McAden of 1753 and Alexander Martin of 1756, or Alexander Macwhorter of 1757 at Queen's Museum, Joseph Alexander of 1760 at Sugar Creek, David Caldwell of 1761 at Greensboro, and Henry Patillo in Orange County—most of them conducting schools which were making honorable history for themselves and for early southern education. At Charleston in South Carolina he would have found Hugh Alison of 1762 beginning his school; and in Georgia he might have heard how Whitefield, seeking a charter for his ill-fated Orphan House at Bethesda near Savannah, had desired one similar to Princeton's.

Without pretending to complete the list of Princeton associations, these names are sufficient to show that throughout the southern communities were to be found graduates of the College of New Jersey consciously exerting on behalf of higher education an influence of which Dr. Witherspoon and the College were to reap the benefit, and which the latter was to repay by the stream of vigorous public-spirited and well-trained men sent back year after year to the South to play leading parts in southern clerical, legal, political and educational circles, or as private citizens to manage their ancestral estates and bear honorably their share of local and untrumpeted responsibility. The genuinely remarkable story of the Princeton tradition in the South is still an unwritten chapter of American social progress; but it will be seen later in these pages that President Witherspoon's energetic support of this tradition was not the least of his legacies to his adopted country.

In his own Province meanwhile he was throwing himself heart and soul into his new work and losing no opportunity to further the interests of the College. He was a man who wasted but little time when a decision had to be reached. An example of his promptness to act is the story of his acquisition of David Rittenhouse's orrery, that remarkable clock-work contrivance for illustrating the motion of the heavenly bodies. The authorities of the University of Pennsylvania had this mechanism under consideration but wished to sleep over their plans before they made a decision. The dismay of the Reverend Provost William Smith when he learned from the newspapers that Dr. Witherspoon had stolen a march on him and had quietly gone to Norriston, where Rittenhouse was living in straitened circumstances, and had closed a bargain for the purchase of the orrery, must have appealed to Dr. Witherspoon's sense of humor quite as much as the two hundred and fifty pounds in hard cash had appealed to the impoverished inventor. Provost Smith could not understand why Rittenhouse "should think so little of his noble invention, as to consent to let it go to a village," when he had within his grasp the opportunity of all the free advertising afforded by the city of Philadelphia. The Governor of Pennsylvania himself declared that the orrery should not leave the state, even if he had to pay for it out of his own pocket; he thought that Pennsylvania ought to have the first orrery, even if the second which Rittenhouse promised to make were a better one; and he went so far as to call a meeting of the trustees of the University on the matter. But he was too late, and the Pennsylvanians had to content themselves with the duplicate, which, be it said in passing, has been much better treated than the Princeton original.

That summer in July (1770) an incident occurred on the college campus, which while unimportant in itself, nevertheless, was significant of a certain wind that was blowing. When the letter of the New York merchants breaking the non-importation agreement and inviting Philadelphia to do likewise, came through Princeton, the undergraduates seized it and burnt it in front of Nassau Hall, "all of them," writes Madison to his father, "appearing in their black Gowns & the bell tolling." [33] A letter from Princeton quoted in the newspapers gives further details:

This afternoon (July 13) the Students at Nassau Hall fired with a just Indignation on reading the infamous Letter from the Merchants in New York, to the Committee of Merchants in Philadelphia, informing them of their Resolution, to send Home orders for Goods contrary to their Non-Importation Agreement, at the tolling of the College Bell, went in Procession to a Place fronting the College, and burnt the Letter by the Hands of a Hangman, hired for the Purpose, with hearty Wishes, that the Names of all Promoters of such a daring Breach of Faith, may be blasted in the Eyes of every Lover of Liberty, and their Names handed down to Posterity, as Betrayers of their Country.[34]

Dr. Witherspoon probably witnessed the whole performance from the discreet shelter of his study window, but if he filed any remonstrance it is not on record. His sympathies were already with New England. At the preceding commencement the College, as we have seen, had honored John Hancock of Boston; in the spring the President had received a copy of the official *Short Narrative of the Horrid Massacre at Boston* on March 5. Whatever he may have thought of the "massacre" he said nothing publicly concerning it, but in a letter to the *Scots Magazine* in May, 1771, he made a passing reference to Dr. Lathrop's sermon "Innocent Blood crying for Vengeance," delivered on the subject of the "massacre," which is not without value in hinting at his position on the incident:

[33] *Writings of Madison*, ed. G. Hunt, vol. I, p. 7, letter of July 23, 1770.
[34] *New Jersey Archives*, I ser. vol. XXVII, p. 203.

As to the author's observations on Dr. Lathrop's sermon, I shall say little; because perhaps it cannot be wholly justified—yet, if all circumstances are duly attended to, there is as little reason to insult or glory over the people of Boston, as there was to excite the public resentment against Captain P.

The College was getting itself in print on the colonial side. In July the *New York Gazette*, commenting on a phrase in a letter from New Brunswick to the effect that "the senior class at Nassau Hall have unanimously agreed to appear at their ensuing commencement, dressed in American Manufactures"—the first known instance of class action at Princeton—, continues:

How happy ought we to esteem ourselves, when we see some of our Youth, who will probably fill some of the highest stations in their Country, when their Fathers have fallen asleep, so early declaring their Love to their Country; and we hope this will meet with the Esteem which is their Due, and that many at this critical Juncture, will follow their laudable Example, in encouraging our own Manufactures.[35]

The appearance of the class a couple of months later at commencement proudly wearing American cloth brought forth still more flattering comment: "That truly noble and patriotic Spirit which inflames the Breasts of those who are real Lovers of their Country," wrote a gentleman in the *Pennsylvania Gazette* after attending the exercises,

seems already implanted in theirs (the students'). I have the Pleasure to inform you, their united Efforts to appear in Cloth manufactured in America, succeeded to their Wish. May I not then say with the young Gentlemen, that the gayest Butterfly in all the Assembly, in all its borrowed Plumes, did not appear more brilliant than his Classmates, who were that Day honored with their Attendance. What too sanguine Hopes can we have of those Gentlemen, and such Principles so early instilled in them?[36]

The exercises themselves more strongly than ever reflected current politics. One of the Latin theses proposed that subjects were bounden to resist their king and defend their liberties if he ignored the laws of the State or treated his subjects cruelly, and

[35] *New Jersey Archives*, I ser. vol. XXVII, p. 209.
[36] *New Jersey Archives*, I ser. vol. XXVII, p. 292.

the discussion though in Latin gathered especial flavor from the facts that His Excellency William Franklin, Governor of the province and representative of His Majesty the King, sat within arm's length of the speakers, and that James Witherspoon, the President's eldest son, was defender of the thesis. Little did this boy dream that before he had been ten years out of college he was to lay down his life in defence of that very proposition. A debate in English followed, declaring that the non-importation agreement reflected a glory on the American merchants and was a noble exertion of self-denial and public spirit. The utility of American manufactures was a corollary, and was the subject of an oration by young Frederick Frelinghuysen, soon to be a leader in the Revolution. A debate in Latin succeeded on the thesis that "All men by law of nature are free." And if the tone of any of the exercises had irritated Governor Franklin, Samuel Witham Stockton of 1767, who delivered the master's oration, did his best to smooth down ruffled gubernatorial plumes by paying him "a particular complimentary address."

The College was growing rapidly. Including the grammar scholars there were one hundred and fifteen boys in Nassau Hall, a larger number than it had ever sheltered. How completely Dr. Witherspoon had won the confidence of his trustees is shown by the compliment with which they repealed a temporary rule passed before his arrival granting each member of the faculty sole authority as to the time and method of recitations heard by him. The board now voted that "the President of the College is invested with the sole direction as to the Methods of Education to be pursued in this Seminary," and that no previous resolution should

exclude him from the Sole Direction whenever he may think proper to interfere in the Conduct & Regulation of the Modes of Instruction; he being chiefly answerable to the World for the particular Steps which are taken in educating the Pupils trained up in this College, and the Trustees have been so fully satisfied from experience of his great Abilities in the Management of the Institution committed to his Care, & with high Pleasure have seen his indefatigable Labours & Success in raising the Reputation of this College; they are clearly of Opinion that all the Authority above declared to be annexed by the said Law to the Office of President of the College, is highly proper to be put into the hands of the Revd Doct^r Witherspoon the new President.[37]

This is the first time that the prerogatives of the Presidency had been defined, and the occupant of that office at Princeton remained an autocrat until the second decade of the twentieth century, when under the leadership of President Hibben a proper share of faculty autonomy, based on the principle of cooperation between the executive and the teaching officers of the University, was inaugurated.

While his personal popularity was daily increasing, opinion in college differed as to the President's power in the pulpit. To some students, like Fithian, his sermons were "almost inimitable," but to others he was "what we call a dull preacher." He himself early perceived that he was not followed so easily in America as in Scotland, which in view of his marked Scottish accent was to be expected; but at best he was not a magnetic speaker. His undergraduates noticed this lack of warmth in his pulpit manner. When a revival of religious enthusiasm sprang up on the campus in the summer of 1770, they invited the Reverend Jedidiah Chapman of Newark to visit them and he spent a week at Princeton preaching three times and meeting inquirers in "praying societies." Early in 1772 there was another outburst of religious interest fostered largely by the effort of Ebenezer Bradford, a student in the Class of 1773 but fresh from Connecticut and the inspiration of the Reverend Dr. Joseph Bellamy of Woodbury, a late follower of Jonathan Edwards' idealistic philosophy. Here again the students sent not across the campus for their matter-of-fact President but this time over to Trenton for the Reverend Dr. Elihu Spencer who preached with "a great deal of warmth and zeal" although, so it was alleged, "not with so much judgment, accuracy, and clearness as could have been desired." The real difficulty with Dr. Spencer was that his doctrine was not sufficiently advanced, but in spite of this he seems to have been successful in making the dry bones of this particular academic valley rattle, for Bradford, whose criticism is the one quoted above, admitted that he roused the attention of most of

[37] Minutes of the Board, September, 1770.

the students. Even college exercises yielded right of way, so Andrew Hunter informed Fithian:

We have had a considerable stir of religion since you went away, he wrote, Lewis Wilson is said to have got religion; and the formerly abandoned Glover is seeking the way to heaven. Our orations are put off lest they should do harm to some under concern.[38]

It was of this revival that the biographers of Colonel Aaron Burr assert that President Witherspoon did not approve. Dr. Ashbel Green, however, took pains to enquire of men who had been students at that period and their statements totally discredited the assertion. The President undoubtedly may have checked imprudences, says Dr. Green, but there is every reason to believe not only that he did not tell Burr that the revival was mere fanaticism, as the story goes, but that he gave the purely religious phase of the episode his entire support.

Of another phase he surely would have disapproved had he known of it, and this phase is of some historic interest in that it is concerned with the most far reaching philosophical event in President Witherspoon's administration—his fight against Berkleyan idealism and his substituting in its place the philosophy of the Scottish common sense school of realism. The Reverend Mr. Chapman had reported to Dr. Bellamy that a number of students had attained "the saving knowledge of the truth; and *the truth* [italics are his] prevails greatly, but not without opposition," adding that several students expected to study divinity with Dr. Bellamy. The "opposition" alluded to certainly came from the President. Bishop Berkeley's philosophy had but recently become popular with a little group of tutors and older undergraduates headed by Joseph Periam,[39] a tutor who was "a steady, zealous friend to truth"—the particular form of truth taught by Berkeley. When President Witherspoon arrived at

[38] Letter of March 1772, Fithian, *Journal*, p. 22. Glover's expulsion a year later for stealing turkeys led Fithian to reflect that "there is no knowing who is converted, only by their after conduct in life."

[39] The influence of Periam, a graduate of the Class of 1762, on the intellectual vagaries of the college at this time may be traced in the philosophical experience of Dr. Samuel Stanhope Smith (1769); and its effects are alluded to in the dedication of Dr. Frederic Beasley's *Search for Truth* where the philosophical history of this period at Princeton is briefly summarized.

Princeton these young enthusiasts were much disconcerted to find that he totally discredited the bishop's views. Those views colored the teaching of Dr. Bellamy and his disciple Bradford, and the "eastward" or "new" divinity they represented met with little or no sympathy from Dr. Witherspoon. In fact when Bradford entered Princeton in 1771 he was advised not to let his sentiments be known, as "it would be of great disservice" to him. He found two or three, however, "who dared think for themselves" and they agreed to promote what they judged to be the truth "in as private and hidden a manner as possible." As the awakening increased, there was inquiry for books, and among the most useful was Dr. Bellamy's *True Religion Delineated* which was loaned under strictest promises of secrecy. "In this manner," says Bradford to Bellamy, "the chief of your books were read over several times by a great number of the students; at last we had societies every evening in which we read something." To those who were hostile to the "new divinity" copies of Bellamy's writings were adroitly loaned with the title pages cut out, and thus disguised were "much admired," and finally two hundred reprints of his *True Religion* were subscribed for in the College. Dr. Chapman reported being invited to return to Princeton where "Mr. Edwards' sentiments make surprising progress." President Witherspoon declared he was neither for nor against the new doctrines on the campus, but, adds Bradford, "he both preaches and converses in contradistinction of them." The President unquestionably would have opposed clandestine propaganda whatever the cause represented, and it may have been his discovery of the facts and his frank protests that led the biographers of Colonel Burr into their misstatement.[40]

After commencement in 1770 Dr. Witherspoon made a trip into New England with Ezra Stiles who had been his guest at Princeton, and visited New Haven, Providence, and Boston. At New Haven he enjoyed the hospitality of Mr. Stiles on whom he

---

[40] The sources of this story are found in the Bellamy Papers in the New Jersey Historical Society containing the correspondence of Chapman and Bradford with Dr. Bellamy. *New Jersey Historical Society Proceedings*, 1 ser., vol. VI, p. 174 ff. The relative importance of this episode in the history of American philosophical thought is indicated in Riley's *American Philosophy*.

appears to have made a deep impression and with whom he was to keep up an intimacy for the rest of his life. After much conversation, Mr. Stiles recorded in his journal the opinion that Dr. Witherspoon was "a very learned divine," and few men in America were better qualified to judge than this encyclopedic Yale professor. He gives a brief but accurate summary of Witherspoon's life to date, and closes his entry with the significant hieroglyph: "£10 Str.," which being interpreted can mean nothing else than Yale's loss and Princeton's gain.

Dr. Witherspoon's increasing importance in Presbyterian councils is easily discernible not only in the New Jersey records of the time but also in those of the Synod. In 1771 his fellow Presbyterian clergy of New Jersey appointed him their spokesman with Dr. Elihu Spencer in petitioning Governor Franklin for a charter to incorporate a proposed "New Jersey Society for the better Support of the Widows and Education of the Children of deceased Presbyterian Ministers," and the document they filed placed the Governor and his legal advisers in a quandary which is amusingly illustrated in the voluminous papers on the case.[41] As for the Synod, it would be expected that he was annually placed on the committee to disburse the Synod's fund for needy but pious youths at the College of New Jersey; but other appointments such as his election to the Synod's treasurership show a marked deference to the position he occupied in that body's esteem. Seven times he was a member of the annual commission which sat between meetings of the Synod; he was frequently deputed to visit and report on David Brainerd's Indian School which was under the Synod's care; with Dr. Rodgers he was ordered in 1771 to draw up the Synod's reply to a letter from the General Assembly of the Church of Scotland and to frame letters to the churches in Holland and Geneva. He was placed on the committee to review all the synodical replies to foreign communications and he seems to have been chosen in particular to interview ministers presenting letters of dismissal from churches in Scotland and Ireland and seeking admission to colonial presbyteries. At his first attendance in the Synod he had been made

[41] *New Jersey Archives*, vol. X, p. 339, etc. S. H. Cobb, *Rise of Religious Liberty in America*, refers to this case as curiously revealing the governmental notion that there was, or ought to have been, a Church of England Establishment in New Jersey.

chairman of a committee to communicate with seceding ministers and seek to bring about a union between them and the
Synod; similarly in 1772 he was appointed chairman of a committee to consider relations with the Associate Presbytery; and
from 1769 until the Revolution he was annually a delegate from
the Synod to the Conventions with the General Association of
Connecticut. It is regrettable that the records of these conventions are so scanty, for one would suppose that President Witherspoon's part in their proceedings was large. But the only inference that can be drawn from the records themselves and from
the failure of his writings to show any allusion to the subject
which gave the conventions their chief reason for existence, is
that he was not active in the movement. The facts follow. The
conventions had been organized in 1766 of representatives of the
Synod and of the associated Congregational churches of Connecticut to meet annually, with the primary object of uniting the
dissenting forces in the Colonies against the introduction of an
American episcopate deriving authority from the Crown, and
also for the purpose of cultivating, by correspondence with dissenting bodies in Great Britain, their support of this object. Dr.
Witherspoon's name occurs in the minutes of the Convention for
the first time in September, 1769. He had been selected by the
Synod to preach the opening sermon, but did not attend. The
Convention appointed him and the Reverend William Tennent a
committee to correspond with ministers in Scotland. No report
of their work was ever made. At the 1770 meeting, it being clear
that the utility of the Convention was not understood by the
ministers of Massachusetts, New Hampshire, and Rhode Island,
the President "now on his journey to the Eastward," was requested to impress them with the necessity of joining the Convention; and the following year, in his absence, it was reported
that he had obeyed his instructions, though with what success
was not known. In 1772 and 1773 he was again a delegate and he
opened the Convention of 1773 with a sermon. Appointed chairman of the meeting he officially signed a letter written by a committee of the Convention to the Committee of Dissenters in England, the only document on the subject of the episcopate that
bears his name; but he was not the author of this paper, nor even
a member of the reporting committee. At this meeting he was di-

rected to obtain information on the state of religious liberty in Canada; but here again there is no evidence that he ever reported.

His name does not occur in the Minutes of 1774 and 1775 although appointed a delegate; the minutes of 1776 are lost; no subsequent sessions were held; and the outcome of the Revolutionary War settled the question of an American episcopate created by the British government.[42]

The Reverend Dr. John DeWitt, in his historical sketch of the College, has noticed the marked contrast between the tone of commencement performances before the Stamp Act controversy and the inspiration of those succeeding that period, and allusion has already been made in these pages to one or two of Witherspoon's early commencement programmes. In 1771 the chief attraction was a poetical dialogue on *The Rising Glory of America* written by Hugh Brackenridge and Philip Freneau, a performance that instantly recalls in contrast the production given a decade earlier entitled *The Military Glory of Great Britain*, and illustrates perfectly the change in tone and inspiration. The Brackenridge-Freneau dialogue received great applause and had the honor of being quoted in the London newspapers. After recounting the story of the discovery of America and the settling of the Colonies, the speakers gaze into the future and see visions of

> A thousand Kingdoms rais'd, cities and men
> Num'rous as sand upon the ocean shore;
> The Ohio shall glide by many a town
> Of note; and where the Mississippi stream
> By forests shaded now runs weeping on,
> Nations shall grow and states not less in fame
> Than Greece and Rome of old.
>
> . . .   .
>
> Hoarse Niagara's stream now roaring on,
> By some great monarch taught a better course
> Or cleared of cataracts, shall flow beneath
> Unnumbered boats and merchandise and men.

[42] "Minutes of the Convention of Delegates from the Synod of New York and Philadelphia, and from the Associations of Connecticut," Hartford, 1843, reprinted in *Records of the Presbyterian Church*. Philadelphia, 1904. Also see A. L. Cross, "Anglican Episcopate and the American Colonies," New York, 1902, *Harvard Historical Studies*, vol. IX.

The fact that not all their dreams came true is no reflection on the authors' poetic skill, and the long poem they jointly wrote on this occasion rises more than once to considerable heights of excellence. Brackenridge and Freneau were leaders of a group of writers in college of whom the American reading public was to hear a good deal before many years elapsed.[43]

There would seem to be nothing in the lines just quoted—and they are typical—that should have hurt British feelings. They were simply a poetic example of the new Americanism of the day, or at worst a somewhat fantastic expression of young America's enthusiastic outlook on her own future. Dr. Witherspoon was not blind to his responsibility as governor of a miscellaneous body of spirited young Americans, and he kept judicious check on all their proceedings.

There are now under my care, he wrote in 1772 to a member of the British aristocracy, many who in a very short time will be at the head of affairs in their several provinces, and I have already and shall continue to temper the spirit of liberty, which breathes high in their country, with just sentiments, not only of loyalty to our excellent sovereign, in which they do not seem to be defective, but with a love of order and an aversion to that outrage and sedition into which the spirit of liberty when not reined is sometimes apt to degenerate.

But the commencement productions of his undergraduates were being taken very seriously by some and at commencement in 1772, the orations cut deeply. In the *Pennsylvania Chronicle* of October 31, they are particularly criticised by "A Friend to Impartiality." Attending commencement he

with many others, was surprised to hear most of the young Gentlemen discussing in their performances the most perplexing political topics. The most difficult and knotty questions, relating to the British constitution, were solved in a jerk. . . . I could almost have persuaded myself that I was within a circle of vociferous politicians at Will's

[43] It was to Brackenridge that the President made his famous reply when the young student on entering college referred to his previous hardships and quoted Juvenal's lines—

> *Haud facile emergunt quorum virtutibus obstat*
> *Res angusta domi.*

"There you are wrong, young man!" retorted the President, "it is only your *res angusta domi* men that do emerge!"

[141]

coffee-house, instead of being surrounded with the meek disciples of wisdom in the calm shades of academic retirement.[44]

The Reverend Jonathan Boucher, who had reason for being critical of Dr. Witherspoon, made caustic comment on the college oratory of the time as exhibited at Princeton and at the University of Pennsylvania.[45] He considered these two institutions the chief nurseries of "all that frivolous and mischievous kind of knowledge which passed for learning in America at this period." They pretended to teach everything without being really competent to teach anything as it ought to be taught; but their chief and peculiar merit was thought to be in rhetoric and belles lettres, a term not easily defined, he says, nor understood; hence in no country were there so many orators, nor so many smatterers; two or three years spent at one of these seminaries were in general deemed sufficient to qualify a person for the gown, and persons so qualified had "pretty generally gotten the churches."[46] A style of oratory not very unlike Princeton's might probably have been heard on one or two other commencement platforms of that day; but the special Princeton brand aroused bitter resentment on more than one occasion during Dr. Witherspoon's presidency. That he himself did not altogether approve of the undergraduate style on the rostrum seems clear from a remark in his *Lectures on Eloquence:*

I believe, he says, it would be a great improvement of the laudable practice in this college of daily orations, if they were chosen with more judgment, and better suited to the performers. Almost all of the pieces we have delivered to us are of the last or highest kind, warm passionate declamations. It is no wonder that some should perform these ill, who have never tried the plainer manner of simple narrative.[47]

[44] *New Jersey Archives,* I ser. vol. XXVIII, p. 277.
[45] *Notes and Queries,* 5 ser, vol. VI, p. 81.
[46] Mr. Boucher adds: "The two colleges of Princeton and Philadelphia manufacture physicians also with great facility." Princeton has never had a department of medicine nor conferred a medical degree. So that half of the reverend critic's slur has no basis of fact. As for the "facility" with which physicians were "manufactured" at the University of Pennsylvania, it can hardly be necessary to do more in refutation of the slander than to point to the brilliant and eminent record of that University's medical school from its earliest day to the present.
[47] *Works,* vol. III, p. 389.

By the close of 1772 the President was receiving a full measure of criticism, and for a publication of his own. He had made another of his southern tours in the autumn of 1771 but his campaigns were now no longer to be limited to the mainland. The college had eighty-five students and forty-five grammar scholars, according to the New Jersey census return in 1772, but the President was casting his eyes longingly on the West Indies as a field for exploitation and when early in 1772 it was represented to the board of trustees that there was fair prospect of collecting money and securing students from the West Indies he was requested to make a tour of the islands. His son James, a graduate of the class of 1770, was planning to go to the Barbadoes and the board commissioned him to receive funds there for the College, and in Antigua or any other of the West Indies. It was thought advisable to appoint an agent to act with the President and this task fell very naturally to the Reverend Charles Beatty, whose early experience as a peddler seems to have developed a talent for money-getting equalled by the natural ability in this direction of the President himself and of the Reverend Mr. James Caldwell. Armed then with credentials from Governor Penn of Pennsylvania and Governor Franklin of New Jersey, Mr. Beatty proceeded to the Barbadoes; but there unfortunately he died before he had made any collections. Dr. Witherspoon never made the trip and whether his son visited the islands is not known. A committee appointed to carry out the project never made a report of its activities, although a number of West Indian students came to Princeton during the end of the eighteenth century.

The President had prepared the way for Mr. Beatty by writing in March, 1772, as a campaign document, an *Address to the Inhabitants of Jamaica and the other West Indian Islands* which was reprinted in October in the newspapers. It was a frank but modest advertisement, an address on behalf of the College. Its preparation arose, says its author, from necessity, not choice; it was against his general method to advertise in print. Exactly how he classed his notices in the newspapers is not quite clear; modern business experts would call them at least excellent "publicity," which is the offspring, if not twin brother, of "advertising." But President Witherspoon says he preferred what he called "private application," and wanted West Indian boys for his school and College. He does not add that he needed West Indian money for his professorships. He claims it is an advantage to West Indian parents to have it in their power to send their sons to approved educational institutions in America for their elementary training rather than to Great Britain. Obviously, such institutions were nearer than those of Great Britain and yet sufficiently distant to remove temptation of running home and lurking in idleness; the climate is better suited to West Indians than that of Great Britain; for the better prosecution of their studies and the better preservation of their morals it is also wiser to send West Indians to America than to Europe, the discipline being firmer, the supervision closer, and a more personal contact with the professors being customary.

Turning then to the College of New Jersey he refers with great restraint to its situation and especial advantages, briefly describing the course of study and the equipment, mentioning the system of prizes which he had inaugurated and devoting a short paragraph to the grammar school. Finally he lays before his readers certain fundamental characteristics of the College which in his opinion should enlist for it the interest of thinking men—its independence of governmental influences, the consequent spirit of liberty that permeates its atmosphere; the esteem it enjoys from those who are nearest to it and therefore know it best; the character of its graduates; its location in a spot "most happily chosen for the health, the studies and the morals of its scholars;" its religious catholicity—every question as to form of church government is so thoroughly avoided that students have been graduated whose denomination he did not know, the whole aim of the College being to make them "good men and good scholars."

The republication of this document in the newspapers called forth at least two severe anonymous rejoinders, one in the shape of a letter to the *New York Gazette* of December 7, 1772[48] signed by "Causidicus," evidently a King's College sympathizer, the other a pamphlet printed in Philadelphia that winter entitled *Candid Remarks on Dr. Witherspoon's Address to the Inhabitants*

[48] *New Jersey Archives*, I ser, vol. XXVIII, p. 345.

of Jamaica, and the other West-India Islands, and commonly said to have been written by the Reverend Thomas B. Chandler of Elizabeth-town.

"Causidicus" gives the President some pretty keen thrusts. He enquires why an address originally intended for West Indians should be obtruded on American readers? Obviously because "the Youth of North America were to be lured by the Charmer's Voice into the Bosom of Nassau-Hall" at the expense of other colleges. As for the alleged independence of Nassau Hall, "turbulence and faction ever have, and probably ever will mark" the proceedings of independents, witness the reign of Charles I and the recent happenings at Boston. The claim that the College of New Jersey is free from political and family influences is a slur directed at King's College in New York; the President's assertion that the spirit of liberty is strong at Princeton is unnecessary, the students in their public exhibitions having dwelt on British politics to such an extent "and in such a Manner, as to give the Greatest Offence to many who were present;" this spirit of liberty deserves a worse name, and in using such an argument the President is playing *ad populum.* He catches Dr. Witherspoon in a slip as to the Princeton enrolment compared with that at other colleges south of New England; he objects to the boast about the prominence of Witherspoon's graduates; he objects to the claims for Princeton's healthfulness; and in conclusion he raises the old and still unsettled question of urban versus rural colleges, proving at least to his own satisfaction that the argument is all in favor of the former.

Dr. Witherspoon replied in the *New York Gazette* of December 28[49] that an anonymous critic deserved no notice, but two of the points made by "Causidicus" he could not let pass unanswered. Therefore he would say first that he had no intention whatever of attacking other colleges in America; he had pleaded the cause of American colleges in general in the principal part of his *Address* and because he had mentioned circumstances deemed by him favorable to Princeton was no reflection, even by implication, on others. Secondly, he had no family in view nor any col-

---

[49] *New Jersey Archives,* 1 ser, vol. XXVIII, p. 369.

lege, when he said that Princeton was free of political ties and family influences. If King's College were controlled by one family it was news to him.

The author of *Candid Remarks* has much the same sort of criticism to make of the *Address*. Scarcely was the design of applying to the West Indies in favor of the college at Philadelphia known "but the Partizans of that at Princeton summoned up their Strength for an attempt of the Same Nature." He admires the "Sagacity and Fertility of Invention" of the President in discovering so many excellencies in the College of New Jersey unknown to others; and he warns the public against imposition. The *Address* has an air of caution and reserve "remote from the easy openness of Honesty." It is sophistry to say that it is better for West Indians to go to American institutions for their elementary and collegiate training than to Great Britain; the academies of Great Britain have advantages not mentioned and the faculties of the British universities are larger and better and have finer equipments at their disposal. He sees in the pamphlet a veiled attack on other American colleges, and in particular the college at Philadelphia and King's College at New York.

Dr. Witherspoon does not seem to have issued a reply to *Candid Remarks*. He could only have repeated the substance of his answer to Causidicus.[50]

College duties, academic polemics, and synodical committees had not been enough to keep the President fully occupied. He had found time to cultivate one of his hobbies and having bought a piece of property on the range of wooded highland a mile north of Princeton, had taken up what he was pleased to call scientific gardening and farming. Thus it was that one summer afternoon in 1772 the itinerant missionary David McClure found him with several of his students reaping in his fields. It appears from a news item in the *Pennsylvania Journal* of February 13, 1772, that the farmhouse on this property had been burned earlier in the year, and probably on its site Dr. Witherspoon built himself

[50] In the *New York Gazette* of January 18, 1773, "Causidico Mastix" prints a "Complete Vindication of a late Apologetical Letter from Princeton," poking fun of a very labored sort at both Causidicus and the President. *New Jersey Archives*, I ser, vol. XXVIII, p. 394.

RES. OF JOHN WITHERSPOON
Mercer Co NJ

TUSCULUM
From an old print

the substantial stone residence which he named "Tusculum"—
"a small but neat house, in a pleasant retired situation surrounded
with woods, in all the simple majesty of their uncultivated
state,"[51] a description which is one of the rare hints of nature appreciation to be found in his writings. The house, in excellent
preservation, is still standing and bears the date 1773 cut in one
of the stones of its massive front wall. He had built the house as
part of his "scheme of improvement" and with no idea of occu-
pying it himself just yet but of retiring thither when his working
days were over. In August, 1773, the *Pennsylvania Journal* advertises for rent "Tusculum," then but lately finished—"within
one mile, and in full view of the front of the College."[52]

It was for joy at rain sadly needed by his "Tusculum" crops
that he at times went through his various tasks "praising, returning thanks, and singing about it," much to the secret amusement of his undergraduates; and on such days, according to
Fithian, even the hymns he chose for college vespers were ones
that had reference, in Mr. Isaac Watts' inimitable words, to
"Those wand'ring cisterns in the sky—Borne by the winds
around." He rather fancied himself as a scientific farmer, and especially as a truck farmer; but his horticulture was purely utilitarian: vegetables he delighted to raise, but never a flower. He
made this clear to a lady who was visiting "Tusculum." "Why
Doctor," she is said to have exclaimed, "you have no flowers in

[51] "The Druid," *Works.* vol. IV., p. 148
[52] "To be Let and entered on immediately at Tusculum, within one mile, and in full
view, of the front of the College at Princeton, New Jersey:
"A neat and elegantly finished house, two stories high, with four rooms on each
floor, besides a garret above, and cellars conveniently divided below the whole house.
It will be very proper for any family who choose to reside for sometime in that agreeable country, for health or pleasure, or who desire to have the education of their children carried on under their own eye. As much garden ground as is necessary, or as
may be desired, will be let with the house; and cows for a family or horses for a carriage will be kept winter and summer at a reasonable price; but the Proprietor being
fond of agriculture and engag'd in a scheme of improvement, will not let any of the
lands for tillage. It is supposed there are persons to whom these circumstances will
render it the more agreeable, as they may have country accommodation without
care, and may make their residence long or short with little or no inconvenience."
Dr. Witherspoon's name does not appear; likely prospective tenants are referred to
"the Proprietor on the spot," or to John Bayard, or Dr. William Shippen, Jr., at
Philadelphia. *New Jersey Archives*, 1 ser, vol. XXVIII, p. 597.

your garden!" "No, Madam," he replied, "No flowers in my garden, nor in my discourses either!"

He also found time to continue his active interest in the subject of Scottish emigration, and to preach charity sermons at which collections were taken for Scottish immigrants—e.g., in January, 1774, at the Old Presbyterian Church in New York when the sum of £70 was gathered.[53] He was never too busy to talk things over with a Scotsman just landed and in need of advice. On his arrival in America he had joined the St. Andrews Society of Philadelphia, a benevolent organization founded in 1749 for the purpose of assisting Scottish immigrants.[54] One of the first he was able to help was a former parishioner Alexander

---

[53] *New Jersey Archives,* 1 ser. vol. XXIX, p. 199.

[54] This is as suitable a point as any other to note that President Witherspoon is said to have been a Mason. It has proved impossible to verify the assertion and its source is untrustworthy. In an address on *Masonry in Rutland* delivered at West Rutland, Vermont, in 1879, and published at Rutland that year, the Honorable Henry Clark stated that Dr. Witherspoon was "at one time master of Alexandria Lodge, No. 1, in Virginia, over which George Washington afterwards presided." The records of Alexandria Lodge, however, fail to disclose the fact that the President was ever a member. Mr. Clark proceeded to tell of a visit to Ryegate made by the President in May, 1774 which extended until July. "He preached in Ryegate and Barnet, and baptized some children. In an extract from his diary furnished me by the late honored and venerable John Dove, Grand Secretary of Virginia, Dr. Witherspoon says: "I have been on a visit to my possessions . . . in the town of Ryegate, and there I convened my Masonic brethren in informal Lodge and held a delightful reunion." Then follows a list of those present. Mr. Clark quoted a further passage from the alleged diary: "June 24, 1782. My Masonic brethren assembled at the tavern, and without working tools or aprons marched to the Presbyterian Church where I endeavored to portray the tenets of the Masonic order as exemplified in the life of our great patron, St. John the Baptist. The Masons marched back to the tavern where we all sat down to dinner." No biographer of the President speaks of him as a Mason. The diary referred to is not mentioned elsewhere unless it be the memorandum book Dr. Green and Dr. J. W. Alexander speak of, and now lost. It is possible but improbable that the President absented himself from his college duties for several weeks in May and June, 1774. As for the list of Masons alleged to have been present, Miller and Wells (*History of Ryegate,* p. 224) call attention to the fact that several of the persons named had not yet settled in Ryegate and that at least two were not yet born. As for the alleged visit in June, 1782, aside from the fact that there was no Presbyterian Church in Ryegate at this time, it will appear in a later chapter that on the twelfth of that month President Witherspoon entered upon his last term of service in Congress, and that on the twenty-fifth the *Journal* of Congress records him as present and voting at Philadelphia. The aeroplane was not yet invented that might have brought him from Ryegate after dinner on June 24 in time to take part in a debate at Philadelphia on June 25.

Thomson, whom he had left tenant in the vicinity of Paisley but who, with his family and the courage of his convictions, had sailed from Scotland to seek better fortune in the new world, and as soon as possible after landing at Boston had made his way to Princeton with letters to Dr. Witherspoon. The latter had started on one of his expeditions to Virginia, but at Philadelphia his fellow countryman caught him and received hearty welcome, with plenty of sound advice—all that he wanted just then. Mr. Thomson's ultimate success may be surmised from the enthusiastic picture of America in the pamphlet *News from America* issued later under his name in Glasgow, and already alluded to in this chapter.

It was with the same unfailing interest in the welfare of his own people that he allowed himself in 1772 to be pressed into a scheme organized by a Glasgow (and Greenock) merchant, John Pagan, for settling land in Nova Scotia with Scottish families.[55] What Dr. Witherspoon's original share in the grant was is not now known, but in 1792 he still held approximately twelve thousand acres. He had consented to the use of his name on condition that no land should be sold at a higher price than he should direct, and Mr. Pagan accordingly inserted his notices in the Edinburgh papers. The scheme was an interesting one. The land was on the Gulf of St. Lawrence about seventy miles from Halifax, with a coast line of some twenty miles, and bounded on two sides by navigable rivers. To the first twenty families going out the company promised to grant in fee simple, at sixpence sterling per acre, one hundred and fifty acres to each man and wife, and fifty acres more to each additional member of the family. To the second twenty families the rate was to be a shilling an acre, to the third eighteen pence, purchase money in all cases to be

[55] The grant had been made in 1765 to a group of men, chiefly residents of Philadelphia, the Reverend James Lyon (1759) heading the list and having associated with him some fourteen others among whom were Mr. Richard Stockton, Judge George Bryan and Colonel John Bayard, trustees of the College, Jonathan Smith (probably the graduate of 1760) and Andrew Hodge, the Philadelphia merchant. This group was known as the Philadelphia Company and their grant, the Philadelphia Grant. The project failed of immediate success because misrepresentation kept prospective settlers away, and in a year or two seven of the original fifteen disposed of their shares. It was these that were obtained by Dr. Witherspoon and Mr. Pagan. (See George Patterson, *History of the County of Pictou, N.S.*, Pictou, 1916.)

payable two years after settling. Transportation at three pounds five shillings was to be supplied by Pagan, children from two to eight at halfprice, and younger children free. The land was no wilderness, twenty families were already on it, and a school of thirty pupils was already running; the proprietors intended asking the Governor of Nova Scotia to grant a charter for a Presbyterian church and offered to give five hundred acres to the first minister who would settle there and one hundred to the first schoolmaster—of itself a significant indication of comparative values.

The scheme was criticised seriously or ironically in most of the Scottish newspapers. One writer mistook the purchase money for yearly rent, another exaggerated the coldness of the climate and the wildness of the country, and many other criticisms were equally unjust. The letter of a "Well wisher to old Scotland" in the *Edinburgh Advocate* was typical of the general objections to the scheme; but the "Bystander" in the *Caledonian Mercury* pointed out that a great part of Nova Scotia would not be more disagreeable to Scottish constitutions than Canada was to the French; and Frenchmen who had emigrated seemed to be living in comfort, if their letters home were to be trusted. The decriers of the scheme had suggested no alternative for poor farmers and mechanics, the weavers and tanners who were out of work or ruined, and "Bystander" suggests that men should rather inquire into the causes of the spirit of emigration than criticise plans to help the poor to better themselves, and he darkly hints that it is the old clerical party antagonism that is casting cold water on the plan because Witherspoon's name is attached to it. The President himself replied to his critics in a letter to the *Scots Magazine*, which that journal, however, did not print.

He was more personally interested in a tract of land in the province of New York. In September, 1763, Governor Wentworth of New Hampshire had granted to a group of proprietors the township of Ryegate consisting of somewhat over twenty thousand acres situated on the Connecticut River in what was to become Caledonia county, Vermont. These men in 1767 conveyed their holdings for a thousand pounds to one John Church of Charlestown, New Hampshire, who prior to 1773 sold the southern half of the township to Dr. Witherspoon, John Pagan and his brother. In February, 1772, a company was formed in Renfrewshire, called the Scotch-American Company, of one hundred and forty members, most of them farmers anxious to emigrate. Articles of association being adopted in February, 1773, James Whistler, a surveyor, and David Allen were commissioned to go to America and buy land for the company. Reaching Philadelphia they ran across Dr. Witherspoon and learned that he would sell his Ryegate tract. They spent five months exploring lands in the north and south and finally returned to Princeton to bargain with the President. The sale, at three shillings New York money per acre, was concluded in October and in the spring of 1774 a party of immigrants arrived.[56] Dr. Witherspoon's influence in the early years of Ryegate's history is believed to have been a large contributor to the sober and patriotic character of the community. He is said to have urged among the Scottish settlers by letter, by visit, and by addresses, the advantages of independence when the cause of the colonies was under discussion. He visited Ryegate himself more than once, on each occasion

[56] The subsequent history of the colony may be followed in the monumental *History of Ryegate, Vermont*, St. Johnsbury, Vermont, 1913, by Mr. Edward Miller and by Judge Frederic P. Wells. The main facts of the Witherspoon association seem to be that, having sold the southern division of the township to the Scotch-American Company in 1773, he purchased in 1774 a tract of 600 acres in the northwestern corner of the township for his son James and in 1776 2760 acres more in the same section. Soon after, his Nova Scotia associate John Pagan bought 5000 acres adjoining. In 1787 Dr. Witherspoon sold the tract bought for his son James to the Reverend Alexander Simpson of Pittenween, Scotland, whose widow eleven years later sold it to James and Abraham Whitehill of Renfrewshire, two brothers who became the ancestors of the well-known Vermont family of that name. In 1793 the President exchanged his 12,000 acres in Nova Scotia for part, and purchased the rest, of the Pagan holdings in Vermont (the deed is filed in the Office of the Register of Deeds, Pictou, N. S.), and later that year disposed of all this property to the New York merchants, Robert Hunter and William Neilson.

The Pennsylvania Historical Society owns a letter of President Witherspoon dated August 28, 1781, to Robert Donald, merchant in Petersburg, Va., and a friend of Pagan, from which it appears that, the latter having fallen upon evil days, the President suggested that he come to America and be admitted to citizenship; he wishes to know more of his situation because of their former partnership; Pagan is likely to lose his Ryegate property by confiscation as a British subject just as he himself is in danger of losing his Nova Scotia lands for a similar reason. This situation probably explains the exchange and purchase of 1793.

preaching and baptizing, and his son James was settled in the northern part of the township for nearly two years.

These transactions have laid the President under more or less severe criticism for what have been called his land speculations. His friend Dr. Stiles, for instance, after noting in his journal on hearsay that the settlers on Dr. Witherspoon's Nova Scotia tract were to occupy and cultivate it for eight years without rent and then were to receive leases from him at sixpence per acre, continues in a lightning calculation as follows:

Allow 2 or 3000 Acres for useless Land & Highways—Raise 6d on 20 Thousand Acres gives a Rental of £5000 ster. annum. The Doctor seems to be taking Care for this World as well as for that which is to come. Is he not laying a foundation for the Ruin of some of his Children and Posterity!

And the late President Maclean in his *History of the College of New Jersey* labored under the similar impression that his distinguished predecessor's interest in Vermont was one of personal gain. Passing over the fact that both of these critics are in error as to details, the main contention that Dr. Witherspoon was a speculator is unfair if any credence whatever is to be given to his own statement. "My having any concern in such an extensive undertaking," he says in his "Letter" to the *Scots Magazine*, "was wholly accidental and unexpected. I was invited and pressed to it, from a motive that was not at all concealed, that it would give the people who intended to come out, greater confidence that they should meet with fair treatment." His aim was to assist as far as he might in alleviating the lot of at least some of his suffering fellow-countrymen. His method was one that would certainly bring about that end at the least cost and peril to the emigrants concerned. It is admitted that he gained nothing financially in the outcome, though to say that he anticipated serious loss is to deny him ordinary common sense. So far as he was concerned his plan was no moneymaking scheme, but rather an eleemosynary enterprise on business principles; and for him at least it was a failure. It is reasonably sure that those who knew him best and understood his motives thought none the less highly of him for his benevolent efforts, and as evidence of the confidence in which he was viewed by his clerical colleagues it may be pointed out that at the meeting of the Synod in 1773 he was elected its treasurer.

The "Letter" to the *Scots Magazine* is more than a reply to the attack on him for supporting Pagan's scheme; it is an essay on emigration, and illustrates not only the alertness of Dr. Witherspoon's observation of conditions as he travelled through the Colonies and the speed of his assimilation of new data, but also the new note—the economic—that permeated so much of his writing after he came to America. This had never appeared in his writings of the Scottish period. Perhaps necessarily so, since all his writing had been theological; yet if he had devoted much study in Scotland to economic questions it is strange that no reflection of that study is found even in his occasional sermons. Once across the Atlantic, however, his essays are strongly marked by his new angle of approach.

In the "Letter" in question he points out that the accusation against him may be reduced to the following argument—emigration from Britain to America is not only hurtful but tends to the ruin of the kingdom, therefore by inviting people to leave Scotland and settle in America he is an enemy of his country. In reply he declares that there is little ground for alarm at migration from Britain to America. The numbers are not of consequence. Any one who reads Montesquieu will know that "when the spirit and principle of a constitution are good, occasional migration, and even war, famine, and pestilence are hardly felt after a little time. The place of those who are removed is speedily filled. Two or three hundred families going abroad make a great noise, but it is nothing at all to the people in Great Britain and will but make way for the settlement and provision of those who stay behind, and occasion them to marry and multiply the faster."

It is probable that the people in Britain imagine that the new settlements in America are wholly filled by those who come from Europe—it is far otherwise. They do not make the fortieth part in any new settlement. Such tracts are peopled from the adjacent settlements at first, with a few stranger emigrants; but their chief increase is from natural generation. . . . America is certainly exhibiting at this time a scene that is new in the history of mankind. It increases in a proportion that no political calculations have yet been able to understand or lay down rules for. The reason of this he thinks is that where colonies were sent out in ancient times, the people and the soil were somewhat similar, and improved by slow degrees; but in America one saw a wild but noble soil taken possession of by all the power, wealth, and learning of Europe, which pushed on its improvement with a rapidity which is inconceivable. Moreover, it should be remembered that "the migration is not all one way." It is said that New England has sent back to England twice as many people as ever came out of it to that section, but with this difference—they commonly come out poor; they go back rich.

But, he proceeds, supposing (what I do not believe) that inviting people over from Scotland to America did tend in some degree to depopulate that part of the world, should a man who does so be called an enemy to his country? What is it for a man to be a friend to his country? Is it to wish well to the stones and the earth, or the people who inhabit it? Can he be an enemy to them by pointing out to such of them as are poor or oppressed, where they may have a happy and plentiful provision, and their posterity be multiplied as the sand of the sea? . . . Is he then the enemy of those who stay behind? Not surely of the multitude, or common people, for there will be but more room made for them, and the more easy access to a comfortable subsistence.

It remains then, that he must be the enemy of the landholders, who may run some risk of being obliged to lower their rents. But is this a liberal way of thinking, to say a man is an enemy to his country, while he promotes the happiness of the great body of the people with a small diminution of the interest of a handful? . . .

I cannot help thinking it is doing a real service to my country, when I show that those of them who find it difficult to subsist on the soil in which they were born, may easily transport themselves to a soil and climate vastly superior to that. Sobriety and industry cannot fail to be attended by independence and abundance. . . .

But after all, I can never admit that the happiness of one class of man depends upon the misery of another, or that it can be any way contrary to the interest of the landholders in Scotland, that a few who find themselves pinched in their circumstances, or who have an active and enterprising disposition should remove to America. . . . I have not said in any part of the above discourse, nor do I believe that there is any hardheartedness or disposition to oppress in the landlords of Scotland. . . . The rise of lands has been the consequence of an increase of trade and wealth, and the disposition to go abroad in the common people, at present is owing to the same cause that made clerks and supercargoes go out, for these fifty years past, viz., the hopes of bettering their circumstances. It is both unjust and impossible to hinder them, if they be so minded.[57] . . . For my own part . . . since Providence has sent me to this part of the world, and since so much honour has been done me as to suppose that my character might be some security against fraud and imposition, I shall certainly look upon it as my duty to do every real service in my power, to such of my countrymen as shall fall in my way, and shall either desire or seem to need my assistance.[58]

Dr. Witherspoon's opinions on colonial politics at this time, though expressed only in private, were approved. After the President's visit to New Haven in the autumn of 1773 to attend the Yale commencement Ezra Stiles makes an interesting comparative statement in his journal that President Locke of Harvard was the most learned of American college executives, excepting Witherspoon in theology; but Locke he asserts would make no stand in politics either for or against the liberty of his country, but rather would "divert himself with the Folly of those who [were] most venturesome & enterprising on both sides." Dr. Stiles was thinking still of Witherspoon when he thus characterized by contrast the President of Harvard. For one reason or another, with the exception of Dr. Witherspoon, the presidents of the American colleges were not distinguished in the history of the Revolution; but there was to be no doubt as to the position of the President of the College of New Jersey on the questions of the day. He was not to linger on the political fence as one President did, nor like another try to flee from the storm, nor yet like a third had he secret longings for British ecclesiastical prefer-

[57] The author of the *Candid Enquiry into the Causes of the Migration from Scotland*, already quoted, points out that emigration from Scotland was not new, but the migration of so many farmers and laborers was new. This had not arisen because of over population—one-fifth of Scotland was not under cultivation and one-half was still in a state of nature, so that strangers wondered at its wildness. Nor was migration due to persecution, or fanaticism, or on religious accounts; it was due simply to the land monopoly, which rendered the condition of the lower classes hopelessly unhappy.
[58] *Works*, vol. IV, p. 287.

ment to give complexion to his politics. His transformation into an American was almost complete, and the hour was fast approaching when he would be enabled to proclaim publicly the position he had already reached privately. Yet, since the Church under whose jurisdiction he had placed himself had not yet raised the ban of silence, as a clergyman he felt bound to respect the tacit convention that in general was keeping politics out of the pulpit.

CHAPTER FIVE

UNDERMINING COLONIAL GOVERNMENT IN NEW JERSEY

DURING the next eighteen months the royal government in New Jersey was undermined and at last overturned, a process in the final stages of which Dr. Witherspoon was to have no small share. By the time he got back to Princeton after his visit to New Haven in the autumn of 1773, a crisis on the tea question was at hand. The October and November meetings at Boston, and the historic Tea Party of December, the fate of the tea consignments at Charlestown and of the tea ships at Philadelphia and New York were incidents which could scarcely have been unheeded by the enthusiastic young gentlemen under his care at Nassau Hall; and there is evidence that the atmosphere of the campus had been growing more and more uncomfortable for stray Tory collegians. One student, whose gentle character in maturer years would not lead us to suspect so much bitterness in his youth, speaks of loyalist undergraduates as "possessed swine" and hopes that when Dr. Witherspoon gets back from New England he will have two or three of them "turned off." [1] Whether the wish became father of the deed, and a steep place going down into the sea was found for these Gadarenes, we are not told. It is quite probable that the college pump was called into requisition, anticipating Civil War days in the next century when the same expedient figured in a very similar episode. The attitude of the campus on the burning question of the day was plainly revealed in the following January (1774) when one fine evening in order "to show our patriotism," says the undergraduate chronicler of the incident, "we gathered all the Steward's Winter Store of Tea, and all the Students had in College and having made a fire in the Campus we there burnt near a dozen pound, tolled the bell, and made many spirited resolves." And in the centre of the bonfire

1 Andrew Hunter to P. V. Fithian, September 6, 1773, Fithian's *Journal and Letters*, p. 42.

was propped an effigy of Governor Hutchinson of Massachusetts, "having a Tea cannister tyed about his Neck." [2]

Dr. Witherspoon and his tutors took no more serious view of this frolic than they had of the bonfire of 1770; but a trustee with a stricter sense for law and order, supposed to have been Mr. Richard Stockton of Princeton, with whose share in persuading Dr. Witherspoon to come to Princeton the reader is familiar, endeavored to stop what he considered riotous and dangerous proceedings, and with more emphasis than elegance was urged by one of the ringleaders, Samuel Leake by name, to go about his business. At the next meeting of the board of trustees when the President read for the trustees' approval the faculty list of commencement honors, Leake's name on the ground of scholarship led all the rest. Thereupon, it being reported to the board that he had been "singularly active in encouraging and promoting some unwarrantable and riotous proceedings among the students," particularly in burning the effigy of Governor Hutchinson and also insulting a member of the board, his proposed appointment to the first honor at commencement was highly disapproved and peremptorily vetoed. A trivial incident perhaps, but showing that the campus was naturally a little ahead of its elders.

As for the province at large, it was beginning to reveal clearly drawn party lines, although having been held so long under the thumb of the Crown administration it could hardly be expected to kindle save slowly to the general cause. During the summer of 1774, however, a distinct change might have been noticed stealing over the spirit of the Colony. Governor Franklin writing on May 31 to the Earl of Dartmouth[3] thought it doubtful if the proposed September congress of colonial representatives would be

---

[2] Charles C. Beatty to Enoch Green, Nassau Hall, January 31, 1774, Library of Princeton University. A few days later the *Pennsylvania Journal* of February 16, 1774, remarked editorially: "We hear from Princeton in New Jersey that the Officers and Students of the College have unanimously agreed to drink no more Tea." Mr. Woods in his biography of the President assumes (p. 117) that the Princeton "Tea Party" was the direct response of the campus to news brought from Boston by Paul Revere in December, 1773, to Burlington and Philadelphia, via Princeton. No record however, has been found showing that Revere came by way of Princeton. Further, the Princeton occasion took place late in January, 1774, and not at the time Revere would have stopped at Princeton.

[3] *New Jersey Archives*, 1 ser., vol. X, p. 458.

held. As to following the example of Virginia and appointing a committee to correspond with other Colonies he had hoped that New Jersey would not go into the measure and had taken some pains with several of the leading members of the Legislature for that purpose, and successfully so he had thought; for although the Assembly had met in November, 1773, and had been frequently urged to bring the question up it had not done so until its February session. And he doubts that it would have considered the matter even then had New York not resolved just before to appoint a committee of correspondence, and New Jersey did not care to "appear singular." The Governor told the assemblymen that the measure was "very absurd, if not unconstitutional;" but notwithstanding, on February 8, 1774, the Assembly had resolved without a dissenting vote to accept the invitation to an exchange of views with sister Colonies and had appointed a standing committee of correspondence and inquiry charged not only to communicate with other Colonies, but also to obtain the most early and authentic intelligence of all acts and resolutions of Parliament affecting the liberties and privileges of the Colonies, and to lay their proceedings from time to time before the House. No trace of the work of this committee is found until four months later. On June 1, the day the port of Boston was closed, six of the nine committeemen met at New Brunswick and sent a letter to the people of Boston stating that they regarded New Jersey as eventually in the same plight with Boston and pledging New Jersey to whatever steps should be agreed on; they further signed a request to the Governor to call a session of the Assembly before August. Governor Franklin informed his petitioners that there was no public business in the Colony to make such a session necessary, and officially he may have been speaking the truth; but privately, a little later, he intimated to the Earl of Dartmouth that affairs in the Colonies were perhaps "worthy of more Attention and Consideration than any Thing that has ever before concerned Great Britain."[4]

And indeed in New Jersey affairs were becoming decidedly worth attention, for through June and July scarcely a week

[4] *New Jersey Archives*, 1 ser., vol. X, p. 464. Letter of June 18, 1774 (misprinted "June 28").

passed which did not bring news of the appointment of some fresh county committee of correspondence, and the fact that most of the public meetings that gave them birth, whatever individuals may have thought, still made a point of declaring their unswerving allegiance to the British Crown, did not make them any less worthy of notice. The first meeting of the kind, sounding a keynote for its successors, was held June 6 by the township of Lower Freehold in Monmouth County only a few miles from Princeton. A few days later (June 11) Essex County met at Newark and appointed the first county committee of correspondence in the province, to meet other county committees and choose delegates to the proposed continental congress in September, and it was suggested that the committees meet for this purpose July 21 at New Brunswick.[5] Bergen and Morris counties were next to fall into line and on July 4 the freeholders and inhabitants of Somerset County met at Millstone, New Jersey, adopted resolutions and appointed a committee of nine members, among them Dr. Witherspoon, to correspond with other counties and to represent Somerset in electing delegates to the congress.[6] We do not know what part Dr. Witherspoon took at the Millstone meeting. Including himself, five of the nine men forming the committee were Princeton citizens.

Writing on June 18 to the Earl of Dartmouth in the letter already mentioned, Governor Franklin had thought it seemed now determined by several of the leading men in most, if not all, the counties of the province to follow the lead of Essex, their aim seeming to be to bring about a congress of deputies from all the Colonies not only to apply to His Majesty for the repeal of the Boston Port Act, but to endeavor to adjust the differences between the mother country and her Colonies; he doubted, however, that New Jersey would agree to non-importation. But he was destined to be sadly disillusioned.

It was a representative body of seventy-two men from eleven

---

[5] *Provincial Congress Minutes.*
[6] *Pennsylvania Journal*, July 20, 1774. The report of the meeting is not in the Minutes of the Provincial Congress, but is reprinted in the *Somerset County Historical Quarterly* of October, 1916, vol. V, p. 242, and *New Jersey Archives*, 1 ser., vol. XXIX, p. 425.

of the thirteen counties of the province that met on July 21 at New Brunswick. Stephen Crane of Essex was elected president and Jonathan Dickinson Sergeant of Princeton, in Somerset County, was made secretary. The minutes of the meeting, or any account of the deliberations, are not known to be in existence. Mr. John Adams informs us, however, that Dr. Witherspoon and William Livingston labored with the convention to have it instruct its delegates to the congress not to pay for the tea, but the matter was not covered by the resolutions adopted and printed. These begin by declaring unswerving loyalty to the King and detestation of the thought of independence; they oppose taxation for revenue without representation as unconstitutional and oppressive; the Acts of Parliament relating to Boston and Massachusetts are characterized as subversive to the rights of American subjects and repugnant to the common principles of humanity and justice; to procure redress the best method is to appoint a general congress of commissioners from the Colonies, empowered to pledge each to the other the public honor and faith of the Colonies to adhere to the determinations of that congress; they recommend a non-importation and non-consumption agreement; they resolve to take collections for the immediate relief of sufferers at Boston and they extend their grateful acknowledgment to the "patrons of constitutional liberty" in Parliament who are endeavoring to avert the storm hanging over the Colonies and to support the "just rights of the King's subjects in America;" and finally they elect as delegates to the Continental Congress five representatives to unite with those of the other Colonies to obtain relief for an oppressed people and the redress of grievances.[7] These resolutions are strongly reminiscent of the seven Somerset County resolutions, covering every one of them and in some cases adopting identical phraseology, thus giving color to the opinion that the Somerset committee headed by Dr. Witherspoon exercised a dominant influence at the New Brunswick meeting.

Whatever his share in the proceedings of the New Brunswick convention, he had very definite ideas of the importance of the approaching Continental Congress, and he went further than the

[7] *Provincial Congress Minutes*, p. 25, and *New Jersey Archives*, 1 ser., vol. X, p. 469.

New Jersey resolves in an essay written that summer, entitled *Thoughts on American Liberty*.[8] The Congress he declared was the representative of the great body of the people of America and was very different from the assemblies of the several provinces, different in mode of election, in purpose, and in term of service. It was, therefore, wrong for some of the Colonies to leave the election of representatives to the assemblies although in certain cases, as for instance Massachusetts and Virginia, there was identity of sentiment between the assemblies and the people at large.

As for the prerogatives of the Congress he was uncertain whether it would be safe, or even proper, to send ambassadors or to petition the King or the Parliament—the Congress might be treated as a disorderly and unconstitutional body, or indeed as criminal. It was certain that the Congress was very different from any regular operation of an approved constitution; "it is an interruption or a suspension of the usual forms," he declared without much danger of contradiction, "and an appeal to the great law of reason, the first principles of the social union and the multitude collectively" for whose benefit all laws and customs in a constituted state are established. That the King and Parliament were resolved to force submission from the Colonies was proved by the repressive Acts. Therefore the great object of the approaching Congress should be to unite the Colonies and make them as one body in any measures of defence, to assure the people of Great Britain that the Colonies will not submit voluntarily, and to convince them that it will be either impossible or unprofitable to compel the Colonies by open violence. And to this end he submitted the following recommendations for the consideration of the Congress:

(1) To profess loyalty to the King, and "our backwardness" to break connection with Great Britain, unless forced thereto;

(2) To declare the firm resolve never to submit to the claims of Great Britain, but deliberately to prefer war with all its horrors, and even extermination, to slavery;

(3) To resolve union and to pursue the same measures "until American liberty is settled on a solid basis," and Massachusetts in particular is restored to its rights;

[8] *Works*, vol. IV, p. 213.

(4) To resolve a non-importation and non-consumption agreement to be entered on immediately;

(5) To take measures to promote industry and manufactures, such as granting premiums in different Colonies for manufactures, appointing public markets for materials, inviting foreign manufacture in every branch and appointing societies in each large city and especially in the seaports to direct and encourage emigrants, whether manufacturers or laborers, and to publish plans of this kind in the British newspapers;

(6) To recommend to the legislature of each Colony to put the militia on the best footing and to urge all Americans to arm themselves "in case of a war with the Indians, French, or Roman Catholics, or in case they should be reduced to the hard necessity of defending themselves from murder and assassination;"

(7) To draw up an address to the British army and navy reminding them of their character as Britons and of the reproach, and perhaps danger, that they will run if they allow themselves to be the instruments of enslaving their country;

(8) To draw up a plan of union for all the Colonies so that as formerly they may correspond how best to cooperate in such measures as shall be necessary to their common defence.

This essay, Dr. Witherspoon's first known writing on the American controversy, marks the completion of his transformation into an American. He was now preparing to take an active part in public affairs. We have his own statement that he did not obtrude politics into his sermons and no published discourse of his at this time alludes in any way to the political crisis; his first printed sermon that can in any way be called political is the one on the *Dominion of Providence*, delivered nearly two years later. His appointment as a representative of the progressive element in the province shows, however, that he had not been silent in private and that the views he had thus expressed were favorable to the colonial cause and were well known at least to his immediate constituents. We have seen that, so far as any published words of his reveal it, he had come to America ignorant that a dispute still existed between the mother country and her Colonies. If he had brought any opinion with him it would have been in all probability that of the great middle class to which he belonged, who silently but doubtfully watched the trend of affairs.

How his eyes were opened on his arrival has already been told. That the American point of view was new to him is indubitable, and that, even after he had grown to understand this point of view, he had never dreamt of independence as the unavoidable end to which the Colonies were drifting cannot be denied, if his oft-repeated statements to that effect are to be believed. Even in the essay just summarized, there is only the vaguest hint at independence; he had not yet reached the point of believing separation inevitable. But he had learned to appreciate the claim of the Americans that they could not submit "in all cases whatsoever to the decisions of a body of the sons of Adam so distant from them." He had heard this claim debated up and down the Colonies during the last six years, and he found himself driven at last into agreement with it. He had learned to realize that the Colonies had enjoyed privileges which had been of such long standing and by which they had so thrived that in his *Letter to Natives of Scotland in America,* written less than two years after the date we have now reached, he was to call them plainly "ancient rights." And the point at issue was that in her progressive imperial views Great Britain would no longer allow the Colonies to enjoy those "rights." Once more he was finding himself face to face with a struggle for personal liberty and popular government, a fight very similar to the old one in Scotland against patronage and privilege. In a sermon at Edinburgh in January, 1758, before the Society for Propagating Christian Knowledge, he had spoken of America as that distant country which "was a refuge to many of our pious forefathers, when flying from the rage of ecclesiastic tyranny,"[9] and in the ordination sermon which he preached at Paisley in September of the same year he had pointed out that "the noble struggle which many in England made, about one-hundred years ago, for their liberties sacred and civil, still bears the name of the Grand Rebellion."[10] These two passages indicate the historical source of his opinions in 1774. His language of 1758 was typical of the attitude toward liberty still held two decades later by colonial dissenting clergy. In the words of an American historian, "they were driven to it in defence of their rebel-

[9] *Works,* vol. I, p. 284.
[10] *Works,* vol. I, p. 326.

lious Puritan ancestors."[11] The *Thoughts on American Liberty* show how far Dr. Witherspoon had advanced in six years. Still loyal to the King, he was nevertheless firmly resolved never to submit to British claims even though that resolution meant bloodshed, and therefore he was insistent that the Colonies put themselves in an attitude to defend their position; he was urgent that they enlarge their sources of supply and that they form a definite and effective union among themselves. Politically he had ceased to be a Briton; he was now an American, but with no sign of bitterness toward the other side. On the contrary he always spoke respectfully of the British government and of British institutions, and one may easily trace in his subsequent writings a tone of regret that separation between the mother country and her Colonies had to occur.

During the summer of 1774, the New England delegates to the Continental Congress came through Princeton on their way to Philadelphia, and few passed unhailed by the President of the College of New Jersey. Two at least have recorded their impressions. Mr. Silas Deane, who passed through on August 30, dismisses Witherspoon and his colleagues with the remark that they waited on his party, "but tutors and scholars are the same everywhere," so he finds it unnecessary to "enlarge" on the Princetonians who welcomed him. He was more impressed by the service he found at the tavern than by any sentiments of liberty he may have heard expressed in the village or on the campus.[12] Mr. John Adams was in a more appreciative frame of mind. He came two or three days before Mr. Deane, arriving on a Saturday and remaining until Monday. He devotes some pages of his diary to his experiences. Piloted by an undergraduate he explored village and College, and under the guidance of Professor William Churchill Houston, the future member of Congress and continental receiver of taxes for New Jersey, he looked over the library, glanced at the philosophical apparatus and waited politely while the professor endeavored to perform an electrical experiment for him. But the chapel bell rang for vespers before the machine could be cajoled into action, and science was compelled to

[11] Van Tyne in *American Historical Review*, vol. XIX, p. 50.
[12] *Connecticut Historical Society Collections*, vol. II, p. 164.

yield to religion. The singing of the undergraduates was another disappointment—they sang "as badly as the Presbyterians of New York." But after chapel Mr. Adams was introduced to Dr. Witherspoon, who escorted him up to the balcony of Nassau Hall to see the view and then down to his house at the corner of the campus to drink a glass of wine. And here the two men had long and free talk. Two points especially struck Mr. Adams. Convinced that British ignorance of the true basis of the American attitude was chiefly responsible for existing strained relations, President Witherspoon urged the advisability of subsidizing writers in the British newspapers, establishing what modern life would call a publicity bureau, to explain the American claims and to remove ignorant British prejudice, a note he struck again and again in his later writings and public utterances. And touching another of his favorite ideas the President further urged the formation in every Colony of a society for encouraging protestant immigration from Great Britain. He accompanied Mr. Adams back to the tavern under the sign of "Hudibras," whose proprietor Jacob Hyer was soon to prove himself, with the rank of colonel, as warm a patriot as he was already popular a boniface. Mr. Adams spent Sunday listening to Dr. Witherspoon, "a clear sensible preacher," and on Monday morning the future President of the United States continued his way to Philadelphia convinced that the head of the College of New Jersey was "as high a son of liberty as any man in America."[13]

But like a war-horse scenting the fray that gentleman could not bear the strain of remaining at Princeton while the Congress of provincial deputies was assembling a scant fifty miles away. Stirring within him again was the blood of the ancient spearmen; it had led him to the field of Falkirk; it had made him the redoubtable champion of the Popular party in the General Assembly of the Church of Scotland, and now it was calling him to Philadelphia. Moreover, he had views on the situation which he felt should be driven home in the minds of those who were meeting there. He could not stay away from a conference which he felt was to debate a national crisis. He had not turned American as one changes a coat,—without deep moral convictions. To

[13] *Life and Works*, vol. II, p. 355.

Philadelphia accordingly he went, and on Saturday morning, September 3, he might have been found at Dr. Edward Shippen's breakfast table, where although Colonel Richard Henry Lee seems to have done most of the talking, Dr. Witherspoon himself nevertheless entered "with great spirit into the American cause," and showed himself to be as heartily for that cause "as any of the natives," thereby strengthening Mr. Adams' impression gained at Princeton that this Scot was an "animated Son of Liberty." And that evening with Adams, Lee, and Harrison of Virginia, the two Rutledges, Dr. Shippen, Dr. Steptoe, and Robert Treat Paine, he was a guest at Mr. Thomas Mifflin's "elegant supper" at which the talk ran high and the company "drank sentiments till 11 o'clock." The following afternoon he preached in Dr. Sproat's church whither Mr. Silas Deane, in more genial mood, went to hear him. How long he remained and what else he did in Philadelphia we do not know. Had Mr. Adams been at the Princeton commencement a few days later he would have secured aural proof of the President's claims for his student's patriotic principles. The Latin salutatory, which Thomas H. MacCaule pronounced in place of the overzealous Samuel Leake, lost nothing of fervor by the change, since it had for its plain unequivocal subject the thesis *"Bellum servituti anteponendum."* Leake himself could scarcely have chosen a more significant text. Another speaker harangued the audience on "Liberty," and a third on the "Horrors of War." The bellicose tone of the exercises was relieved by Hugh Brackenridge's "Poem on Divine Revelation," delivered as a Master's oration on taking that degree;[14] and to the Commencement audience Dr. Witherspoon preached a special sermon at which a collection was taken for the Society for Relief of Widows and children of deceased Presbyterian Ministers.[15] But it must be admitted that the campus was living up to its bellicose reputation.

Meanwhile all over the Province of New Jersey the movement toward the adoption of patriotic principles was slowly going forward. Essex County had led the way in calling the convention of

[14] Advertised for sale by Samuel Loudon, Rivington's *New York Gazette*, November 17, 1774. *New Jersey Archives*, 1 ser. vol. XXIX, p. 527.
[15] *New Jersey Archives*, 1 ser. vol. XXIX, p. 474.

July, and the grand jury of the county now took the occasion of a reply to Chief Justice Smyth's charge from the bench the first Tuesday in November, to express in unmistakable language the attitude of the community. The county lost little time in obeying the resolutions of the Articles of Association agreed to by the Continental Congress of September. In November a committee of observation was appointed and it was recommended that every county in the province do likewise, so that any citizen found violating the articles might be held up to public notice as unfriendly to the liberties of the country and all dealings with him broken off. At Elizabeth on December 1 the committee of correspondence and freeholders met, elected a fresh committee, resolved to petition the Assembly to appoint delegates to the next Continental Congress and then, adjourning to the front of the courthouse, publicly burned two recent pamphlets "calculated to sow the seeds of disunion among the good people of America." The new committee consisted of six members, three of whom were the Princeton trustees, William Peartree Smith, Elias Boudinot, and William Livingston. Elsewhere, men who failed to appear and answer charges of disloyalty to the cause were blacklisted; users of tea were reasoned with, or boycotted until they submitted to public opinion; criticism of the resolutions of the Congress was not tolerated, and publications of that color were given a coat of tar and buzzard's feathers and nailed to the pillory as monuments to "the indignation of a free and loyal people against the author and vendor of publications so evidently tending to subvert both the liberties of America and the Constitution of the British Empire." James Rivington, the New York printer, received especial attention, being branded "as a noxious exotick plant, incapable either of cultivation or improvement on this soil of freedom and only fit to be transported." And it was resolved to have nothing to do with him while he continued to retail such "dirty, scandalous, and traiterous performances." At Burlington, although a centre of Tory influence, a meeting of patriot freeholders and inhabitants was held at which the Articles of Association were approved and a committee of observation was appointed for the city and county. In this wave of feeling the opposition was almost lost sight of, but here and there it organized, put itself on record, and promptly got into trouble. Such was the fate of Shrewsbury and Staten Island whose inhabitants according to the Elizabeth committee were manifesting an unfriendly disposition to the liberties of America and had neglected to join the Association. Even in Bergen county's patriotic ointment there lurked a Tory fly. The town of Hackensack declared that petitions to the Throne were the only salutary means of removing grievances, disavowed all riotous mobs, refused to be concerned in any unconstitutional measures, resolved allegiance to the Crown and decided to support His Majesty's civil officers in all lawful proceedings. Opinion, however, differed in New Jersey as to what constituted lawful proceedings and what did not, and the seriousness of the outlook brooked no dallying. Therefore volunteers were being raised; men who knew the manual of arms were being hired to teach raw recruits; supplies of powder were being laid in; leaden clock and window weights and even family heirlooms of pewter were being run into bullets. The day after the news of Lexington and Concord reached New Jersey the Newark committee advised its constituents to give all possible support to Massachusetts, to drill their military companies at least once a week, to see that the men were properly equipped, and to request all heads of families and masters of prentices to encourage those of proper age to learn military exercises, and to allow them time to perfect themselves. At Freehold by March, 1775, companies had already been formed and the militia was making good progress.

In December, 1774, Somerset County had met on call of the committee of correspondence chosen in July and had unanimously approved the proceedings of the Continental Congress, elected a new committee of correspondence to serve until July, 1775, and instructed it to meet other county committees and appoint delegates from the province to the next Congress, if the assembly failed to do so. Dr. Witherspoon was one of the new committeemen.[16]

The provincial legislature was convened in regular session and the council in January, 1775, had returned a brief and perfunc-

[16] *New York Gazette*, December 26, 1774, in *Somerset Historical Quarterly* vol. V, p. 244. *New Jersey Archives*, 1 ser. vol. XXIX, p. 554.

tory reply to the Governor's opening address, assuring him that with sincere loyalty to the King, they would endeavor to prevent those mischiefs which seemed to threaten, and by their zeal for the authority of government on the one hand and for the constitutional rights of the people on the other, would aim to restore the health in the body politic that every one desired. But there was a new note in the assembly's address, the note of new-found power although its protestations of loyalty seemed just as earnest. The proceedings of the Continental Congress of September were approved and the delegates from New Jersey were thanked for their faithful discharge of their duties, and were reappointed. This action was somewhat of a shock to Governor Franklin. He had hoped that the proceedings at Philadelphia would not be approved, and had in fact framed a paragraph of his speech to this end; but according to his account William Livingston, Mr. DeHart, and Mr. Elias Boudinot, three of the delegates, came down and lobbied for the resolution of approval; and by what the governor unluckily termed "artful management" succeeded in forcing a vote the very morning the resolution was made, although several members desired postponement for further consideration.[17]

Such was the general condition in New Jersey when the news of Lexington and Concord was carried across the province on the night of April 23, 1775. The rider reached Princeton from New Brunswick at six o'clock in the morning of the twenty-fourth; his dispatch was endorsed by Dr. Thomas Wiggins and Mr. Jonathan Baldwin of the local committee, one a trustee and the other the steward of the College, and was forwarded at once to Trenton and Philadelphia. By breakfast time its contents were known to the campus and throughout the village and neighborhood. A town meeting was at once called, of which Mr. Jonathan Dickinson Sergeant was made secretary, and from which emanated the first call for a provincial congress of New Jersey. Who were the leaders of this meeting is not known, but under the circumstances there can be no doubt that Dr. Witherspoon was not only present but took part in the proceedings. The following

[17] *New Jersey Archives*, 1 ser., vol. X, pp. 537, 575.

copy of the call in the handwriting of Mr. Sergeant and dated April 24, 1775, is in the Library of Princeton University:

To the Committee of Correspondence for the Borough of Elizabeth. Gentlemen:

The very alarming Intelligence we have just received induces us to fear that the Friends of American Liberty will be compelled to resort to the last Appeal for the Protection of their Rights. In this Extremity when no Time should be lost from Preparation we think that a Communication of Sentiment from the different Parts of our Province should take Place; and that no mode of doing this is so proper as that of a Provincial Congress. Should our Brethren concur with us in this Opinion, we would be glad that the Members of the Committees of Correspondence for the Province, to whom it seems to belong, would together with the Chairman, appoint a speedy Day for such Convention. These Sentiments, should they even appear to be erroneous, will need no Apology as They come from Persons who would wish not to be wanting to the common Cause; and the Suddenness of the Occasion hardly admits of formally convening the different Committees. Several of the Committee of Correspondence are in your Neighbourhood or within your influence, which is the Reason of our addressing ourselves to you in this Way.

The above is taken as the Sense of a Meeting of the Inhabitants of Princeton and the Neighbourhood, together with some of the Members of Committees of Somerset & Middlesex and Hunterdon. It is further desired of our Brethren to consider whether it may not be proper to fix some Day shortly before the meeting of the Continental Congress and not too early to be notified to the more distant Parts of the Colony. We have thought of Friday 5 May.

By order of the Meeting

Jonathan D. Sergeant clk

P.S. It is requested that the Contents of this Letter may be communicated on the Passage to the Committees of N. Brunswick & Woodbridge.

That night, April 24, another express with the news of Concord and Lexington in duplicate traversed the province and at half past three in the morning was received by Dr. Wiggins and Mr. Baldwin, and sent on. New Jersey had needed some shock like this to startle it into real activity.

The Princeton letter went the rounds and the proposal it contained met with instant favor, but the date suggested was too early and on May 2 the committee of correspondence for the province directed the congress to convene at Trenton on the twenty-third, and issued a call to that effect. On the eleventh, the freeholders of Somerset County, Dr. Witherspoon's county, met at Somerset Court House in answer to a call of the county chairman and resolved that "the steps taken by the British ministry to enslave the American Colonies and especially the late alarming hostilities call the people of the province to decide what their part shall be."[18] The meeting readily agreed to the proposed provincial congress and elected nine delegates to endorse all measures necessary for the preservation of their constitutional rights and privileges, and they resolved to join other county representatives in forming such plans for a provincial militia as might seem proper and to arm such a number as they should be ordered to raise. At Princeton the committee of observation was spending money for various patriotic purposes, and furnishing equipment to several rifle companies, expenses for which it was later reimbursed by the Continental Congress, while the New York and Philadelphia papers commented on the martial spirit pervading Somerset County where men were drilling daily.

Governor Franklin had meanwhile received dispatches from England which he believed were calculated to restore harmony, and late in April he issued a proclamation convening the Assembly for May 15. On this date accordingly at Burlington the Assembly met and the next day listened to His Excellency's message laying before the house the plan of reconciliation resolved upon by the House of Commons in February. But it was too late. Mr. Tucker of Hunterdon had a countermove ready and promptly laid beside the message a pamphlet recently received from Great Britain containing an extract of Governor Franklin's letter to the Earl of Dartmouth of February 1 in which he had alluded to the "artful management" by which the last Assembly was induced to endorse the action of the Continental Congress of the preceding September. After debating the address and appointing a committee to frame a reply, the extract of the Gov-

[18] *Provincial Congress Minutes*, p. 114.

ernor's letter was taken up and it was resolved to ask him whether or not he acknowledged its authorship. As for the plan of conciliation the Assembly informed him that as the Continental Congress was sitting to consider the general situation and the Assembly of New Jersey had already appointed delegates to the Congress, until the latter was heard from the Assembly could do nothing but give the Governor its own sentiments, assuring him, however, that it would abide by the decision of the Congress. The Assembly then declared it did not see that the present plan at all differed from the one offered the year before the Stamp Act was passed, and there seemed no reason for accepting now what was declined then. The Assembly further hoped it was unnecessary to assure His Excellency that the province did not mean to throw off all dependence on Great Britain and get rid of every control exercised by the British legislature. To which the Governor replied that the question whether the plan was old or new was not in point—the question was whether it ought or ought not to be approved; and he professed surprise that the Assembly of New Jersey did not consider itself competent to settle the matter, but must rely on another body for decision. The House merely recommended its delegates to lay the government's plan before the Continental Congress. After which the Governor replied as to the authorship of the "artful management" letter; the Assembly's question he declared was merely another of those personal affronts to which he was becoming accustomed; the Assembly had no right to pry into his correspondence with the King's ministers; but to satisfy curiosity he would say that the extract did not "contain a true representation of the words and substance" of his letter. The Governor was sailing perilously close to the wind; the only change made in the extract was the substitution of the word "every" for the word "several." The House came back with the parting shot that far from being an affront, the inquiry ought to have been a real service to His Excellency by giving him an opportunity to exculpate himself from the charge of writing the letter if the charge were groundless; and after resolving to consider the message on the authorship of the letter at the next session, on May 20 the Assembly adjourned until June. To close this unhappy episode it may be said here that at the November session the committee on the address reported and the House, in view of the critical situation of affairs and the necessarily controversial nature of the report, postponed consideration.

Three days after the legislature adjourned, the first provincial congress of New Jersey met at Trenton. Its personnel was almost totally different from that of the Assembly, only seven of its eighty-seven members belonging to the regular body. While Dr. Witherspoon was not a member, his attitude had full representation, nine of the nineteen delegates from Somerset and Middlesex counties, on whose common border-line Princeton lay, being either citizens of the village or connected with the College. Hendrik Fisher was elected president, and to Jonathan Dickinson Sergeant once more fell the duties of the secretaryship, while William Paterson and Frederick Frelinghuysen were appointed his assistants. The four came from Somerset and all but Fisher were graduates of Princeton.

While the members of the Congress fully realized their responsibility they did not realize their powers. It was the first session of such an assembly in the province, the convention of the preceding July having met for the sole and comparatively easy task of electing delegates to the Continental Congress. The new body owed its existence to the acuteness of the stage that the controversy with Great Britain had now reached. No definite powers had been entrusted to it; it had been given the task of providing such ways and means for the security of the province as the exigencies of the time might require; no limitations had been set and its members saw plainly that the business on which they were now assembled might affect the life, property, religion and liberty not only of themselves but of their posterity. They resolved to open each day's session with prayer. Then Mr. Fisher addressed them on the importance of the occasion, counselling the utmost deliberation in all measures pursued in defense of their rights and privileges, and advising the utmost care to support established civil authority for the maintenance of order and the undisturbed administration of justice, as far as was consistent with the preservation of their fundamental liberties. The Congress then declared its profound veneration for, and allegiance to, His Majesty the King, following this perfunctory resolution with one more truly sincere, endorsing the delegates appointed by the Assembly in January to represent the province in the Continental Congress, and thanking the Assembly for its attitude toward the general situation. And here the members paused.

Having no precedents or definite instructions, and no constructive instrument wherewith to be guided, and wishing to take no measures inconsistent with the plans of the Continental Congress which was then in session, they turned to it for advice as to the line of conduct they should follow and thus avoid marring or obstructing general views or disappointing the hopes of the more experienced and more widely representative body. They, therefore, sent Mr. William P. Smith and Mr. Elias Boudinot to Philadelphia to secure the advice of the Congress. But the Congress had none to offer. So, feeling their way carefully, the Jerseymen resolved adherence to the resolutions of the Congress refusing exportations to the British fisheries, to Quebec, and to other Canadian British possessions on American coasts; it opened correspondence with New York and Connecticut; it drew up articles of association according to the direction of the Congress and ordered copies distributed through the province; it laid down rules to govern the formation of a militia; and it authorized and directed the raising of ten thousand pounds proclamation money for the use of the province; and appointing a committee of correspondence of fourteen to act in its stead, with power to convene the entire provincial congress if necessary, it adjourned on June 3.

Governor Franklin, though ignorant of the actual transactions of the provincial congress, was perfectly aware of the new spirit abroad in his domain. Since the news of Lexington and Concord the Colony had been in the "utmost commotion;" he had seen his people arming themselves, forming companies, and taking "uncommon pains" to perfect themselves in military discipline; he had seen a Freehold band of militia pass his very door "with Colours, Drum & Fife" returning—after a false alarm—from an expedition to secure the colonial treasury and records before the crew of a British man-of-war could seize them; all legal authority and government seemed to be drawing to an end, and that of "Congresses, Conventions and Committees establishing in their Place;" the colonial militia officers were all resigning their commissions in the hope of getting others from the Continental Congress; government was "nearly laid prostrate" and public officers were "now only on Sufference as it were;" the Governor thought they would be well off if allowed to remain even on suffrance, and he remarked a little fearfully that there was not a single warship off the Jersey coast on which the governmental officials might take refuge; if General Gage should beat the provincials in an open engagement he did not doubt that all the governors in America and all the crown officers generally would be seized as hostages in retaliation.[19] When the lawyers of the province in their May term adopted resolutions to do all in their power to prevent unnecessary litigation, since the state of the Colonies required every man for public service, the loudest Tory scoffer must have perceived that New Jersey was becoming thoroughly in earnest.

Things had now reached such a pass that the Synod of New York and Philadelphia was compelled to give them attention at the annual meeting that May. A committee, of which Dr. Witherspoon was chairman, was appointed to draw up a pastoral letter on the situation addressed to the ministers in the Synod to be read to their flocks. He reported a document whose dignity and restraint, no less than its patriotic and statesmanlike tone, rank it among the most striking pronouncements of the period. However the members of the Synod had hitherto avoided the subject in their pulpits, they could no longer make pretence of concealing their private opinions on present public affairs. Now that the controversy seemed inevitably about to be decided by recourse to arms, they are to remember that there is no soldier so undaunted as the pious man, no army so formidable as one whose members are superior to the fear of death. With this introduction Dr. Witherspoon urges his readers to express allegiance to the King at every opportunity, to maintain the union of the Colonies and to support the Continental Congress, to be strict and vigi-

[19] Letter to Earl of Dartmouth, May 6 and June 5, 1775. *New Jersey Archives*, 1 ser. vol. X, pp. 590, 601.

lant in private life and morals, to pay their debts and do their utmost to serve one another, to practise humanity and mercy on the field of battle, meekness and gentleness of spirit which is the noblest attendant on true valor, and to pay strict attention not only to general fasts but to the habitual exercise of prayer. It was altogether such a letter as one might expect from the pen of a former member of the Scottish Popular party. Five hundred copies were ordered to be issued for the use of the Synod. Dr. Gillett says that "they were thus scattered throughout all the congregations contributing in no small measure to kindle and sustain the patriotic zeal of the country;" but not a single copy seems to have been preserved.

In President Witherspoon's appointment to the chairmanship of this important committee may be found not only evidence that his position at this juncture was perfectly assured, but also testimony to his prominence in Presbyterian circles. Besides having been made the Synod's treasurer he had frequently been appointed its representative on public errands, and annually he had been delegated to the joint convention with the New England churches; but now, as author of the Synod's Pastoral Letter at this turning point, he found himself the spokesman of American Presbyterianism in its declaration on the political situation confronting the Colonies.

At a meeting of the freeholders of Somerset County in July, 1775, he was reelected to the county committee of correspondence to serve until May 1776, and he now became its chairman. The provincial congress met again in August and devoted its session of two weeks principally to putting itself on a permanent basis by providing for the election of future congresses, deciding the term of service of delegates, organizing the militia, devising the machinery for raising funds, and arranging for the appointment of standing committees of observation and correspondence to act in its stead between sessions. The only permanent official needed under its simple system was one to handle its meagre funds, and Mr. Jonathan D. Sergeant of Princeton found himself elected provincial treasurer. Appointing a committee on safety to act in its place the Congress on August 17 adjourned until September.

This committee shared the conservatism of its parent. It was loath to take any very active steps or else to permit them to be recorded. The printed extracts of its minutes contain entries under only four dates and its most important acts were to resolve that hunting frocks should be the uniform of New Jersey's minute men, and that the proceedings of the provincial congress and of the committee of safety should be printed. The dislocation of government was having its effect on the province, tramps and vagabonds, under the picturesque name of "strollers," were abounding, servants were running away from their masters, horse stealing and robberies had become frequent, and the committee recommended all good people to challenge and strictly examine suspicious characters, and if satisfactory account were not given to turn them over to the authorities. It is significant that the meetings of the committee were all held at Princeton.

The college commencement that September had a stamp of its own. The President took for the text of his baccalaureate sermon to the graduating class the twelfth verse of the second chapter of St. Paul's first epistle to the Thessalonians. His subject was "Christian Magnanimity," that greatness of mind which would constrain his hearers to act as the apostle had exhorted his readers to act, suitably to the dignity of their character and the challenge of their privileges. Save in his opening sentence where he admitted that the times were a continual trial to Christian faith and constancy, he made no allusion to the struggle on which the Colonies had entered, a struggle in which he frankly hoped that his graduates would take their full share; but it is easy to read between the lines both what he was thinking of and also the wider message he intended his sermon to bear when he pointed out some of the duties that belong to Christian great-mindedness —to attempt great and difficult things, to aspire after great and valuable possessions, to encounter danger with resolution, to struggle against difficulties with perseverance, and to bear suffering with fortitude and patience. This time he said nothing about allegiance to the King.

The address to the senior class with which the baccalaureate ended was striking, but the original version has disappeared. It was in substance repeated by him every year until 1787 and the

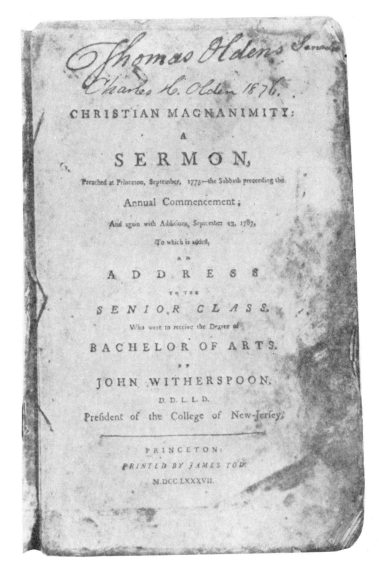

CHRISTIAN MAGNANIMITY:

A

SERMON,

Preached at Princeton, September, 1775—the Sabbath preceeding the

Annual Commencement;

And again with Additions, September 23, 1787,

To which is added,

AN

ADDRESS

TO THE

SENIOR CLASS,

Who were to receive the Degree of

BACHELOR OF ARTS.

BY

JOHN WITHERSPOON,

D. D. L. L. D.

President of the College of New-Jersey.

PRINCETON:

PRINTED BY JAMES TOD.

M.DCC.LXXXVII.

SERMON ON CHRISTIAN MAGNANIMITY

version then published contains no reference to the events of 1775. Beginning with a plea for religion he proceeds to urge the further prosecution of studies begun in college; college education is intended only to give the elements and first principles which should whet the appetite for more; the life of a graduate should be one of diligence and application, firmness of mind, and steady perseverance. He urges his hearers to maintain their friendship with one another and to keep up the intimacies of college life: "Man, made for society, derives his chief advantages of every kind from the united efforts of many conspiring to the same end;" piety itself consists of love of God and fervent charity to all men; those who deserve the name of Christians "are said to be pilgrims and strangers in the earth; therefore they ought to keep together, lest they lose their way." No less is this true in respect to literature; he has observed that the eminent men in every nation have appeared in clusters, for the reason that mutual intercourse invigorates natural talents, and here America suffers by the paucity of learned men and the poverty of her libraries.

Then he urges prudence in management of business affairs, order and exactness in dress, books, furniture, and the keeping of accounts; a certain humility, the government of passions and of the tongue, a kindly cheerful interest in the affairs of others—"it is no inconsiderable legacy for a man to leave to his children, that he had always been a friend to others, and never refused his assistance to those who stood in need of it." This leads him to speak once more of friendship—not friendship based on weakness, as in those who seem obliged to have recourse to some other upon whom they may lean and without whom they seem unable to think, act, or even exist, but friendship that is based on judgment as well as affection.

It is one of the greatest comforts of life as well as one of the greatest ornaments to human nature, and its genuineness may be discerned by the following mark; that though it is particular, it is not exclusive. When there is a great but virtuous attachment to a person who deserves it, it will make a man not less but more friendly to all others.

And the final advice is to preserve sacred and inviolable a regard for sincerity and truth:

So very sacred a thing indeed is truth, that the very shadow of departure from it is to be avoided. . . . Let me therefore recommend to you a strict universal and scrupulous regard to truth; it will give dignity to your character, it will put power into your affairs, it will excite the most unbounded confidence, so that whether your view be your own interest, or the service of others, it promises you the most assured success.

The commencement programme borrowed some of the elevation of the President's baccalaureate and farewell. "Civil liberty promotes virtue and happiness," "*Pax nationis summa felicitas*" —these were only two titles, and the valedictorian sent his auditors away with the echoes of an oration on "Magnanimity" ringing in their ears. Dr. Witherspoon looked over all, and rewrote some, of the orations that his students delivered on commencement platforms. The coincidence between the valedictory and his own baccalaureate is possibly not altogether accidental.

The provincial congress met again on October 3, 1775, at Trenton, devoting the rest of the month almost entirely to military and financial matters. The committee of safety which it left in its place on adjournment found more to do and assumed more power in doing it. Five of its members had served on the former committee and had learned their business. It assumed a practical dictatorship over the province, ignoring entirely the existence of the constituted legislature and usurping all the authority of that body, going so far as to confiscate the provincial barracks for the housing of its own troops and the guarding of its own prisoners of war; and after an exciting and active session it adjourned in the middle of January 1776, calling the provincial congress to assemble again on the thirty-first.

Although there were but one or two crown officers left to whom he could talk confidentially about public affairs, Governor Franklin had been doing what he could to keep up some semblance of government; but it was quite clear that the province had now got far beyond his control. He had nevertheless called the General Assembly to meet in November. Up to that time, so he testified in his address, except in one or two instances, none of the royal officers in New Jersey had met with insult or improper treatment; nevertheless, as he went on to say, if he were to take the advice of friends he would seek asylum on one of His Majesty's ships; but he proposes to stay. If the Assembly advises differently he would like to know it; in view of the talk of independence by persons "of present consequence" it is high time that each man should know what to expect; if crown officers are in danger, all he asks is to be told so plainly. The Assembly resolved that the government of the province be honorably supported for another year. Petitions from loyalist centres praying the House to enter into resolves discouraging independence and supporting the civil government having been received, the House after debate went on record to the effect that reports of the movement for independence were groundless and the delegates to the Continental Congress were directed to use their utmost endeavors to obtain redress of grievances but to reject any propositions tending to "separate this Colony from the Mother Country, or change the form of Government thereof." On the last day of the month the House delivered its humble address to the Governor in reply to his opening address. Officially speaking, and therefore with some latitude of meaning, it informed him that it conceived his person to be in no danger whatever; officially it knew of no sentiments for independence openly avowed by any "men of consequence," nor did the members approve of any efforts to encourage such measures. They reiterated their "detestation of such opinions" and claimed that in view of their record they should be "exempt from all suspicions of this nature." The irritated Governor knew better, and returned a somewhat caustic reply; one week later the legislature of the province was prorogued—and for the last time.

How different in complexion was the body that now completely took the legislature's place may be surmised from the fact that when the provincial congress in February, 1776, took up the question of new delegates to the Continental Congress and objection was made to the election of a certain member because he favored independence, a vote being demanded, eleven of the twelve counties present approved his election, thus corroborating information that had reached the Governor's ears to the effect that a majority of the Congress favored independence. The new delegation to the Continental Congress was William Livingston, John DeHart, Richard Smith, John Cooper, and Jonathan Dickinson Sergeant.

The Governor's correspondence had already embroiled him with his legislature; it was to get him into more serious trouble a little later. Lord Stirling, having intercepted a dispatch to the Earl of Dartmouth, forwarded the packet to Congress, and, fearing that the Governor would now flee the province, caused his arrest, and with the aid of Chief Justice Smyth secured much against the Governor's will a parole that he would not leave his house. Here, then, he remained conducting government as best he could, with a continental sentry posted at his gate, until the last hour of his falling out with his people, a story which belongs to a subsequent chapter.

As chairman of the Somerset County committee Dr. Witherspoon had been attending to his duties. The county had been at great pains to arm its militia but was short of powder, and a letter of the President's is extant seeking in February, 1776, to buy a ton from Philadelphia.[20] His committee was sending frequent suggestions to the provincial congress. It petitioned, for example, that householders and tax-payers in the province be given a vote for county delegates to the Congress, democratic principles which were not generally shared as a counter petition showed, praying that the suffrage be restricted to freeholders. Another suggestive resolution looked to the fortification of Perth Amboy which was defenceless and therefore a likely spot for British attack by water. The papers of February also contained an important proposition announcing county fairs for the sale of linen and other textile goods which is signed by Dr. Witherspoon as chairman of the committee and will be recognized as advocating one of his favorite projects. Considering the importance of promoting manufactures in the county, the committee appointed fixed markets for the sale of linen and woolen goods in particular and of the instruments and materials of their manufacture. The idea was that whatever would make it easy for each person to do a little and turn it to immediate advantage would ultimately be

[20] New York Public Library, Emmet Collection.

beneficent at large and thus useful in promoting industry and the beginning of manufactures which might grow to be large and hence of service to the whole country. The schedule of these fairs was so arranged that virtually every week in the year there would be a fair at some town in the county.[21] But as the late learned editor of the *New Jersey Archives* points out, however much Dr. Witherspoon, coming from a linen manufacturing centre in Scotland, may have hoped to establish a similar manufacture in New Jersey, his project failed. In the main effort of his life during the winter of 1775–1776, however, that of bringing New Jersey into line with other Colonies and inducing it, in spite of its hesitation, to show a fairly solid front, there can be little doubt of his success, although the direct evidence of his work is difficult to secure.

While he received credit at home and abroad for a larger share of responsibility in moulding public opinion and in shaping the events of the next few months than can now be definitely traced, evidence is nevertheless not entirely lacking. For example the vitriolic pen of the Reverend Dr. Jonathan Odell of Burlington devoted five stanzas of his satire *The American Times*, to Dr. Witherspoon's activities from which it is sufficiently clear, even after due allowance is made for their author's bias as a loyalist Anglican, that the President did not limit his efforts to presiding over meetings of county committees or writing proposals to the press or to the provincial congress:[22]

> Ye priests of Bael, from hot Tartarean stoves
> Approach with all the prophets of the groves.
> Mess-mates of Jezebel's luxurious mess,
> Come in the splendour of pontific dress;
> Haste to receive your chief in solemn state;
> Haste to attend on Witherspoon the great.
> Ye lying spirits too, who brisk and bold
> Appear'd before the throne divine of old,
> For form, not use, augment his rev'rend train;
> The sire of lies resides within his brain.

[21] *New Jersey Archives*, 2 ser., vol. I, p. 45.
[22] Sargent, *Loyalist Poetry of the Revolution.*

PRESIDENT WITHERSPOON

Scotland confess'd him sensible and shrewd,
Austere and rigid; many thought him good.
But turbulence of temper spoil'd the whole,
And show'd the movements of his inmost soul.
Disclos'd machinery loses of its force;
He felt the fact, and westward bent his course.

Princeton received him, bright amidst his flaws,
And saw him labour in the good old cause;
Saw him promote the meritorious work,
The hate of kings, and glory of the kirk.

. . .   .

Return we to the hero of our song.
Who now but he the darling of the throng;
Known in the pulpit by seditious toils;
Grown into consequence by civil broils.

Three times he tried, and miserably fail'd,
To overset the laws—the fourth prevail'd.
Whether as tool he acted, or as guide,
Is yet in doubt; he conscience must decide.
Meanwhile unhappy Jersey mourns her thrall;
Ordain'd by vilest of the vile to fall;
To fall by Witherspoon—O name the curse
Of sound religion and disgrace of verse.

Disgrace of verse or not, the reverend poet was to contrive a
rhyme for the abominated name, for he proceeds—

Member of Congress we must hail him next;
Come out of Babylon was now his text.
Fierce as the fiercest, foremost of the first,
He'd rail at kings, with venom well-nigh burst;
Not uniformly grand—for some bye end
To dirtiest tricks of treason he'd descend.
I've known him seek the dungeon dark as night
Imprison'd Tories to convert or fight;
Whilst to myself I've hummed in dismal tune
I'd rather be a dog than Witherspoon.
Be patient reader—for the issue trust,
His day will come—remember Heav'n is just.

Even had these verses lacked their undeniable cleverness, the allusion to four separate occasions on which "Witherspoon the great" tried to overset the laws is of itself sufficient to deserve the attention of the most "patient reader." But the identity of these occasions except perhaps in two cases, is now beyond even conjecture. If Dr. Odell's chronology is correct they all antedate President Witherspoon's congressional service and therefore are to be placed before July, 1776. Two of them have completely baffled identification; one other would seem to be an incident described by Mr. Elias Boudinot, the Princeton trustee, in his *Journal*,[23] and the last and successful effort alluded to is certainly the President's share in the deposition of Governor Franklin, to be described in the next chapter.

Mr. Boudinot's story is this: After the adjournment of the provincial congress in March, 1776, an anonymous notice appeared in the newspapers requesting the county representatives of the province to meet at New Brunswick on the nineteenth of April. It happened that the regular spring meeting of the trustees of the College of New Jersey had been set for the seventeenth. The session usually lasted two days. At the end of the first day's business the board adjourned until the morrow; but when it reassembled, much to its surprise the President was absent and nothing was known of his whereabouts. Business accordingly was concluded without him. The next morning Mr. Boudinot and his friend Mr. William P. Smith, journeying home to Elizabeth, halted at New Brunswick to freshen their horses and were reminded by a friend of the meeting of county delegates set for that day, and to their amazement learned that Dr. Witherspoon that morning had appeared and had informed his audience that he was author of the anonymous notice and that the object of the meeting was to "consider the peculiar situation of the Province, and the propriety of declaring a separation from Great Britain and forming an independent Constitution." That they might not be too precipitate, he had proposed an adjournment until the afternoon when he would state his reasons for advocating separation and in the meantime his hearers might think

[23]Privately printed, Philadelphia, 1894.

the matter over. Mr. Boudinot and Mr. Smith decided to remain over and hear what was said. Accordingly in the afternoon Dr. Witherspoon delivered "a very able and elegant" speech of an hour and a half duration, showing the absurdity at that late day of professing full allegiance to Great Britain and support of her courts of justice. The speech, the position of the speaker, his known sympathies with the American cause, and the ability with which he presented his case, created a profound impression. The conservative Mr. Boudinot found himself in an embarrassing position. The meeting of the trustees, all Presbyterians, Dr. Witherspoon in the front rank of that denomination and author of the famous *Pastoral Letter*, leaving Princeton to come to this meeting, Mr. Smith and himself arriving apparently to lend their countenance to the proceedings—it looked as if the move were concocted at Princeton and carried out by Presbyterians. So when the chance came to reply to Dr. Witherspoon's speech, much to the President's surprise and concern Mr. Boudinot boldly declared that the proposal lacked wisdom and prudence; a Continental Congress had been elected to consider public affairs, its members knew the exact condition of the country in regard to finances, cooperation, and the chance of reconciliation with Great Britain as well as in regard to its relation to Europe. New Jersey had no right to force the hand of Congress or drive that body into measures of so delicate a nature until it should give some cue, or advise the Colonies as to procedure. Seasoned debater that he was, Dr. Witherspoon speedily recovered from the shock of this unexpected opposition on the part of a man so prominent in colonial affairs, and started to reply, when two or three gentlemen intimated to Mr. Boudinot that if the speaker continued they would not be responsible for his safety. But Mr. Boudinot knew the rules of debate and properly answered that the Doctor had a right to reply and that if they did not approve of his proposal they should say so openly before the meeting. The President had spoken about twenty minutes in his rebuttal when someone whispered to him and he immediately desisted, telling the chairman that he understood he was giving offence and therefore would say no more on the subject, but hoped each one would go back and consult his constituents. Mr. Boudinot demanded a vote which Witherspoon naturally opposed as the debate had not been concluded, but a vote being taken, of thirty-six votes cast, only three or four favored the proposition, the rest rejecting it, according to Mr. Boudinot, "with great warmth." How many did not vote Mr. Boudinot does not say. And thus ended the earliest recorded attempt to feel the pulse of New Jersey on the question of independence.

Apart from Dr. Odell's allusion, if indeed he does refer to it, this curious story finds corroboration in two facts, first, that a meeting of the board of trustees was scheduled for April 17, 1776, and second, that a conference of county committees was called for April 18—not April 19, as Mr. Boudinot remembered it; the slip of memory is negligible. The meeting of the board was held, but the rough minutes were never engrossed in the permanent minute book and have not been preserved, so that we have no means of knowing whether Dr. Witherspoon absented himself from the second day's session. The board was accustomed to assemble at an extraordinarily early hour in the morning and it was quite possible that the second day's session, particularly in the President's absence, closed early enough in the forenoon to allow Mr. Boudinot and Mr. Smith to reach New Brunswick soon after midday. That a call for the conference of county committees at New Brunswick was issued is proved by a notice in the *Pennsylvania Packet* for April 1, 1776, (and apparently in no other newspaper,) emanating from the Somerset county committee of which Dr. Witherspoon was chairman.[24] The notice is dated Hillsborough, N. J., March 27, 1776, and reads:

The Committee of Observation and Correspondence for the County of Somerset, in the province of New-Jersey, having taken into their consideration the present state of public Affairs were unanimously of opinion, That it would be highly expedient to have a conference with the Committees of the other counties, previous to the election of members to the Provincial Congress; They did therefore resolve to

[24] The notice has escaped inclusion in the newspaper extracts printed in the *New Jersey Archives* covering that year.

invite the Committees of all the counties in this province to a conference on some matters of great importance, at Brunswick, on Thursday the 18th day of April, at 10 o'clock.

Published by order of the Committee

JOHN LAFFERTY, Secretary.

N.N. Letters are sent to every county; but in case of miscarriage, this
notice is given.

The notice was, therefore not anonymous as Mr. Boudinot asserts but was signed by the secretary, Witherspoon's name not
appearing. However, one of the letters referred to in the postscript—addressed in the hand of a clerk to the chairman of the
Monmouth County committee—is in the Library of Princeton
University. It contains the resolutions of the Somerset committee as printed in the *Packet* with a note subjoined, in the same
clerk's hand:

Sir

Above is a Coppy of the Minute of the Committee of Somerset
County which I undertook to transmit to you & do Earnestly Request that you will meet the Committee without Delay. Compliance
with our Request we cannot Doubt in the present Posture of Affairs.

I am Sir

your Very Humb. Servt

JOHN WITHERSPOON praeses.

A coppy.

Hence it would appear that, while Dr. Witherspoon's name
does not occur in the call itself, it was signed to the added personal note accompanying each copy of the call. His appearance
at New Brunswick accordingly could hardly have been as surprising to all of his audience as it was to Mr. Boudinot. Granted
that the latter's story is true, even if Mr. Boudinot did not write
it down until his old age, the incident would have leaked out inevitably, and in due time would have reached the willing ears of
Dr. Odell at Burlington, himself a graduate of the College and so
a doubly interested observer of the course being pursued by his
alma mater's president. The most striking feature of the story is
the evidence it contains that Dr. Witherspoon was far in advance
of his province even in April, 1776, in his effort to "overset the
law."

Among the President's papers Dr. Ashbel Green found a fragment of an undated letter prepared for the press on the *"Controversy about Independence,"* which does not seem to have been
published until Dr. Green included it in his edition of Witherspoon's *Works*.[25] It contains the President's summary of the situation just before the colonies declared their independence. After
pointing out that "when the claims of the British Parliament
were openly made and violently enforced, the most precise and
determined resolutions were entered into, and published by
every Colony, every county, and almost every township or
smaller district, that they would not submit to them," he says
that for his own part he would never have signed these resolves
if he had not been convinced "that acquiescence in this usurped
power, would be followed by the total and absolute ruin of the
colonies. They would have been no better than tributary states
to a kingdom at a great distance from them." For this reason he
declared it was his meaning, and he knows it was the meaning
of thousands more, "that though we earnestly wished for reconciliation with safety to our liberties, yet did we deliberately prefer, not only the horrors of a civil war, not only the danger of
anarchy and the uncertainty of a new settlement, but even extermination itself to slavery, rivetted on us and our posterity."

In spite of peaceable efforts on the part of the Colonies to obtain relaxation of oppressive Acts, these followed one after another; the constitution and government of Massachusetts were
"subverted to their very foundation" and curiously enough the
King, Parliament and people of Great Britain in their several
public expressions never failed to extol their leniency. He does
not infer from this that they were barbarians—"the inference is
unnecessary and unjust." But he does infer the misery of the
people of America if they must submit in all cases to the dictates
of such a body of men.

It has been my opinion from the beginning, he continues, that we did
not carry our reasoning fully home, when we complained of an arbitrary prince or of the insolence, cruelty and obstinacy of Lord North,
Lord Bute, or Lord Mansfield. What we have to fear, and what we

[25] *Works*, vol. IV, p. 205.

have now to grapple with, is the ignorance, prejudice, partiality and injustice of human nature. Neither king nor ministry could have done, nor durst have attempted, what we have seen, if they had not had the nation on their side. . . . I am firmly persuaded, that had the wiser heads in America met together to contrive what measures the ministry should follow to strengthen the American opposition and defeat their own designs, they could not have fallen upon a plan so effectual as that which has been steadily pursued. . . . Nothing is more manifest, than that the people of Great Britain, and even the king and ministry, have been hitherto exceedingly ignorant of the state of things in America. For this reason, their measures have been ridiculous in the highest degree, and the issue disgraceful.

Some will not believe this. How could the government have been ignorant when they have multitudes in this country to give them intelligence from the beginning? Because they would trust none but so-called official intelligence, "that is to say, from obsequious, interested tools of government; many of them knew little of the true state of things themselves, and when they did would not tell it, lest it should be disagreeable." As for private correspondents, "they thought the friends of American liberty much more inconsiderable, both from weight and numbers, than they were. They conversed with few, but those of their own way of thinking, and according to the common deception of little minds, mistook the sentiments prevailing within the circle of their own acquaintance for the judgment of the public." And here the letter abruptly ends.

A briefer essay on *"Conducting the American Controversy"* dates also from this period and, like the letter on the *"Controversy about Independence,"* was prepared for the press, is incomplete, and does not appear to have been published until Ashbel Green placed it in his edition of the President's *Works*.[26] It reiterates his belief that more accurate information in Great Britain would have prevented this disagreement. Dr. Witherspoon begins by declaring his respect for George III and his belief that the King wishes the prosperity and happiness of his people in every part of his dominions. "Nay, I have still more to say, I do not think the British ministry themselves have deserved all the

[26] *Works*, vol. IV, p. 209.

abuse and foul names that have been bestowed on them by political writers." Their steps, which have been "unjust, impolitic and barbarous to the highest degree," are due to two chief causes: (1) ignorance or mistake occasioned by the misinformation of interested and treacherous persons employed in their service, and (2) the prejudice common to them, with persons of all ranks in Great Britain.

Taking up the second of these first, he declares that the newspapers contain evidence in plenty "that it was not the King and the ministry only, but the whole nation that was enraged against America." The tide is beginning to turn but he doubts whether it has fairly turned yet

upon any larger principle than a regard to their own interest. . . . It can hardly be expected that the eyes of a whole nation should be at once opened upon the generous principles of universal liberty. It is natural for the multitude in Britain, who have been from their infancy taught to look upon an act of parliament as supreme and irresistible, and to consider the liberty of their country itself as consisting in the dominion of the house of commons, to be surprised and astonished at any society or body of men, calling in question the authority of parliament, and denying its power over them. It certainly required time to make them sensible that things are in such a situation in America, that for the house of commons in Great Britain to assume the uncontrolled power of imposing taxes upon American property, would be as inconsistent with the spirit of the British constitution, as it appears at first sight agreeable to its form.

And because the people of Great Britain have not seen immediately is not to stamp them "destitute of honor and truth." He therefore grieves to hear pleaders of American liberty mixing

so much of abuse and invective against the ministry in general, as well as particular persons, with their reasonings in support of their own most righteous claim. I have often said to friends in America, on that subject, it is not the king and ministry, so much as the prejudices of Britons, with which you have to contend. Spare no pains to have them fully informed. Add to the immoveable firmness with which you justly support your own rights, a continual solicitude to convince the people of Britain, that it is not passion but reason that inspires you. Tell them it cannot be ambition, but necessity, that makes you run an evident risk of the heaviest sufferings, rather than forfeit for your-selves and your posterity the greatest of all earthly blessings.

It gave him still more uneasiness, he said, that many Ameri-can patriots seemed to think themselves "interested in the pros-perity of that most despicable of all factions that ever existed in the British empire, headed by the celebrated John Wilkes." He is glad that no American has ever gone to such extremes as the people of Britain in this connection. "Far greater insults were offered to the sovereign within the city of London, and within the verge of the court, than ever were thought of or would have been permitted by the mob in any part of America." But dutiful and respectful as the people of America are, some things pub-lished seemed to intimate "that we had one and the same cause with the author of the North Britain No. 45. . . . Nothing could be more injudicious than this conduct in the Americans; and it arose from the most absolute ignorance of political history. The Stamp Act, that first-born of American oppressions, was framed by the chief men of that very faction; and it is plain from their language to this hour, that they make no other use of Amer-ican disturbances, but as engines of opposition, and to serve the mean purposes of party or of family interest." He does not mean by this statement to take any part with or against the present ministry; he has seen many changes of ministry, without any sensible change in the state of public affairs. The present ques-tion is greater than the mere matter of who is in or who is out of court favor:

I look upon the cause of America at present to be a matter of truly in-expressible moment. The state of the human race through a great part of the globe, for ages to come, depends upon it. Any minister or ministry, who is in or out of court favor, at a particular juncture, is so little a matter, that it should not be named with it.

The preparation of articles for the press, and the distractions of a busy public life, coupled with the unceasing round of college duties, did not prevent Dr. Witherspoon from keeping in close touch with absent members of his family and especially with his youngest and most brilliant son, David. His three sons had now graduated and his oldest daughter had married. Nine of his letters to David written during 1776 and 1777 have been saved in Dr. Green's *Christian Advocate*, the only family letters from the President's pen that are known. Besides family references and the latest news of the war, they contain fatherly counsel which reveals as nothing else can the tenderer side of the President's character. One of the originals, here quoted in full (Dr. Green printed it only in part), is in the Library of Princeton University; the manuscripts of the others have disappeared. David Witherspoon had been graduated at the age of fourteen and now was teaching at Hampden-Sidney Academy in Virginia, under the direction of his brother-in-law Samuel Stanhope Smith.[27]

[27] David Witherspoon was born at Paisley, Scotland, September 22, 1760. Entering the Nassau Hall Grammar School in 1768, at commencement in 1769 he delivered the Latin salutatory opening the school's graduation exercises. Proceeding into the freshman class of the College in 1770, at commencement in 1771 he shared with Henry Brockholst Livingston the freshman prize in Latin. Although precocious he was graduated in 1774 without honors. His brother-in-law Samuel Stanhope Smith in 1775 offered him a modest position in the newly organized Hampden-Sidney Academy, his father continuing him an allowance and even sending him shoes (of which, however, he only guessed at the size). "*Je n'oublierai pas ma promesse que je vous donnerai vingt cinque ou trente livres par an*" is a sentence in a letter of October, 1776, which was followed by a letter in Latin wherein occurs this: "*Mitto ad te unum par calceorum quanquam incertus sum an sint pedibus tuis apti & idonei.*" In 1777 David was a lieutenant in the company of Hampden-Sidney students who volunteered. Shortly afterwards he began the study of law but in March, 1780, was acting as secretary to Mr. Huntington, President of the Continental Congress. In October, 1788, he married Mary (Jones) Nash, widow of Governor Abner Nash of North Carolina. He settled at or near New Bern, N. C., practised law, and subsequently represented Wilkes County in the North Carolina legislature. He seems to have prospered as his will disposes of property and slaves. He was a Mason, being companion in the Royal Arch Chapter at New Bern. Seven years after the President's death David revisited Princeton for the benefit of his health and brought with him his young son. His will, dated October 24, 1801, was drawn and witnessed at Princeton on this visit. Less than two months later, in December 1801, the clerk of Craven County, North Carolina, certified in court that David Witherspoon had died. Depositions of the witnesses to his will were taken and the will eventually was probated. The exact date and place of death have not been found. He was buried, it is thought, in the Nash family vault on Pembroke Plantation, near New Bern, but during the Civil War the spot was desecrated and the vault obliterated.

His son John Nash Witherspoon (b. 1792, d. 1853), whom he had intended to send to Princeton, was graduated at the University of North Carolina, but received the honorary degree of Master of Arts from Princeton in 1815 and that of Doctor of Divinity in 1836, when he was moderator of the General Assembly.

Princeton, May 6, 1776.

My dear David

I have received your three letters regularly & am obliged to you for writing so punctually. The one from Baltimore of March 31 I received April 5. The one from Portroyal of April 6 I received April 21 & the last by Mr. Spencer of April 23 I received last night. It gives us great Pleasure to know of your Safety & arrival at your Brothers. I shall be glad to be informed of as many particulars of your Situation as possible—How much did it cost you to complete the Journey? What have you done with your horse? I think it would be best to sell him for what he would fetch & not to buy another unless you can easily maintain him without being burdensome to Mr. Smith.

It gives me much pleasure to see by your last that you propose to teach the French. If you do this with Care & Application it will soon perfect you in that Language. Take particular pains to prepare & fit yourself for any thing you do. Take pleasure in doing things with Accuracy & Perfection. To see you a complete Scholar will be the greatest Delight you can give to me except your being a good Man which is of more Consequence still but I hope they will both go together. I beg it of you not to forget the particular Advices I gave you at parting & have often recommended. Keep pen & Ink always about you or by you & take Notes of many things as well as your Expenses. In writing your Letters keep black Lines till you can write Straight and neatly without them. To write Latin well & with Spirit is a great Accomplishment & I desire that you would write to me as often as possible. Mr. Smith is mistaken as to the Miscarriage or opening of Letters, I believe it was owing to my not writing so frequently as I ought to have done. But if you write to me often you may depend upon it your Letters shall not be henceforth long neglected.

As you are now among strangers take particular Care of your behavior for a Character is soon formed & often easily lost. If you mind your Business with Diligence every body will approve & applaud you and on the Contrary Idleness is soon observed & always blamed. Be obliging and friendly to all. I do not know so general or so excellent a Rule for good Manners as to think concerning others as every good Man ought to think. If you wish them well in your heart you will certainly be civil to them in your Behavior.

I would be happy that you would write to me sometimes a Letter in Latin or french but you may delay that till you receive one from me in one or the other of these languages by way of Example. La

[194]

première Lettre que Je vous écrirai sera en françois ou en Latin ou peut être en tous les deux.

We are all in our Ordinary health here & remember you all kindly. You may easily Suppose we were made very happy by hearing of Mrs. Smith's safe Delivery without ever having heard of her being with Child. I sent a Letter to Mr. Smith from Philadelphia last week by a private hand who has promised to take particular Care of it. With him I sent 2 pair of shoes & one of slippers for Annie which I wish may get safe there & answer in point of size.

Your Brother James was here lately a few Days & has returned to Ryegate. John Ross who has married Jean Hyndman has bought up his Time & engaged to go with James & work with him this Summer. Alex. Inglis is to go likewise James [torn] to you or his Sister or both before he went away. Professor Houston [torn] to Jenny Smith.

Mr. Reid late our Schoolmaster now Lieutenant & Charles Beatty past this place for Quebeck both of them learned a little French with me & it is likely to be of great service to them. Spare no pains to make yourself Master of that language.

I think it would not be amiss to make some Acquaintance with Mr. Purdie Printer at Williamsburg for books. I will write to him soon. I write by this Post to Mr. Smith. Make my Compliments to John Smith & write to me what he proposes to follow.

I am Dr David your affec^t Father

JNO. WITHERSPOON[28]

Later in the summer of 1776 the President wrote

I am glad to perceive that you are endeavouring to make yourself master of the French; continue in it carefully, and be sure to read through, and be well acquainted with the dialogues and conversation phrases in the Grammar. . . . Make yourself as useful as possible to Mr. Smith and perfect your classic learning. . . . It gives me great pleasure to see that the school increases so fast. I hope no pains will be spared to make the scholars as complete as possible. You ought to exercise them well in the grammar and syntax. It would be a great advantage if they were kept some part of their time to writing and arithmetic. If among you you can bring it about that the boys write their letters to their parents neatly and sensibly, it will give them great pleasure. Many of them are not judges how far they profit in Latin and Greek; but if they write their letters well they will perceive their

[28] Mrs. Smith was the President's daughter Ann; James Witherspoon was graduated in 1770, Charles Clinton Beatty in 1775, and John Smith in 1770.

improvement; and on the contrary, if they write nothing home but blotted, ill-spelled nonsense, they will suppose they have learned nothing, though you take ever so much pains. Your letters which are before me, please me better than any you have written. . . . Remember, my dear boy, to fear God, and serve him in sincerity and truth. Let this be your first and highest care, and accomplish yourself as much as possible for usefulness in life.

That autumn, receiving a letter from David in French, the President replied:

Votre frère Smith par la lettre et M. Jean Smith par la conversation m'ont rendu tout à fait heureux en m'assurant de votre diligence et bonne conduite. Ils m'ont dit que vous enseignez dans l'école avec prudence et assiduité, et que vous ne vous mêlez point avec les folies & badinages des jeunes gens; enfin que vous êtes respecté & aimé des écoliers, et vous appliquez aussi à vos autres études. Continuez mon cher fils d'être sage et diligent. C'est le tems dans votre jeunesse de cultiver vos talents, d'acquérir des connoissances, et de vous rendre capable des plus hauts et honorables emplois. Vous savez bien avec quel ardeur je souhaite votre progrès dans les arts et votre bonheur pour toute la vie . . . Soyez diligent; écrivez souvent et avec tout le soin et précaution possible, afin que vous soyez perfectionné dans cet art. . . . Votre lettre françoise est bien écrite . . . Vous apprendrez bientôt à parler quand vous aurez opportunité et occasion. Pour cet effet lisez souvent les phrases familiales dans la grammaire. Je souhaite aussi que vous lisiez beaucoup en Latin, afin que vous pouviez lire les livres classiques avec plaisir. Sitôt que vous entendiez fort bien Horace & Virgile vous les lirez & répéterez avec le même plaisir qu'une poème Anglaise.

And a few days later he sent David a letter in Latin:

Gaudio quam maximo affectus fui, per fratris literas & per amicorum vestrum Joannem Smith, audire te esse modestum, diligentem, & studiis debitum. Optime dixit Solomon, 'Sapiens filius Patrem loetum efficit.' Perge obsecro, mi fili, amato libros, incumbito studiis, ut sis doctus, & ideo carus amicis, amabilis omnibus . . . Cupio plurimum quam saepissime a te audire.

On May 17, 1776, the fast day appointed by the Continental Congress, Dr. Witherspoon in a ringing sermon seized the chance at last to come out fairly for the cause in which he was so deeply

The Dominion of Providence over the Passions of Men.

SERMON
PREACHED
AT PRINCETON,
On the 17th of May, 1776.
BEING
The GENERAL FAST appointed by the CONGRESS
through the UNITED COLONIES.

TO WHICH IS ADDED,

An ADDRESS to the NATIVES of SCOTLAND residing in
AMERICA.

BY JOHN WITHERSPOON, D.D.
PRESIDENT OF THE COLLEGE OF NEW-JERSEY.

PHILADELPHIA:
PRINTED AND SOLD BY R. AITKEN, PRINTER AND
BOOKSELLER, OPPOSITE THE LONDON COFFEE-
HOUSE, FRONT-STREET.
M.DCC.LXXVI.

SERMON ON THE DOMINION OF PROVIDENCE
OVER THE PASSIONS OF MEN

involved. Whatever he may have hitherto written anonymously for the newspapers, or have expressed in private, we have his definite word that this sermon preached in Nassau Hall was his first political utterance from the pulpit. Its subject was "The Dominion of Providence over the Passions of Men,"[29] and the text was taken from the tenth verse of the seventy-sixth Psalm. In view of the contest in which the Colonies were engaged, a contest "the length of which it is impossible to foresee and the issue of which it will perhaps be thought presumptuous to foretell," Dr. Witherspoon applies the spirit of the text to the Colonies and to the plague of war. "The ambition of mistaken princes," he declares, "the cunning and cruelty of oppressive and corrupt ministers and even the inhumanity of brutal soldiers, however dreadful, shall finally promote the glory of God." For the first time, he says, he is introducing politics into his pulpit; the cause that has led him to this action is the cause of justice, of liberty, and of humanity. But his audience shall not hear from him in the pulpit what they have never heard from him in conversation; he will not rail at the King, or at his ministers and the Parliament and people of Great Britain, as barbarous savages. "Many of their actions have probably been worse than their intentions." He refuses submission to their unjust claims because they are men and therefore liable to the bias inseparable from human nature. He calls unjust the British claims of making laws to bind the Colonies in all cases, because the distance separating Great Britain from the Colonies renders a wise and prudent administration of American affairs as impossible as the claim is unfair. Such is the ignorance of Great Britain as to the real state of affairs in the Colonies, so much time must elapse before a mistake can be seen and remedied, and so much injustice and partiality must be expected from the misrepresentation of interested parties, that "for these Colonies to depend wholly upon the legislature of Great Britain would be, like many other oppressive connexions, injury to the master and ruin to the slave." The colonists' opposition to

---

[29] *Works*, vol. II, p. 407, separately printed late in July, 1776, by Robert Aitken of Philadelphia and dedicated to John Hancock, president of Congress. Two editions were published at Glasgow in 1777, and another in London, 1778. See also *Scots Magazine*, vol. XXXIX, p. 96.

the claim of the British ministry does not come from a seditious and turbulent spirit, or a wanton contempt of legal authority, but from a concern for the interest of their country and the safety of themselves and their posterity. And if to the justice of their cause and the purity of their principles his hearers add prudence of conduct they will have the greatest reason to hope for final success. Prudence in conducting the struggle implies union, firmness and patience; and by these he means obedience to those chosen to lead, adherence to duty, and fortitude in adversity. And he concludes by recommending first, attention to religion, for "he is the best friend of American liberty who is most sincere and active in promoting true and undefiled religion and who sets himself with the greatest firmness to bear down profanity and immorality of every kind." Next, he exhorts all who do not go into the field to devote themselves to works of industry with the utmost diligence, so will they not only supply the necessities but also add to the strength of their country. Therefore he urges on all the virtues of frugality and temperance. And finally he begs his hearers to remember that their duty to God, to their country, to their families, and to themselves, is the same—it is the man of piety and inward principle that we may expect to find the uncorrupted patriot, the useful citizen, and the invincible soldier. "God grant that in America true religion and civil liberty may be inseparable and that the unjust attempts to destroy the one may in the issue tend to the support and establishment of both."

It was one of the few occasions on which President Witherspoon approached real eloquence. On that May morning at Princeton he spoke from a heart whose feeling had long been pent up. It was no academic occasion, not even a routine Sabbath sermon; the gates were lifted and for once the liberty-loving soul within him supplanted the calculating logician. To appreciate the noble dignity of this great discourse one should read in contrast some of the raving effusions that found their way into contemporary print—such for example, to point the criticism with only Princetonian sins of commission, as the Reverend George Duffield's parallel between George III and Pharoah, or Dr. Nathaniel Whitaker's *Antidote to Toryism* wherein things are reduced to a series of violent elemental principles of which the conclusion, in mild paraphrase, is that the Almighty demands that people struggling for their liberties shall treat as open enemies, and shall reject as unworthy the privileges others enjoy, those members of the community who do not join them, a doctrine which the frenzied preacher found wrapped up in the very bowels of his volcanic text "Curse ye Meroz . . . because they come not to the help of the Lord."

While preparing his fast-day sermon Dr. Witherspoon was also planning an appeal to a wider audience than the one he addressed at Princeton. There were certain broad points of view, certain fundamental concepts of society and life that he feared were in danger of being lost in the immediate glare of open hostilities and these he wished to set before the reading, thinking public. He was one of the promoters of the *Pennsylvania Magazine*, a periodical started in January, 1775, by his compatriot and protégé Robert Aitken, the Philadelphia printer. Aitken was employing as his editor Thomas Paine, at that time still a lately arrived seeker after the fame that lay before him. The fact that this Englishman had actually experienced the hardships of life among the lower classes which Dr. Witherspoon felt to be the shame of the British nation; the knowledge that he had come to America to seek a fairer chance at life's possibilities; his warm-hearted enthusiasms and his ability to express them on paper, these were some of the factors that originally enlisted the President's sympathy for this young man "with genius in his eyes." During 1775 Dr. Witherspoon under the pen-name of "Epaminondas" had been contributing to the *Magazine* among other essays a series of "Letters on Marriage" and also one of "Letters on Education," or more accurately, the education of children in "the principles of religion as well as every branch of polite literature." In the last letter on education (January, 1776) he speaks as though he intended to continue the series, but 1776 demanded sterner, timelier stuff. *Common Sense* had burst upon the public that month and had crystallized the sentiment for independence. Dr. Witherspoon must have known the secret of its authorship; he must have seen the pamphlet before he made his unsuccessful attempt to force New Jersey's declaration; he certainly had read it before his fast-day sermon was written. Now that the Colonies were actually fighting for their liberties he felt that he had a deeper message for the times and he began his "Druid" papers, issuing the first group of three in the May, June and July numbers respectively of the *Pennsylvania Magazine*.

In the opening paper after explaining that his pseudonym was suggested "by the place which is now, and is likely to be, my residence while I continue on earth"—"Tusculum" is meant of course—, and after touching lightly on his own attitude toward life, now having reached the age of fifty—he was fifty-three, to be exact—"a cool and contemplative season when men of education or business have generally seen as much of the world as satisfies their curiosity," he announces that his general subject is to be the philosophy of human nature and human life. "Literature and morals, arts, and industry, shall be my chief themes; and under one or other of these, every thing may be introduced, that can in the least contribute to the happiness of social or private life." In the treatment of these subjects he will "have a particular view to the state and interest of this rising country." And to those who may think that the present (May, 1776) is a time for action rather than speculation he begs to say that this is a mistake. He looks not with solicitude but with unshaken confidence on the present struggle for the liberties of mankind and he is much mistaken if "the time is not just ripe at hand when there shall be greater need than ever in America for the most accurate discussion of the principles of society, the rights of nations, and the policy of states," all of which shall have a place in these essays.

In the June number he discusses the waging of war. Natural rights and the cause of liberty in general have been explained in unnumerable treatises, ancient and modern, and the application of these principles to the American controversy has been handled by writers of the day with the greatest clearness and precision, and even the nature of government and the methods of balancing a civil constitution have been discussed though less ably. He will, therefore, leave these topics for the present and as the country is engaged in a war "somewhat singular in its nature" he will discuss the manner of carrying on war. It had been asserted that the enemy in their conduct of the war have acted contrary to the rules of war, but no one has yet pointed out what these rules are. When independent nations disagree they have no court of last resort to which they may appeal save that of the sword. In this extremity is there any law by which their acts are controlled? And if there is, to whom shall appeal be made when that law is broken.

That there is such a law—the law of nature and of nations—he considers evident not only from universal acknowledgment but from the very nature of the thing. If there be any duties binding on individuals in a state of natural liberty the same are binding between independent nations. Bodies politic do not differ in this circumstance from individuals. The single purpose of society is to protect the individual. To whom, however, shall appeal be made when this law is trampled on? The sanction of the law is nothing else than a sense of duty and accountableness to the Supreme Judge together with the sense of fear that a breach of the law will bring upon the offender reproach and infamy among all the nations and probably resentment and indignation by common consent. Hence a recourse to arms is often called an appeal to heaven and is generally accompanied by some public declaration to convince other nations of the justice of the cause.

How may war be carried on? By all manner of force or open violence except acts agreed by common consent of modern times to be cruel and inhuman, such as refusing quarter to those who surrender, killing or torturing prisoners, women, and children, indiscriminate destruction of property, the use of poisoned weapons, and the poisoning of springs and provisions, the principle underlying these restrictions being "that all acts of cruelty which have no tendency to weaken the resisting force are contrary to reason and religion and, therefore, to the law of nature and nations." As examples of the breach of this law he cites the undeniable attempt of the British to set the Indians upon the back settlements. This is an act of unjustifiable barbarity because of the well-known method of warfare employed by the Indians. Another instance is the effort made by the British to liberate slaves and stir them up to rebel against their masters. This is as base and treacherous an act and as universally condemned as to suborn the servants of a military leader to assassinate him privately

although to aim at his life in open battle is not only fair but "prudent." The principle above laid down will make us judge how to
view acts of violence and depredation. When an army can avail
itself of the goods and property of the members of an hostile
state, or reduce them to surrender, not only the seizure but the
reduction may both be justifiable; but when men can only destroy and not possess and the destruction can only fall upon helpless people, it is not only inconsistent with greatness of mind but
for the most part works against the interest of the destroyer,
since it operates as an inflammatory principle.

For these reasons he believes that the burning and destroying
of houses where there is no fortress, as has in some instances been
done, is barbarous, savage, and inhuman.

In the "Druid" of July, 1776, the third and last of the first
series, Dr. Witherspoon discusses the distinction between foreign
and civil wars and the two varieties of the latter; insurrection of
disorderly citizens against law and order, and resistance of part
of a monarchy or republic against the constituted authority on
the ground of suffering under oppression and with the purpose of
a redress of grievances or of a complete reorganization of government. History has dignified such as are successful by the name of
Revolutions; if unsuccessful, they are called Rebellions. But success is no criterion of justice.

The author then discusses the conduct of civil war and concludes that only in the first case may behavior be different from
that which governs in war between independent States. But
when the grounds of the quarrel are plausible on both sides, and
when persons of strictest honor and integrity may be found in
both parties, all are bound to candor in judgment, and humanity
and mercy in their conduct toward one another. And pointing
his essay with the present controversy he sees the perfect justice
and great importance of the claims on the one hand, and as easily
appreciates the power of prejudice on the other. There was not
the most distant thought of subverting the government, or of
hurting the interest of Great Britain nor the least desire of withdrawing allegiance from the common sovereign until it became
necessary and indeed was the result of that sovereign's deliberate
choice. On the other hand he readily understands that the Brit-

ish people who have long been accustomed to subjection, and from whom subjection is due, cannot easily enter into the reasons for exempting from the same burdens a people otherwise situated. Finally, he lays down the precept that humanity is the noblest attendant of true valor and he will probably fight most bravely who never fights until he has to, and who ceases to fight as soon as the necessity is past.

Here the "Druid" essays came to an end, with the periodical that contained them. The summer of 1776 and the next few years were to be far too busy a time for magazine writing, however edifying. When Dr. Witherspoon resumed the series in 1781 it was to take up a totally different topic.

CHAPTER SIX

INDEPENDENCE

THE "Druid" essays were anonymous although their authorship was probably no great secret; but the sermon on the "Dominion of Providence" had thrust Dr. Witherspoon into the glare of public notice, and from this time on for the next six years he was to remain a public character. Just now he was plunging deeper into New Jersey's political struggle. There was no time to be wasted; everything was sacrificed to public service; as usual of late he missed the opening exercises of the Synod meeting that May, and when he arrived it was only to ask permission to be allowed to go home at once. There was work to be done in Jersey where he had been elected a delegate from Somerset County to the provincial congress which was to meet in June. Before that date arrived the first of the swiftly successive incidents occurred that marked the closing hours of British rule in New Jersey.

On May 30 Governor Franklin had issued a proclamation calling for a special session of the Assembly, giving as his indefinite but sole reason that he had "matters of great importance to the public welfare" to communicate. No hint was offered as to what these matters were. The next regular session was not due until October. Perhaps less than anyone in the province did the Governor realize that his action would strain to the breaking point the storm-cloud that had been settling down about his head and was to sweep him from the exalted position he had occupied for twelve years. He had given Lord Stirling his word of honor that he would not leave the province without the knowledge of the revolutionary party, and his word was that of a gentleman. Since his arrest in January, therefore, he had lived an uneventful if uncertain life. Had he not issued his proclamation of May the leaders of the June provincial congress would have been compelled to devise some direct pretext for his deposition. A stroke of his pen gave them what they wanted. No sooner was the proclamation issued than from Somerset County appeared (June 6) unsigned, but containing strong indications of President Witherspoon's authorship, an open letter entitled "Reflections on Public Affairs recommended to the Perusal of the Members of the New Jersey Assembly."[1] The writer calls attention to the fact that the Governor, contrary to custom in calling special meetings of the Assembly, had given no intimation of the nature of these alleged "matters of importance." Assemblymen would, therefore, have to exercise the spirit of divination or else come totally unprepared to discuss them; at any rate they would be unable to consult their constituents, and as things were now circumstanced these matters might be of the greatest magnitude and could with propriety be determined only by ascertaining the sentiments of the people at large. The present move on the Governor's part looked like nothing else than an

insidious design to lay hold on the present combination of apparently unfortunate circumstances to distract and divide our counsels and thereby to throw us into so much confusion and disorder as that we may the more readily be induced to submit to any terms they may think fit to propose, or perhaps to give ourselves up entirely to the old Government as the readiest way out of our present difficulties.

Some weak and many willing minds thought that the resolution of the Continental Congress on May 15 was a final bar to reconciliation and it was held up by adherents to the Crown as the test whereby to distinguish those who wished independence and those who desired reconciliation, whereas many who advocated compliance with Congress sincerely hoped for ultimate reconciliation. By taking this attitude the Crown's advisors had divided the people into two classes, for and against independence, thus hoping to divide the Colonies against themselves, for if they could get one Colony from the rest, especially one of the middle Colonies, they would consider their work well done; the Colonies would soon be fighting one another and thus fall an easy prey to their oppressors' machinations.

Whether this warning had any share in the outcome or not, it turned out that the Governor's call had come too late and the special meeting of the Assembly never took place. The provincial

[1] *American Archives*, 4 series, Vol. VI, p. 723.

congress which was to assemble ten days before that meeting had yet to be reckoned with. The delegates were slow in appearing at Burlington on the tenth of June. No quorum was obtainable until the afternoon of the next day when the reading of certificates of election was the only business transacted. Business proper began at the evening session which Dr. Witherspoon opened with prayer. One distinctly new element appeared in this congress—that of clerical members. The clergy of the province had come out as public leaders and were assuming their share of responsibility. To conservatives like Mr. Boudinot this fact was deplorable. "Our clergy unhappily have gone distracted," he wrote to another Princetonian, the Reverend James Caldwell,[2] on June 19, 1776,

and have done us more injury than I am afraid they will do us good, in a great while. They have verified what our Enemies have so often prognosticated. We have been quarreling with the Ch. of England these 40 years past, about uniting Civill and Ecclesiastical Power, and now at the moment we have the shadow of Power in our Hands, we are running into the same extreme. Six, or seven clergymen set up for candidates at the late election among whom three were elected viz: Dr. Witherspoon (who is at the Bottom of it) Mr. Green and Dominie Hardenburg. This has given amazing offence and has raised a cry agt our clergy that must ruin their influence in every station.[3]

Throughout this period of uncertainty Mr. Boudinot, who had not forgotten Dr. Witherspoon's performance at New Brunswick, appears to have been extremely cautious; but he was to live long enough to have the leisure to revise his opinion as to the ruin of the clergy's influence because of their political activity.

The complexion of the new provincial congress was in another respect also very different from that of its predecessor. In the congress that had adjourned in March, twenty-five per cent of the fifty-two members had failed to appear and this neglect of duty was not forgotten. Of the sixty-five delegates to the June

[2] Events proved that Mr. Caldwell was to be anything but a conservative. He is the hero of Bret Harte's ballad *Caldwell of Springfield*, and whether this poem is based on fact or not, at least Mr. Caldwell's tragic history admits of no doubt as to his unhesitating support of the colonial cause.
[3] *Henkel's Catalogue*, March 14, 1912, Lot 1057.

body only twenty-five had been members of the earlier session. Burlington and Somerset Counties had totally new delegations, while in each of those from Middlesex, Essex, and Salem, only one man had served before. The most striking group was the quintet sent down from Somerset. At Dr. Witherspoon's side was the Reverend Jacob Hardenburgh, the Dutch reformed minister of Raritan, an honorary graduate of Princeton, and later so keenly "wanted" by the British that he is said to have kept a loaded musket by his bedside in readiness for self-defence. He was to become a leader in New Jersey's constitutional deliberations and later to be the first President of Queen's College, at New Brunswick. Two college-mates, fellow soldiers in Lord Stirling's Somerset militia, were James Linn who was graduated from Princeton in 1769 and whose later legislative record well sustained his early reputation, and Frederick Frelinghuysen, one of the Princeton commencement orators of 1770, who had just turned his twenty-third birthday but had already served a term in Congress and was destined to serve again. The future associate justice of the United States Supreme Court William Paterson, another Princetonian, was the fifth delegate and was elected secretary of the Congress.

There is no evidence that this group or any other controlled the majority, but there can be no doubt that the Somerset men exercised the strongest sort of influence. Their voting was unflaggingly along one line and toward one end. In the previous sessions votes had been cast by counties and it is impossible from the printed record to follow individual votes; but thanks to a resolution of this session that yea and nay votes should be recorded if any member so moved and were seconded, we can follow each delegate's action on leading questions.

The convention was by no means unanimous. To Bergen county unexpectedly enough seems to belong the honor of leading the conservative party. The first test of strength came on the morning of the twelfth when it was moved by the conservatives that not less than two-thirds of the whole body constitute a quorum; but it was no time for possible filibustering and the motion was defeated by a vote of more than two to one, Dr. Witherspoon and his Somerset colleagues voting solidly against it as might be expected. A resolution for majority rule accordingly prevailed. This preliminary skirmish over, the vital question of the day was approached, whether or not New Jersey should comply with the recommendations of the Continental Congress of May 15, that government under the Crown ought to be suppressed since it could no longer be supported, and that each Colony, therefore, should adopt such form of government as would conduce to the happiness and safety of its constituents in particular and of America in general. Two petitions from the south ward of Perth Amboy looking toward these ends were read that day, but Perth Amboy, seat of the official residence of the Governor, was a city divided against itself, for three days later—on Saturday the fifteenth (misprinted "sixteenth" in the minutes) —arrived a belated petition from the north ward praying that the government be not changed. Shrewsbury in Monmouth County filed a petition to the same effect, but the hour for appeals of that color was past. The progressive party was in the saddle and these petitions were laid on the table.[4]

The Governor's proclamation came up for discussion on Friday the fourteenth, and the process of battering down the last vestige of colonial government in New Jersey was begun. In view of the recent recommendation of the Continental Congress, the provincial congress boldly resolved by a vote of thirty-eight to eleven that Governor Franklin's call ought not to be obeyed. Following this direct blow at constituted authority it was resolved on Saturday the fifteenth that Governor Franklin had by his proclamation acted in direct contempt and violation of the resolution of the Continental Congress, on which proposition the yeas and nays were not called. Next it was voted that he had shown himself an enemy to the liberties of the country and measures ought to be taken for his arrest, a motion which was carried by a vote of forty-two to ten. And finally it was voted that his salary be stopped forthwith, the vote being forty-seven to three. The trio of negatives on this motion had voted bravely for the

---

[4] A similar petition signed by a number of inhabitants of New Jersey is in *American Archives*, 4 series, vol. VI, p. 788.

Crown throughout the debate. For their courage at least they deserve to be recorded.[5]

It is said that on this date, Saturday, June 15, William Livingston, William Paterson, John Mehelm, and Dr. Witherspoon were appointed a committee to arrange the details of the governor's arrest and deposition.[6] The procedure to be followed would certainly have been left to a committee to decide, but the minutes show no such appointment, no manuscript corroboration of the assertion has been found, and Mr. Livingston was not even a member of the congress. At any rate, the committee, if appointed, lost no time in reporting, for that very day it was resolved that to Colonel Nathaniel Heard of the First Middlesex Battalion be assigned the delicate task of offering to the Governor a parole, giving him choice of Princeton, Bordentown, or his own estate at Raucoco, as a place of retirement, within six miles of which he was to remain during the war unless otherwise directed. He was also to engage not to give information to the enemy or do or say anything in opposition to or in prejudice of the proceedings and measures of the Continental Congress during the present trouble. If he refused to sign the parole he was to be kept under close guard until further orders.

On Monday the seventeenth, petitions from the villages of Windsor and Maidenhead (now Lawrenceville) came in praying that a new form of government be established, and the congress resolved that on the following Friday it would consider the propriety of forming a new government, would elect new delegates to the Continental congress and would draft instructions for their guidance. That morning at Perth Amboy Colonel Heard, armed with an order signed by president Tucker of the provincial congress, had presented the parole to the Governor. The latter promptly refused to sign it and forbade the colonel at his peril to execute the alternative of the congress. Heard at once appealed to his new superiors for instructions and the next day was ordered to bring the Governor to Burlington to face his judges, and

[5] John Allen of Hunterdon, Daniel Isaac Brown of Bergen, (Princeton, 1753) and Thomas Potts of Sussex.
[6] Mellick, *Old Farm*, p. 300.

a report of the whole proceeding was sent to the Continental Congress at Philadelphia. This body recommended that the New Jersey convention proceed with the Governor's examination and report to the Continental Congress, and the recommendation was forwarded to Dr. Witherspoon by Mr. Hancock, President of the Congress, in a personal letter dated Saturday, June 19. The fact that Mr. Hancock transmitted the resolution to Dr. Witherspoon rather than to an officer of the congress suggests clearly the prominence of Dr. Witherspoon in its councils. On Friday the twenty-first accordingly, Franklin was brought before the provincial congress to be examined on such parts of his conduct as were "hostile to American liberties," and the curtain rose on the most dramatic scene in New Jersey's political history. The province had reached her parting of the ways and had made her choice. At best, the examination of the Governor could have been little more than a form. Even had he been able to make out a case for himself, his official usefulness was at an end. He was well aware of his predicament but he faced his doom unflinchingly, maintaining to the end the bearing of an undaunted and loyal officer of the Crown. Beneath the surface there was something very sobering and almost pathetic in the scene, for it marked the final passing of an old established order with all its historic associations, its power, and its rich prestige. The confrontation of this splendidly representative figure of a British colonial governor—William Franklin was marked as one of the handsomest men in America—by a heterogeneous body of humbler and homelier persons bent on freeing themselves from the government he represented, meant that in his person once more the world was to see a mighty empire brought to bay and forced inevitably to pay the price of mistakes in judgment, blunders in policy, blindness to opportunity.

Six questions were put to him; had he issued the proclamation of the thirtieth; did he know of the resolution of May 15 passed by the Continental Congress; what was his authority for calling the Assembly; what was the alleged "important business;" did he write to the British ministry encouraging them to proceed against the country and especially calling attention to the defencelessness of the coast; what did he mean by the threatening words he had used to Colonel Heard, as for example: "It is your turn now, but it will be mine another day"?

The governor refused to answer; he denied the authority of his inquisitors; he declared with obvious truth that they had usurped lawful government in the province; and he furthermore asserted that they had not treated him with gentlemen's courtesy but had resolved that he was an enemy to his country, had made him a prisoner, and had robbed him by depriving him of part of his salary; and he ended his speech with a flash of anger: "and now do as you please, and make the best of it!" Altogether, wrote Mr. Tucker to Mr. Hancock, the Governor's conduct was "gross and insolent," and it was the opinion of the New Jersey body that he ought to be confined, but not in the province he had been ruling. "Only one thing we beg leave to add, that in our opinion the sooner the Continental Congress take him in charge the better."

There is no doubt that the Governor lost his temper, and, under the circumstances, excusably. Dr. Ashbel Green, quoting his father, the Reverend Jacob Green, who was a member of the congress, corroborates the tradition that the Governor reminded his hearers of their lack of administrative experience and their probable unfitness to devise and carry on a new form of government; but the further tradition that he so far forgot his manners as to taunt his inquisitors with their humble birth is questionable. Dr. Green does not mention it in his narrative of the occasion obtained from his father and used in his manuscript biography of Dr. Witherspoon, although he refers to the story in his own autobiography written later. If, however, the Governor alluded sneeringly to the common characteristic of a large majority of his judges he made a blunder which he speedily regretted. For only a few feet away, nervously plucking at his bushy eyebrows as was his habit when excited, sat the head of the College of New Jersey. The Governor might have foreseen that the President would reply; he could not have been ignorant of his activity in the political crisis. President Witherspoon was angry; and Ashbel Green has left it on record that at such times "the Doctor's aspect was truly awful." Witherspoon's anger must have been worth hearing as well as seeing, even if he did fall back so completely into his native Scotch that the torrent of his invective was difficult to follow. What was his reply to the Governor is not known although it is said—by tradition—to have caused the boldest to hold his breath in astonishment.[7] The Reverend Jacob Green used to relate that the President ended his tirade with the sarcastic fling "On the whole Sir, I think Governor Franklin has made a speech every way worthy his exalted birth and refined education." Evidently Dr. Witherspoon too had lost his self-control; for, whatever mistakes Benjamin Franklin's natural son may have made during his tumultuous career, he was hardly to blame for the irregular circumstances of his entrance into this difficult world. It is said—and it is probably true—that Dr. Witherspoon regretted his ungenerous thrust and later sought, but never found, opportunity to apologize.[8]

The rest of the Governor's story is quickly told. He had hit off pretty accurately what the future held in store for him when some months before this he intimated to the Earl of Dartmouth that it would be extremely mortifying to be "seized upon and led like a Bear through the Country to some place of Confinement in N. E." His New Jersey inquisitors received from the Continental Congress instructions to send him to Hartford, Connecticut, under close guard; and thither, a captive Ichabod, he was escorted. In November, 1778, he was exchanged, and going back to England resided there until his death in 1813.

Having disposed of their Governor, the Jerseymen turned their attention to their representatives in the Continental Congress. With the exception of William Livingston and Jonathan Dickinson Sergeant, the New Jersey delegation elected in February had not kept abreast of the movement for independence. Even Livingston, undoubted patriot though he was, had by no means yet convinced himself of the necessity of that measure. John Cooper seems to have taken part in nothing but a studied

[7] Mellick, *Old Farm*, p. 300.
[8] Messler, (*First Things in Old Somerset* p. 37) reports a modified version of the incident; when the Governor demanded by what authority he was so treated, Dr. Witherspoon on whom all eyes were turned, says Messler, replied that it could not be expected that a plain body of farmers and workingmen should treat the governor with all the politeness and respect which his illustrious birth and refined education would demand, but his judges meant to treat him civilly.

silence. Richard Smith had requested leave to resign on the score of ill health and was followed by John DeHart who for the time relinquished his seat for family reasons. On June 21, the provincial congress appointed Livingston, much against his will, to the command of state militia; he would have preferred to remain in Congress. The following day, Sergeant, having wisely decided that he was more needed at home and could there do better work for the cause, also resigned. Cooper was tacitly ignored and an entirely new delegation was elected consisting of Abraham Clark, John Hart, Francis Hopkinson, Richard Stockton, and John Witherspoon. It was well known how each of these men stood on the question of independence, and what their instructions would be. A week before their election Sergeant had assured Mr. Adams that Jersey's new delegation would "vote plump" for independence. Hereafter there was to be no mistake.

For a Colony that was not supposed to value education any too highly,[9] it was a very creditable delegation. Three of its members, Witherspoon, Stockton, and Hopkinson, were college graduates, had been in Europe, and had rubbed elbows with a wider society than that bounded by Jersey province lines. Born at Princeton in 1730 and graduated from the College of New Jersey in 1748, a member of the provincial council, a judge of the provincial supreme court, Mr. Stockton was at the zenith of his powers as lawyer, scholar and gentleman. It was an odd turn of fortune that he should be sitting beside the man whom he had brought ten years ago from the other side of the Atlantic for a very different purpose, and that both should now be engaged in overturning the government which at that time they had loyally supported.

Mr. Stockton's junior by seven years, Francis Hopkinson was English by parentage and Philadelphian by birth. He had received his bachelor's degree from the College of Philadelphia in 1757, like Stockton a member of the first class sent out by his alma mater; six years later Princeton had made him an honorary alumnus. As musician, as a writer of light verse and lover of art, as a lawyer, as director and secretary of the Philadelphia Library

[9] Dr. Witherspoon used to say jokingly to Ashbel Green that he was the most popular man in the State that had any learning.

Company, and as collector of customs at Newcastle on the Delaware, he was probably the most versatile member of the Congress, and had got into his small shrewd head—the head that John Adams made fun of—a world of experience that gave an edge to his natural fund of wit and imagination. His slight figure had been for two years a familiar one in New Jersey congresses.

Abraham Clark was a self-made man of fifty, a Jerseyman born and bred. He was a surveyor by profession,and had been sheriff of Essex county and clerk of the colonial Assembly. A warm adherent of the cause, he had served on the committee of observation in 1774 and in the provincial congress of 1775.

"Honest" John Hart of Hunterdon county, the oldest member of the group—he was baptised in March, 1714—was a farmer of little or no education. He was as rough a diamond as Stockton and Hopkinson were polished; but his simple, rugged character had so commanded the affection and trust of his neighbors that it had won him his nickname, had elected him to numerous offices, and for a decade past had sent him to the colonial Assembly. He had already served in the Continental Congress and in both the provincial congresses of New Jersey, and he was vice-president of the body that returned him to Philadelphia in June, 1776.

Thoroughly representative of their constituents in most ways though this group was, their departure from Burlington deprived the province of the presence of men whom it could ill spare from its own congress. We find a hint of the scarcity of experienced leaders in New Jersey in a letter which Jonathan D. Sergeant wrote to Mr. Adams some weeks later: he feels the want of wisdom in the state's councils; raw, young, and inexperienced as he is, he finds himself forced to bear a principal part; "would to Heaven," he cries, "that I could look round here, as when with you, and see a number in whose understanding I could confide." But in New Jersey he finds a "miserable prejudice against men of education . . . plain men are generally returned, of sufficient honesty and spirit, but most of them hardly competent to the penning of a common vote."[10]

[10] Adams, *Life and Works*, vol. IX, p. 425. Letter of July 19, 1776.

[214]

Competent or not, there was no mistaking New Jersey's meaning when she did finally, with Sergeant's aid, get her thoughts into writing, as the instructions given on June 21 to her delegates to the Continental Congress amply prove. And Sergeant himself was forced to admit that New Jersey was "mending very fast." East Jersey he told Mr. Adams had always been firm and West Jersey would now move with vigor. The Tories in some parts of the province had impeded the work of the Congress by delays and "an infinity of hearings," but a quick remedy had at last been provided by framing an ordinance against "treasons, seditions and counterfeitings," which Sergeant thought would effectually tie Tory hands and in any event check Tory tongues.

Dr. Witherspoon's appointment prevented him from serving New Jersey on the committee that drafted the state constitution and secured its adoption on July 2. It is generally asserted in histories of New Jersey that he took an active part in preparing this constitution, but the only evidence brought forward consists of the marks of clerical influence that the instrument bears. These may be more reasonably credited to the Reverend Jacob Green who was chairman of the drafting committee. Dr. Witherspoon was perhaps consulted, but his absence from New Jersey must have debarred him entirely from any active participation in the discussion and adoption of the constitution. It is a tradition that the document was drafted at "Constitution Hill," Princeton.

On Friday, June 28, 1776, Francis Hopkinson appeared before the Continental Congress at Philadelphia and produced the credentials of the New Jersey delegation reading as follows:

In Provincial Congress New Jersey.
Burlington June 21st 1776.

The Congress proceeded to the Election of Delegates to represent this Colony in Continental Congress when Richard Stockton, Abraham Clark, John Hart, and Francis Hopkinson, Esquires, and Doctr John Witherspoon were elected by Ballot to serve one Year unless a new Appointment be made before that Time

Resolved, that the following Instructions be given the Delegates elected as aforesaid:

To Richard Stockton, Abraham Clark, John Hart, and Francis

Hopkinson, Esqrs. and the Revd Doctr John Witherspoon Delegates appointed to represent the Colony of New Jersey in Continental Congress.

The Congress empower and direct you, in the Name of this Colony, to join with the Delegates of the other Colonies in Continental Congress, in the most vigorous Measures for supporting the just Rights and Liberties of America and, if you shall judge it necessary or expedient for this Purpose, we empower you to join with them in declaring the United Colonies independent of Great Britain, entering into a Confederacy for Union & common Defence, making Treaties with foreign Nations for Commerce and Assistance, and to take such other Measures as may appear to them and you necessary for these great Ends, promising to Support them with the whole Force of this Province; always observing, that, whatever Plan of Confederacy you enter into the regulating the internal Policy of this Province is to be reserved to the Colony Legislature.

| Extract from the Minutes | By Order of Congress |
| Wm Paterson, Secy | Samul Tucker, president.[11] |

The minutes of the Continental Congress do not state that Mr. Hopkinson's fellowmembers were with him when he presented the credentials, but there seems to be no reason to misconstrue Mr. John Adams' statement in his autobiography that on this date (June 28) "A new delegation appeared from New Jersey,"[12] and we may be sure that Dr. Witherspoon had not needed more than a week to arrange matters at Princeton for his absence. It seems indubitable that he appeared at Philadelphia as soon as the rest of the delegation although the first autographic evidence of his presence in Philadelphia is a letter he wrote July 3 to President Tucker of New Jersey in regard to Governor Franklin.[13]

The Jerseymen arrived at an important moment. Not only was Congress, in committee of the whole, on the point of adopt-

---

[11] The credentials are among the Papers of the Continental Congress in the Library of Congress and are printed in the *Journal of the Continental Congress* edited by Worthington C. Ford. (V. 489). The original is in Paterson's handwriting except the signature of Mr. Tucker. It is endorsed by Paterson "Copy for Mr. Hopkinson" and by Charles Thomson, secretary of Congress, "Credentials of New Jersey," and is dated in another hand "21st June 1776."

[12] *Life and Works*, vol. III, p. 53.

[13] *New England Historical and Genealogical Register*, vol. XXX, p. 313.

ing a resolution of independence, but Friday morning, June 28, the special committee appointed to prepare a declaration of that independence brought in a draft which was read and ordered to lie on the table over Sunday. On Monday, July 1, the draft was referred also to the committee of the whole. The latter reported that it had agreed to the resolution of independence but desired leave to sit again. The resolution was then read again, but "at the request of a Colony," says the *Journal*, final disposition was postponed until the next day. It was also resolved that on the morrow Congress would in committee of the whole consider further "the declaration respecting independence." This agrees in general though not in detail with John Adams' statement under that date (July 1) that "before the final question (i.e., on the resolution) was put, the new delegation from New Jersey came in, and Mr. Stockton, Dr. Witherspoon and Mr. Hopkinson, very respectable characters, expressed a great desire to hear the arguments." The main debate had taken place; Mr. Dickinson had made his speech summing up against independence and Adams had replied. The house was weary of discussion, but Mr. Rutledge urged Mr. Adams to satisfy the Jerseymen, which he did concisely, giving the arguments pro and con. The Jerseymen declared themselves ready to vote, and on July 2 the vote was taken by which it was resolved "that these United Colonies are and of right ought to be free and independent States." Congress then went into committee of the whole on the declaration of this independence, discussion proceeded, lasting through July 3 to culminate on the fourth in the adoption, by the committee, of a declaration, which on being reported to the house was agreed to as "the unanimous Declaration of the thirteen United States of America."

What share did Dr. Witherspoon have in the proceedings of these four memorable days? Lacking contemporary or autobiographical data on this point, the best source available at present is Dr. Ashbel Green's manuscript biography of the President. Referring to the part played by his revered teacher in the debate on independence, he says that the substance of a statement made by Dr. Witherspoon in his hearing was to the following effect:

That the principal argument relied on by those who wished to post-pone for a time the Declaration of Independence was that a number of new members had recently entered Congress who had not heard the whole of the previous discussion, and who could not therefore judge correctly of the reasons for and against an immediate declaration, which had been so ably advocated and urged before they took their seats and that the country at large needed more time for reflection and was not yet ripe for so important and decisive a measure. To this the Doctor took the opportunity to reply that, although there were some members who had recently come into Congress, it did by no means follow that they had not examined this important subject in all its bearings and weighed the arguments fully for prompt action on the one side, and for delay on the other; that this had certainly been done by himself, and he doubted not by others to whom the objection applied; nor had they wanted ample means of information on the merits of the question, although they had not been favored with hear-ing all the debate by that house. As for the country at large, it had been for some time past loud in its demand for the proposed declara-tion and in his judgment, it was not only ripe for the measure but in danger of becoming rotten for the want of it.[14]

We have nothing in the shape of a more personal record. That there is discrepancy between the Adams and the Green state-ments is obvious. Dr. Green is either confusing the declaration of the fourth with the resolution of the second, or is using the word "declaration" to mean the action of the second. The Presi-dent's entire speech plainly refers to the resolution of the second, and not to the declaration of the fourth. It seems also clear that when the New Jersey delegates put in their appearance at the end of the debate on the resolution of independence, the point was made by the conservative party that there were a number of new members in Congress who had not heard the debate and for whose benefit, therefore, it should be recapitulated. Mr. Stockton and Mr. Hopkinson may have "expressed a great desire" to hear

[14] Green MS. The same statement, in almost identical words, occurs in Dr. Green's autobiography (p. 62). It is fair to state that Dr. Green's biography of Dr.Wither-spoon was written from 1836 to 1840 and that the passage in the autobiography was written probably in 1843, assuming that the date heading (July 20, 1848) of the chapter is a misprint inasmuch as its author died in May 1848. The accuracy of Dr. Green's recollections in incidents which are capable of exact verification leads the present writer to accept the reliability of his statement in this case.

the arguments, as Mr. Adams has it; he declares twice that New Jersey desired recapitulation and there is evidence in the biography of Mr. Stockton that he at least was undecided until he heard Mr. Adams;[15] but Mr. Adams must be entirely mistaken in including Dr. Witherspoon with those desiring further debate. That he would have opposed longer delay his previous record sufficiently proves. It was certainly on July 1 or 2 that he made the speech of which Dr. Green has preserved the outline.

The way being cleared for the declaration which already had been under discussion for two days, President Witherspoon is said to have protested against the use of the word "Scotch" in the phrase "Scotch and foreign mercenaries,"[16] used in the original draft and omitted in the final form of the declaration; and he protested, as he always did, against calling the King a tyrant, etc., as being false and undignified.

That on the fourth of July, at an alleged critical moment in the debate, he stepped into the breach and delivered the "nick of time" speech, traditionally credited to him and inscribed on his monuments in Fairmount Park, Philadelphia, and at Washington, is a legend. There is no trustworthy evidence that he spoke on the declaration of independence save to criticize successfully some of its original phraseology.[17]

[15] Sanderson, *Signers*, p. 192. There is also evidence elsewhere that imprisonment and ill health later sapped his courage for the cause.

[16] Lee, *Life of R. H. Lee*, vol. I, 176.

[17] The tradition has become so firmly entrenched in the popular mind that a disbelief in its authenticity deserves more than mere assertion. The problem of this speech has been made the subject of a close and able study by Dr. Louis F. Benson, Honorary Librarian of the Presbyterian Historical Society, published in the *Journal* of the Society for June, 1916. The conclusions reached by Dr. Benson are with slight exception identical with those reached by the present writer some years since and suggested in a local address. Since then this chapter has lain in manuscript awaiting the completion of the volume of which it is a part. The delay has happily given it the benefit of useful details from Dr. Benson's later researches.

The grounds for disbelief in the tradition are that the alleged pivotal appeal by President Witherspoon was unknown to his contemporaries and unmentioned by himself, is not in his manner, does not ring true, and owes its existence to a confusion and distortion of facts. In what is perhaps its most familiar form the alleged speech is found in Dr. William P. Breed's *Presbyterians and the Revolution*, published at the time of the Centennial in 1876. Dr. Breed's source was a sermon entitled *Merciful Rebukes* delivered in 1841 by Dr. John M. Krebs and published in New York that year. Dr. Krebs himself, however, was also quoting, as reference to his sermon proves; but he did not name his source. Dr. Thomas Smyth's *Ecclesiastical Republicanism*, printed in 1843, also uses the Krebs version. A footnote in the Philadelphia 1846 edition of Graydon's *Memoirs*, not found in earlier editions, quotes a highly colored passage in an address "by the Reverend S. S. Templeton," which contains the speech. Mr. Templeton's oration has not been traced, but the identity of his version with that of Dr. Krebs leads to the conclusion that the latter was also his source.

The *Presbyterian* for September 21, 1867, states that the speech is found in an oration by the Reverend Hooper Cumming delivered July 4, 1824, at Morristown, N.J. This is an error both of date and place, for the oration was delivered at Newark, N. J., on July 4, 1822. The report there given constitutes the earliest form of the alleged speech at present known. Comparison of the texts shows that it is almost certainly the source used by Dr. Krebs. Like those who followed him, however, Dr. Cumming was quoting or at least paraphrasing. For he only claims to have been "credibly informed" that Dr. Witherspoon uttered the speech he proceeds to report, and it is fairly evident, therefore, that he is not trying to repeat the exact language.

The passage runs as follows (he is speaking of the Continental Congress): "And it must be a source of proud exultation to a Jersey man that one of the Representatives of his native State by a laconick speech signalized for its energy, its disinterestedness, and its burning patriotism, turned the scale which was at that moment equipoise, and decided the passage of the Declaration of Independence. 'There is,' as I have been credibly informed, 'there is,' said the venerable Witherspoon, when he perceived the house wavering, 'there is a tide in the affairs of men—a nick of time.— We perceive it now before us. To hesitate, is to consent to slavery. That noble instrument upon your table, which ensures immortality to its author, should be subscribed this very morning by every pen in this house. He who will not respond to its accents, and strain every nerve to carry into effect its provisions, is unworthy the name of freeman. For my own part, of property I have some—of reputation more. That reputation is staked on the issue of this contest—that property is pledged. And although these gray hairs must soon descend into the sepulchre, I had infinitely rather they would descend thither by the hands of the public executioner, than desert, at this crisis, the sacred cause of my country.' The Declaration was signed by every member present—and the heart of the illustrious Jefferson palpitated with joy."

Comparison of the later versions with that of Mr. Cumming shows that it supplies all the necessary hints for the fanciful touches found in those versions. Dr. Krebs for example embroiders the Cumming reference to the scale being at that moment "equipoise" and the "house wavering" into this: "The House hesitated, wavered, and for a while liberty and slavery appeared to hang in even scale." To which Mr. Templeton adds: "Silence, deep and solemn silence, reigned throughout the spacious Capitol," which seems to refer prophetically to Washington, D. C. The "venerable Witherspoon" and his "burning patriotism" is expanded into: "An aged patriarch arose, a venerable and stately form, his head white with the frosts of many years . . . the hue of age was lost in the flush of burning patriotism that fired his cheek." Then follows the speech, Templeton omitting two sentences but otherwise without change from Krebs. The improvements on Mr. Cumming may be dismissed without further ado since they spring from his unwitting temptation of his followers and because they contain their own refutation. One example will suffice. The characterization of President Witherspoon as an "aged patriarch" whose head was "white with the frosts of many years" becomes ridiculous when we remember that he had but recently passed his fifty-third birthday, and even though it be admitted that he looked older than he was.

But the Cumming original itself lacks conviction. Mr. Cumming was a graduate of Princeton in the Class of 1805 and therefore could not have obtained his information from the President himself. He may have received it from one of the President's colleagues of July 4, 1776; in which case it is not difficult to understand why the recollection of this supposed contemporary was confused. He makes a mistake similar to that of Dr. Green and assigns to July 4 a speech which if made at all was delivered on July 2. At best it cannot be and is hardly intended to be an exact reproduction of Dr. Witherspoon's words; its style is in every way markedly unlike that of any used by the President in his authentic speeches. The allusion to the noble instrument lying on the table ensuring "immortality to its author" is too prophetic for 1776, the historic action in contemporary eyes being that of July 2 and not any action taken on the fourth. Dr. Witherspoon could scarcely have spoken of deserting the sacred cause of his adopted country at this juncture; he had already voted for the vital resolution of independence and his position toward the cause as shown by his recorded speech and vote was now beyond recall, and the question at the moment did not involve desertion; that Rubicon, in the well-known words of Mr. Adams, had been crossed on July 2, and now it was merely a question of public declaration of the reasons leading to that action. Finally, Dr. Witherspoon must have been sufficiently familiar with the procedure of the Congress to have been aware that the declaration as a committee report would, if adopted, be signed only by the president and attested by the secretary of Congress unless the Congress should order otherwise, and Congress had not yet so ordered. The declaration was not signed generally until the engrossed copy was brought in some weeks later for that express purpose and according to subsequent resolution of Congress, Witherspoon himself signing in August.

The alleged incident, which Cumming would have us believe swung the vote in favor of the declaration of July 4, is not mentioned in any account of the debate written by a contemporary; it is not hinted at in Ashbel Green's autobiography nor in his manuscript life of Witherspoon both of which contain the latter's own account of his part in the final debate; and no such speech is preserved in Dr. Witherspoon's printed writings. It is incredible that so important an utterance, if made, should have been overlooked by those who were present and who recorded the proceedings, or that Green should not only have failed to hear of it but should have failed to take note of it.

Mr. John Adams' statement in 1815, in a letter to Governor McKean, that Dickinson and Witherspoon each printed a speech delivered in Congress on the declaration of independence (Stille, *Life and times of Dickinson*, vol. I, p. 193) seems to be inaccurate as regards Mr. Dickinson and is erroneous as regards President Witherspoon.

The speech is most probably a vague recollection of President Witherspoon's remarks on July 2 opposing further delay in adopting the resolution of independence, but so distorted by oral tradition, the passage of time, and the gradual magnifying of the proceedings of July 4, that it had become unrecognizable when it reached Mr. Cumming's willing ears and was transformed into a supposed speech of July 4. The story has every quality of misguided information or misinformed enthusiasm and is an excellent example of the growth of legend around ascertained facts. In this case the facts are two: first, the arrival of new delegates in Congress at the end of June, 1776, delayed until July 2 a vote on the resolution of independence while the preceding debate was recapitulated for their benefit; and second, President Witherspoon spoke at the beginning of this delay denying its necessity and urging an immediate vote.

The Declaration of Independence reached Princeton on July 9 and that night the undergraduates once more placed tallow dips in every window of Nassau Hall so that the building was "grandly illuminated," and amid triple volleys of musketry "Independence was proclaimed with universal acclamation for the prosperity of the United States. The ceremony was conducted with the greatest decorum."[18]

Dr. Witherspoon's recent actions had not been unnoticed by the other side. In New Jersey he was known to half the inhabitants by sight; in Philadelphia he had long been a familiar figure; his opinions and his readiness to utter them anywhere outside of the pulpit were commonplaces; British troops on Long Island showed an unexpected sense of humor when they prepared for their bonfire of July 30 an effigy of him haranguing similar effigies of Generals Washington, Lee, and Putnam, standing before him mutely in a row; and Dr. Odell's estimate was not an extreme example of loyalist attitude toward him; but his severest critics were his own countrymen abroad. In 1775 he had been attacked in the Edinburgh *Caledonian Mercury* by a writer, hiding behind the pseudonym of "Historicus," who, having read a British reprint of Provost Smith's sermon at Philadelphia on June 23, sent to the *Mercury* a long account of the preacher's varied career up to that time, in the course of which he asserted that, next to his countryman Dr. Witherspoon, he was generally considered to be the clergyman who in the middle provinces had taken most violent part in the present differences between Great Britain and her Colonies. This is one of the earliest European references to Witherspoon's share in the shaping of affairs that has been found, and it would hardly occur to any one now to place the two Presidents in the same category on this score. The Reverend Dr. John Erskine in the *Mercury's* next issue took up the cudgel in defence of his absent friend Witherspoon. The American clergy he declares have not influenced the people nor urged them to violence; they have neither printed nor preached on political topics; Witherspoon's letters to Erskine and to others have been couched in terms of great restraint and modera-

[18] Letter from Princeton July 10 in *New Jersey Archives*, 2 series, vol. I, p. 142.

tion and show instances of his having done all he could to allay animosities and disorders. The issue of the *Scots Mazagine* that quoted this letter from the *Mercury* prints the "Pastoral Letter" of May, 1775, which we know came from Witherspoon's pen, and is certainly not an inflammatory document.

From his foreign critics President Witherspoon's fast day sermon of May, 1776, on the *Dominion of Providence* received close attention. When he published it late in July he took the opportunity to add as an appendix an *Address to the Natives of Scotland residing in America,* which is invaluable in its revelation of his political views at this time.[19] Besides indicating that he now considered the controversial phase of the situation closed and its decision irrevocable, the *Address* contains much of the cool reasoning that had led him to his present position. It shows how little he had been carried off his feet by mere emotionalism and suggests more fully than even his then unpublished essay *"On the American Controversy about Independence,"* the views he held as to the significance of the struggle in which the Colonies were now embarked.

The *Address* is composed very largely of ideas, and in part of phraseology, borrowed from his unfinished *Reflections on the Present State of Public Affairs*. It had given him great uneasiness to hear the word "Scotch" used as a term of reproach during the American controversy, "which could be explained only upon the supposition that Scotsmen were more generally opposed to American liberty than the English or the Irish." Admitting that possibly in some provinces, the natives of Scotland have been "too much inclined to support the usurpations of the parent State," he proposed first to "endeavour to account for it, by assigning some of its probable causes, and then offer a few considerations which should induce them to wipe off the aspersion entirely by a contrary conduct."

[19] The fact that he deemed it wise to address this large group of colonial inhabitants shows that he feared for their adherence to the colonial cause. He may have heard of the formation of Highland regiments in the Colonies to serve the Crown, and he may have had an inkling of the situation in Scotland where scores of loyal addresses were showered on the Crown at this time—one from his former parish, Paisley. J.P.Maclean, *Historical Account of Scotch Highlanders in America,* (1900) pp. 299–300.
[20] *Works,* vol. IV, p. 201.

The first and radical cause was the confusion in the minds of friends of liberty in many places in America between the American cause and that of John Wilkes. It is clear, he avers, that "till very lately" those who seemed to take the part of America in Parliament never did so on American principles. The truth was that

by far the greater part of the countenance given in Britain to the complaints of this country, was by those who had no other intention in it, than to use them as an engine of opposition to the Ministry. . . . Some have now learned to reason very justly, and upon the most liberal principles; but their number is not great, and it was not the case with any one speaker or writer whose works I have had the opportunity of perusing, till the very last stage of the quarrel.

The Wilkites used the American troubles to sharpen their own tirades against the government. The effect of "Wilkism (if I may so speak)" on the Scotch is easily explained: Wilkes and his party had ever hated and insulted the Scotch and had stirred up jealousy between Scotland and England. Hence the supposed Scotch apathy, to call it by no harsher name, toward the American cause. He is far from admitting this a good reason "for any man's being cool to the American cause, which was as different from that of Wilkes as light is from darkness." It was doing great dishonor to a noble struggle "to suppose it to have any connection with—who should be in or out of court favour at London." "In order to justify the American opposition, it is not necessary to show that the persons in power have invaded liberty in Britain; it is sufficient to say that they, with the concurrence of the whole nation, have refused to suffer it to continue in the Colonies."

This brings him to the second part of his plan—to lay before his readers the reasons which in his opinion should induce every lover of justice and of mankind, not only to be a well wisher, but a firm and steadfast friend to America in this contest. The progress of the British Colonies has been far greater than that of settlements of other European nations. This cannot be ascribed to climate, for they are of all climates; nor to the people, for they are a mixture of all nations. "It must, therefore, be resolved singly into the degree of British liberty which they brought from home, and which pervaded more or less their several constitutions." It had been repeatedly said "by mercenary, short-sighted writers in favour of submission to, or re-union with, Great Britain, that we have thriven very much in past time, by our dependence on the mother country and therefore we should be loath to part. These writers forget that the very complaint is that she will not suffer us to enjoy our ancient rights." He challenges such reasoners to prove that in exercising these rights "we have thriven by our dependence, and not by the degree of independence we have hitherto enjoyed." On the contrary, those provinces have thriven most which have enjoyed the freest form of government. Hence how can any person of liberal mind wish "that this great and growing country" should be brought back to a state of subjection to a distant power? "It ought in my opinion to meet with the cordial approbation of every impartial person, as I am confident it will of posterity, that they [the Colonies] have united for common defence, and resolved that they will be free and independent because they cannot be the one without the other."

He next proposes to show that independence was necessary, that it will be honorable and profitable, and that in all probability it will work not injury but a real advantage to Great Britain. Independence was necessary because reconciliation except upon terms of unconditional submission had been refused by Great Britain; things had gone so far that it was impossible to lay down a scheme by which Great Britain should be sure of our dependence, and the Colonies at the same time secured in their liberties. Independence will be both honorable and profitable to the country—he passes over commerce and other material advantages, in order to "dwell a little on the great and leading benefit, which is the foundation of all the rest. We shall have the opportunity of forming plans of government, upon the most rational, just, and equal principles." He had long looked upon this "with a kind of enthusiastic satisfaction." The case never happened before, since the world began.

All governments we have read of in former ages were settled by caprice or accident, by the influence of prevailing parties or particular parties, or presented by a conqueror. . . . But to see a government, in large and populous countries, settled from its foundation by deliberate counsel, and directed immediately to the public good of the present and future generations, while the people are waiting for the decision with full confidence in the wisdom and impartiality of those to whom they have committed the important trust, is certainly new.

And so far there has been great unanimity and public spirit. The inhabitants of every province and persons of all denominations had vied with one another in zeal for the common interest. In England at the time of the Civil War if the Parliamentary party "had settled on a regular form of Government as soon as the parliament had obtained an evident superiority their liberties would never have been shaken and the Revolution would have been unnecessary. But by delaying the thing too long they were broken into parties, and bewildered in their views, and at last tamely submitted, without resistance, to that very tyranny against which they had fought with so much glory and success." Hence he rejoices at the measures lately taken by the States of America and especially at the declaration of independence, "as it will not only give union and force to the measures of defence while they are necessary, but lay a foundation for the birth of millions, and the future improvement of a great part of the globe."

Thirdly, the independence of America will be a real advantage to Great Britain partly in trade, but most in the influence Great Britain will have in peopling and enriching this great continent. "Trade is of a nice and delicate nature; it is founded upon interest. It will force its way wherever interest leads, and can hardly by any act be made to go in another direction." If American trade has been valuable in the past how much more valuable may it become to Great Britain when the country shall be still more highly improved? There is not now, nor has there ever been, among Americans any aversion to the people to Great Britain, "so that they may be sure of our trade if they treat us as well as others; and if otherwise, they do not deserve it."

These in brief are the principles on which he thought the cause of the American Colonies ought to be pleaded; and on the principle of majority rule, there was a time when it was not only just and consistent but needful that every one should speak his mind freely and fully on the necessity or expediency of resisting Great Britain; but that time is gone long ago, and now America is no place for the half-hearted man or the neutral—in a leaking ship the half-hearted man who will not help at the pumps but only carps and hinders, should be thrown into the sea "in less time than I have taken to state the case." He himself has been abused in the papers at home for the part he has taken and this *Address* is partly in reply to those criticisms. He hopes that an honest and faithful support of liberty and equal government in this part of the world will be no just reproach to his character as a scholar, a minister, or a Christian, and that it will be perfectly consistent with an undiminished regard for the country that gave him birth.

The sermon on the *Dominion of Providence* with the *Address* was reprinted at Glasgow twice in 1777, with an introduction and notes signed by "S.R.," the publisher's and printer's names not being given. The editor calls attention to the belief among "many persons of the best intelligence" that the trouble in the Colonies has been "considerably promoted, if not primarily agitated, by clerical influence," and none has had a greater share in this commotion ascribed to him than Witherspoon, "though not credited by many of his favourites in this country." To justify the allegation and silence the President's friends is the editor's object in reprinting the sermon and its appendix. In the former are blended "the most rebellious sentiments with the most sacred and important truths;" the author had "the audacity to affirm, that not only the temporal but eternal happiness of the revolted colonists depends upon persevering in their independence, and undauntedly opposing the arms of their lawful sovereign." Witherspoon proves himself the most inveterate enemy of his King and country; he stretches every nerve to induce his countrymen to imbibe his political sentiments; and that his rebellious tenets may be diffused through the different Colonies his sermon and address "must be printed and published, and dedicated to the chief of the rebel faction;" he exerts his utmost abilities to instigate the deluded colonists to persevere in their rebellious course; he labors to inflame their minds against the determinations of Parliament; "the best of Kings hath the most vile and unjust

[227]

epithets ascribed to him; the salutary and equitable Acts of the British parliament are pronounced unjust and tyrannical; the ablest of ministers are represented as corrupt, cruel, and oppressive; the most lenient measures of the government are flouted at and treated with contempt; the mildest of commanders and the best disciplined army are painted out as barbarous, inhuman, and brutal"—and so forth, ending with the warning that if Witherspoon "falls into the hands of Government and meets with the demerit of his offence, he hath justly and deservedly procured it to himself." The notes scattered copiously through the reprint are as extreme in tone as the preface.

At London the sermon and *Address* were reprinted separately and show interesting contrast to the Glasgow editions. Notes are designedly omitted, says the anonymous English editor of the sermon, the purpose being not

to inflame the minds of readers against present measures of Government but to inculcate the great moral and religious instructions which the sermon contains for persons of all parties who if they will read without prejudice must acknowledge that whatever the truth with regard to the present unhappy contest between Great Britain and America, the discourse contains many admirable hints of advice, which if properly regarded will tend to the prosperity of both sides. And it is hoped, that the decency and moderation which so warm and interested an advocate on the part of the Americans discovers, may tend to promote the same spirit in those readers on this side of the Atlantic, who have made themselves parties in the same cause, as well as to moderate the resentment of their most zealous opponents; and to promote in good men, on both sides, (for such there are on both) an hearty disposition "to seek the things which make for Peace" and above all to promote the Righteousness "which alone exalteth a nation."

The London edition of the *Address* likewise contained a brief but not unfriendly preface. While many of Dr. Witherspoon's readers and friends in Great Britain who wish well to American liberty will be disgusted at his pleading the cause of American independence, others will wish America independent though utterly disapproving the measures taken to make it so. As far, however, as the *Address* has a real tendency to the honor of the

Crown and the interests of the British empire, which is one of Dr. Witherspoon's objects in pleading for independence, so far it has the good wishes of the editor. Which was a kinder introduction, one suspects, than Dr. Stiles of New Haven would have written; for in the latter's diary for August 15, 1776, he takes note of President Witherspoon's assertion that American independence would redound to the advantage of Great Britain, and that after peace had been restored the Colonies would resume trade with the mother country, and adds the comment: "I doubt. Too much Scotticism! He wants to save his countrymen, who have behaved most cruelly in this American conflict."[21]

If the London reprint is neutral, the *Monthly Review's*[22] comment is distinctly friendly.[23]

Dr. Witherspoon is a character well known. He is a man of considerable abilities, a little tinctured with fanaticism of the Whitfieldian complexion. Some years ago we had frequent occasion of mentioning his writings published while he was a minister in Scotland, his native country. He is now become an eminent preacher among the Americans. This discourse, however, has nothing in it irrational or illiberal. It abounds more in piety than politics; though by no means destitute of the latter; but his doctrines in both respects breathe a spirit so candid and so agreeable to the moderation of the Christian character that, excepting few passages tending to encourage the Americans in their scheme of independency, this animated and pious discourse might have been delivered with great acceptance and possibly with good effect before any Fast Day audience in the Kingdom without subjecting the preacher to the imputation of disloyalty or disaffection to the government.

The *Scots Magazine* for February, 1777, quotes in seven columns, without comment, the political passages of the sermon, and must have contributed largely to the interest that demanded

---

[21] *Literary Diary*, vol. II, p. 41.
[22] *Monthly Review*, vol. LVIII (1778), p. 246.
[23] In the volume for 1757, p. 185, the *Review* had concluded a two page synopsis of his *Essay on the Connection between the doctrine of Justification and holiness of life* with this pleasant remark: "Judge for thyself, Reader, whether this rant savours anything of the genius of Christianity, and what share their author has of that amiable spirit of candor and charity which the Christian religion so strongly recommends and enforces."

a second edition of the Glasgow reprint in the same year. The March number of the *Scots Magazine* reprints the *Address* in full and again without comment but giving it the leading place in that issue, and following it with a further extract from the sermon, consisting of Witherspoon's note attacking the author of *Common Sense* for representing the doctrine of original sin as "an object of contempt or abhorrence." A subtler, although unsuccessful, bid for Scottish favor could not have been selected. In the issue of the *Scots Magazine* for October, 1777, a correspondent ironically endorses the passage in the *Address* in which Witherspoon had intimated that Chatham's plan of reconciliation would not have been acceptable to America, remarking that Chatham and other noble lords might have saved themselves much trouble if they had only had the advantage of perusing Dr. Witherspoon's essay before they framed their plan. The correspondent also objects to the President's ethics:

St. Paul says the damnation of those who do evil that good may come is just. Dr. Witherspoon on the contrary says that if the colonists were wrong in the present contest it would be the part both of generosity and justice, in a certain class of persons, to support them effectually in it. The Apostle condemns evil when done that good may come; the Doctor would justify evil even when done in support of what is wrong.

These quotations indicate the feeling stirred up by the *Fast Day Sermon* and its accompanying *Address*; but probably the most curious example of the mood in which some of his countrymen viewed Dr. Witherspoon's American activities is found in the shape of a nineteen page quarto pamphlet entitled *The XLV Chapter of the Prophecies of Thomas the Rhymer, in Verse*, written by Hugo Arnot,[24] published anonymously at Edinburgh in 1776, and sold at sixpence a copy. Arnot was a well-known Edinburgh character, a local historian of repute, and an Advocate with a caustic tongue. The introduction, in the form of a dedicatory letter to "Dr. Silverspoon, Preacher of Sedition in America" and

[24] So pencilled note on the title page of the unique copy in the Advocates Library at Edinburgh.

written in prose that is infinitely cleverer than the poetry it introduces, informs him that

the design of this publication is to arouse my sleeping countrymen, to alarm them with imaginary dangers, to blast and eradicate harmony and loyalty, which at present unhappily flourish among this deluded people; to clog the wheels of government, nay, to join hands with our brethren in America, and overturn the system.

These being the laudable and professed intentions of this work, I should be insensible to your merit, and ungrateful for your services, did I hesitate a moment in laying it at your feet, and acknowledging your eminence in influencing the people to take arms against government.

The author then proceeds to explain "the whole mystery of rebellion." Rebellion is due to drunkenness, and drunkenness in turn is of two sorts, natural and political, the former due to liquor, the latter to zeal. Political drunkenness

is distributed by those of desperate fortune and counsel, by the victims of disappointed ambition, by discontented pretenders to patriotism in the Houses of Peers and Commons, by needy authors; but above all by seditious Preachers, who gain an honest livelihood by exerting their respective endeavours, conducive to the same end, namely the destruction of their country.

Now, there are two ways of dissipating this drunken zeal; by a hearty drubbing, or by being crowned with success. If we shall attain the latter of these alternatives, our honourable purpose, if we shall no longer have Britain, to contend with, it is to be dreaded that the delirium will cease, that the people will turn sober, will perceive the nakedness of their situation, exposed to internal dissention and foreign invasion, and following the example set them in the Scriptures, will say, "I will arise and go to my Father, etc."

The author wishes he could send Dr. Silverspoon more agreeable news from this "deluded kingdom." "We are not, however, totally destitute of friends; a majority of smugglers are in favour of us, and some high-flying clergy in a certain city have betrayed their affection to our cause." He entreats the doctor to continue his correspondence "with the wizard brethren;" they will publish letters in the *Caledonian Mercury* until they get a magazine of their own, "replete with inflammatory stores; and in these letters they will applaud his 'great temper and moderation on the present melancholy state of affairs' and will assure the public, that he has 'neither preached nor printed on political subjects.' "

We need quote but a few lines of the poem itself—which is completely equipped with a panoply of notes and commentaries, in ironical respect to "the genius of the age."

> In distant climes in days of yore,
> Four holy wizard Brethren bore
> Descent, of horrible conjunction,
> Of parent Gods, reverse in function.
> Lord Mercury, after might pother,
> Seduced Discordia their mother,
> The breth'ren hence were famed for lies,
> Sedition and malignant eyes,
> Practised their mother's cheating arts,
> And threw their mother's rankled darts,
> To blast the concord of a nation
> Whose laws they held in destestation.

The four wizards meet, and borrowing from an obvious source sing an incantation, each muttering a stanza, of which the first is a sufficiently fair example:

> In a brazen pulpit boil,
> Of flaming zeal the holy oil;
> Throw the seeds of harsh pretensions
> Tongue of Preacher on damnation,
> To a snoring congregation:
> Cimeter that with a blow
> Laid the tyrant Charles low.

And each stanza is followed by a chorus:

> Double, double, toil and trouble
> Make our brazen pulpit bubble.

As the last chorus ends "a monster huge" flies out of the pulpit—

> Its wings expanded dully flew,
> Scattering sharp corrosive dew.

Sedition springs up wherever this dew falls, and the wizards continue their song:

> We shall rejoice when good kings bleed,
> When to change administration
> We embroil the British nation,
> Holding kings in detestation
>   More firmly than our creed.
> But see, thro silver moonlight gliding,
> Horrid hags in triumph riding,
> Bringing news of joyful tiding,
>   From Discord's dreary dome.
> Lo they bring from coast Atlantic,
> Where fears ideal, yet gigantic,
> Have render'd a whole nation frantic,
>   The gentle Silverspoon.

> But now, that we open so splendid a vein,
> Our verse must assume an heroical strain,
> To you our Apostle, all hail, and all hail,
> Who with red flaming fire-brands a people assail.
> Sure no man (this century) has trumpeted further
> Our favourite causes of treason and murther;
> You have boldly supported the doctrine we hold
> "That our King and our God were made to be sold"
> We shall justify both by the gallant behaviour
> Of the people who murder'd their king and their Saviour.
> A king should be kill'd, says historic description,
> When his right to the throne is fix'd by prescription:
> Besides, shall we ever incur the disgrace,
>   To raise no rebellion for thirty years space?
>   To arms, to arms, sound Discord's alarms:
>   Our pen and our pulpit shall rouse us to arms.

One skips willingly several pages of similar verse, and at length finds the production ending with a song in celebration of the approaching downfall of "Thistle, Crown and Rose," due chiefly to the efforts of the American Apostle of Sedition.

President Witherspoon's writings of this period were not confined to sermons and addresses. It will be remembered that Dr. Jonathan Odell accused him of attempting to convert Tories languishing in patriot jails. There is no evidence that he followed so patient a procedure. On the contrary, two or three of his productions show feeling of just the opposite sort. His "Supplication of James Rivington"[25] is an alleged plea by the well-known Tory printer of New York for the protection of Congress when the British evacuated the city, and is full of the most biting satire. He had even less sympathy for turncoats, and therefore more personal still is his "Recantation of Benjamin Towne,"[26] printer of the *Pennsylvania Evening Post*, a newspaper for which the President used to write. This companion piece to the "Supplication" was composed in Aitken's bookshop at Philadelphia when Towne, on the return of Congress after the British left the city, asked Witherspoon to continue his contributions. The doctor refused, says Isaiah Thomas,[27] the historian of American printing, unless Towne, who had gone over to the British side, would publish an acknowledgment of his fault, make profession of repentance, and ask forgiveness of his fellow countrymen. Towne willingly agreed to print such a statement if Dr. Witherspoon would write it, whereupon the President dashed off the "Recantation." But Towne did not carry out the bargain and Dr. Witherspoon published the document in the *New York Packet*.[28]

Towne is represented as admitting that he used to print the *Pennsylvania Evening Post* and professed to be a firm friend of American liberty; that when the British took Philadelphia he turned completely around and called Congress and its adherents rebels, rascals, ragamuffins "and several other unsavoury names;" that now he wishes to turn once more in favor of the United States, "which are likely to be uppermost." He never pretended to be "a man of character, repute, or dignity," hence his change of sides is not surprising; had a Hancock or an Adams changed they would deserve no quarter; but to pass judgment on an obscure printer is "miserable reasoning." Therefore he suggests that he be not hanged. For after all, he printed for Congress purely from love of gain, not for love of liberty; he had no

[25] *Works*, vol. IV, p. 359.
[26] *Works*, vol. III, p. 607.
[27] *History of Printing in America*, vol. II, p. 75.
[28] Issue for October 1, 1778.

more regard for General Howe than for Congress, and it was not true that he had printed bigger lies for the British than for Congress; he should be given a chance to show what he can do. And he therefore concludes: "I do hereby recant, draw back, eat in, and swallow down every word that I have ever spoken, written, or printed to the prejudice of the United States of America."

Dr. Witherspoon's bitterest and boldest satire, however, was his *Caspipina's Catechism*, directed against the celebrated Rev. Jacob Duché, author of the *Caspipina Letters* and chaplain of Congress until the British reached Philadelphia when he, like Towne, became a supporter of the Crown. The *Catechism* was unpublished in Witherspoon's lifetime and is found among his papers now in the Library of Congress. According to Mr. Woods, who first printed it in part in his biography of the President, the latter was not suspected of its authorship. The complete text reads:

Question. Who is a Fop ?
Answer. The Rev. J. Duché.
Q. What is your Reason for that Opinion ?
A. Because he walks the Street in the Habit of a Clergyman with the Gestures of a *Petit Maître*.
Q. Who is a Turncoat ?
A. The Rev. Jacob Duché.
Q. What is your Reason for that Opinion ?
A. Because the late Chaplain of the Congress has entered with Zeal into the service of Sir Wm. Howe.
Q. Who is a Robber ?
A. The Rev. etc.
Q. What is, etc. ?
A. Because he pocketed the Money of the United States when of his own Shewing he was an Enemy to their Cause.
Q. Was he Singular in that Practice?
A. I do not say that he was, but though there are more Robbers than one, any Robber deserves the Gallows.
Q. Who is a Hypocrite ?
A. The Rev. etc.
Q. What is, etc. ?
A. Because he accepted his Office as Chaplain after the Declaration of Independence.

Q. Who is a Fool ?

A. The Rev. etc.

Q. What is, etc. ?

A. Because he attempted to Shew that his Conduct was not absurd and inconsistent.

Q. What else could he do ?

A. He should have alledged Necessity or confessed his Roguery.

Q. Who is a Blasphemer ?

A. The Rev. etc.

Q. What is, etc. ?

A. Because for a long Tract of Time he solemnly called upon Almighty God conscious of the Insincerity of his own Heart. A Citizen & Traitor is to blame, a Soldier & Traitor is a Rogue, a Chaplain & Traitor is a Blasphemer.

Q. Who is a Pedant ?

A. The Rev. etc.

Q. What is, etc. ?

A. We ought to judge thus of him from the Book which he published & all the Sermons which he preached, Yet ought we most chiefly so to do from his lofty & sonorous Congress Prayers against the british Tyrant.

Q. Who is a Sychophant ?

A. The Rev. etc.

Q. What is, etc. ?

A. Because he used to lick the Feet of Mr. Hancock & the New England Delegates whom he has abused.

Q. Who is a vain conceited Creature ?

A. The Rev. etc.

Q. What is, etc. ?

A. Because he thought he had Authority, Interest & Eloquence sufficient to persuade Gen. Washington to wound his own Honour & betray his Country's Cause.

Q. Who is a Liar ?

A. The Rev. etc.

Q. What is, etc.?

A. Because he affirms that the Committee's Acct. of their Conference with L. Howe is not true although it is justified by the London Gazette.

Q. Who is an Ass ?

A. The Rev. etc.

Q. What is, etc.?

A. Because he set his Name to his Letter. He was a Rogue to conceive it, a Coxcomb to write it, but an Ass to set his Name to it.

Q. How comes it that so many Inconsistencies meet in one Man ?

A. I can give no other Account of it but that if God Almighty has given a Man a topsy turvy understanding, no created Power will ever be able to set it right End uppermost.

Q. What was your Opinion of him before?

A. That he was a weak superficial—& his empty Flashes hardly merited Attention.

Q. What is your Opinion of him now ?

A. That he is a Wretch without Principle, without Parts, without Prudence, & that by an unexpected Effort he has crept up from the Ground Floor of Contempt to the first Story of Detestation.

PRESIDENT WITHERSPOON

VOLUME TWO

LONDON: HUMPHREY MILFORD

Oxford University Press

PRESIDENT

WITHERSPOON

A BIOGRAPHY

BY

VARNUM LANSING COLLINS

VOLUME TWO

PRINCETON

PRINCETON UNIVERSITY PRESS

1925

PRINTED AT THE PRINCETON UNIVERSITY PRESS
Princeton New Jersey United States of America

CONTENTS

VOLUME TWO

ILLUSTRATIONS

VOLUME TWO

PRESIDENT WITHERSPOON

VOLUME TWO

CHAPTER ONE

THE MEMBER OF CONGRESS

DR. WITHERSPOON left no journal or other personal record; his extant private letters are very few in number; and excepting a *Memorial of Facts* written by him, and now in the Library of Congress, describing the circumstances that led to the much discussed "Instructions" given in 1781 to the American commissioners for negotiating peace, comment of his own on his career in Congress is non-existent, and the story of his work as a member rests entirely on the barren *Journal* of that body, on the few speeches carefully prepared by him for important debates and preserved in his *Works*, and finally on allusions to, or summaries of, his remarks, found in the writings of his colleagues, the most useful being the notes of John Adams, Thomas Jefferson and Charles Thomson. The record of his share in congressional deliberations is therefore at times unavoidably scanty. To a certain extent his course after August, 1777, when it was decided to record yeas and nays on demand, may be followed in the tally of votes, but here one is necessarily suspicious that voting was sometimes governed by the exigencies of parliamentary tactics and not solely by the merits of the questions at issue.

Elected to Congress in June, 1776, to serve one year, he remained three years and a half, or until December, 1779; then at his urgent request released for the year 1780 by his constituents, he allowed himself to be returned for 1781, and finally in May, 1782, he was sent back again to serve until November.[1]

President Witherspoon had the good fortune to be in Congress during many important episodes of its early history; he voted for both the Resolution and the Declaration of Independence;

[1] The exact terms of Dr. Witherspoon's five years in Congress were the following: June 21, 1776, to serve one year; November 30, 1776, reelected under the state constitution to serve one year; November 20, 1777, reelected to serve one year or until December 1, 1778; November 6, 1778, reelected to serve one year or until December 1, 1779; November 24, 1780, reelected to serve one year from December 1, 1780; May 30, 1782, reelected to serve until November 5, 1782.

took active part in the succeeding debates on the Articles of Confederation; shared in the formation of the new government's foreign alliances; witnessed that government floundering in a bankruptcy of which he had given it plain warning; assisted in organizing the executive departments that superseded the earlier committee plan; was a leader in the discussion of the perplexing problem of the western lands, helping to prepare for future legislation on statesmanlike and non-provincial lines; and when peace with Great Britain was impending he was conspicuously prominent in directing the preliminaries in selecting the American commissioners, and actually dictated himself their most important instructions. In addition to these major concerns he was occupied with a multitude of lesser activities which may be classed under the head of humanitarian endeavors—such as the kindlier treatment of prisoners, the checking of cruelty in warfare, the better administration of military hospitals, the improvement of health and morals and therefore of discipline, in the army. It was to be expected also that for drafting fast-day and Thanksgiving Day proclamations and other appeals to the public consciousness, for the codification of parliamentary rules to govern congressional debates, or for the preparation of official publications such as the *Journal* of Congress, his experience and training should be largely drawn upon. Furthermore, he served on many interesting special committees appointed to act in emergencies outside the routine of congressional business and calling for particular tact and firmness, such as the capture of Henry Laurens by the British, the New Hampshire Grants controversy, and the mutiny of the Pennsylvania Line.

He was a member of three standing committees of which at least two—the Board of War and the Committee on Secret Correspondence, or Foreign Affairs—were of supreme importance, while to the other—that on Clothing for the Army—he at least brought good intentions and some knowledge of the weaving industry gained from his residence at Paisley. During the five years of his life as a Congressman he served on more than one hundred and twenty committees. The continuity and length of his attendance gave him an advantage of familiarity with past actions and circumstances which few others enjoyed and which

on more than one occasion was of distinct service to his colleagues.

His strong sense, says Judge Wharton, his resolute courage, his high
moral and religious tone, were of immense value. He at once saw the
necessity of a strong executive, both in the military and civil side of
the government, and he uniformly gave his support to whatever
measures were calculated to strengthen Washington and to sustain
Franklin, and afterward Livingston and Morris. Of the necessity of a
punctilious fulfilment of our obligations to France he was a firm
champion; and perhaps his Scotch blood may have added somewhat
to his conscientiousness and his tenderness in whatever related to our
dealings with France.[2]

To trace his congressional career in detail is needless and this
chapter will endeavour to follow only the main lines of service to
which President Witherspoon devoted himself—the stabilizing
of the national government, the solution of its internal and in
particular its financial problems, the creation of its international
status, and the direction of the preliminaries to the peace it won.
If here and there the narrative shall touch upon matters of less
public concern, it will be only because they supply to the portrait this book attempts to draw their measure of the human
values in which the President's personality was so rich.

His name appears in the *Journal* of Congress for the first time
on June 28, 1776, when Francis Hopkinson presented the credentials of the New Jersey delegates; it is not found again until October 2 when he received his first committee appointment. Although he was not given any responsibilities during the summer,
he was no mere onlooker. As shown in the preceding chapter, he
spoke on the resolution of independence and voted on July 2; he
protested against certain phrases in the original draft of the
the declaration of July 4, and secured the deletion of at least one
objectionable sentence, and in the debate on the Articles of Confederation his definite convictions quickly found utterance.
While he firmly believed in a strong central executive, as Judge
Wharton has intimated, he nevertheless was just as insistent on
the rights of the individual States and on their equality under

[2] *Diplomatic Correspondence*, vol. II, p. 470.

the confederation, steadily opposing any action which would give one State undue advantage over another. If he was a champion of France in foreign affairs, in domestic affairs he was no less the champion of the smaller Colonies or "landless" States, those which held no claim to vast territories west of the mountains, the ultimate disposal of which lay behind so much of contemporary discussion and action.

His course in the debate on the Articles of Confederation was typical of this attitude. When in July, 1776, the committee appointed to prepare articles brought in a draft, Dr. Witherspoon at once figured in the discussion that ensued. In connection with Article XI, proportioning to population the money quota to be paid by each State into the common treasury, he gave it as his opinion, says Mr. Jefferson, that the true barometer of a nation's wealth is to be found in the value of its lands and houses and not in its population; any estimate based on population was imperfect of itself and unequal between the States. It had been argued, he said, that negroes ate the food of freemen and therefore should be taxed; but horses ate the food of freemen and therefore they too should be taxed. It had been asserted, he continued, that by counting slaves in the estimate for taxes Congress was proposing to do no more than the States themselves did—slaves being always estimated in the tax levies. But the cases were not parallel, for in the Southern States slaves were ubiquitous, whereas they were not so found in the North. Finally, the original resolution of Congress to proportion quotas according to population was a temporary measure and related to monies heretofore emitted, whereas the States were now entering into a new compact and were standing on fresh unbroken ground. But he could not at this time induce his hearers to agree with him and the Article went back to the house unchanged.

His first stand for the landless states was made when Article XVII came up giving each State but one vote. Franklin had warmly opposed the Article; he wished the vote to be according to the taxable population; let the smaller Colonies pay the same quotas as the larger, he is reported to have said, and then they shall vote equally; but if they received an equal vote without bearing equal financial burden he for one believed a confederation based upon what, according to Mr. Adams, he called "so iniquitous a principle" was doomed to short life. He cited the history of England and Scotland; at the time of the Union Scotland had made the same objection that the smaller States were making now; whereas experience had proved that no unfairness had ever resulted to Scotland; her advocates had prophesied that as in times of old the whale would swallow Jonah, but he thought the prediction had been reversed in the event and Jonah had swallowed the whale, "for the Scotch had in fact got possession of the government and gave laws to the English." He regretted the original agreement of Congress to vote by Colonies and was for voting in all cases according to the number of taxables.[3]

Dr. Witherspoon rose at once to the double bait of Biblical and Scottish allusions, and the more quickly because he was opposed to Franklin's general view, however important the grain of truth lurking in his allusion to Scottish infiltration of English politics. Following his custom, and in anticipation of the difficulty of harmonizing so many varying opinions of what the confederation should be, he had prepared a speech on the necessity of such a compact and was watching for an opportunity to deliver it. Franklin's reference to the futility of the present fundamental Article gave him his chance. The opening portion of the speech is in his *Works*[4]; it is summarized at some length by Jefferson[5] and briefly by Adams,[6] both Jefferson and Adams indicating that in the debate Dr. Witherspoon added extemporaneously to his prepared remarks. In spite of Franklin's assertion that a confederacy based on equal votes without equal burdens would not last, President Witherspoon opposed any alteration of the Article and believed a lasting confederation would be made. To confess it unlikely was to dampen the ardor of the people and weaken their hands.

I confess, said he, it would to me greatly diminish the glory and importance of the struggle, whether considered as for the rights of man-

[3]Jefferson, *Writings*, I, 44, 46; Adams, *Works*, vol. II, pp. 496, 501.
[4]Vol. IV, p. 253.
[5]*Writings*, vol. I, p. 47.
[6]*Works*, vol. II, pp. 496, 500, 501.

kind in general, or for the prosperity and happiness of this continent in future times. What would it signify to risk our possessions and shed our blood to get ourselves free from the encroachments and oppression of Great Britain, with a certainty, as soon as peace was settled with them, of a more lasting war, a more unnatural, more bloody, and much more hopeless war among the colonies themselves?

Some of us, he declared, consider ourselves as acting for posterity at present, having little expectation of living to see all things fully settled and the good consequences of liberty taking effect. But how much more uncertain the hope of seeing the internal conflicts of the colonies settled upon a lasting and equitable footing!

The chief danger lay at present, he believed, in dissension among the Colonies and bribery from outside. But what a force would be added to the arguments of seducers if they could say with truth that sooner or later "we might be subjected, the greatest part of us, to the power of one or more of the strongest or largest of the American States?" If the Colonies were to be independent States, separate and disunited after this war, "we may be sure of coming off for the worse."

Citing the Helots of Sparta and the fate of the Roman provinces as examples in his contention that the weaker inevitably became the vassals of the more powerful, he named in illustration of his preference the East India Company which voted by individuals and not by proportion of stock, and the Provinces of the Netherlands which also voted individually. In questions of war, said he, the smaller States were as much interested as the larger and therefore should have equal voice. As for Franklin's historical allusions, he declared that the union between England and Scotland was an incorporating and not a federal union, and Scotland had suffered in that her inhabitants had been drawn from her by hopes of places of employment; nor was it an instance of equality of representation, because while Scotland was allowed nearly one-thirteenth of representation her people paid only one-fortieth of the land tax. But whatever differences of opinion as to details might exist he insisted that a confederation be agreed to quickly. There would never again be an opportunity like the present one when common danger gave a common ground of union.

If we shall find it impossible to agree upon the terms of this confederacy, what madness is it to suppose that there will ever be a time, or that circumstances will so change, as to make it even probable that it will be done at an after season? . . . So certain is this, that I look upon it as on the repentance of a sinner—every day's delay, though it adds to the necessity, yet augments the difficulty and takes from the inclination.

What if the confederacy were later altered or did not last? Shall we establish nothing good, he demanded, because we know it cannot be eternal? Shall we live without government because every constitution has its old age and its period? Because we know that we shall die, shall we take no pains to preserve or lengthen life? Nay, rather, "it only requires the more watchful attention to settle government upon the best principles and in the wisest manner that it may last as long as the nature of things will admit."

And then came this strikingly forward-looking conclusion which the speaker begged leave to present, though at the risk, as he said, of being called "visionary and romantic:"

I do expect, Mr. President, a progress, as in every other human art, so in the order and perfection of human society, greater than we have yet seen; and why should we be wanting to ourselves in urging it forward? . . . There have been great improvements not only in human knowledge but in human nature, the progress of which can be easily traced in history. Everybody is able to look back to the time in Europe when the liberal sentiments that now prevail upon the rights of conscience would have been looked upon as absurd. It is but a little above two hundred years since that enlarged system called the balance of power took place; and I maintain that it is a greater step from the former disunited and hostile situation of kingdoms and states to their present condition, than it would be from their present condition, to a state of more perfect and lasting union. It is not impossible that in future times all the states in one quarter of the globe may see it proper by some plan of union to perpetuate security and peace; and sure I am a well planned confederacy among the states of America may hand down the blessings of peace and public order to many generations. . . . Every argument of honor, interest, safety, and necessity, conspires in pressing us to a confederacy, and if it be

seriously attempted I hope, by the blessing of God upon our endeavours, that it will be happily accomplished.

Dr. Witherspoon's conception of the doctrine of the Balance
of Power as evidence of the improvement of human nature may
be open to question, and his belief in the theory of human per-
fectibility is somehow difficult to reconcile with Scottish theology as the wayfaring man understands it; but at least his vision
of an international union for the perpetuation of security and
peace in one quarter of the globe is a flash of idealism, as unexpected as it is interesting, in a mind hitherto so sternly practical.
It marks a new phase in the President's thought, developed since
taking sides in the American quarrel.

A year later Congress was still debating Article XVII and on
the afternoon of October 7, 1777, the old arguments on representation were once more advanced; but Dr. Witherspoon clung to
his point and fought proposals to allot one vote to each 50,000
white inhabitants, or to each 30,000; he opposed a substitute
that votes be based on taxes levied and paid; and finally when
the original form of the article was reported—each State to have
but one vote—he at last recorded himself in the affirmative and
had the satisfaction of seeing his position adopted.

A week after this when Article IX was debated again and it
was moved that the share of public expenses to be borne by each
State be proportioned to the value of all land within each State
granted to or surveyed to any person according as such land and
its improvements should be estimated under whatever plan Congress might direct, President Witherspoon voted with the Southern members in the affirmative and successfully against the New
Englanders, whose eyes were set on their western claims. That
afternoon his jealousy for the smaller States came to the front
once more when it was proposed that no State be represented by
less than two nor more than seven members. Here he voted on
the negative and losing side. It is plain that he felt that the time
would come, as indeed it did come within the month, when New
Jersey might find herself with only one representative present
and he did not propose to lose that solitary voice.

The same watchfulness for the interests of the weaker members of the confederation is evident in his vote on Article XIV. He opposed the attempt made to compel each State to place before Congress a description of its territory and a summary of the grants and treaties on which that territory was claimed, so that the Articles of Confederation might lay down the territorial jurisdiction of each State. He opposed at this time the attempt to authorize the United States to fix the western boundaries of States claiming to the Mississippi, and to lay out new States in the territory beyond the boundaries as circumstances and population might require. He could not admit the premised claims to the western land and he felt that the whole subject would better be postponed until it could be taken up as a separate problem and settled equitably for all. And it was because of the same fundamental position that he refused for the present to agree to the proposition that the United States in Congress assembled should be the last court of resort in boundary disputes and that the procedure in case of such disputes should now be laid down. He asserted that Congress was not yet in a position to assume such a responsibility.

On the other hand he was just as sure of himself regarding the specific rights of the central executive authority. When it was moved later in the same month that no treaty of commerce be made whereby the legislative powers of the respective states should be restrained from imposing such duties as foreigners or their own people were subjected to, he voted with the minority against what he deemed an encroachment on federal prerogative.

President Witherspoon was absent during November, 1777, and therefore did not witness the adoption of the Articles of Confederation.

His speech in July, 1776, on the confederation had indicated his trust in the potential destiny of the new government. A few weeks later—in September—he gave additional evidence of his firm belief in its permanency, in a speech delivered in opposition to any consideration of reconciliation with Great Britain until the independence of the Colonies was formally acknowledged,[7]

[7] *Works*, vol. IV, p. 245.

which with him was a fundamental premise in all dealings with Great Britain and the other continental powers.

It will be remembered that Lord Howe had arrived from England with a curiously ill-fashioned olive branch. When he capped the climax of a blundering policy by sending General Sullivan to invite Congress to a conference, President Witherspoon opposed acceptance of the invitation. He could not be deceived as to the real object in view—the unconditional surrender of the Colonies; Lord Howe had not yielded one iota; he had not given General Washington his title; he would not treat with Congress as such but had sent a prisoner to tell the colonial representatives that he would be glad to confer with them as private gentlemen; in his eyes they were still rebellious British subjects. What advantage then, asked the President, is there in such a conference? None; for everyone is agreed that we cannot admit a thought of yielding independence. This has been called boasting, while our troops are fleeing before the redcoats; but, continued he, "I found my hopes of success in this cause not on the valor of the Americans or the cowardice of the British, but on the justice of the cause." He rather wondered at the success of the American arms up to this time. Lord Howe spoke as if the contest would be decided by one blow; which was a prodigious mistake—the President instanced the Scottish rebellion of 1745 when the British broke and fled at Prestonpans, and he recollected that he had seen the same thing happen at Falkirk. There was nothing to fear from the first few engagements; on the contrary, Lord Howe had made a tactical error in proposing a conference at this late date—it really looked as if he were afraid. The improbability of the conference leading to peace was shown by several arguments of which he would mention only one, Lord Howe's explicit declaration that he would not acknowledge American independence. There was a time when the Colonies were contending for the restoration of certain principles under the government of Great Britain and were praying for reunion, but early in July they had declared themselves free and independent. Shall this question be re-opened, he demanded. The acknowledgment of independence is a first and indispensable preliminary, and the fact that it is not so recognized by all shows that we have not yet acquired the whole idea or habit of independence. Lord Howe himself had said that the Declaration of Independence had rendered his mission abortive—he wished he had arrived ten days earlier. Obviously, any conference with him under present conditions would inevitably compromise the action of July 2.

It had been asserted, however, that the conference was advisable in order to show the public that we were ready to hear anything that might lead to peace. Now, said the President, the contemporary American public consisted of three classes—Tories, Whigs, and the army. Naturally the Tories desired the conference; they were already presuming on it; the proposal had given them renewed vigor, and in cases where the expediency of any measure was doubtful, if he had an opportunity of knowing what his enemies wished him to do, he would on general principles do the opposite. As for the Whigs, multitudes are clear that no conference should be held and those who are in doubt need only to learn the full circumstances to be of the same opinion. As for the army, nothing is more likely to deaden its patriotism; it would impute the conduct of Congress to fear and jealousy; a timorous and despondent spirit would be produced and thus only add to present discouragement.

But in spite of these plain words, and many like them, that fell from other lips in Congress, the conference was held, with what result everyone knows. In Lord Howe's presence Franklin and Adams found excellent occasion for a little courteous sarcasm, and the war proceeded.

A month later President Witherspoon was appointed on his first congressional committee, a minor appointment, but one that must have had singular appeal to him as a Jersey farmer and the owner of valuable live stock. He found himself one of three members to consider plans for providing wagons for public service so that any demands might be speedily complied with and oppression of private persons be effectually prevented. On this committee's report it was agreed that quartermasters in each department be ordered to avoid as much as possible impressing horses and vehicles and that as soon as service would admit they return all horses and vehicles impressed and that no violence be done any persons, or their property, who came to camp voluntarily to sell provisions or for other purposes.

On the same date Congress resolved to increase the standing committee on clothing and President Witherspoon was chosen as one of the additional members. This was his first appointment to a standing committee. Subsequently he was able to turn the matter of clothing for the troops to the advantage of a protégé, James Finley, a Paisley weaver who had emigrated from Scotland and had settled at Princeton. To him Dr. Witherspoon gave the use of a vacant floor in Nassau Hall to fill his contracts with the state clothier for New Jersey.

Meanwhile a far more important appointment was awaiting the President. Vergennes, the French foreign minister, had for months been counselling his royal master at Versailles to aid the revolting American Colonies secretly, for political motives, and at last in May, 1776, Louis XVI had authorized the transfer of funds for the purchase of supplies for the Colonies through the interesting medium of Hortalez et Cie., or in other words through Beaumarchais. By midsummer in 1776, Silas Deane had already reached France on a mission to secure a loan and supplies; instructions to further commissioners from Congress were agreed upon; in September, Franklin and Jefferson were appointed with Deane, and when Jefferson declined, Arthur Lee, then in England, had been given Jefferson's place. With Franklin going abroad and other changes taking place in the personnel of Congress, the Committee on Secret Correspondence found itself in need of enlargement, and on October 11, 1776, with Richard Henry Lee and William Hooper, President Witherspoon was added to the committee. As a member of this committee, when it presently became the Committee on Foreign Affairs, he was to perform his greatest service in Congress. Dr. Franklin himself carried to Deane and Dumas the first letters written abroad by the reorganized committee, with Dr. Witherspoon as a signer, informing them individually of Franklin's appointment with Lee, and announcing the new membership of the committee.

President Witherspoon was a warm admirer of Dr. Franklin and throughout the latter's difficult years of service abroad was

his staunch friend and supporter at home against the petty jeal-
ousies that sought often to deprive him of his place as tacit head
of the American mission in Europe. Careful scrutiny of the votes
in the *Journal* of Congress shows that Dr. Witherspoon carried
into the young republic's diplomacy his adherence to the idea of
centralized authority, advocating a system with one central diplomatic executive, while other members of the committee continually strove for individual envoys responsible directly to Congress under a de-centralized system.[8]

The situation in Congress during the winter of 1776 is briefly
summarized by Dr. Witherspoon in his *Memorial of Facts*. In his
opinion, looking back over the whole course of events, the Colonies were never in more critical situation than in December,
1776, when Congress left Philadelphia on the approach of the
British and went to Baltimore. There was never greater need for,
nor greater anxiety to obtain, foreign aid. Membership in Congress had shrunk and the outlook was worse than dark, but Dr.
Witherspoon did not remember "one word of despondency to
have fallen from any member or the most distant hint of a desire
to make submission to England; but the means of persuading
France to interpose effectually were the great subject of deliberation and discussion." It had been already growing clear to the
commission in France that secret aid through commercial channels was insufficient for the purposes of the Colonies, and acting
on their own judgment they were soon to propose a formal alliance, without waiting for instructions. Meanwhile on this side of
the Atlantic, Congress had been coming to the same view. The
reasoning as recorded by Dr. Witherspoon in his *Memorial* is
that it was plain the Colonies could not be supported without
foreign aid; there was no country except France to which application with any probability of success could be made; she
was disposed to assist but we had given her no sufficient inducement to intervene; proposals to offer France exclusive trade
or freedom from imposts were discarded as contrary to the spirit
of independence which meant independence not only from Great
Britain, but from every other nation; the reasons for France's
delay in assisting America were believed to be due to other

[8] Wharton, *Diplomatic Correspondence*, vol. I, p. 461.

causes. Dispatches from France strengthening these views, at length, the day before Christmas, 1776, at Baltimore, a special committee of which the President was a member, was appointed to draw up a definite plan for securing the additional foreign assistance so desperately needed. On the twenty-eighth, the very day that the American commissioners at Paris were receiving their first formal audience with Vergennes, this special committee reported and its plan was immediately debated, Congress sitting also the following day, a Sunday, and finally adopting on the thirtieth the plan to send commissioners to Vienna, Spain, Prussia and the Grand Duchy of Tuscany; to induce France to assist the United States openly for certain considerations; and to have the commission to France prepare treaties of commerce and alliance with Spain and Russia.

What part Dr. Witherspoon had in the discussions that led to the steps outlined in the preceding paragraph is not known; but it is safe to assume that his *Memorial of Facts* fairly represents the point of view he advocated, and that he supported vigorously the new instructions that were immediately dispatched to the commissioners at Paris.

Busy though it may have been, the Committee on Secret Correspondence had not absorbed all his time during that winter, and we may consider for a moment some of his other activities. Early in November, 1776, he received leave of absence to take to Princeton for safe-keeping four prisoners recently arrived in Philadelphia, a congressional action difficult to explain save on the supposition that the prisoners were Scotsmen—two at least bore Scottish names—in whom Dr. Witherspoon was interested, and that he paroled them, offering himself as surety and putting them to work on his farm at Princeton.[9] Reference has been made to the large share of committee work dealing with prisoners that fell to his lot. In December, 1776, he was deputed to investigate the case of loyalist prisoners from New Jersey with the result that a number were released from jail; in January and February, 1777, in August, 1781, and July and August, 1782, similar assignments were given him. In January, 1778, he was

[9] In January, 1777, he was allowed expenses for two prisoners he had been supporting at Princeton; and later he had a farmhand who was a former British soldier.

appointed chairman of a committee to prepare a manifesto on the treatment American prisoners were receiving at the hand of the enemy, and in March of the same year he offered himself as surety for two British officers, prisoners at Princeton, who desired passes to New York or Philadelphia in order to arrange exchanges for themselves. During the war, Princeton, besides sheltering a military hospital, was also a prison camp, and references to the President's dealings with individuals detained there are constantly turning up, invariably in the way of amelioration of conditions. It appears to have been agreed by his congressional colleagues that his experience as governor of a body of young but chronic objectors at college had in some subtle way equipped him for settling the very real grievances of older and more genuine captives.

It was probably for a similar reason that he was given so much committee work dealing with discipline in the army. In view of the disastrous campaign of 1776 and the consequent thinning out of Washington's army, Congress appointed in November a committee of three, among whom was Dr. Witherspoon, to repair to headquarters and assist General Washington in filling up his ranks, and at the same time to make particular enquiry why the troops were not being paid and to redress to the utmost of their power the just grievances of the soldiers. The committee was further charged to enquire into alleged abuses in the medical department and report to Congress. What the committee did at headquarters does not appear; but they lost little time in instituting reforms at Princeton where a hospital was being maintained. Two days after setting out for camp they had appointed an assistant quartermaster and a commissary to take care of the military stores sent to Princeton and especially to look after the sick. They reported to Congress January 4, 1777, on their doings and the report was referred to the Medical Committee.

President Witherspoon's most delicate mission in connection with the morale of the army was performed when the Pennsylvania Line mutinied in 1781 and he was made head of a congressional committee of mediation. He had the good sense to allow General Joseph Reed, President of Pennsylvania, to treat directly with the mutineers—they were encamped at Princeton on the edge of the college campus—and to accept his findings, acting only in an advisory capacity.[10] The detailed report of the committee is in Dr. Witherspoon's handwriting and was delivered in Congress on January 24. The disturbance, he wrote in concluding, however unhappy and threatening at first had now afforded an undeniable and pleasing proof of the firm attachment of the soldiers and of the country in general to the American cause; notwithstanding the hardships the army had suffered, and the Pennsylvania Line in particular, there was not the least appearance or evidence of concert with the enemy nor any disposition to listen to overtures from that quarter. The committee suggested that British deserters be prevented from enlisting in the American service and recommended that every State be urged to pay the strictest attention to supplying the wants of the army. Less stereotyped was a further comment: "The inferior officers of the army should be directed in their treatment of the soldiers never to separate severity from justice and to temper severity with mercy." At this point the college president seems to have been reminded by his unacademic fellow-members that a congressional committee report was not the best medium for the expression of abstract principles; and the paragraph was ruthlessly stricken from the version finally presented.

Immediately after his reelection to Congress in November, 1776, Dr. Witherspoon had been appointed chairman of a committee to prepare an address to the inhabitants of America and a recommendation to the States for a day of fasting, humiliation, and prayer. The confusion and alarm caused by the approach of the enemy is plainly reflected in the numerous and hurried resolutions of Congress during the week of December 9, and the committee presented the address within twenty-four hours, and on the next day its recommendation for a fast. The address is framed especially "to excite the inhabitants of Pennsylvania, New Jersey and the adjacent States to an immediate and spirited

---

[10] According to Alexander Garden (*Anecdotes of the American Revolution*, 2d series, p. 213), when the committee was first considering its procedure in the matter, Dr. Witherspoon said he would commence by giving the mutineers a sermon—"religious admonition might be attended with powerful effect." But the suggestion did not appeal to his colleagues.

exertion in opposition to the army that now threatens to take possession of this city" (Philadelphia). No manuscript copy of either document is to be found among the Papers of the Continental Congress but style and temper of the recommendation as published strongly indicate that Dr. Witherspoon was its author.

Whereas, the war in which the United States are engaged with Great Britain, has not only been prolonged, but is likely to be carried to the greatest extremity; and whereas, it becomes all public bodies, as well as private persons, to reverence the Providence of God, and look up to him as the supreme disposer of all events, and the arbiter of the fate of nations; therefore,

Resolved that it be recommended to all the United States, as soon as possible, to appoint a day of solemn fasting and humiliation; to implore of Almighty God the forgiveness of the many sins prevailing among all ranks, and to beg the countenance and assistance of his Providence in the prosecution of the present just and necessary war.

The Congress do also, in the most earnest manner, recommend to all the members of the United States, and particularly the officers civil and military under them, the exercise of repentance and reformation; and further, require of them the strict observation of the articles of war, and particularly, that part of the said articles, which forbids profane swearing, and all immorality, of which all such officers are desired to take notice.

It is left to each State to issue out proclamations fixing the days that appear most proper within their several bounds.

Tory cynics were accustomed to allege that the high moral tone of this and similar resolutions of Congress were not ingenuous but were planned for effect. It is related that one such observer remarked, when Washington forbade card playing in the army, that the American rebels like all other rebels claimed especial favors from Providence and seldom issued a proclamation "without a pious sentence bringing up the rear." But, continued this gentleman, however easily General Washington "may bait old Witherspoon . . . and some of the other pious ones who are hanging on the rear of his moral forces, when the time comes he'll find he can't fool the Lord with pretended piety or Presbyterian general orders." This choice bit of militant moral criticism in Moore's *Diary of the Revolution* broaches the old question as to how far "Presbyterian general orders" or other moral forces played a part in the conduct of the Revolution, a question which it is not the province of this book to consider further than to point out that to Dr. Witherspoon the American Revolution was quite as much a moral movement as the struggle between the Popular and the Moderate parties in the Scottish Church had been. It can hardly be out of place, however, to add that while he never claimed Presbyterian responsibility for the Revolution yet these pages set forth at least the story of the significant share that he, a leader of that denomination in America, had in making the claim so plausible.[11] And it is surely unnecessary at this stage of the narrative to do more than suggest that, baited or not, President Witherspoon did his own thinking and hardly depended on Washington or anyone else for his conclusions.[12] Typical as this slur is of much contemporary misunderstanding and intentional misrepresentation of Dr. Witherspoon's actions, it is nevertheless a striking commentary on the spiritual qualities of many official public documents of the period; and in those which the President and "other pious ones" helped to compose in the next few years, the crusty British officer quoted above doubtless found little cause to change his opinion of what might be termed Congressional proclamatory style.

The British military successes in the campaign of 1776, which had made Vergennes in France stay his hand and had driven Congress from Philadelphia in December, gave President Witherspoon a task of which the fulfilment swept the country with a wave of indignation at the facts presented. Reports of the conduct of the enemy in its victorious campaign through New York

[11] The question has been discussed with his usual brilliance and charm by Trevelyan in his *American Revolution*, part II, vol. I, chap. XVI, and is treated in Dr. W. P. Breed's little book *Presbyterians and the Revolution*, the seventh chapter of which on "Presbyterian zeal and suffering" is composed chiefly of a quotation from the tenth chapter of Gillett's *History of the Presbyterian Church*, vol. I, and reads like a catalogue of eighteenth century Princetonians.
[12] As illustrating his fearless independence of mind may be cited an incident in April, 1779, when the appointment of a French officer as inspector of Southern troops came before Congress. Dr. Witherspoon alone of thirty-one members of Congress voted in the affirmative.

and New Jersey had reached Congress, and in January, 1777, a committee was appointed to institute enquiry and take testimony. The committee, of which the President was the most active member, proceeded at once to New Jersey and made Princeton its headquarters. Its report delivered in April was spread on the minutes and ordered published in the newspapers in full, with the affidavits.[13] Much of the actual testimony was gathered by Dr. Witherspoon himself and is in his handwriting, the documents being still among the Papers of the Continental Congress; and he wrote most if not all of the report. Congress later voted that four thousand copies of the latter be printed in English and two thousand in German for distribution through the States, but no copy is known to exist and it is doubtful that the report was ever so published.[14]

Congressional life even in those dark days had its occasional hours of relaxation and Mr. Adams' diary gives us one or two glimpses of his New Jersey colleague in lighter mood. At Baltimore in February, 1777, for example, he was a dinner guest at Mr. Lux's estate "Chatworth," about half a mile out of town where his host "lived like a prince." A little later on a Saturday night at "Mrs. Page's over the bridge" he was one of a group consisting of the two Princetonians, Dr. Rush and Jonathan D. Sergeant, the two Lees, Mr. John Adams, Dr. Brownson and Elbridge Gerry, who had supper together in a room with George III's picture hanging on the wall upside down, a contemporary Baltimorean fashion, says Mr. Adams, in families that owned a copy of the monarch's portrait. Under this "topsy turvy king" at Mrs. Page's were tacked lines whose conclusion ran as follows:

---

[13] See *New Jersey Archives*, 2 ser., vol. I, pp. 347, 363, for examples.

[14] Mr. Ford, *Journal*, vol. IX, p. 1085, has noted an interesting comment by Franklin in a letter to David Hartley, February 2, 1780, in which he states he was expected to make a school reader of the report with illustrations, but balked at the idea. Aside from the general reprehensibility of the enemy's conduct, Dr. Witherspoon's personal activity had been enlisted by the fact that New Jersey had suffered most by enemy conduct. The whole matter had come to a head in the brutal murder of the Reverend John Rosborough, a chaplain in the Continental Army and a graduate of Princeton in the Class of 1761. Governor Livingston of New Jersey addressed his legislature on the subject in February, 1777. (*New Jersey Archives*, 2d ser., vol. I p. 301.)

PRESIDENT WITHERSPOON

                              —See his head
          Placed where the meanest of his subjects tread.
          Like Lucifer the giddy tyrant fell;
          He lifts his feet to Heav'n, but points his head to Hell.

The talk that evening in the presence of upset royalty must have
been as "high" as on that morning in September, 1774, around
Dr. Shippen's breakfast table at Philadelphia. The next day
President Witherspoon preached on the edifying text "redeem-
ing the time," with some of his fellow Congressmen among his
hearers. The effort is not included in his collected writings but
Mr. Adams' comment as usual is interesting:

An excellent sermon. I find that I understand the Doctor better since
I have heard him so much in conversation and in the Senate; but I
perceive that his attention to civil affairs has slackened his memory;
it cost him more pains than heretofore to recollect his discourse.[15]

The sermon was unquestionably an old one and it should have
occurred to Mr. Adams that in view of the preceding night's con-
viviality the preacher had scarcely had sufficient opportunity to
review his notes—if he possessed any.

    Whether or not Dr. Witherspoon grew a little rusty in the pul-
pit as a result of his new occupations, he seems to have been at
no loss when lecturing to his colleagues in Congress on the elements of economics. Dr. Rush in his *Historical Notes*[16] has recorded some of the President's views on the subject. Congress
was debating in November, 1779, whether it should recommend
to the States the plan for fixing the prices of labor, manufactures,
imports, and provisions, which had been adopted by a convention of four New England States. Dr. Witherspoon opposed the
proposal. The enemy he said, had published the Connecticut
Act for Regulating Prices, as it was called, to show in what distress the Colonies found themselves and he for one always
avoided doing the things an enemy wished him to do. To recom-

[15] *Works*, vol. II, p. 435.
[16] *Pennsylvania Magazine*, vol. XXVII, pp. 137, 140.

mend the adoption of the Act to all the States would be to spread further the impression of distress. Prices would be just if the quantity of money and the scarcity of supplies bore an exact proportion to one another; the increase of prices began first with luxuries, next with necessaries, third with manufactures, and then with grain; and the reason that grain was last was because it was plentiful compared with money. It is beyond the power of despotic princes, said the President, to regulate prices; laws are not almighty; tea and salt are higher in proportion to other commodities because the supply is more limited; in Pennsylvania salt was regulated at fifteen shillings per bushel, but was sold at sixty; in Virginia, where there was no limitation, it sold at ten. If the price of one commodity were regulated, he declared that Congress would have to regulate the price of all. As a matter of fact, Congress exempted only salt and military stores from limitation of price. Salt being "of indispensable necessity to all ranks of people and often difficult to be procured," it was recommended that "well disposed and public spirited" citizens who were "blessed with plenty and affluence" form voluntary associations to procure "a plentiful supply of the said article" and to reduce its price, "that the poor may be furnished therewith on the most reasonable terms"—a recommendation that curiously anticipates, at least in spirit, the measures taken to meet the scarcity of certain staples during the period of the recent World War, and one that obtained as little real success.

The views on price-fixing which Dr. Witherspoon expressed in this debate, he advanced at greater length and anonymously as a "Jersey Farmer" in a letter to General Washington on the latter's plan for a market in camp.[17] He was disappointed in the plan because it proposed to fix prices, and he set forth arguments against the proposal not very different from those used by modern antagonists of government price-fixing.

Fixing the price of commodities has been attempted by law in several states among us, and it has increased the evil it was meant to remedy, as the same practice ever has done since the beginning of the world.

[17] *Works*, vol. IV, p. 281.

To punish men for selling at higher prices than legal, and to confiscate their goods if they will not sell at all, has some meaning to it though little wisdom; but to publish a list of fixed prices as an encouragement to a weekly market is a new strain of policy indeed. If people are willing to sell at these or lower prices is not that enough? If they are not willing to sell how shall they be made willing to come to the market? Perhaps the prices listed were believed to be reasonable, but what constitutes a reasonable price? If it be that which is proportioned to the demand on the one side and the plenty or scarcity of goods on the other, I agree to it; but I affirm that this will fix of itself by the consent of the buyer and seller better than it can be done by any politician upon earth. If Washington meant anything else, it would not matter whether it was reasonable or not; for if it is not *agreeable* as well as reasonable, you might have one market day, but not a second.

There are some things, continued the Jersey Farmer, which are not the object of human laws, and such are all those that essentially depend for their success upon inward inclination. . . . It would be much to the advantage of many lawgivers and other persons in authority if they would carefully distinguish between what is effected by force and what by persuasion, and never preposterously mix these opposite principles and defeat the operation of both. Laws and authority compel; but it is reason and interest that must persuade.

Price-fixing by authority is not only impolitic but it is in itself unreasonable and absurd; so many circumstances are to be taken into account to secure equality or justice that they cannot all be attended to—the plenty of one kind of provision and the scarcity of another, the distance of one place and the nearness of another, changes of conditions in the course of a few days or weeks, good or bad roads, good or bad weather—these and a hundred other things which cannot be foreseen actually govern "and ought to govern" prices at markets. . . . if "tenpence per pound is a just price for veal at present I am certain it must be too much a month hence when veal will be much more plentiful; and the grass not yet come on. . . . If it is reasonable to pay one shilling per pound for any meat on a good day, I shall expect more if I go out in a storm; if not, I will stay at home on a bad day, and so you must starve one week and pamper the next."

"Such are restraining circumstances. He who is nearest and has goods in plenty, by selling cheap will moderate the demands of him who comes from far. If you pay very dear for an article one day, the news spreading brings in large quantities and the price falls; and so it happens in every case. Thus it is out of one's power to tell what is a reasonable price and by attempting to do it we not only refuse to gratify expectations but treat them with injustice. To fix the prices of goods, especially provisions in a market, is as impracticable as it is unreasonable."

The year 1777 had dawned hopefully enough with the success at Princeton following close on the surprise at Trenton, but the occupation of New Jersey by the enemy had spelled its devastation. It was not surprising then that in February the President asked for a brief leave of absence; "Tusculum" has been occupied by the British, and "the situation of his private affairs," he said, "required his returning home." Soon after his reappearance, Congress voted that the Committee on Secret Correspondence be henceforth called the Committee for Foreign Affairs, and that it have a secretary. Thereupon Mr. John Adams nominated Thomas Paine, supposing him "a ready writer and an industrious man."[18] To this appointment, Dr. Witherspoon immediately objected with an earnestness that surprised Adams. He gave his reasons: he knew Paine and his writings; when he first came over he was on the other side of the controversy; he had later been employed by Robert Aitken and, following the tide of popularity, had turned to the side of the Colonies; he was very intemperate and could not write "until he had quickened his thought with large draughts of rum and water; in short, he was a bad character and not fit to be placed in such a situation." No one, says Mr. Adams, confirmed Dr. Witherspoon's criticism at the time "though the truth of it has since been sufficiently established." According to Mr. John Jay,[19] Paine, as Aitken's reader for the *Pennsylvania Magazine*, in which Dr. Witherspoon had more than a mere contributor's interest, had struck out several passages in articles by the Doctor as being "too free." Apparently Dr. Witherspoon's views had been further advanced than those of the editor. Mr. Jay alleged moreover that Paine's attachment to the American cause was under suspicion more than

---

[18] *Life and Works*, vol. II, p. 509. The date is erroneously given as 1775 or "not long after." The incident took place April 17, 1777.
[19] William Jay, *Life of John Jay*, vol. I, p. 97.

once until his indiscreet revelation of secret arrangements between France and the United States placed France in a compromising situation, forced the hand of Congress, and eventually led to Paine's resignation as secretary of the Committee on Foreign Affairs. Mr. Conway[20] quotes Adams' suggestion that some of Paine's earlier writings had been unfavorable to the Colonies but can find nothing to justify the view. The only printed comments on Paine coming from Dr. Witherspoon's pen are a thrust at a vulgarism in *Common Sense*, a criticism of a reference in the same production to the doctrine of original sin, about which Paine theoretically knew little, and an allusion in his essay signed "Aristides" defending the purpose, though not the style, of *Common Sense* against *Plain Truth*, *Cato's Letters* and similar contemporary productions for all of which together, it may be added parenthetically, he said he "would not give a rush."[21]

Dr. Witherspoon's first important appointment on a committee having to do with finances came in May, 1777, when he was one of three members to whom was given the cheerless task of devising ways and means to defray national expenses for the current year. On this committee he began his close association with Robert Morris, who was also a member, and whom he was to support strongly from that time on. In 1778 he was one of the committee to re-organize the Board of Treasury and was also a member of the committee on finance whose comprehensive and constructive report delivered in September was debated almost daily until the end of the year. In October, 1779, he was appointed to address the States on the subject of finances and to devise further ways and means; and when he returned to Congress in 1781 he was constantly employed with financial problems—exchange, commercial regulations, raising money for military campaigns, depreciation, and bills on Europe; and he it was who suggested that an expert accountant be sent to Europe to bring order out of the chaotic books of the American commissioners. His speeches, save in two cases—payment of loan office certifi-

[20] *Life of Thomas Paine*, 3d edition, vol. I, p. 92.
[21] *Works*, vol. IV, pp. 184, 316, 317.

cates and the state of finances—are not preserved, but it is said that on them was based his *Essay on Money*, published anonymously in 1786, a little volume which was put together at the request of those who had heard the speeches delivered and felt that their clearness and sense would work for the good of a public at that time deluged with worthless pamphlets on the financial situation.

His views seem to have been sound. He vigorously endorsed Robert Morris' effort to control army expenditures and substitute a contract system for the expensive commission method of supply; but it was only after bitter experience had proved the wisdom of his position that his ideas prevailed. He maintained that paper money could not preserve its credit unless kept within bounds and unless its redemption were properly assured. So earnest was he in this contention that for a time his popularity was endangered. After the second emission of paper money he steadfastly opposed any further issue unless supported by corresponding measures for maintaining public credit.

When payment of interest on loan office certificates defaulted, he delivered a speech which contained the following passages:[22]

Public credit is of the utmost moment to a state at any time, but it is all in all in a time of war. Public credit among us has been reduced to the lowest ebb, first by a monstrous and unheard-of emission of paper money, next by an act of bankruptcy, reducing it to sixpence in the pound; then by a table of depreciation. There remained but one thing which preserved us some degree of respectability, that the promises made to lenders of money before a certain period had been kept for three years. But now as a "last and finishing stroke, this also is broken to pieces and given to the winds."

We are endeavouring, he said, to borrow money in Europe; is it not possible, is it not probable that our treatment of our creditors here will soon be known there? Must not this repeated insolvency, neglect, and contempt of public creditors prevent loans in Europe? It is ignorance of our situation and past conduct that alone will make them trust us. "I confess," he frankly admitted, "that if I were at Amsterdam now and had plenty of money, I would give what I thought

[22] *Works*, vol. IV, p. 239.

proper to the United States but would lend them none" . . . By making some payment to public creditors immediately we should obtain a dignity and weight abroad that would procure money wherever it could be found.

Let us consider next the effect upon credit at home. If our security were good and our credit entire we should find plenty of lenders. Everything of this kind proceeds upon principles which never fail in their effect. We should be much better off for loans at home which in their nature are preferable to those abroad; therefore whatever leads utterly to destroy credit at home does essential injury to the public cause and has an unhappy influence on every internal temporary operation; people will not seek your service but fly from it.

If this proposal is enforced, it will be a hindrance to the payment of taxes and raising supplies. He would not insist on his suggested payment in order however that it would enable many to pay their taxes, but because it would give dignity to public spirit, animate the people, and give them better thoughts of their rulers and prevent murmuring. In a free state much depends on holding the esteem and attachment of the people. They say we are now paying prodigious taxes but what becomes of the money? The army is two years in arrears of pay; public creditors get none of it. A small payment would be much talked of because it would be general, and because of its general good influences would be worth all and more than all the sum spent. In similar cases he had heard it said you must sometimes throw a little water into a pump in order to bring a great deal out of it.

On the other hand what would be the effect of refusal? Creditors have been told we have no funds in Europe; they will speedily hear however of the Dutch loan and it will increase their indignation; they may combine to refuse their taxes; if such an association were formed it would spread and if it became general it would put an entire stop to our proceedings. This prospect is not conjectural; there have already been meetings to enter into concert to refuse payment of taxes. Can we employ the sum mentioned in the motion to better advantage than in satisfying a deserving body of men and preventing evils of so alarming a nature?

Possibly some are comforting themselves that ultimately they will resolve to pay all; they have taken or are taking measures to do so— the five per cent impost, for example. But it will be long before such measures bring money into the treasury and meanwhile the late step of refusing to draw bills had dealt such a blow to loan office certificates that their value is fallen to a trifle. The inevitable consequence will be that necessity, incredulity, ill humor will make holders part with them for a mere nothing and thus the greater part will really be in the hands of speculators, and when that time comes it will not be surprising to find someone in Congress proposing a new scale of depreciation and thus public faith will once more be trodden under foot and the few remaining original holders of the certificates will lose them entirely.

President Witherspoon reverted to the subject in his speech on the state of public finances when it was proposed to cease drawing bills on Europe to pay interest on loans, as Congress had pledged itself to do, by its Act of September 10, 1777.

He had little to say against the resolutions as reported by the superintendent of finance; perhaps they were unavoidable. But he wished to see whether anything could be added which might in some degree prevent the evils apprehended or at least exculpate Congress and convince the public that the resolutions are the effect of absolute necessity.

The resolutions are a deliberate deviation from express stipulations and will give the last stab to public credit. The stipulation of Congress as to how the interest was to be paid had been an additional security; the promise of giving bills upon Europe if broken or withdrawn must operate to national prejudice. Consider the state of those who held loan office certificates drawing interest on France; they were without exception the country's firmest, most active, and generous friends and many of them had advanced hard money to help the cause. And the class of people who had lost their money were widows and orphans, corporations and public bodies. Of these he could speak from good knowledge; the trustees of the College of New Jersey in 1777 had directed their committee on finance to put into the loan office all the money that should be paid to them and now they had nearly invested all. Payment of interest had given these early investments value; had lenders suspected that they would be cut off they could have disposed of their holdings for something but as it now stands the country's best friends are being reduced to beggary. What faith can be placed in the governments promises?

He wishes the house would weigh the consequence of this resolution; enemies will accuse Congress of oppression and the grossest fraud; they will have the fairest opportunity to make Congress ridiculous and contemptible. As for friends—their disappointment and suffering have already been mentioned; whether they will proceed to violence and disorder is impossible to say; but he would very much dread such efforts of despair. Even though they should not take such steps he is certain the measure will produce hatred and contempt for Congress. . . . Undoubtedly it will greatly lessen the respect due from the public to this body and thus weaken its authority in all other directions.

It will lay the foundation for greater and more scandalous steps of the same sort; it will ruin the certificates; multitudes will sell them for next to nothing; when ultimately holders apply for their money it is highly probable that Congress will issue a scale of depreciation. . . .

What would be the effect abroad? Many of the certificates are held abroad and other sovereigns will not suffer their subjects to be plundered. Letters from Vergennes are on file concerning our former depreciation in which he says that whatever liberty we take with our own citizens we must not think of treating the subjects of France in the same way; and it is possible that we may hear upon this subject when the terms of peace are settled. We shall be called upon to pay at its full value all the money, as well as the loan office certificates, held in France, Spain, and Holland. Some may even be in the hands of British subjects; will they not demand payment? . . . By their punctuality in paying interest Great Britain has been able to support an enormous debt; have they ever thought of presenting holders of her certificates when they came to be paid, with a scale of depreciation? The very idea would knock the whole system of public credit to pieces. But the importance of the matter will be felt before the end of the war. We are soliciting foreign loans; with what face can we expect credit in foreign parts or in future loans after so notoriously breaking every engagement hitherto made?

A disposition to pay and visible probable means of payment are absolutely necessary to credit; where that is once established it is not difficult to borrow. If Congress would but lay down a foundation of credit, enough money could be borrowed in this country . . . to purchase property in the cultivated parts of the country is not nearly so profitable as interest on money; anybody knows that it is almost universal in this country, when a man dies leaving infant children, the executors sell all his property to turn into money and put it into securities for equal and easy division. These things proceed upon certain and indubitable principles which never fail of their effect. Therefore you have only to make your payments as soon, as regular, and as profitable as borrowers and you will get all the money you want; and by a small advantage over others it will be poured in upon you so that you need not go to the lenders, for they shall come to you.

The President did not follow Congress in its peregrination of September, 1777; perhaps he realized that his colleagues would assemble merely to adjourn; and besides, affairs at Princeton needed his attention. He did not answer a roll call until October 7. Three days before, at the battle of Germantown, the oldest of his three sons, James, a major in the New Jersey Brigade, had been killed in action. President Witherspoon's loyalty to the American cause needed no further evidence of its sincerity.[23]

[23] James Witherspoon was born at Beith on November 17, 1751, matriculated at the University of Glasgow in 1764, and on his father's removal to Princeton in 1768, had entered College as a Junior, graduating in September, 1770. His occupation during the next three and a half years is uncertain; he seems, however, to have been in Savannah part of this period; but in the spring of 1774 he went to Ryegate and settling on a tract of 600 acres which the President had bought for him, and which is still known as the "Witherspoon Tract," he cleared some 25 acres and erected a dwelling and other buildings. In May, 1776, he was in Princeton for a short visit. During that summer, after returning to Vermont, he probably joined the northern army, for with two other Ryegate men he went north through the woods to obtain intelligence for the American commander at Ticonderoga, penetrating as far as St. Johns, Quebec, according to a letter he wrote to the President describing his adventure and especially, his narrow escape from capture by the British and the hardships endured on the way back. He then seems to have returned to Princeton and later in the year to have joined Washington's army, for in February, 1777, the President informed David, his youngest son, that James was now aide to General Maxwell "and if his life is spared, will be sufficiently provided for in the army." In August he was in camp at Germantown, and there on October 4 he was struck by the cannon-ball which also gave General Nash his mortal wound.

Wrapped in a blanket the young officer was buried with six other American soldiers in a common grave on the main road through the village of Germantown. The remains were disinterred a little later in the presence of his sister Ann and a brother (probably John). They had made arrangements to take the body back to Princeton, but this proved impossible and it was reburied in St. Michaels' churchyard, in Germantown, where a simple headstone marks the grave, bearing this inscription:

HERE

LIES THE BODY

OF MAJOR

JAMES WITHERSPOON

OF THE JERSEY BRIGADE

WHO FELL IN THE BATTLE OF

GERMANTOWN, OCT. 4TH 1777.

Watson, *Annals of Philadelphia*, vol. II, p. 59; *Christian Advocate*, vol. II, pp. 398, 399, 444, 445; Miller and Wells, *History of Ryegate, Vt.*, pp. 39, 40, 239, 567; *New Jersey Archives*, vol. XXVII, pp. 267, 276.

He was placed on the Board of War during the same month, and on his reelection to Congress that winter was added (December 26, 1777) to the committee appointed to investigate the causes of the evacuation of Ticonderoga, and the conduct of the general officers at the evacuation. Six months later this committee recommended the court martial of General St. Clair.[24]

The ominous color given to the situation by the disaster in the northern department, by the successful approach of the enemy to Philadelphia, and by Washington's defeat at Brandywine and failure at Germantown, was suddenly brightened by the news of Burgoyne's surrender at Saratoga. The wretched sequel to that surrender, the needless difficulty and even hardship to which an equivocating Congress subjected the captured army, and more particularly Dr. Witherspoon's share of responsibility therein, admit of no defence and only partial excuse. It is plain that, either in nervous panic over a reckless utterance of Burgoyne, or seizing upon that remark as a welcome chance to repudiate the generous terms of the convention, Congress attached ridiculous weight to the British commander's words. That Dr. Witherspoon deliberately sought the repudiation of the convention is unthinkable. He had given the whole question careful consideration and had prepared on the subject a long speech which, excepting its conclusion, is preserved in his writings.[25] This speech clearly reveals how he argued himself into a position at variance with his better impulses, his jealousy for the safety of the coun-

[24] At his court martial St. Clair publicly accused President Witherspoon of malicious misrepresentation in regard to operations at Fort Mercer. In order to "set the public right with respect to that matter, and to show the baseness of those who have endeavored to turn them to my prejudice," he filed a copy of the directions he issued at the time. He believed the principal agent was "a very reverend gentleman, a Member of Congress, Doctor Witherspoon I mean, who, forgetting the strict regard to truth his clerical character required, and the impropriety of a Member of Congress publicly pre-judging a matter that must ultimately be referred to Congress, has been taking every opportunity (and has had the meanness to do it in taverns as he has been passing through the country) to misrepresent the whole of my conduct, and so far as in him lay, to prevent a fair trial and acquittal should that follow, from wearing off the prejudices against me, which I have good reason to think were raised in the same manner." (Trial of St. Clair, *N. Y. Historical Society Collections*, 1880, p. 169.) Dr. Witherspoon's alleged conduct had no effect on the court martial, for St. Clair was unanimously acquitted of all charges.

[25] *Works*, vol. IV, p. 273.

try overcoming his private judgment. It is of much moment that every nation preserve its faith and honor in its solemn contracts, he said, and especially for the United States "just beginning to appear upon the public stage;" he therefore hoped Congress would do nothing which would appear "mean, captious, or insidious, whatever advantage may seem to arise from it." On the other hand it was their duty to see to it that the country suffer no injury by deception, or abuse, or insult. It was his opinion on the first of these two principles that Congress should vote that the convention be not broken although he recognized certain irregularities on the part of the surrendered army—colors and minor equipment had not been given up as stipulated; but he would not consider them "such breaches of the convention as would authorize us in justice to declare it void."

Here the President should have stopped; but having eased his mind of these sentiments, he then viewed the situation from the angle of his second principle—justice and caution. He finds Burgoyne declaring that the convention has been broken by the American general because adequate quarters had not been provided for the surrendered officers as stipulated. And he proceeds to extricate himself from his first position in the following manner:

We have here the declared opinion of one of the parties, that the public faith is broken by the other. . . . Therefore we have reason to conclude that if General Burgoyne is of opinion that the convention is broken on our part he will not heed it on his. He would act the part of a fool if he did. . . . If it is really his opinion (and we should wrong his sincerity to doubt it) the consequences are the same with respect to us. . . . What are we to expect from him as soon as he shall receive his liberty and the power of doing mischief?

But it is said that he did not mean us to dread such consequences. All this I believe to be strictly true. It probably fell from him in passion—and very unadvisedly. . . . His folly in this instance is our good fortune. . . . He evidently is a man showy, vain, impetuous and rash. . . . Do you think that such a man would not take the advantage of this pretended breach of the convention to wipe off the reproach of his late ignominious surrender by some signal or desperate undertaking?

The printed speech ends at this point; but no reader can fail to guess the conclusion. Because of Burgoyne's statement Dr. Witherspoon would take him literally at his word and vote that the convention had been broken. As a member of the committee in charge of the conduct of the war, he advocated the strictly prudent course perhaps, but one that posterity very generally has marked as a blot on the history of the young republic; and he voted for the resolution of January 8, 1778, that the embarkation of General Burgoyne and his troops be suspended until "distinct and explicit" ratification of the convention should be transmitted to Congress by Great Britain, a ratification which of course was an impossibility until the independence of the Colonies should be conceded.

President Witherspoon was absent when the news of the signing of the French treaties reached Congress in April, 1778, and when they were ratified in May. In fact he was absent during most of that spring; but in view of the new alliance, on his return one morning in June he must have served with increased zest as member of the committee into whose care was given a dispatch from General Washington enclosing letters from Lord Howe and General Clinton which accompanied three recent Acts of Parliament and suggested that the latter paved the way to immediate peace. The committee was a safe and trusted one—William Henry Drayton, Richard Henry Lee, Gouverneur Morris, Samuel Adams and Dr. Witherspoon, to whom during the year were referred numerous matters touching upon foreign affairs. Retiring to an adjoining room as ordered by Congress, the committee promptly composed the perfect answer expected. It was brief, formal, and conclusive: the new Acts of Parliament were not essentially different from others on which Congress had already expressed its sentiments; when the King should seriously desire an end to the "unprovoked and cruel" war he was waging, Congress would readily consider such terms of peace as might "consist with the honor of independent nations, the interest of their constituents, and the sacred regard they mean to pay to treaties." The position of the Colonies could have hardly been summed up more tersely or more plainly.

To the same committee was entrusted on June 13 a task

closely akin to the one just accomplished. On that day an express arrived with a letter from the new British peace commission which was headed by the Earl of Carlisle and accompanied by Dr. Adam Ferguson, professor of moral philosophy at Edinburgh University, as secretary. Two days later, after postponement of a motion that Congress could not "hear any language reflecting upon the honour" of the "good and faithful ally" of these States, the letter was referred to the committee named and its answer, declining to negotiate with the commission, was unanimously adopted and General Washington's action in refusing Dr. Ferguson a passport to deliver the communication from the commission was approved. A by-product of this episode, and more interesting than the foregone conclusion of the committee itself, was the opinion the professor of moral philosophy at Edinburgh entertained of the professor of moral philosophy at Princeton, now turned Congressman. This is found in a paragraph from a letter he subsequently wrote to Dr. Witherspoon's boyhood friend and collegemate, Alexander Carlyle:

It is the fashion to say that we have lost America. . . . I am in great hopes that nothing will be lost, not even the continent of North America. We have 1200 miles of territory occupied by about 300,000 people of which there are about 150,000 with Johnny Witherspoon at their head, against us—and the rest for us. I am not sure that if proper measures were taken but we should reduce Johnny Witherspoon to the small support of Franklin, Adams and two or three more of the most abandoned villains in the world, but I tremble at the thought of their cunning and determination opposed to us.[26]

Dr. Witherspoon would have been flattered by the distinction conferred upon him in these lines, for not even his most enthusiastic American admirers claimed him as leader of the revolting Colonies, although they would have been prompt to admit that he moved in fairly good company even if it were that of "abandoned villains." Professor Ferguson was also misinformed as to the proportion of colonials who were against his government—and his generally inaccurate knowledge of the situation in America is characteristic. But in another respect his statement reflects

[26] Charles Rogers, *Social Life in Scotland*, vol. III, p. 121.

an opinion not confined to adherents of the Crown but shared by many foreign observers. The assertion that Dr. Witherspoon belonged to a junto in Congress is frequently found in contemporary records. It is implied by Ferguson, besides being referred to in contemporary newspaper correspondence, and was implicitly believed in British circles in New York whence probably Ferguson derived his faulty information. M. Gérard, the first French Minister to the United States, in a passage which is curious enough to merit summarizing, reported it to Vergennes as a fact. Writing from Philadelphia just after his arrival in America Gérard, who sniffed intrigue everywhere, quoted information given him by *"plusieurs personnages principaux"* and told his chief that before the arrival of the French treaty that spring there was a faction in Congress which might have become the more dangerous because it could not have been accused of disloyalty; it was composed of clever and ambitious men, but of mediocre influence, whose plan was to maintain a certain equilibrium so as to be indispensable when capitulation to the British took place, for there were few people then who thought the quarrel could be terminated without some sort of capitulation; a Scotch minister named Wederspun (Witherspoon), the only man of his profession in Congress, was the soul of this party; he united in high degree two qualities seemingly opposed, extreme forcefulness of character and the greatest pliability of mind (*souplesse d'esprit*); Mr. Samuel Adams also belonged to this party; but since everyone is now persuaded that the issue of the quarrel will be honorable and lasting, no further suspicion of them exists.[27] To appreciate how wide of the mark Gérard's information was it is only necessary to remember Dr. Witherspoon's repugnance to the slightest hint of capitulation or compromise. If he belonged to any marked group at all it was the group that refused to consider any proposal short of complete independence. That he was party to a private understanding or held the views he did with expectation of personal advantage either in power or in position, or of becoming "indispensable" at the close of the war, is manifestly absurd. He had been driven into politics by a

[27]H. Doniol, *Histoire de la participation de la France à l'établissement des Etats Unis d'Amérique.* vol. III, p. 267.

sense of duty and against his preference; he was to quit public life at the earliest opportunity; and it is difficult to see what advantage of power or position was obtainable outside of public life.

At the end of July, 1778, the report of the Board of Treasury advocating a re-organization was considered and after debate referred to a committee of which Dr. Witherspoon was a member with Gouverneur Morris, Mr. Gerry, Mr. Telfair and Richard Henry Lee. Two weeks later these gentlemen reported a plan and after a month's debate further their report with amendments was referred to a reconstituted committee, in which Robert Morris and Samuel Chase succeeded Mr. Gerry and Mr. Telfair. Their revision was adopted by Congress on September 26. To the lay mind, unskilled in the dark matters involved, it would seem as if the difficulty with the new plan was its cumbrousness; it appears to be little else than an over-elaborate system of checks and counter-checks which must have been vexatious in the extreme both to the checkers and the checked. A machine containing so many wheels within wheels could scarcely have been expected to run satisfactorily and it is not surprising, therefore, that three years later Robert Morris was freed entirely from the Board's hindering presence by its abolition.

During the autumn and early winter of 1778 the report which Dr. Witherspoon helped to draw up for the committee appointed in August "to consider the state of money and finance of the United States" was debated almost daily in committee of the whole. The *Journal* necessarily contains no details of the discussions, the committee merely reporting progress, but it must be believed that the President was constantly engaged in defence and explanation of the committee's proposals.

While these debates were proceeding his name occurs frequently enough in connection with matters relating to the country's new ally. When the French envoy, M. Gérard, transmitted to Congress the speech he intended to deliver at his first audience the document was handed over to Dr. Witherspoon, Gouverneur Morris and Richard Henry Lee to draft the reply the president of Congress should make. Their draft proving unsatisfactory, it was passed to a fresh committee in which Colonel

Joseph Reed and Francis Dana supplanted Lee and Morris, Dr. Witherspoon retaining the chairmanship, and the version the new collaborators produced was used by Henry Laurens as presiding officer at the audience on August 6. When Lafayette sought permission in October, 1778, to return to France the favorable answer he desired and the resolution of thanks for his zeal and services which Congress added were framed by Dr. Witherspoon and Messrs. Drayton, Lee, Morris, and Adams. On Franklin's election in September, 1778, as minister plenipotentiary to France the same committee, with the exception of Dr. Witherspoon, had been again appointed to draft his credentials and instructions; but in October the *Journal* records the fact of President Witherspoon's restoration to the committee, so that he ultimately shared in preparing the papers adopted on the twenty-second and twenty-sixth.

In January he had been appointed chairman of a committee to prepare a manifesto on enemy treatment of prisoners. The committee gathered evidence during the year and at length reported; but there is no draft of the manifesto among the Papers of the Continental Congress, nor does the *Journal* record any formal action. The text of the manifesto is found nevertheless in the manuscript *Journal* for October 30, 1778, in the handwriting of Charles Thomson, the secretary of Congress, and ending with the words "done by unanimous consent." Under the circumstances it is impossible to assign authorship definitely; but the document is full of passages which have ear-marks of Dr. Witherspoon's composition. The closing paragraph is a typical example:

We, therefore, the Congress of the United States of America, do solemnly declare and proclaim, that if our enemies presume to execute their threats, or persist in their present career of barbarity, we will take such exemplary vengeance as shall deter others from a like conduct. We appeal to that God who searcheth the hearts of men, for the rectitude of our intentions; and in his holy presence we declare, that as we are not moved by any light or hasty suggestions of anger or revenge, so, through every possible change of fortune, we will adhere to this our determination.

During this year the President was also chairman of the special committee to design seals for the Treasury and Navy Departments; and it was fitting that it should fall to his lot on behalf of the State of New Jersey to ratify the Articles of Confederation.

He allowed himself to be returned to Congress for the year 1779 against his will. Attendance was costly and in addition he felt that his presence was sorely needed at Princeton. He accepted reelection on the understanding with his constituents that he would come and go as he pleased. When in his seat he took most active part in the proceedings, but he seldom remained long enough to figure consistently in the debates.[28]

Absent during the latter half of January and a fortnight in February he surely made especial effort to be present on Monday the fifteenth, when M. Gérard held a most important conference with Congress dealing with peace terms. No votes are recorded in the *Journal* of that date so that it is not possible to verify attendance, but Dr. Witherspoon could have left Princeton early enough that Monday morning to reach Philadelphia in time for the audience, and thus have avoided travelling on Sunday. That he was present the next day is shown by the record of votes. To him and four other members were referred on the seventeenth letters from Arthur Lee together with the communications of M. Gérard at the conference, and also the draft of a treaty of commerce with Holland received from William Lee, Dr. Arthur Lee's brother. The committee reported within the week that it was of opinion that Spain was disposed to enter into alliance with the United States and that eventually the independence of the United States must be acknowledged by Great Britain and negotiations for peace be set on foot. If so, the American commissioners would require fresh instructions and the committee therefore submitted a list of articles as essential conditions to be insisted upon in the negotiations and others to be yielded or required on terms of mutual compensation. The President's ab-

[28] He was absent from January 9 to the middle of February; a week at the end of that month; three weeks in May; from June 4 to August 25 he was present only one week but after that was fairly regular in attendance.

sences prevented him from sharing to any appreciable extent in the protracted discussion of these "ultimata" and in particular the bitterly contested one concerning the Newfoundland fisheries, although in his *Memorial of Facts* he recounts the conferences held with Gérard and the latter's advice that the United States be not "too high in their demands." He even missed seeing the ultimata finally adopted.

Present one day in March, however, he characteristically seconded Gouverneur Morris' resolution that a committee of three be appointed to prepare an account of so much of European intelligence as was proper to publish, and to him accordingly with Mr. Morris and William H. Drayton the task was given. He was a firm advocate of publicity; he believed that much of the British misunderstanding that had brought about the Revolution would have been avoided if Great Britain had been properly informed; he had urged publicity on Mr. John Adams when the latter passed through Princeton in 1774 on his way to the first Congress; in 1778 during the Deane investigation when the Committee on Foreign Affairs was directed to lay before Congress all its papers, he was unwilling that the members should pledge themselves not to mention outside of Congress matters that might appear in the documents. During the debate on the ultimata of 1779 Mr. Jay told Washington that there was as little secrecy in Congress "as in a boarding school," and he alluded to the rules of Congress as being "far too general and perhaps for that reason more frequently violated." Mr. Jay would have classed President Witherspoon among the violators, if a remark by that inveterate chronicler, Dr. Ezra Stiles, may be trusted. The latter records in his diary of this period meeting a Bostonian "so toryfied" that he had not heard "what Dr. Witherspoon communicated at General Washington's table" respecting "the Friendship of Spain, the King of the 2 Sicilies, Holland and Petersburg." This "friendship" was the subject of the long debate in Congress then proceeding.

On May 4, 1779, the President was one of the committee chosen, a member from each State, with the President of Congress, to wait upon the French Minister and offer the congratulations of Congress on the birth of a princess to the King of France; and he was one of the committee of three who prepared the letter in reply to His Majesty's announcement.

Absent during the unpleasant discussion of the dissensions among the American commissioners in Europe, his attitude on the matter may be inferred perhaps by his seconding, on his return to his seat, Richard Henry Lee's resolution that Congress now proceed to hear evidence exculpating the commissioners. The resolution is undated but is inserted in the *Journal* by Mr. Ford under date of June 10, 1779. If this date be accepted, color is also lent to an interesting tale printed in the newspapers towards the end of June, in an anonymous letter emanating from Philadelphia.[29] It repeats the old fiction that Dr. Witherspoon belonged to a junto, dating back to the First Congress, to control congressional action. For the past year, so the story ran, a club had been formed of New England, New Jersey, Pennsylvania, and two or three Southern members who had met regularly to arrange proceedings in Congress; and as an illustration of their activity it is alleged that the night before Arthur Lee's recall was to be voted upon (June 10) an express was sent off for Dr. Witherspoon and Mr. Scudder, who made posthaste to Philadelphia "each of them with as much expedition as if they had been flying before the enemy." Mr. Scudder is recorded in the *Journal* as present on June 10, but Dr. Witherspoon's name does not appear, although he was present if Mr. Ford's dating of the resolution mentioned above is accepted. Both he and Mr. Scudder had voted in May against the recall of Arthur Lee when the house was equally divided; and there is no question as to President Witherspoon's friendliness to the Lee family. His references to Arthur Lee are uniformly favorable, speaking of him in 1781, for example, as "one of the most able, faithful and active servants we ever had, and certainly one of the most disinterested"[30] —high praise with which not everyone agreed then, or will agree now.

[29] *Silas Deane Papers*, vol. III, p. 490, N.Y. Historical Society Collection 1888. The letter was reprinted in the *Baltimore Advertiser*, the *New York Packet*, and the *Virginia Gazette*.
[30] *Works*, vol. IV, p. 269.

Placed on a committee to take up the New Hampshire Grants controversy he was absent through the rest of June and the whole of July, and on his return from Vermont he resumed his seat only long enough to present a report for the committee and then at once went to Princeton, thus missing the debate in August on instructions for the American peace commissioner, for the commissioner to negotiate a treaty of commerce with Great Britain, and for the American minister at Versailles. The instructions for the minister at Madrid could not be prepared at the time for want of final determination on the part of Congress; but when at length in September it was agreed to send Mr. Jay as minister to Spain, the President evidently sensed the difficulties the envoy would encounter at Madrid, for, a few days before Jay sailed, he offered (October 13) a resolution that the minister be "privately instructed" to recede from the claim of free navigation of the Mississippi if such proved an insuperable bar to the proposed treaties with Spain. The motion was lost, receiving but four votes; and yet a few months later Dr. Witherspoon's defeated proposal was exactly what Congress authorized. There appears to have developed as the war proceeded a difference of opinion as to the value of Spain's services, and modern historians share that difference. Professor Corwin considers Spain's assistance in the light of results, save in 1781, to have been negligible, "when indeed it was not worse."[31] Dr. Witherspoon however, speaking on the floor of Congress in 1782 thought the services of Spain underrated. She had done much, he asserted; she entered the war with the common enemy and the Colonies had derived as much advantage from her exertions as if she had agreed to the treaty of alliance; she aided the Colonies with money, opened her ports to American ships, and admitted the United States to trade at Havana. We are not perfectly satisfied with the reception Mr. Jay received, concluded the President, but "we must not tease Spain with solicitations," and should leave her to judge the time when she will think it proper to comply with our engagements.[32]

Dr. Witherspoon seems to have made a special trip to Phila-

[31] *French Policy and the American Alliance*, p. 211.
[32] *Thomson Papers*, N. Y. Historical Society Collections, 1878, p.90.

delphia to be in his seat on September 17, 1779, the day M. Gérard took formal leave of Congress. He had been absent for some time before, and was away for a month immediately after, this date. He was present when Gérard's successor, La Luzerne, on November 17 was given his first public audience with Congress; but his attention for the rest of the session was devoted chiefly to finances.

In October, 1779, he had been added to a committee chosen a month earlier to address the States on finances. The report urged the necessity of punctual payment of the state quotas recently assigned and expressed the belief that the "operation of taxes and other salutary measures" would reduce prices and enable Congress to lessen the quotas or apply a portion of them to the public debt. The recommendation was to prove to a large degree futile, and Dr. Witherspoon seems to have had speedy premonition of this result. On November 17, after La Luzerne had been received in audience, and, as the *Journal* puts it, "had been conducted home," and Congress, plunging once more into finances, had authorized a fresh emission of bills of credit, Dr. Witherspoon moved the appointment of a committee of five to devise further ways and means for supplying the treasury. He was a member of the committee which accordingly reported two days later. But the report found Congress engrossed with the idea of fixing prices and checking a continued rise attributable to "engrossing and advancing," contemporary synonyms for modern "profiteering." It was at this time that the President made the speech in opposition to price-fixing which Dr. Rush recorded, as already quoted, and to which Congress merely gave polite attention. The report of the Committee on ways and means was taken from the table four or five days later and the plan of drawing bills of exchange on Mr. Jay and Mr. Laurens, to be sold at the current rate of exchange, was adopted, and a fresh committee appointed to carry it into effect.

Reference has been made to Dr. Witherspoon's appointment to a committee on the New Hampshire Grants controversy. The task of this committee must have been of more than ordinary interest to him, not merely because by an odd chance three of his four associates were graduates[33] of the college whose shattered fortunes he was directing *in absentia,* but rather because the committee's duty would take him northwards and might pave the way to stable political existence for the state of Vermont where his settlement of Ryegate lay. The States of New York and New Hampshire were both claiming the whole of the Grants, part of whose people had formed the commonwealth of Vermont and were acting as an independent State. Congress at this juncture had finally overcome its reluctance to interfere in the triangular controversy and after protracted discussion had voted in the first week of June (1779) that a committee of five repair to the district and find out why the citizens thereof refused to continue citizens of the States hitherto exercising jurisdiction over them. That Dr. Witherspoon fully appreciated the delicacy of the situation is shown by the resolution which he left behind him for presentation on the floor of Congress and which was adopted after he had started on the mission, stating

That it was not the intention of Congress, by their resolution of the first instant nor ought the same or any part thereof, to be construed to hold up principles subversive of, or unfavorable to the internal policy of any or either of the United States.

Dr. Witherspoon and Colonel Atlee made their way to Bennington, Vermont, but Judge Edwards having resigned his seat in Congress could not serve, while Root and Ellsworth arrived only after Witherspoon and Atlee had started home, so that the committee never met as a whole or even in quorum. During their stay in Vermont, however, Dr. Witherspoon and his colleague persuaded Governor Chittenden of Vermont to urge his adherents to abstain from violence and to raise their quota of troops whenever their neighbors were called upon to do so; they "conversed at great length" with all persons of weight at Bennington and made many enquiries to secure a clear understanding of the conflicting claims, to learn the disposition of the people, and to persuade them to an amicable settlement. So runs the report

[33] Jesse Root (1756), Oliver Ellsworth (1766), and Pierpont Edwards (1768). The fifth member was Colonel Atlee.

which Dr. Witherspoon wrote and delivered to Congress on July 13. As a matter of fact the Congressmen did nothing, and under the circumstances could do nothing, save act as mediators and pacifiers. They had visited Governor Clinton of New York on their way north and a remark of his that he had found Atlee particularly receptive, by inference suggests that Dr. Witherspoon's mind was less open on the subject. He had in fact definite ideas on the fundamental problem at the heart of the whole difficulty which were not favorable to the New York claim and which he had already given hint of and was soon to exploit fully in connection with the question of the western lands. The committee was discharged in September, on the obvious ground that no quorum had met. The Vermont controversy was destined to occupy much attention during the rest of Dr. Witherspoon's membership of Congress and he was to serve on more than one committee in that connection. Statehood, however, was not acquired by Vermont until long after he had returned to private life.

President Witherspoon left Congress in December, 1779 at the end of his term, not expecting to return. In a letter to a friend in Scotland he gives the reasons:[34]

I have now left congress, not being able to support the expence of attending it, with the frequent journeys to Princeton, and being determined to give particular attention to the revival of the college. Professor Houston, however, our professor of mathematics, is a delegate this year; but he tells me he will certainly leave it next November. I mention this circumstance to conform what I believe I wrote you formerly, that the members of congress in general, not only receive no profit from that office, but I believe five out of six of them, if not more, are great losers in their private affairs. This cannot be otherwise; for as none of the delegates are allowed to have any lucrative office whatever, either in their own state or for the United States, though their expences should be fully borne, their time is taken up, and their own private estates are neglected. At the end of the year 1778, I gave notice to our legislature that they must either not chuse me at all, or leave me at full liberty to attend only when I could conveniently. They chose me however, and I made a good deal of use of that liberty in the year 1779; and this year all the delegates were changed but one.

[34] *Works*, vol. IV, p. 335. Letter of March 20, 1780.

Regarding the general situation in America, he has these comments to make:

As to public affairs, it seems to be yet uncertain whether we shall have peace soon. Greatly do I and many others in America desire it; and yet, were our condition ten times worse than it is, nothing short of the clear independence of this country would be accepted. I observe, by your letter of the 19th of March last year, that you had a high opinion of your successes at St. Lucia, in Georgia, and against the French trade. I believe before the end of the campaign, there was little reason to boast of your success upon the whole. I mentioned to you in my last how obstinately the court of England continued in erroneous opinions respecting America; and now I think that obstinacy has become incurable. It is plain that they still harp upon the same string, that a few leading men in congress stir up the people, and persuade them to continue the contest. Allow me to assure you that this is one of the most absurd and groundless opinions that ever was formed. The congress is changing every day. There is no instance in the whole contest, in which the public opinion did not go before their resolutions. To go back to the very beginning—the declaration of independence was forced upon the majority of the then congress, by the people in general; and, in consequence of subsequent elections, every six months that I have been in congress has weakened the party that was suspected of coldness upon that subject; and now perhaps I may say it is annihilated.

I am not only fully sensible, by a general knowledge of the country in this and other states, that the public mind is entirely on the side of liberty, and for the independence of America—but I could mention a great many facts and circumstances as evidences of it, stronger than could well be imagined, and indeed which have turned out stronger than even my expectations. One circumstance is alone decisive upon this subject, which is well known to yourselves, that the moment your army leaves any part of the country, it is not only lost to you, but returns so strongly to the interest of congress, that all the persons known to have been attached to you are obliged to fly with terror and confusion. But there is another strong circumstance, the universal attachment of the people to the French alliance. In vain have your partisans endeavored to alarm the people with the fears of popery and arbitrary power. It makes not the least impression even upon the common people.

Please to attend to the circumstance I am going to mention; because it surprised myself when I observed it. There are always, you know, little feuds and contentions, jealousy and emulation, in every society and in every association. Both in congress and in the country, I have observed that when one set or faction wants to make the other odious, they charge them with being cold to the French alliance, and ungrateful to them for their services. This to my knowledge has been the subject of mutual reproaches, when I do not believe there was any truth in it on either side. Would you think it—some have seriously attempted to persuade me that the New-England delegates were cold to the French, and inclined to the English; to which I answered, that I well knew the contrary, but that they were of an independent spirit, and would not easily submit to unwarrantable influence, either from the French or the English. I mention all this singly with this view, to shew you the bent and inclination of the public mind.

I will mention another circumstance to you. The distress of this country by the depreciation of the money, has been very great. Many have suffered great losses; not a few have been utterly ruined. Yet I never could perceive that this altered the inclination of the people as to the public cause in the least. Nay, notwithstanding the dreadful complaints made against particular classes of men, such as forestallers and engrossers, commissaries and quartermasters, yet I am persuaded that any body who should but propose to return to submission to England for relief from their depredations, would be torn in pieces.

During the year 1780 he devoted himself to his college duties and also served in the New Jersey State Council or Senate, and in December, 1780, he was returned to Congress. How he was induced to accept reelection is not recorded, but it is safe to surmise that on the one hand New Jersey felt, from the point of view of her own interests, that his experience and sagacity rendered his presence in Congress imperative, while on the other hand the President realized that vital questions of administration at home and of diplomacy abroad, on which he had pronounced views as representing his State, were approaching settlement, and that therefore it was his duty to accept reelection. Events proved that the year 1781 was one of the most important in the period. The Bank of North America was founded; national powers for Congress were proposed such as it had not possessed under the Confederation as interpreted up to that time; the formation of government executive departments was agreed to, and an effort at a federal judiciary was made; while the mission to France was enlarged and historic instructions were framed for it —in the formulation of which the President was to play a most extraordinary part.

He had not been back in Congress a week before he was given the task of drafting, with his old pupil James Madison and with Mr. Duane, a commission and a set of instructions for an envoy to Russia which were promptly laid before Congress and adopted, Francis Dana being appointed to the post.

In support of the plan for the coming campaign agreed upon by General Washington and the French commanders, Congress had voted to send an envoy extraordinary to the Court of Versailles to seek the needed funds, a decision Dr. Witherspoon sought to have reconsidered, involving as it did inevitable confusion, if not conflict, with the mission already at Paris. Congress declined to reconsider and a few days later selected young Colonel John Laurens for the task,—one to which he was inadequately fitted by his youth and lack of experience. Dr. Witherspoon's opposition must have had weight however, for presumably with the object of reconciling his fears to the wishes of Congress, he was made chairman of the special committee sent to confer with La Luzerne regarding young Laurens' mission, and to secure his advice.

Meanwhile news had been received of the capture on the high seas by the British in the autumn of 1780 of Henry Laurens, and his imprisonment in the Tower of London on the charge of high treason. Dr. Witherspoon seconded the resolution calling for a committee to consider the case and, as a member thereof, wrote the report presented in March, 1781, pointing out that Mr. Laurens, a former President of Congress, instead of being treated as a prisoner of war had been placed in close confinement; that the United States "are and of a right ought to be free and independent" and their citizens ought to receive the same treatment when taken prisoners as subjects of other independent States, and that the independence of the United States had been virtually acknowledged by Great Britain so far as treatment of prisoners and the conduct of war were concerned; and that, therefore, Congress should at once express its resentment against the present infraction of rights and take effectual measures to prevent its recurrence. The committee accordingly proposed in reprisal that (an unnamed prisoner) be put "into secure and close confinement" and be treated as Laurens.[35] This retaliatory report was referred to General Washington and eventually Congress voted to table its recommendation. The incident illustrates nevertheless the President's keen jealousy for the dignity and rights of the new government. Indeed, his jealousy for the national dignity is marked in all his congressional work during this year (1781), so far as that work can be traced in the *Journal*. In his financial proposals especially is this evident. Late in January Congress in committee of the whole had resolved to recommend

[35] The President did not resort to Congress when his son John was captured at sea in the following year. John Witherspoon, Jr., was born at Beith, Scotland, July 29, 1757. He was graduated from the Nassau Hall Grammar School in September, 1769, delivering the Latin Valedictory. Entering the freshman class that year, at commencement, 1771, he won as a sophomore in open competition, the first prize for reading Greek and Latin, Aaron Burr, Jr., the future Vice-president, and Henry Lee, Jr., the future "Light Horse Harry," winning second and third prizes respectively. In his junior year he took the second prize for Greek and Latin reading, but at graduation in 1773 won no honors.

He studied medicine and in the summer of 1775 entered service, accompanying General Washington when the latter went to Boston. In July and August, 1776, he was stationed at New York at the General Hospital and in August, 1777, was at the hospital at Trenton. He is listed as a surgeon in the hospital department from 1778 to 1780. In September, 1779, the French minister Gérard, asking Congress to allow the young physician a leave of absence to go to France, speaks of him as "a surgeon in the service of the United States." He sailed in October to purchase medicines and instruments. He next appears as surgeon on the American privateer *De Graaf* which was captured by the British early in 1781, and he was taken to England as a prisoner on the man of war *Celemene* and was severely treated. President Witherspoon wrote in June, 1781, to Franklin at Paris to procure his release and supply him with enough money to get home. The ensuing correspondence is among the Franklin papers in the Library of Congress. Franklin was able to arrange the release in September, young Witherspoon reaching Paris the next month and receiving, with a charming letter from Franklin to his father, the additional funds the latter had forwarded.

On return to America he made Princeton his residence, and was placed on a town committee in the summer of 1782 to carry out resolutions to prevent trade and intercourse with the enemy. He was still in Princeton in the fall of 1783. By the curious ill-fortune that seems to have beset the President's children, an estrangement took place between this son and his father, the causes of which are not known. It is said that he settled in St. Stephens Parish, South Carolina, where connections of the family lived, but no traces of him have been discovered. He was named by the President in 1794, when drawing his will, as one of his remaining children, but is believed to have been lost at sea in 1795.

that the States levy a tax of five per cent on all imports, the tax to be paid, however, to federal agents and not to state officials, and the revenue accruing to be used for public purposes by Congress. This resolution was amended a few days later to ask the States to pass laws granting to Congress the power to levy such a tax and was still under discussion when Dr. Witherspoon, with mind made up on the real issue underlying these timid resolves, offered a motion that went to the heart of the difficulty, moving that it was necessary that Congress be vested with the right to oversee the commercial regulations of each State so as to avoid discriminations and partiality, or injury to the national interest; and that furthermore Congress should be vested with an exclusive right to lay taxes on imports within a certain period and for a specified purpose. But this attempt to provide a national revenue was too advanced and his ambitious motion secured the support of only four States. The original form of the resolution of January prevailed.

At least, however, he was recognized as a man of fearless ideas, and that spring in May (1781) he was appointed chairman of a committee to devise further ways and means to defray the expenses of the ensuing campaign and for the better regulation of public finances. He reported on the fourteenth proposing that the States repeal their laws making any kind of paper money legal tender, that the Treasurer of the United States draw on the several States for arrears, that debts of the United States be liquidated as might be or funded as loans if creditors preferred, that the States issue no more bills of credit upon their own account and recall as soon as possible what were still outstanding, that the superintendent of finance obtain a sum of hard money "for the most pressing exigencies of the public affairs," and finally and most important of all, that the United States take into consideration the line which they would guarantee to each State as its western boundary and declare the remainder the property of the United States as a fund of credit for the common interest and defence. Here again were constructive proposals which if adopted were likely to start the government on the road out of its financial quagmire. Little progress toward rehabilitation of national credit, or the creation of national funds would be made as long as each State handled finances in its own way and disregarded the claims of the United States; but meanwhile if sovereignty could be gained over the vast western land vaguely claimed by various States, it was obvious that the government would have at hand an imposing source of revenue. After several days of debate, and after the report had been returned to the committee for further consideration, it was adopted by Congress, with the exception, however of the potentially vital paragraph as to the western boundaries. On this point Dr. Witherspoon had again been in advance of his time. The hour had not yet arrived when the majority of his colleagues should bring themselves to face that particular problem.

Late in the same month the committee reported approval of Robert Morris's plan for a national bank of the United States, whereupon Congress gave the proposal its endorsement, at the same time recommending to the States to forbid the establishment or existence of other banks during the war, and voting that the notes of the national bank should be receivable for all taxes, payments, duties, and debts, and that it be a felony to counterfeit them or to convert any of the bank's funds or other property to private ends.

But Dr. Witherspoon was not willing to let the question of the western lands be lost to sight, and on June 27, as chairman of the committee on ways and means already mentioned, he reported a resolution[36] on the Virginia, New York and Connecticut cessions and the memorials of the Illinois and Wabash companies, that owing to the conditions annexed and to other circumstances the committee felt it inexpedient for Congress to accept the cessions as they stood. Therefore, repeating the earlier suggestion, the committee proposed that Congress name a date on which to consider the western limits beyond which it would not extend its guarantee to the States, and to ascertain what vacant lands belonged to the United States in common for the general benefit. It was in addition recommended that as soon as this were done a committee should be appointed to prepare a plan for dividing and settling the said territory, and for disposing of it so as to discharge the debts of the United States contracted in the war.

[36] The resolution in his handwriting is among the Papers of the Continental Congress.

Without further ado Congress pigeonholed the resolution by postponing consideration. And here the problem of the western lands rested for the time being.

The culmination of President Witherspoon's work in the Continental Congress was now approaching, in the preparation of the famous Instructions of June, 1781, whereby the United States, to use Professor Corwin's phrase, "surrendered to France their diplomatic autonomy." When the President remarked during the debate that "what we do now will be often mentioned in after times," he was more than prophetic. The Instructions and the policy creating them have not ceased to be attacked and defended from that day to this.[37]

The *Journal* of Congress reveals plainly enough that the President guided the debate leading to the Instructions;[38] the latter are in his handwriting; he defended them not only at the time of their adoption, but repeated his support of them whenever they were discussed during the remainder of his stay in Congress; and so controversial did the whole episode seem to be to him that he subsequently took the pains to write the *Memorial of Facts*, explaining how Congress was induced to direct the American commissioners to be ultimately guided by the Court of Versailles. Unfortunately this document, like so many of the Witherspoon papers, is incomplete, but what it lacks can be supplied from records of his speeches.

Professor Corwin has analysed the complicated circumstances leading to the Instructions and the finesse with which La Luzerne persuaded Congress, without dissent but not without misgivings, to adopt his suggestions. For the French Minister the vote was a personal triumph; but for President Witherspoon it was no less a victory. Mr. Corwin gives as the chief reason governing the decision, besides confidence in France, the common American belief that the fate of the United States rested

[37] The most recent and scholarly consideration is found in Professor Corwin's authoritative *French Policy and the American Alliance*. It is a pleasure to acknowledge the indebtedness of this chapter to several passages in that book.

[38] Another witness is Madison. Recalling two years later, the debate on the Instructions of 1781, he names in a note to his manuscript the personnel of the committee that framed them, and adds "Mr. Witherspoon was particularly prominent throughout." *Writings*, vol. I, p. 417.

THE INSTRUCTIONS OF JUNE 1781

Original Manuscript of President Witherspoon

almost entirely with France and therefore Congress could hardly do better "than vest France outright with the trusteeship of American interests."[39]

Whatever the continental diplomacy underlying La Luzerne's efforts, President Witherspoon appears to have reached his own conclusions after the coolest sort of consideration. It was a case of facing embarrassing but undeniable facts and framing a course of action accordingly. His personal sentiment for France played little or no part in the process. That he was in constant communication with La Luzerne must be taken for granted; he was one of the few members who could converse with the French Minister in his native tongue; and there are indications that more than once he gave close heed to suggestions made during the debate by the representative of France; but by no manner of means can it be said that he blindly followed La Luzerne's leading, or was merely his mouthpiece.

In his *Memorial of Facts* he enumerates the indebtedness of the Colonies to France for recognition, for troops, and money; Mr. Adams, charged with the peace negotiation, had fallen into a difference of opinion with Vergennes in which he was at fault; Congress had either to recall him or restrict his powers, and of the two evils Dr. Witherspoon chose the latter as less of a reflection on the national dignity; he was satisfied that the national security at least could not be injured; France was bound only to maintain our independence in government and commerce; beyond that she had the right to judge whether she would or would not continue the war for other objects claimed by the United States; the American ministers were not restrained from urging anything they thought proper in order to obtain all that the United States wished; could they have done more, asks the President, if they had been left quite at liberty? Finally, Congress did the only thing in its power to safeguard the various sectional interests that emerged by adding more members to the commission and from different parts of the country, thus removing suspicion and fear that the interest of one part would be sacrificed to that of another as might have been the case had one plenipotentiary alone been retained to conduct the negotiations for

[39] *op. cit.*, p. 306.

[53]

peace. As will appear later, Dr. Witherspoon ridiculed this last idea when it was first brought forward. Madison's version of the controlling reasons agrees with Dr. Witherspoon's in the main and is found in his report of the debate of December, 1782, on a motion to revise the Instructions of June, 1781, and release the American commissioners from the obligation to conform to the advice of France.[40]

These being the considerations governing the President's course, the debate itself may now be followed.

On May 28 a committee of which Dr. Witherspoon was a member, and which had been appointed at the request of La Luzerne to receive important communications he wished laid before Congress, reported in great detail the substance of its interviews with the Minister, announcing that a further loan had been agreed to by France and that there was strong probability of mediation by the courts of Vienna and St. Petersburg, urging the necessity of meanwhile placing a curb on Mr. Adams' use of his plenipotentiary powers, and emphasizing the need of the greatest exertions at this time on the part of the American federation, inasmuch as every success now gained by the American army would infinitely facilitate the negotiations of the American plenipotentiaries. Pending the conclusion of the conferences with the French Minister the report was re-committed.

A few days later (June 1) the committee reported the draft of a letter to the several States, which Congress agreed to, proclaiming the welcome news of overtures for peace and calling upon the States for their final supreme exertion, an exertion proportionable to the truly critical situation and complying unequivocally with the demands of Congress for provisions, men, and money. If these are supplied, said the draft, "we have the most pleasing prospect of putting a speedy and happy issue to the war, by driving the enemy out of their present possessions in every part of these States." The committee was confident the States would put forth strenuous efforts to accomplish such results and be prepared to accept peace on no other terms than independence. On June 5 and 6, the committee's report on La Luzerne's announcements was further considered and Congress

[40] *Writings*, vol. I, p. 298-9.

voted that the mediation proposed by Russia and Germany be concurred in, but that no treaty of peace be considered which did not effectually secure the independence of the United States, and leave in full force and validity the existing treaty with France. In view of the proposal of mediation President Witherspoon drew up a "Memorial and Manifesto of the United States of North America"[41] addressed to the mediating and other powers in Europe. It is a dispassionate and carefully framed presentation of the case of the American Colonies and reveals how fully the President had assimilated the American point of view during the twelve years of his residence in the New World. A native born colonial perhaps would have allowed himself more rhetoric, more feeling; but his statement could not have been clearer or more dignified. The document is the President's apologia for the American Revolution and for that reason, besides being one of the few political papers among his writings that has come down to us entire, is important enough to summarize.

It begins with a brief statement of the causes that led to the planting of the Colonies in America, "the spirit of curiosity and enterprise which was so prevalent in Europe in the sixteenth and seventeenth centuries," the hope of riches, and lastly, "the iron rod of sacerdotal tyranny" at home. The settlers solicited charters and formed their governments on different principles, but in one factor they all agreed: "they considered themselves as bringing their liberty with them and as entitled to all the rights and privileges of freemen under the British Constitution." The foundation stone of that liberty was that freeholders or proprietors of the soil should have the exclusive right of granting money for public uses, and they proceeded upon that plan. "With respect indeed to the whole of their internal government, they considered themselves not as directly subjects to the British government, but as separate independent dominions under the same sovereign, and with similar coordinate jurisdiction. . . . This was their opinion many years before the late unjust claims and oppressive acts which gave birth to the bloody conflict not yet finished."

They willingly "submitted to Britain's enjoying an exclusive right to their commerce, though several of the acts of the British Parliament upon this subject they always looked upon as partial and un-

---

[41] *Works*, vol. IV, p. 217.

just. Some of these . . . would not probably have been submitted to, but that the rigid execution of them at this distance was in its nature impossible." In the opinion of the Colonies, the benefits to Great Britain from exclusive commerce with America and the taxes thus raised on her own subjects were more than their share of the common treasure necessary for the defence of the empire. Notwithstanding, in extraordinary emergencies they complied with requisitions and advanced sums which in one or two instances Britain herself considered above their ability and made restitution or compensation.

The reason for this long and patient acquiescence was the attachment the inhabitants of America had to Great Britain as their parent country:

"They gloried in their relation to her; they were zealous for her honor and interest; imbibed her principles and prejudices with respect to other nations; entered into her quarrels, and were profuse of their blood for the purpose of securing or extending her dominion. Almost every city and county in Great Britain had its counterpart which bore its name in the new world; and those whose progenitors for three generations had been born in America, when they spoke of going to Britain, called it going home."

Such was the state of affairs when unwise counsellors to the British King thought of raising revenue without consent of American legislatures. The first attempt was the Stamp Act, so odious over the whole land that in short time it was repealed. Parliament by the Declaratory Act, however, showed it intended to maintain the so-called right, and it was not long before an Act was passed imposing duty on tea, glass, etc., which by the smallness of the duties was "plainly designed to steal upon us, gradually and if possible imperceptibly, the exercise of their pretended rights." The Colonies rose against its execution. "Not only every Colony, by its representative body, but every county and almost every corporation or other subordinate division, publicly declared that they would defend their liberty at the risk of their estates and lives." Meanwhile the British government was determined on unconditional submission and thus the rupture took place.

As to the justice of the cause, "if any impartial person will read the Declaratory Act stating that . . . Parliament has the right to make laws binding upon the Colonies *in all cases whatsoever*, and which is now producing its proper fruit, he must be convinced that . . . we should have been in no respect different from conquered tributary States, subject to a foreign country, and the Colonial Assemblies would have become both useless and contemptible." Writings in England that the Colonies were represented in Parliament are and will remain "a disgrace to reason as well as an insult to American understanding."

The troubles in America were said to have been raised by a few seditious persons and the consequences of a scheme to set up an independent rule: "This unjust and indeed absurd accusation may be refuted by a thousand arguments—the predilection of the people of America for the people, fashions and government of Britain, the absence of any person or persons in America of sufficient influence to effect it, the state of the Colonies when they began to grapple with the power of Britain, no step taken to obtain foreign aid, no provision of arms, ammunition, or warlike stores of any kind, the country exposed, naked, and helpless, before the enemy."

Reconciliation, with the security and preservation of our rights, was the wish of every soul; but each succeeding petition was treated with fresh and greater insult and was answered by new Acts of Parliament which will be a stain upon the annals of the kingdom. To crown all, the last petition sent by Congress to the King, beseeching him "to appoint some mode by which our complaints might be remedied and a way paved for reconciliation, was treated with absolute contempt and no answer given to it of any kind . . . We were declared rebels; and . . . no alternative left us but either to go with ropes about our necks and submit ourselves not to the King but to the kingdom of England, to be trampled under foot, or risk all the consequence of open and vigorous resistance."

The latter alternative was chosen and independence was declared, with the full approbation and at the ardent desire of the people at large. "The extent and growth of the Colonies seemed in the nature of things to call for such a separation long before; yet it would not probably have happened for many years if it had not been forced upon us by the conduct of our unkind parent herself."

After the Declaration of Independence, Lord Howe brought a commission for giving peace to America, but as he had not the liberty to acknowledge us by open treaty so the substance of what he offered was pardon upon submission. So important a step as the Declaration of Independence could not be recalled and the armament sent against us in 1776 rendered it more necessary than ever.

Dr. Witherspoon was sorry to take notice of the conduct of the war: "It would be for the honor of humanity that it could be buried in oblivion. The many instances of persons murdered in cold blood, the barbarous treatment of prisoners, multitudes dying of starvation, many impressed on British ships of war or sent to Britain to rot in prison, houses and towns wantonly burnt and the country devastated, to which may be added hiring the Indians to fall upon the back settlements."

At last it pleased God to incline the heart of the French King to give relief by entering into a treaty with the United States which gave "a new turn to our affairs, and a new dignity to our cause." The terms of that treaty, favorable to us and honorable to our ally, "cannot fail to add the bond of gratitude to that of justice and make adherence inviolable." Soon after, commissioners came out to offer terms; we were offered freedom from taxes and even "a species of independence itself," upon condition of breaking our faith with France and uniting our force with that of Great Britain. These proposals were ample confession that the demands of America were just and the circumstances and time of their making show they could not be accepted with any regard to justice, gratitude, or policy. Could we be guilty of a direct breach of faith when the ink was hardly dry on the treaty with France? Could we instantly forget favors so earnestly solicited and so generously bestowed? Could we, who had not entered an offensive and defensive league with France except for the present struggle in our own behalf, throw ourselves into the arms of an hostile nation and promise to make war with her against our benefactors?

"Upon the whole, since the American Colonies were, from their extent and situation, ripe for a separation from Great Britain, and the nature of things seemed to demand it; since their growing power added to that of Great Britain would give her such a dominion of the sea as must be dangerous to the liberty and commerce of other nations; since by her own acts of oppression she has alienated the minds of the Americans and compelled them to establish independent governments, which has now taken place; and since these governments, which are distinct though confederated, wholly settled upon republican principles, and fit only for agriculture and commerce, cannot be an object of jealousy to other powers, but by free and open intercourse with them are a general benefit to all; it is hoped that the revolution which they have effected will meet with universal approbation."

From La Luzerne, whose chief, Vergennes, had with difficulty secured Spain's active participation in the war, Dr. Witherspoon must have received, in addition to what Gérard had told Congress, fresh light on Spanish territorial claims in case the Colonies won their independence; for immediately after the passage of the motion accepting mediation he moved on June 6,[42] seconded by his colleague from New Jersey, Professor William C. Houston, further to instruct the Minister negotiating on behalf of the United States that as to disputed boundaries reference was made to previous instructions from which "the desires and expectations of Congress" would be easily perceived; but, continued the further instruction "we think it unsafe *at this Distance* to ty you up by absolute and peremptory Directions upon any Subject than the two essential Articles above mentioned" (i.e., independence, and the integrity of the French treaty). "You will therefore use your own Judgment and Prudence in securing the Interest of the United States in such Manner as Circumstances may direct. . . . " Further, the minister was "to make the most candid and confidential Communications upon all Subjects to the Ministers of our generous ally the King of France, to *undertake nothing without their Knowledge and Concurrence*, and make them sensible how much we rely upon his Majesty's Influence for effectual support in every thing that may be necessary to the present Security and future Prosperity of the United States." The italics are in the manuscript motion in Dr. Witherspoon's handwriting. But Congress did not approve the additional instruction as to boundaries; it failed of adoption and in further debate was with the entire report recommitted. The next day (June 7) Dr. Witherspoon, for the committee, resubmitted the motion with the following "Additional and secret Article of Instructions with Respect to the Boundaries of the United States:" first, the Minister was to use his utmost endeavors to secure the limits fixed by descriptions in previous instructions; second, failing this, peace was to be made without fixing the northern and western boundaries, leaving them for future discussion; and third, if that too proved impracticable and boundaries must be ascertained, as advantageous a settlement as possible in favor of the United States was to be obtained. Of these additional and

[42] The resolution in his handwriting is among the Papers of the Continental Congress.

secret instructions, which also are in Dr. Witherspoon's hand-writing, the first was adopted unanimously, the second was safely carried, while the third, receiving the votes of only five States, was lost.

The debate was continued on June 8 and the first part of President Witherspoon's original motion of the sixth being again reported by the committee, Virginia through the mouthpiece of Madison offered an additional provision that the Minister do not recede from the former instruction of Congress as to boundaries except so far as a western line was concerned, which the mover proceeded to describe; but his State was the only one to favor his proposal. Undaunted, Madison offered another amendment which provided that the Minister do not agree to any cession of territory lying on the southeast side of the Ohio and this met the fate of its predecessor. Then Mr. Bland, also of Virginia, took up the fight for his State and moved to strike out all after the phrase "desires and expectations" of the United States in Dr. Wither-spoon's motion, but was no more successful than Madison.

The original Witherspoon instructions of June 6 were then adopted; and an attempt to reconsider the vote on the third ad-ditional and secret instruction having failed, the President, per-ceiving that he now controlled a majority, promptly had the first and second secret instructions of the day before reconsid-ered and voted down, and the original form of the instructions adopted. June 9, on the President's further motion, another ad-ditional instruction was passed unanimously to the effect that if difficulty arose in the course of the peace negotiations on account of Great Britain's reluctance to make formal acknowledgment of the independence of the United States, the American nego-tiator was at liberty to agree to a truce or to any other conces-sion as might not affect the substance of what the United States were contending for, and "provided that Great Britain be not left in possession of any part of the thirteen United States."

At this point (June 9) came the suggestion from the commit-tee that additional plenipotentiaries be joined to Mr. Adams, a proposal for which Dr. Witherspoon was prepared and which he combatted in a speech preserved in his writings. With the purport of this speech Congress agreed, declining at the time to increase the personnel of the commission.[43]

Dr. Witherspoon's *Memorial of Facts* gives the confidential history of the transaction at this point. La Luzerne had intimated to the committee that the secret instructions, although made more definite at his request, were not yet sufficient for the present emergency; he read to the committee letters from Vergennes "upon the subject of Mr. Adams, complaining of him in the strongest terms and expressing fears of the negotiations being marred by his stiffness and tenaciousness of purpose;" it was even suspected by the committee that France wished Congress to recall Mr. Adams and appoint someone else, although no hint of this was made by Vergennes or suggested by La Luzerne; Mr. Adams' unfortunate disagreement with Vergennes, says Dr. Witherspoon, was due to an excess of well meant zeal, and the sacrifice of "a Minister of unquestionable integrity could not be submitted to merely because he had had more zeal than good manners." Therefore it had been proposed that a clause be added "that he *do nothing without the consent and approbation of the Court of France*" (italics are Witherspoon's). But La Luzerne was still unsatisfied; the new clause was merely negative; Mr. Adams might indeed now do nothing himself, but he might still obstruct every measure and effectually prevent anything else being done. When this was reported to Congress, continues the *Memorial*, "the matter appeared exceedingly delicate and diffi-

[43] The President after alluding to the warmth of the debate, insisted that the appointment of only one commissioner would conduce to "more precision, more expedition, more uniformity, and more certainty of agreement with others and consistency with himself." Mr. Adams having long been in Europe had no doubt "been turning his thoughts, and making enquiries upon the subject ever since he went there, so that we may suppose him pretty ripely advised." As for the alleged advantage in the council of several as against one, he felt that this meant only distribution of responsibility and possibly a division of opinion which would of itself be the cause of danger. As for the necessity of representation from various parts of the country he could not see what circumstances could "be peculiar to one part of the country more than another" in a negotiation of this kind. If it concerned internal government, taxation, or interstate commerce, it would be different; but when "it is only to make peace for the liberty and protection of all, there seems to be little right in it," (*Works*, IV, 267). Professor Corwin has pointed out (p. 302) how this question after all did concern various groups in Congress representing various interests; and President Witherspoon himself very soon discovered sufficient grounds for changing his mind.

cult. It was discussed at great length. All the objections against removing Mr. Adams were argued in their full force; but on the other hand, it appeared humiliating if not dangerous to deliver ourselves entirely to the Court of France. However, after full deliberation it was agreed that he should *be ultimately guided by the opinion and judgment of the Court of France"* (italics again Witherspoon's).

On June 11 Dr. Witherspoon's committee reported that it had conveyed to the French Minister the substance of the Instructions of June 9, and now wished to incorporate certain amendments, all of which were approved. The debate thereon, if any, is not recorded, but the effect of these amendments was without exception to place the American representative more completely than ever under the direction of the French Foreign Office, and La Luzerne's hand is plainly discernible.

It is regrettable that Dr. Witherspoon's *Memorial of Facts* is not complete, for he might then have explained his change of attitude on the question of enlarging the commission. It is quite evident that further conference with La Luzerne had won him over to a compromise, for on June 11 his committee moved reconsideration of the question of enlarging the mission, and in the light of fuller information, so easily was Congress induced to reverse itself and add others to Mr. Adams as negotiators for peace, that the yeas and nays were not even called for.[44] As a result Jay, Franklin, Henry Laurens and Jefferson were added to the mission and at length on June 15 the famous Instructions as a whole, framed in the first instance by Dr. Witherspoon to control Mr. Adams, were adopted to govern the new commission.[45]

The President was absent the first three weeks of July, 1781, but when he returned was immediately made chairman of a committee appointed to receive further important communications which the French Minister informed Congress he wished to make. On July 23 he reported the substance of the audience with the Minister. The latter explained the causes delaying the meas-

[44] See *Journal,* XX, 626.
[45] It may be well, as Professor Corwin reminds his readers, to remember that the Instructions had no influence after all on the negotiations leading to the peace of 1783. Their fate may be followed in his volume.

ures the King of France had taken for a naval campaign; he intimated that Holland was open to approach and offered his services as an intermediary; he suggested that Congress send an envoy to Holland with suitable instructions: and he alluded to the favorable attitude of Russia. This report was referred back, and early in August Dr. Witherspoon reported resolutions expressing the gratitude of Congress to the King of France for his friendship and regard, accepting his offer of interposition with Holland, and directing Mr. Adams to go to the Hague to propose a treaty of amity and commerce, consistent with the terms of the treaty with France. The committee was ordered to frame definite instructions for Mr. Adams and on August 16 these were introduced by Dr. Witherspoon and approved.

The Board of War injected academic matters into Congressional diplomatic deliberations that summer by presenting to Congress bills from Dr. Witherspoon and Colonel George Morgan of Princeton for tuition and maintenance of three Indian students at the College of New Jersey. They were sons of Delaware chieftains and had been at Princeton since the spring of 1779 attempting, under the guardianship of Colonel Morgan and at government expense, to assimilate an education in the college grammar school. The curious and pathetic story of this totally unsuccessful educational venture may be found in the *Princeton University Bulletin*[46] for May, 1902, and mention of it here has place chiefly as illustrating the inefficiency of the government's financial administration and of the predicaments in which Dr. Witherspoon's multiplied activities often placed him. The report of the Board of War was referred July 31 to the Board of Treasury "to devise ways and means for furnishing Colonel George Morgan with the sum of one hundred and thirty-seven pounds currency of New Jersey in specie," for the settlement of the bills. But the Board of Treasury was not so easily to be parted from its money, and a week later retorted that Dr. Witherspoon was holding a "large sum in specie" due the United States which had been deposited with him in 1778 by exchanged North Carolina prisoners of war to discharge demands of the United States in return for subsistence, and the Board suggested that this money

[46] vol. XIII, p. 101, etc.

be applied to the bills in question. Dr. Witherspoon promptly returned the warrant with a protest and several letters, which action was duly reported to Congress in September and was referred to a fresh committee, which in its turn reported in October; and after consideration by Congress the whole matter with the accompanying file of documents was referred to the superintendent of finance to whom Dr. Witherspoon was ordered to account for and pay over the monies he had received from the prisoners, the superintendent of finance thereupon to "take order for the support and education of the Indian youths at Princeton College under the care of Colonel George Morgan, out of the said moneys, or otherwise as he may think expedient"— which action plainly shifted the whole matter on to his already overburdened shoulders. The controversy seems to have been amicably settled in a manner now not quite clear, but the records show that Colonel Morgan thereafter received fairly regular reimbursements from the superintendent of finance for expenses incurred by the government's wards at Princeton. No papers, however, have been found relative to Dr. Witherspoon's accounting for the funds he was alleged to be holding.

Except for this comedy, the College of New Jersey figures seldom in the Congressional record of the time. One or two petitions for relief from quartering of troops in Nassau Hall, or for reimbursement for rentals, or to excuse the officers of the College from military duty are the only occasions when the institution formally appears in the record. But in debate Dr. Witherspoon did not hesitate to use his college experience. For example, in 1777 he pointed his objection to leaving the election of five major generals in the army to the vote of the general officers, by telling his colleagues that once—and only once—he had allowed his Seniors at College to elect their own commencement honormen, and the election had produced so much ill-feeling and confusion that he had ever since kept the appointive power himself. Congress followed the hint.

The condition of national affairs that autumn externally looked so favorable that a day of thanksgiving seemed appropriate, and on September 15 Dr. Witherspoon was appointed chairman of a committee to report a proclamation. Before he brought

THANKSGIVING PROCLAMATION OF OCTOBER 1781

Original Manuscript of President Witherspoon

it in, however, Cornwallis surrendered at Yorktown on October 19, and when the President reported his proclamation on the twenty-sixth, it was more than ever timely. The rapidity with which he usually produced compositions of this sort makes one wonder why he delayed this particular paper six weeks. Had he possibly some inkling of important developments in the South? Washington had reported the arrival of the Count de Grasse in the Chesapeake with ships, men and money; and Dr. Witherspoon had seen Washington and Rochambeau leave Philadelphia the first week of September marching south. Is it an unreasonable conjecture that they had dropped a hint as to the prize for which they were playing, and that the President before penning the proclamation had calmly waited to see whether fortune—or rather Providence—would crown their plans with success.

Whereas, it hath pleased Almighty God, father of mercies, remarkably to assist and support the United States of America in their important struggle for liberty, against the long continued efforts of a powerful nation: it is the duty of all ranks to observe and thankfully acknowledge the interpositions of his Providence in their behalf. Through the whole of the contest, from its first rise to this time, the influence of Divine Providence may be clearly perceived in many signal instances, of which we mention but a few.

In revealing the councils of our enemies, when the discoveries were seasonable and important, and the means seemingly inadequate or fortuitous; in preserving and even improving the union of the several States, on the breach of which our enemies placed their greatest dependence; in increasing the number and adding to the zeal and attachment of the friends of Liberty; in granting remarkable deliverances, and blessing us with the most signal success, when affairs seemed to have the most discouraging appearance; in raising up for us a powerful and generous ally, in one of the first of the European powers; in confounding the councils of our enemies, and suffering them to pursue such measures as have most directly contributed to frustrate their own desires and expectations; above all, in making their extreme cruelty to the inhabitants of these States, when in their power, and their savage devastation of property, the very means of cementing our union, and adding vigor to every effort in opposition to them.

And as we cannot help leading the good people of these States to a retrospect on the events which have taken place since the beginning of the war, so we recommend in a particular manner to their observation, the goodness of God in the year now drawing to a conclusion; in which the Confederation of the United States has been completed, in which there have been so many instances of prowess and success in our armies; particularly in the Southern States, where, notwithstanding the difficulties with which they had to struggle, they have recovered the whole country which the enemy had overrun, leaving them only a post or two on or near the sea; in which we have been so powerfully and effectually assisted by our allies, while in all the conjunct operations the most perfect harmony has subsisted in the allied army; in which there has been so plentiful a harvest, and so great abundance of the fruits of the earth of every kind, as not only enables us easily to supply the wants of the army, but gives comfort and happiness to the whole people; and in which, after the success of our allies by sea, a General of the first Rank, with his whole army, has been captured by the allied forces under the direction of our Commander in Chief.

It is therefore recommended to the several states to set apart the thirteenth day of December next, to be religiously observed as a Day of Thanksgiving and Prayer; that all the people may assemble on that day, with grateful hearts, to celebrate the praise of our gracious Benefactor; to confess our manifold sins; to offer up our most fervent supplications to the God of all grace, that it may please Him to pardon our offences, and incline our hearts for the future to keep all his laws; to comfort and relieve all our brethren who are in distress or captivity; to prosper all husbandmen, and give success to all engaged in lawful commerce; to impart wisdom and integrity to our counsellors, judgment and fortitude to our officers and soldiers; to protect and prosper our illustrious ally, and favor our united exertions for the speedy establishment of a safe, honorable and lasting peace; and bless all seminaries of learning; and cause the knowledge of God to cover the earth, as the water covers the seas.[47]

The New York *Gazette* that winter printed in its columns an alleged speech by the President on Cornwallis's surrender. It was copied by the Edinburgh *Gazette* of January 8, 1782, and reprinted in 1809 in Sergeant Lamb's *Original and authentic Journal of Occurrences during the late American War*. The speech is

[47] In Dr. Witherspoon's handwriting—Papers Continental Congress, vol. 24, 463— printed in *Journal*, vol. XXI, p. 1074.

original, but by no possibility authentic; it sneers at Washington and his army; it curses the French alliance; and either of these features alone is sufficient to stamp it as fraudulent. One or two passages—such as the dark picture of the country's general condition, and the suggestion that overtures for peace might now be made—may be genuine; but except for these and similar scattered paragraphs neither content nor style admit of any belief whatsoever in the authenticity of the speech as a whole.

President Witherspoon's term came to a close that December and he returned to Princeton probably confident that the surrender of Cornwallis had brought the end of the war actually within sight. In February, 1782, the House of Commons voted against continuing offensive warfare in America, an action promptly followed by the resignation of Lord North and the appointment of his successor Lord Rockingham; in April the Dutch Republic recognized American independence; in May Sir Guy Carleton superseded Sir Henry Clinton in command of the British forces in America and quickly indicated that further active hostilities would not be undertaken; and on the last day of that month, New Jersey returned Dr. Witherspoon once more to Congress to serve until November. He had just been attending the annual meeting of the Synod of New York and Philadelphia at which, as chairman of a special committee appointed for the purpose, he had drafted and brought in a letter[48] from the Synod to the French Minister and had accompanied the moderator of the Synod in presenting it to La Luzerne. The letter began with these words:

The Synod of New York and Philadelphia beg leave to address your Excellency on the auspicious birth of a Dauphin of France and by your means to communicate to your sovereign the interest which they take in every event with which his honour or happiness is connected.

The wish is then expressed that this address may be considered as testimony of the Synod's approbation of the French Alliance; and the assurance is given that the Synod will

[48] The manuscript is in the President's handwriting.

not cease to pray to the God of all grace that the illustrious ally of these States and his posterity to the latest ages may be distinguished at home and abroad as the supporters of liberty and justice, as the friends of mankind and deliverers of the oppressed.

In its letter of May, 1779, with which it will be remembered Dr. Witherspoon was also concerned, congratulating His Majesty on the birth of a princess, Congress had expressed the prayer that the "Supreme Disposer of events" would long continue to France "the blessings resulting from the administration of a prince who so nobly asserts the rights of mankind." It is a curious speculation whether the President recollected these phrases of his when, ten years from that summer, the news reached America of the tragic fate of the French ruler and his little children, whose entrances upon their pitiful histories Dr. Witherspoon had helped to commemorate. There is no known expression of his feeling toward the French Revolution, although, as a subsequent chapter will show, that event did not pass unrecognized by the republicans of the Princeton campus.

Dr. Witherspoon took his seat in Congress June 12 and immediately proceeded (June 17, 1782) to push the question of peace negotiations by moving that a committee be appointed to report the information and instructions proper to be transmitted to the American Ministers the better to enable them to support the claims of the United States not included in their ultimate demands of June, 1781. But Congress was unready to follow his lead and voted the resolution down, and it was not until midsummer that the proposal at length was adopted, when the great debate on the western lands came on. It was an easier matter to gain his colleagues' approval of the better regulation of the business of the government and he secured the passage of a resolution appointing committees semi-annually to enquire fully into and report on the condition of the various executive departments. He was able also to secure consideration of an important resolution bearing on the finances of the country. The superintendent of finance had reported that every loan Congress could command for the year had already been anticipated and he could not meet the loan office obligations without further funds. The situation was referred to a committee of which Dr. Witherspoon. was chairman. The resulting resolution penned by him reads:

Whereas the drawing Bills upon Europe for the Payment of Interest due on Loan Office certificates has been attended by many Inconveniences and the Continuation of it would be inconsistent with the Public Service.

Resolved that the Superintendent of Finance be directed to draw no more Bills on Europe for the payment of Interest due or that may become due on monies lent to the United States, but that he take Measures in future for the seasonable Payment of the Interest on all Loans and of the Duties laid or to be laid on imported Goods in the several States at the Disposal of Congress.

This was referred to the superintendent of finance who in turn reported a similar resolution which was referred to a fresh committee of which Arthur Lee was a member. This committee's concurring resolution being under debate in July, Lee presented a memorial asking that his account against the United States for service in Europe be honored in bills of exchange as in the case of other Ministers. The memorial was referred back to Dr. Witherspoon and Messrs. Lowell and Middleton, who earlier in the month had approved Lee's claim. In the pointed language of Charles Thomson, the veteran secretary of Congress,

notwithstanding the information that there were no funds on which bills could be drawn, notwithstanding a report of a Committee . . . was then before Congress . . . for putting a stop to the drawing of any more bills and notwithstanding the clamours of the holders of certificates which would naturally be increased when they found their interest stopped under pretence that Congress had no funds in Europe . . . and at the same time drawing in favour of one of their members for a sum equal to one fortieth of their whole interest, notwithstanding all this the Committee on July 19 reported that the superintendent of finance draw on Dr. Franklin for the full amount of Lee's claim.

Dr. Witherspoon had written the previous resolution of reference to the superintendent who evidently gave it at least his acquiescence if not approval, and returned it to Congress July 12, when it was handed once more to Dr. Witherspoon's committee to frame the order at length adopted July 19.[49]

On July 31 a grand committee, Dr. Witherspoon representing · New Jersey, appointed to report the most effectual means for supporting the credit of the United States, bluntly informed the House that in its opinion Congress should come to a decision on the land cessions of Connecticut, Virginia and New York. The question was plainly uppermost in men's minds at this time, however they may have preferred to avoid it. The difficulty of obtaining money from the States either by recommendation or pleading had long been chronic; even the federal five per cent tax was not being collected; and the vacant western lands now seemed to offer the only possible solution to a financial situation that brooked no further tolerances. More than a year had elapsed since Congress had declined to consider Dr. Witherspoon's report on the cessions. But Congress as a body was still unwilling to take the question up, and when on July 31 after much discussion, most of which was aside from the point, President Witherspoon moved that a week later the report of the grand committee be considered, he failed by the vote of one State to carry his motion.

Before the matter was next considered the ever rankling question of the Instructions of June, 1781, was reopened and on August 8 a motion was offered that a committee be appointed "to consider and revise the instructions given to our Ministers for negotiating a peace with Great Britain." Madison made a long speech against any alteration of the Instructions; if any member wished to secure further the several objects claimed by

[49]Was this a further illustration of Dr. Witherspoon's friendliness to the Lees? Mr. Lowell, one of the committee, had been opposed to the action but was over-ruled by his colleagues (*Thomson Papers* 68). Mr. Thomson shows how Lee had placed himself on the footing of other public creditors and had no right therefore "to any peculiar favor or indulgence." By passing the matter to the superintendent of finance with power, Congress shifted on to his shoulders the dilemma of incurring either the odium of the public creditors by drawing in favor of Mr. Lee, or the resentment of the latter by a refusal. This is Mr. Thomson's conclusion (*Papers*, 69). It should be added, however, that Lee asked only what had been accorded to other ministers whose accounts had been settled, with the difference that he had complicated his accounts by expenditures on behalf of the state of Virginia.

the United States he had no objection to consider them, provided there was no encroachment on the Instructions; and he gave notice that he would move postponement of the present motion and in its place offer another to the effect that a committee be appointed to consider and report the best means to secure the objects claimed by the United States, but not included in the Instructions of June, 1781. In this attitude Madison was supported by President Witherspoon who in seconding the motion to postpone made the speech already referred to, recalling the circumstances in 1781 leading to the adoption of the Instructions, reminding Congress of the dilemma in which it had found itself at that time through Mr. Adams' conduct, and how in order to save its dignity it had increased the number of the commissioners; and he concluded with the observation that as American confidence placed in France was a mere compliment and not a discard of any real security, he opposed withdrawing it and therefore supported Madison's motion. Postponement being agreed to, Madison then offered his resolution to appoint a committee on the further claims of the United States, being again seconded by his former preceptor. It was now the opposition's turn to move postponement of consideration, but Dr. Witherspoon warmly defended Madison's proposal. He seemed to admit, says Mr. Thomson's record, which is followed here, that France had desired the committee to fix the boundaries but that it could not be done at the time so as to satisfy all the States; he observed that the happiness of the people on this side of the Allegheny Mountains had been a sufficient object to induce them to enter into the war; that some of the States had their boundaries fixed and determined; that the State he had the honor to represent was one of these; that it had not entered into the war, nor would it, he believed, be willing to continue, for the sake of boundless claims of wild uncultivated country; especially as they were a matter of dispute and would undoubtedly occasion much contention among the States to whom the country, if ceded, would of right belong; that what related to a treaty of commerce would come within the objects of the present motion, however, and that he was therefore against postponement. He carried his point; the postponement was negatived, and Madison's motion to appoint a committee coming up was carried and both he and Dr. Witherspoon found themselves so appointed.

They reported a long resolution on August 15 the purport of which was that a file of documents, collected by a former committee in support of claims not included in the peace ultimatum of 1781, be turned over to the Secretary for Foreign Affairs to transmit to the commissioners for their use to communicate to the King of France so much as they saw fit, representing to him that Congress had caused the compilation of the documents in the belief that he would find in them clear proofs of the validity of the American claims.

The intention of the committee was that the documents should be forwarded without having Congress pass any opinion on their contents, by which procedure they would not go as instructions, but merely as materials of evidence, and the conduct of the ministers would be influenced by them no farther than their judgment directed. Contrary to the committee's plan, however, the file, known as "Facts and Observations in support of the several claims of the United States not included in the Ultimatum of the fifteenth of June, 1781," was called for and read the next day. When the secretary, reaching the end of the citation of grants and charters, came to a clause reading

if the vacant lands cannot be demanded upon the preceding grounds, that is upon the titles of individual states, they are to be deemed to have been the property of His Britannic Majesty immediately before the revolution and now to be devolved upon the United States collectively taken.

he was interrupted by Mr. Lee with a motion to expunge; and the match was set to the fire. Heated debate was at once precipitated.

Professor Corwin has shown the evolution of contemporary American opinion regarding the disposal of the western lands. At the outset favoring the view that these lands were subject to the disposal of Congress, with the rise of the principle of state sovereignty opinion veered to the narrower view that the lands were the property of particular states; but from 1781 on, "the prospect developed that States credited with ownership would surrender their claims to the Confederacy at large. Once more the interest of all States in seeing the American title established became what it originally had been." For this change back to the broader national sentiment it may be fairly claimed that no member of Congress was more responsible than President Witherspoon. The broad national view had marked his attitude toward all questions of policy from the very beginning of his presence in Congress; it was a view he had never lost an opportunity to emphasize. To him the disposal of the western lands was a question of national policy and not a question merely of individual state claims or rights. According to him, at the declaration of the independence of the Colonies the title to the western lands had devolved on the American people as a nation, and this position he with members of other States, whose boundaries like New Jersey's were fixed and determined, forcefully reiterated in the present debate. Members whose States claimed territory to the Mississippi, or whose western boundaries were undefined, just as forcefully opposed him. Finally, a vigilant parliamentarian on the floor raised the point of order that the reading of the report was for information only and not for debate and that, therefore, both the motion of Mr. Lee and the present debate were out of order and no vote could be taken until the entire file of documents was read. The reply was made that this technical objection should have been raised earlier and it was now too late to inject it. But to put an end to discussion for the present adjournment was called for and carried.

On the twentieth, the "Facts and Observations" having been read to their end, the report of Dr. Witherspoon's committee was amended to read that the documents be referred to the Secretary for Foreign Affairs to be transmitted to the Ministers negotiating peace, for their information and use. Mr. Lee then moved to except the passage already quoted and the main debate came on. Mr. Lee's arguments were those of the individual States; the claims to the western territory rested solely on the titles of the individual States; Congress had no authority but what it derived from the States; these individually were sovereign and independent and upon them alone devolved the rights of the Crown within their respective territories; the sovereignty of the Crown could not devolve upon the United States in Congress assembled since no such body legally existed; whence was the sovereignty of the United States derived? did it really exist? Finally, should Congress put an argument in the mouths of the Ministers which they might use to their own advantage? One of the Ministers had a claim on some of the lands in question and one of the Ministers of France was likewise interested. Dr. Witherspoon at this point sought to have a vote taken without further debate; the Ministers in supporting the American claims to the western lands were first to urge the titles of the several States; failing this they were to urge the argument of the clause to which Mr. Lee objected; to omit this clause meant that if the claims could not be supported on the stated grounds they were to be relinquished entirely. Mr. Lee repeating that the amendment was intended to remove an argument which the ministers might use to their own advantage, Dr. Witherspoon came gallantly to the defence of the absent representatives of the nation. He challenged the suggestion that the Ministers would be unfaithful; if Franklin, to whom Lee had referred, was interested and would take advantage of it, let his recall be moved; he (Witherspoon) would second the motion. The "Facts and Observations" as they stood required that the Ministers should in the first place urge the titles of the several States; if these prevailed the end was obtained and the argument in question would not be brought forward. But if arguments "drawn from old charters, charters granted at a time when the extent and limits of this country were without charters and titles interfering with one another, whose limits were so extravagant that it was thought proper to curtail them in a former treaty, if arguments from this source should be found of no weight with the mediating powers of Europe (and he believed this would prove to be the case), would anyone wish to preclude our Ministers from using an argument which would carry weight, an argument drawn from general security, the force of which had been admitted in former treaties and would be admitted by every disinterested power in Europe?"

The several States, he went on to say, were known under the style ⁊ and title of the United States. This nation was known to be settled along the coasts to a certain extent; if any European power was admitted to establish colonies or settlements behind them, what security could they have for the enjoyment of peace? What a source of future wars! Was not this the principal argument urged by Great Britain against France at the breaking out of the last war? Whether the uncultivated wilderness on the frontiers should belong to one state or another was a matter of little concern to the European powers. The only argument that would weigh with them was whether it was necessary for the security of the United States that other nations should be excluded from that country, and particularly Great Britain, the enemy of these states. He was, therefore, against the amendment.

Further discussion followed, and notice having been served that the yeas and nays would be called for by the proposers of the amendment, a parliamentary manoeuvre by which the whole of the "Facts and Observations" would go into the *Journal* and Congress would have to take action upon them, thus making them instructions and not merely information as the committee had desired, on motion of Dr. Witherspoon the report was referred to a fresh committee of which again he and Madison found themselves members.

Before they reported however, the question emerged from a totally unexpected quarter. A petition signed by "a number of inhabitants of a tract of Country called Kentucky" was read, setting forth that they had settled a tract west of the Alleghenies, that Virginia had recently granted tracts there, claiming jurisdiction, and had undertaken to form them into counties, that owing to the distance—eight hundred miles from the seat of government at Richmond—jurisdiction could not be exercised with justice and energy, that they were in danger of losing their rights if they had to appeal to Richmond to contest the last grantees, that they had taken oaths of allegiance and considered themselves citizens of the United States and not of Virginia, that the charter under which Virginia claimed the country had been dissolved and that in consequence the country belonged to the Crown, and that by the Revolution the rights of the Crown devolved upon the United States, and that therefore they prayed

Congress to erect them into a separate and independent State and admit them into the Union.

Lee was on his feet at once; the countenancing of such a petition was an insult to Virginia; the only thing now to do was to refer it to Virginia; the petitioners were citizens of Virginia and the Legislature of that State was their proper court of appeal. What right, he asked, had Congress to interfere? The assertion that the rights of the Crown had devolved upon Congress was a groundless, extravagant, and idle supposition; Congress had no powers or rights but what the Confederation gave it; the United States individually were in existence before Congress was; they were sovereign, free, and independent States except in what they voluntarily gave to Congress by the confederation; the rights of the Crown to the vacant lands within any State could not devolve upon Congress, but upon the individual States within which the lands lay.

Mr. Lee was supported by Madison who described the provisions made by Virginia to care for the particular grievances complained of; Virginia and not Congress was the rightful judge in the case; the dissolution of the charter did not break the social compact among the people; the charter was an agreement between the King, the proprietors, and the people; the King by dissolving the charter might succeed to the rights of the proprietors but not to those of the people; these remained untouched. The supposition that the right of the Crown devolved upon the United States was so extravagant that it could not enter into the thoughts of any man; if the right of soil devolved, why not the right to the quit rents and to confiscated estates?

Other members sensed the dangers involved in the question under discussion and hoped it could be put off indefinitely; its further consideration might be attended with the most portentous consequences—one gentleman thought the sword alone could settle it; (and he was not far wrong). Others however, while recognizing the serious nature of the question, were not for leaving it to posterity, but for thrashing it out at once. If the people of Kentucky, said Mr. McKean of Delaware, had sworn allegiance to the United States he would take them by the hand; he was not afraid of Virginia; he hoped no state in the Union would ever become so great as to give laws to the rest, nor that any would be suffered to acquire so much power that the others could not control it. Such sentiments were in accord with the feelings of President Witherspoon who seems to have been saving himself while the debate grew more heated. He now at last arose with a speech which is not preserved in his *Works*, but luckily was saved by Mr. Thomson; it is his summing up for the landless States, and marks his broad conception, not only of the rights of the United States, but also of the powers of Congress.[50]

One of the gentlemen from Virginia, he began by remarking, had said that it could not enter into the thoughts of any man that the rights of the Crown devolved on the United States; he supposed this was intended only as a figure of rhetoric, not as an assertion that would be admitted. It certainly could enter into the thoughts of men and had actually entered into his thoughts, and it had entered the thoughts of the petitioners and into the thoughts of very many sensible men at the beginning of the present controversy. The western uncultivated and unappropriated lands belonging to the Crown were considered and spoken of early in the controversy as a fund for discharging the debts that might be contracted by the United States in the war. It would appear a strange whim if a sentiment which occupied and engrossed the minds not only of speculative but of illiterate men and the bulk of the inhabitants of many of the states had not some solid foundation to rest on.

For his part he thought it founded on truth, on justice, on the nature of things, and was warranted by the laws of society. The revolution had been begun and the war carried on by the united and joint efforts of the thirteen States. By their joint exertions and not by those of any one State the dominion of Great Britain had been broken and consequently the rights claimed and exercised by the Crown devolved on all and not any individual States. Why should one State reap more advantage than another? He admitted the consequence that not only the right of the unappropriated soil but also of the quit rents and confiscated estates devolved on the United States. As to the quit rents it seemed to be the general opinion that they should no longer be collected, but that each man should enjoy the portion of land he was possessed of, clear of all incumbrance of quit rents and therefore they were not made an object; with respect to confiscated estates, they

[50] *Thomson Papers*, p. 149.

were too inconsiderable to excite attention. Had a major part or even one-half of any State joined the enemy and their estates thereby become confiscated he apprehended it would have been a matter of serious discussion whether they should belong to the United States or be appropriated to the sole benefit of the other half of the citizens of the State.

With regard to the powers of Congress, or of the United States collectively taken, they could not be exactly defined in the articles of the Confederation. Cases would arise for which no previous provision could be made. These came under and were decided by the great law of necessity which was admitted as a law of nations. It might happen that a State would grow so powerful and so ambitious as to be dangerous to the other States in the Union. In such a case the law of necessity and of self-preservation might compel the others by a sovereign act of authority to abridge the power of that State and even to divide it into two or more distinct and independent States. He would not undertake to say that the petitioners were within or without the bounds of Virginia, or that it was proper or improper to grant their prayer; but he saw no impropriety in letting the petition remain on the files of Congress and should therefore vote in favor of that question.

Adjournment again put an end to the debate temporarily, but in the first week of September Congress resumed the discussion. After several attempted amendments serving special interests, it became evident to all parties, as Madison wrote to Edmund Randolph describing the debate,[51] that unless a compromise were effected no advantage could ever be derived by the United States "even if their right were ever so valid." The number of States holding the doctrine of individual titles rendered a vote in favor of a federal title impossible to reach whilst the individual States "having both the will and the means to avail themselves of their pretensions" might open land offices, issue patents, and "if necessary, protect the execution of their plans." This situation had its effect on even the most temperate advocates of the federal title and President Witherspoon, himself the leader of the federal group, moved a set of resolutions to the effect that if the States claiming exclusive ownership would cede the western lands to the

[51] *Writings*, vol. I, p. 232.

United States, such action would create "an important fund for the discharge of the national debt." He recommended that the States which had made no cession consider the matter as soon as possible, that those which had made cessions "not entirely agreeable" to the above recommendations reconsider and report, and that in case States claiming lands had ceded them, none of their Acts regarding private property should be reversed or altered without their consent. These resolves were naturally referred to a committee and the latter reported September 25 virtually in Dr. Witherspoon's words and after amendment in the debate, Congress at length declined the report. When the question was eventually decided in the direction of the President's views, he was no longer in Congress.

During the summer of 1782 the effect of the news of approaching peace on the morale of the country seems to have been feared in Congress and particularly by President Witherspoon and his colleagues on a committee to which had been referred correspondence between General Washington and the British commanders at New York, Sir Guy Carleton and Admiral Digby. Afraid that the country might think Congress had received authentic information announcing peace, it was resolved August 15 on the advice of the committee that the correspondence be published, that Congress consider it "as mere matter of information, inexplicit as to the nature and extent of the independency" to be proposed by Great Britain, and that as Congress had no information on the subject from the American commission in Europe no action could be taken upon it. The committee recommended further that the States be urged "not to remit of their exertions for carrying on the war with vigor, as the only effectual means of securing the settlement of a safe and honorable peace" —a clause with which sounds very like Dr. Witherspoon. Meanwhile, however, it was suggested that General Washington propose to the British commanders the appointment of commissioners to arrange partial exchange of prisoners.

In the midst of the tension caused by the debate on the western land Dr. Witherspoon had reported (September 12) on the project of his friend Robert Aitken, the Philadelphia printer, to issue an edition of the Holy Bible; and on his recommendation it was voted that the United States in Congress assembled highly approved the pious and laudable undertaking of Mr. Aitken "as subservient to the interest of religion as well as an instance of progress of arts in this country;" and hereby authorized him to publish this recommendation in the manner he should think proper. The committee had watched his work from time to time —he had memorialized Congress in January, 1781, on the subject—and had secured recommendations from the chaplains of Congress, the Reverends William White and George Duffield, who certified that his edition of the scriptures contained "as few grammatical and typographical errors as could be expected in an undertaking of such magnitude," and that in view of the demand for this "invaluable book" they rejoiced in the prospect of a supply and hoped it would be as advantageous as it was honorable to the printer who was risking his private means in the enterprise. Half of the committee's hope was realized, but unfortunately it was the wrong half from the commercial point of view, and Mr. Aitken lost the money he spent on his venture.

In the well-known Lippincott-Huddy case which jeopardized the whole movement for peace, and was debated so warmly late that summer, Dr. Witherspoon as a member of the committee, to which the matter was at length turned over, voted for temporizing, meanwhile suspending execution of the sentence of retaliation, until eventually Vergennes asked clemency for the English officer selected to suffer Huddy's fate, and secured his release a few days after Dr. Witherspoon had ceased to be a member of Congress. Shortly before the committee on this difficult case reported, the President had brought in what was to be the last of his proclamations recommending a day of thanksgiving. The text is in his handwriting:[52]

It being the indispensable duty of all nations, not only to offer up their supplications to Almighty God, the giver of all good, for his gracious assistance in a time of distress, but also in a solemn and public manner to give him praise for his goodness in general, and especially for great and signal interpositions of his Providence in their behalf; therefore the United States in Congress assembled, taking into their

[52] Papers Continental Congress, 24*ff*, 471; *Journal* vol. XXIII, p. 647.

consideration the many instances of divine goodness to these States, in the course of the important conflict in which they have been so long engaged; the present happy and promising state of public affairs; and the events of the war in the course of the year now drawing to a close, particularly the harmony of the public councils, which is so necessary to the success of the public cause; the perfect union and good understanding which has hitherto subsisted between them and their allies, notwithstanding the artful and unwearied attempts of the common enemy to divide them; the success of the armies of the United States and those of their allies, and the acknowledgment of their independence by another European power, whose friendship and commerce must be of great and lasting advantage to these States; do hereby recommend it to the inhabitants of these States in general, to observe, and request the several States to interpose their authority in appointing and commanding the observation of Thursday, the twenty-eighth day of November next, as a day of solemn thanksgiving to God for all his mercies; and they do further recommend to all ranks and testify their gratitude of God for his goodness, by a cheerful obedience to his laws, and by protecting, each in his station, and by his influence, the practice of true and undefiled religion, which is the great foundation of public prosperity and national happiness.

CHAPTER TWO

THE years of Dr. Witherspoon's congressional service were years of bitter hardship for the College over which he presided. Receiving almost a deathblow at the very beginning of this period, its condition for seven months (November 29, 1776, to July 8, 1777), was one of suspended animation; and its history, while its President was fulfilling the higher duty of national service, is a story of struggle to regain from military occupants the possession of its property, to secure from the Congress at least partial remuneration for the destruction caused by that occupancy, and despite staggering financial losses to repair damage and make collegiate residence and a semblance of academic life once more possible. Before attempting to reconstruct the history of those years, it is well to sketch the condition of the College when the President left it in the summer of 1776.

During the period between his arrival at Princeton in 1768 and his election to Congress in 1776, the College of New Jersey had made creditable progress. The new President had more than fulfilled the expectations of his friends and the experiment of his importation had proved a success. Whatever may be the proper criterion today for judging the vigor of an institution of learning, certainly in the eighteenth century the growth of the student body was one of the fairest tests. And on this score Dr. Witherspoon's administration had fully held its own. There are no eighteenth century printed annual catalogues of students, nor are there any manuscript class rolls prior to 1787, the date of the first volume of the minutes of the faculty in which matriculations were recorded. The only sources for estimating the enrolment of the period are the printed triennial catalogues of graduates, a few official reports, and casual references in correspondence, diaries, and similar personal records.

In the eight years preceding Dr. Witherspoon's arrival, the annual graduation lists had contained on an average nineteen names. During the first eight years of his Presidency (1769–1776 inclusive) the average size of the graduating class was twenty-two, ranging from twelve in 1771 to twenty-nine in 1773.[1] As for undergraduate enrolment, in November, 1770, it had been eighty-one, in addition to some twenty-five grammar scholars;[2] in 1772 there were eighty-five undergraduates and forty-five scholars;[3] in the following year the undergraduate body had "considerably increased" and there were thirty-nine in the grammar school.[4] In July, 1773, James Whitlaw, to whom it will be remembered Dr. Witherspoon sold the Ryegate land, and who as a surveyor may be supposed to have been fairly accurate in statements of figures, reported that the college "at present contains upward of 100 students, besides about 80 Latin scholars,"[5] the latter of course being the grammar school pupils. Dr. Witherspoon himself in his description of New Jersey prepared for M. Marbois[6] says that the College "was in a flourishing state before the war, having about one hundred and fifty undergraduates and other scholars." "There are at this time under my tuition," he wrote in 1772, "young gentlemen of the first fortune and expectation from almost every province on the continent as well as several of the West India Islands."

The grammar school had become one of the best in the Colonies—beyond question it was the best in New Jersey—and those at Hackensack, at Baskinridge, at Elizabeth-town and at Freehold conducted chiefly by Princeton graduates, were of no mean reputation. The Nassau Hall Grammar School had possessed a reputation before Dr. Witherspoon's coming; it enjoyed the unique distinction of being the only school in the Colonies of sufficient importance and permanence to have a Latin grammar

---

[1] During the following five years (1777–1781 inclusive) the average was six; during the next six years (1782–1787 inclusive) it was eighteen; and during the last seven years of his administration (1788–1794 inclusive) it was twenty-one. These figures show the steady recuperation after the war.
[2] Fithian, *Journal*, 10.
[3] New Jersey Census. *New Jersey Archives*, 1 ser., vol. XXVIII, p. 325.
[4] Fithian, 36.
[5] Vermont Historical Society *Proceedings*, 1905–1906, p. 133.
[6] *Works*, IV, 305.

printed for its own especial use,[7] and one which ran into several editions; but on Dr. Witherspoon's taking charge it had gained greater reputation not only for the efficiency of its teaching, but particularly for the emphasis it laid on the study of English. The method introduced by the President was British and superior to that of American schools both in the amount of ground covered and the thoroughness with which the work was done. What that work was is most easily gathered from the President's public notices which have been already quoted. Its principal quality seems to have been its liveliness and its constant emphasis on accuracy and mental alertness. Drill and exercise were so constant that fluency for example in the use of Latin was in the end almost inevitable. And accuracy and mental alertness were the winning qualities in the prize competitions which Dr. Witherspoon had instituted in 1771.

The college curriculum had also been strengthened, and chiefly in the upper-class years. The emphasis laid on English in the grammar school had been carried on up into the College; the President's lectures on eloquence, which included taste, criticism, and composition, were giving the curriculum a distinction it had never possessed. He had introduced the study of history and French, and in his lectures on moral philosophy—another inclusive term covering ethics, government, politics, and international law—was giving the first course in any American college to expound a definite philosophical system. He was seriously formulating and directing graduate studies, offering special courses for graduates and guiding their reading; and at the same time as professor of divinity he was lecturing to candidates for the ministry. He had failed, it is true, to secure the additional professorships that had been anticipated and so had not strengthened the faculty to any great extent except in so far as he was himself a whole staff of instructors. There were the usual tutors, for the most part freshly graduated from college; but for lack of adequate endowment only one professor, William Churchill Houston, had been appointed. Nevertheless, under the spur of

[7] Ross, *Complete Introduction to the Latin Tongue.* This was a revision of President Burr's *Newark Grammar.*

the President's example and constant supervision, the teaching in the college had probably never been better.

The equipment and the finances of the institution just before the outbreak of war had been in encouraging condition and it seemed as if funds might soon be obtained for professorships. The report of a committee of the board of trustees dated April, 1775, the last to be made before the beginning of hostilities, shows that besides the four and a half acre lot on which Nassau Hall stood, the College owned part of a lot adjoining the Presbyterian Church in Princeton, two hundred acres of woodland outside the village, one lot in the city of Philadelphia, one hundred acres in Essex County, New Jersey, and one hundred and twenty-eight acres in Morris County. No values are assigned to these parcels of real estate nor to the buildings on the campus. The orrery, one of the marvels of the age, was valued at two hundred and eighty-four pounds and the philosophical apparatus which Dr. Witherspoon had imported from London, at four hundred and sixteen pounds. The library is not assessed nor is its size given, but we know that Dr. Witherspoon brought one consignment of books with him and that two more followed. In a report of losses during the war, made some years later, it is asserted that the library lost two thousand volumes, not including broken sets. These figures show a substantial increase over the 1300 given in the printed library catalogue of 1760.

During the preceding five years (1770–1774 inclusive) Dr. Witherspoon had gathered for the College the respectable sum of £7,468; receipts from college fees and room rents had netted in round figures £2,450; interest, cash, and old lottery accounts received had amounted to £2,167, which sums added to the capital owned in 1769, £3,762, reached the total of £15,847. Salaries during the same period had absorbed £4,191 and some £3,300 had been spent on the orrery, old debts, and "the apparatus" (which seems to have included books for the library). The clear assets of the College in 1775 were estimated to be double what they were when he assumed the Presidency. It was further claimed that a balance of £625 and a few shillings was still due from Dr. Witherspoon, a claim of which we shall hear again.

In general then it seemed in 1776 that the College was in

better condition than ever before, with good prospect of continuing progress. But whatever dreams its friends may have had at that time were soon to be shattered. In the fourteen years covering the War and the period immediately following, the resources mentioned in the 1775 report were to suffer through depreciation, bankruptcies, and bad debts, a shrinkage of sixty-six per cent, and this in spite of fresh donations. Equally severe was to be the damage suffered by the buildings and equipment.

As rental for the occupation of Nassau Hall by continental troops the College in 1779 received from the government seven thousand two hundred and fifty pounds in depreciated paper currency, estimated to be worth in hard money only one hundred and eighty-seven pounds; in 1796, after the President's death, the New Jersey Legislature voted a grant of six hundred pounds per annum for three years; but beyond these sums the College received no compensation whatever for the losses it sustained during the Revolutionary War. That it recovered as well as it did, or indeed that it recovered at all, during the decade following the war—the last decade of Dr. Witherspoon's life—is eloquent testimony not only to the generosity of its friends and their confidence in the President, but also to his own splendid energy and unflagging courage.

When Dr. Witherspoon rode away from Princeton in June, 1776, to take his seat in Congress he left the College in charge of Professor Houston and two tutors, and for the next few years, although he kept as closely in touch as he could with it, his attention to its affairs was necessarily sporadic. Fortunately his duties in Congress instead of totally preventing visits to Princeton often facilitated them. During the whole period of his service in Congress he contrived never to miss a Princeton commencement nor a trustees' meeting, and he was usually on hand for term openings. During the second half of the year 1777 Professor Houston and one tutor with the President's periodical assistance conducted the little teaching that was done; in 1778 Houston and a tutor were alone; in 1779 either the President or Mr. Houston was on hand, and a tutor was engaged for the winter term. Samuel Stanhope Smith joined the faculty in December, 1779, and in 1780 he and Witherspoon were alone, Houston having taken the latter's place in Congress; in 1781 the instruction of the College was maintained by Smith and Houston with the President's occasional assistance, and after that year tutors were again added to the staff. During these years the enrolment was never too large for two instructors to handle.

The disaster that the closing days of 1776 had in store for the College and village was scarcely a bolt from the clear sky. Princeton, town and gown, was marked for trouble. The first call for a New Jersey provincial congress had been sounded here in April, 1775; in August and September of that year the committee of safety representing the usurping provincial government had its headquarters at Princeton, and after the adjournment of the provincial congress the committee had resumed its sessions at Princeton in January, 1776. At the tavern stables express riders were kept in constant readiness to relay dispatches between Congress and General Washington. In August of 1776 the organization of a new state government took place at Princeton and the first legislature under the new state constitution convened in Nassau Hall, holding its sessions in the college library room; here in September William Livingston was inaugurated first Governor of the State; and here in October the Great Seal of the State was adopted—the earliest of all the American state seals, antedating even that of the United States. Happenings like these were sufficient to stamp the village as the rebel capital of New Jersey.

As for the College, the name of whose building was a parole among American troops,—with a President who had taken so active a part in the measures leading to independence, who had voted for separation, who was as notoriously keen on the colonial side as any man in America, who had sons actually in American service, and whose trustees, faculty, pupils and friends had thoroughly earned a reputation for disloyalty[8]—such an institution could anticipate nothing but the severest retaliation when once the enemy should reach it.

American troops had been stationed at Princeton in Septem-

[8] For example, of fifteen leading Presbyterian ministers named by Dr. Charles A. Briggs (*American Presbyterianism*, p. 352) as taking an active part in the Revolutionary struggle, thirteen were either graduates or officers of the College.

ber, 1776, and had probably been passing through the village all summer.[9] The presence of the State Legislature and of the soldiery, the clatter of hard-riding messengers, and the constant military traffic on the high road outside the college gate, must have been sufficiently distracting to boys in classrooms; but when, at commencement that year, the undergraduates learned that a quorum of the board could not be obtained "on account of the difficulty of public affairs" (as the trustees, minutes explain it), and that degrees accordingly could not be conferred, they must have begun to realize that they were living in perilous times. A private commencement was held; the candidates went through the programme without an audience, no account was published, and the handful of trustees present agreed to accept the faculty's recommendations for degrees and to confer them at the next meeting, set for November but not held, as it turned out, until May of the following year.

Dr. Witherspoon presided at this commencement and was in Princeton again during October and the beginning of November. While there, he issued his customary notice regarding the opening of the next term,[10] and on November 6 the annual assigning of rooms took place as if nothing were happening that was likely to put an end to the peaceful pursuit of learning. But the term was destined to be short. By the eighteenth the American army was in full retreat across New Jersey; every rider galloping past Nassau Hall with dispatches from General Washington was the bearer of bad news; and it required no abnormal gift of prophecy to guess that the day of reckoning was at hand. The village lay in the very path of the oncoming British.

It will be remembered that early in November a congressional committee of which Dr. Witherspoon was a member had been sent to Washington's camp to devise some method of filling up his fast thinning ranks. The President found Washington at Newark retreating, with the British at his heels. On his return, halting at Princeton he reluctantly chose the prudent course de-

[9] H. C. Alexander in his *Life of J. A. Alexander*, vol. I, p. 15, is manifestly in error in asserting that on July 22, 1776, "two stories of the college were full of Hessian soldiers."

[10] *New Jersey Archives*, 3 ser., vol. I, p. 217.

scribed in the diary of an anonymous undergraduate in this language:

On the twenty-ninth of November, 1776, New Jersey College, long the peaceful seat of science and haunt of the Muses, was visited with the melancholy tidings of the approach of the enemy.

This alarmed our fears and gave us reason to believe we must soon bid adieu to our peaceful Departments and break off in the midst of our delightful studies; nor were we long held in suspense, our worthy President deeply affected at this solemn scene entered the Hall where the students were collected, and in a very affecting manner informed us of the improbability of continuing there longer in peace; and after giving us several suitable instructions and much good advice very affectionately bade us farewell. Solemnity and distress appeared almost in every countenance. Several students that had come 5 and 600 miles, and just got settled in College, were now obliged under every disadvantage to return with their effects or leave them behind, which several through impossibility of getting a carriage at so confused a time were obliged to do, and lost their all.

As all hopes of continuing longer in peace at Nassau were now taken away, I began to look out for some place where I might pursue my studies, and as Mr. J. Johnson had spoken to me to teach his son, I accordingly went there and agreed to stay with him till Spring. Next day I sent my Trunk and Desk to his house and settled all my business at College.[11]

Despite the warnings of the summer and early autumn, despite even the private commencement, it was in all probability the first time that the reality of war had struck home in most of those boyish minds. It had been easy during recent years to face commencement audiences of admiring friends and favor them with patriotic orations; it had been highly diverting to turn out with the local militia company in May, 1775, and salute the cavalcade of New England and New York delegates to the Continental Congress as they passed through Princeton; even the presence of the State Legislature in Nassau Hall and of Ameri-

[11] The complete diary is published in the *Princeton Standard* for May 1, 8, and 15, 1863. The experience of only a few days proved to the young student the impossibility of remaining in the neighborhood, and casting his educational plans aside he joined the army and saw immediate service.

can troops in the village earlier in the year had been little more than an added excitement, a welcome relief from the monotony of college routine; but having to flee for one's life was a very different matter. It need not be thought that Dr. Witherspoon's students had failed to live up to their oratory. His political prominence in the spring and summer of 1776 had not gone unheeded by them, nor had they allowed their actions to fall short of their ambitious platform declarations. Taking literally the President's own dictum in the *Druid* for May that "when liberty, prosperity, and life are at stake, we must not think of being scholars but soldiers," under the leadership of a Senior, William Richardson Davie (afterwards a general, and eventually the Governor of North Carolina) a company of volunteers, whose muster roll has not come down although some of the names are known, had been formed from the undergraduate body and had marched to Elizabeth, New Jersey, to enlist. President Witherspoon and his faculty had not sanctioned the step, so Alexander Garden recalls,[12] as it did not seem that the country yet needed the services of college boys. But as Professor Houston himself had in February accepted a captaincy in the Second Battalion of the Somerset militia, the President perhaps did not feel like adopting drastic measures to restrain undergraduate truancy. He believed that several of the company had enlisted in a spirit of adventure and he expected to see many of them return to college in due time, as in fact they did when they found themselves discharged at camp. It was perhaps in view of this incident and in response to Dr. Witherspoon's own motion that Congress in August, 1776, voted that the members of the college faculty should be excused from military service and should devote themselves to their college duties. Houston resigned his commission in August because of his increased college responsibilities owing to the President's absence.

For many of the students, however, who had gathered at Princeton in November for the winter term, the closing of the College so shortly after the session began presented a serious situation. Eighteenth-century undergraduate letters show how transportation was ordinarily arranged; horses used to be en-

[12] *Anecdotes.*

gaged months ahead; James Madison in piping times of peace had even considered having his horse sent up from Virginia. But in the prevalent panic of November, 1776, farmers were hiding away their live stock and would not hire out their horses; private individuals were securing their valuables; the village was being deserted; and the student diarist already mentioned tells of the attempts made to impress Mr. Johnson's wagons and horses for public service. Having dismissed the College, President Wither-spoon gathered up a load of his belongings and with his family hurriedly left Princeton. "We carried nothing away of all our effects," he wrote in January to his son David, "but what could be carried upon one team. Benjamin Hawkins drove your mother in the old chair, and I rode the sorrel mare, and made John Graham drive the four young colts."[13] The cavalcade made its way to Pequa in Pennsylvania where Dr. Witherspoon left his wife for the winter with the family of the Reverend Robert Smith, father of Professor S. S. Smith who had recently married Ann Witherspoon, while he pushed on to rejoin his congressional colleagues at Philadelphia.[14] As it was, the students, and as-suredly the President, got away none too soon. One boy of six-teen, James Ashton Bayard, son of Colonel John Bayard, of Philadelphia, was caught by the British on his way home, and it was only through the intercession of his mother and the inter-vention of Washington himself that he escaped being hanged.[15] In the old graveyard at Princeton is a stone with this inscription:

In Memory of
Guy and Paul Rupert
Students of the College of New Jersey
who departed this Life January, 1777
Their Blood is on the Hands of the British.

[13] *Christian Advocate*, II, 443. Letter dated Baltimore, January 8, 1777. Dr. Wither-spoon in this letter mentions "a very full and particular account" of his flight which he had written to his son-in-law, Professor S. S. Smith of Hampden-Sidney; but this has not survived. He repeats the news of Washington's coup at Trenton and the rumor that he had defeated the British at Princeton. Benjamin Hawkins, mentioned above, was at this time a Senior in College; he was the future Governor of North Carolina.

[14] Frances, the younger daughter, later in the winter joined her brother David at Hampden-Sidney, Va., whither he had accompanied Professor Smith. Her two older brothers were in service.

[15] *New York Genealogical and Biographical Record*, vol. XVI, p. 60.

Indeed, able-bodied collegians seem to have been safe from neither friend nor foe. John Trottman, a seventeen year old fellow-student of Bayard, spending his vacation in Philadelphia that September had been seized by an American pressgang and forced on board the "Andrew Doria," an armed brigantine in the service of the Continental Congress. In the roadstead of St. Eustatius in the Dutch West Indies, this young Princetonian a few weeks later had at least the satisfaction of hearing and seeing what was probably the first foreign salute to the American flag.[16]

On the morning of December 2 Washington and his broken army came hurrying through Princeton, leaving a rear-guard of 1200 men who rejoined the main army five days later. For on the seventh the British arrived, quartering themselves in the empty college building, the church, and most of the houses in the village and neighborhood, and posting batteries at every country road that entered the main street. Then began what an anonymous eye-witness called their "twenty days tyranny."[17] A brigade consisting of the 17th, 55th and 40th regiments constituted the British force in Princeton, the 40th being quartered in Nassau Hall. It is said that the basement was used as stables. A brigade of Hessians arrived on December 28. but could have had little share if any in the ravages suffered by the community, and the damage done cannot fairly be charged to them. The enemy remained until early in the morning of January 3, 1777, and by that time, as Dr. Benjamin Rush wrote from Princeton four days later to Colonel Richard Henry Lee, the place was

indeed a deserted village; you would think it had been desolated with the plague and earthquake, as well as with the calamities of war; the college and church are heaps of ruin; all the inhabitants have been plundered; the whole of Mr. Stockton's furniture, apparel, and even valuable writings, have been burnt; all his cattle, horses, and hogs, sheep, grain, and forage, have been carried away by them; his losses cannot be less than five thousand pounds.[18]

[16] His story is found in the *New England Magazine* for July, 1893.
[17] *Brief Narrative of British and Hessian Atrocities*, Princeton, 1906.
[18] Lee, *Memoir of R. H. Lee*, vol. II, p. 164. Dr. Rush was Mr. Stockton's son-in-law and presumably had accurate sources of information.

The last phase of the battle of Princeton on January 3 took place at a little ravine half a mile southwest of Nassau Hall. Retreating toward the rear campus, part of the British forces sought refuge in Nassau Hall whence they had so confidently issued early that morning; and when, as it is said, Captain Alexander Hamilton's artillery fired a few round shot at the building and a small band of American militia burst open one of the rear doors, the occupants promptly surrendered. Washington burned the store of hay he found in Nassau Hall and having destroyed "such other things as the shortness of the time could admit," moved on eastward leaving behind him the British wounded.[19] Cornwallis arriving later in the morning from Trenton detailed five privates and a surgeon to tend them and shortly after, from New Brunswick by a flag of truce sent an additional surgeon with medicines.[20]

Late in January as chairman of the congressional committee on British and Hessian atrocities Dr. Witherspoon made Princeton his headquarters and found ample opportunity to estimate the damage suffered by the community. Obtaining leave of absence from Congress in February to give his private affairs some needed attention, it was after this visit that he wrote to his son David a letter describing the damage his property sustained.[21] He found he had suffered what he later characterized as a "dreadful stroke;" all his sheep were destroyed, although some fourteen of his cattle had been saved; not many of his books, however, were gone, and but little of his standing furniture. Whether soldiers were quartered at "Tusculum" or not is not known, but evidently Dr. Witherspoon's man had been so faithful and careful about the farm that although the President was, as he said, "the object of the enemy's distinguished hatred" he had escaped on the whole better than he expected. There is no evidence that his residence suffered pillage as Sir George Trevelyan picturesquely alleges.[22] He never filed a claim for damages although the Somerset Book of Damages in the State Library at Trenton con-

[19] Letter to President of Congress, January 5, 1777.
[20] Washington to Cornwallis, January 7, 1777; Rush to R. H. Lee, January 14, 1777.
[21] *Christian Advocate*, II, 443. Letter of February 2, 1777.
[22] *American Revolution*, vol. II, Part 2, page 31.

tains the claims of many other Princeton citizens. Had he fallen into the enemy's hands there is little doubt, as he remarked in his letter to David, that he would have suffered the fate of another Princetonian, the Reverend John Rosborough who at Trenton was struck down in cold blood by Hessians, under the misapprehension that they were settling scores with the President of the College of New Jersey; but his own casual report of his losses does not leave one with the impression that "Tusculum" suffered to any very large extent. Dr. Rush had not greatly exaggerated conditions in Princeton, and is corroborated by the records in the Somerset Book of Damages and by the comments of the anonymous eye-witness already mentioned. Fences were gone, orchards and standing timber had been levelled or burned, houses and barns were wrecked.[23] And Trevelyan's account in general of the damage done to the College is not inaccurate. As for Nassau Hall, the whole building was wrecked and polluted. It had suffered to some extent during the summer and autumn of 1776 by visitations of American troops; Washington's rearguard undoubtedly used it in December; the three weeks stay of the British had furthered the injury which the last phase of the battle and the subsequent American occupation of the building had completed. General Putnam reached Princeton late in January, 1777, with a considerable force; in May, General Sullivan arrived with 1500 men, to which body additions were made from the south, and Nassau Hall remained a military post until June. Despite the resolution of the board of trustees that Dr. Witherspoon should move in Congress "that troops shall not hereafter be quartered in the College," in the following October Nassau Hall was taken over as a military hospital and was so used until the end of November, 1778, for besides being a center for the distribution of clothing and other supplies, Princeton was also a most convenient point for the concentration of British prisoners and captive loyalists. Quartermaster Robert Stockton of Princeton reported that between November, 1778, and September, 1780, excepting two rooms assigned by Dr. Witherspoon to the tailors of the New Jersey Brigade and occupied by them from October, 1779, to April, 1780, Nassau Hall was seldom used

[23] *Brief Narrative.*

by troops; but not until 1782 did the college authorities regain sole and complete possession.[24]

No contemporary description of the condition of the building after the battle has come to light save Dr. Rush's figurative assertion that it was a heap of ruins. The most detailed accounts are those given by Dr. Ashbel Green in his manuscript biography of the President, in his own autobiography, and in his address on Witherspoon's administration delivered before the Nassau Hall Alumni Association in 1840. These accounts, it should be remembered, describe the building as it was in May, 1782, when Green entered college and after Nassau Hall had been for five years and a half occupied by the military. From his statements it is clear that the brief cannonading to which Nassau Hall had been subjected by the American artillery at the battle of Princeton had contributed greatly to the ruinous appearance reported by Dr. Rush. The destruction wrought by at least three shots from Hamilton's efficient battery, was plain even in Green's day, while "the whole building" he says, exhibited the effects of the American artillery. One ball had made a conspicuous hole in the south wall in or near the projection containing the prayer-hall; another had entered the window of a room on the south side of the building west of the projection and had pierced the partition wall separating the room from the long corridor or "entry" running through the length of the building; a third had entered the prayer-hall and, according to a tradition well accredited in 1782, had struck out the head of the portrait of George II—that it destroyed the picture admits of no doubt.[25]

But Hamilton's artillery was responsible for only part of the damage done. The furnishing and other contents of Nassau Hall and of the kitchen building were virtually a total loss; even the

[24] Library Princeton University, Report of Robert Stockton; *Princeton Press*. August 13, 1858, letter of Robert Stockton accompanying report; petition of board of trustees July 15, 1777; minutes of the board May 30, 1781; *New Jersey Archives*, 2 ser., vol. II, contains numerous references to the use of Nassau Hall for military purposes.
[25] The statement made by the Marquis de Chastellux, who visited Princeton in 1780, that the British had carried off the portrait, is unquestionably a foreign traveller's misunderstanding. The local version of the portrait's destruction is given official stamp by the trustees in their resolution of September, 1783, ordering the Peale portrait of Washington to be placed in the frame that had held King George's likeness.

college pump had to be rebuilt. Woodwork of every kind had been used for kindling; the library of over 2000 volumes, many of them quartos and folios, had been rifled,[26] some of the books being subsequently found in North Carolina carried thither, we are asked to believe, by British troops. The majority of the lost volumes were burned or otherwise destroyed by the troops during the winter of 1776–1777. The valuable experimental apparatus which Dr. Witherspoon had imported was reduced to a few jars, a small telescope, and an electrical machine. The Rittenhouse orrery at first had escaped harm, for Cornwallis intended to carry it back to England as a prize of war and had set a guard over it; but his American successors in Nassau Hall had been less considerate and in clumsy curiosity to see the wheels go round had ruined the delicate mechanism.[27] The prayer-hall was wrecked; its benchlike pews, the rostrum, the high pulpit, all had vanished in smoke. As for the organ, fingers more accustomed to musket triggers than to ivory keys had not only crushed the life out of the instrument but had torn away its very vitals; nothing was left but the case, and we wonder why that was spared.[28] The portrait heads of British sovereigns given by Governor Belcher had disappeared and the Governor's own full length portrait, another of his gifts, was likewise missing.[29] His carved and gilded coat of arms, originally surmounting the picture, still hung on the wall. The basement and the third floor when Ashbel Green first saw Nassau Hall in 1782 were "entirely uninhabited and unhabitable," except that in the east end of the basement on the north side Dr. Witherspoon had fitted up a room for the grammar school and opposite it on the south side another room for the college dining room. The kitchen was in the steward's house

[26] Sergeant Thomas Sullivan of the British 49th Regiment of Foot, speaking of the College says: "Our army when it lay there spoiled and plundered a good Library that was in it." (*Pennsylvania Magazine of History and Biography*, vol. XXXII, p. 54).
[27] Sir George Trevelyan (*American Revolution*) is mistaken in ascribing the destruction of the orrery to British vandalism. Its own friends were its worst enemies.
[28] "There was an organ and a nice Chapel in the College," says Sergeant Sullivan, with a fine sense for his tenses.
[29] "The trustees, being extremely sorry that the picture of his Excellency Governor Belcher which hung in the college Hall, has been destroyed during the late war," etc., is the language used by the Board in October, 1783, when ordering a committee to secure either another original or a copy.

adjoining the east end of the building. Moreover, on the third floor in the projection over the main entrance a small room was being used by the Cliosophic Society. The American Whig Society was not revived until later. The library room on the second floor contained in 1782 the remnant of the library and the fragments of the experimental apparatus. Enough rooms had been repaired on the first and second floors to accommodate the two score students then in college; but the rest of the building lay waste, a desolation of soiled walls, gaping windows, broken partitions, fallen ceilings, and heaps of plaster and filth; and this probably had been the condition of the building in January, 1777, when Dr. Rush saw it after the battle.

Dr. Witherspoon visited Princeton again in March, 1777, and undauntedly set about plans for reopening the College whether Nassau Hall were fit or not to receive students. From Philadelphia he issued notice that undergraduates should hold themselves in readiness to assemble punctually on May 10,[30] the regular date for the opening of the spring term, proposing "by assiduous application to recover what had been lost by the public confusion," but warning students that the opening session would probably not be held at Princeton but at some safer place, notice of which would be issued. The term, however, did not open on May 10, and two weeks later the trustees met at Cooper's Ferry (Camden), New Jersey, to consider whether it was expedient or not to collect the students and endeavor to proceed with their instruction, finally resolving that if the enemy left the State Dr. Witherspoon was to gather his flock at Princeton and continue their education as best he might, and if more students came than he could instruct himself he was to obtain such assistance as was needful. With Mr. Stockton and Dr. Spencer he was also to determine what repairs were indispensable for the convenience of the students and to have them made, but to go no further than absolutely necessary to save the building and to accommodate such undergraduates as might respond to the call; and the President was again instructed to move in Congress that hereafter no more troops be quartered in the building.

He accordingly drew up the following memorial a few weeks

[30] *New Jersey Archives*, 2 ser., vol. I, p. 322.

later and presented it in Congress, where it was referred to the Board of War:

To the honorable The Congress of the United States of America—
    The Memorial of a Committee of the Trustees of the
College of New Jersey—
        humbly sheweth,
        That your Memorialists were lately appointed by the Board of Trustees to inspect their public Building at Princeton, to make what repairs might be absolutely necessary, and to collect the Students in order to their proceeding in the course of their studies; That your Memorialists have already collected a number of the Students who have begun their course; but your Memorialists are discouraged from proceeding in the repairing on the College, for that every party of the Continental Troops, marching thro' this place, take possession of it as Barracks; and partly thro' wantonness, and also under pretence of not being supplied with fire Wood, are daily committing the greatest ravages upon the Building, in breaking up the floors, and burning every piece of Wood they can cut out of it; Your Memorialists do therefore most humbly pray, for the sake of promoting the public education of the youth of this and other States, who come here, that your honorable House will be pleased to add that no Continental Troops do hereafter presume to enter the sd College & use the same as Barracks; but that to supply the want of this public Building, the Quarter Master (whom we hope will be appointed to be resided in this place) be directed to hire some of the vacant Houses & out Houses of the Owners thereof for the reception of the Troops, in their Marches: and that the Legislature of this State be requested by their honble House, to make provisions for the payment of the rents; whereby the public burthens will fall more equally on the inhabitants.
    And your Memorialists shall ever pray &c
Princeton 15th July 1777   JNO WITHERSPOON
                                            ELIHU SPENCER
                                            RICHD STOCKTON[31]

A resolution in the President's handwriting among the Papers of the Continental Congress seems to have been adopted by Congress at this time although not appearing in the *Journal*:

[31] *Papers Continental Congress*, 41, vol. VII, p. 6.

That a Person be elected at Princeton to act as an Occasional Quarter Master & Commissary for forage with Directions to hire empty houses & otherwise with the Assistance of the Magistrates to provide quarters for any troops that may be passing through that Place so that none may be suffered to quarter in the College unless one or more Magistrates find it absolutely necessary and in that Case said quartermaster shall take effectual care that no Damage be done.

John McComb and Colonel Jacob Hyer, both of Princeton, were suggested and in August it was voted that the former

be authorized to act as quartermaster at that place, for such detachments of the army as may be passing that way, till the quartermaster general shall give further directions on this subject; and that he take care that no damage be done to the college at that place.[32]

In June 1777, once more from Philadelphia, the President had summoned his pupils to meet him at Princeton, this time on July 8. They were to take all possible pains to bring textbooks, and he sanguinely hoped they had been pursuing their studies privately as well as circumstances would allow and that on their arrival at Princeton they would apply themselves "with extraordinary diligence to recover the ground that had been necessarily lost." July 10, from Princeton,[33] he announced that the College had been duly re-opened as advertised and college exercises had been resumed for the first time since November, 1776. Tardy undergraduates were asked to bring their books with them as none could be bought at Princeton. Professor Houston and himself were both on hand, although the President did not remain more than a few days.[34] Recitations were held in his house inasmuch as repairs on Nassau Hall were at a standstill, not even the broken windows having been replaced. The building was moreover being used as a hospital. A tutor having been engaged, he and Mr. Houston carried on instruction when the President was away. The President was back for a week in August as his absence from Congress and a letter to his son David show.[35] In accordance

[32] *Journal of Congress*, vol. VIII, p. 615, August 6, 1777.
[33] *New Jersey Archives*, 2 ser., vol. I, p. 408.
[34] *New Jersey Archives*, 2 ser., vol. I, p. 427. Textbooks were supplied ordinarily by the steward; but there was no steward at this time.
[35] *Christian Advocate*, vol. II, p. 245.

with previous decision, in September no public commencement exercises were held and degrees were conferred at the following meeting of the board.[36] In April, 1777, the board had adjourned until April, 1778, thus indicating that it had no expectation of sitting in September, 1777. Recitations continued to be held in the President's house through the winter of 1777–1778 and the spring and summer of 1778, while the few attending students boarded in the village. In the announcement of commencement 1778 it was stated that the residence requirement for a bachelor's degree would be waived, and not only those who had attended "constantly or occasionally, but those who had studied at home," provided they sustained examination, would be admitted, if qualified, to their degrees. The class of 1776 had been graduated twenty-seven strong; that of 1777 had numbered only seven; that of 1778 only five.

The director general of the hospital had assured the President in August, 1778, that all the sick would be removed from Nassau Hall in a few weeks, and it was hoped by the college authorities that students might then again occupy their rooms. The sick were removed as promised but the building was left "in so ruinous a state as to be very unfit for accommodating the scholars."[37]

The grammar school had been re-opened in April and had been running ever since. Commencement exercises that September were held in the prayer-hall in the presence of the Governor, the state council and assembly. Only a handful of trustees was present; the programme, however, was as timely as ever, the Latin salutatory being on "Civil Discord," and another oration having "Horrors of War" as its subject; Dr. Witherspoon delivered an exhortation to the class, and degrees were conferred.[38] The next term opened in November with a complete schedule of recitations although full college orders were not resumed until 1782.

Taking advantage of his arrangement with his constituents Dr. Witherspoon seems to have spent most of the spring of 1779

[36] *New Jersey Archives*, 2 ser., vol. II, p. 436.
[37] *New Jersey Archives*, 2 ser., vol. II, p. 325, 437.
[38] *New Jersey Archives*, 2 ser., vol. II, p. 488.

at Princeton. The board resolved in April to apply to the State Legislature for a reduction of the quorum of the board from 13 to 11 and for permission to change the amount of clear annual income the corporation was allowed to hold, from £2000 sterling, to the value of 30,000 bushels of wheat, and it was further resolved to petition that the faculty and students be exempted from military duty, Dr. Witherspoon being commissioned to draw up and present the petition.[39] It was agreed to continue to the President and Mr. Houston their antebellum salaries, while they in turn were to give as much attention to the course of instruction as they could, until the building were repaired and the state of public affairs permitted them to conduct classes "in a more compleat manner." It was agreed to repair the roof of Nassau Hall as soon as possible and glaze the broken front windows—a concession to appearances,—and then to repair the rooms on the main floor; but nothing more than essential repairs to the roof was to be undertaken unless the board were successful in obtaining payment from Congress for damage done by American troops.

Dr. Witherspoon's own statement of the situation is worth quoting at this point:[40]

Nassau Hall, Princeton, New Jersey.
April 23, 1779.
The many inquiries that have been made by Gentlemen at a distance, render it necessary to give information to the public of the past and present state of the College here. Every promise in former advertisements has been fulfilled. In the summer of 1777, as soon as the enemy

---

[39] *The New Jersey Gazette* of January 14, 1778, contains a letter by "Cato" protesting against compulsory military service for undergraduates in the College of New Jersey. After stating his reasons for this attitude the author, who it is suspected was Dr. Witherspoon, continues "Considering these things, I flatter myself that our superiors will not, for the comparatively trifling service which the collegians are capable of rendering the public in the capacity of soldiers, continue the present embargo upon the seat of muses; nor compel the arts and sciences, against which none ought to wage war, to wage war against any." *New Jersey Archives*, 2 ser., II, 14.

In the preceding issue of the *Gazette* "Cato" had announced his intention of writing from time to time his opinions on public affairs, and in that issue published his conception of the duty of representatives in the New Jersey Assembly. No article by "Cato" appears in Dr. Witherspoon's collected works.

[40] *New Jersey Archives*, 2 ser., vol. III, p. 324.

left the State, the instruction agreeably to notice was begun: the Trustees having empowered the President to employ such teachers occasionally as should be necessary. Accordingly such of the scholars, as conveniently could, returned, and were carried on according to their standing and the Seniors of that year received their Degree of Bachelor of Arts at Commencement, as usual. The same was the case through the winter following and the summer of 1778, when there was a private Commencement; but the attendance was difficult and inconvenient, the College being occupied by the Publick as a barrack or hospital, and the recitations from necessity in a room of the President's house. Last summer the College was entirely given up to us, but in so ruinous a state as to be very unfit for accommodating the scholars. Several, however, lived in it all the winter session, and the recitations were in College. Now we have the pleasure of acquainting the Publick that tradesmen have been at work for some time repairing the fabrick; that a good part of the windows are put in; that we expect the roof will be made entirely sound in a few days; and that chambers will be fitted up sufficient, it is supposed, to receive those who may come for the summer session, which begins on the tenth of May. As to boarding, it is not yet practicable to get a steward for the College, but boarding for those who lodge in College may be had in families in town at such rate as the times will admit. The Publick may depend upon the instruction being carried on and that always one or other of the Subscribers, if not both, will be upon the spot.

The Grammar School which was begun in April last year, has continued ever since, and is in a thriving condition, there being near thirty boys in it. The school, after a vacation of two weeks, nearly elapsed, will be opened on Monday next the twenty-sixth instant. Great care is taken in this school to make the scholars accurate in the grammar and syntax, and by frequent periodical exercises to perfect them in reading, spelling, and pronouncing the English language; a branch of education of the first importance and yet often shamefully neglected.

To encourage the early and punctual attendance of the Students, the same rule will be observed as in former times at the end of every vacation, viz., that after the first day of meeting no regard will be paid to the standing of the scholars in the distribution of the chambers, but those who come first will have their choice of such as are vacant.

JOHN WITHERSPOON
WILLIAM CH. HOUSTON

From Dr. Witherspoon's financial statement for the year 1779 it would appear that in May of that year he received from Charles Pettit, continental deputy quartermaster general, the sum of twelve hundred and fifty pounds, and in September and November further sums of three thousand pounds each. These amounts are described by a committee of the trustees as rental for Nassau Hall and in no sense reimbursement for the damage done; furthermore the payments were made in depreciated money which in November, 1778, was worth twenty-six to one, having steadily fallen from twelve and a half to one in May, and sixteen to one in August. These payments nevertheless enabled Dr. Witherspoon to take up repairs. His accounts for January, 1779 show that a beginning had been made with the windows, nearly three hundred pounds being spent for glass and labor. For nails alone during the spring of that year he paid out close upon four hundred pounds, for carpentering some six hundred and seventy-five, and for lime for plastering three hundred and fifty. Since the death in January, 1777, of Mr. Sergeant the treasurer, a committee of the board had managed the finances of the institution, but in April, 1779, Professor Houston was elected to add the treasurer's duties to his own, and the trustees pledged themselves to exercise their utmost efforts to obtain benefactions. Emissaries were sent through New England and Pennsylvania, and a memorial for their use was drawn up by the President and Mr. Stockton, of which no copy has been kept. In September, 1779, the President paid for six hundred pounds worth of boards, significant of the damaged flooring of Nassau Hall, while for glass, putty, and brushes he disbursed in September and November over fourteen hundred pounds. The labor of "glazing the college" is charged at two hundred and fifty-five pounds, and in December "nails and oyl" absorbed another six hundred.[41] All payments were of course in depreciated money.

For the greater part of the year there were not more than ten undergraduates in attendance but commencement was held as usual and six were graduated.[42] At the commencement meeting of the board Dr. Witherspoon's son-in-law, Samuel Stanhope

[41] MSS., Princeton University Library.
[42] Stiles *Diary*, vol. II, p. 384, and *New Jersey Archives*, 2 ser., vol. III, p. 671.

[103]

Smith, was elected professor of moral philosophy and in December he arrived at Princeton to take up his work. To him Dr. Witherspoon relinquished half of his own salary of four hundred pounds and gave him the president's house on the campus, while he himself moved out to "Tusculum." In Dr. Smith's hands he also left the administrative details and duties to which his own absence prevented him from giving proper attention.[43]

Dr. Witherspoon left Congress, as we know, at the end of 1779 with the intention of devoting himself henceforth to the College and to his farm; and in February, 1780, he marked his return to academic life by issuing in the *New Jersey Gazette* an open letter to the public which, besides being an advertisement of his grammar school, is one of his most important statements of the principles of elementary education and methods of instruction.

It looked, he said, as if the College were once more set straight on its way. With the grammar school recovering from the desolation of war and pupils coming in from various parts of the country and even from the West Indies, he thinks that public attention may once more be directed into educational channels,

[43]Dr. Smith was born March 16, 1750, at Pequa, Pa., where his father, the Reverend Robert Smith, conducted a well-known academy. After graduation from Princeton in 1769, he taught for a year at Pequa, then returned to Princeton as tutor, remaining three years and studying theology under the President. Contemporary college verse indicates that his courtliness and elegance puzzled the undergraduates, such qualities being unexpected of tutors and theological students.

Receiving his license he went in 1774 to Virginia and was instrumental in organizing Hampden-Sidney Academy, being elected first principal in 1775. Before leaving Princeton he had married Ann Witherspoon, the President's oldest daughter. He had the physical graces that Dr. Witherspoon lacked, being unusually tall, with a sonorous voice and a handsome face. A strikingly beautiful pastel portrait of him in his prime was bequeathed to the University by the late General Alfred A. Woodhull of Princeton. He was famous for his oratory, fashioning his style after the elaborate French manner. He succeeded Dr. Witherspoon in the Presidency of Princeton and held office until 1812. In his administration the sciences of chemistry and natural history were introduced into the curriculum, the chairs then created being the first of their kind to be founded for undergraduate instruction in an American college. Besides this impetus to scientific studies, Dr. Smith's administration was marked by important additions to the faculty, by the erection of new buildings, and by a large increase of enrollment. He was extremely popular with his students, and maintained correspondence with them after their graduation and even after he resigned the presidency.

He preserved his erect stature and his good looks, and is mentioned in contemporary letters, and was long remembered, as one of the stateliest figures that ever headed a Princeton academic procession. He died at Princeton in August, 1819.

SAMUEL STANHOPE SMITH
From the Pastel by James Sharpless

and there are things of much importance to be said to school masters and to parents. "This would not have been done in a newspaper if it had been possible to find any other way as easy, speedy, and effectual."

Schoolmasters are entreated to be as careful as possible to make the boys intended for college accurate in their preparatory studies; if boys enter college "ill founded in classic learning," it will be impossible to remedy their defects, and often it will seem very hard "to reject them for the fault of their teachers, and not their own." There is greater need than ever of attention to this point, as students may now enter the junior class, when they devote most of their time to the sciences, and although "they are kept reading a part of their time in the higher classics" yet it is plainly impracticable to devote attention to grammar and syntax. Therefore it is desired that "effectual pains be taken, and early," to teach the rules of syntax, for which he suggests Rudiman's *Grammatical Exercises* for beginners, and Mair's *Introduction* for the more advanced. But any book

will do well enough in the hands of a skilled master. It ought to be remembered that it is of much more consequence to make them understand the grammar and structure of the language well, than to make them by force of memory or application, translate passages of the classics either in poetry or prose.

Secondly, "it were to be wished that masters, instead of pushing boys forward to the higher classics, or making them change their books often," would not only perfect them in construction, but at the same time give them extended vocabularies by using easy books that they can understand such as Corderius, Erasmus, Aesop and Selectae Veteri Testamenti Historiae, "all of which were written or collected by great men, in order to facilitate the instruction of youth." In addition to this, there should always be translating from English into Latin as well as from Latin into English.

For want of this, nothing is more common than to meet with boys who say they have read Vergil or Horace who yet cannot speak three sentences in Latin upon the most common subjects, and cannot explain two pages of Corderius or Erasmus unless they have read them lately; nay, will very simply answer, if they be desired to do it, that they have not read them of a long time. This is just as absurd as if in arithmetic they should say they could do the rule of three, but had forgot numeration and addition. . . . I am persuaded that were boys taught the whole construction of the Latin Language from such books as Corderius or Erasmus' Colloquies, and could they express everything readily in classic Latin that might be expressed by the words to be found in these books, they would be better Latin scholars than many who have finished their college course.

Thirdly, he urges masters to teach boys to read and pronounce Latin properly. "They should from the beginning be made to lose their place in the class as certainly for a false quantity as for a wrong word."

Fourthly, masters are requested, by frequent or rather periodical exercises in reading, spelling, speaking and writing, to make the scholars accurate in their knowledge of their mother tongue.

Certainly this is of the first importance, and will be thought so by all parents whose approbation is worth seeking for. You will say this ought to be done in English schools; undoubtedly it ought; but what knowledge they acquire there ought to be preserved and increased in every stage of their progress. There is an advantage in a grammar school and college for this purpose.

He concludes his lecture to schoolmasters by remarking that

the art of teaching any science whatever to advantage, is built upon two great principles. 1. That the learner should be made as perfect as possible in one thing before he be carried forward to another. 2. That the steps of transition should be as easy and gentle as possible. The first will not be disputed by anybody; but there are masters who carry boys through the grammar with anything less than half learned, so that in their lessons they are stammering and guessing, saying one word right and two wrong, by which the master's time is wasted, and yet the profit of the scholar very small.

The second principle is as just as the other, "but of much greater compass, variety, and difficulty in the application." And he illustrates by the method "now frequently taken in teaching the art of writing." Writing masters have analyzed the whole into a series of simple strokes, and after these are learned perfectly they are joined together

with the utmost facility as well as accuracy. Something of this kind should be constantly in the view of the master of a grammar school, and he is the most accomplished teacher who can make the steps by which the pupil proceeds the most easy, natural and obvious.

Dr. Witherspoon then proceeds to give to parents "a few advices." First, they should not attempt to force their children. The general desire with parents seems to be to have their children "taught in as little time as possible in the grammar school, and entered as high as possible in the classes in college." Nothing can be more preposterous; it is "more honourable as well as pleasant" for a boy to be at the head of one class than to be at the bottom of one immediately superior to it. Besides it makes their work difficult, and their improvement or success uncertain. If parents wish their children's education to be soon finished "that they may not arrive at the stature of men before they have completed the work of boys, it is a most laudable purpose; but the true way to obtain it is to begin early, that they may have time to be taught in a proper and effectual manner." If it is too late to do this he recommends altering the object of instruction, and instead of giving them a regular course, "making them perfect in some of the most essential branches and omitting others."

Secondly, children should be regular and constant in attendance. They should not be called home on trifling occasions or allowed to go home on frivolous pretences. It gives them an idle turn, takes their minds off their books, breaks the thread of their instruction, and throws them behind their class, which "extinguishes their emulation, and often produces a despondent indifference and sloth." They casually say "that they will study hard to make up the time . . . but experience tells me that the very reverse is commonly the case."

Lastly, parents are urged to support the moral discipline of the college. "I look upon it as certain that the past prosperity and success of the College has been capitally owing to the strict attention paid to this circumstance by the trustees from its first foundation." If home discipline differs from that of the College it is obvious how harmful this is for the boys:

We say they shall not be suffered to play at cards or dice, to swear or speak profanely, or take their diversion abroad on the Lord's Day, and withal endeavour to persuade them that these causes are the road to perdition. But when they return home to their parents, all these things are done frequently, openly, and without reserve. Perhaps I shall hereby expose myself to the reproaches of that honourable class of men the Free thinkers of the age; this gives me very little concern.

Some parents even admit that children and youth should be kept from these practices in a seat of learning, though they make no scruple of defending the same indulgences in persons of riper years:

The consistency of this I leave them to make out at their leisure, and shall only say, that at any rate those parents who approve of the system of education practised, should for their own sakes, be very cautious of counteracting or defeating it either by discourse or example.

In the summer of 1780 two articles signed by "Aristides" appeared in the *New Jersey Gazette*,[44] one on the murder of Mrs. Caldwell, wife of the Reverend James Caldwell of Elizabethtown, New Jersey, by a British sentry, and the other on the alleged humanity of the English nation. These two papers bear strong indication of having come from Dr. Witherspoon's pen, besides being signed by one of his pseudonyms. His knowledge of the bitterness with which the British army had waged war in New Jersey, the abundant historical references, the quotation from Montesquieu and the repetition of arguments confessedly his, together with the general style, all support the theory that Dr. Witherspoon was the author of these two articles. They do not appear, however, in his collected *Works*.

The Marquis de Chastellux visiting Princeton that summer has left an interesting account of the institution and its President. On reaching Princeton, a town of "about sixty or eighty houses, all tolerably well built," his attention was

[44] *New Jersey Archives*, 2 ser., vol. IV, p. 531, 660.

immediately attracted by an immense building which is visible at a considerable distance. . . . As this building is remarkable only for its size, it is unnecessary to describe it; the reader will only recollect . . . that it is situated towards the middle of the town, on a distinct spot of ground, and that the entrance to it is by a large square court surrounded with lofty palisades. I dismounted for a moment to visit this vast edifice, and was soon joined by Dr. Witherspoon, President of the University. . . . In accosting me he spoke French, but I easily perceived that he had acquired his knowledge of the language from reading, rather than conversation, which did not prevent me, however, from answering him, and continuing to converse with him in French, for I saw that he was well pleased to display what he knew of it. . . . I conversed therefore with him the President and from him I learnt that this college is a complete university.

Then follows a partly erroneous description of the course of study and a statement of expenses, as the Marquis remembered them.

This useful establishment has fallen into decay since the war; there were only forty students when I saw it. A handsome collection of books had been made; the greatest part of which has been embezzled. The English even carried off from the chapel the portrait of the king of England, a loss for which the Americans easily consoled themselves, declaring they would have no king amongst them, not even a painted one.[45] There still remains a very beautiful astronomical machine; but as it was then out of order, and differs in no respect from that I saw afterwards in Philadelphia, I shall take no notice of it.

Being anxious to follow the traces of General Washington in a country "where every object reminded me of his successes," the Marquis passed

from Parnassus to the field of Mars, and from the hands of the President Witherspoon into those of Colonel Moylan. They were both equally upon their own ground; so that while one was pulling me by the right arm, telling me, Here is the philosophy class; the other was plucking me by the left, to show me where one hundred and eighty English laid down their arms.[46]

[45] This is the erroneous account of the fate of the picture already mentioned.
[46] *Travels in North America*, London, 1787, vol. I, p. 160–4.

At the celebration of the Fourth of July in 1780 at Princeton, after the outdoor exercises "the company adjourned to the College Hall where a discourse was delivered by the President, in which he considered: (1) The importance and the necessity of Independence at the time it was declared; (2) The events of providence in the course of the contest; and (3) The duty of all ranks in the present crisis."[47] The address has not been preserved but this outline printed in the newspapers indicates that Dr. Witherspoon used most of his material again at the Thanksgiving Day exercises of 1783.

Elected in 1780 to the state legislative council or senate, he took his seat at the opening of the session late in October and during the month that followed was actively employed. His most important assignment was the preparation of the draft of a memorial to Congress on finance, pursuant to the resolution of a joint conference of the two branches of the legislature. The draft was brought in on November 18 and agreed to by the council. It is a frank statement of New Jersey's constant acquiescence in and support of public measures; the hope is expressed, however, that Congress will suggest to other states the propriety of a uniform ratio between continental currency and the "new money" of Congress of the preceding March. New Jersey has constantly supplied its share of supplies for the army, but has seldom received anything but certificates in return, and as the population of the State consists principally of farmers this situation works a hardship. Moreover, New Jersey is always called upon first for supplies although the citizens have reduced their private stores to a very scanty allowance and are often compelled to see provisions and forage impressed and taken from them and their families reduced to want. It is hoped that Congress will require the other states to forward their full share of supplies and thus relieve New Jersey of a burden which will otherwise become intolerable.

Reelected to Congress a few days later Dr. Witherspoon was present in the Council on November 23 for the last time, and his seat was declared vacant. Meanwhile he had been leaving no stone unturned to fill up his college rolls. While at Trenton, for

[47] *New Jersey Archives*, 2 ser., vol. IV, p.506.

example, he wrote the following letter of condolence to the widow of General Woolford, and it was through no fault of his that the characteristic suggestion it contains proved fruitless:

By Major Nevil passing this Way I beg leave to express my Sympathy with You & Your Family on the Death of my Worthy Friend of which I am just informed. I pray that God almighty who has said he will be a Father to the Fatherless, & a Husband to the Widow may not only support You under this heavy Trial but sanctify it to You & Your Children for your present & future Benefit.

Major Nevil informs me it was the particular Request of General Woodford that his Son should finish his Studies if therefore you see it proper to send him back here You may expect all possible Attention from me & my Son in Law Mr. Smith to his Improvement. I wrote You before upon this Subject & therefore shall only refer you to the Bearer, and am

Madam, Your most obedt. humble Servant

Jno. Witherspoon[48]

A plan to regulate the work of graduate students and lead them to the higher degrees was brought before the board of trustees in May, 1781. It proposed to confer the higher and intermediate degrees in theology and law after some method similar to that practised in European universities. The plan has not been preserved. Although presented by Dr. Smith and Mr. Houston, its provisions without doubt received the sanction and supervision of the President if he did not actually draw them up himself, being the only man on the ground who had any first hand knowledge of European higher instruction, and having instituted graduate study at Princeton as early as 1768. The plan was referred to a committee which reported favorably a few months later; but further consideration was desired and for the next three years the plan was discussed intermittently by the board but definite action deferred. Undoubtedly it required better financial equipment than the College yet controlled and the administration clearly saw that its first duty lay toward the undergraduate department, and nothing came of the movement to formulate these, the earliest plans for organized graduate

[48] Presbyterian Historical Society.

work at Princeton. Dr. Witherspoon had sought graduate students as soon as he assumed the Presidency, and his desire was not without a certain measure of fulfillment. Although Princeton in his day did not confer, and since his time has not conferred, degrees in course in theology,[49] and the only degrees in course ever granted in law were those conferred during the brief existence of the Princeton law school in the middle of the nineteenth century, yet during Dr. Witherspoon's time graduate students in both law and theology were commonly in attendance. Because of the absence of annual catalogues of the period it is impossible to give the exact total but the names of at least a score are known. Evidence of the presence of such students is found in Fithian who writes in his *Journal* in November, 1770, that "resident graduates" assisted at his entrance examination; in February, 1773, Oliver Reese, a theological student writes to Fithian that he has preached before Dr. Witherspoon "and the graduates," and a note to a sermon by Dr. S. Stanhope Smith of January, 1795, preached a few months after Witherspoon's death, informs us that the discourse is published "at the request of the students in theology and law."

Militia being still quartered in Nassau Hall, in May, 1781, the board petitioned the State Legislature to put an end to the practice, coupling the petition with one further to reduce the trustees' quorum:

> To the Honorable the Council & Assembly
> for the State of New Jersey now met in
> general Assembly at Princeton.

The Petition of the Trustees of the College of
New Jersey

Sheweth

That your Petitioners have long had the Charge and Care of an important Seminary of Learning at Princeton in this state, known by the name of the College of New Jersey—

That the derangement of the Funds as well as destruction of the costly and valuable Building erected for the reception of the Students

[49] Save apparently in the case of the Reverend John Joachim Zubly of Charlestown, S. C., who presented in 1774 for the doctorate in divinity a learned but curious "Exercitatio Theologica de Nuptiis Virginis superadultae" (Charlestown, 1775).

(occasioned by the invasion of this State by the Enemy) requires the immediate and careful attention of the Trustees to prevent the entire ruin of the Corporation, to the great Injury of the State in one of its most essential interests—

That from the scattered situation of the individuals of this Corporation, their Meeting is often prevented by means of the large quorum required by the Charter of Incorporation—

Your Petitioners therefore humbly pray the Interposition of the Legislature to reduce the Number of the Quorum to Nine Members, whereof the Governor of the State for the time being to be one, and in case of his absence, the President of the College, or in case of his Death or removal, the oldest Trustee always to be one, or to provide such other remedy as to your Honorable Houses shall seem meet—

Your Petitioners further show that they have laid out large Sums of money for the repairs of Damages done by the Enemy to the Building, but by the continual quartering of our own troops, especially the Militia passing from Time to Time through the town in the sd Building the said repairs have been again thrown down and destroyed, wherefore your Petitioners farther pray that a penalty may be laid on any Civil or Military officer who shall hereafter Quarter or suffer to be quartered any Troops in the sd Building and its appurtenances or to grant your Petitioners such other remedy as in your wisdom you shall think fit.

> Signed in the Name of and by Order of the
> Board, in full Meeting
> JNO WITHERSPOON[50]

Dr. Witherspoon was finding time to resume writing. The *Pennsylvania Journal* reprinted in February and March, 1781, his three *Druid* papers of 1776, and beginning with the issue of April 11, the President started a fresh series of four. The first of the new essays is a discussion of common sense and lacks the interest of its three successors, which concern another of the President's hobbies, and contain his speculations on the future of the English language in America.[51]

Opening his fourth essay with a paragraph on the manifest improvement made by writers during the past century in their use of the English language, he warns his readers that the situa-

[50] Princeton University Library.
[51] *Works*, vol. IV, p. 168.

tion of America in this respect is such "as to require peculiar attention." America is at a great distance from Great Britain "in which the standard of the language is as yet supposed to be found."

Every State is equal to and independent of every other; and I believe none of them will agree, at least immediately, to receive laws from another in discourse, any more than in action. Time and accident must determine what turn affairs will take in this respect in future, whether we shall continue to consider the language of Great Britain as the pattern upon which we are to form ours, or whether, in this new emprise, some centre of learning and politeness will not be found, which shall obtain influence and prescribe the rules of speech and writing to every other part.

His expectation is that "being entirely separated from Britain we shall find some centre or standard of our own, and not be subject to the inhabitants of that island, either in receiving new ways of speaking or rejecting the old." Pending the settlement of this point, however, it had occurred to him "to make some observations upon the present state of the English language in America and to attempt a collection of the chief improprieties which prevail and might be easily corrected."

He thinks that the reason the common people in America speak much better than the same class does in Great Britain is that they move more frequently from place to place and are not so liable to local peculiarities of accent or phraseology. On the other hand he finds a marked difference between the "public and solemn Discourses" of gentlemen and scholars in Great Britain and those of Americans of the same social standing.

I have heard, he asserts, in this country, in the senate, at the bar and from the pulpit, and see daily in dissertations from the press, errors in grammar, improprieties and vulgarisms, which hardly any person of the same class in point of rank and literature would have fallen into in Great Britain.

He then gives examples from the collection which curiosity had led him to make, and which he had named "Americanisms," a word which he claims to have coined and which he defines, a claim and a definition accepted by the New English Dictionary.[52] He has classified them into vulgarisms, local phrases or terms, common blunders, cant phrases, personal blunders, and the pedantic use of technical terms. He warns his readers not to expect his enumeration under any of these heads to be complete—this was "not necessary to my purpose, which is by specimens to enable every attentive and judicious person to make observations for himself." Neither is it necessary to the purpose of this book to do more than note that the accuracy of many of the observations the President makes in the rest of the *Druid* series is supported by the work of later and far more scientific investigators. As typical of his "specimens" may be cited "improve" in the sense of "to use," "chunks" meaning blocks of half-burned wood, "considerable" in the phrase "he is considerable of a surveyor," "tote" for "carry," "mad" for "angry," and the American meaning of "clever" which he declares would certainly "be mistaken when heard for the first time by one born in Britain."

The last *Druid* essay announces that one more was planned to conclude the series; but this was never published. The *Pennsylvania Journal* for June 20, 1781, contains a communication to the *Druid* listing additional Americanisms, and the *Journal* for June 30 prints a letter from the inevitable disgruntled and critical reader taking the *Druid* to task for inaccuracies and for "Scotticisms" which were just as objectionable as so-called "Americanisms." The President decided to carry his investigations no further—at least in print.

Meanwhile, the board of trustees was continuing its canvas for funds. Dr. Robert Smith of Pequa collected in the Forks of Brandywine some £238, and the indefatigable Mr. Caldwell, £200 in gold and silver; the trustees ordered certain lots owned by the College to be sold for another £200 and the money applied to repairs. The chief payment on this account during 1780 was £1357 for carpentering made in continental money which Dr. Witherspoon notes in his statement was worth "in hard money at 75 for one," or roughly £18 sterling. Philadelphia and its neighborhood had proved to be the most fruitful campaign soil, the collection in May, 1779, being £663, in December 1779,

[52] Though with inaccurate date—"about 1794," instead of 1781.

£391, and 1780, £765. But repairs were a bottomless pit and the committee in charge reported but little progress. A guinea entrance fee was next required from each new student, the proceeds to be used in borrowing further funds.

This increase in the cost of education did not deter applicants, and at the opening of the winter term in 1781 the *New Jersey Gazette*[53] gave the honor of its first column to a long notice signed by Dr. Witherspoon which contains signs of improving conditions. The College is filling up fast, and it is the belief of the authorities that all the former regulations may now be re-established. Therefore, since a large part of Nassau Hall is already repaired and the rest is expected to be restored without delay, hereafter all students will be required to live in college, and strict compliance with college orders will be expected as regards attendance at prayers, daily recitations, and being in their rooms at night. Grammar scholars will as formerly be permitted to reside with private families. Board at commons is ten shillings a week and no one may board out save by special permission. Tuition is six pounds and room rent two per annum. The grammar school tuition is the same as that of the College, and a matriculation fee of one guinea is required. A student entering college from another grammar school into a higher class than the freshman will be called upon to pay the tuition for as many terms as he thus "slipped over," but a student entering from another college would be admitted to the same standing. All fees and charges are payable in advance semi-annually, and the President's own pocketbook has suffered so much from arrearages and unredeemed pledges made by parents and guardians living at a distance, that he can no longer repeat "so expensive and dangerous a contrivance." He hopes that parents will entrust the management of boys' accounts and expenses to some one in college or in the neighborhood. Students in the past have run into extravagance of dress and incidentals and have set a bad example, have been imposed upon by the unscrupulous, and have brought reproach upon the institution.

Twenty years later during the Presidency of Dr. Smith the same situation led to the enactment of sumptuary laws. It is

[53]October 10, 1781.

difficult to get any exact idea as to the extravagances to which allusion is made. But an extremely polite letter to young Stephen van Rennsalaer, student at Nassau Hall in the summer of 1780, from a Mr. William Pollard of Philadelphia, does not owe its astonishing figures solely to the fact that the prices quoted are in terms of depreciated currency. Mr. Pollard, who seems to have been a tailor, sends to van Rennsalaer some green cloth, some shalloon, and some buttons. The cloth "is not Superfine, but it is the best that is to be got in Town," wrote Mr. Pollard. Naturally one could not expect the son of the famous New York patroon to wear anything but the best that Philadelphia could provide, especially when he had come to college, so it is said, in his own chaise and with the most luxurious wardrobe that had yet been aired in the frugal atmosphere of Nassau Hall. At any rate, for one and a half yards of the cloth he paid two hundred and twenty-five pounds, for three yards of shalloon seventy-five pounds, and for one and a half dozen buttons sixty-seven pounds, ten shillings, making a total of three hundred and sixty-seven pounds ten shillings for the materials of a single piece of raiment.[54] One shudders to think what the final "ready to wear" cost was. It would also seem that Ashbel Green himself, a minister's son, might have got along with a somewhat less valuable coat than the one he wore during his first year at college in 1782. It had been made for a British officer and had been left on its importer's hands, so that this bargain hunting student secured it for a thousand dollars in depreciated money,[55] which perhaps was cheap for so fine a garment, but appears otherwise. The *Journal of 1786* does not give evidence of undergraduate extravagance, and as the group of students mentioned in it belonged to what must have been the social set in college, it is possible that extravagance had by this time been fairly checked.

The restoration of Nassau Hall, in spite of the best endeavors and promises of the board and its president, was still far from complete. By the spring of 1782 or five years after the battle of Princeton, as we have seen from Ashbel's Green statement, only the middle portion of the first floor and a room or two in the

[54] Princeton University Library.
[55] *Autobiography*, p. 71.

basement had been rendered habitable. Nevertheless, that autumn it was announced that all college orders were re-established as they had been before the war. A further increase had been ordered in the matriculation fee which now was to be one pound fifteen shillings, while board was correspondingly raised to fifteen shillings a week.[56] The public seemed ready enough to respond to the President's desire for pupils and to pay whatever college fees were demanded; to look after them when they got to Princeton was still the problem. By the time Dr. Witherspoon returned to Princeton in the winter of 1782 after his congressional service was definitely ended he found the funds of the College cut in half, the college enrolment shrunk to a quarter of its former self, and besides having a half-ruined building on their hands which they had no funds to repair, the trustees owed him nearly nine hundred pounds for salary and various official expenses; and he himself was badly out of pocket as the reward of his absence in national service.

[56] *New Jersey Gazette*, October 9, 1782.

CHAPTER THREE

THE condition of the College described in the last chapter and the prominence which Dr. Witherspoon had attained during the Revolution were responsible for the fact that although he had planned otherwise the final decade of his life showed but little decrease in his activity. He was sixty years old at the close of the Revolutionary War; his life had been anything but peaceful, the last six years in particular had been years of peculiar strain; and it had long been his cherished purpose, so he wrote to a friend in 1780, to spend the remainder of his days *in otio cum dignitate*. With dignity in the abstract he was adequately equipped, and of honors he had received his full share during the fourteen years of his residence in America, and he was to continue to be the recipient of recognition and distinction; but ease, under whatever interpretation, was not to mark his closing days.

In the first place, he was so seriously handicapped financially that he was compelled to live in strict economy and was often criticised for not meeting his obligations more promptly.[1] In common with other members of Congress he had found public life a grave expense. Ashbel Green believed that the chief source of his embarrassment was the loss he suffered in connection with his Ryegate property. As far as can now be judged, it is certain that none of the exchanges and sales connected with that venture brought any appreciable profit to Dr. Witherspoon, especially in view of the length of time during which he held the property. The fate of one of his Ryegate tracts is alluded to in a letter from his son-in-law, Dr. Samuel S. Smith, to an agent in 1798, and was probably not an exception:

I have bought 1200 acres of land near Newbury of Mrs. Witherspoon being the same that Mr. W. Wallace some time ago bought at collec-

---

[1] Documents in Princeton University Library show that sales of land were made by his widow to satisfy debts of his, one in particular being of £2000 incurred in 1785.

tor's sale for taxes and re-conveyed to her for a certain sum. It was formerly the property of Dr. Witherspoon. But he was negligent and forgetful in his latter years & it slipped from him.

Similarly the story of the land he had bought for his son, James, and which he held for ten years after the boy's death at the battle of Germantown, is one of gradual decline. It will be remembered that James Witherspoon had gone to Ryegate in the spring of 1774, and had cleared 25 acres of the 600 in his tract and had erected some sort of dwelling and other buildings. The Vermont wilderness soon won back his clearing and twenty years later few traces of his work remained. In 1798 the ruins of one building could still be seen, half hidden in the dense undergrowth. This tract and a lake in Ryegate township bearing the Witherspoon name now constitute all that is left of the President's association with the place.

He seems to have suffered from a chronic shortness of ready funds. A letter of his in 1775 to the Hon. Daniel Clymer of Philadelphia, enclosing a student's account, asks Mr. Clymer to advance cash beyond the amount of the bill—"as you will understand by this time on Account of my Daughter's marriage which is at hand & my son's setting out in the World, I stand very much in need of Money & it could scarce at any time be a greater favour;" and a postscript adds: "If you will send the money by Monday's Stage, it will be a particular favour."

It is tolerably evident that however much Dr. Witherspoon may have known of the theory of finance he was not successful in its application to his own business. He was speaking from grim experience when he remarked in the *Druid* that "some who are even connoisseurs in economy never can keep their own affairs in tolerable order." For a man whose mind was distinctly practical in most of its workings he seems to have been singularly unpractical and even careless in business dealings where he himself was concerned. We are told by Ashbel Green, that, returning once from Ryegate with a drove of cattle received in payment of rent, Dr. Witherspoon was met by an affable individual who volunteered for a consideration to bring the cattle down to New Jersey for him and thus allow their owner to hasten homeward. The proposal was accepted and the President went on to Princeton. But the cattle never reached the shelter of his Tusculum barns and he did not hear of them again. He had even neglected to get the swindler's name.

A similar neglect of elementary business principles is said to have involved his estate in heavy financial loss. Signing a bond for Robert Morris when the latter borrowed money from a person named Leslie for the use of Congress, Dr. Witherspoon made a verbal agreement to pay in cash and not in continental money, for which consideration Mr. Leslie was to waive interest on the loan. After the President's death Leslie claimed and took both principal and interest, no written statement of the agreement having been made.

Even loyalty to old friends seemed to involve him in unfortunate financial complications. An example was his effort to save "Castle Howard," a fine estate on the outskirts of Princeton, belonging to the widow of Captain William Howard, a retired British army officer of wealth and strong pro-colonial feelings. The details of the transaction are not altogether clear, but apparently with a view to evading the New Jersey Confiscation Act this lady and her second husband, Captain Ibbetson Hamer, also a British veteran, on being compelled to leave "Castle Howard" when the British retreated to New Brunswick in 1777, gave the President a power of attorney to sell the property. But the place was seized by the State, its contents sold (the inventory mentions family portraits, a library, and a large organ) and the house rented. Dr. Witherspoon regaining possession, in 1785 sold a portion of the property for £900, of which sum only one installment, £60, appears to have been paid by the purchaser, the Reverend Philip Stockton. In 1788 the Hamers had not yet received a penny and were blaming the President for gross mismanagement, to call it by no worse a name. In 1793, the year before his death, he bought the property back under an Act enabling creditors to recover their just debts from absconders, and part of it was purchased in 1794 by Colonel Erkuries Beatty of Princeton. Whether Captain and Mrs. Hamer ever received their money, investigation has not yet revealed.[2]

Leaving out of consideration the drain on his pocket continually caused by his interest in impecunious strangers, particularly if they happened to be Scotsmen, he was a constant sufferer in his financial relations with the College owing partly to unavoidable conditions and partly to his own generous nature. That he contrived to keep the College from total disintegration through the discouraging period of the war and in spite of a national monetary system of which he totally disapproved, was a feat to be marvelled at; and the personal sacrifices which repeatedly marked his administration of the institution's finances and enabled it to tide over desperately hard times can never be too highly praised. In 1779 he had voluntarily relinquished half his salary to secure the services of Dr. Smith, an arrangement which in 1783 he offered to make permanent; for at least two years he accepted depreciated currency instead of the gold the board of trustees had voted he should receive; for several years he allowed himself to suffer by the rule that the President must either dismiss students in arrears for tuition or else make up their deficits himself; and at last he was forced in self-defence to issue warning, as we have seen, that he would no longer meet arrearages but would adopt the other alternative. How many young men he helped though college will never be known, but the frequent references to this characteristic lead one to suspect that few boys had to leave Princeton for lack of means to pay their college bills when Dr. Witherspoon knew the circumstances. A sheet of accounts in his handwriting headed "Notes of Arrears given in to the Com," and evidently the fragment of a report drawn up for one of the trustees' investigating committees, contains ample evidence of the President's generosities as well as his lack of strict business method. The list contains the names of eight students in classes from 1789 to 1791, seven of whom are acknowledged as directly chargeable in part or in whole to himself. One

[2] For the documents relating to this affair grateful acknowledgment is here made of the researches of E. Alfred Jones, Esq., M.A., of the Temple, London, among the loyalist archives of the Public Record Office, the results of which have been most generously transmitted. The deed of sale to Col. Beatty is in the Library of Princeton University.

boy was to be charged to him for the summer of 1787, so the Doctor's own comment runs, "after that he was to answer for himself & is not now under my Care. Yet if the Winter session of that year is not paid I will assume it." Another name has this note attached: "Joseph Caldwell is a charity Scholar. I do not recall whether I had then determined to support him. Yet I will assume it." A further entry reads: "Will Perrie (Perry) was a charity Scholar at my Expense if his entry is not paid I will assume it." In an earlier list of delinquents whose overdue bills, reached the respectable sum of four hundred pounds, individual accounts to the amount of eighty pounds were later marked as paid off by "Dr. W."

Owing to transactions like these, of which the bookkeeping was obviously careless, and to the President's prolonged absences from Princeton amid the confusions of the war—Ashbel Green entering in 1782 did not see him until six weeks after the term had opened—and also partly because of the unbusinesslike system of handling college funds that was in operation when he assumed office and which he had not been able to change, the financial management of the College during his Presidency easily laid itself open to criticism. When board bills were paid to the steward, tuition bills to the President, and room rent and other monies were handed to the treasurer; when no adequate system of vouchers was maintained and virtually any officer of the College could without warrant from higher authority contract debts, purchase supplies, or order repairs and look to the treasurer for settlement, it is small wonder that the financial affairs of the institution bordered on the chaotic. The following exchange of brief communications between the President and the treasurer, preserved in the Princeton manuscripts, shows that even before the war the payment of salaries was dependent entirely on the state of the treasurer's petty cash. On November 22, 1774, Dr. Witherspoon wrote to Mr. Sergeant:

Sir
    I have a written Order for the whole that is due to me to the 29th of September therefore desire to know when I may expect it
                                        JNO. WITHERSPOON

The treasurer replied on the same sheet:

My being able to pay money I suppose will very much depend on Mr. Woodruff's [the steward] paying in tuition money. He has answered considerable in paying Messrs Houston and Grier [the tutors]. I hope to settle with Mr. Woodruff Soon but doubt whether he will have much more Cash to pay or not.

Your most humble Servt

JNO. SERGEANT

Under the circumstances the management was probably as efficient as it ever had been. The trustees enjoyed no reputation as financiers long before Dr. Witherspoon's election; and for that matter to be in a financial condition other than stringent was even then, as it still seems to be, incompatible with the nature of American institutions of learning. But the fact remains that had Dr. Witherspoon's personal accounts not been in such confusion he would have been spared the mortifying position in which he found himself during the last year of his life when a committee of the board, in belated effort to straighten out the tangled money matters of the College, found itself for a time unable to agree with his claim that he did not owe the College several hundred pounds. Fortunately the situation was cleared to everyone's satisfaction before Dr. Witherspoon's death, but the controversy must have weighed hard on him in his blindness and ill health and after his twenty-five years of devoted and generous service.

Even had no controversy arisen over college finances and had he escaped the pinch of private embarrassment, Dr. Witherspoon would not have been allowed to live the peaceful closing years he sought. When he left Congress he immediately took up his share of instruction in college, resuming his lectures, and by way of variety holding some of his classes at "Tusculum;" he continued to preside at Commencement, and once more he occupied the College pulpit in his regular turn. But he was not one of those public figures who lay aside their harness and pass gradually and unnoticed from the scene of contemporary history. Rather was he one of those whose conspicuousness ends only with their lives. Calls to important service in Church and State were still to come to him, and he was to remain the best illustration of his own firm conviction that public service is one of the chief ends of education and one of the principal duties of the educated citizen.

His first recorded public utterance after the conclusion of hostilities was at the Princeton celebration of the declaration of peace on the official Thanksgiving Day, April 19, 1783, a day spent, according to the cheery reporter of the occasion, "with that festivity, decency, and good order which we hope will ever characterize a free and virtuous people."[3] After the proclamation of peace had been read at the village flagstaff Dr. Witherspoon delivered in the college prayer-hall a thanksgiving sermon on the text "Salvation belongeth unto the Lord," which as his final word on the American Revolution is worth examination.[4] His enthusiastic survey of the war was excusable; he could find many reasons for viewing it through rosy glasses; and it was of course consistent with his calling and with the view of history which he entertained to lay his stress on the providential aspects of the contest. As a sermon, therefore, the effort is admirable; but it is disappointing in its failure to indicate in any way its author's matured political opinion of the Confederation, his attitude toward its present problems, his hopes of its future. Instead, he calls attention to dispensations of Providence shown in the unexpected successes and favors enjoyed by the United States during the war, in the preservation of the Confederation from the difficulties and evils besetting its path, and in the confounding of the enemy's councils so that they actually hastened the very changes they sought to prevent. That the Colonies were unjustly charged with a deliberate concerted plan to break with Great Britain and set up an independent government he proves by the facts that until they had declared themselves independent there was no pre-contract between them, no attempt to enlist foreign aid, and above all no laying in of munitions of war.

---

[3] *The New Jersey Gazette* of April 23, 1783, contains a full account. The people met at noon at the village flagstaff "on which the American flag was beautifully displayed;" at one o'clock they adjourned to the college hall for Dr. Witherspoon's sermon; at three o'clock public dinners were served at the taverns of Colonel Hyer and Mr. Beekman; at seven the village was illuminated; and at eight the local infantry company fired a salute of thirteen guns.
[4] *Works*, vol. II, p. 451.

The cooperation of the French he considers a special favor of Providence, and if he ever suspected the existence of any of the age-long underlying reasons for the alliance he gives no indication thereof, although as a member of the congressional committee on foreign affairs during that exciting time, he must have been cognizant of part of the intrigue that went into the formation of that alliance. Above all, the appointment of Washington as commander in chief of the American forces was in his opinion the work of divine intervention. With brief apology, but without mentioning Washington's name, he delivers a calm eulogy of his friend in terms whose truth modern appreciation of the General's character has only emphasized.[5]

As for perils avoided by the Confederation, even the emission of paper money, an expedient which he did not consider himself "obliged either to justify or approve," had not been fatal. Another danger successfully surmounted had been that of anarchy and confusion when government under the Crown came to an end and each State had to frame its own new constitution,—it was done as quietly and calmly, he avers, as the moving of family and furniture from one house into another. The chief peril avoided, however, was internal dissension, a source from which he had apprehended more danger than from any other. Here his fears had been wholly disappointed and his hopes greatly exceeded. It may be taken as perhaps a reflection of Dr. Witherspoon's unswerving faith in the future of his adopted country, and his buoyant breadth of view that ignored petty details, coupled to some degree perhaps with a latent inability, through foreign birth and association, to appreciate fully all the hidden causes of sectional friction in America, that we find him telling his audience that "in our public councils, no mark of dissension in matters of importance has ever appeared; and I take upon me further to say that every year has obliterated colonial distinction and worn away local prejudices, so that mutual affection is at

[5] In contrast with the restraint and sanity of his remarks on Washington one should read the rhapsody of Dr. Stiles on the same occasion at New Haven (Tyler, II, 334.) Dr. Witherspoon used passages from this part of his sermon again in August when he wrote the address of welcome to General Washington from the College and village of Princeton. Other portions of the sermon were also used by Mr. Boudinot as President of Congress in his address at the audience given to Washington at the same time.

present more cordial and the views and works of the whole more uniform than ever they were at any preceding period." To cite no other contravening facts, the very hall in which he uttered these overoptimistic words was to hear, before the year was ended, a congressional debate on the location of a federal residence which intimated that local prejudices were far from dead or worn away, and that "mutual affection" did not conspicuously mark congressional relations.

He then proceeded to show how the councils of the British had been confounded and how they had hastened their own undoing. Once more he insisted on the ignorance and error under which the British ministry had labored as to dispositions and things American. Failing to see the "strong and rooted inclinations of the people themselves, such as no address or management of interested persons could have produced," those at the head of the government had sincerely believed that the great body of the colonists were on their side and were misled into rebellion by a few factious leaders. They were further led astray by American loyalists. He ventured to assert that "time will constrain everybody to confess that the partisan friends of the English in America have done more essential injury to their cause than the greatest and boldest of their enemies." Of the sufferings and hardships meted out to loyalists he says nothing save to admit in one casual sentence that the adherents to the Crown were "sometimes roughly handled by the multitudes at the beginning of the controversy"—which, to say the least, is scarcely an adequate summary of the treatment they received.

Then he offers his subtlest reason for the failure of Great Britain's advisers. They thought that they had only a few malcontents to punish, and an army to conquer in no way comparable with their own; they forgot that they had the lost affections of a whole people to recover. Every measure taken by Great Britain instead of tending to regain the hearts of the American people had a most powerful influence in producing the contrary effect. As an example he cites the cruelty and severity with which the war was conducted by the enemy—the barbarous treatment of American prisoners—

we in this State, through which they passed to their homes, can never forget the appearance of the emaciated spectres who escaped or were exchanged from British dungeons or prison ships. Neither was it possible for the people in general but to be struck with the contrast when exchanges took place and they saw companies of British prisoners going home hale and hearty, bearing every mark of their having been supplied with comfortable provisions and treated with humanity.

In the same vein he speaks of the needless devastation and ruin that marked the path of the British army across the country. Upon the whole, nothing to him appeared more manifest than that the separation of the Colonies from the mother country was an act of Providence; every step the British took to prevent it only served to accelerate it, "which has generally been the case when men have undertaken to go in opposition to the course of Providence and to make war with the nature of things." And so he calls upon his hearers to thank God for the present promising state of affairs and he lays it down as their civic duty to testify their gratitude by usefulness in their several stations:

This is the duty of every person, even of the lowest station, at all times. Even the meanest and most unconnected hath still some small bounds within which his example and influence may be useful. . . . In free States where the body of the people have the supreme power properly in their own hands and must be ultimately resorted to on all great matters if there be a general corruption of manners there can be nothing but confusion. So true is this that civil liberty cannot long be preserved without virtue. A monarchy may subsist for ages, and be better or worse under a good or bad prince; but a republic once equally poised must either preserve its virtue or lose its liberty and by some tumultuous revolution either return to its first principles or assume a more unhappy form.

A double duty therefore results—that of the people who choose their rulers, and that of the representatives to whom is entrusted the exercise of this delegated authority. The people must choose men of high principles; while those chosen are under the strictest obligation to do their utmost to promote religion, sobriety, industry, and every social virtue. And the sermon closes with a series of exhortations which, as time has passed, have lost but little of their force:

Let us endeavour to bring into and keep in credit and reputation everything that may serve to give vigor to an equal republican constitution. Let us cherish a love of piety, order, industry, frugality. Let us check every disposition to luxury, effeminacy, and the pleasures of a dissipated life. Let us in public measures put honor upon modesty and self denial which is the index of real merit. And in our families let us do the best by religious instruction to sow the seeds which bear fruit in the next generation. We are one body of federated States. For many reasons I shall avoid making comparisons at present but may venture to predict that whatsoever state among us shall continue to make piety and virtue the standard of public honor, will enjoy the greatest inward peace, the greatest national happiness, and in every outward conflict will discover the greatest constitutional strength.

In May, 1783, Dr. Witherspoon attended as usual the annual meeting of the Synod, and a report on the slender salaries of Presbyterian ministers coming up, he was ordered with Dr. Elihu Spencer and Dr. S. Stanhope Smith to draft a pastoral letter to the congregations of the Synod urging an increase. The letter was adopted and ordered printed, and Dr. Witherspoon published it in the *Pennsylvania Packet* of May 29, 1783, where it appears over the signature of the Moderator John McCrery. It is included in the second edition of Dr. Witherspoon's works.[6] Recalling that the Synod had addressed a Pastoral Letter to its congregation in May, 1775, the opportunity now afforded by the cessation of hostilities to express the Synod's "sentiments on this happy occasion and its advice as to the duty incumbent upon all ranks," was inescapably convenient. After congratulating the congregations "on the general and almost universal attachment of the Presbyterian body to the cause of liberty and the rights of mankind," the letter calls upon its readers to render thanks to Almighty God "in a particular manner" for establishing the independence of the United States of America. The illustrations of divine intervention are those Dr. Witherspoon had used in his sermon at Princeton in April, and the advice as to

[6] Philadelphia, 1802, vol. III, p. 9.

civic duty is phrased in the same language. But the document as a whole does not rank with its predecessor of 1775. The call to increase pastoral salaries is relegated to one sentence.

As soon as the Synod adjourned Dr. Witherspoon went to Vermont where he seems to have endeavored to expedite the disposal of his Ryegate property by giving General Whitelaw and another representative a power of attorney to sell all his holdings. On his way back in July he stopped at New Haven to visit Dr. Stiles. Had he known what was going on at Princeton he would have halted only long enough to water his sorrel mare. For the members of the Continental Congress, frightened for their lives by a band of mutinous soldiers, had hastily fled from Philadelphia to re-assemble at Princeton. After Colonel George Morgan of Princeton had given the fugitive legislators the hospitality of "Prospect," his farmhouse at the edge of the campus, Vice-president Smith and tutor Riddle offered the Congress the use of Nassau Hall. Here, on his return to Princeton a few days later, Dr. Witherspoon found the government of the United States installed; and here it remained until November.

The visit of Congress metamorphosed the quiet little village into a gay and brilliant capital where on the one hand not unwelcome academic occasions relieved the monotony of official life, and on the other rural hospitalities adopted new standards to suit imported metropolitan tastes. Young Ashbel Green, then a Senior, describing for his father the joint celebration of the Fourth of July by college, town, and Congress, at which he was one of the orators, refers to the general effect of the presence of Congress on the community:

The face of things is inconceivably altered in Princeton within a fortnight. From a little obscure village we have become the capital of America. Instead of almost silence in the town, nothing is to be seen or heard but the passing and rattling of wagons, coaches, and chairs, the crying about of pine apples, oranges, lemons, and every luxurious article both foreign and domestic.[7]

[7] H. C. Alexander, *Life of J. A. Alexander*, I, 16. The detailed history of the stay of Congress at Princeton during the summer and autumn of 1783 may be found in Collins, *The Continental Congress at Princeton*, Princeton, 1908.

In August, when General Washington came to Princeton in answer to the summons of Congress, the faculty of the College and the inhabitants of the village presented to him the following congratulatory address of which President Witherspoon was the author.[8]

TO HIS EXCELLENCY GENERAL WASHINGTON, &C, &C, &C,—

The inhabitants of Princeton & neighbourhood with the president & faculty of the college beg leave to embrace this opportunity of congratulating your excellency on the late glorious peace on your meeting with congress in this place & the present happy & promising state of public affairs.

As the college of New Jersey devoted to the interests of religion & learning was among the first places in America that suffered by the ravages of the enemy so happily this place & neighborhood was the scene of one of the most important & seasonable checks which they received in their progress. The surprise of the Hessians at Trenton & the Subsequent victory at Princeton redounded much to the honour of the commander who planned & the handful of troops with him which executed the measures. Yet were they even of greater moment to the cause of America than they were brilliant as particular military exploits.

We contemplate & adore the wisdom & goodness of divine providence as displayed in many instances in favour of the United States during the course of the war, but in none more than in the unanimous appointment of your excellency to the command of the army. When we consider the continuance of your life & health the discernment prudence fortitude & patience of your conduct by which you have not only sacrificed as others have done person & property but frequently even reputation itself in the public cause choosing rather to risk your own name than expose the nakedness of your country—When we consider the great & unabated attachment of the army & the cordial esteem of all ranks of men & of every state in the union which you have so long Enjoyed & when we consider in contrast the british leaders who have been in Succession opposed to you their attempts to blast

[8] The original is among the Washington Papers at the Library of Congress (Letters to Washington 110, folio 7) and appears to be in the hand of James Riddle, the college tutor; it was published in contemporary newspapers such as the *Pennsylvania Packet*, August 30, and the *Pennsylvania Gazette*, September 3, 1783; a curiously altered version appears in Ashbel Green's editions of Witherspoon's *Works*; the correct text taken from the original manuscript, as given above, may also be found in Collins, *Continental Congress at Princeton*, pp. 103–5.

each others characters & the short duration of their command we cannot help being of opinion that God himself has raised you up as a fit & proper instrument for establishing & securing the liberty & happiness of these states.

We pray that the Almighty may continue to protect & bless you & that having survived so much fatigue & so many dangers from traitors & in the field you may enjoy many years of repose in the bosom of your grateful country.

Signed in behalf of the whole in a public meeting by

JNO WITHERSPOON
ROBT STOCKTON
JONATHAN DEARE
JAMES RIDDLE
JAMES M'COMB
ENOS KELSEY
FRANCIS J. JAMES

Princeton August 25, 1783

To this address Washington at once replied.[9]

TO THE INHABITANTS OF PRINCETON AND NEIGHBOURHOOD TOGETHER
WITH THE PRESIDENT & FACULTY OF THE COLLEGE
Gentlemen:
I receive, with the utmost satisfaction and acknowledge with great sensibility your kind congratulations.

The prosperous situation of our public affairs, the flourishing State of this place, and the revival of the Seat of Literature from the ravages of War, encrease to the highest degree, the pleasure I feel *in visiting* (at the return of Peace) the Scene of our important Military transactions, and *in recollecting* the period when the Tide of adversity began to turn, and better fortune to smile upon us.

If in the execution of an arduous Office, I have been so happy as to discharge my duty to the Public with Fidelity and success, and to obtain the good Opinion of my fellow Soldiers and fellow Citizens, I attribute all the Glory to that Supreme Being who hath caused the several parts, which have been employed in the production of the wonderful events we now contemplate, to harmonise in the most perfect manner and who was able by the humblest Instruments, as well as by the most powerful means to establish and secure the Liberty and happiness of the United States.

[9] Collins, *Continental Congress at Princeton*, pp. 105–6.

I now return to you, Gentlemen, my thanks for your benevolent wishes, and make it my earnest prayer to Heaven, that every temporal and divine Blessing may be bestowed on the Inhabitants of Princeton on the Neighbourhood, and on the President and Faculty of the College of New-Jersey, and that the usefulness of this Institution, in promoting the Interests of Religion and Learning, may be universally extended.

I am, Gent'n, &c,

G. WASHINGTON

Rocky Hill, 25th August 1783

But it was at commencement in September that Dr. Witherspoon's cup of pride was filled. On the platform in the church where the exercises were held sat the entire Congress, adjourned in special honor of the occasion, the executive officers of the government, the French Minister La Luzerne, and General Washington. Ashbel Green, who was valedictorian of the day, has recorded the President's evident satisfaction with the brilliance of the scene. That this commencement had very definite political significance was the firm belief of at least one person in the audience and probably of others. An English officer named Michaelis who had come from New York to what he called "the Princetown Athens" and was present at the exercises incognito, a few days later wrote out his impressions, which document reached Sir Guy Carleton and by him was transmitted to Lord North.[10]

After paragraphs on the unpopularity of Congress, and on General Washington, Michaelis sketches the influence of President Witherspoon:

An account of the present face of things in America would be very defective indeed, if no mention was made of this political firebrand, who perhaps had not a less share in the Revolution than Washington himself. He poisons the minds of his young Students and through them the Continent.

He is the intimate friend of the General; and had I no other arguments to support my ideas of Washington's designs, I think his intimacy with a man of so different a character with his own (for Washington's private one is perfectly amiable) would justify my suspicions.

[10] A copy is in the New York Public Library among the Bancroft Transcripts, Carleton Papers, America 1783, vol. II, p. 225, etc.

The commencement was a favourable opportunity for conveying certain sentiments to the public at large (for even women were present). . . . This farce was evidently introductory of the drama that is to follow. The great maxim which this commencement was to establish was the following:—"A time may come in every Republic, *and that may be the case with America*, when anarchy makes it the duty of the man who has the majority of the people with him, to take the helm into his own hands, in order to save his country; and the person who opposes him deserves the utmost revenge of his nation, deserves —to be sent to Nova Scotia. Vox populi vox dei."

These were the very words of the Moderator who decided on the question,—was Brutus justifiable in killing Caesar? Or they thought us all who heard them blockheads, or they were not afraid of avowing their designs. This was plainer English still than the pactum confederationis of the Cincinnati. When the young man who with a great deal of passionate claquerie defended his favorite Brutus extolled the virtue of the man who could stab even his father when attempting the liberties of his country, I thought I saw Washington's face clouded; he did not dare to look the orator in the face who stood just before him, but with downcast look seemed wishing to hide the impression which a subject that touched him so near, had I thought very visibly made on his countenance. . . . The orations of the younger boys were full of the coarsest invectives against British tyranny. I will do Mr. Wetherspoon the justice to think he was not the author of them, for they were too poor indeed; besides they evidently conveyed different sentiments; there was one of them not unfavorable to liberal sentiments even towards Britons. But upon the whole it is but just to suppose that Wetherspoon had read them all.

The Minister of France was not present, though expected; but I have a right to think that *all* or almost all the members of Congress and all the Cincinnati in the neighborhood assisted at this entertainment. The Cincinnati sat together en corps.

Michaelis was one of those who saw in the unpopularity of Congress at this period unmistakable indications of the desire for a revolt against Congress and the formation of a new government of which Washington was to be the head. This was the alleged plan of the so-called "aristocratic junto" which was said to be broadly hinted at, if not openly discussed, in Princeton taprooms that summer. Michaelis claims that it was in a tavern that he heard the significant retort to the objection that Baltimore was too warm for the federal residence: "By the time it grows warm Congress will sit *nowhere.*"

This revolution is near at hand, says he, but I do not venture to affirm that it will affect all America. There is an opposition to it in Congress: (a weak one I believe in number and power, tho' not in abilities, for I think Thomson is at the head of it) besides all the eastern provinces oppose it. The junto Washington, Wederspan [Witherspoon] Marbois, and the Cincinnati beside the clear majority of the people in Congress, and I am confident a majority of the people at large, will certainly carry the point.

Michaelis would have alleged further proof of a secret understanding between President Witherspoon and General Washington had he seen the minutes of the Board of Trustees of the College for that day and the next. It is somewhat remarkable that the Board at no time took official notice of the presence of Congress in Princeton; but on returning from the church after the conclusion of the commencement exercises, the trustees testified their respect for Washington in the following terms:

The board being desirous to give some testimony of their high respect for the character of his excellency general Washington, who has so auspiciously conducted the armies of America.

Resolved, that the Rev^d–Drs Witherspoon, Rodgers & Jones, be a committee to wait upon his Excellency to request him to sit for his picture to be taken by Mr. Charles Wilson Peale of Philadelphia— And, ordered that his portrait, when finished be placed in the hall of the college in the room of the picture of the late king of Great Britain, which was torn away by a ball from the american artillery in the battle of Princeton.

Adjourned till to morrow morning 9 o'clock.

25th day; the board met accordingly to adjournment.

Dr Witherspoon reported that his Excellency Genl. Washington had delivered to him fifty guineas which he begged the trustees to accept as a testimony of his respect for the college.

Resolved, that the board accept it; & that the same committee who were appointed to solicit his Excellency's picture, at the same time present to him the thanks of the board for this instance of his politeness & generosity.[11]

[11] Minutes of the Board of Trustees, vol. 1, p. 236, September 24 and 25, 1783.

A year later, the portrait, having been completed, was hung in the prayer hall in the old gilt frame which had held the unlucky likeness of George the Second. There it still hangs, Princeton's most valued and historic painting.[12]

At this commencement meeting of the board Dr. Witherspoon suggested that his proposal of 1779, giving half his salary to Dr. Smith, be made permanent, a suggestion which the board accepted "as an act of generosity toward this corporation." At this time also the report of a special committee on the finances of the institution showed that there was owing to the President the sum of eight hundred and eighty-one pounds, thirteen shillings and three pence.

Although Dr. Witherspoon had no open share in the proceedings of the Congress during its residence in Princeton, he had been too recent a member and was too deeply interested in the government he had helped to create not to have been consulted. We lack documentary evidence, however, save the curious fact that the official congratulatory address from Congress to General Washington extending to him the thanks of the nation for his part in the conduct of the war contains sentences unblushingly borrowed from Dr. Witherspoon's thanksgiving sermon of April. At "Tusculum" the Dutch Minister, Peter van Berckel, was entertained during his brief but exhilarating stay at Princeton in October, and it was Dr. Witherspoon who drew up for the board of trustees the congratulatory address to the Minister which, with the exception of the reference to Washington's gift and the Peale portrait, is the only allusion the College records contain to the presence of that summer's distinguished guests. The text reads:

May it please your Excellency—The Trustees of the college of New Jersey beg leave to congratulate your Excellency on your arrival in this country. The name by which the building is distinguished in which our institution is conducted, will sufficiently inform your Excellency of the attachment we have ever had to the States of the United Netherlands. And the friendship, countenance, & assistance,

[12] "Mr. C. W. Peale having executed a portrait of his Excellency Gen[l.] Washington, according to the order of the board—Ordered that it be hung up in the college Hall agreeably to a former resolution." (Minutes, vol. I, p. 245, September 29, 1784.)

which we have received from Holland call upon us, in the most particular manner to express our gratitude to your constituents, by wishing you all happiness, comfort, & success in your present important mission.

Signed in the name & by order of the Board

JOHN WITHERSPOON, Presdt.

Octo. 22. 1783[13]

Meanwhile Somerset County had elected Dr. Witherspoon to represent it in the State Assembly, an election which he accepted in the hope, so Ashbel Green says, of being able to secure State aid for the College. Before he could make any effort toward that worthy object, however, he found himself deputed with Mr. Thomas Henderson to prepare new legislation defining the grounds for divorce and conferring power on the judges of the state supreme court to grant divorce. More in keeping with his legislative experience was his appointment on a committee to prepare a bill for raising and appropriating revenue to pay interest on the national debt, in accordance with congressional recommendation of April. Finally in November he presented a memorial from the trustees of the College setting forth the damages it had sustained not only by injury to its buildings, and the destruction of its library and equipment, but also by the virtual annihilation of its funds, and praying the Legislature to take the College into consideration. No copy of this valuable document has come to light. On its second reading, a committee was appointed to prepare a bill to appropriate to the use of the College such funds as might be levied in the several county courts of the State for the term of two years. That this novel plan did not meet with altogether cordial reception may be inferred from its adoption by the vote of fourteen to thirteen. Evidently the State was not ready to assume the protection of the College. A bill was brought in, however, by Mr. Henderson, who was an alumnus, and was ordered a second reading which was heard on December 10 in Dr. Witherspoon's absence, when it was laid over until the next session and nothing further was done with it. Ill luck had also attended Dr. Witherspoon's effort to regulate divorce. He brought in a bill late in November but it was ordered filed, and

[13] Minutes of the Board of Trustees.

although the question was raised again six years later, ten years were to elapse before the first New Jersey divorce law was adopted.

Dr. Witherspoon ceased to attend the Legislature on the last day of November. His service had been unexpectedly cut short, and on December 8 his letter of resignation was laid before the House announcing that he was about to sail for Europe. It has been seen how slow in results had been the effort of the board to rehabilitate the College. Money seemed almost impossible to obtain in America. British coin had built Nassau Hall and it was thought that, if properly approached, those in Great Britain who were charitably inclined toward education and the cause of religion, as well as those who had opposed the government's American policy, would be willing to come to the rescue of an institution whose British affiliations were so strong; and it had been resolved, therefore, to send a mission over to Europe to solicit benefactions. This ill-judged decision was reached against Dr. Witherspoon's approval. But he and General Joseph Reed of Pennsylvania, whose English wife and earlier London associations presumably should have made his way easier, were commissioned to undertake the trip.

Their commission, dated October 22, 1783, was as follows:

The Trustees of College of New Jersey in North-America To the Honble & Revd John Witherspoon, D.D., President of the said college, late member of the Honble Continental Congress, & representative in the General-Assembly of the said State

And to the Honble Joseph Reed Esqr late President & Commander in chief of the State of Pennsylvania, Adjutant General of the Army of the United States, a member of the Continental Congress, & one of the Trustees of the said college—

And to each & every of you—Greeting—

Whereas the college of New Jersey was founded by private liberality for the promotion of religion & learning, & had, by the blessing of Heaven, arisen to an eminent degree of reputation & usefulness before the late unhappy war; but being occupied as barracks by the contending armies, its library & philosophical apparatus destroyed, the funds for the support of professors & masters, in consequence of the ravages & events of war, sunk & almost annihilated, the very existence of this benevolent & useful institution is become doubtful, unless some certain & effectual relief can be obtained from the friends of virtue & literature, who have not been exposed to such dreadful calamities.

For these reasons, & confiding in your abilities, character & zeal for the said institution, we have authorized & appointed, & by these presents, do authorize & appoint you & each of you to receive from all public bodies & well disposed individuals, such benefactions as they may be pleased to make, for the purpose aforesaid; of which you will render to us a due & regular account—And we do hereby recommend you & each of you to the notice & favour of all generous friends of religion & learning, in every part of Europe which you may visit, for the benevolent purpose herein contained.

Given under the hand of his Excellency William Livingston Esq. Governour & Commander in chief of the said State of New-Jersey & president of our board of trustees, & under the corporate seal of the said College at Princeton the 22ᵈ day of October & in the year of our Lord one thousand, seven hundred & eighty-three.

Following the procedure of Samuel Davies and Gilbert Tennent in their memorably successful trip on a similar errand twenty-five years earlier, Dr. Witherspoon and General Reed drew up a memorial for general use which is said by Ashbel Green to have been a striking presentation of the condition and need of the College, but of which he neglected to see that a copy was preserved. They sailed from Philadelphia in December, 1783, and after a tempestuous voyage reached London at the end of January, 1784. The British government had been warned of their coming; the London papers announced their arrival; and the rumor got back to America that Dr. Witherspoon had been openly insulted in the streets of the city. But he told Dr. Green that he had never received a formal insult in London or elsewhere, although he had overheard a conversation at the London Coffee House one day in which he was being vituperated, but as he did not know whether the speaker intended his remarks to be heard or not he took no notice of the language. At London Dr. Witherspoon prepared his campaign of personal solicitation by writing to all his old friends, informing them of the object of his trip and seeking their advice as to its best accomplishment. If all the replies he received were of the same tenor with those which have survived he must have quickly realized that his fears as to the success of the mission were only too well grounded; for with but one exception the extant replies express wonder that such a mission should have been thought of at that time. His friends assured him that they would be personally glad to see him again, but none save a stranger gave him any hope of securing aid for the cause he represented. Dr. Jo' Fre' ne wrote that all whom he had approached on the subject declared it "utterly imprudent" not to have consulted friends in Scotland before undertaking the mission. Dr. Rush had enquired six months before as to the advisability of seeking benefactions for his newly established Dickinson College, and had been told that he would not collect enough money to pay his passage. And he goes on to quote Witherspoon's old friend, Dr. Charles Nesbit, to whom he had written in regard to the present project. Nesbit doubted whether there was such a spirit of reconciliation with America as would give any encouragement to Dr. Witherspoon's business; it seemed a great abasement of the dignity of the United States to send a late member of Congress "a-begging in England for any purpose whatever," and Nesbit even raises the interesting question as to the legality of contribution to a foreign seminary of learning unless it were authorized by the Crown. At any rate, he suggested that Dr. Witherspoon be cautious when referring to his losses or to "the Gothic burning of his library." To Witherspoon himself Nesbit wrote in March when the President was contemplating a visit to Scotland. He called attention to the poverty of the country, the stagnation of trade, the rise in rents and taxes; hundreds were willing to emigrate; the court of landholders was doing all it could to prevent emigration; if Witherspoon came to Scotland he would receive innumerable applications from eager would-be emigrants; during the war Nesbit himself had been persecuted as a friend of America, but now he was beset by people who thought he had American connections and who wished to leave Scotland for the new country. In the same vein an old parishioner of Dr. Witherspoon's, after the most tender enquiry for the various members of his family, points out the utter unseasonableness of his visit; had he come to encourage emigration he would have received attentive hearing, but to come from plentiful America, the Mecca of poverty-stricken Scotland, to beg money seemed a reversal of things that was both curious and undignified. Dr. Snodgrass of Paisley wrote that the temper of the people was unfavorable for contributions to Witherspoon's object; and the friend of his youth, Miss Anna Hogg, in an otherwise charming letter had no more substantial encouragement to offer than a welcome back to Britain—where he would receive no heartier greeting nor find a sincerer friend than at her threshold.

It remained for a stranger, the Reverend Brian Bury Collins, an English clergyman at Bath, to sound the only hopeful note in the chorus of discouragement. He had never met Witherspoon, but had been converted by reading his writings; and he actually collected between fifty and sixty pounds for the President, in the face of great obstacles—"all the persons I have applied to," said he, in a puzzled way, "seem restrained from showing their usual kindness by prejudice or fear."

Dr. Witherspoon had hesitated to visit Scotland for fear of bodily harm, but Nesbit reassured him; beyond the importunity of prospective emigrants "I think I can be positive you will be in the most perfect safety from insult or ill manners." To Scotland, therefore, Dr. Witherspoon went, visiting Edinburgh, Glasgow, Paisley, Beith, and Greenock, but preaching only in his former parishes. At Paisley he occupied several times the pulpit of his friend, Dr. Snodgrass, drawing on each occasion large audiences.[14] He must have also visited Gifford where were the graves of his parents and where the scenes of his boyhood recollections lay, but we have none of his letters to America of this period. At Edinburgh he did not appear in any pulpit, although there are indications that several would have been open to him. His former rival Dr. Robertson, now His Majesty's historiographer for Scotland, was at the head of the University and, as government friends shaped public sentiment at the Scottish capital, it seemed unwise to court open antagonism. The Moderates still controlled the affairs of the Church, and although many of the participants in the fray of earlier days in which Dr. Witherspoon had taken part had passed away during the last eighteen years, nevertheless, as Dr. Ashbel Green phrases it, "there was still working a portion of the old leaven of ecclesiastical enmity quickened into

[14] Thomas Crichton, *Memorial of Findley*, Paisley, 1821.

powerful action by strong political resentment." Dr. Witherspoon, therefore, so far as we know, neither asked nor obtained a single donation in Scotland. The visit was purely private and sentimental, and prudence hinted that it must be brief; he remained across the border only two weeks.

It was also evident by this time that he would have to look elsewhere than in Great Britain for the money he was to get and he, therefore, turned his attention to the Continent. Of Franklin and Jay, American commissioners at Paris, he enquired as to the possibility of securing subscriptions in France. Franklin sent back a cool reply utterly discouraging the plan and citing the failure of Dr. Eleazer Wheelock in his effort to secure donations for Dartmouth College the year before. Franklin's chief argument, however, was the one Dr. Witherspoon had heard touched upon by Nesbit—the revelation such a mission made of America's neglectful attitude toward educational affairs:

The very request would be disgraceful to us, and hurt the credit of responsibility we wish to maintain in Europe by representing the United States as too poor to provide for the education of their own children.

For my part, I am persuaded we are fully able to furnish our Colleges amply with every means of public instruction, and I cannot but wonder that our Legislatures have generally paid so little attention to a business of so great importance.[15]

Mr. Jay's reply was less judicial in tone but quite as definite in its deprecation of any plans like those Witherspoon was contemplating. The rank of the United States implied ability to provide for all the common objects of governmental interest, and among these he placed schools and colleges; they should be no longer regarded as private corporations; the government should extend to them its constant care; if the French court should take up the case of the College of New Jersey and make it the fashionable fad of the day, sufficient temporary interest might be awakened to secure some money, but the interest would be brief. As for books, Witherspoon might obtain a few, but as for apparatus the best was manufactured in England. However, if Witherspoon in-

[15]Franklin, *Works*. The original is in the Presbyterian Historical Society.

sists on visiting Paris, Mr. Jay assures him a hearty personal welcome:

we have been fellow-laborers in the same field, and if you come we will rejoice together in celebrating harvest home.[16]

Whether Dr. Witherspoon crossed the Channel and joined Mr. Jay in a celebration or followed his whimsical suggestion and attempted to make the puritanical College of New Jersey an eighteenth century Parisian fad, we do not know. No record of his movements during the spring of 1784 has been found. But while in London at least he yielded to a London fad and took the opportunity—or was it a touch of vanity?—to sit to James Tassie, the popular Scottish cameo maker, at that time settled in the British capital; and he brought home with him two copies of the medallion likeness reproduced as the frontispiece of this book.[17]

Late in July, 1784, convinced of the futility of his errand and leaving the matter in the hands of friends (who never reported) he sailed once more from Greenock and on September 11, 1784, after a voyage of forty-five days reached New York harbor. When his accounts were examined by an expectant committee of the board of trustees a few days later they found a balance in favor of the College of exactly five pounds and fourteen shillings, and even this could not be called clear profit as the board had borrowed money to pay the President's passage. General Reed had met his own expenses; he was in bad health when he sailed from America and derived no benefit from the voyage; he seems to have been unable to do any work on arriving in England, and he returned to America to die a few months later. Dr. Witherspoon met with an accident on board ship which ultimately destroyed the sight of one eye; and the only pleasant feature of the unfortunate trip was the opportunity it afforded him of revisiting old haunts and of seeing old faces once more.

[16] *Writings*, ed. Johnston vol. III, p. 120, and *Life and Writings*, ed. William Jay, vol. II, 153.

[17] Tassie's cameos were not cut, but were modelled in a paste of which he alone had the secret. A collection of the moulds from which he produced his final works is in the National Portrait Gallery at Edinburgh, and his art was of sufficient importance to give him place in the *Dictionary of National Biography*.

The board at its meeting in September, 1784, heard "with extreme affliction," as well it might, the unsuccessful result of the European mission and determined to make one more application to the charity of the people of America "for whose general use," it declared, "the institution had been founded and to which it was still faithfully dedicated." It was proposed to memorialize all presbyteries in the Synod of New York and Philadelphia, asking that in whatever way they deemed best they would solicit the aid of the people under their respective charges, and agents were appointed to collect the monies thus obtained.[18] But the results were not encouraging, and although eventually enough funds were scraped together to pay the salary of a professor of mathematics, Dr. Witherspoon, like every other college president, never realized the dreams he cherished of seeing the institution he governed amply provided with funds, faculty, and facilities. To cap the climax of this unluckiest year in his life, Christmas Day brought him one of the saddest trials he had yet

---

[18] A note of desperation lurks in the terms of the memorial drawn up by Dr. Witherspoon and dated October 1, 1784:

> "The memorial of the trustees of the college of New Jersey to the several Presbyteries composing the synod of New York and Philadelphia

Shewth

That, among the ruinous consequences of the late war is the depreciation of the continental money, & destruction of the college buildings, the funds & revenues under the care of your memorialists have been almost annihilated. That in order to reestablish these & repair their buildings & to carry on the designs of the institution, application hath been lately made to obtain assistance from the friends of literature in Europe; but, unhappily, your memorialists have from sundry unexpected causes, failed in their foreign sollicitation, & have not obtained even so much as to defray the expences of the undertaking—It is, therefore, become absolutely necessary to make a general application to the friends of religion & learning in the country, who wish success to an institution of such importance to our civil & religious interests—Your memorialists have in consequence deemed it a proper measure to apply themselves to the respective presbyteries belonging to the Synod of New York and Philadelphia, wishing to impress them with a lively persuasion of the necessity of a general exertion throughout all our churches for the support of this college under its present state of depression. Your memorialists must refer to your wisdom the methods most proper & prudent to be pursued in sollicting the aids of the people under your respective charges, & in making such personal, or public applications, throughout your several churches & districts, as shall be judged best & likely to be the most effectual.

By order of the board of Trustees

John Witherspoon President."

been called upon to suffer—the death of his favorite daughter and youngest child, Frances, wife of Dr. David Ramsay of Charleston, South Carolina. President Witherspoon had ridden in that Sunday morning to preach in the college chapel, and had found a letter from Dr. Ramsay awaiting him; he read it silently at Vice-president Smith's house and, as he read, the tears rolled down his cheeks. Then he spoke quietly to those around him, re-mounted his horse, and slowly rode home to "Tusculum." Dr. Green says it was the only time that the President was known to break a preaching engagement. Mrs. Ramsay had been married but a year and had died five days after confinement. Dr. Green recollects that shortly after this bereavement Dr. Witherspoon preached a series of sixteen impressive sermons on submission, from the text found in Luke xxii, 42. None of these was preserved, but Green considered them the best series he ever heard and after forty years still remembered their general scope.[19]

The canvas of the congregations in the Synod having virtually failed, another special meeting of the board was called in August, 1785, to adopt measures for reimbursing those who had advanced funds to pay Dr. Witherspoon his arrears in salary, and to defray the expenses of his European trip; and fresh subscription papers were issued asking for contributions in cash, in public securities, or in annual interest thereon, the principal to be paid up in five years; and in the following month the board "pressed with the difficulties of supporting the necessary officers of the College" and considering that tuition and room rent had not been raised in any proportion to the increased cost of living, resolved to raise room rent to two pounds. Money was reached for in all directions, and came in driblets. The Reverend William Tennent was appointed collector for Maryland only to return a year later empty-handed; one Stephen Cook was appointed collector in Bermuda and never reported. Under such conditions the honorary degree of Doctor of Laws which Yale College at the hands of President Stiles conferred on Dr. Witherspoon that September, returning the compliment Princeton had paid her the year before when the College of New Jersey exuberantly conferred two honorary degrees at once on Dr. Stiles, was an honor

[19] *Christian Advocate*, vol. II, p. 350.

which Witherspoon would gladly have exchanged for the cash he needed so badly.

In April, 1786, it seemed likely that in the distribution of western lands Congress might be induced to make a grant to the College, and President Witherspoon, Dr. Rodgers and Dr. Beatty were appointed a committee to petition Congress to that effect when they thought it most prudent; but their petition was no more successful than its predecessor of eighteen years earlier, and the discouraging hand-to-mouth existence went on.

But the picture of those days of reconstruction has its pleasanter side. With the quick recovery in enrolment after the war, the normal life of the campus seems to have been easily resumed. As we have seen, Dr. Witherspoon had announced the re-establishment of all college laws and orders. This meant that the characteristic threads of Princeton campus life, unravelled and scattered by the war, would now be re-gathered; the undergraduate's resilient, carefree nature, unconcerned with the burden of responsibility resting on administrative shoulders, made him a willing cooperator; and it came to pass that, before long, the only reminders of the lost years were the proud scars borne by Nassau Hall and the hidden pinch of precarious finance suffered by the administration; the life of the place was completely restored.

Comparison of a letter of Samuel Beach in 1783 with one by Fithian thirteen years earlier shows a daily routine almost identical—rising bell at 5 a.m., chapel at 5:30, breakfast at 8, recitations from 9 to 1, dinner at 1, recitations again from 3 to 5, vespers at 5, supper at 6, and curfew at 9 p.m., when each student was expected to be in his quarters, a rule which even the village taprooms seem to have respected—at least, couplets scribbled by Philip Freneau in his copy of Horace testify regretfully to its observance by Mr. Enos Kelsey, local merchant and tavern-keeper:

> Then what my thoughts design to do,
> My hands with all your might pursue,
> Since Kelsey neither Rum nor Wine will sell
> When once they've rung the ev'ning bell!

Before Dr. Witherspoon's coming to Princeton, campus life had gone far in the process of making; it had been organized by President Burr when the College removed from Newark and occupied its first buildings at Princeton; and during Dr. Witherspoon's long term of office it was wisely fostered and strengthened until it became moulded in the lines it was to follow, and acquired a quality and color it has never lost.

In most respects, life in Nassau Hall after the Revolution still retained its earlier simplicity and almost monastic austerity. There is evidence, however, that undergraduates, as a result of the spirit of the times, took unto themselves more liberties than formerly. Dr. Green says that this was especially noticeable after the French Revolution, when discipline became still harder to maintain. For one thing, more time seems to have been given to exercise, or at least there is more frequent mention of it. "Baste ball" and "prison baste" were played on the campus, shuttle cock in the prayer-hall, hooprolling in the basement. Stony Brook afforded skating in winter and in the hot summer term gave sweltering undergraduates their only chance for bathing. But the attitude of the authorities toward sports in general was expressed in an edict of 1787 forbidding shinny—"a play at present much practised by the small boys, among the students, and by the grammar scholars with balls and sticks;" it was "low and unbecoming to gentlemen and scholars," besides being attended with danger from "sudden and alternate heats and colds," not to mention "disfiguring and maiming."

College law required that gowns be worn at all academic exercises such as chapel and recitations, thus reducing the undergraduate body, rich and poor alike, to a common external standard. For appearances on the rostrum of the prayer-hall, or of the societies, elaborate dressing seems to have been the rule, but the ordinary informal garment of the campus was a dressing-gown whose weight and texture varied with the seasons, thin flowered calico or cotton being worn in summer and heavily padded cloth in winter.

When a boy entered the grammar school in Nassau Hall, he came immediately under the strictest sort of system. At the back of the Latin grammar which he used he found a set of rules of conduct which, with the code of college laws, governed his daily life. If very young he roomed and boarded in approved lodgings in the village, where he received better personal care than in the less domestic precincts of Nassau Hall, and he was excused from the chief bane of undergraduate existence, morning chapel. But if he roomed in college, he was subject to all college regulations, eating his frugal meals in the refectory at a special table, attending chapel regularly, and seeking his recreation on the campus. The only known account of the grammar scholar's life is to be found in the autobiography of Dr. Joseph Caldwell. There are no records of the school in the University archives; its graduation exercises, however, were reported in the newspapers with the college commencements to which they formed the preliminaries, and at least two grammar school valedictories have been preserved. Graduation from the school constituted entrance into the freshman class of the College and Dr. Witherspoon asked entering students from other schools to come up for examination at the grammar school commencements. Entrance into higher classes lacked uniformity of method. John Leake of 1776 wrote to his guardian that he and they who were examined with him received admission into the junior class, but were afterwards told that they should have been examined in Roman Antiquities "if it had not been forgotten."

Aside from his studies, the Princeton undergraduate of that day found his life controlled by four leading factors, three of which were also unfailing points of controversy—compulsory chapel, which he had to attend twice a day, compulsory commons, where he ate if he ate at all—unless surreptitious meals at the taverns be counted—proctorial oversight by tutors who policed him all day and even dropped in on him after he was safely in his room at night, and finally the life of the two literary societies, of one of which he was inevitably a member. He found relief for his animal spirits in spasmodic exercise, in constant practical joking, and in breaking the rules as often as he dared and could escape detection.

Compulsory chapel was as old an institution as the College itself, appearing in the original set of laws. Its value from a religious point of view was negligible, but its value as a discipline was indubitable. The author of the anonymous *Journal of Nassau Hall*,[20] like the majority of his fellows, was a young gentleman to whom this ancient rule of worship was usually irksome and never a joy; but without it he would seldom have got out of bed before noon. His nearest approach to satisfaction with chapel was expressed one spring morning in a note to the effect that it was "a sweet day indeed—do not shiver in the Hall at Prayers as formerly." Invariably he lay abed until the last moment, reaching his bench in the dark unheated prayer-hall half dressed and more than half asleep. "Lie till the second bell," he writes one day, "return from Hall half asleep and am not able to keep awake to study." Another winter morning "do not wake till [roused] by the noise of students running thro' the entry—spring up; half give over dressing soon enough to get there, however persist, & have just time enough." And once more:

Hear the knocking in the morns but get asleep again, waked by the 2d bell, scramble up in the dark, James [his roommate] dont attempt to get up & dress [though] time enough, but I resolve not to miss prayers & huddle on my cloathes any how & push into Hall all open & unbuttoned, tho by far the coldest morning of the season and escape being tardy.

Philip Fithian, more piously inclined, found no objection to the discipline he faced and after his first week in college assured his parents that the rules were "exceedingly well formed to check & restrain the vicious & to assist the studious, & to countenance & incourage the virtuous." He even admitted that, "through divine goodness," he was very well and "more reconciled to rising in the Morning so early, than at first."[21]

Although he did but little studying, the diarist of 1786 carefully obeyed the schedule of study hours during which a tutor made frequent rounds; but he was always one of the first to welcome the bell releasing him from his imprisonment in Nassau Hall. His time was frittered away with friends as little studious as he, and when examinations loomed perilously near he was wont to reproach himself bitterly for his lack of concentration.

[20] Library of Congress.
[21] *Journal and Letters*, p. 7.

Dr. Witherspoon was a pitiless examiner: "Our Quarterly Examination," said a boy in 1774, "was about two weeks ago, when the Doctor not only used me ill, but near 15 more clever fellows, which we in no wise deserved." And in 1786 the ordeal was just as fearsome: "Find it necessary to employ every moment," wrote the diarist, "and lament that I did not began to review sooner—think the time lost in going to meals & prayers—study very hard." The next morning he arises "after 4 hours sleep, feel examinations very near—fall to strenuously . . . near 10 o'clock take my clothes out to dress—but suddenly shocked with the bell—begin to tremble." The bell proving to be a false alarm, "return to room and have time to dress myself before 10 o'clock. At that time We march in like so many criminals, Faculty take their Seats formally & we extend in a great circle round the room, 26 of us."

Before the Revolution, final examinations—at least of the senior class—began at a much earlier hour, those of 1773 being set for seven o'clock in the morning, to which a formal invitation to the public was issued by the clerk of the board of trustees. Examinations took place in the college library room and the final examination of the junior class, with which the *Journal* closes, had a touch of ceremoniousness all its own. The class acquitted itself brilliantly:

After withdrawing we returned & rec^d our Sentences from the old Dr. [Witherspoon]. No distinctions could well be made—but the whole class prettily complimented—& the Dr. reminding us of what was incumbent on us being promoted to the Senior Class, dismissed us with his good wishes & still better advice.

The dormitory floors of Nassau Hall were admirably adapted to the frequent visiting from room to room and the consequent inevitable loafing without which no ordinary evening seemed to be complete, according to the record of the *Journal*:

Come to my Room positively to do something clever either to study some of props [propositions of Euclid] write part of my Religion [a Sunday required composition] or write &c—but spend the whole time till the Bell without doing a single thing but joining in a foolish lottery for Breast pins & broaches in which I lost 3/5. . . . I go into Abiel's room, find a number of Lads collected & a blessed scene. . . . after supper invited to drink coffee with Read—also to eat oysters with Graham &c by Abiel—decline—both Lads in room prevent me studying—lose 1/1 more by the bad lottery.

Likewise, on evenings when the resident tutor was known to be out, the long and unlighted corridors or "entries" that ran through the building gave every opportunity and incentive to disorder:

Meet a lad in the entry this evening—seizes me—I lay hold of him and he runs, afterwards have a chase after him upstairs in the dark, but do not find out who he is. . . . Go to Brown's Room to hear Bob Hughes play his violin, the Room full as usual, Whigs & Clios promiscuously—after that go to the upper entry with Ab. Woodruff, find Bob there who draws over a negro with a violin also—the fellow playing very well & Reed & myself have glorious exercise dancing up & down the entry & joining in the noise & confusion of 20 students hallowing & tearing about. GILBERT NOT IN COLLEGE. Come down at 8—reading part of my lesson, go to bed 10 Clock.

The gentleman in capitals was the resident tutor, Gilbert Tennent Snowden, who was fond of village society and was frequently absent from the building where his proctorial duties lay.

Students were always ready to supplement the fare offered in the college dining hall, although that fare was not without its surprises:

Chocolate Tea & bread & butter for supper tonight for a wonder but not to be continued for it was only because they could not give us Mush conveniently.

A year or two before, a student had complained

I believe in my soul they will turn me into a line of veal, or a chocolate cake, for we have had nothing else scarcely since I have been here.

Proper formalities laid down by college law were supposed to govern conduct in the dining hall, but if no tutor were present the customary conventions were lost in the riot that prevailed:

Furman & I run as hard as we can drive to get to dinner & arrive just time enough—Gilbert said to be gone a-riding & the lads rush in & seize everything—while in confusion, Gilbert comes & going round to see who had taken butter &c on their plates, he orders those out. . . .

Just get down before dinner—no Tutor comes & we rush in as if storming the Room I am pitched over & 1 or 2 over me. . . . Pot Pie for dinner & by the time I get to it all is swept off, some of the lads seizing near 1/3 of the whole that they may not miss taking enough.

In those lean years the college appleman was a ministering angel, especially when he added a basket of eggs to the legitimate wares he brought to Nassau Hall, and initiated his purchasers into the mysteries of egg-nogg—"for tis a glorious Liquor, he says," adds the diarist. Many a joyous evening, however, was staged far less insidiously; indeed the rarity of references to drinking is one of the characteristics of this remarkably frank diary; coffee was the favorite undergraduate beverage and tea a distinct luxury. The most hilarious party described was keyed up by nothing more dangerous than coffee and toast:

about 9 sit down to 2 good potts of it & a fine plate of toast & the worst was that there were too many to divide it among; however have pretty near 3 dishes a piece if we had had dishes to drink it from—all [in] good humour & all join in singing several good songs both before & after supper—knowing Gilbert was out of College—come down to our Room at 1/2 after 12.

With the Revolution a new holiday appeared on the calendar, and in the *Journal* the national festival receives the honor of a full page with a much decorated heading. It is a fair record of the manner in which the Fourth of July was celebrated in President Witherspoon's time:[22]

How are the mighty fallen! This day for 3 or 4 years past has been celebrated with the greatest elegance & festivity. Literary as well as many other entertainments—the day entirely devoted to relaxation & pleasure—Professors, tutors, students partaking in common of a most elegant dinner previously provided—But this year the latter

---

[22] The *Pennsylvania Packet* for July 11, 1787, contains the account of the celebration at Princeton in that year with an almost identical program, so far as the formal exercises were concerned. The college participation dated from the summer of 1783.

part of the celebration was knocked in the head—the Faculty having determined it *high treason* for any students to breakfast, dine or sup out of the Stewards Hall who was anyhow within reach of it—This by the by the Steward would willingly have dispensed with. For it is very currently reported & as generally believed that his feelings were much hurt, his conscience much strained and his Purse much impaired by the Punch, ham & green peas which (mirabile dictu) were had on this memb^{le} day—The orations del^d in the morn^g by S. Snowden & Ed Graham were very well spoken & in all other respects well conducted, —a good audience—polite & attentive—the speakers complimented by Dr. Smith—In the afternoon partake with 3 or 4 select students of a nicely elegant repast, fruit, preserves, punch, &c. At 5 o'clock 6 other orations were deliv^d by Students 3 from each Society & concluded with 2 very humorous ones which terminated the Literary exercises of ye Day—The Day was ushered out by the discharge of 13 rounds from a cannon in the campus which seemed to defuse more gen^l satisfaction than had been felt before.

No occasion was suffered to pass without appropriate oratory, and few without music—indeed, music instrumental and vocal seems to have been a feature of life in Nassau Hall. Moreover, however formal the exercises, the collegian's unfailing sense of humor was always keenly on the alert and never failed to make the most of its slender opportunities. A passage from the letter of a sixteen year old Sophomore of 1785 to his mother, describing the college Christmas celebration that winter, affords an illustration:

We had a very agreeable Christmas, the Senior Class spoke orations of their own Composing and we had a numerous Assembly, but I fancy their pieces rather solemn to gratify the ladies' expectations; we had musick also but it was only a hand organ, and whenever the Steward (who is a very corpulent man, and has a remarkable large head) reached over the Gallery to play, he created a laughter and especially as he went more like the bagpipes than anything else.[23]

Evidently the organ which had been eviscerated by the British during their occupancy of the building had been replaced by some sort of instrument, which, however inadequate musically,

[23] *Princeton Alumni Weekly*, December 22, 1915.

at least gave the overworked steward an additional task in life and added materially to the joy of undergraduate existence.

The paternalism of Dr. Witherspoon's government of the College is apparent on perusal of the first minute book of the faculty. It dates from November, 1787, when the faculty consisted of the President, two professors and a couple of tutors. The faculty seldom met save to take disciplinary measures—there are but half a dozen exceptions in seven years—and the record is therefore a mirror of contemporary academic penology. The gradations in punishments were finely drawn and sometimes odd; insolence to tutors was punished by admonition before the entire College; disorder or absence from chapel or classroom, by suspension and sentence to coventry; swearing, and abusing a fellow student, by apology and asking pardon of the faculty; visiting a house of ill-fame was punished by "serious" admonition; but the heinous crimes of refusing to open a door when commanded, or to appear before the faculty when called, met with summary expulsion.

Procedure in cases of discipline was formal, the defendants being served with written charges and a list of witnesses. If at the trial the culprits confessed, the findings of the faculty were read at evening chapel, not infrequently concluding with some such phrase as "it is their confession which has prevented any very pointed or severe punishment." A group of students, after eating and drinking to excess in a tavern, tethered a calf in the prayer-hall pulpit and "also overset the college necessary;" they were cited to appear for trial, with the result that the leaders were ordered to leave college instantly; others pleading not guilty were likewise expelled without ado; but the rest, having confessed, were admonished, and soon after even those who had been expelled were allowed to return on confession and apology. An "improper" use of a sword cane—a weapon which seems to have succeeded the dress sword—having been made in a personal encounter between two undergraduates, there resulted private admonition for both, and the adoption of a new rule by the faculty:

Whereas disorders have arisen in college by some of the students making an improper use of swords and pistols, the Faculty unanimously ordain that in future no student shall be permitted to use any such instruments, under pain of high censure or expulsion as to the Faculty shall seem proper.

On another occasion the faculty met to investigate a rumor that several students had played cards on the Sabbath. The investigation resulted in public confession at evening prayers, the "more guilty" from the rostrum, the others from their seats; and all were ordered to return their winnings. The minutes fail to explain whether or not the size of the winnings was the criterion of the degree of guilt.

The part that oratory played in the daily life of the College was preponderant; orations were delivered in the prayer-hall every afternoon after vespers, and when the better speakers in college were scheduled even the careless author of the *Journal* came in to listen. In due time his own turn arrived; he waited impatiently until nearly five o'clock for the college barber to come and dress his hair, with its ear-curls and its ribboned queue—

at last obliged to run out of College to his house, return just time enough before the bell, not so much perturbed as I expected, go into the Hall, Green prays, after I mount first & but once prompted, after [me] Pollock a good deal prompted, and after him Jas. Read who misses so much is obliged at last to make his bow & come off the Stage without going thro' with it.[24]

The constant stream of oratory was varied now and again by dramatics. For, however much Dr. Witherspoon in theory may have objected to the stage, there is ample evidence that he permitted the production of plays in the prayer-hall. At Commencement in 1772 the boys of the grammar school acted a Latin play which perhaps had academic excuse; but some years later the prayer-hall saw the Reverend John Home's tragedy *Ormisanda and Alonzo* handsomely produced—"our dress was silk and elegant and every circumstance to render it noble was strictly adhered to," says the undergraduate chronicler; "it was so affecting that it caused tears to flow from many." Dr. Witherspoon was away in Congress at this time, but he must have known of the

[24] James Read's misadventure was identical with the one that happened to a classmate of Philip Freneau and was gleefully celebrated by the latter in his *Distrest Orator*.

production of this play by the author of *Douglas*. In 1782 Nathaniel Lee's *Rival Queens* was given, followed by Fielding's version of Molière's *Médecin Malgré Lui*, young Ashbel Green, the future divine, scoring, as Alexander the Great in the *Rival Queens*, a hit that was the talk of the campus for months.[25]

Besides these reliefs to monotony and the customary Fourth of July celebration, unexpected incidents such as the visit of the Continental Congress to Princeton, or the news of the founding of the French Republic added their measure of welcome variety. The news from France was celebrated at Princeton in January, 1793, with a public dinner at the tavern, but the account of the proceedings contains only a list of the toasts which included, besides those to the new Republic, the United States, the State of New Jersey, and the College, one to Lafayette, one to Poland, one to the Colonies of South America, and one to "a millenium of universal liberty, peace, and virtue." No reference is made to any especial academic function. The celebration on July 14 of the same year had, however, a distinctly collegiate note, for the campus republicans marked the anniversary of the fall of the Bastille by a brilliant ball in one of the taverns, where French and American flags, liberty caps, and cockades of the national colors figured prominently among the decorations, and the "Marseillaise" was the only song sung during the supper—a supper at which one toast, "a very patriotic one but I do not remember the words," sent the company into ecstasy,—"Good Heavens how it was clapped, I thought the room would have come down with the stamping," writes the young lady whose letter has recorded the affair. Nassau Hall was handsomely illuminated with clusters of lights in each window with "a fine transparency of the American and French colours in the form of arms" over the main entrance, and in front of the door a large tree of liberty around which the French gentlemen stood "singing the Marseilles Hymn with great enthusiasm" amid the crackle and glare of fireworks and rockets.[26] What the January civic dinner lacked in gaiety was more than supplied by the abandon of the July celebration. Citi-

[25] An account of Eighteenth Century Dramatics at Princeton may be found in the *Princeton Alumni Weekly*, December 6, 1916.
[26] *Princeton Alumni Weekly*, November 3, 1915.

zen Genet had reached this country, and college republicanism was bent on making itself conspicuous, without pondering too deeply the awkward problem of neutrality confronting the national government.

It will be gathered that the social graces were not neglected by these undergraduates, although such waste of academic time was not universally approved. In spite of faculty protest, dancing and fencing masters maintained in the village well attended classes for students. "We have a dancing master in town and a fencing master," wrote Zadoc Squire in 1783 to his friend John Croes, the future bishop of New Jersey, "and I do not know what other animals, but I believe it would be better for us if these frenchmen were all where they came from; for a republic cannot subsist by such useless accomplishments; it must subsist only by simplicity and frugality." And Dr. Witherspoon's trustees seemed to agree with this solemn young philosopher, if not as to the proper disposal of French visitors, at least as to the value of their instruction, for an edict was issued in September in the following terms:

It being represented, that permitting the students to attend a dancing school in the town is useless to them in point of manners, they being generally past that period of youth in which the manners are formed & it being represented that their attendance in such school involves them immediately, or by consequence in considerable expences, to the injury & ill report of the college, & it being held in a tavern & often late at night, circumstances unfriendly to the order of good government of the institution—it was unanimously resolved, that from henceforth the students shall not be permitted to attend a dancing school, during the sessions of the college, under any pretense whatever.

However lightly the eighteenth-century Princetonian took his academic work he was almost sure to fulfil scrupulously his duty to his Society. As the Well Meaning and the Plain Dealing clubs, the two societies had been suppressed by the faculty just before Witherspoon's coming, because of the bitterness of their rivalry. It was not merely to satisfy undergraduate whim that the new President permitted their reorganization with more imposing names—the Cliosophic Society and the American Whig Society. Their value was too obvious not only as safety valves for undergraduate energy but also as adjuncts to the curriculum which he intended to emphasize. He must have sensed here the possibility of moulding and developing a latent power, and if the opinion of the Princeton makers of America like Madison, Ellsworth, Paterson, and their fellow Nassovians, could have been recorded, there is little doubt that among the strongest influences these men carried from Princeton, next to the personal influence of Witherspoon himself, they would have placed that of the two Societies. President Witherspoon dignified them, gave them headquarters in Nassau Hall, and official recognition on public occasions such as Commencement and the Fourth of July. Their importance in organizing campus life is a striking feature in every allusion to them in eighteenth-century Princeton documents. They formed the backbone of that life; they were the centre of college loyalties, the promoters of college friendships; even their "paper wars"[27] and wordy wrangles over foolish trivialities had their part in giving life at Princeton its distinctiveness. Under Witherspoon they became serious organizations, almost as serious as they were in the next century when they had made history, had built their own halls, and had gathered traditions unto themselves. They were the unique feature of life at Princeton, constituting an activity in which even academic loafers really worked, compelled by the force of campus opinion. Their influence was not merely formal, nor confined to style and manner of literary effort. Here, beside the production of poems, essays, and orations and the satisfaction of the personal partisanships of the campus, the deeper feeling of the 1760's that had seen the end of the French and Indian War and had led collegiate political temper to stage at commencement *The Military Glory of Great Britain*, now was turned to the local questions which had grown into national problems; here were discussed the proud ideas of young America which in 1772 found partial expression in Freneau's and Brackenridge's commencement poem on *The Ris-*

---

[27] This was the name given to the practice of posting on the walls of Nassau Hall anonymous attacks and equally scurrilous replies. "The two societies have been quarreling with each other so warmly," writes Ashbel Green in the summer of 1782, "that Mr. Smith (Professor S. S. Smith) interposed and put an end to the contention, not, however, till about twenty pieces were written." Specimens are still extant.

ing Glory of America, and in the ultra-patriotic orations of successive commencement platforms. In the rooms of the Cliosophic and Whig societies on the top floor of Nassau Hall, eighteenth-century Princetonians practised not only the formal side of the art of written and spoken expression on which the President lectured in the classrooms downstairs, but thrashed out with probably more earnestness than formality the new politics of the day and spun their shining dreams of the future. Here Philip Freneau —and how many others we do not know—advocated independence of the Colonies long before it became a public matter; here was shaped the spirit that in 1770 burned the New York letter breaking the non-importation agreement, that later decided to wear no other than American cloth at commencement, and that burned the college tea in 1774. It cannot be questioned that the training afforded by the weekly sessions of the Societies contributed largely to the impression made by Princeton undergraduate oratory and conduct on the American public of the eighteenth century. In purely educational lines Dr. Witherspoon may have exerted a more evident influence; but in no way did he better foster the spirit of the new nationalism than in the open support he gave to Princeton's two historic literary societies.

While his undergraduates were thus continuing the cheerful tenor of their way, the last great achievement of Dr. Witherspoon's life was looming up over the struggle and routine of his presidential duties. One of his three great rôles, that of the constructive statesman, was virtually completed; the second, that of the educator, ended only with his death; the third, that of the ecclesiastic, was now to reach its crowning point. He had been far too busy to be able to devote much time to the Presbytery of New Brunswick to which he belonged; indeed the records of the Presbytery show that he seldom attended its deliberations save when he had some special business to put through, or when it met at Princeton. He was absent from fifty-two of the eighty-eight stated meetings held by the Presbytery during his membership. But his attendance at the Synod was somewhat more regular and his presence was usually marked by his appointment to important tasks. The most important was the one assigned to him shortly after the end of the war. Dr. John DeWitt, of Princeton Theological Seminary, has pointed out the elements making for the spirit of union in the Presbyterian Church in America at this time and aiding to eliminate the provincialism that marked it when Dr. Witherspoon first landed in America. To the President was to fall the task of guiding, in the work of reorganizing the Church on national lines, the ready hands he at last found about him. The actual work began at the meeting of the Synod in 1785 when he was appointed chairman of a special committee to consider the constitution of the Church of Scotland and other Protestant churches and, agreeably to the procedure for presbyterian government, to compile a system of general rules for the government of the Synod, the presbyteries under its inspection, and the people in its communion, and to report at the next meeting of the Synod. It being clear that the Church had outgrown its colonial organization, a further step in the direction of reorganization was taken when Dr. Witherspoon proposed at this meeting of 1785 an overture looking toward the breaking up of the Synod into three or more, and erecting a General Assembly of delegates from each. This overture was made the order of business for the 1786 meeting, when a committee was appointed which drew plans increasing the number of presbyteries from twelve to sixteen, grouping them into four Synods with provision as to the number of ministers and ruling elders each presbytery was to send to the proposed Assembly. Three hundred copies of the plan were ordered printed and distributed among the presbyteries for discussion. A committee of which Dr. Witherspoon was also chairman was appointed to prepare a book of discipline and government. At the 1787 meeting of the Synod Dr. Witherspoon resigned the treasurership as it was deemed more convenient to have the treasurer resident of the place where the Synod met. His plan of government was reported and discussed, the criticisms of the single presbytery that had any comments to offer were considered, and after debate and amendment the plan was ordered to be printed in an edition of 1000 copies for further distribution and discussion. In the following year, 1788, after several days of debate the whole plan, with the confession of faith, the two catechisms, the directory for worship, and the form of government and discipline, was adopted and it was resolved that the first meeting of the General Assembly of the Presbyterian Church in the United States of America be held on the third Tuesday of May, 1789, in the Second Church at Philadelphia, Dr. Witherspoon to preach the opening sermon and to preside until a moderator should be elected. The selection of the radical New Side Second Church as the first meeting place of the Assembly instead of the conservative Old Side First Church, was indicative of the new spirit of harmony. Noting the debates that led to this historic conclusion one cannot help remembering that the Constitution of the United States was under discussion at the same time, and that the new organization of one branch of the Christian Church in America was (to borrow the phrase of one of its historians) but the "fruit of the same great national impulse of the time to give the social life its complete expression by a policy of national dimension and spirit."[28]

Manassah Cutler has left a portrait of the President at this time. He met him at Dr. Rodgers' house in New York City in the summer of 1787 and heard him preach in Dr. Rodgers' church:

He is an intolerably homely old Scotchman, and speaks the true dialect of his country except that his brogue borders on the Irish. He is a bad speaker, has no oratory, and had no notes before him. His subject was "Hypocrisy." But, notwithstanding the dryness of the subject, the badness of his delivery, which required the closest attention to understand him, yet the correctness of his style, the arrangement of his matter, and the many new ideas that he suggested rendered his sermon very entertaining. The attention of the congregation strongly marked their regard for good sense and clear reasoning, rather than the mere show at oratory and declamation.[29]

This description of Dr. Witherspoon's personal appearance tallies with the Trotter engraving of 1785, which without question is an intolerably homely picture, and which it is claimed was drawn from life. It flatly contradicts the Tassie cameo of 1784 which we know was modelled from life and resembles the Peale portrait.

[28] R. E. Thompson, *History of the Presbyterian Church in America*, p. 67.
[29] W. P. Cutler, *Life of Manassah Cutler*, vol. I, p. 236.

Possibly the cameo and the painting flatter their subject; but the engraving is almost a caricature.

The meeting of the first General Assembly in May, 1789, was the climax of Dr. Witherspoon's ecclesiastical career. As moderator he presided and opened the session with a sermon on I Corinthians iii, 7, the same sermon that he had delivered twenty years before, when he occupied for the first time his Princeton pulpit. What changes he made in its contents we do not know as the printed version is the earlier one; but it was characteristic of the man that, on this crowning occasion of his life—for one must believe that he so considered it—, he should have chosen a sermon whose keynote was humility. For himself, if he looked back over his varied labors of the past twenty years he might justly have claimed some satisfaction. Surely he must have known, if he ever allowed himself the thought, that although others might be more accomplished or more brilliant, he was by his very office that morning the most distinguished Presbyterian minister in America and his influence in the councils of the Church correspondingly greater than that of any other minister in it. Dr. Ashbel Green is authority for the statement that most of the published acts of the Synod of New York and Philadelphia had been from Witherspoon's pen, and that in framing the constitution of the Church his opinions were all but dominant. He had suggested the publication of the principles of the Synod in forming that constitution and the draft he brought in was adopted with scarcely an alteration, if we may believe Dr. Green, who was present. Benjamin Rush's unpresbyterian dream had come true. Dr. Witherspoon had become the veritable "bishop of the churches."

When the Assembly voted at the meeting of 1789 to present an address to President Washington, Dr. Witherspoon was the logical chairman of the committee in charge and author of the document it prepared;[30] when the Assembly resolved to publish selections from its minutes, he was appointed chairman of the committee to make the selection and print five hundred copies of it; and when it was agreed to commission Isaac Collins, the

[30] Text in *Minutes of the General Assembly*, Philadelphia (1842), pp. 11–12. Washington's reply is in the *Minutes*, p. 24, and also in his *Writings*, Sparks edition, XII, 152.

Trenton printer, to issue an edition of the Holy Bible, not only was Dr. Witherspoon placed on the committee to act with similar committees from other denominations or synods to choose the text and to correct the proof, but the preface which takes the place of the "Dedication to King James" in the English bibles was prepared by him, being "a short account of the translations of the Old and New Testaments from the original Hebrew and Greek in which they were written." The edition appeared in 1791 and the preface is Dr. Witherspoon's last piece of published writing on non-secular subjects.

The efforts of the board of trustees of the College to put the institution back on its feet were still meeting but meagre results. In 1786 a sensible and long needed step toward method was taken when a standing committee was appointed to assume general charge of the corporation's finances. It was furthermore ordered for the first time that all monies whatsoever paid to the College should be turned in to the treasurer and that henceforth he should disburse only on order of the board. Treasurers had found their task anything but easy. When Professor Smith was appointed Vice-President in 1786 and therefore resigned the treasurership he had held only six months, he was out of pocket over three hundred pounds. This was nothing new, and the deficit was made good, but the trustees found great difficulty in finding his successor. Dr. John Beatty, the eminent surgeon, who was finally prevailed upon to accept the office conducted matters so well, and subscriptions came in so opportunely, that at the end of the following year he was able to report a deficit of only eleven pounds. This improvement and the steady growth of the enrolment emboldened the board to fill the chairs of mathematics and natural philosophy left vacant by the resignation of young Ashbel Green, and to call to the professorship the first incumbent of any chair at Princeton, save that of divinity, who was by his previous training especially prepared for his task. Even Dr. Smith who was elected in 1779 to the chair of moral philosophy cannot be said to have had any particular training in his subject save as a teacher since graduation, and as an ordained minister. The new member of the faculty was Walter Minto. The board's resolution of September 26, 1787, in connection with his election is interesting:

The board considering the importance to the interest & reputation of the institution of perfecting the course of mathematical & philosophical science—Resolved that this board will establish a professorship of Mathematical & Natural Philosophy in the faculty of the College, & that its appointment at present, till the funds of the College may enable the board to make a more liberal provision, shall be two hundred pounds current money of New Jersey per annum.

Dr. Minto was then elected by ballot, with the further proviso that, if he would reside in Nassau Hall and perform certain proctorial duties, his room and board should be free.[31]

The Federal Convention had by this time completed its labors and the Constitution of the United States was awaiting ratification by the individual States. Somerset County, New Jersey,

[31] Born in Scotland in 1753, Dr. Minto had been educated at Edinburgh University and on graduation had devoted himself to literature. As tutor in the family of the Hon. George Johnstone, who during the American Revolution achieved notoriety by attempting to bribe General Joseph Reed, Minto had visited the Continent and during a residence at Pisa had become intimately associated with Professor Slop, the astronomer at the University, who seems to have turned the young man's serious attention to science. On his return to Edinburgh he taught mathematics, corresponded with scientific men, and published several minor writings on astronomical subjects, some of these appearing in the publications of the Royal Society. Aberdeen conferred on him the honorary degree of LL.D. His most important work was published jointly with the Earl of Buchan, being an *Account of the Life, Writings, and Inventions of John Napier of Merchiston*, which appeared the year of its author's appointment at Princeton. In 1786 he had come to America and had accepted the headship of Erasmus Hall, an Academy at Flatbush, Long Island. The Pennsylvania Historical Society owns a letter from President Witherspoon to the Earl of Buchan written soon after Professor Minto's transfer to Princeton, expressing the satisfaction he was giving in every respect, "so that we look upon him as a great Acquisition to our Seminary & to America." At the time of his death he had several mathematical treatises ready for the press with the plates engraved, but his death halted their publication. These manuscripts were still in existence in 1850, but are now lost. His Princeton inaugural address *On the Progress and Importance of the Mathematical Sciences*, was published at Trenton in 1788. One of the two Princeton copies of his *Researches into some Parts of the Theory of Planets*, published at London in 1783, was a presentation copy to Benjamin Franklin. Dr. Minto is said to have been one of the most distinguished younger mathematicians of his time. The *Princeton Magazine* (1850 pp. 38-47) contains an extended sketch of him. An unflattering portrait of him is in the University's collection.

sent to Trenton, as its representatives at the state ratification convention held in December, 1787, three of the men who had helped to depose Governor Franklin in 1776, Colonel Frederick Frelinghuysen, Dr. Jacob Hardenburgh and Dr. Witherspoon; and the latter was also a member of the committee finally elected to draw up the form of ratification.

The financial condition of the College in September, 1788, had been still wretched; the roof of the President's house in which Vice-President Smith now lived was leaking badly; the foundation and other parts of Nassau Hall were found to be in a "decaying state;" but the committee on repairs reported that for lack of funds to pay workmen it had not been able to get the necessary work done, and funds were ordered to be advanced from interest accruing from public securities belonging to the College. The board, confessing its inability to discharge its debt to Colonel Bayard and Mr. Snowden, ordered that the education of their sons and others under their charge be credited to them. Matters improved in 1789, for at the annual meeting in September the treasurer's report showed a balance of one pound and a few shillings, the first time such a condition had appeared for many years. But the board was not permitted to enjoy this novel sensation for more than a few moments. Professor Minto informed the trustees that he was contemplating matrimony and therefore petitioned for an increase of salary, a bond for arrearages, and permission to live outside of the college building. All of his requests, save the supreme one of increase in salary, were gladly and promptly granted.

That spring General Washington passed through Princeton on his way to his first inauguration and visited his old friend at "Tusculum." Town and College united in framing an address[32] of congratulation of which Dr. Witherspoon was the author.

TO HIS EXCELLENCY GEORGE WASHINGTON, ESQUIRE—
    PRESIDENT GENERAL OF THE UNITED STATES OF AMERICA
Sir,
    The President and Faculty of the College of New Jersey, and the Inhabitants of Princeton beg leave to join in the general joy, and con-

[32] *Princeton Bulletin*, vol. XI, p. 54.

gratulate Your Excellency on your appointment to the first office in confederated America.

The unanimity with which you have been destined to this Station does honor to the citizens of the United-States, as it Shows they retain a just and grateful Sense of your eminent Services during the late war in council and in the field; and we are of opinion that you have hardly an opportunity, even in your own life, of discovering greater self-denial and devotedness to the public good than by relinquishing your peaceful retirement with fulness of honor; and again submitting to the toils and cares of public life.

That Almighty God may direct your counsels, and prosper your undertakings; and that your life may be long continued as a blessing to your country, is our sincere and fervent Prayer.

Signed in name and by appointment of the Faculty of the College and Inhabitants of Princeton

JNO WITHERSPOON
JOHN BEATTY

On October 8, 1789, Dr. Witherspoon's wife died at "Tusculum" at the age of 68. Ann, the wife of Dr. Smith, was now the only member of his family left in Princeton. Little is recorded of Mrs. Witherspoon. Her attitude at the time of her husband's call to Princeton has been described earlier in these pages. Ashbel Green, who knew her well, says she was of distinguished piety, devoted to the promotion of her husband's comfort and usefulness, a peculiarly fond parent, amiable in temper, social in her habits and universally beloved. She was buried in the Princeton graveyard but her tomb is now unmarked save by a tablet bearing her name and set into the end of the President's stone.

Dr. Witherspoon found relief in active work. Somerset County sent him to the State Assembly and he was immediately given important committee duties. Entrusted with the correction of the journal and the examination of the documents accompanying the Governor's message, from which he was to select those that needed the urgent attention of the House, his choice was characteristic, a resolution to provide for the safe keeping of prisoners committed under the authority of the United States to the various jails of the State, a proposed amendment to the Constitution of the United States, an act to pay invalid pensioners of the United States, and a letter to the Secretary of the Treasury on the order of Congress regarding public debts. He served on the committees appointed to take up the first two of these matters, and he was also placed on the joint committee of the two Houses to draw up a congratulatory address to the President of the United States, the text of which he reported November 19. It was also natural that he should be a member of the joint committee to report what was proper and competent for the State Legislature to do to promote interest in religion and morality among the people of the State. The old question of divorce was also turned over to him but, as in the case of the bill reported in 1783, his report led to no action although it reached a second reading. His varied financial experience brought him also appointment on a committee to consider the state of paper money in New Jersey and to raise its value. This time he secured the passage of a bill. Another committee of which he was a member brought in a bill dividing the state into districts and requiring registers of marriage, birth, and deaths to be kept; the beginning of the recording of vital statistics in New Jersey. Another bill looking toward progress and for which he was jointly responsible, planned the relief of prisoners languishing indefinitely in jail for debt; and one of his favorite hobbies met with encouragement when a committee was appointed to report the most feasible mode of encouraging manufactures in the State.

The second session of the Legislature (1790) found him on two interesting committees, one to ascertain the cause of depreciation in New Jersey copper currency, and another, to which was referred the petition of Essex and Morris counties praying the Legislature to take steps to abolish slavery. As chairman of the latter committee Dr. Witherspoon reported that the law already in force forbade the importation of slaves except actual servants of immigrants from other States, or of transient residents; that the exportation of slaves was likewise forbidden; that the law as it stood encouraged voluntary manumission of slaves; and that by it, moreover, slaves were protected from violence. He then offered the suggestion that New Jersey might enact a law that all slaves born after its passage should become free at a certain age, as for example 28;[33] but in his opinion "from

[33] He was thus anticipating by several years the law adopted in Pennsylvania in 1804.

the state of society in America, the privileges of the press, and the progress of the idea of universal liberty," there was little reason to believe that there would be any slaves at all in America twenty-eight years from that time, and experience seemed to show that precipitation in such a matter might do more harm than good not only to the citizens of the State in general but also to the slaves themselves. With these laudable but over-sanguine opinions the house entirely agreed, and did nothing further.

In May, 1791, the General Assembly placed the President on a committee to devise measures for collecting materials for a history of the Presbyterian Church in America, and he was also appointed a delegate to the General Association of Connecticut for the Promotion of Religious Harmony. Dr. Archibald Alexander has recorded the impression made on him by Dr. Witherspoon at this meeting of the Assembly. Speaking of his presence on the floor he says:

He immediately participated in the business, and evinced such an intuitive clearness of apprehension and correctness of judgment, that his pointed remarks commonly put an end to the discussion. . . . Dr. Witherspoon was as plain an old man as I ever saw and as free from any assumption of dignity. All he said, and every thing about him bore the marks of importance and authority.[34]

Dr. Witherspoon had cause to feel in good spirits at this meeting of the Assembly, plain and old though he may have appeared to be. For, a week after the Assembly adjourned, Dunlap's *American Daily Advertiser* for Thursday, June 2, 1791, contained the following brief but startling notice:

On Monday evening was married in this city, by the Reverend Dr Nesbit, President of Dickinson College, the Reverend Dr. Witherspoon, President of New-Jersey College, to Mrs. Ann Dill, widow of the late Dr. Dill, of York County in this State.

Dr. Armstrong Dill had been a pupil of Dr. Witherspoon at Princeton. Up at New Haven, Dr. Stiles in his diary notes the incident with a touch of pointed finality:

[34] J. W. Alexander, *Life of Archibald Alexander*, 98, 99.

On 30th May Reverend Dr. Witherspoon aet 69 was married to Mrs. Dill of Philada Widow aet 24.

The hint of something more than surprise contained in this entry is also found in Ashbel Green's cryptic reference to the event when he says that the Doctor's elevated station and ministerial character "rendered his second marriage the occasion of much observation and remark, but when his mind was made up and satisfied few men lived who were less moved by popular opinion or gossip."[35] Dr. Caldwell, who was an undergraduate at this time, in his *Autobiography* recalls the occasion and relates an incident which supports Dr. Green's comment. It was rumored in college one morning after prayers that Dr. Witherspoon had set out early for Philadelphia in the old family chaise harnessed to four horses, some of which "had been called to their higher service from the more humble function of the car or the plough." He breakfasted at Trenton with his friend the Reverend Dr. Armstrong who knew the nature of the President's errand to Philadelphia. As Dr. Witherspoon was leaving, his host, glancing at the incongruous team, said by way of pleasantry: "Doctor, you do not seem to be well matched." The President, construing the remark as a veiled allusion to the disparity of age between himself and his bride-elect, gruffly retorted: "I neither give advice, nor do I take any!" and clambered into his carriage.

When he returned to Princeton two or three days later with his young wife, the students sent a delegation out to "Tusculum" to beg a holiday to celebrate the event. With a greater show of feeling than he usually manifested, the President invited the committee in to drink the lady's health, to which toast the wily collegians coupled the name of the groom, and when they asked for one day's holiday, he gave them three. At the close of the

[35] Green records (*Autobiography* 241) that in July, 1791, he went to "Tusculum" one afternoon to take tea with Dr. Witherspoon and to pay his respects to Dr. Witherspoon's new wife: "I had heard her represented as very handsome. She is comely; but to my apprehension, nothing more. The doctor treated me with great politeness." By this marriage Dr. Witherspoon had two daughters, Frances, (born November 9, 1792, died November 18, 1793) and Mary Ann born in 1793, who became the wife of the Reverend J. S. Woods and the ancestress of one branch of the present Witherspoon family in America descending from the President.

third day, the revolutionary cannon lying on the campus was dragged to the front of Nassau Hall and fired the signal for lighting up all the front windows of the building. Six hundred candles were used in the illumination which lasted an hour, while an orchestra of students in the belfry entertained the crowd with appropriate selections.[36]

At the spring meeting of the trustees in 1793 the committee appointed to apply to Congress for re-imbursement of losses suffered through the war reported that any application for that object was without prospect of success, and the committee was discharged. The trustees subsequently turned their efforts to the State, with better success.

During the summer of the same year an interesting movement was set on foot to unite the College of New Jersey and Queen's College at New Brunswick, and a unanimous agreement was reached that such a union would tend to promote learning in the State, that, therefore, a new charter should be applied for naming twenty-eight trustees, thirteen from each college, the President of the College of New Jersey and the Governor of the State to serve ex-officio, all the trustees to be residents of New Jersey, the grammar school at Princeton to be given up and a preparatory department to be maintained at New Brunswick in its place, the present officers of the College of New Jersey to become the officers of the new institution, and finally that these recommendations be laid before the two boards for approval. A bare quorum was present at Princeton when Dr. Witherspoon laid the proposal before the meeting of his board in September, and it was decided to postpone consideration until a larger representation should be present. At the December meeting Dr. Witherspoon placed before the board a letter from the trustees of Queen's College wholly rejecting the project and no further action was therefore taken at Princeton, thus ending a plan which in the circumstances could scarcely have resulted successfully.

During this interlude the efforts of the finance committee to bring order out of college books were reaching a conclusion that seemed ungenerous. Colonel John Bayard, whose mercantile

[36] *Gazette of the United States*, June, 1791. Quoted in the *Princeton Alumni Weekly*, October 15, 1919.

training had been called into requisition, had been appointed in 1790 to systematize the accounts, open a new set of books, and inaugurate a more business-like method of keeping them. Vigorous efforts were made to collect the overdue subscriptions of 1785, the price of the board in the college commons was raised, and students were ordered hereafter to supply their own furniture. Repairs were still imperatively demanding attention; the kitchen in the President's house was now in a "ruinous condition;" the new roof of Nassau Hall on which hundreds of pounds had already been spent needed further patching. But in April, 1793, the committee reported that it had digested the college books from 1766 to date, and had collected and arranged the documents. To its surprise it had discovered that a similar committee had been appointed in 1774 and had reported certain recommendations; this committee's accounts had been examined in 1775, approved, and ordered spread on the minutes of the board; but this had never been done, and the report and even the rough minutes of that session had been missing. At that date Dr. Witherspoon had claimed a balance due him, but the report had declared him in debt to the college to the amount of six hundred and twenty-five pounds and some shillings. In 1778 a special committee had re-examined his statement and with fuller evidence had allowed his claim. Now among loose papers turned over to it, the present committee had found a copy of the missing report. It, therefore, asked direction whether it should accept the findings of the earlier special committee or ignore them. The board ordered the previous report to be disregarded. Concerning some special funds in the President's hands the committee also sought instruction, the disposition of the monies involved being in dispute. In December Dr. Witherspoon asked for a certified copy of the report and it took him long to clear up the tangle, for in April, 1794, the committee, by way of reporting progress, informed the board that it had employed accountant after accountant: one had to relinquish his work for private reasons, another had fallen a victim of the yellow fever epidemic, a third had been seized with sudden illness; it hoped, however, that Dr. Witherspoon would turn in his statement and explanation, if he had any, before the final report was made. At last Dr. Witherspoon's statement was received, and in September, 1794, the committee announced finally that the balance due from him up to 1788 was only one hundred and eighty-six pounds, nine shillings and eight pence, which could be easily and satisfactorily explained. Beyond that date the report had not been carried as the President's ledger showed all accounts thereafter.

As Dr. Maclean has devoted a chapter to the committee's report and its unfortunate controversy with the President,[37] there is no necessity for repeating the details except as the documents throw light on the financial condition of the College during Dr. Witherspoon's presidency. The prevalent unbusiness-like practices and methods in the financial administration of the College have already been mentioned; in addition to these, however, the death, at the beginning of the war, of Mr. Sergeant who had been treasurer for over twenty-five years, the frequent changes in his successors, the consequent scattering or loss of papers, and above all the chaos into which the war threw not only the affairs of the College, but also the finances of the country, complicated the situation almost inextricably. The treasurer's books and in particular the one most frequently referred to in the documents as "the college ledger" have disappeared, and for data on the situation we are restricted to the reports of special committees made in 1775, 1794, and 1795, the last three being continuations, and to Dr. Witherspoon's own transcripts for the years 1778 and 1789 inclusive, complied apparently for the information of the committees from his now lost private ledger.[38] According to these reports, the total capital of the corporation in 1769 was about three thousand pounds and in 1774, when the 1775 report closed, a little over six thousand pounds. During this period donations and subscriptions had been received amounting to roughly seven thousand seven hundred and eighty pounds. On October 1, 1777, when depreciation first became apparent, the resources of the College exclusive of property at Princeton amounted to eight thousand one hundred and fifty-two pounds eighteen shillings and eight pence. On October 1, 1781, when depreciation, except

[37] *History of the College of New Jersey*, vol. I, p. 368.
[38] The various papers are now in the University Library, and in the Office of the Secretary of the University.

in state paper money, had virtually ceased, this amount had fallen in value to four thousand eight hundred and fifty-four pounds one shilling and eleven pence. And by October 1, 1791, in spite of donations the resources were estimated at only two thousand four hundred and eleven pounds six shillings and two pence. From 1768 to 1795 the College had received in subscriptions over twenty-two thousand pounds, part of which—the amount is not stated—was in depreciated money. The report of 1795 censures the corporation, and of course this in reality means the President, for allowing current expenses to be paid out of monies which it is claimed should have been applied to capital; but the fact is disregarded, as Dr. Maclean very pertinently remarks, that most of the subscriptions secured during the war were frankly sought not for endowment, but to meet current salaries and make necessary repairs. The committee's further criticism is fairer; that interest and arrears were often permitted to remain for years uncollected, that interest was allowed on debts of the institution, while a large proportion of debts due the corporation were received without interest, and that large sums were often held in bank without being applied to capital, so that current expenses had swallowed them up, and arrears due on outstanding debts had been totally lost for want of timely collection. The committee accordingly opened new books and laid down a number of regulations to govern the handling of college funds, the vital feature being a reiteration of the 1786 rule that hereafter all monies should be received exclusively by the treasurer, and that all payments should be made by him and that no other vouchers would be honored by the board. In its September 1794 report of progress the committee remarked that it had felt it a duty

not to close the report without declaring that whereas it appears to have been apprehended that some enquiries, heretofore made by this committee were intended to implicate the character of Dr. Witherspoon, no such design was ever in the contemplation of the committee. And they do now most cheerfully report that these enquiries are answered to their entire satisfaction from papers furnished by the President himself and in such a manner as must convince every person who understands the subject, that there is no foundation whatever for any impeachment or suspicion of the president's integrity.

In glad anticipation of this much desired conclusion of the whole disagreeable matter the entire faculty asked for an increase in salary, the funds for which were to be raised by increased tuition, so as not to encroach on monies assigned to other purposes. And the trustees, content to let well enough alone, just as cheerfully tabled the petition.

Despite his increasing infirmities, which had induced him to give up his ministerial duties as pastor of the Presbyterian Church at Princeton,[39] Dr. Witherspoon's interest in current events remained unflagging. He was a subscriber to three newspapers and read several others. His concern over a tendency in American life induced him to dictate to his amanuensis his last letter for publication and shows how keenly he watched the press. Soon after the New Theatre was built at Philadelphia and was beginning to draw a large patronage, Philip Freneau in the *National Gazette* quoted a paragraph from a French source to the effect that formerly a stigma was attached to the theatrical profession, especially when compared with the professions of the Law and the Church: He hoped that now the improvement in the status of actors due to their merit would contribute not a little to the improvement of public culture. In reply to this Dr. Witherspoon dictated his *Letter on Play Actors*[40] explaining why a stigma was attached to the stage, a document so severe in its tone that no newspaper editor, says Dr. Green, would accept it, and it remained unpublished until he placed it in his edition of Witherspoon's Works. The article shows that the President had not modified by one whit the attitude he had held at the time of *Douglas*, nor lost any of his mental vigor. It contains of course, the stock arguments—players have so often been persons of loose morals; their profession leads to corruption of heart; whoever acts human passions is prone to become their victim, and "will soon become" what he had "so often seemed to be;" players by always appearing in assumed characters must lose all sense of sincerity and truth; love is the most conspicuous passion on the stage—"a play without intrigue and gallantry would be no play

[39] See Petition of the congregation to declare the church vacant. Hageman, vol. II, p. 93.
[40] *Works*, vol. III, p. 94.

at all"—and yet love is the passion that has produced the most misery in the history of mankind; hence the futility of sending young persons to the theatre "to form their manners." No cognisance is taken of the attractive, or even of the noble, characters in dramatic literature. And in conclusion he deprecates the acting of pieces by young persons in schools or private families, as a means of obtaining grace in deportment or propriety in pronunciation. And yet he permitted dramatics in his own prayer-hall.

The college enrolment was increasing, but the physical appearance of the institution reflected the gaunt poverty of its exchequer; the place looked seedy; Dr. Witherspoon's administration was running out—gallantly, but none the less forlornly. Pitiful and graphic, even though lacking in sympathy, is the last description we have of the College in his time. In May 1794, the French traveller Moreau de Saint Méry passed through the village and recorded his impressions.[41] After describing the exterior of Nassau Hall, which he confesses is in all respects a striking building "for America," he continues:

In front of it is a vast court enclosed on the street side by a brick wall bearing at even distances wooden urns painted gray.[42] This front court is dirty, covered with the dung of cattle that come there to graze, and in its centre lies an old four pounder minus its carriage. The cannon, the bad condition of the wall, many of whose urns have fallen to the ground, all reflect a lack of care, and one reaches the building sorry that the students should have so unfortunate an example before their eyes.

The building, which is called Nassau Hall, is entered by three doors of equal size, of which one is in the middle of the front projection and two others at the sides. One goes up by means of wooden steps with-

[41] *Voyage aux Etats-Unis de l'Amérique*, 1793–1798. Edited by S. L. Mims, New Haven, 1913, pp. 114–117.
[42] The wall enclosing the campus was built in September, 1770. It was of brick on stone foundations with a fence of wooden palings topping it. These palings were probably consumed as firewood during the military occupancy of Princeton in the Revolution. It is not known when the urns were put up.

While the wall was being erected the entire front campus from Nassau Hall to the street was graded down about two feet so as to make the basement rooms in the building more habitable. The latter then acquired and long retained the name of "the barracks" and continued to be the most undesirable rooms on the campus.

out balustrades. . . . On the lower floor are a chapel, a refectory, a library of about 2000 books where one may see the justly famed orrery of Dr. David Rittenhouse. . . . On this floor opposite the main entrance door, but at the rear, is a vast hall furnished with benches, like a school room. On entering one perceives on the right hand a picture about 8 feet high. It is a full length portrait of General Washington. . . . Behind the College is a very large yard, dirty, and lying fallow, so that it all looks neglected. Although 120 students can be lodged in the building, it has ordinarily about 80, most of whom come from Virginia and the two Carolinas.

It would be pleasant to approve the government of the institution, but when one has not been raised in American fashion it is very difficult to do so. A system which makes children subject to no restraints, humors the carelessness of masters, and flatters so strongly the indolent American disposition, must produce a vicious system of government. Its effects are apparent at the college at Princeton where, it is said, gambling and licentiousness occupy the students more than study.

That the students did not overstudy was probably as true then as it is now; but the charge that they were addicted to gambling and licentiousness can, under the strict system of surveillance in operation, have had little or no basis of fact. It is not supported by the records of the faculty, or by any other source.

The President maintained until the end his perogative of examining candidates for admission to college. When young Titus Hutchinson of the class of 1794 entered Princeton in 1793, he recorded in his diary an experience which was typical. Directed to "Tusculum," he reached the house at about sunrise; his letter of introduction was taken by Mrs. Witherspoon up to the President who presently came downstairs, "feeling his way along." After family prayers and breakfast, the President went up to his study with the lad and there questioned him as to his reading in Greek and Latin, testing him pretty severely in the latter tongue. He then said he would see him later at the village tavern. About eleven o'clock the Doctor came into the village, Mrs. Witherspoon driving the chaise, and the new student led him over to Vice-President Smith's house, where the President and Dr. Smith held a private consultation in such loud tones that young Hutchinson in an adjoining room plainly heard his fate being settled.

But pathetic evidence of the President's growing infirmity is found in his trembling signature of January, 1794,[43] compared with that of February 26, 1790, which was still firm and flowing. In May 1794 he appeared once more in the General Assembly, but his useful days were over; blind and feeble, he was given no work to do. His last appearance at a meeting of his faculty was on September 25, 1794, and two days earlier he had presided over a meeting of the board of trustees for the last time. Death came suddenly, although in his poor state of health it could not have been unexpected. Besides being blind, he was suffering from dropsy, but his mental faculties remained unimpaired; his last request was for the newspapers. He died on the evening of Saturday, November 15, 1794, at "Tusculum," in the seventy-second year of his age.

Dr. Ashbel Green, who was not in Princeton at the time, and secured his information many years later,[44] says in his biography of the President that he died in his bed suffering but little. An undergraduate's Sunday letter home, written the day after the President's death, seems more trustworthy and is so circumstantial that it may be quoted in full. The letter is from William Eltinge, a Junior in College, to his father under date of November 16, 1794:

We have lost our president Doctor Witherspoon, he was found dead in his chair, he was very desirous to hear the last news read, they had sent for Doctor Smith that Night and when he came they read the news of the last paper they had, but Doctor Witherspoon was still desirous to send for the last paper. They sent for it but before the boy had arrived with the paper, they found him dead sitting on his chair, and but a little before his wife was with him in the room, but going out into another room upon some business and when she returned he was dead.[45]

Eltinge's account is corroborated by Joseph Warren Scott of the class of 1796, writing to John Henry Hobart of 1793, on the following Monday, in a letter of very different style.

[43] Library of Princeton University.
[44] *Autobiography*, 460.
[45] Library of Princeton University.

Nassau Hall Princeton Nov. 17, 1794

My Dear Friend

What melancholy tidings does this bear? It is the death of our Good & worthy president.

On Saturday evening in his chair, this good old [man] met the common enemy of man, with joy and cheerfulness. And why should he not? It would set a final period to trouble and suffering, and land him in that haven of eternal peace, which is the reward of his labours, and his fidelity to his Master's trust. Full of days and full of honors, this venerable sage left us to deplore his loss as a father and a protector, but he has also left us an example, truly worthy to be imitated.

Tomorrow his body is to be committed to the silent grave. Doctor Smith I believe is to pronounce his funeral sermon, no doubt it will be a moving and a feeling discourse.[46]

On the eighteenth of November, early in the morning, the President's body was brought from "Tusculum" to Nassau Hall where it lay in state and was viewed by the undergraduates. Years after, Richard Rush, of the Class of 1797, told of seeing the President thus, and Judge Herring, of the Class of 1795, at a Princeton alumni meeting in New York in April 1868, described how the President looked in his coffin, especially recalling "his massive head, high cheek bones, and almost interminable nose."[47]

From Nassau Hall, the body was carried to the Presbyterian Church where the Reverend Mr. David Austin of Elizabeth, New Jersey, preached a discourse which has remained unpublished. Then, accompanied by eight clergymen as pall-bearers and followed by the faculty, the trustees, the treasurer, the steward, and the undergraduates as mourners, and a large throng from town and neighborhood, President Witherspoon was borne to the Princeton graveyard, a stone's throw down the street now named after him, and was laid beside his predecessors in the Presidents' Lot.[48]

[46] *Archives of the General Convention, Hobart Correspondence*, vol. I, p. 102. Seventy-four years later, the writer of this letter and a classmate, Judge Elbert Herring, sat on the platform as the two oldest and most conspicuous alumni guests at the inauguration of Princeton's other great Scotsman, Dr. McCosh.

[47] J. W. Alexander, *Familiar Letters*, vol. II, p. 119, and *Nassau Literary Magazine*, June 1868, p. 33.

[48] *American Daily Advertiser*, November 24, 1794. His death was noticed in the *Scots Magazine*, the *European Magazine*, and the *Gentleman's Magazine*.

The faculty's Minutes do not mention his death. The trustees also took no formal action at the time, but at a special meeting on May 5, 1795, resolved, according to a previous understanding, to ask the President's old friend, Dr. Rodgers, to preach a commemorative sermon in the church the next day. This is the discourse published under the title of *The Faithful Servant Rewarded*. The biographical sketch in this sermon was supplied by Dr. Smith, who also wrote the epitaph carved on the tombstone ordered by the board.[49]

Dr. Witherspoon's will is filed in the Secretary of State's office at Trenton. It was drawn on September 15, 1793, with a codicil dated November 11, 1794, and was proved November 28. It appoints his wife Ann his executrix, and to each of his surviving children by his first wife, John, David, and Ann, who had already received sums from him, besides their education "in the best manner," he gives £50. To his grandsons, John Witherspoon Smith, John Witherspoon Ramsay and John Nash McPherson, he leaves £200 each; of the balance of his estate, one-half is left to his daughter Frances "and any other child or children which may be born to me," and the other half to his wife. A codicil was signed November 11, 1794, substituting the name of his infant daughter Mary for that of his daughter Frances, since deceased, in the provision disposing of the first half of his residuary estate.

The inventory of Dr. Witherspoon's "Goods, chattles & Credits wares & merchandise" was drawn up at "Tusculum" by Daniel Agnew, the college steward, Professor Walter Minto, and Derrick Longstreth, on November 28, 1794, and filed with the will. It reveals nothing—and the tastes and manner of life of Dr. Witherspoon reveal nothing—to substantiate the implication of luxury in Sir George Trevelyan's statement[50] that Dr. Witherspoon had endeavored as far as might be done at that distance from Italian antiquarian shops and Birmingham and Leipsic printing houses, to render "Tusculum" worthy of the name by the character and value of its decorations and contents. On the contrary, the furniture and decorations listed in the inventory consist of little but the most necessary articles. The four

[49] See opposite page.
[50] *American Revolution*, Part Two, vol. II, p. 31.

RELIQUIAE MORTALES
JOHANNIS WITHERSPOON, D.D., LL.D.
COLLEGII NEO-CAESARIENSIS PRAESIDIS, PLURIMUM VENERANDI,
SUB HOC MARMORE
INHUMANTUR.

NATUS PAROCHIO YESTERNENSI SCOTORUM,
NONIS FEBRUARII, MDCCXXII. V. S.
LITERIS HUMANIORIBUS IN UNIVERSITATE EDINBURGENSI
IMBUTUS.

SACRIS ORDINIBUS INITIATUS, ANNO MDCCXLIII.
MUNUS PASTORALE
PER VIGINTI QUINQUE ANNOS PERFUNCTUS EST,
PRIMO APUD BEITH, DEINDE APUD PAISLEY.

PRAESES DESIGNATUS AULAE NASSOVICAE, ANNO MDCCLXVII.
IN AMERICAM MIGRAVIT, ANNO MDCCLXVIII.
IDIBUS SEXTILIS.

MAXIMA EXPECTATIONE OMNIUM,
MUNUS PRAESIDIALE SUSCEPIT.

VIR EXIMIA PIETATE AC VIRTUTE
OMNIBUS DOTIBUS ANIMI PRAEELLENS
DOCTRINA, ATQUE OPTIMARUM ARTIUM STUDIIS,
PENITUS ERUDITUS,
CONCIONATOR GRAVIS, SOLEMNIS.

ORATIONES EJUS SACRAE
PRAECEPTIS ET INSTITUTIS VITAE
PRAESTANTISSIMIS,
NECNON EXPOSITIONIBUS SACROSANCTAE SCRIPTURAE
DILUCIDIS
SUNT REPLETAE.

IN SERMONE FAMILIARI COMIS, LEPIDUS, BLANDUS,
RERUM ECCLESIAE FORENSIUM
PERITISSIMUS.

SUMMA PRUDENTIA,
ET IN REGENDA, ET INSTITUENDA JUVENTUTE,
PRAEDITUS.

EXISTIMATIONEM COLLEGII APUD PEREGRINOS
AUXIT:
BONASQUE LITERAS IN EO MULTUM PROVEXIT.
INTER LUMINA CLARISSIMA, ET DOCTRINAE ET ECCLESIAE,
DIU LUXIT.

TANDEM, VENERATUS, DILECTUS, LUGENDUS OMNIBUS,
ANIMAM EFFLAVIT, XVI. KAL. DECEM.
ANNO SALUTIS MUNDI, MDCCXCIV.
AETATIS SUAE LXXIII.

prints owned by the President were valued at only a dollar each, a Wilton carpet at thirteen dollars, seventeen mahogany chairs at two dollars apiece, one clock and case at thirty-six dollars. His plate weighed but one hundred and fifty-two ounces and was valued at one hundred and sixty-two dollars. The number of volumes in his library is not stated but the collection was appraised at six hundred and forty dollars. Two slaves were valued at a hundred dollars each; and the whole inventory amounted to only $2495. This, of course, does not include the house itself nor its buildings and farmland, although the standing grain on its seventy-three and a half acres is included. The President's live stock consisted of seven oxen, six cows, one bull, five heifers, ten horses, twelve pigs, thirteen hogs, and twenty-four sheep. He also owned a sleigh, a riding chair, two waggons and one cart. Judged by the standard of even that day, he was far from wealthy.

CHAPTER FOUR

FOR once in the world "a man of extraordinary force, versatility, and charm had found the place exactly suited to give full swing and scope to every element of power within him. He seems to have come at the right moment, to the right spot, in the right way."[1] This conclusion, by a scholar whose special study of the period will hardly be superseded, must remain unchallenged. If few men have been fortunate enough to justify such an estimate of their careers, it is because as the Philadelphia *American Daily Advertiser* phrased it, few have filled with greater dignity, or with more eminent and extensive usefulness the several places Dr. Witherspoon occupied in life. Still rarer was the man who could have touched the imaginations of as many different groups of contemporaries as he did—the general public who read his printed writings and found them easy to understand and profitable to remember; the scores who listened to him on the floor of Congress or in ecclesiastical assemblies and never forgot the dry humor and zest of his debating; the crowds who heard him in the pulpit and bore away the memory of his clean-cut, telling phrases; and finally the hundreds of undergraduates who carried from his presence into their lives as public servants, ministers of the gospel, lawyers, doctors, teachers, or heads of families already historic, the unfailingly pungent stimulus of their association with his dominant personality.

That President Witherspoon was lucky in the opportuneness of his coming to America for the work he was to do is an assertion that scarcely needs defence. For if, to borrow Professor Becker's words, by the time of his arrival the mantle of Samuel Davies the preacher had fallen upon Patrick Henry the political orator, and something of the moral conviction of the Great Awakening had passed into secular activities, it was given to President Witherspoon to weld the two strains together not only by send-

[1] Tyler, *Literary History*, vol. II, p. 321

JOHN WITHERSPOON
By Charles Willson Peale

ing out from Princeton what Mr. Becker recognizes as a new leaven to work itself through the processes of the American Revolution, but also by typifying in himself the amalgamation of the older power of Calvinistic religion and the newer political spirit. Other clergymen may have been as active as he in fostering the spiritual temper of Revolutionary days; but he was the only clergyman in America to cap that activity by serving the country in the Continental Congress, and by aiding it to shape its new national individuality.

A more fortunate spot, moreover, could scarcely have been chosen for the headquarters of his great emprise. Set as Princeton was, midway between New England and the South, and in a buffer province between the dominating cities of New York and Philadelphia, a province that was almost a no-man's land in its political balance and denominational variety, a province that at the same time was perhaps somewhat less worldly than most of its neighbors, President Witherspoon came thither politically unaffiliated and unprejudiced, save as a Presbyterian fresh from Scotland (if that qualification does not deny all others), and wisely non-committal until he perceived that this particular spot had long been preparing to play a national part and was but waiting for the call. One has only to read the history of the College of New Jersey up to Witherspoon's time to see the signs clearly written. Given its antecedents, the College in his day could hardly have done other than it did.

If one adds to these fortuities of time and place the nature of the man himself, the more firmly convinced does one become that, as the *Daily Advertiser* said, usefulness to his day and generation was the impelling characteristic of the President's philosophy of life, and he could not have taken a different course on coming to America. Fame, wealth, position, none of these influenced him in accepting the opportunities thrust upon him, opportunities that were never of his own seeking. His leadership of the Popular Party in Scotland, his election to the presidency of the College of New Jersey, his advancement in American political circles, his elevation in the American Church, were accepted by him only because they seemed inevitable calls to the practical service of his fellowmen. It is safe to assume that at heart he would have preferred the quiet of his hillside farm at "Tusculum" to congressional wrangles at Philadelphia, the guiding of young enthusiasms in Nassau Hall to dull sessions of a peripatetic State Legislature; but he never shirked what he conceived to be a present duty. Usefulness to the society in which one lived was his own motto and the great outstanding lesson he taught his students. Among his parting advices to his graduating classes occur these words:

Avoid sloth as a dangerous enemy. Fear it, hate it, and despise it. It is a common saying that men do not know their own weaknesses; but it is as true, and a truth more important, that they do not know their own strength. . . . Multitudes of moderate capacity have been useful in their generation, respected by the public, and successful in life; while those of superior talents from nature, by mere slothfulness and idle habits, or self-indulgence, have lived useless and died contemptible.[2]

Of course, his definition of usefulness to society was bounded by the sternness of his religious views. His conceptions on the subject found their grimmest expression in his essays dealing with the influence of the stage. Here he went so far as to assert that any talent, however excellent in itself, was beneath notice when devoted only to entertainment or pleasure; even music, if used only for amusement, was "wholly contemptible." He was willing to admit that natural talents were gifts of God, but "the instances of their being eminently useful are exceeding rare."[3] He would not actually condemn all human accomplishments that had no "immediate reference to our religious improvement;"[4] but he affirmed that they ought to be kept in "subordination and subservience to the great and chief end of man."[5] For similar reasons he cared but little for pure scholarship as such and for its own sake, or for intellectual ability that produced no really useful results. Great genius, he was wont to say, is often like a fine flower —to be wondered at, but of slight use for food or medicine.[6] The

[2] *Works*, vol. II, p. 617.
[3] "Serious Enquiry," *Works*, vol. III, p. 61.
[4] *loc. cit.* p. 88.
[5] "Letter on Play Actors," *Works*, vol. III, p. 97.
[6] "Lectures on Eloquence," *Works*, vol. III, p. 384.

mere beauty of a flower appealed but little to him; his comment on his garden has been already quoted. Similarly, he dismissed novels with a sentence—they were "a class of writings to which the world is very little indebted."[7] And elsewhere he declared that "romance and fabulous narrations are a species of composition, from which the world hath received as little benefit, and as much hurt, as any that can be named, excepting plays themselves."[8] Therefore, we are not to be surprised that the eighteenth-century British novelists find no place in his lectures. Here too may be found the key to his lack of appreciation of poetry—it was an unnecessarily ornamental mode of expression. It is significant that the paragraph mentioning a beautiful poem, in the third lecture of the printed edition of his *Moral Philosophy*, does not appear in the manuscript student copies of his lectures made under his own dictation; it was doubtless inserted by a later lecturer, using his outlines.[9] No undergraduate copyist of Witherspoon's time would have omitted the allusion had the President made it.

Hence, too, he saw nature only with utilitarian eyes and although he was perhaps in a general way conscious of beautiful scenery it scarcely appealed to him from an aesthetic point of view. There is not a free appreciation of nature in all his writings. But, "the beauties of nature," he wrote, "are greatly heightened by adding to their delightful appearances a reflection on their utility and the benevolent intention of their author."[10] A Beith tradition of his curling days illustrates this attitude of mind. One of his ministerial friends taking him to task, solemnly asked if he thought curling was becoming in a clergyman. The unequivocal reply shot back: "When God Almighty makes Kilbirnie loch to bear, He intends us to use His blessings with thankfulness in this most rational recreation."[11]

And naturally he held similar views with regard to feminine beauty. He complained in his *Letters on Marriage* that almost every writer on the female sex overrates the charm of outward

[7] "Letters on Marriage," *Works*, vol. III, p. 577.
[8] "Serious Enquiry," *Works*, vol. III, p. 71.
[9] See his *Moral Philosophy*, edited by V. L. Collins, Princeton, 1912, p. 22.
[10] "Eloquence," *Works*, vol. III, p. 494.
[11] Dickie, *John Witherspoon, Patriot*, p. 3.

form; in plays and novels "the heroine for certain, and often all the ladies . . . are inimitably beautiful;" whereas, he remarked in the *Druid*, "I have not seen any killing eyes these several years," adding, with a quiet chuckle, that he would rather have "the exalted and rapturous phrases of Arcadia" brought down to the level of "the composed discourse of a quiet man and wife in Philadelphia."[12] Even though he maintained a correspondence with the lady whom he had not been able to persuade to marry him, the utilitarianism of his maturity had carried him bravely over his youthful infatuation for the other sex. "Men may talk in raptures," he wrote in his *Letters on Marriage*,[13] "about youth and beauty, wit, and sprightliness, and a hundred other shining qualities, but after seven years of co-habitation not one of them is to be compared to good family management which is seen at every meal and felt every hour in the husband's purse." It must not be hastily inferred, however, that Dr. Witherspoon was unobservant of feminine charms. Far from it. He admired extremely, so we are told, the brilliant complexion of that radiant American beauty, Mrs. John Jay, although he doubted its genuineness; and it was just as well that his cloth forbade him to back his doubts with his dollars, or, like the French Minister, who shared his suspicions and placed a wager on the question, he would have lost his money. It is clear, however, that there was little of the sentimentalist about him. In most matters the practical bent of his mind prevailed; he did not preach the philosophy of common sense without practising it. Dr. Smith aptly summed up the case when he spoke of the President's "cool and simple" character.

The development of President Witherspoon's Americanism may be traced in the series of essays, letters, and sermons, that came from his pen during the years 1774–1778, and in his progressive participation in public service. Sent by Somerset to the New Jersey convention to elect delegates to the Continental Congress in 1774 he gave, in his *Thoughts on American Liberty*, his opinion of what that Congress should be and what it had to do; unbidden he went to Philadelphia when the Congress met,

[12] *Works*, vol. III, p. 577 and vol. IV, p. 153.
[13] *Works*, vol. III, p. 581.

and mingled with its members endeavoring to force home certain notions of his own; a few months later he voiced the attitude of American presbyterianism in the *Pastoral Letter* of May, 1775; in July, war having begun, he accepted minor public service on the Somerset County committee of correspondence, and in September, 1775, preached his baccalaureate sermon on *Christian Magnanimity*; in April 1776, seeing independence looming up inevitably he futilely urged New Jersey to accept the logical and unavoidable conclusion; at about this time he wrote his essays on *Conducting the American Controversy* and on the *Controversy about American Independence*; in May 1776 he preached his fast day sermon on the *Dominion of Providence*, and began his first group of *Druid* papers; probably in June he wrote his *Reflections on Public Affairs*, and it was in this month that he was elected to the New Jersey provincial congress, helped to depose Governor Franklin, and was sent by his colleagues to the Continental Congress to vote for independence; his *Letter to the Natives of Scotland in America* appears with his fast day sermon shortly after; in 1777 he was too busy to put pen to paper, but in 1778 was written his letter on the *Contest between Great Britain and America*; and by 1781, when he drew up the *Memorial and Manifesto of the United States* and the Instructions of June for the American peace commissioners, he had become spokesman for the nation.

His writings on the controversy rest on four main contentions which he continually repeated; separation was not sought by the Colonies but was forced by the ignorance and blundering of the British government; under the circumstances separation was inevitable; it was the visible intention of Providence; and finally, the great need and duty of the Colonies was union. He differed from many of his contemporaries in his invariable protest against vituperating the King and his Ministers. We have seen that he held the more discriminating view that at worst they, as well as the British nation at large, were misguided. "The wise and valuable part of the British nation," he wrote in 1776 in the *Address to Natives of Scotland in America*, "were and as yet are, in great measure ignorant of the state of affairs in this country." British ignorance of American geography he had flayed in a letter to the *Scots Magazine* as early as May, 1771.[14] But when he realized that an understanding was impossible—and he realized it early—he did not hesitate to accept the consequence of that impossibility. While he probably did not endorse every phrase in the final form of the Declaration of Independence, he advocated independence itself because it was the only solution unattended with sacrifice of self-respect or annihilation of the whole colonial political fabric—the converse of John Adams' remark made twenty years before, that "the only way to keep us from setting up for ourselves is to disunite us." Independence the President, therefore, advocated not only because it was inevitable, but because it would give unity and strength to colonial self-defence and because of the world-destiny it involved. No other point of view would he tolerate. Ezra Stiles, voicing current opinion of Scottish responsibility for the war, of course read Dr. Witherspoon's attitude differently. Writing in his diary in July 1777, he said:[15]

There are only two Scotchmen in Congress viz., Dr. Witherspoon Presid^t of Jersey College, & Mr. Wilson, Pennsylv^a, a Lawyer. Both strongly national & can't bear any Thing in Congress which reflects on Scotland. The Dr. says that Scotland has manifested the greatest Spirit for Liberty as a nation, in that their History is full of their calling Kings to account & dethroning them when arbitrary and tyrannical. But Dethronization & Revolution are constantly taking place at Constantinople, Isphahann, & Delhi; no one however thinks that this will prove the Policies of Persia & the Mogul & Turkish Empires friendly to Liberty. The Policy of Scotland & all the governmental Ideas of the Body of that People, are abhorrent to all Ideas of civil Liberty & are full of rigorous tyrannical Superiorities & subordinations. But Dr. Witherspoon goes all lengths with the Congress both in the War, independency & foreign Alliances. Because he had Discernment to see from the beginning that America would be inevitably dismembered, & then acted as all Scotchmen would do under such a conviction, determined to rise & figure in the Dismemberment & p^{hps} lay a foundation of reconciling the Americans to the Scots so far as at least to forgive them. The Dr. is a politician. We may use him as far as he is for America—but scorn to be awed by him into an

14 *Works*, vol. IV, p. 295.
15 *Literary Diary*, vol. II, p. 184.

[188]

ignominious Silence in the subject of Scots Perfidy & Tyranny & Enmity to America. Let us boldly say, for History will say it, that the whole of this War is so far chargeable to the Scotch Councils, & to the Scotch as a Nation (for they have nationally come into it) as that had it not been for them, this Quarrel had never happened. Or at least they have gloried in the Honor of exciting & conductg these Measures avowedly by their Earl of Bute behind the Curtain.

This was Dr. Stiles' reply to the *Address to the Natives of Scotland*, and in all probability even as late as 1791, when President Witherspoon visited his New Haven friend for the last time, the matter had not been settled to Dr. Stiles' satisfaction. He shared the ineradicable and erroneous opinion of the majority of colonials who ignored the fact that the Earl of Bute had been out of office since 1763, and still considered him the responsible agent behind the scenes pulling the wires of his marionnettes on the stage.[16]

Dr. Witherspoon's conception of the political struggle into which he found himself plunged was mainly practical; the separation of the Colonies from the mother country was not only providential and inevitable—according to his view that would have to be conceded—but it would work to the mutual advantage of both sides. If there was little of the sentimentalist about him there was less of the reckless enthusiast, and least of the ranting demagogue. He had matured too soon to see visions, and if he dreamed dreams he was too matter-of-fact to relate them. Therefore his writings contain scarcely any hint of his expectations for the future of the United States, unless they are revealed in his belief that the War of the Revolution was no petty insurrection but an epoch-making struggle in the history of mankind and one upon which hung the fate of unborn millions. In his *Reflections on the Present State of Affairs*, which it will be remembered was in part the basis of his *Address to the Natives of Scotland resident in America*, he speaks of this belief as an "august idea" and becomes almost enthusiastic over the vastness of the American continent and its wonderful development in a century —"a country, growing every year in beauty and fertility, the

[16] See Trevelyan, *American Revolution*, Part II, vol. II, pp. 183*ff.*

people growing in numbers and wealth, arts, and sciences carefully cultivated and constantly advancing, and possessing security of property and equal laws, which are the true and proper source of all the rest." But even in this incompleted essay, with all its warmth, it is clear that Dr. Witherspoon based the Revolution in the last analysis on economic causes, the need of unhindered material and social expansion; it was not merely a revolt against an alleged deliberate political tyranny. And economic causes in his vocabulary were synonymous with providential design. He readily perceived, however, that the period immediately after his entrance into Congress was one in which men of vision around him were not only struggling to maintain the national independence but were also striving in a subtler fight to crystallize the idea of nationality into the concrete shape of a strong central government, and it was for the conservation of this sentiment that he was most concerned. Yet it is odd that he left behind him no clear expression of his thought on the ultimate greatness of the new nation. In 1790 he was still able to believe that a country, as territorially vast as this was even then, really needed no capital or abiding seat of government. In a letter opposing the discussion of the location of a federal city, he admits that if one were decided upon he would wish its buildings to be as magnificent as "the dignity of the empire" demanded; but he hoped,—indeed, he seems to have expected—that the annual sessions of Congress would become shorter as the years went by; he appears to have thought that the republic in the main would somehow run itself. Of course he had no notion of the future enormous and complicated machinery of the national government. His jealousy for the rights of the individual States colors his statement:

If the American empire comes to be consolidated government I grant it would be of some consequence that the seat of government and source of authority should be not too distant from the extremities. . . . But if the particular States are to be preserved and supported in their constitutional government, it seems of very little consequence where the Congress, consisting of representatives from these States, shall hold their sessions. There is not only little profit in their being fixed and central, but perhaps some advantage might arise from their being unfixed and ambulatory. This last seems to be more suitable to the equality of rights of the several States.

The discussion of a federal city he considered inopportune, because all intelligent people, he believed, were of the opinion that "bringing order into our finances, restoring and establishing public credit, is the most important business which the Congress had to do." Just how Congress was to accomplish this without permanent headquarters is not explained.[17]

While his writings show scarcely any forecastings of the future, he occasionally made them in conversation, as when he was told one day by Ashbel Green of the completion of the turnpike between Philadelphia and Lancaster, and replied: "You are not to be surprised if you live to see a turnpike road that shall extend from Philadelphia to the Pacific Ocean." Patriarch though he became, Ashbel Green did not live to see that day; but it is a curious fulfilment of his master's prophecy that the old postroad past Nassau Hall should now be a part of the Lincoln Highway stretching from coast to coast.

Dr. Witherspoon was deeply impressed by the development of the country immediately after the Revolution. Writing to the Earl of Buchan in the spring of 1788, after remarking that there was no news of moment except the approaching adoption of the federal constitution, he continued:

to a scholar & Philosopher it may be more worth while to observe this —the Rapidity with which the immense extent of Territory to the westward fills is most astonishing. To know or be informed of the Numbers that migrate would make a man suppose that the former settlements must be laid waste; yet it is not so.

There is no place with which I am acquainted in which they are not building new Houses. Princeton is very nearly double to what it was in 1776 & it is much more than double what it was when I came here in 1768. This is far from being all owing to an influx from Europe though to be sure this has some Effect, but the Increase of Mankind

---

[17] His arguments against a federal city are contained in "A few reflections humbly submitted to the consideration of the public in general, and in particular to the Congress of the United States," an article evidently prepared for the newspapers. (*Works*, vol. IV, p. 231.)

when the far greatest part of them live a simple country Life is vastly greater than has been generally supposed. The Principles of Dr. Wallace's book on the Numbers of Mankind are clearly illustrated & fully confirmed by the present & past state of America.

Ashbel Green asserts that the President lamented the ambition and jealousy of the States in the formation of the Confederation, and passed judgment on the inefficiency of that compact at the time of its adoption. He complained, says Dr. Rodgers, of the petty spirit of the individual States which opposed the strong central government he advocated. His attitude toward the disposal of the western lands is only one illustration of this feeling. Especially did he remonstrate against the total inadequacy of the method of providing for public exigencies and debts by requisition on the States. He insisted that the government should hold in its hands the entire regulation of commerce and the revenues derived therefrom. This he had believed would have been sufficient for the needs of the United States in time of war; he was certain it would suffice in time of peace, and he had the satisfaction later of seeing the country swing to his view. He heartily rejoiced to see the adoption of the Constitution, as it embraced principles he had long advocated.

The respect President Witherspoon commanded in deliberative bodies, as we have already seen, was not due to his possession of any tricks of the oratorical trade. The untranslatable French of one of La Rochefoucauld's maxims—*La vraie éloquence se moque de l'éloquence*—expresses Dr. Witherspoon's case exactly; he was never eloquent in the ordinary sense of that word—he showed no warmth, or color of language, when he spoke. We know that he did not even have the orator's voice. Alexander Carlyle's description of his voice in early days is repeated by every later recollection of him, save Benjamin Rush's first rapture. But in spite of its weakness, that voice could be easily heard in the largest auditorium if there was silence. The secret of his success on the platform is revealed by Ashbel Green. Although a fair extempore speaker Dr. Witherspoon preferred to listen to debates in legislative and ecclesiastical courts and then, in the quiet of his room, to prepare a speech which he memorized and, when opportunity arose, delivered in apparent reply to a previous speaker. By this simple device he used to surprise his hearers with the orderliness of his ideas, when he was merely carrying out the advice he urged on his divinity students—the wisdom of careful preparation. His close dependence on memorized material perhaps deprived his utterances of spontaneity; but in part this lack of style was inborn. "After you have learned the theory of oratory in the most perfect manner," he said to his students, "there is still the nameless something which nothing but experience can bestow;"[18] but he did not add that experience at best bestows only a small portion of this "nameless something" if the would-be orator is not to some degree its born possessor. And it was just this that he lacked and which all his experience never gave him.

In part also, his total lack of oratorical fervor was due to the restraint he carefully adopted after his nerves were shattered at Castle Doune. That experience left his whole nervous system extremely tense, and it was for this reason that in his delivery he substituted gravity for fervor. This studied self-repression left indelible traces in his style. Here evidently was a man who never let himself go; one is conscious that he must have felt deeply, keenly, perhaps passionately; but he kept himself closely in hand. The emotionalism of Ezra Stiles was not to be found in him; and Stiles' thumb-nail sketch of Dr. Finley, President Witherspoon's predecessor at Princeton, that he was a "boisterous" preacher who filled his sermons "with too much Gall and Invective,"[19] could never have been made of Witherspoon. Reading through his sermons and speeches one finds oneself on a level of high thinking and clear expression, a plateau as it were, elevated, but still a level. In vain one looks for the peaks thrusting up into the sky; the ringing phrase shot with immortality, the one inspired line that outlives a dozen pages of solid reasoning. This is wanting. He held his hearers by the sheer clarity of his thought and by his constant reversion to simple fundamental principles, the inferences from which were inescapable. That keen psychologist, Dr. Rush, his youthful impulsiveness

[18] *Works*, vol. III, p. 388.
[19] *Literary Diary*, vol. II, p. 337.

outgrown, wrote of him as "a man of great and luminous mind. He seemed to arrive at truth intuitively. He made use of his reasoning power only to communicate it to others."[20] The peculiarly mature judgment which we are told marked him as a boy became the chief quality of his mental processes as man. Dr. Rodgers, for example, gave it as his opinion that Witherspoon's ability to seize upon the heart of every question, his skill to disentangle the most complicated subjects, his clearness and conclusiveness in reasoning were due to this innate soundness of judgment, and enabled him to conduct a discussion to the most speedy and decisive termination.[21]

Already conspicuous on his first appearance in the Synod of New York and Philadelphia, his position of intellectual leadership as President of the College of New Jersey added to this conspicuousness; the phenomenon that he speedily illustrated, a Briton turned completely American, capped the growth of his prominence and gave double weight to his views when he entered politics. If the attention he commanded owed nothing to any oratorical ability, still less was it due to any deference to his age, for although there were but seven or eight members of Congress older than himself—and the average age of the men who debated the Declaration of Independence was about forty-five—yet, he was only fifty-three. It was due to his known experience, his British birth and education, his breadth of learning, and his reputation for a certain mellow weightiness of mind. Ashbel Green, who knew by sight if not personally most of the great Americans of the Revolution, asserts moreover that President Witherspoon had more "presence" than any public character he knew, save Washington—and he did not have Washington's advantage of physique. Dr. Witherspoon's "presence" was not a physical quality; on the contrary it was what the brilliant Frenchman already quoted defined in one of his gentler moods as "a loftiness that does not depend on fortune, a certain air that distinguishes its possessor, compels the deference of others, and places him

[20] Biddle, *Memorial of Rush*, p. 29.
[21] It is pertinent to note in this connection that he discarded logic as a formal study in college, insisting that thorough drill in the elements of Euclid was the finest possible training in logic.

higher above his fellows than birth, honors, or even merit." The judicial sanity and the practical common sense of the President's views, and the directness and cogency of argument with which he urged them, kept him in the forefront of attention during his congressional service. Men felt that here was a person whose judgment could be trusted, who could think straight, and who voted as he thought. He himself appreciated the respect with which he was treated, although he explained it with his accustomed modesty:[22]

A person educated in the old countries, he wrote in 1778, had a degree of rank and credit from the circumstance independent of any other. I think the Americans were even partial in this respect. I believe had I myself been born and educated in America, I should have met with a degree of acceptance and success in my station far inferior to what actually happened.

Dr. Rush, however, considered that President Witherspoon's usefulness in Congress was hampered by his cloth and that he did not cut the figure there to which his ability entitled him. The President always sat in gown and bands,[23] and this practice is said to have spared him liberties of speech on the part of his colleagues which might have wounded his sensibilities; but it is difficult to see how he was hampered, or how he could have been more active. His presence in Congress added a novel and a distinctly picturesque personality to that assembly. If his isolation as a clergyman placed him at any disadvantage with his colleagues, the latter in return conceded him a compensating advantage in his fresh reading of the authorities for his college courses in international law, politics, government, reviews which he did not hesitate to use before his maturer audience. Whether his cloth hampered him or not, had his fellow-members slighted the value of his judgments he would not have been appointed to the committee work that fell to him; and had he been a negligible figure he would not have drawn upon himself the constant attention of foreign observers. We have seen what his own hostile compatriots in Scotland thought of him; what the British officer

[22] "Letter on the Contest between Great Britain and America," *Works*, vol. IV, p. 300.
[23] He never used the clerical wig, but wore his hair buckled at the back.

at the 1783 commencement reported; and what Professor Adam Ferguson's opinion was. Horace Walpole is said to have remarked that the Colonies had run away after a Presbyterian parson, and even if the remark has repelled all attempts at verification, it represents pretty accurately the thought of no small portion of the British public. The British spy, Paul Wentworth, in his "Minutes concerning some characters in America" describes the President as "an able—Indefatigable—cunning—well informed Person—great talents and address—a Zealot, a Republican, but prone to the love of Power & Riches."[24] In 1777 Wentworth had already named him to William Eden as a leader on the anti-British side,[25] and Lord Carlisle's list of American leaders in June, 1778, similarly includes him.[26] We know that when with General Reed he was sent to Europe in 1783 the British authorities in New York City thought it worth while to warn the home government. And in a *Liste des Membres et Officiers du Congres*, dated 1783 and preserved in the archives of the French Foreign Office, his name occurs, with a curious confusion as to his Scottish career, to the effect that he was a *"vieillard intéressant par son zèle qui l'obligea de quitter l'Ecosse où il avoit embrassé le parti du Prétendant. Il a dit au commencement de la révolution que ce seroit la dernière fois qu'il se mèleroit de rebellion."*[27]

But after all, Dr. Witherspoon's political service was incidental to the main current of his life, a day's task fulfilled to the best of his ability, and laid aside when that day was done. His chosen work, that of the clergyman and educator, was a task he never put down, and it is there that his true power must be sought. Had he lived in the present time he would have been a natural supporter of church institutionalism. There was in his make-up a gift of leadership and a vigorous interest in life at large that had to find expression no matter where he was or what his official duties were. He had preached that ministers should keep out of politics, chiefly perhaps because of his objection to a state-con-

[24] Stevens, *Facsimiles*, 487 f⁰ 30.
[25] Stevens, 3.
[26] Stevens, 71.
[27] *Min. Aff. Etr.*, Archives. Etats Unis, Corresp. Supplément, 2e serie, XV, f⁰ 328. This reference was given to the writer by Professor Max Farrand.

trolled Church, but the first thing he himself had done on entering the ministry had been to lead his militaristic parishioners in a purely political enterprise; later this strain found vent in ecclesiastical politics and his militant interest in the relation of the Scottish church to Scottish life. In Scotland, however, he was primarily a pastor; when he came to America he found his opportunities enlarged to an extraordinary degree. His clerical office was eclipsed by the very nature and prestige of his new position. Pre-eminent though his influence was in American ecclesiastical councils, like later American clerical heads of colleges he found it impossible to divest himself of his academic rôle when he appeared in the pulpits of the day; he was first and always President of one of the leading colleges of the land at a time when colleges were not yet as thick as leaves. After his coming to America he was never again in the full sense pastor of a church. He sorely missed this relation, however much his new approaches to society may have satisfied certain other needs of his nature, and he never outgrew the feeling of utter loss that swept over him when he first faced his Princeton congregation and bethought him of the parish he had left behind "at home."

It is true that in his opening lecture on divinity he admitted that the chief comfort of his coming to America and sacrificing the work he had been doing in Scotland was the hope that he "might be instrumental in furnishing the minds, and improving the talents, of those who might hereafter be the ministers of the everlasting gospel."[28] But he did not allow this hope to outweigh all others. In his *Address to the West Indies* he said that boys had been graduated from Princeton whose church affiliations he did not know. The non-sectarian atmosphere of the College is further indicated by the fact that in his administration specially printed versions of the Episcopal Catechism and of the Shorter Catechism were used as college texts for Sunday study. He harbored no fancy that piety, whether Presbyterian or Anglican, was a universal panacea. "Some pious persons believe that religion is better than all the learning in the world, and have come to despise learning itself," and of them he did not approve any more highly than of those who, "promising well in early life" become

[28] *Works*, vol. IV, p. 10.

"enamored with human wisdom," and think "themselves such great scholars that they are too proud to be Christians." He warns his divinity students that "intellectual pride is perhaps as dangerous a distemper as any we are liable to."[29]

He held one "great and leading view" ever before his eyes when teaching:

to unite together piety and literature, to show their relation to, and their influence one upon another, and to guard against any thing that may tend to separate them, and set them in opposition one to another.[30]

Accordingly, the religious life of the campus during his administration in general reflected the sanity of his attitude. It was marked by restraint rather than by any sensationalism. He was open-minded enough to allow Dr. Jedidiah Chapman to remain a week on the campus, nor did he resent the invitation to Dr. Spencer, who was a better exhorter; but, while he permitted the youthful enthusiast Bradford to spread a new doctrine among the students, he did not muzzle himself.

The Revolutionary War was destructive to strict piety in Nassau Hall and Dr. Green tells us that in his senior year he was the only "professing Christian" among the students, "and a number were grossly profane."[31] The first part of this statement is hard to believe, but if it be true, the solitariness of Green's religious experience gives relative significance to the acquaintance with Rousseau's writings revealed by the grammar school valedictorian of 1783. Ten years later, so it is said, the works of Voltaire, Volney, and Thomas Paine were in everyone's hands, and, according to some observers, infidelity was spreading

[29] *Works*, IV, 11. The same thought occurs in his *Address to the Senior Class*: "We see sometimes the pride of unsanctified knowledge do great injury to religion; and on the other hand, we find some persons of real piety, despising human learning, and disgracing the most glorious truths, by a meanness and indecency hardly sufferable in their manner of handling them." *Works*, II, 617.

[30] *Works*, vol. IV, p. 10.

[31] Nevertheless, they checked their tongues under circumstances that would have tested the patience of more experienced natures; for Green goes on to admit that the College behaved perfectly well at five o'clock morning prayers, when in the absence of the President, the Vice-president and the faculty he, as a pious Senior, used to conduct that compulsory so-called devotional exercise. (*Autobiography*, p. 133).

throughout the College.[32] Apparently toward the end of President Witherspoon's administration, in spite of the advantage the philosophy of realism enjoyed it had proved unable to keep Princeton undergraduates locked in "intellectual dormitories," as Professor Riley puts it, "safe from the dark speculations of materialism or the beguiling allurements of idealism."[33]

There is no doubt that President Witherspoon established at Princeton its traditional and almost official philosophical doctrine. His life in America was too varied and active to allow him the leisure to be a creative philosopher, even if he had possessed that type of mind. He was a man of action rather than meditation, practising his philosophy rather than writing about it; he left behind him no philosophical work; even his lectures on philosophy consist of the merest outlines, were never intended for publication, did not receive his correction, and acquired an authority of which he had not dreamed. But through these lectures, repeated to several college generations, he gave firm rootage in America to the doctrine he had brought with him from Scotland. He came over with his philosophical mind somewhat rigidly made up, as Professor Riley has remarked, and at his age possessed ideas more conservative than those of his predecessors. These ideas were the tenets of Scottish realism and the common-sense school of Reid and others. He used to claim that before Reid or any other writer had criticized idealism he had written against it in the essay in the *Scots Magazine* mentioned in an earlier chapter, a production which modern critics consider at best but a dubious refutation of Berkleyanism.[34] Certain it is that Dr. Witherspoon had no patience with early American idealism, as the group of advanced thinkers at Princeton discovered when he set about checking their influence.

His substitution of the firmer though less alluring Scottish philosophy in place of Berkleyanism was not without its disad-

[32] Joseph W. Scott (of 1795) writes in November, 1794, to the future bishop John Henry Hobart (of 1793) forwarding a message from Joseph Caldwell (of 1791), to the effect that "if you are coming, be expeditious, or otherwise we will not have a sufficient barrier against infidelity, which is spreading its dominion far and wide." *Archives of the General Convention, Hobart Correspondence*, vol. I, p. 107.

[33] J. W. Riley, *American Philosophy*, p. 477.

[34] Riley, *American Thought*, p. 128.

vantages. While the College became a point of strategic importance between the idealists of the North and the materialists of the South, continues the historian of American philosophy, "the victory over the opposing forces was gained only at considerable expense, the loss of a certain spirit of liberality due to the replacement of speculation by dogma, of philosophy by theology."[35] It may be true that contemporary philosophical tendencies elsewhere in America had more of the breath of intellectual liberty in them, although they were not more safe or sound, but if these tendencies were chilled to their death by the Princeton doctrine —and this seems to have been particularly true with regard to the French philosophical influence in Virginia and the Carolinas —the fact constitutes striking evidence of the remarkable power exercised by a man who after all was only incidentally a philosopher.[36]

If Dr. Witherspoon was hardly a creative thinker, he was still less a formal theologian. His unrivalled position in American ecclesiastical circles, which may have proved to be one compensation for his loss of the purely pastoral relations he had so dearly prized in Scotland, was based not so much on his doctrine as on his perfect familiarity with the historic principles, discipline, and forms of Presbyterianism. His theology was plainly one which would find favor with his American ecclesiastical colleagues, being essentially that of the Old School Presbyterians on the fundamental Calvinistic dogmas. His general sermons, framed on the conventional lines taught at Edinburgh, are purely evangelical. He once said that if they had any particularly valuable feature it was that they emphasized the essential principles of the subjects they treated. Dr. Benjamin Rush on the other hand set it down as his deliberate and mature opinion that "there was nothing in Dr. Witherspoon's sermons to recom-

[35] There is a suggestion of this in the continuation of Scott's letter to Hobart mentioned in an earlier note. He is still referring to Caldwell's message about the spread of infidelity: "This stroke I apprehended is meant for me: he knows I have been reading Hume and is frequently giving me sharp strokes about my beliefs. I have said that reading the above named I thought rendered any person less bigoted; Caldwell supposes that I believe all that is said by Hume."

[36] See review of his *Moral Philosophy* in New York *Evening Post*, November 23, 1912; also H. B. Adams, *Jefferson and the University of Virginia*, p. 28 (United States Bureau of Education, Circular of Information No. 1).

mend them but their uncommon good sense and simplicity,"[37]—
which was pretty close to the truth and does not necessarily con-
tradict the President's words. The principles referred to by Dr.
Witherspoon are discussed in his group of doctrinal sermons and
essays published before he came to America and constitute his
sole and slight contribution to a system of theology.[38] To them
he added nothing during his American career, save as his divinity
lectures, incomplete though they are, developed some of his
points. In this connection it should be said that he seems to have
prepared for publication a volume of essays intended to promote
church unity, but this project came to naught, and his manuscripts on the subject have been lost.

The President's influence as an educator is to be sought in his
upbuilding of the Grammar School, his broadening of the college
curriculum and his provision of graduate courses, in the wide
variety of pupils he attracted to Princeton, and in their subsequent careers. The school was the first department of the College to feel the new vigor he brought to Princeton, and the stress
he laid on it in his announcements and in his administration was
not a selfish one, even though the school was a presidential perquisite. He was constantly emphasizing the importance of early
education. His British belief in disciplinary fundamentals and in
the necessity of beginning them while a boy was still young, was
the point, as we have seen, on which he broke with the Reverend
Mr. Boucher. Especially interesting is his full appreciation of the
fact that the education some of his scholars received in the basement of Nassau Hall would be the only formal instruction they
would ever get, and his consequent planning of special courses
for boys intending to go no further in their studies. As early as
1771 he announced, for example, that they could have French
and the practical parts of mathematics if they desired. Clearly
he was here anticipating one of the problems of the modern
American public school and meeting it in not a very different

[37] *Rush Memorial*, p. 86.
[38] Professor Lyman H. Atwater of Princeton estimated Dr. Witherspoon as a theologian in the *Biblical Repertory* for October, 1863, vol. XXXV, p. 596. His material is
drawn entirely from these sources.

way, except that he did not discard the immemorial foundations and the tested training to be gained in classical studies.

The President's theories on education are scattered through his essays and lectures and are most definitely expressed in his newspaper announcements. His *Letters on Education* deal only with moral upbringing of children and are negligible in the present connection. First of all, he did not believe in forcing higher education upon the unwilling or the ineducable; "it is not only difficult to instruct those who have a radical incapacity for any study, but sometimes they are much worse for application just as fine clothes and a courtly dress upon a clown renders him unspeakably ridiculous."[39] Book learning amounts to nothing of itself: "we find many who learn the dead languages to great perfection, who learn arithmetic, geometry, natural philosophy, rhetoric, politics, who even become eminent in some of these and tolerably skilled in all, whom yet we reckon greatly inferior to more ignorant persons, in clear, sound common sense."[40] It has already been shown that Dr. Witherspoon placed but little value on merely acquisitive scholarship. In his lectures to his divinity students he pointed out that:

To excel in any particular branch of science, and to know everything upon that branch that may be known, is the work of a life-time. Grammar, mathematics, astronomy, oratory, history, law, physic, poetry, painting, statuary, architecture, music; nay, the subordinate divisions of some of these sciences, such as anatomy, botany, chymistry, are all of them sufficient to employ a life, to carry them to perfection. It is therefore plainly in itself improbably, that almost any man can attain a high degree of perfection in all, or indeed in many of these branches of study. There is something more to be observed: the person who addicts himself to any one of those studies so as to be an adept, or really a complete master in it, cannot be a man of extensive knowledge; and it is but seldom that he can be a man of a liberal or noble turn of mind, because his time is consumed by the particularities, and his mind narrowed by attending to one particular art. He is likewise apt to esteem his favourite study so much, as to confine all excellence and even all capacity to it. . . . Hence you may observe

[39] "Eloquence," *Works*, vol. III, p. 383.
[40] "Druid," *Works*, vol. IV, p. 171.

that all who are devoted to the particular study of one small branch, are generally considered as pedants. . . . But I observe that the most reasonable pedants and the least to be blamed are those whose hearts are set upon what is their business in life. Therefore though a schoolmaster can scarcely speak without citing Virgil or Horace, he is to be indulged; and though he may not make the most distinguished figure in public or polite life, yet he is useful in his generation, and fit for the discharge of his trust.[41]

But Dr. Witherspoon appreciated true learning applied to the service of mankind and realized clearly the need his adopted country was under of stimulating intellectual life. Nothing, he declared, was holding America back in point of general knowledge so much as the lack of large libraries, where "thorough researches" might be made, and the small number of learned men "to assist in making research practicable, easy, and complete." The enlargement of the Princeton library had been his first care even before he set foot on American soil. After its depletion in the Revolutionary War he at once set about replenishing it by inducing English and Scottish authors to present their works, enlisting in particular the aid of the Earl of Buchan in Scotland. His own library must have been large for his day; its remnant still contains about nine hundred titles. The constant bibliographical references in his lectures show the importance he attached to the use of books. "Reading a few books well chosen," said he to his divinity students, "and digesting them thoroughly, together with the frequent exercise of reflection, will make a knowing and intelligent man: but to make what the world calls a learned man, or a great scholar, requires a very general knowledge of authors, books, and opinions of all kinds."[42]

Not only did he constantly urge his students to continue their reading after college days were over, but those who cared to have his counsel as to further study he was only too glad to advise. John Read, after commencement in 1787, returned home bearing to his father, the Hon. George Read, the Delaware statesman, a typical letter from the President, in which the latter testified to the great satisfaction the young man had given to the college

[41] *Works*, vol. IV, pp. 18, 19.
[42] *Works*, vol. IV, p. 17.

authorities—he had talked with him about his future—"if he cannot return here I shall willingly write him my opinion upon the subject of future studies."[43]

His letters to his son David show how solicitously he watched over the lad's further development after graduation:

I received your favour of the 20th past, with pleasure, he wrote in January, 1777. When I cast my eye on the back of it, I thought it was somebody that wrote very distinctly and neatly and did not think of you, till I saw with satisfaction your name at the bottom. There are however still some small inaccuracies—be ambitious of improving every day.

A little later he wrote:

I need hardly tell you that our greatest comfort now is to hear of the welfare of our children. It gives me unspeakable pleasure to hear that you apply to your studies, both in teaching and reading. . . . Be as accurate as possible in writing your letters, and take pains to improve your hand.

It having been reported that David was "lusty and grown much," the President wrote to him:

That is a pleasing but very inconsiderable circumstance, compared with the accounts I had before and confirmed by him of your applying diligently to your business. I wish you to be sensible how much joy I have had from this information, and therefore often repeat it. My first concern is that you should fear God . . . now that you are at a distance, I pray you to remember that the fear of God is the beginning of wisdom. Next to the *one thing needful*, you know I am chiefly concerned for your improvement in useful knowledge, and fitness for the duties of active life; and I am persuaded by the taste you have taken, you will find the highest pleasure and the greatest honour by attending to your duty.

And once more:

I hope, my dear boy, if you continue to keep the path which I have chalked out for you, you will be useful, happy, and successful in life. Give great application to your studies, but above all be attentive to

[43] W. R. Read, *Life of George Read*, p. 459.

your moral conduct. . . . Remember, my beloved child, that those who have been trained up in the fear of God, cannot sin at so cheap a rate as others, and that the great advantages which you have had, and do still enjoy, must be accounted for. I wish your accomplishment in every respect, and therefore bear with me while I put you in mind to prevent at any rate a habit of holding down your head, or keeping it on one side, or any other ungraceful habit. Let there be decency in your outward carriage, reserve and modesty in your conversation, and humility in your heart.[44]

He must have been gratified by the increasing number of young men who did not think their studying days were done when they received their diplomas, but who came back to Princeton, like James Madison, to read for a year or so longer under his guidance. No one regretted more than he the failure of the effort made in 1781 to systematize the graduate department of the College.

Most of all did he seek to make his divinity students well-read men, and here in all probability is the explanation of the influence his clerical graduates exerted. "Piety without literature, is but little profitable," he said in his introductory lecture, "and learning without piety, is pernicious to others, and ruinous to the possessor." And in his second lecture he says: "There is no branch of literature without its use. If it were possible for a minister to be acquainted with every branch of science, he would be more fit for public usefulness . . . I may also say, therefore, it were good if a minister were a person of extensive knowledge."[45] He strongly recommended as helpful in the ministerial calling not only eloquence, belles lettres, and moral philosophy, but also history sacred and profane, the classics, Hebrew, and French. The remains of the ancients were still the standard of taste, and all literary persons should be familiar with them. He, therefore, advised the reading of the classics with the best critics.

It is to be lamented that many spend a great part of the time of their education in learning Latin and Greek, and yet few ever attain them to that perfection, which alone can make the learning of a language of great moment, so that they can read the authors with pleasure, and

[44] The letters quoted above are from the *Christian Advocate*, vol. II, pp. 443–5.
[45] *Works*, vol. IV, pp. 11, 17.

profit for the matter which they contain. This might easily be attained by almost any student after his grammar school and other education.[46]

French was both useful and ornamental:

There is hardly any such thing as a learned education in Britain, where the French language is omitted. . . . And though there are some branches of writing in which there are English authors not inferior to any of the French that I am acquainted with; yet, in general, there is to be found a greater purity, simplicity and precision in the French authors than in the English.[47]

But what had chiefly disposed him to recommend the French language was the "sound calvinistic, reformation divinity" to be read in that language: "There are many more able and elegant writers in that language than in English;" and he was broadminded enough to admit that there were admirable treatises by popish divines in French, not to mention the writings of the Jansenists.

It will be recalled that he had offered French as a graduate study on his arrival in 1768, and had introduced it into the undergraduate curriculum as an elective subject as early as 1770, and into the grammar school in 1771, teaching the language himself. That he spoke and read French easily we know, although the Marquis de Chastellux's comment on his pronunciation is sufficient authority for the conclusion that the President's accent was far from Parisian. Parisian or not, his knowledge of the language proved of great service in his congressional days. On the arrival of Baron Steuben at Yorktown in 1777, Dr. Witherspoon found that he alone of the committee of which he was chairman could converse with the Baron, who knew no English, but could speak French. He acted as interpreter in the interview which sought to learn the terms of Steuben's service, and was called as a witness for the Baron when the latter's claim came up. It was because of the increasing usefulness of the language in the new country that he made such a point of its study.

[46] *Works*, vol. IV, p. 20.
[47] *Works*, vol. IV, p. 21.

You will find a vast advantage in the French (language) now, he wrote in February, 1777, to his son David, for there are multitudes of Frenchmen come over and almost everybody is ambitious of learning the French. I am often employed as interpreter to those who come to Congress, and have many visits from them.[48]

A letter from him to M. Marbois, secretary of the French mission in America, throws light on his effort to popularize the language in college; it is dated from "Tusculum" July 18, 1783:

I am just favoured with your Letter of the 14th by Mr. Delandes to the Education of whose son I shall pay the strictest Attention. We have now several young french Gentlemen which gives me much Pleasure & I hope will be attended with happy Effects.

As to Mr. Lavalette he came to Princeton of his own Accord to teach the French Language. I was well pleased with it & gave him all the Encouragement in my Power as I had done much before the War to introduce the Knowledge of the French Language and Writings among our Students & indeed taught the Language myself as well as I could for some years. . . . I believe the Reason why he removed was that all he could gain was not a sufficient support.[49]

Dr. Witherspoon's own reading in French seems to have been limited chiefly to the Port Royalists and the French Calvinistic writers. Fénelon appears to have been studied carefully by him and is easily his favorite French author after Montesquieu. To the latter he refers again and again with admiration, and for a few years the *Spirit of Laws* was used as a textbook in his courses. Other classical Frenchmen, Molière and Pascal, Fontenelle and Boileau are barely named, while La Rochefoucauld is scored in the *Address to the Senior Class*. Although Voltaire was being read surreptitiously in college toward the end of his administration, the President himself had in his library only a copy of the London (1784) edition of Voltaire's memoirs;[50] and the deist receives but a sentence in his printed lectures—like David Hume, Voltaire's enmity, he says, appears to be directed against religion in general and not against the gospel, save that Voltaire "deals very

---

[48] *Christian Advocate*, vol. II, p. 444.
[49] Pennsylvania Historical Society.
[50] Bearing the autograph "D. Witherspoon"; possibly David.

much in particular cavils, and of the most silly kind."[51] He owned a copy of Hume's account of his controversy with Rousseau published at London in 1766, and Rousseau's theory of the degeneration of society was quoted by the grammar school valedictorian in 1783, but the President's lectures contain no allusion to the author of the *Social Contract*.

Dr. Witherspoon's college courses were the first to establish a tradition at Princeton. Other lecturers had preceded him; and several had been more eloquent; but they were scarcely more than temporary, while he had the advantage of lecturing for a quarter of a century on the same group of subjects. With a personality like his the establishment of a tradition was inevitable. His pupils carried away their carefully copied notes and many used them as the basis of their own lectures when in turn they found themselves teaching in after years. Until his time the curriculum had been chiefly confined to three fields—the classics, mental philosophy, and natural philosophy, with daily practice in oratory. While he strengthened the whole course in these fields, and was a pioneer American college lecturer on history and on philosophy, he was more conspicuously the first to give particular attention to the cultivation of the English language, which as a study had been neglected. "The education must be very imperfect in any seminary," he declared in the *Druid*, "where no care is taken to form the scholars to taste, propriety and accuracy, in that language which they must speak and write all their life afterward."[52] Accordingly, "great pains have been taken," he said in October, 1773, in announcing the opening of the next college term,

to introduce a taste for the study of the English Language, not without considerable success, and it is earnestly recommended to all masters of schools, that they be at pains, not only to make their pupils well acquainted with the Grammar and construction of the Greek and Latin Languages, but with the Orthography, Punctuation and Grammar of their own Language, in which, if they be defective, when they come to enter College it is extremely difficult afterwards to remedy.[53]

[51] *Works*, vol. IV, p. 24.
[52] *Works*, vol. IV, p. 180.
[53] *New Jersey Archives*, 1 ser., vol. XXIX, p. 60.

His influence in this direction is said to have done much to correct contemporary speech and purify contemporary taste in literature. The literary criticisms which he put forth for more than a quarter of a century not only in his college lectures but in the public press did not fail of effect. In the opinion of many, his most important influence was to be found here, Dr. Rush going so far as to allege that in this respect Dr. Witherspoon "gave a new turn to education and spread taste and correctness throughout the United States" so that it was possible to pick out his pupils whenever they wrote or spoke. While this statement may be an exaggeration, nevertheless it appears to be generally conceded that he gave fresh impetus to literary style and appreciation in those centers where such an influence would have most weight. As Dr. Rodgers puts it, the mode of learning was changed by Dr. Witherspoon and literary inquiry and improvement became more liberal, more extensive, more profound, because of the influence that emanated from Nassau Hall. This was particularly true of the Middle Colonies and Dr. Rodgers' implication that the College in Witherspoon's day was a fountain of new literary vigor in those Colonies is corroborated by Professor Tyler.[54] The movement centered about a little group of undergraduates of whom Philip Freneau and Hugh Brackenridge were the leaders, the former the first true lyric poet the country saw, the other America's earliest dramatist and novelist. Their undergraduate adventures into literature have been noted by Professor Pattee in his edition of Freneau's *Poems*, and included not only poetry but fiction.

Oratory and the classics had been the backbone of the Princeton curriculum when President Witherspoon arrived and he left oratory even more firmly entrenched. The attention that Princeton undergraduate platform utterances attracted in his day has been sufficiently referred to. He found when he came to Princeton that the prevailing style of public speaking was the persuasive and he urged his pupils to cultivate the narrative style as lying better within their powers, but it does not appear that they made much use of his advice. Senator William B. Giles of the Class of 1781, replying in 1827 in the Virginia Legislature to

[54] *Literary History*, vol. I, pp. 11, 187.

what he called a "jingling sonorous" speech of Henry Clay, recorded two fundamental rules he had learned at Princeton:

It happened to be my fortune in early life, he said, to be placed for my education under the care of the late celebrated Dr. Witherspoon of Princeton College. The Doctor although highly learned, was as much celebrated for the simplicity and elegance of his style and for the brevity of his orations, as for the extent and solidity of his erudition. He lectured the class of which I was a member upon eloquence and criticism and was delighted with the exercises in that branch of science. . . . He commenced his lectures in the simplest style of conversation. "Lads, if it should fall to the lot of any of ye, as it may do, to appear upon the theatre of public life, let me impress upon your minds two rules in oratory that are never to be departed from upon any occasion whatever—Ne'er do ye speak unless ye ha' some thing to say, and when ye are done, be sure and leave off." Frightful restraints upon modern oratory! The Doctor would proceed most methodically to impress upon the class the sacred inviolability of each of these rules and the indispensable necessity of their strict observance by every pretender to oratory.

Dr. Witherspoon gave his personal attention to his students' productions, in some cases writing their orations himself. There is, for example, extant in his handwriting, a Latin oration delivered by one of his boys on the very subject he had used for his inaugural; a commencement dialogue on "Civil Liberty" by two other undergraduates and published in the *Pennsylvania Magazine* for April, 1776, was written for them, says Dr. Green, and was taken from the President's lectures; the British officer who attended commencement in 1783 incognito expresses more than current opinion when he speaks of the President's hand visibly coloring the orations of the day, for a college law required all commencement performances to undergo his correction. The emphasis at Princeton on oratorical and English training led to the selection of that college for the education of John Randolph of Roanoke. His mother wished him to become an orator and he was, therefore, sent to what he later called "the noisy wretched grammar school kept for Dr. Witherspoon's emolument," where the prizes for elocution were borne away by "mouthers and ranters," to the utter disgust of this superior Virginian of fourteen, who, in his own estimation at least, was a better scholar than any of his fellows and just as good as his master.[55] Public speaking being the chief object of the American Whig and Clio-sophic Societies, it is no wonder that facility in that art was a characteristic of the men who graduated under Witherspoon.

A distinct novelty introduced into the curriculum by the President was the study of history, which his announcement asserted was "easy, pleasant, and profitable, and by a peculiar happiness of this age, fashionable"—a craftily worded advertisement whose allurements must have appealed to every type of undergraduate mind. Instruction in history was given by means of lectures, but Dr. Witherspoon's notes have not been preserved. Dr. Green reports that they were fragmentary and that he, therefore, "suppressed" them, when he prepared the President's writings for publication.

The single manuscript student version (and no other is known save an outline by Fithian) in the Library of Princeton University, a quarto of twenty-four leaves stitched together, is likewise fragmentary, containing only six lectures. It was made by Abel Johnson of the Class of 1784 and was copied from either the President's notes or from another undergraduate version. Gaps occurring where words in the original were illegible, and in particular one amusing error, prove that young Johnson was merely a copyist. He makes the President assert that Noah's Ark is supposed to have rested on the mountains of "America"—not the first time, nor the last, that Armenia has been mishandled.

The study of history, says the President in his opening sentence, "is, first, honorable being at present in high repute especially in our country, 2^d useful, 3^d delightful, 4th very much connected with and subservient to the interest of religion."[56]

[55] H. A. Garland, *Life of John Randolph of Roanoke*. It was this lad's valuable conviction that "nowhere is there such foul play as among professors and schoolmasters, more especially if they are priests." Which disposes completely, and once for all, of Dr. Witherspoon, his grammar school, and the local brand of oratory!

[56] In his *Serious Enquiry into the Nature of Effects of the Stage* he had already remarked that the knowledge of history was "necessary for proving the truths of natural, and confirming those of revealed religion; for repelling the attacks of adversaries, and giving us such a view of the plan of Providence, as may excite us to the exercise of the duties of adoration, thankfulness, trust, and submission to the Supreme Disposer of all events. Real facts only are proper for this purpose."

Two lectures deal with chronology and the remaining four cover the period from the providential creation of the world (4003 B.C.) out of previously non-existent matter to the death of the patriarch Jacob (1690 B.C.). How far the entire course extended cannot be said, and it is perhaps unfair to try to form an estimate of the whole from the opening group of lectures. Their outstanding feature is the attempt made in the last three lectures to describe, "the state of religion in that period . . . the state of civil society, and the improvements of the human mind." Under these heads the President discussed the origin of laws and government, the progress of manufactures, commerce, and the arts, the beginnings of science, the development of the art of warfare, and finally, general manners and customs. The peoples described are the Egyptians, Assyrians, and Phoenicians, with constant reference to the Old Testament. Dr. Stiles considered the President a good historical scholar and the reader is at once struck by the numerous historical allusions in his essays and speeches; but the fragmentary notes on his lectures would indicate that his outlines were more curious than well formulated.

From Dr. Witherspoon's lectures on "Eloquence," imperfect though they also are in their printed form, we can reach some judgment as to the scope of his own reading and taste in general literature. His inevitably high opinion of the value of the classics is apparent in all his academic pronouncements, but he was no mere classicist. In an allusion to the famous French Quarrel of the Ancients and Moderns, like his much admired Fénelon he takes the middle ground. A better Latinist than Grecian, whenever he quotes from the classics it is from a Latin author. In the same mention of the French Quarrel he passes judgment on "great and excellent patterns to form upon, both ancient and modern;" and thus among the Greeks he names Demosthenes, "simple, close, nervous, rapid and irresistible," and Xenophon "superior to almost every author in dignity, elegance and sweetness in the narrative." Of the Latins he names Cicero— "flowing, fervent, ornate, somewhat vain and ostentatious, but masterly in his way;" Livy, who has "a bewitching knack of telling a story," Sallust, who "excels in giving characters, which he strikes off in single epithets, or very concise remarks;" and Tacitus, "remarkable for judicious and sagacious observations on human life." Among the moderns he names Addison, whose *Spectator* he knew intimately, as a "noble pattern of elegance, dignity, and simplicity;" Swift in his political pieces is "a pattern of style which has scarcely been exceeded since his time;" and his old rival Dr. Robertson, turned historian, he generously declares "has as just a mixture of strength and elegance, as any other author I know in the English language." Just here Dr. Witherspoon cannot help cautioning his hearers against

one modern author of some eminence, Johnson, the author of *Rambler*. He is so stiff and abstracted in his manner and such a lover of hard words, that he is the worst pattern for young persons that can be named.[57]

In his closing lecture on "Eloquence" he considers the alliance between the various kinds of written and spoken composition and the fine arts, poetry, oratory, music, painting, sculpture, and architecture. He believed in a standard of taste—that set by leading authors on aesthetics; but evading himself a definition of this alleged standard, he declares that the way to state it is to quote the opinion of these authors, as for example, Addison *On the pleasures of the imagination*, Longinus *On the Sublime*, Crousaz *Traité du beau*, Hogarth *Analysis of Beauty*, Burke *On the Sublime*, Gerard's *Essay on Taste* and the French author of the *Theory of agreeable Sensations*.

As we have seen, Dr. Witherspoon's interest in poetry was of the slightest, and the few poetical quotations he made in his lectures are used only to point some moral. Here Horace is his commonest source, with Vergil a distant follower. Butler, Young, Swift, and Pope are infrequent English sources, although he is said to have been thoroughly familiar with the seventeenth-century British poets. His life-long antipathy to the stage explains

[57] "Lectures on Eloquence," *Works*, III, 386, 387. Dr. Witherspoon's opinion of Robertson was not shared by Dr. Johnson, who disliked him for what he called his "verbiage," although as Mr. Boswell hints, the dislike was more probably based on Johnson's general antipathy to the Scotch. Incidentally, it is interesting to find that Dr. Witherspoon had in his library a copy of Boswell's Edinburgh graduation dissertation, or *Disputatio Juridica* (Edinburgh, 1766), which fact suggests the possibility of an acquaintance.

his neglect of the drama. To Shakespeare he refers but three times—twice to *Julius Caesar* and once to *Hamlet*. Molière is the only French dramatist he names and in his one allusion to him, he merely calls attention to the ecclesiastical opposition aroused by *Le Tartuffe*. For poets as a class he had but slight regard, if a passage in one of his *Druid* essays may be trusted; he has known "youths of bright genius, in their own esteem," he says, "who have looked down with contempt on the plodding boys, and yet the latter have become men of spirit, and capacity, while the others have turned out to be rakes and bullies and even block-heads," or "taking the road to Mt. Helicon have become poets, fools, and beggars."[58] And yet the prizes offered in his grammar school commencement competitions were the works of English authors, in prose "and poetry." But if his interest in poetry was negligible, he was imaginative enough to have interesting ideas on simplified spelling, on the influence of climate on style, on the value of a central authority in language such as the French Academy, on the probability of an American school of English speech distinct from, and as authoritative as, the British; and on punctuation—"a thing the scholar should strive to understand a little, tho' few gentlemen and scholars use it much in their letters or in their composition." And in this respect Dr. Witherspoon was both a gentleman and a scholar; for his amanuensis asserts —and is fully corroborated by the President's remaining manu-scripts—that the only punctuation mark he used was the period.

When Dr. Ezra Stiles, estimating the sixteen college presi-dents he had known, laid down the opinion that Dr. Wither-spoon's mathematical and scientific training was inferior, he was not far from the truth. The President's acquaintance with the higher mathematics, with astronomy, and with physical science in general, was little more than elementary. He once undertook to criticize an essay on the Cartesian and Newtonian theories published in the *Pennsylvania Magazine* by Dr. Matthew Wilson who enjoyed reputation as a physicist. In the next issue of the magazine the President found himself somewhat tartly answered by David Rittenhouse himself; and wisely refrained from ven-

[58] *Works*, vol. IV, p. 178.

turing again into that field of polemics.[59] But he appreciated the value of the physical sciences and extended and emphasized their place in his curriculum. The experimental apparatus he purchased in London for the College was considered, before the Revolution, one of the best in the country; his acquisition of the Rittenhouse orrery was a step in the same direction; lack of funds alone kept him from strengthening his faculty on the scientific side earlier than he did, and after the war, with his apparatus wrecked, he called to the faculty Walter Minto, a genuine mathematician and physicist. Dr. Green declares that there was a distinct change in the upperclass curriculum after the war, by which juniors and seniors spent their whole time "in mathematics, philosophy, natural and moral, belles lettres, criticism, composition and eloquence," resulting in the virtual elimination of the classics. This post-war materializing or commercializing of the curriculum, as Dr. Green would have called it, came to such an unheard-of pass that in his own class (1783) there was one individual who did not even know the Greek alphabet and yet received his degree, while the Latin salutatorian, whose oration was written by Dr. Witherspoon, was such a poor Latinist that he came to Green for a translation of the President's composition. On the other hand there was criticism of the equipment in science toward the end of Dr. Witherspoon's administration,[60] but he had no funds to secure both a professor and a new equipment and he wisely chose the former, when he appointed Minto.

Dr. Witherspoon was a great teacher not because of any remarkable quality in his scholarship; he had not been trained as a scholar. His greatness as a teacher lay in his thoroughness, his personality, his sympathetic understanding of young men, and in his ability to make them share with him his enthusiasm for the subjects he taught. While therefore it is true that he vitalized instruction in college it is nevertheless inaccurate to say, as the chief speaker did at the dedication of the Witherspoon statue in

[59] Dr. Green does not include Witherspoon's effort in his edition of the *Works*. It may be found in the *Pennsylvania Magazine* for May, 1776, and Rittenhouse's reply in the issue for June, 1776. See also Riley, *American Philosophy*, p. 492.
[60] "Our education at Princeton," wrote Charles W. Harris, of the Class of 1792, "was shamefully & inexcusably deficient in experimental Philosophy." (*Harris Letters* in University of North Carolina *Sprunt Historical Publications*, vol. 14, p. 32.)

Washington, that on coming to Princeton the President found the college "sleeping over its books;" on the contrary, he found it only too wide awake to the new philosophies of the day. But he did give a touch of what was modern and liberalizing to the studies of the curriculum. He constantly sought to awaken the intelligence of his listeners and to induce them to read beyond the mere boundary of daily recitations. And he did not confine his attention to his upper-classmen; for several years after the Revolution he heard the freshman and sophomore recitations in the classics, and it was the sophomore class in Xenophon that he had to tramp out to "Tusculum," where the informal surroundings and the intimacy of the hour must have made those recitations far off prototypes of the twentieth-century Princeton preceptorial method of instruction. He was at his best, however, in his upperclass and graduate courses. Here he combined the lecture and recitation methods. He used no textbook save his own lectures, and each student was required to make a copy from the President's original outlines, of which the text was then all but learned by heart. At recitations on this text he would expand at great length, illustrating the point at issue by his wealth of anecdote and experience. This procedure will explain the meagreness of his printed lectures; they are summaries or syllabi rather than complete lectures; in them none of his subjects is treated minutely; and in his course on divinity he was accustomed to lecture on topics rather than follow any definite system.[61] Whatever we may think of these outlines, when we are reminded by Ashbel Green that they were originally prepared during the first four years of Dr. Witherspoon's presidency, while he was crowded with other new duties, we must be struck by the activity of his mind, the comparative breadth of his knowledge, and the facility and speed of his composition.

It should not be supposed that because he drew so many of his students from leading families of the country, such as the Lees, Madisons, Randolphs, and Washingtons, of Virginia, the Clymers and Hodges of Pennsylvania, the Morrises, Bruyns and Van Renssalears of New York, the Macons and Hawkins of

[61] Fithian, p. 29.

North Carolina, the Reads of Delaware, and the Stocktons, Patersons and Livingstons of New Jersey, that Princeton was chiefly a rich man's college. The democracy of its enrolment is proved by the scores of pupils he attracted from humbler families neither boasting of pedigrees nor blessed with accumulations of wealth. The autobiography of Dr. Joseph Caldwell furnishes an example; and the reference, in an earlier chapter, to his generosities toward impecunious collegians affords abundant evidence. He took likely students wherever he found them, and they came from various kinds of families; but they left him all singularly alike in spirit and outlook, and purpose in life. Fithian in 1772 said that almost every province in the country was represented in college, a statement which Dr. Witherspoon himself corroborates.[62] He had students from the West Indies, and French boys after the Revolution; in 1774 two free negroes, Bristol Yamma and John Quamine, sent by the Missionary Society of Newport, Rhode Island, were enrolled at Princeton for a couple of years of preparation for work in Africa; and in 1783 he accepted three Delaware Indians, whose tuition bills, it will be remembered, were the subject of Congressional action. A little later the rolls contained the names of two direct descendants of Pocohontas, and also that of another young Indian; and Dr. Witherspoon states in his description of New Jersey written for M. Marbois, that Indian boys from New Jersey had been educated at Princeton. None, however, was graduated.

The most remarkable of his pupils in this group was John Chavis, a negro sent to Princeton as an experiment, who became famous as a schoolmaster and preacher in North Carolina.

His students seem to have had a genuine affection for him, John Randolph's jibe being conspicuous by its isolation as well as its ill-nature. Ashbel Green's love of him is patent in every line he wrote about him. But it was an affection marked by no familiarity. Dr. Witherspoon was not a man with whom to take any liberties. Although he was known on the campus as "the old Doctor," there was a certain aloofness about him which compelled respect. One of his maxims was "never to praise a man to his face, and never to speak evil of him behind his back, unless

[62] *Letter to a Noble Lord*, Woods, p. 144.

called to do so as a matter of obvious duty and for a useful purpose." Green recalls his own experience of this maxim. His maiden sermon was delivered in the Princeton church with Dr. Witherspoon in the pulpit behind him; "After the worship was over, he tapped me on the shoulder and said 'Well, well, continue to do as well as that and we'll be satisfied'—the only praise he ever gave me to my face."[63]

Episodes in Dr. Witherspoon's pastorate at Paisley suggest that he was by nature a strict disciplinarian, and several later incidents in his life give evidence of his love of orderliness and rule, and his reputation for authority. An odd bit of testimony to this repútation is reported by Dr. Green who tells us that, during the President's voyage to Great Britain in 1783, he was asked by his fellow-passengers to draw up a set of rules to govern their conduct on shipboard.[64]

The Minutes of the faculty have been quoted to show that his government of the College was paternal and strict,[65] but marked by a sane tolerance. Ashbel Green was of the opinion that after the war and especially after the French Revolution a very noticeable spirit of independence permeated American colleges and made government more difficult and delicate than teaching; but Dr. Witherspoon seems to have had little real trouble with discipline. Knowing personally as he did the family of nearly every boy under his charge he was able to find in the intimacy of his

[63] *Christian Advocate*, vol. XII, p. 613.
[64] The sequel as related by Dr. Green is characteristic. All agreed to the code save one man who declared "in a profane manner" that he would do as he pleased. A storm arising and there being danger of the ship foundering, the lawless passenger staggered across the cabin and sat down beside Dr. Witherspoon, seeking consolation. "This," continues Green, "Dr. Witherspoon was by no means disposed to administer, but wished rather to increase his fear. The following dialogue then took place:
Mr. Lawless: 'Doctor, a most tremendous storm!'
Dr. W.; 'It is indeed dreadful.'
L.: 'I am afraid we shall be lost.'
Dr. W.: 'There seems much reason to apprehend that we shall.'
L.: 'The captain says he thinks the ship cannot live!'
Dr. W.: 'Well he certainly knows best.'
L.: 'Oh, we must go down! I hope we shall all go one way!'
Dr. W.: 'There, Sir, you must excuse me.———I hope *we shall not!*'
[65] Mr. Adams in 1774 learned on his visit to Princeton that "the government of this college is very strict, and the scholars study very hard." *Life and Works*, II, 356. That his informants were undergraduates, it is almost superfluous to add.

relation with his undergraduates a satisfaction that meant more
to him than even his ecclesiastical conspicuousness. The many
glimpses we get of this intimacy—students reaping his fields,
classes going out to "Tusculum," the celebration in honor of his
second marriage, his letters to parents, his sponsorship for penni-
less boys—all point to the conclusion that he was more the
friend and counsellor than pedagogue. Senator Giles of Virginia,
in the reference to Dr. Witherspoon already used in part, tells us
that "the Doctor generally approached his class in great familiarity, with a 'How do ye do, lads?' to which the reply was always
in kind: 'Brawly, sir, brawly!' " In an earlier chapter, a letter of
his to Colonel Lee was quoted as evidence of the parental oversight he exercised in college. The following letter to Mr. Thomas
Fitzsimmons, the Philadelphia merchant, is an additional illustration of his personal interest in his pupils:

Princeton May 12, 1788

Sir

I have now to inform You respecting Mr. John Ferguson that after
I had conversed fully with him about 10 days ago he agreed that if he
did not hear from Mr. Gadsden by the End of last Week he would
then proceed to Charlestown by the first Opportunity. He dined with
me to Day & having heard Nothing he seems quite desirous to go &
I think as discreet & sensible in his Behavior and Designs as ever I
saw him. Therefore you will please to take a Passage for him in the
first Vessel for Charlestown. I may also inform You that I had told
him before that it was the Opinion of many People that he was hurting his younger Brother Billy by his Example. This seems to have
deeply impressed him & I find he has been at much pains to advise his
Brother to be regular & stick to his Studies. Accordingly as the Session of the College began on Saturday Billy has gone into College &
seems to be ambitious to apply to his Books.

I shall probably see you in Philadelphia next Week & then fully
inform you of their Affairs & in the mean Time shall not be wanting
in giving John my best Advice as to his future Conduct. I shall be
glad to hear when any vessel is to sail.

I have the Honour to be Sir your most obedt humble
Servant[66]

[66] Princeton University Library.

From the paternalism of his college discipline it may have resulted that, no matter what a student's offence was, if he confessed, apologized, and promised to do better, he was certain of ultimate pardon; but the scarcity of severe punishments recorded in the faculty's Minutes was not due to any laxity of discipline. Dr. Witherspoon had very definite theories as to the government of his undergraduates. When Ashbel Green and Samuel Beach were appointed tutors on their graduation in 1783, the President invited them out to "Tusculum" to dine, and gave them some pertinent advice on their new duties. Govern always, he said, but beware of governing too much—a piece of advice that the early nineteenth-century authorities at Princeton, and especially Dr. Green, would have done well to follow. Convince your pupils, he continued, for you may convince them, that you would rather gratify than thwart them, that you wish to see them happy, and that you desire to impose no restraints but such as their real advantage and the order of the College render indispensable. Put a wide difference between youthful follies and foibles and those acts which show a malignant spirit of intentional insubordination; do not even notice the former except it be by private advice; overlook them entirely unless they occur in such a public manner that it is known that you must have observed them. And he told them that one day he was walking down the long corridor of Nassau Hall when he heard soft footsteps behind; suddenly turning his head he found one of his students tip-toeing after him, shaking his fists at him. He said nothing: the fellow slunk away; and expecting to be called to account, was politeness itself from that time on. On the other hand, continued the President, be exceedingly careful not to commit your authority or that of the College in any case that cannot be carried through with equity; but having pursued this system in every instance where there is manifest intention to offend or to resist authority, make no compromise whatsoever; put it down absolutely and entirely; maintain the authority of the laws in their full extent and fear no consequences.

Even when he was the sufferer by some thoughtless prank, if a frank acknowledgment was forthcoming the President was quick to forgive. The story of the bowlful of soapy water tossed from an upper window of Nassau Hall which accidentally drenched him as he stepped out of an entry is an example. To the stammering apology of the dismayed perpetrator of this breach of the college law that forbade the casting forth of anything from the windows, he merely replied—"Yes, but why did ye do it at all? Ye knew it was unlawful," and passed on.

The autobiography of Dr. Joseph Caldwell tells of a hunger strike in College toward the end of Dr. Witherspoon's administration because bread and milk became the regular fare at supper. The College refused to eat and even went so far as to "clear the tables with a volley of stones," despite the presence of the Vicepresident and tutors. Recitations were suspended until discipline was restored, when Dr. Smith met a deputation of the strikers and effected a compromise, saving them from a sterner fate. Fithian tells of a tamer revolt in his days against the brand of butter that the steward served, but mentions no punishment, threatened or inflicted. Perhaps the President had tasted the butter. But when necessary, he was firm and merciless. There was but one serious combination against his authority during his entire administration. Learning of it, he summoned the students together in the prayer-hall before anything actually had happened, and lectured them sternly on the situation. Then calling up the ringleader he demanded: "Now what have you to say?" Undaunted, the lad replied: "I have only this to say, that I am no more guilty than twenty others, and we are resolved to share the same fate." "Then," said the President, "you shall know it and share it without delay, even if your number should include the whole college. You, sir, are expelled; and go you immediately out of the hall." Then turning to the rest, "And now follow him, just as many as please, and take part in his disgrace!" Not another individual moved, and the rebellion was broken. Dr. Green cites, as another instance of the President's personal authority, the case when several of his best students began to board out of College, and the President, reminding them of the rule requiring all students to board at the refectory, ordered them to give up their new eating place. The following day, as he was leaving Princeton he learned that his injunctions had not been obeyed, and proposed to dismiss the group instantly. Green persuaded him to delay action until his return, and in the President's absence warned the seceders of their impending doom. When the President got back, each was in his proper place at the refectory, meekly making the best of his plainer fare.

One of the purposes of the founding of the College of New Jersey had been to provide an educated ministry for the middle and southern provinces and until the end of President Finley's administration in 1766 this had remained a leading function of the College. The Presbytery of New Brunswick, in a memorial drawn up in April, 1769, for the use of its members in collecting funds for the College, had stated that the object was "important & interesting to Church and State;" and while the Presbytery had observed with pleasure "some very eminent Departments of a civil Nature already filled with sons of this college," yet in 1767 not less than eighty Princetonians were Presbyterian ministers of the Gospel throughout the Colonies. The majority of vacant churches especially in New Jersey and the South, the memorial said, looked to Princeton to supply them with incumbents who would also make a stand "against any such as might be glad to abridge our Liberties and bring us under the Yoke of Ecclesiastical Power—instruments to plead the Cause of Religion & Liberty & to make our Body Respectable."

Of the 313 graduates in classes from 1748 to 1768 inclusive, 148 or 47% had entered the ministry. The next twenty-six classes, from 1769 to 1794 inclusive, covering Dr. Witherspoon's administration, graduated 478 men of whom only 114, or 23%, entered the ministry. Until the war the previous average was fairly well maintained; in the classes from 1769 to 1776 inclusive 117 were graduated, of whom 75, or slightly over 42%, became ministers. But in the classes from 1777 to 1794, of 301 men graduated only 39, or 13%, entered the ministry. Part of the responsibility for this marked contrast may be laid to the war and the new national conditions it brought about, but part must also be laid to the President's conviction, hinted at in his first announcement and driven home upon his students, that the College should prepare its members for constructive citizenship—leadership not only in Church but also in State, in education, at the Bar, and in less conspicuous walks of private life.

Although the number of candidates for the ministry under Witherspoon fell below previous averages, their quality remained high (if membership in the General Assembly was a criterion), and the President still had cause to congratulate himself. Leaving an Assembly in company with Ashbel Green one day, so the latter reports, he said:

You can scarcely imagine the pleasure it has given me in taking a survey of this Assembly to believe that a decided majority of all the ministerial members have not only been sons of our college, but my own pupils.

The occasion must have been the third General Assembly as the following table shows:

ASSEMBLY	NO. OF MINISTERS	PRINCETON GRADUATES	WITHERSPOON PUPILS
1789	22	10	3
1790	22	10	6
1791	36	28	16
1792	50	15	11

The President need not have confined his boast to the General Assembly's rolls. The Assembly's minutes for 1789, in a report on the "State of the Presbyterian Church at the time of the organization of the General Assembly," contain a roster of one hundred and eighty-eight Presbyterian ministers from ten States. Of these, ninety-seven are Princetonians, fifty-two being men of Witherspoon's training.

Aside from the fact that he was constantly being called upon to name tutors for wealthy families, or teachers for struggling academies, or instructors for new colleges, it was chiefly through his clerical graduates, because so many of them were teachers as well as ministers, that the President's influence made itself felt in the spread of education. Over eleven per cent of them became Presidents of colleges in eight different States of the Union. Princetonians of his breeding were first Presidents of Union College, New York; Washington College and Hampden-Sidney College in Virginia; Mount Zion College in South Carolina; Queen's College and the University of North Carolina in that State, and of Washington, Greenville, Tusculum and Cumberland Colleges and the University of Nashville in Tennessee. Two of his own graduates succeeded him at Princeton. With first Presidents should be classed founders like Thaddeus Dod (1773) of Washington College, Pennsylvania, John Macmillan (1772) of Jefferson College, Pennsylvania, and Caleb Wallace (1770) of Transylvania College in Kentucky. The second presidents of Hampden-Sidney in Virginia, Jefferson College in Pennsylvania, the University of North Carolina, and Franklin College and Oglethorpe University in Georgia were also his graduates.

It is true that the educational success of Dr. Witherspoon's clerical graduates was due in part to causes with which he had little to do. The Scotch-Irish dwellers in the Shenandoah Valley, as Mr. Becker has remarked, were through racial and religious prejudice more disposed "to give credit to ministers trained at Princeton than to clergymen ordained by the Bishop of London,"[67] and especially if they had been trained by Dr. Witherspoon. Organizing schools in connection with their churches these men had prepared the way for the stream of men he sent forth in Revolutionary days to preach the doctrine that education and religious freedom went hand in hand with civil liberty. The log college erected by the Reverend John Brown of 1749 at New Providence in Virginia was matched by the simple cabin at Chartiers in Western Pennsylvania in which John McMillan of 1772 held the first Latin school established west of the Alleghanies. If McMillan, big of frame, heavy voiced, and rough as the stone benches in his school, was typical of one sort of Princeton frontier preacher and schoolmaster, his collegemate, Thaddeus Dod of 1773, represented the other type. Slender and graceful in figure, with a winning personality, a mathematician and classical scholar who had a passion for music and poetry, Dod gave up the certainty of a comfortable career for the hardships of a missionary's life in the west and founded his school at Amity in Washington County, Pennsylvania. Subsequently, these two

[67] *Beginnings*, p. 184.

contrasting products of Dr. Witherspoon's teaching were associated as trustees of the academy which became Washington College. In schools like theirs, rude in equipment, but hearths of unquenchable fires, many of the elder institutions of learning in the South and on this side of the Ohio found their beginnings. For the stream did not exhaust itself in the fertile and congenial Valley of Virginia, but passed on down into the Carolinas and Georgia, whence here and there a pioneer, bolder than his fellows, turned westward into Kentucky and Tennessee.

The Witherspoon influence in Virginia centered in Hampden-Sidney College which, under the name of Prince Edward Academy, was opened in 1776 with Samuel Stanhope Smith, Dr. Witherspoon's pupil and son-in-law, as rector. Here it was that young David Witherspoon was an instructor. When Dr. Smith went back to Princeton in 1779, he was succeeded at Hampden-Sidney by his brother, John Blair Smith of 1773, also a pupil of Witherspoon. Through these brothers the early curriculum and administration of Hampden-Sidney took on a cast distinctly Princetonian. Those were days when religious liberty was the absorbing issue and it is said that the younger Smith's defence of this claim before the Virginia Assembly was an appeal which for astuteness and eloquence Patrick Henry could scarce have equalled. Both the Smiths were orators of the first order, speakers with physical gifts that President Witherspoon had trained. John B. Smith, moreover, was not only a defender of religious freedom; to aid the fight for civil liberty, he formed at the outbreak of the Revolution a company of students of Hampden-Sidney and marched away to Williamsburg to place them at the service of the revolutionary government.

The private school of the Reverend John Brown, 1749, was the germ of the more ambitious Augusta Academy, founded in 1776 by the Presbytery of Hanover at Timber Ridge with William Graham of 1773 as rector and John Montgomery of 1775 his assistant, both pupils of President Witherspoon. Removed to Lexington in 1779, the Academy was renamed Liberty Hall and nearly a century later became Washington and Lee University. Like his classmate, John B. Smith, Graham was a militant Christian, and when the necessity arose assembled pupils and parishioners and marched out to dispute the passage of the Blue Ridge with Tarleton's British dragoons. Some years later he appeared in a different rôle as author, on behalf of the Presbytery of Hanover, of the very remarkable memorial to the General Assembly of the Commonwealth of Virginia, protesting against a proposal to support religion by an assessment on all the people. His argument was based on a fundamental proposition which reminds one of Dr. Witherspoon's manner of thought in its assertion that

religion is altogether personal, and the right of exercising it inalienable; it is not, cannot, and ought not to be, resigned to the will of the society at large; and much less to the legislature which derives its authority wholly from the consent of the people and is limited by the original intention of civil association.[68]

Madison and John B. Smith supported the protest and carried the day against Patrick Henry.

Whether President Witherspoon ever travelled further south than Virginia will probably never be known; there is no evidence now that he did. But on his several trips to Virginia he must at one time or another have visited the school at Bladensburg in Maryland, founded shortly before the Revolution by the Reverend James Hunt of the Class of 1759; and there is fairly clear indication that he was personally instrumental in sending two of his more brilliant, though perhaps less pious, non-clerical graduates, the restless classmate poets, Hugh Brackenridge and Philip Freneau of 1771, to the famous Washington Academy in Somerset County, Maryland, a school, says Freneau, that was attended by boys who belonged to the best families in the State, but who preyed on him like leeches. Dr. Witherspoon failed dismally in his attempt to make a schoolmaster out of Freneau; the dreamer later fled in desperation from Erasmus Hall, Flatbush, whether he had gone on leaving Maryland, and so found his way back to his beloved Princeton to make a fresh start in life. He was succeeded at Washington Academy by William Linn of 1772, his college-mate but a better pedagogue, and destined to become President of Washington College, Maryland.

[68] Foote, *Sketches of Virginia*, vol. I, p. 342.

Had Dr. Witherspoon visited South Carolina after the Revolution he would have found at Charleston, besides the schools presided over by Princetonians of the older generation, the Reverend Thomas H. McCaule of 1774, a Princetonian of his own making, re-organizing the famous Mount Zion College in that city, along the plans of his alma mater.

The College of New Jersey was well-known in Georgia in Witherspoon's day. But his influence in that State seems to have been felt more through social affiliations with families like the Macons and Hawkins, than through pioneer educators, although a graduate of his training, the Reverend Robert Finley of 1787, became President of the University of Georgia early in the nineteenth century.

The Reverend John Todd of 1749 had secured in 1780 the Act of the Legislature incorporating Transylvania Academy in Kentucky, but Dr. Witherspoon's graduate, Caleb Wallace of 1770, was responsible in 1783 for a further Act naming the trustees and actually founding the institution, which became Transylvania University, and it was in the house of a third Princetonian, David Rice of 1761, that classes were begun. Kentucky Academy near Lexington was organized by Rice and Wallace in 1794 and a few years later amalgamated with the older institution. This was the Caleb Wallace who wrote the memorials of the Presbytery of Hanover in 1774 and 1776 to the Virginia Assembly claiming equal rights of freedom of conscience for dissenters, and it is suggested that Thomas Jefferson, as a member of the Assembly, was strongly influenced by these documents in his advocacy of religious liberty.

Thomas B. Craighead of 1775 came to Nashville, Tennessee, in 1785 and soon was elected principal of the Davidson Academy, whose classroom was the rough stone meeting house erected for him, where for more than twenty years he taught on week-days and preached on Sundays. Later on, this academy was chartered as Cumberland College of which Dr. Craighead was elected first President. To this college Philip Lindsley of Princeton eventually was called as President when it became the University of Nashville.

The first school in Tennessee and the first literary institution in the Mississippi Valley was founded by one of the most remarkable of Dr. Witherspoon's students, Craighead's classmate Samuel Doak, who, after serving as instructor at Hampden-Sidney for two years, on receiving his licentiate had pushed into the Southwest, settling first in what later became eastern Tennessee. The pioneer spirit in him could not be satisfied and he soon moved westward settling at Salem, in Washington County, Tennessee. He was the first preacher and teacher in that beautiful wild region. His log cabin school was incorporated by the legislature as Martin Academy and later chartered as Washington College, and it was for the library of this institution that he obtained gifts of books while in Philadelphia in 1798 attending the General Assembly, carrying them back with him on a packhorse, five hundred miles across the mountains. He gave up the Presidency of Washington College in 1818, and in Greene County, mindful of his old Princeton associations, he opened another school which he called "Tusculum" and which under the name of Tusculum College was consolidated with Greeneville College, founded by Hezekiah Balch an older Princetonian. The spirit of President Witherspoon, passed on by President Doak, is marked to this day in the history and achievement of the College in Tennessee named after the President's home at Princeton.

When the story of Princeton's influence in the South is written, no chapter will be more remarkable than the one narrating the service to higher education performed in North Carolina by Dr. Witherspoon's graduates.[69] In Mr. C. L. Smith's history of education in that State, published by the United States Bureau of Education, is given a list of thirty-six Princetonians who furthered the cause of higher education in North Carolina, and of these no less than twenty-three had been pupils of Witherspoon. When Queens College, the successor of Joseph Alexander's school at Sugar Creek, changed its name to Liberty Hall and was chartered in 1777, ten of the fourteen trustees besides the President were Princetonians, and six of the ten, with the President, were

---

[69] It was in some lonely region in North Carolina, according to the tale, that the suspicious owner of a wayside house declared to a stranger seeking shelter: "I allow no man to sleep under my roof but a Whig." "Then let me rest in peace," replied the other, "for I graduated under Witherspoon."

Witherspoon's students. Clio's Nursery or Academy of Sciences, at Snow Creek, the first scientific school in North Carolina, was opened by James Hall of 1774, who supplied his own apparatus, wrote his own text-books, and taught. Zion's Parnassus, the classical school of Samuel E. McCorkle of 1772, at Thyatira, was the first institution in North Carolina, and perhaps in the United States, to have a separate normal department. Warrenton Academy, incorporated in 1786, had as its three most prominent trustees, Princeton non-graduates, Henry Patillo of President Davies' time and Benjamin Hawkins and Nathaniel Macon, who were Seniors when Dr. Witherspoon closed the doors of Nassau Hall on that eventful day in November 1776. There were five Princetonians among the trustees of the University of North Carolina when it was chartered in 1789, three of whom were at Princeton under Witherspoon, and the two first Presidents of the University were also his pupils.

One of his layman graduates, James Madison became President of the United States, and Aaron Burr, a Vice-president; and ten became cabinet officers. Young though they were at the time, six were elected members of the Continental Congress. Thirty-nine became United States Representatives and twenty-one were United States Senators; twelve were Governors of States and fifty-six were chosen to State Legislatures. Thirty became judges, three others being appointed Justices of the United States Supreme Court. Of the twenty-five college graduates in the Federal Convention, nine were Princetonians and six of these had President Witherspoon's signature on their diplomas. It will never be known how many Princetonians, nor even how many of Witherspoon's own students, served in the War of the Revolution; the lack of any class rolls previous to 1787 renders an exact count impossible. But when allowance is made for the fact that he came to Princeton only eight years before the outbreak of the War it is startling to note that, even if commissions were cheap, among these young graduates of his were eleven captains, six majors, four colonels, and ten lieutenant-colonels. Four of these officers died in service. Of the eleven army chaplains found among his students of theology seven gave up their lives on the same altar.

These are records of President Witherspoon's graduates only. The records of his non-graduates are almost non-existent; there is not even a list of these men, and with few exceptions their histories are still unwritten. But the summary contained in the preceding pages of the part played in after years by some of the lads who came under his influence in the closing quarter of the eighteenth century shows how well his lesson of service bore fruit.

Until the latter part of his life Dr. Witherspoon preached in the college chapel regularly twice on Sunday in summer and once on Sunday in winter. Later, he preached only every third Sunday or on special occasions such as the baccalaureate. He never carried notes into his pulpit; all his sermons being delivered memoriter, and when blindness overtook him so that he could no longer see to write new sermons and even had to be led up into his pulpit, his remarkable memory stood him in good stead; he never failed to deliver verbatim the old discourse his amanuensis had read to him the day before. He once told Ashbel Green that when he had recently written a sermon he would engage, after reading it over three times, to repeat what he had written, "to an 'of' and a 'the.' "[70]

Ashbel Green, temporarily victim of a nervous complaint somewhat similar to that from which Dr. Witherspoon suffered, wished to resign his Philadelphia charge. But the President would not listen to such a step: "Take care how you do that," he said, "if you do that, it is my opinion you are likely to do little good while you live. There is no other alternative but to do as I did, or to consent to be useless the remainder of your days. Go you down to Philadelphia and do as well as you can, and God will help you. Take everything with moderation: but with this abatement do everything just as if you were well and after a while you will be so." It would seem, however, that the President never really got over his own nervousness. According to Dr. Green, his "olfactory and auditory nerves were morbidly excitable." He could not stand the odor of a small stove in the pulpit where he was preaching. Any sudden noise or accident would upset him. One Fourth of July, when he was presiding at the

[70] *Christian Advocate*, vol. II, p. 350.

exercises in the prayer-hall, at the close of a speech the college cannon was fired close outside the building. He sprang forward as if in a convulsion and only with difficulty regained his composure. On another occasion while Congress was at Princeton, the preacher of the day was a young clergyman who clung closely to his manuscript. A belated Congressman entering the hall, the preacher raised his eyes, lost his place, and in his confusion re-read a whole sentence. Dr. Witherspoon, sitting in one of the front pews, started up from his seat muttering, and then recovered himself. His nervousness showed itself in company by his restless changing of position, his constant shifting of hands and feet. He suffered from insomnia and was drowsy by day—especially after dinner, innocently adds Dr. Green; and he was even known to nod in the pulpit behind a dull preacher. In view of this failing he endeavored, when a member of the New Jersey Legislature, to get the daily sessions held in one sitting before dinner, but was outvoted. He accepted his defeat good-naturedly, and adroitly prepared for future quiet naps, with this apology: "Mr. Speaker, as you will have this matter in your own way, permit me to remark that there are two kinds of speaking that are very interesting—the one is perfect sense, and the other is perfect nonsense. When there is speaking in either of these ways I shall engage to be all attention. But when there is speaking, as there often is, half-way between sense and nonsense, you must bear with me if I fall asleep."

For several years he suffered from fits of sudden dizziness. The first seizure of this sort occurred one day while he was preaching in the college pulpit, and he fell headlong into the pew where his family was seated. These turns left him with a swimming in the head, he says, and a sense of dread and uncertainty when about to deliver a discourse. They began, however, to leave him, so he continues in the letter here quoted, after an eruption appeared on his temples and forehead in 1780; and after 1782 he was never troubled again.

His blindness in one eye, as we know, was the result of a fall on board the ship that took him to England in 1783. He told Dr. Green that he had no idea the eye was seriously injured, until after his arrival in London, when, putting his hand to the other eye to dislodge a grain of dust, to his dismay he found himself in total darkness. The second eye was injured by a fall from horseback in Vermont. Cataracts forming, in the spring of 1793 the celebrated surgeon Dr. Tilton of Delaware operated on him; but confinement in a cold room bringing on a chill and other complications, the operation was unsuccessful. Ashbel Green was with him in Philadelphia before he underwent the operation. The President had but little hope of its success and agreed to it only at the insistence of his friends. He said he had had the use of his eyesight a long time, and if it pleased God to take it away it gave him but little concern; he then compared the privations suffered by the blind with those experienced by the deaf and decided that those of the blind were less trying; the blind could still enjoy the cheering influence of the human voice, the pleasure of free conversation, and of books read aloud, all of which was denied to those who had lost their hearing.[71]

Methodical and systematic in the management of his library and papers, he knew, even after he became blind, if a single volume or document were misplaced, and it would cause him to fret and pluck at his eyebrows with both hands, exclaiming "They use me verra ill, verra ill!" In connection with his Scotch accent Green notes Dr. Witherspoon's odd pronunciation of his own name— "Wotherspoon"—although he spelled it in the usual way. Routine even in minor details marked the conduct of his household; morning and evening prayers were part of that routine; the last day of the year was always a day of fasting and self-examination; on Tuesdays Scotch barley broth was always served at his table; and Saturdays invariably saw a fish dinner. In the summer he retired at nine, in winter at ten; and he rose as soon as it was light enough to see to read or write. When he had

---

[71] The Reverend Professor W. Brenton Green of Princeton Theological Seminary records in the *Princeton Book* on the authority of Dr. Witherspoon's granddaughter, the late Mrs. Joseph A. Williamson of Georgetown, D. C., that the President experienced a few days before his death a remarkable restoration of sight. His wife brought his little daughter into his room. He looked at her for some time and turning to his wife, said: "Why, Nannie, the bairn has eyes like yours!" "Why, Dr. Witherspoon," she exclaimed, "can you see?" "As well as ever I could in my life," was the reply.

guests at his table he served wine—he was particular about his wines[72]—and his first toast was invariably "our absent friends," itself indicative of a dominant trait in his character, and his second was always "the land we live in;" and if he proposed a third it would be either the health of the President of the United States, or the prosperity of the United States itself. There was a charming note of old world dignity in all his hospitality.

During the last two years of his life he employed as an amanuensis his third cousin, John Ramsay Witherspoon, who entered college in November 1792 as a Sophomore. It is to him, next to Ashbel Green, that we owe most of our knowledge of Dr. Witherspoon's personality. The boy used to go out to "Tusculum" at least once a week, and sometimes oftener, to devote the whole day to the President's correspondence. The hardest work he did, however, was to read to the President on Saturday afternoon the sermon selected for Sunday, for apart from the fact that it deprived him of his half-holiday, the manuscripts were often so old that the ink had faded, and as the Doctor in his prime wrote a rapid hand, with a gentleman and scholar's shortcomings and seldom dotted an "i" or crossed a "t," the sermons were sometimes scarcely decipherable.[73] President Witherspoon's fund of anecdotes, and the interesting play of his mind, at one moment full of humor and at another serious and contemplative, made him one of the most companionable of men. Of warm though unobtrusive affections, he was a sincere and loyal friend. His affec-

[72] There is a letter in the Emmet Collection (No. 4192) from him to Mr. William Semple, a Philadelphia merchant; he finds that the "spirits" Mr. Semple has sent him have been tampered with; as this is the third occurrence of the sort he will cease to buy in Philadelphia unless Mr. Semple can devise some safe method of transportation. Another letter to Mr. Semple (in the Pennsylvania Historical Society) expresses the hope that the spirits ordered will be sent up to Princeton soon—"the sooner they come the better as we are almost quite out."

[73] In earlier days this hasty penmanship often got the President into difficulty when his pupils were copying his lectures. They would have to wait for him to decipher passages and he was often puzzled himself. Indeed, once after careful examination of a particularly illegible passage he had to confess that he "supposed he knew what it was when he wrote it, but he could not tell now what it was." He prudently never used his own manuscript when hearing recitation, but borrowed the best written copy in the class. This story will remind a later generation of Princetonians of the occasion when President Patton, lecturing on ethics, looked up from his notes and remarked that when he wrote the sentence he had just read he probably knew what it meant, but that he could not understand it now.

tion for his own people never cooled. A letter of his written in 1786 to an old friend at Paisley states that his remembrance of his former flock is unabated, he has often said he would willingly add to all his other labors to ride ten miles any Lord's Day morning to have such a congregation as he used to preach to; he will not cease to pray for them. "I have accustomed myself to such forms of expression as to include them morning and evening in my family prayers."[74] We know that more than once during the Revolution he took British prisoners to Princeton and those he took usually had Scottish names. Robert Aitken, the Philadelphia bookseller and publisher, James Tod, the first printer in the village of Princeton, James Finley, the Paisley weaver who settled at Princeton on his urging, and Mrs. Isabella Graham, whose name is associated with the beginnings of child welfare work and other organized charity in the United States, are illustrations of the permanent interest Dr. Witherspoon felt in old friendships. He was a man of many friends. It is significant and characterisitc that his commencement address to the senior class, delivered first in 1775 and repeated several times thereafter, should have contained an earnest plea for friendship, urging the young men before him to keep up the associations they had formed while pursuing together the common social aim of education.

His amanuensis has recorded the unforgettable impression of Dr. Witherspoon that he carried away with him when the time came to leave Princeton after commencement in September 1794. He went to "Tusculum" to pay his graduation fee and bid farewell to the blind President. The Doctor gently refused the money, but, placing his trembling hands on the lad's head, with tears in his eyes gave him his blessing. It always seemed to him, so he wrote many years later, that Dr. Witherspoon's manner at that moment had combined the simplicity of a child, the humility of a patriarch, and the dignity of a prince.

FINIS

[74] Crichton, *Memoir of John Findlay*, 52.

APPENDIX A

PRESIDENT WITHERSPOON'S WRITINGS

THE only manuscripts of President Witherspoon's published writings that have been preserved are his *Caspipina's Catechism* (Library of Congress) and a portion of one of his *Druid* essays (Library of Princeton University). It is recorded that shortly before his death the younger Mrs. Witherspoon at his direction destroyed a quantity of his papers. The remainder were for some time in the possession of his son-in-law, Dr. Smith, who sent part of the collection to the Woodwards of Philadelphia for Dr. Green's edition of the President's *Works*. It is said that all of the collection eventually passed into the hands of Dr. Smith's grandson, John Witherspoon Smith, of New Orleans. Its fate has not been traced.

The President's commonplace books, two little volumes of extraordinary interest containing memoranda, notes, outlines of sermons, etc., were seen by James W. Alexander (*Familiar Letters*, I, p. 83) in the Princeton Library in 1825; they are there no longer. The series of sermons and essays containing a "comprehensive view of divine truth," of which Dr. Witherspoon wrote to the Reverend Brian Collins in 1783 as if it were ready for the printer, seems to have disappeared before the President's death. Dr. Green heard him preach regularly during four years; but not one of these discourses (which included the series on submission preached after the death of Mrs. Ramsay) was found with his papers. They were probably among those destroyed by Mrs. Witherspoon.

Soon after the President's death Dr. Green wrote to Dr. Smith with regard to the possibility of publishing by subscription an edition of Dr. Witherspoon's writings. Dr. Smith's reply of March 20, 1796, now in the Library of Princeton University, reveals his utter discouragement; the printers informed him that subscribers were a "very uncertain reliance," the labor of transcribing the President's posthumous papers "without which they would be almost useless to a printer" would be immense; and without subscribers the book would not sell at all, "religion and morals have been so effectually supplanted in this country by politics, infidelity, and frivolous entertainment." Ashbel Green, however, did not abandon his effort to perpetuate the memory of his beloved teacher and within a year or two had arranged with the Woodwards to undertake the publication. To that firm accordingly Dr. Smith gave full use of the papers in his possession. In November 1799 he wrote to Green (Library of Princeton University):

I have furnished Mr. Woodward with all of Dr. Witherspoon's manuscripts that I have been able to find. There is a bundle of essays chiefly political, a great part of which very probably deserve to be published; but I confess I never read them and therefore judge only from the character of the writer. There are twelve sermons written in a tolerably fair hand. Three or four appear to have been cut out after Mr. Austin had possession of the volume. Dr. Witherspoon was very much displeased at him for publishing one or two & attempting to publish others that he had desired him not to do. The bundle of manuscripts that my brother took with him shortly before he died will require great selection as a large part of them I imagine were not intended, and are probably not fit, for publication.

This statement indicates a curious lack of interest on the part of Dr. Smith in his father-in-law's writings and also suggests that the President's manuscript sermons were kept together in volumes which Mr. Austin, editor of the *American Preacher*, a collection of discourses by American divines, mutilated, even failing to exercise critical care with the portions he published. It also appears that Dr. Smith's brother, John Blair Smith, had already taken a portion of the manuscripts south with him. These possibly were the papers Dr. Green speaks of in the preface to the fourth volume of the first edition as having been sought for "at many miles distance."

The first edition of the *Works* finally appeared at Philadelphia in 1800 with a list of 900 subscribers. It had been planned in three volumes, but a fourth volume, the most interesting of the set as it contains the President's political papers, was issued in 1801. A second edition, revised and corrected, came out the next year.

Dr. Green had not published all the material sent to him. For example, there were several pieces of satire, two in verse, which he considered might well be suppressed—possibly one of them was the fragment published by Mr. Woods in his biography of the President. Thirty years later he still had in his hands "nearly the whole" of the President's unpublished manuscripts, as well as a "large number of letters addressed to him by correspondents in Europe and America," and he proposed (*The Presbyterian*, April 3, 1835) a third edition of the *Works* which should be more nearly complete than its predecessors. He was in possession of a "considerable number of articles in the Doctor's own handwriting numbered and endorsed by himself, perhaps with a view to publication. From these a selection will be made for the new edition; and there will be a republication from the *Christian Advocate* of a few short pieces which have appeared in that work." Moreover it had long been his wish, he says, to write and publish the life of "his early and best friend, his venerated teacher, counsellor and patron," which had never yet been done in a manner at all worthy of the subject. The biographical sketch now among the manuscripts of the New Jersey Historical Society at Newark was the result, and was intended to be the introduction to the new edition; but, although a publisher had been selected, Dr. Green's proposal came to naught and the third edition never appeared. What became of the Witherspoon manuscripts then in his hands is not known.

In the following chronological list of the President's writings all the known editions of any work are recorded under the date of the original publication, with cross references under the dates of later issues.

1739

DISPUTATIO PHILOSOPHICA, quam favente numine Ut in artibus liberalibus & disciplinis Philosophicis magister rite renuncietur, ex Auctoritate Reverendi admodum Viri, D. Gulielmi Wishart, S.T.D. Academiae Edinburgenae Praefecti, nec non Amplissimi Senatus academici, & nobilissimae Facultatis artium decreto, Publico erudi-

torum examini subjiciet, ad Diem 23 Februarii, hora decima antemeridiana, Joannes Wederspan, A & R.
    Edinburgi: In Aedibus Jo. Paxton, M.DCC.XXXIX.
pp. (4) 10, (1) 4to.

1753

REMARKS ON AN ESSAY ON HUMAN LIBERTY
    In *Scots Magazine*, vol. XV, April 1753, pp. 165-70
    Signed by J. W.

ECCLESIASTICAL CHARACTERISTICS: or, the Arcana of Church Policy.
    Glasgow, 1753. Not found.
(Published in October, 1753. See Note to 3d edition).

The same. Second Edition. Not found.
(Published in December, 1753. See Note to 3d edition).

The same, Ecclesiastical Characteristics: or, the Arcana of Church
Policy, being an Humble Attempt to open up the Mystery of Moderation. Wherein is shewn a plain and easy Way of attaining to the
Character of a Moderate Man, as at present in Repute in the Church
of Scotland. The Second Edition, Corrected and Enlarged.
    Glasgow: Printed in the Year, MDCCLIV. Price Six-pence
pp. xii, 7-49. 12mo.
Either the second edition dated 1754 but published in December 1753, or really a
third edition published in 1754. See Note to 3d edition.

The same. The Third Edition, Corrected and Enlarged.
    Glasgow: Printed in the Year, M.DCCLIV.
pp. xii, 13-62. 8vo.
Contains an "Additional Maxim." Verso of title bears this "Advertisement. The First
Edition of the Characteristics was published in the beginning of October 1753; the
Second, the middle of December following; and this Third, the end of May 1754."

The same. Another edition. London 1754. Not found.
Announced in the *Gentleman's Magazine* as having been issued in September, 1754.

The same. The Fourth Edition, Corrected and Enlarged.
    Glasgow: Printed in the Year, MDCCLV.
pp. xiv, 15-71. 12mo.
The Advertisement of 1754 is repeated with the additional fact that the present 4th
edition was published in February, 1755.

The same. The Fifth Edition.
    Edinburgh: MDCCLXIII.
pp. xii, 17-68. 8vo.

The same. Kenschets van het bestaan en gedrug der Kerklyken.
Utrecht. Wed. J. J. van Poolsum. Rotterdam, P. Holsteyn. n.d
(1763?).
8vo. Not found.

The same. The Sixth Edition.
In "Essays on Important Subjects." London, 1765.

The same. The Seventh Edition. London: Printed, Philadelphia; Reprinted, by William and Thomas Bradford at the London Coffee-
House.
M,DCCLXVII.
pp. 60. 8vo.

The same. Reprints of Scarce Tracts connected with the Church of
Scotland. No. 1 Ecclesiastical Characteristics. By J. Witherspoon,
D.D. Originally published 1753. New edition with an introductory
preface (by Alexander M. Dunlop.)
Edinburgh, 1842.
8vo.

1754

ECCLESIASTICAL CHARACTERISTICS. Second edition.
See 1753.

The same. Third edition.
See 1753.

The same. Another edition.
See 1753.

1755

ECCLESIASTICAL CHARACTERISTICS. Fourth edition.
See 1753.

1756

ESSAY on the Connection between the Doctrine of Justification by
the imputed Righteousness of Christ, and Holiness of Life: With
some Reflections upon the Reception which that Doctrine hath generally met with in the World. To which is prefix'd, a Letter to the
Rev. Mr. James Hervey, Rector of Weston Favell, Northampton-

shire, Author of Theron and Aspasia. By John Witherspoon M.A., Minister of the Gospel in Beith.

Glasgow: Printed by John Bryce and David Paterson. M,DCC,LVI.

pp. vi, 3–72. 12mo.

The same. The Second Edition.

Edinburgh: Printed by T. Lumisden and Company; sold by Gray and Peter, at their shop in the Exchange. M,DCC,LVI.

pp. 74. 12mo.

Christ mis-printed *Chrirt*, and *Reflections* spelled *Reflexions*.

The same. Third Edition.

In Essays on Important Subjects. London, 1765.

The same. Proeve over het verband tusschen het Leerstuk van Christus toegerekende geregtigheit en de heiligheit des levens.

Utrecht, 1764, Wed. J. J. van Poolsum.

8vo. Not found.

The same. See Treatises on Justification and Regeneration. 1815.

1757

A SERIOUS ENQUIRY INTO THE NATURE AND EFFECTS OF THE STAGE. Being an Attempt to show, that contributing to the Support of a Public Theatre, is inconsistent with the Character of a Christian. By John Witherspoon, M.A., Minister of the Gospel in Beith.

Glasgow: Printed by J. Bryce and D. Paterson. MDCCLVII.

pp. (iv), 72. 12mo.

The same. Ernstig onderzoek aangaande de Toneelen zynde ingeregt om aan te toonen dat het begunstigen en bevorderen van een openbaar Toneel onbestaanbaar is met het Karakter van een Christen.

Utrecht. Wed. J. J. van Poolsum. 1772.

8vo. Not found.

The same. A Serious Inquiry into the Nature and Effects of the Stage: and A Letter respecting Play Actors. By the Rev. John Witherspoon, D.D.L.L.D. Late President of the College at Princeton, New Jersey. Also a Sermon, on the Burning of the Theatre at Richmond, &c. By Samuel Miller, D.D. Pastor of the first Presbyterian Church in New York. Together with an Introductory Address by several Ministers in New-York, &c.

New-York: Published by Whiting and Watson, 96 Broadway. 1812.

pp. 199(1). 12mo.

The same. A Serious Inquiry into the Nature & Effects of the Stage (Originally Published in 1757); with a Letter respecting Play-Actors, (First published in 1793), by the Rev. John Witherspoon, D.D., sometime minister of the gospel at Paisley, and late President of Princeton College, New Jersey. With a preface by the Rev. D. T. K. Drummond, B.A. Oxford, and memoir of the author, by the Rev. William Moffat, M.A., Cairnie.

Edinburgh: Lyon & Gemmell, George IV Bridge, 1876.

pp. xxxvi, 100. 12mo.

The preface (pp. ix–xxvi) is an essay against the stage, followed by a Note (pp. xxvii–xxix) on certain novelists. pp. xxxi–xxxvi is the memoir. The title page is in error in stating that the Letter on Play Actors was published in 1793.

1758

CASE OF THE MAGISTRATES AND TOWN-COUNCIL OF PAISLEY, the Minister and Session of the Laigh Church, and the Minister of the High Church of that Town, Appellants; the Reverend the Presbytery of Paisley, Respondents. The Appellants Case. To be heard at the Bar of the Venerable Assembly met at Edinburgh in May 1758.

n. t. p. [Paisley, 1758?]. pp. 8. 4to.

Signed at end, by "Ja. Baine & Jo. Witherspoon."

THE CHARGE OF SEDITION AND FACTION AGAINST GOOD MEN, especially faithful Ministers, considered and accounted for. A Sermon preached in the Abbey-church of Paisley, on Thursday, September 7, 1758. At the Ordination of Mr. Archibald Davidson, as one of the Ministers of that Church. To which is subjoined, the Charge to the Minister, and the Exhortation to the People. By John Witherspoon, A.M. One of the Ministers of Paisley. Published at the desire of those that heard it.

Glasgow: Printed by J. Bryce and D. Paterson. MDCCLVIII.

pp. 52. 12mo.

The same. Belfast: Printed for Robert Johnston, Bookseller in Bridge-street. MDCCLVIX (*sic*).

pp. 40. 12mo.

The same. In *Christian's Scholar's and Farmer's Magazine.*
Elizabethtown. 1789.

vol. I, pp. 38–40, 179–181, 428–430.

The same. Boston: Reprinted and sold by Lincoln and Edmands. No. 53 Cornhill. 1811.

pp. 36. 12mo.

APPENDIX A
1758

THE ABSOLUTE NECESSITY OF SALVATION THROUGH CHRIST. A Sermon, preached before the Society in Scotland for propagating Christian Knowledge, in the High Church of Edinburgh, on Monday, January 2, 1758. By John Witherspoon A.M., Minister of the Gospel at Paisley. To which is subjoined, a short Account of the present State of the Society.

    Edinburgh: Printed for W. Miller. 1758.

pp. 90. 12mo.

The same. [Second Edition?].

In the expansion of a note on the Scripture meaning of Charity, appended to this sermon, Mr. Witherspoon states that criticism of the note induced him "on notice of a second edition being intended, to offer a few reflections on this subject." No copy of the second edition has been found. The expansion of the note constitutes his Inquiry into the Scripture meaning of Charity. See under 1768.

PRAYER FOR NATIONAL PROSPERITY and for the Revival of Religion inseperably (*sic*) connected. A Sermon Preached on Thursday, Feb. 16, 1758. Being the Day appointed in Scotland for the late Publick Fast. By J. Witherspoon, A.M. Minister of the Gospel in Paisley.

    London: Printed for Tho. Field, at the Wheatsheaf. The Corner of Pater-noster-Row Cheapside. MDCCLVIII.

pp. 38. 12mo.

1759

THE TRIAL OF RELIGIOUS TRUTH BY ITS MORAL INFLUENCE. A Sermon, preached at the opening of the Synod of Glasgow and Ayr, October 9th, 1759. By J. Witherspoon, A.M. Minister of the Gospel in Paisley.

    Glasgow: Printed for James Wilken, Bookseller in Paisley. MDCCLIX.

pp. 45. 12mo.

THE CHARGE OF SEDITION AND FACTION.
See 1758.

1760

CASE OF THE TOWN-SESSION OF PAISLEY, Appellants from a Sentence of the Synod of Glasgow and Ayr, at Glasgow, October 15, 1760, disapproving a Plan for uniting the Offices of English Schoolmaster and

Session-Clerk in the Town of Paisley. To be heard at the Bar of the Venerable Assembly met at Edinburgh in May 1761.
n. t. p. [Paisley, 1760?]. pp. 8. 4to.
Signed "John Witherspoon."

1762

SEASONABLE ADVICE TO YOUNG PERSONS: A Sermon on Psalm i:1. Preached in the Laigh Church of Paisley, on Sabbath, Feb. 21st, 1762. To which is prefixed, An Authentic Narrative of the disorderly and riotous Meeting, on the Night before the Celebration of the Lord's Supper in that Place, which gave occasion to the Discourse. By John Witherspoon, A.M. One of the Ministers of Paisley.
   Glasgow: Printed by Robert Urie. Sold by [names of thirteen booksellers in nine cities.] MDCCLXII. Price Six-pence.
pp. vi, 41. 8vo.

The same. On the sin of scoffing at things sacred.
In Sermons, Edinburgh 1798. A reprint of the Seasonable Advice with the notes and local references omitted.

1763

A SERIOUS APOLOGY FOR THE ECCLESIASTICAL CHARACTERISTICS. By the real Author of that Performance.
   Edinburgh: Printed by Sands, Murray, and Cochran. For William Gray, in front of the Exchange. MDCCLXVII.
pp. vi, 5-45. 8vo.
ECCLESIASTICAL CHARACTERISTICS. Fifth edition.
See 1753.

The same. Dutch translation.
See 1753.

1764

ESSAYS on Important Subjects.
   London: Dilly. Three volumes.
Advertised in the *Gentleman's Magazine* for September 1764, and in the *Scot's Magazine* for November 1764; noticed in the *Monthly Review* for December 1764; but no copy has been found bearing date of that year.

The same. Essays on Important Subjects. Intended to establish the Doctrine of Salvation by Grace, and to point out its Influence on

Holiness of Life. By John Witherspoon, D.D. To which are added by the Publishers, Ecclesiastical Characteristics, or the Arcana of Church Policy, with a Serious Apology; which have been generally ascribed to the same Author.

London: Printed for Edward and Charles Dilly, in the Poultry, near the Mansion-House. M.DCC.LXV.

2 vols. pp. 279, (5); 290. 12mo.

The preface signed "J.W." is dated London, June 1764, and speaks of the Treatise on Regeneration as "now first published." Contents of the series: Vol. I Essay on the Connexion between the doctrine of Justification . . . and Holiness of Life, 3d edition; Absolute necessity of salvation through Christ; Trial of religious truth; Charge of sedition . . . against good men; Prayer for national prosperity. vol. II. Serious enquiry into the . . . stage; Ecclesiastical characteristics 6th edition; Serious apology. vol. III. A Practical Treatise on Regeneration.

The same. Essays on Important Subjects. By John Witherspoon. D.D. Sometime minister of the Gospel at Paisley, and late President of Princeton College, New Jersey. In four volumes.

Edinburgh: Printed for Ogle & Aikman, J. Pillans & Sons; J. Ritchie; and J. Turnbull. 1805.

12mo.

The same. A New Edition.

Bungay: Printed for the editor, by C. Brightly. 1800.

2 vols. pp. viii, 249; vii, 407. 8vo.

Editor's name not given. Introduction dated "Northwood Place, near Beccles, 1800."

A PRACTICAL TREATISE ON REGENERATION. By John Witherspoon, D.D.

London: Printed for Edward and Charles Dilly. M.DCC.LXIV.

pp. (4), 281, (3). 12mo.

Apparently the first edition referred to in preface to the 1765 edition of the Essays on Important Subjects.

The same. [Second Edition. Not found.]

The same. [Third edition. Not found.]

The same. [Fourth edition. Not found.]

The same. The fifth edition.

London: 1815.

pp. 211. 8vo.

The same. Regeneration, or the New Birth: extracted from Dr. Witherspoon by the Rev. George Burder. [Quotation: John iii:3.]

London: Printed by J. Dennett, Leather Lane, Holborn. Sold by

Williams & Son, Stationer's Court, Ludgate Street. Price Two-pence.

n.d. pp. 16. 16mo.
This abridgement appeared first in the Protestant Dissenter's Magazine, vol. II.

The same (Extracts only.) In the Christian Advocate.
vol. VIII (1830) pp. 118, 177, 228, 287, 341, 397, 453, 505, 560, 616; vol. IX (1831) pp. 6, 63, 115, 172, 229, 285, 349, 404, 460.

The same. Verhandeling over de Wedergeboorte met eene Voorede van Prof. Chevalier.
Gröningen. A. Groenwolt. 1776.
8vo. Not found.

The same. An Address to six classes of persons: the rich and the poor: the young and the old; the self-righteous and the chief of sinners. By Dr. Witherspoon.
London n.d. [1830].
pp. 8. 12mo.
No. 358 of Vol. 10 Religious Tract Society, The First Series of Tracts. A reprint of the conclusion of Dr. Witherspoon's Treatise on Regeneration, with a few omissions. The date is that assigned by the British Museum Catalogue.

The same. Traité Pratique sur la Régénération, par John Wither-spoon, D.D. [Text from John iii:3].
Toulouse, Delhorve, Libraire, rue du Lycée, 14. Paris, Librairie Protestante, rue Tronchet 2. 1850.
pp. 432. 12mo.

The same. See Treatises on Justification and Regeneration. 1815.
TREATISE ON JUSTIFICATION.
See 1756.
A PRACTICAL TREATISE ON REGENERATION. By John Witherspoon, D.D. Principal of Princeton College, New Jersey.
n.p.n.d. (London 1844?).
pp. 68. 8vo.
In the Christian Treasury. London, 1844.

The same. Reprint of the above. In the Christian Treasury. London, 1855.

1765

THE HISTORY of a Corporation of Servants Discovered a few Years ago in the Interior Parts of South America. Containing some very Surprising Events and Extraordinary Characters.

Glasgow: Printed for John Gilmour, and sold by him and the other Booksellers in Town and Country. MDCCLXV.

pp. 76. 8vo.

The same. In sermons, Edinburgh, 1798.

Essays on Important Subjects.
See 1764.

Ecclesiastical Characteristics. Sixth edition.
See 1753.

1767

Ecclesiastical Characteristics. Seventh edition.
See 1753.

1768

Practical Discourses on the Leading Truths of the Gospel.
Edinburgh: Kincaid and Bell and Gray. 1768.

Advertised in the *Scots Magazine* for June 1768; reviewed in the *Monthly Review* for April 1769. Contains 13 sermons and forms with Sermons on Practical Subjects (Glasgow 1768) two of the five volumes of Essays and Sermons on Important Subjects (Edinburgh and Glasgow 1768).

The same. Another edition.
Philadelphia: W. and T. Bradford. 1770.

Hildeburn 2618 and Evans 11944, but seen by neither. Not found.

The same. Practical Discourses on the leading Truths of the Gospel. By John Witherspoon, D.D. President of the College of New Jersey. Second Edition.
London: Printed for C. Dilly in the Poultry. MDCCXCII.

pp. viii, 355. 12mo.
The "Advertisement" dated Paisley May 16, 1768, is signed "J.W." and states that the sermons are selected to form "a little system of the truths of the gospel, to point out their relation to one another, and their influence on practice . . . an attempt to illustrate the scripture-doctrine by experience and observation on human life."

Sermons on Practical Subjects: to which is added, a Farewel (*sic*) Discourse Delivered at Paisley in April and May 1768. By John Witherspoon, D.D.

Glasgow: Printed by A. Duncan and Company, for James Duncan

Bookseller, opposite the Main Guard, Trongate; and William Walker, Bookseller, Head of the Salt-Mercat. MDDCCLXVIII.

pp. vii, 323, (1). 12mo.
Contains nine sermons and forms the last volume of the set of five volumes of Dr. Witherspoon's writings advertised in the *Scots Magazine* for June 1768. When found with the Practical Discourses and the three volumes of essays already published it carries an additional title-page: Essays and Sermons on Important Subjects. See below.

The same.
  Edinburgh. J. Turnbull for Ogle & Aikman. 1804.

pp. 318. 12mo.

ESSAYS AND SERMONS on Important Subjects: intended to establish the doctrine of Salvation by Grace, and to point out its influence on Holiness of Life. By John Witherspoon, D.D. President of the College of New Jersey. In Five Volumes.
  Edinburgh: Printed for A. Kincaid & J. Bell, and W. Gray, Edinburgh; and J. Duncan, & W. Walker, Glasgow. MDCCLXVIII.
12mo.

AN INQUIRY INTO THE SCRIPTURE-MEANING OF CHARITY. By John Witherspoon, D.D. Formerly Minister of the Gospel at Paisley. Now President of the College of New Jersey.
  Edinburgh: Printed for A. Kincaid & J. Bell, and W. Gray. MDCCLXVIII.

pp. 28. 12mo.

THE NATURE AND EXTENT OF VISIBLE RELIGION. A Sermon. By John Witherspoon, D.D. Formerly Minister of the Gospel at Paisley. Now President of the College of New Jersey.
  Edinburgh: Printed for Kincaid & Bell, and W. Gray. MDCCLXVIII.

pp. 36. 12mo.

The same. In Liberality in Religion, taken from the *Christian's Magazine*, edited by the Reverend Dr. Mason of New York, together with "An inquiry into the Scripture meaning of Charity," extracted from the writings of the Reverend Dr. Witherspoon.
  Portland: Published and sold by A. Lyman & Co. Insurance buildings, Exchange street. J. McKnown, printer, 1811.

pp. 40. 16mo. The Inquiry begins on page 22.

APPENDIX A

1769

[REPORT to the Synod of New York and Philadelphia on the affairs of the College of New Jersey. 1769.]

At the meeting of the Synod on May 23, 1769, Dr. Witherspoon was appointed chairman of a committee, consisting of himself and Messrs. Blair and W. P. Smith, to draw up a statement of the affairs of the College; on their report the next day, he was ordered to have five hundred copies printed. No copy has been found.

1770

PRACTICAL DISCOURSES ON THE LEADING TRUTHS OF THE GOSPEL.
See 1768.

1772

ADDRESS to the Inhabitants of Jamaica, and the West-India Islands, in Behalf of the College of New Jersey.
Philadelphia: Printed by William and Thomas Bradford, at the London Coffee-House. M.DCC.LXXII.
pp. 27. 12mo.

The same. Reprinted in the *Pennsylvania Gazette*, October 28, 1772, and the *New York Gazette*, November 16, 1772.

The same. In New Jersey Archives, vol. XXVIII, pp. 289–308.

1775

A COMPARISON OF THE PASSIONS OF PRIDE AND VANITY.
In *Pennsylvania Magazine*, vol. I, January 1775, pp. 12–15.
Unsigned, but admitted to be by Epaminondas, Dr. Witherspoon's pseudonym, in the next essay. Not in Dr. Witherspoon's Works.

ON FIRMNESS AND OBSTINACY.
In *Pennsylvania Magazine*, vol. I, March 1775, pp. 115–119.
Signed by Epaminondas. Not in Dr. Witherspoon's Works.

ON PUBLIC SPEAKING.
In *Pennsylvania Magazine*, vol. I, June 1775. pp. 262–263.
Signed by Epaminondas. Not in Dr. Witherspoon's Works.

A PASTORAL LETTER from the Synod of New York and Philadelphia, to the Congregations under their Care; to be read from the Pulpits on Thursday, June 29, 1775, being the Day of the General Fast.

New York: Printed by Shober and Loudon, at the Newest Print-ing-Office, the corner of Maiden-Lane and Nassau Street. M.DCC.LXXV.

pp. (8). 8vo.
Signed by Benjamin Hart, moderator, New York, May 22, 1775. Written by Dr. Witherspoon for the committee of which he was chairman.

The same. In Records of the Presbyterian Church in the United States of America. (Minutes of the Synod of New York and Philadelphia). Philadelphia. 1841.

pp. 466–469.

LETTERS ON EDUCATION.

In *Pennsylvania Magazine*, vol. I (1775). pp. 149–153, 197–202, 245–249, 399–405. April–June, and September and vol. II (1776) January.

Prefaced by a note signed "X.Y." stating that the letters were from a minister to a gentleman of rank, and had not been intended for publication. Letter No. 1 (April 1775) is dated "P— Oct. 2, 1765. To Mr. S."

The same.
In *The American Museum*, vol. IV (1788) July–November, inclu-sive, pp. 25–27, 108–111, 217–220, 310–315, 397–401.

The same. A Series of Letters on Education. Ascribed to J. Wither-spoon, D.D. President of Princeton-College, N. J.
New-York: Printed by J. Buel, for C. Davis. 1797.

pp. 108. 32mo.
pp. 99–108 are a poem "Education intended to fortify the mind against criminal excess in all enjoyments, as exhibited in the Vision of Pleasure," by Dr. Cotton.

The same.
Bristol: Printed by J. Rose, for I. James, North-Street; and sold by W. Button, Pater-Noster Row, London. 1798.

pp. 2,196. 32mo.
The two-page introduction is dated Bristol November 9, 1798, and is signed by Isaac James, stating that the volume is a reprint of the New York 1797 edition, and that he has no authority for ascribing it to Dr. Witherspoon, but that he is "fully of opinion, that it would not disgrace the pen of any one."

The same. A series of Letters on Education. By John Witherspoon, D.D. President of Princetown (*sic*) College New Jersey.
Southampton: Printed & sold by Baker & Fletcher. Sold also in London by Longman, Hurst, Rees, & Orme, Paternoster Row; and Williams and Smith; Stationers' Court. 1808.

pp. viii, 108. 16mo.

The same. A series of Letters on Education. Ascribed to J. Witherspoon, D.D. Formerly President of Princeton-College, N. J.

Morris-Town: Printed by Henry P. Russell. 1815.

pp. 84. 12mo.

The same. Letters on Education. By John Witherspoon, D.D.L.L.D. Late President of the College in Princeton, New-Jersey. Also, Letters on the same subject, from the Christian Observer.

Salem, N. Y. Printed by H. Dodd and Co. Sold by them at the Salem Book Store; also by Collins and Co. New York, and W. W. Woodward, Philadelphia. 1822.

pp. 167. 32mo.

The same. Letters on the Education of Children, and on Marriage. By the Rev. John Witherspoon, D.D. L.L.D. President of Princeton College, N. J. (Quotations from Solomon).

Andover: Printed by Flagg and Gould. 1817.

pp. 81. 12mo.

The same. Four Letters on Education. By John Witherspoon, D.D. Late President of the College of New Jersey. [Quotation from Proverbs xix:20.]

Glasgow: Printed by Napier and Khull, Argyle-Street. For M. Ogle, Glasgow; J. Ogle, Edinburgh; R. Ogle, London; J. Fowler, Paisley; G. Charles, Hamilton, and R. Nairn, Renton. 1799.

pp. 58, (2) 12mo.

The titlepage is in error as the series contains the usual five letters. These end on page 55 and are followed by three pages of verse: "A parent's prayer," "Obedience to parents," and "Love between brothers and sisters."

LETTERS ON MARRIAGE.

In *Pennsylvania Magazine*, vol. I, September 1775, pp. 408–413, December 1775, pp. 543–548; vol. II, March 1776, pp. 109–114. In vol. I, pp. 557–559 and vol. II, pp. 319–323 are his replies to questions he had received with regard to these letters.

The same.

In *The American Museum*, vol. IV (1788) July–September inclusive, pp. 21–25, 105–108, 213–217. The issue for October 1788 contains (pp. 315–316) a series of questions respecting marriage from an anonymous correspondent with Dr. Witherspoon's replies.

The same.
   In A Series of Letters on Courtship and Marriage. Hartford:
Lincoln and Gleason. 1806.
16mo.
The Letters on Marriage are pp. 59–94.

The same. In Letters on Courtship and Marriage. By various authors.
   Trenton: published by Daniel Fenton and James J. Wilson. James
J. Wilson, Printer. 1813.
16mo.
pp. 99–158 are: Letters on Marriage ascribed to the Rev. John Witherspoon, Late
President of Princeton College.

SERIOUS INQUIRY INTO . . . THE STAGE (Dutch translation).
See 1757.

1776

DIALOGUE ON CIVIL LIBERTY, delivered at a Public Exhibition in
Nassau Hall January 1776.
   In *Pennsylvania Magazine*, vol. II, April 1776, pp. 157–167.
Said by Dr. Ashbel Green to have been written by Dr. Witherspoon and to be based
on his lectures.

A FEW THOUGHTS ON SPACE, DIMENSION, AND THE DIVISIBILITY OF
MATTER IN INFINITUM.
   In *Pennsylvania Magazine*, vol II, May 1776. pp. 225–229.
Signed "J.W." and written in reply to M[atthew] W[ilson's] "Proposal for reducing
Natural Philosophy to a System" etc., which appeared in the *Pennsylvania Magazine*
for March and April 1776.

THE DOMINION OF PROVIDENCE OVER THE PASSIONS OF MEN. A Sermon preached at Princeton, on the 17th of May, 1776. Being the
General Fast appointed by the Congress through the United Colonies. To which is added, An Address to the Natives of Scotland residing in America. By John Witherspoon, D.D. President of the College of New Jersey.
   Philadelphia: Printed and sold by R. Aitken. Printer and Bookseller, opposite the London Coffee-House, Front Street.
M.DCC.LXXVI.
2 leaves, pp. 78, 1 leaf. 8vo.
Leaf 1 is title; leaf 2 is dedication "To the Honourable John Hancock, Esq." etc; the
leaf at the end is: "Erratum. Page 61, line 13 & 14 *for* reformation of letters, *read*
revival of arts and letters."

The same. The Second Edition, with Elucidating Remarks. Philadelphia Printed: Glasgow Re-printed; Sold by the Booksellers in Town and Country. MDCCLXXVII. Price Six-pence.

pp. vi, 7–54. 12mo.
The notes are signed by "S.R."

The same. The third Edition, with Elucidating Remarks. Philadelphia Printed: Glasgow Re-printed. MDCCLXXVII.

pp. (7), 8–56.
Contains an Appendix of 2 pages signed by "S.R." who also signs the notes.

The same. [The fourth edition.] Philadelphia printed; London reprinted, for Fielding and Walker, No. 20 Pater-noster Row. M,DCC,LXXVIII.

pp. iv, 44. 8vo.
Date in title is misprinted May 17, *1775*. Does not contain the Address to the Natives of Scotland, this being separately printed.

The same. [The fifth edition]. London 1779. [Not found].

Samuel W. Stockton writing to Dr. Witherspoon from London April 14, 1779 (Stevens Facsimiles 938), says he sees a fifth edition of the sermon is announced in London.

THE DRUID.

In *Pennsylvania Magazine*, vol. II, May, June, and July 1776, pp. 205–209, 253–257, and 301–305.

This first series of three essays was reprinted in the *Pennsylvania Journal* for February 14, March 14 and 21, 1781, and was followed by four more essays: No. 4 in *Pennsylvania Journal* for April 11 and 18, 1781; No. 5, *Pennsylvania Journal* May 9, 1781; No. 6, *Pennsylvania Journal* May 16, 1781; No. 7, *Pennsylvania Journal* May 23 and 30, 1781. The closing paragraph of No. 7 announces a forthcoming final essay which did not appear. The *Pennsylvania Journal* for June 20, 1781, contains additional examples of Americanisms contributed by an anonymous correspondent. In the issue for June 30, 1781 another anonymous writer takes Dr. Witherspoon to task for "inaccuracies and Scotticisms."

[ADDRESS TO THE PEOPLE.] The Representatives of the United States of America in Congress assembled, to the People in General, and particularly to the Inhabitants of Pennsylvania, and the adjacent States . . .

[Philadelphia: John Dunlap. 1776.]
Fo. Broadside.

Dr. Witherspoon was chairman of the Congressional Committee reporting this Address.

The same. Die Repräsentaten der Vereinigen Staaten von America, im Congress versammelt, An das Volk uberhaupt, und an die Ein-

wohner Pennsylvaniens, und der angrenzenden Staaten insbesondere. Gegeben in Philadelphia, den 10ten December, 1776.
    [Philadelphia; Heinrich Miller 1776.]

Fo. Broadside.
In German script.

[PROCLAMATION FOR FAST DAY.] In Congress. December 11, 1776. Whereas, the just war into which the United States of America have been forced by Great Britain, is likely to be still continued by the same violence and injustice which have hitherto animated the enemies of American freedom . . .
    Baltimore: John Dunlap [1776].

Fo. Broadside.
Dr. Witherspoon was author of this proclamation and chairman of the Congressional Committee reporting it.

The same.
    Hartford: Printed by Ebenezer Watson [1776].

Fo. Broadside.

PRACTICAL TREATISE ON REGENERATION. Dutch translation.
See 1764.

1777

THE DOMINION OF PROVIDENCE. Two editions.
See 1776.

1778

[ON THE TREATMENT OF AMERICAN PRISONERS BY THE BRITISH; resolutions of Congress of December 19, 1777, and January 21, 1778.]
    [Philadelphia: 1778.]

pp. 2, Fo.

[REPORT on Currency and Finance delivered September 19, 1778.] Your Committee to whom it was referred to consider and report on the Currency and Finance of these United States, begs leave to report . . .
    [Philadelphia: September 19, 1778.]

Fo. Broadside.
Only 60 copies printed. Dr. Witherspoon was a member of the Congressional Committee reporting.

THE HUMBLE CONFESSION, declaration, recantation, and apology of Benjamin Towne, Printer in Philadelphia.
    In the *New York Packet.* Fishkill; Samuel Loudon. October 1, 1778.

The same.
[Philadelphia: Robert Bell. 1778.]
pp. 5, (1). 8vo.
At the head of the first page is the following: "Some truth, much wit, with a sufficient quantity of satire intermixed, entitles the following laughable composition, which hath been handed about in manuscript at Philadelphia, to preservation in print with other works of greater magnitude. It is reported to be written by J—n W–th–sp–n D.D. one of the Members of the American Congress." The unnumbered page at the end is a list of "Miscellanies for Sentimentalists" for sale at Bell's bookstore "next door to St. Paul's Church, in Third-Street, Philadelphia," and contains in addition to the Towne item the Life of David Hume by himself, the Travels of a Philosopher by Le Poivre, Chesterfield's Principles of Politeness, La Rochefoucauld's Maxims, Murray's Travels of the Imagination, and Freneau's American Independence.

The same. Appended to James Murray, Sermons for Ministers of State.
Philadelphia: Robert Bell. 1783.
pp. 76–79. 8vo.

[Manifesto on the conduct of the War.] By the Congress of the United States of America. A Manifesto.
[Philadelphia: Printed by John Dunlap. 1778.]
Fo. Broadside.
Issued by order of Congress, October 30, 1778. Signed by Henry Laurens, president, and Charles Thomson, secretary. This manifesto, threatening reprisals, was reported by Dr. Witherspoon, chairman of the Congressional Committee appointed to frame it.

The same.
New York. 1778.
pp. 4, 8vo.

An Address to the Natives of Scotland residing in America. Being an Appendix to a Sermon preached at Princeton on a General Fast. By John Witherspoon, D.D. President of the College at New Jersey.
London: Printed for Fielding and Walker. No. 20, Paternoster-Row. M,DCC,LXXVIII. Price Six-pence.
pp. iv, 24. 8vo.
pp. iii–iv is "Advertisement" signed by "The Editor."

The same. Another edition.
London. Fielding and Walker. 1779.
8vo.
Title taken from Reid, Bibliotheca Americana. London 1789. p. 199.

The same. In Sermons.
Edinburgh. 1798.

APPENDIX A

DOMINION OF PROVIDENCE.
See 1776.

1779

DOMINION OF PROVIDENCE.
See 1776.

ADDRESS TO THE NATIVES OF SCOTLAND.
See 1778.

1781

[PROCLAMATION naming December 13, 1781, thanksgiving day].
Whereas, as it hath pleased Almighty God, the Father of Mercies, re-
markably to assist and support the United States of America . . .
Done in Congress this twenty-sixth day of October in the year of Our
Lord one thousand seven hundred and eighty-one.
  [Philadelphia: D. C. Claypoole, 1781.]
Fo. Broadside.

The same.
  [Exeter. Zachariah Fowle, 1781.]
Fo. Broadside.

THE DRUID.
See 1776.

1782

[PROCLAMATION naming November 28, 1782, thanksgiving day.] It
being the indispensable duty of all nations, not only to offer up their
supplications to Almighty God . . .
  [Philadelphia: D. C. Claypoole. 1782.]
Fo. Broadside.

The same.
  Printed at Exeter [1782].
Fo. Broadside.

1783

PASTORAL LETTER to the Congregations of the Synod of New York
and Philadelphia on salaries.
  In *Pennsylvania Packet*, May 29, 1783.

Signed by John McCrery, Moderator, but reported by a committee of which Dr. Witherspoon was chairman. This Letter does not appear in the first edition of Dr. Witherspoon's Works but was included in the second.

The same.

In Records of the Presbyterian Church in the United States of America (Minutes of the Synod of New York and Philadelphia) 1841.

pp. 466–469.

The same.

In *Journal of the Presbyterian Historical Society,* vol. V (1909), pp. 127–131.

HUMBLE CONFESSION . . . of Benjamin Towne. See 1778.

1786

A DRAUGHT of a Plan of Government and Discipline for the Presbyterian Church in North America. Proposed by a Committee for that purpose.

Philadelphia: Printed by Francis Bailey, at Yorick's Head, in Market Street. MDCCLXXXVI.

pp. (6), 47. 8vo.

On May 23, 1785, the Synod of New York and Philadelphia ordered a committee of which Dr. Witherspoon was chairman to consider the constitution of the Church of Scotland and compile a system of rules for the government of the Synod. This committee reported May 22, 1786 and on May 23 a new committee of which Dr. Witherspoon was also chairman was ordered to print 300 copies of their digest of the report.

The same. A Draught of the Form of the Government and Discipline of the Presbyterian Church in the United States of America. Proposed, by the Synod of New-York and Philadelphia, for the consideration of the Presbyteries and Churches under their care.

New York: Printed by S. and J. Loudon, No. 5 Water-Street. M,DCC,LXXXVII.

pp. (145). 8vo.

On May 28, 1787 the Synod ordered an edition of 1000 copies printed of this revised and amended draft.

ESSAY ON MONEY, as a Medium of Commerce; with Remarks, on the Advantages and Disadvantages of Paper admitted into general Circulation. By a Citizen of the United States.

Philadelphia: Printed by Young, Stewart, and McCulloch, the Corner of Chesnut (*sic*) and Second-Streets. M.DCC.LXXX.VI.

Leaf 1, pp. 60. 12mo.

The same. By a Citizen of the United States, said to be John Witherspoon D.D.L.L.D. President of the College of New-Jersey.

Charleston: Printed and for and sold by A. Timothy. 1786.

The same. An Essay on Money as a Medium of Commerce, with Remarks on the Advantages and Disadvantages of paper admitted into general circulation. By John Witherspoon, D.D.

New-York: Printed by S. and J. Loudon, 1787.

The same [Extracts].

In *The American Museum*, vol. II (1788). pp. 47–73.

1787

SERMONS, By James Muir, A.M. Minister of the Presbyterian Church, Bermuda.

[Princeton, N. J.] Printed for the Author by James Tod. M.DCC.LXXXVII.

pp. 228. 8vo.

Page 4 is a notice "To the Reader" signed by Dr. Witherspoon, stating that the sermons were submitted to his perusal with the desire that he superintend their publication. The author was son of the Rev. Dr. George Muir of Paisley. Dr. Witherspoon in all probability not only edited them for the press but financed the venture. The volume is the most ambitious product of the press of James Tod, Princeton's first printer.

The same. Sixteen sermons, chiefly on Practical subjects, enforced from our Saviour's Parables. By James Muir, A.M. late of Bermuda. With an Introduction, by Dr. Witherspoon.

New York: Printed for Robert Hodge. 1788.

8vo.

ESSAY ON MONEY.

See 1786.

DRAUGHT of the Form of Government of the Presbyterian Church.

See 1786.

CHRISTIAN MAGNANIMITY: A Sermon, Preached at Princeton, September, 1775—the Sabbath preceeding (*sic*) the Annual Commencement; And again with Additions, September 23, 1787. To which is added an Address to the Senior Class, who were to receive the Degree of Bachelor of Arts. By John Witherspoon, D.D.L.L.D. President of the College of New-Jersey.

Princeton: Printed by James Tod. M.DCC.LXXXVII.
pp. iv, 44. 8vo.

The same. In The Youth's Companion; or a Safe Guide to Eminence. Compiled by Amator Virtutis.

Andover: Printed by Flagg and Gould. 1820. Price 62$^1/_2$ cents.
pp. xii,13–159, (3). 16mo.
Pages vii–44 Sermon on Christian Magnanimity; pp. 45–96 Address to the Senior Class.

1788

AN ADDRESS to the Senior Class of Students, who were to receive the Degree of Bachelor of Arts, and leave the College. Sept. 25, 1787. By John Witherspoon, D.D.L.L.D. President of the College of New Jersey.

Paisley: Printed by Peter M'Arthur. M.DCC.LXXXVIII.
pp. 23, 12mo.

The same. In the Youth's Companion.
Andover. 1820.
See 1787.

The same. In Sermons.
Edinburgh. 1798.

The same. In Lectures on Moral Philosophy.
Philadelphia. 1822.

SIXTEEN SERMONS. By James Muir.
See 1787.

ESSAY ON MONEY.
See 1786.

LETTERS ON MARRIAGE.
See 1775.

LETTERS ON EDUCATION.
See 1775.

1789

A SERMON on the Religious Education of Children. Preached in the Old Presbyterian Church in New York, to a very numerous Audience, on the Evening of the second Sabbath in May. By the Rev. John Witherspoon, D.D. President of Princeton College.

Elizabeth-town: Printed by Shepard Kollock. M,DCC,LXXXIX.

pp. 23. 8vo.

The same.

New York: Printed and sold by Archibald McLean, Franklin's Head, Hanover-Square, and Hodge, Allen, and Campbell. 1789.

8vo.

The same. The Religious Education of Children. A Sermon, on Mark x: 13, 14, 15, 16. [Quotation.] Preached in the Old Presbyterian Church in New-York, on the second Sabbath in May, 1789. By the Rev. John Witherspoon, D.D. President of Princeton College, New-Jersey, in America, and late Minister of the Gospel in Paisley.

Paisley: Printed by J. Neilson, for G. Caldwell. M,DCC,XC.

pp. 16. 12mo.

CHARGE OF SEDITION AND FACTION.

See 1758.

1790

SERMON on the religious education of children.

See 1789.

1791

[NINE SERMONS.] In *The American Preacher*. Edited by David Austin. Elizabeth-town, N.J. Shepard Kollock. 1791–1793.

The sermons are: Ministerial Character and Duty (vol. I, pp. 9–25).

Man in his natural State. (vol. I, pp. 27–41).

An Inducement to come to Christ. (vol. I, pp. 43–55).

On the Purity of the Heart. (vol. I, pp. 343–364).

Seeking a Competency in the Wisdom of Providence. (vol. II, pp. 365–377).

The Danger of Prosperity. (vol. II, pp. 379–390).

The Danger of Adversity. (vol. II, pp. 391–403).

Trust in God (2 sermons). (vol. III, pp. 199–212, 213–230).

The same In *Select Discourses from the American Preacher* . . .

Edinburgh: Printed by Adam Neill and Co. and sold by W. Laing and J. Ogle. 1796.

8vo.

Reprints of the sermons: Ministerial Character, Purity of Heart, and Trust in God.

APPENDIX A

1791

THE HOLY BIBLE, containing the Old and New Testaments: Translated out of the original Tongues: and with the former Translations diligently compared and revised.

Trenton: Printed and sold by Isaac Collins. M.DCC.XCI.

4to.

An Address "To the Reader" by Dr. Witherspoon (unsigned) takes the place of the usual Dedication to King James. This edition is sometimes found in two volumes. O'Callaghan "List of Editions of the Holy Scriptures" notes the following reprints of the Collins Bible: quartos; Trenton 1807, New York 1814, New York 1815; stereotype editions, quarto, New York 1816, New York 1817, New York, 1819, New York 1821, Boston 1824, Boston 1831, New York 1856. Two editions were issued in octavo, Trenton 1793 and Brookfield 1815; and three editions in duodecimo, New York 1817, New York 1818, and New York 1821. In all of these reprints Dr. Witherspoon's address "To the Reader" is substituted for the dedication.

1792

PRACTICAL DISCOURSES on the leading Truths of the Gospel.
See 1768.

1796

SERMONS from *The American Preacher*.
See 1791.

1797

SERIES OF LETTERS ON EDUCATION.
See 1775.

1798

SERMONS by the late John Witherspoon, S.S.T.D. President of the College of New Jersey. A Supplementary volume including such sermons as are not already published in his works. To which are added, by the same author, the History of a Corporation of Servants, and other Tracts.

Edinburgh: Printed for J. Dickson, J. Fairburn, and J. Ogle. 1798.

pp. xx, 381. 12mo.

The preliminary matter is "Some Account of the Life and Character of the Author" extracted from Dr. John Rodgers' sermon on his death. In addition to the History of a Corporation of Servants, the tracts reprinted are the Address to the Natives of

Scotland residing in America, and the Address to the Students of the Senior Class. The sermons are twelve in number of which nine are taken in consecutive order from "The American Preacher," followed by the Dominion of Providence (1776), the Seasonable Advice (1762) which appears under the new name On the Sin of Scoffing at Things Sacred, and Christian Magnanimity (1787).

ADDRESS to the Natives of Scotland.
See 1778.

LETTERS ON EDUCATION.
See 1775.

1800

THE WORKS OF THE REV. JOHN WITHERSPOON, D.D.L.L.D. Late President of the College, at Princeton New-Jersey. To which is prefixed An Account of the Author's Life, in a Sermon occasioned by his Death, by the Rev. Dr. John Rodgers, of New York. In Three Volumes.

Philadelphia: Printed and Published by William W. Woodward. No. 17 Chesnut (*sic*) near Front Street. 1800. Copyright secured.

4 vols. pp. 604, 632, 611, (10). 8vo.

The first edition of Dr. Witherspoon's complete works. The fourth volume has the same title-page as the others, except "In Four Volumes" and dated 1801, pp. (8), 9–368.

The same. Second Edition, revised and corrected.

Philadelphia: Printed and Published by William W. Woodward. No. 52 South Second Street. 1802. Copyright secured.

4 vols. pp. 569 (2); 586; 592; 475 (6). 8vo.

THE WORKS OF JOHN WITHERSPOON, D.D. Sometime Minister of the Gospel at Paisley and Late President of Princeton College, In New Jersey. Containing Essays, Sermons, &c on Important Subjects; intended to Illustrate and establish the Doctrine of Salvation by Grace, and to point out its Influence on Holiness of Life. Together with his Lectures on Moral Philosophy Eloquence and Divinity; his Speeches in the American Congress; and many other valuable Pieces never before published in this Country.

Edinburgh: Printed for Ogle & Aikman; J. Pillans & Sons; J. Ritchie; and J. Turnbull. 1804–1805.

9 vols. pp. 331, 351, 318, 340, 288, 354, 317, 331, 304. 8vo.

The same.

Edinburgh: Printed for J. Ogle, Parliament-Square; M. Ogle,

Glasgow; Ogles, Duncan & Cochran, London; and T. Johnston, Dublin. 1815.

9 vols. 8vo.

ESSAYS ON IMPORTANT SUBJECTS.
See 1765.

1803

THE MISCELLANEOUS WORKS OF THE REV. JOHN WITHERSPOON, D.D.L.L.D. Late President of the College of New Jersey.
Philadelphia: Printed and Published by William W. Woodward. No. 52 Corner of Second and Chesnut (*sic*) Streets. 1803.

pp. 368. 8vo.
Merely the fourth volume of the 1800 edition of the Works with a new title page.

1804

THE SELECT WORKS OF JOHN WITHERSPOON, D.D., late President of Princetown (*sic*) College, New Jersey. Containing his most admired and popular Treatises, Essays, and Sermons: viz. [follows a list of contents]. To which is prefixed The Life & Character of the Author, by John Rodgers, D.D. In Two Volumes.
London: Printed by W. Nicholson, Warner Street, for W. Baynes, 54 Paternoster-Row. 1804.

pp. xvi, iii–viii, 346; v, (2), 407. 8vo.
The unpaged leaves at beginning of Volume II are the Contents of Volume I. The printer was C. Brightly of Bungay, whose imprint is found on the last page of each volume.

1805

ESSAYS ON IMPORTANT SUBJECTS.
See 1765.

1806

LETTERS ON MARRIAGE.
See 1775.

1808

LETTERS ON EDUCATION.
See 1775.

APPENDIX A

1810

LECTURES ON MORAL PHILOSOPHY, AND ELOQUENCE. By the Rev. John Witherspoon, D.D.L.L.D. Late President of the College at Princeton, New-Jersey. Published by the American Editor for the Benefit of Schools and Academies. Woodward's Third Edition.

Philadelphia: Printed by and for William W. Woodward, No. 52 South Second Street. 1810.

pp. 304. 12mo.

1811

CHARGE OF SEDITION AND FACTION.
See 1758.

INQUIRY INTO THE SCRIPTURE MEANING OF CHARITY.
See 1768.

1812

SERIOUS INQUIRY IN TO THE STAGE.
See 1757.

1813

LETTERS ON MARRIAGE.
See 1775.

1815

AN ESSAY ON JUSTIFICATION, and a Treatise on Regeneration. By John Witherspoon, D.D. Sometime Minister of the Gospel at Paisley, and late President of Princeton College, in New Jersey. To which is prefixed some Account of the Life of the Author.

Edinburgh: Printed for J. Ogle, Parliament-Square; M. Ogle, Glasgow; Ogles, Duncan & Cochran, London; and T. Johnston, Dublin. 1815.

pp. xxxiii, (34)-331. 12mo.
The biographical sketch is unsigned but is dated Canongate, Edinburgh, August 1804, and states that the material was obtained from Dr. Rodgers' funeral sermon on the President.

The same. Treatises on Justification and Regeneration. With an Introductory essay by William Wilberforce.

[263]

Glasgow: Printed for [follows a list of booksellers in Edinburgh, Dublin, and London]. 1823.

pp. 319. 12mo.
In series "Select Christian Authors."

The same. Treatises on Justification and Regeneration. By John Witherspoon D.D. Sometime Minister of the Gospel at Paisley, and late President of Princeton College, New Jersey. With an Introductory Essay, by William Wilberforce, Esq., author of "Practical View of Christianity." Third Edition.
   Glasgow: Printed for William Collins: [follows a list of booksellers in Edinburgh, Dublin, and London]. MDCCCXXX.

pp. xviii, 19–308. 12mo.

The same. [Another edition.]
   Amherst. 1830.
12mo.
Listed in Roorbach, Bibliotheca Americana I, 592.

PRACTICAL TREATISE ON REGENERATION.
See 1764.

LETTERS ON EDUCATION.
See 1775.

THE WORKS OF JOHN WITHERSPOON.
See 1800.

1817

LETTERS ON EDUCATION.
See 1775.

1820

CHRISTIAN MAGNANIMITY.
See 1787.

ADDRESS TO THE SENIOR CLASS.
See 1788.

1822

LECTURES ON MORAL PHILOSOPHY. By the Rev. John Witherspoon, D.D.L.L.D. Carefully revised, and freed from the errors of former editions. To which is added, by the same author, An Address to the Students of the Senior Class, and Letters on Education and Marriage.
   Philadelphia: Published by William W. Woodward, No. 52, South Second Street. 1822.

pp. 298. 12mo.

The same. Lectures on Moral Philosophy. By John Witherspoon, D.D., LL.D. President of the College of New Jersey. Edited under the auspices of the American Philosophical Association by Varnum Lansing Collins.

Princeton, N. J. Princeton University Press. 1912.

pp. xxxii, 144. 8vo.

The frontispiece is a reproduction of the Woodhull copy of Peale's portrait of the President. The Introduction is a biographical sketch, followed by a Check-list of his published writings.

LETTERS ON EDUCATION.

See 1775.

ADDRESS TO THE SENIOR CLASS.

See 1788.

1823

TREATISES ON JUSTIFICATION AND REGENERATION.

See 1815.

1830

TREATISES ON JUSTIFICATION AND REGENERATION.

See 1815.

ADDRESS to six classes of persons. (Regeneration).

See 1764.

1842

ECCLESIASTICAL CHARACTERISTICS.

See 1753.

1844

REGENERATION.

See 1764.

1850

REGENERATION. French translation.

See 1764.

1855

REGENERATION.

See 1764.

APPENDIX A

1876

SERIOUS INQUIRY INTO THE STAGE.
See 1764.

1912

LECTURES ON MORAL PHILOSOPHY.
See 1822.

NOTE ON "A LETTER FROM A BLACKSMITH"

An anonymous pamphlet entitled *A Letter from a Blacksmith*, which has been ascribed to President Witherspoon since the end of the eighteenth century, is omitted from the foregoing list of his writings. The *Letter*, which was a protest against prevalent conditions in the Scottish Church, first appeared in London in 1759 and was reviewed in the *Gentleman's Magazine*, the *Critical Review*, and the *Monthly Review*. Its popularity was extraordinary, no less than thirteen editions coming out in Great Britain and the United States between 1759 and 1845, nine of them being issued during Dr. Witherspoon's lifetime. It was not until 1791 that its authorship was ascribed to him. The *Monthly Review* noticing a new London edition published that year—it had reviewed the first edition thirty-two years previously—remarked: "This pretended letter from a blacksmith was written, as we have heard, by Dr. Witherspoon, formerly a minister of some eminence in Scotland, and there distinguished for his uncommon abilities; but he has since made a greater figure in America where, if we mistake not, he obtained the honor of a seat at the board of Congress." On the basis of this hearsay ascription Halkett and Laing credited the pamphlet to the President, and have been followed by the British Museum Catalogue and by Sabin, Hildeburn, and Evans. Horne's Catalogue of the Library of Queen's College, Cambridge, on the other hand names the "Reverend Mr. Hume" as author, while the Bodleian Catalogue gives the credit to the "Reverend Mr. Buchanan of Somersetshire."

The pamphlet is not mentioned by Ashbel Green or other biographers of the President. Had he been its author, it is incredible that a production, of which so many editions were published in Great Britain and America before his death, should have remained unassociated with his name in the minds of those most intimately acquainted with him; there is no adequate evidence that he wrote it; and the style and content of the pamphlet reinforce the conclusion that he was not its author.

[266]

APPENDIX B

WITHERSPOON ICONOGRAPHY

PAINTINGS, STATUES, ETC.

PRESIDENT Witherspoon's portrait was painted by Charles
Wilson Peale. This is believed to be the portrait formerly
owned by the late General Alfred A. Woodhull of Princeton,
N. J., the President's great-great-grandson. It descended directly in the family from Ann Witherspoon, to her daughter Mrs.
Dirck G. Saloman, to the latter's daughter Miss Caroline Saloman, and from the latter to her nephew General Woodhull. It is
now owned by Princeton University and hangs in Nassau Hall.
Copies are in Madison Hall, Princeton University, in Independence Hall, Philadelphia; and a further copy by Rembrandt
Peale is owned by Mr. S. S. Woods of Lewistown, Pa., having
descended from the President's daughter by his second marriage.

Another and earlier portrait by an unknown artist was owned
by the Slidell family, formerly of Princeton, and is believed to be
at present in Paris. It has proved impossible to trace the origin
of this painting.

The President's likeness is in Trumbull's celebrated "Signing
of the Declaration of Independence," owned by Yale University.
An enlarged copy is in the Capitol at Washington. While planning the enlargement the artist wrote to Thomas Jefferson that
the portraits "were done by myself from the Life, being all who
survived in 1791." Dr. Witherspoon was still living at this time
and it is, therefore, to be assumed that his likeness in the Trumbull group is from life.

The Presbyterian Historical Society at Philadelphia owns a
modern watercolor painting of the President.

Another modern portrait is in the New Jersey Room, Memorial
Continental Hall, Washington, D. C.

James Tassie, the Scottish cameo maker, modelled Dr. Witherspoon's likeness in 1784. Two copies of this are in America, one
owned by Princeton University and the other by Mrs. J. M.
Spindle of Norfolk, Va. Mrs. Spindle's copy belonged to David

Witherspoon. The original matrix is in the Tassie Collection, National Portrait Gallery, Edinburgh.

There are three heroic statues of the President, one in bronze by J. A. Bailly, at Fairmount Park, Philadelphia, unveiled in 1876; a second also in bronze by William Couper, in front of the Church of the Covenant, Washington, D. C., unveiled in 1909; and the third of stone, by J. Massy Rhind, over the arch of the Library of Princeton University, erected in 1897.

An heroic bust in marble of the President by an unknown artist was presented to the University in June, 1876, by the Class of 1876 and is in the University Library. A bust is mentioned in Breed's *Witherspoon* as being owned in 1876 by the family of John Knox Witherspoon of Camden, S. C. Its history and present whereabouts have not been traced.

A life-size bronze bas-relief medallion of the President by an unknown artist is in Nassau Hall, Princeton University.

Engraved Portraits

1. TROTTER

Stipple; full bust turned to the left; right hand resting on edge of standing book. Oval; h. 2 1-8 in.; w. 1 11-16 in. Surrounded by border with bow of ribbon at top and ornamental clasp.
Inscription
"Drawn from the Life, and Engraved by T. Trotter."
"John Witherspoon, D.D. President of New Jersey College in America." "Published as the Act directs April 1st 1785. (from the Drawing in the Possession of the Revd Dr Simpson) by J. Simco."
Nothing is known of the artist or of the drawing on which this unflattering portrait is based.

2. D. EDWIN

Stipple; bust, full face. Oval; h. 3 in.; w. 2½ in.
Inscription (at top of plate)
"The Evangelical Intelligencer;"
Signed
"D. Edwin, sculpsit."
"Doct. J. Witherspoon." "Engraved for W. P. Farrand & Co. No 185 Market Street Philadelphia." "Page 17."
Frontispiece to Vol. I, No. 1 (January 1805) of the "Assembly's Missionary Magazine," or "Evangelical Intelligencer."
Stauffer No. 917.

3. RIDLEY AND BLOOD
Stipple. Oval in line frame; H. 3¼ in.; w. 2½ in.
Inscription
"Ridley & Blood, sculp."
"Revd J. Witherspoon, D.D. President of Princeton College, New Jersey, America." "Published by Williams and Co. Stationers Court. March 1, 1808."
    Frontispiece to the "Letters on Education" Southampton, 1808.

4. ILLMAN AND PILLBROW
In rectangular ruled frame; H. 3 5-8 in.; w. 2 7-8 in.
Inscription
"Illman & Pillbrow sc."
Facsimile signature "Jno Witherspoon."
    Frontispiece to the "Lectures," Philadelphia 1810.

5. J. SCOTT
The Trotter engraving with architectural design, ornamented with flowers and fruit; figure of child resting on books at base of the design. The whole 4 5-8 in. in H., by 2¾ in. in w.
Inscription
"Eng^d by John Scott, Glasgow."
"John Witherspoon D.D." "Published by William Collins, Glasgow."
    Frontispiece to the "Treatise on Justification and Regeneration," Glasgow, 1830.

6. Unsigned.
Stipple; full bust. H. 3 5-8 in.; w. 3 in.
Inscription
"John Witherspoon, D.D."
"From a Painting by C. W. Peale."
"Pub^l. for the American Quarterly Register."
    Frontispiece to the November 1836 issue of the "American Quarterly Register," Volume IX, facing p. 105.

7. J. B. LONGACRE
Stipple. Oval; H. 3 in.; w. 2½ in.; in rectangular ornamental frame.
Inscription
"John Witherspoon."
"Engraved by J. B. Longacre from a painting by C. W. Peale."
    In Sanderson, "Biography of the Signers of the Declaration of Independence," Vol. II facing page 205, Philadelphia 1838.
Stauffer No. 2127.

8. A. H. RITCHIE

Rectangular; H. *3 6-8 in.;* W. *3 in.*
Inscription
"A. H. Ritchie."
"Rev. John Witherspoon, D.D."

In the Presbyterian Magazine *Vol. I* (1851); *frontispiece to the December issue which contains a sketch of the President.*

Also used in 1858 as frontispiece of Sprague, "Annals of the American Pulpit," *Vol. III.*

Also used in 1879 in Hageman, "History of Princeton and its Institutions," *Vol. II, facing p.* 261.

A photogravure of this engraving, without the artist's signature, but with a facsimile of Dr. Witherspoon's signature replacing the title, was used as frontispiece to D. W. Woods "John Witherspoon," *Philadelphia* 1906.

9. O. PELTON

In rectangular frame; H. *3 1-8 in.;* W. *2½ in.*
"Painted by C. W. Peale. Eng^d by O. Pelton, Boston."
With poor facsimile of signature of Dr. Witherspoon.
Stauffer No. 2535.

10. PRINCETON BOOK

Heliotype; from the Peale portrait in Nassau Hall; H. *6 in.;* W. *5 in.*
In "The Princeton Book," *Boston* 1879, *facing p.* 45.

11. SESQUICENTENNIAL BOOK

Copper plate of the Peale portrait in Nassau Hall; H. *6½ in.;* W. *5 in.*

In "Memorial Book of the Sesquicentennial Celebration of the Founding of the College of New Jersey," *New York* 1898, *facing p.* 382. *The plate was considerably retouched by the artist.*

WOODCUTS

Woodcuts of the President are in "Harper's Magazine" *Vol. III,* (1851), *p.* 155; "Harpers' Magazine" *Vol. VII* (1853), *p.* 154; "Potter's American Monthly" *Vol. IV* (1875), *p.* 505; "Potter's American Monthly," *Vol. IV* (1875), *p.* 510 (*the Fairmount Park monument*); *facing p.* 48 *of W. P. Breed,* "Witherspoon. Proceedings and address at the . . . unveiling of the statue of John Witherspoon," (*in Fairmount Park*), *Philadelphia,* 1877, (*the cloth cover of this booklet bears a reproduction of the statue stamped in gold*); *Duykinck,* "Cyclopedia of

American Literature," *New York* 1856, *Vol. I, p.* 277; "Scribner's Magazine," *Vol.* XIII (1877), *p.* 629; "The Church at Home and Abroad," *Philadelphia* 1888, *p.* 529. "Harpers Weekly," *Vol. XXXII, p.* 360; *E. T. Giddings,* "American Christian Rulers," *New York,* 1889, *facing p.* 575; "McClure's Magazine," *Vol. XVII,* (1901) *p.* 235.

OTHER PORTRAITS

Photogravures of the President are found in William H. Michael, "Declaration of Independence," *(Washington, Government Printing Office), facing page* 38; *in the printed proceedings (Washington* 1909,*) at the dedication of the Witherspoon Statue at Washington, (the statue and pedestal; in the programme of the dedication of the Witherspoon Statue at Washington* (the statue only)); *in the* 1912 *reprint of the* "Lectures on Moral Philosophy," *(the Woodhull copy of the Peale portrait), and in the* "Catalogue of the Portraits in Independence Hall," *(Philadelphia,* 1915) *p.* 167 *(the Independence Hall copy of the Peale portrait.)*

APPENDIX C

BIBLIOGRAPHY

THE principal manuscript source on President Wither-spoon's life is Dr. Ashbel Green's sketch preserved in the New Jersey Historical Society's Library at Newark, N. J. This manuscript, which was planned to be the introduction to Dr. Green's proposed third edition of the President's *Works* but was never issued, consists of 250 quarto pages and contains the best extant account of the President's personality by one who was intimately acquainted with him. Virtually all the reports presented by Dr. Witherspoon as a congressional committee-man are among the Papers of the Continental Congress now in the Library of Congress. In the libraries of the Pennsylvania Historical Society, the Presbyterian Historical Society, and Princeton University are a few of his letters, but the President's correspondence, which was said to have been extensive, has disappeared. The anonymous "Journal of Nassau Hall in 1786," describing college life at Princeton in Witherspoon's time, is owned by the Library of Congress.

The only extended printed biography of Dr. Witherspoon is that by David Walker Woods, Jr. (*John Witherspoon*, Fleming H. Revell Co., 1906), a volume to be used with caution. The most satisfactory account of the President's congressional career is to be found in Sanderson's *Biography of the Signers* for which both Dr. S. Stanhope Smith and Dr. Ashbel Green supplied material. Professor Moses Coit Tyler in the *American Historical Review* (I, 671) sketched the President's congressional service, quoting largely from his printed speeches and essays. The second volume of Professor Tyler's *Literary History of the American Revolution* contains a sympathetic and delightful chapter on the President. Of great interest is the Reverend J. F. Dickie's pamphlet *John Witherspoon, Patriot* printed without date at Detroit (?). It contains allusions to local traditions connected with Dr. Witherspoon's charges in Scotland. *John Witherspoon and his Times* (Presbyterian Board of Publication, 1890) by ex-President James McCosh is an address delivered before the Presbyterian Historical Society and the Presbyterian Ministers Association of Philadelphia. It is merely a re-working of the printed material.

Of more value is a chapter in Dr. McCosh's volume *Scottish Philosophers* (New York), although the only genuine attempt to assign Dr. Witherspoon his place in the history of philosophical thought is found in Professor Woodbridge Riley's *American Philosophy: the Early Schools* (New York, 1907). His work as a theologian is discussed by Professor Lyman H. Atwater in the *Biblical Repertory* (vol. XXXV, p. 596 etc.)

The fullest account of Dr. Witherspoon's administration at Princeton is in ex-President John Maclean's *History of the College of New Jersey* (Philadelphia, 1877). It is followed by a brief memoir which, however, contains no new material. His administration was entertainingly described by Dr. Ashbel Green in an "Address before the alumni at Commencement in 1840," printed in 1854 in the *Presbyterian Magazine* (vol. IV, p. 467 etc.).

Besides his booklet *Presbyterians and the Revolution* (Philadelphia, 1876), written primarily to create public interest in the erection of a statue of the President, Dr. William P. Breed also compiled and edited the *Proceedings and Addresses at the laying of the corner stone and at the unveiling of the statue of John Witherspoon in Fairmount Park, Philadelphia* (Presbyterian Board of Publication, 1877). This little volume contains a particularly spirited oration by Governor Joseph D. Bedle of New Jersey which has minor errors of fact, but in the main is an excellent portrayal of the President.

The proceedings at the unveiling of the statue in Washington were published in a pamphlet with illustrations, *The Witherspoon Memorial. Sketch of the Association and Unveiling of the Statue* (Washington, 1909). The oration, then delivered by President Woodrow Wilson of Princeton, was a strikingly phrased estimate of Dr. Witherspoon's character, but not intended to be a careful study.

A good account of the President's life and character, based

upon the biographical portion of Dr. Rodgers' Sermon and upon Dr. Green's manuscript sketch, is found in Sprague's *Annals of the American Pulpit*, vol. III, pp. 288–300.

The funeral sermon by Dr. John Rodgers, "The Faithful Servant Rewarded" is not notable. The biographical portion of the sermon was supplied by Dr. S. Stanhope Smith.

The scattered magazine articles on the President are principally re-statements of one another. The chief exception is the article in the *Christian Instructor* (vol. XXVIII, Oct., 1829) by Thomas Crichton, of Paisley, who signed himself "A Presbyterian of the West."

The Edinburgh *Quarterly Register* for May, 1923, (vol. XII, pp. 581-6) commemorates, under the title "The Witherspoon Bi-centenary," the two hundredth anniversary of the President's birth, in two articles, "John Witherspoon in Scotland," by the Rev. A. Mitchell Hunter, M. A., Librarian of New College, Edinburgh, and "Witherspoon in America," by Professor Frederick W. Loetscher, D. D., LL. D., of Princeton Theological Seminary. These articles, although unavoidably brief, are suggestive and useful surveys of the President's career.

INDEX